Reality: *Your mid-sized business ($200 million–$800 million) must compete and expand on a global scale.*

Conflicting Reality: *You lack the time, staff, and/or knowledge to explore international business opportunities and competition in depth.*

Here is the complete, one-stop guide for executives who are doing business globally, or researching such moves. A few hours spent with *Global Gold* will reap years of rewards. It will steer you toward your company's best foreign opportunities . . . and away from the costly mistakes that so many expanding companies make. It also gives you an international directory of contacts that will prove invaluable.

Make no mistake—this is not a global etiquette handbook, but a fact-packed resource designed to position you for long-term international profit. The author distills her experience with scores of mid-sized companies and her business dealings in 80+ countries to help you identify and fulfill your global expansion priorities. You will learn:

- Which countries and regions offer the highest potential for your products and services

- Who has succeeded and failed in these countries, and why

- Whether your company has taken the seven essential steps that ensure global success

- How to measure the expense of entering a new market against sales potential

(Continued on back flap)

beyond your country's borders.

GLOBAL GOLD

Panning for Profits in Foreign Markets

GLOBAL GOLD

Panning for Profits in Foreign Markets

Ruth Stanat

AMACOM

American Management Association

New York · Atlanta · Boston · Chicago · Kansas City · San Francisco · Washington, D.C.
Brussels · Mexico City · Tokyo · Toronto

This book is available at a special
discount when ordered in bulk quantities.
For information, contact Special Sales Department,
AMACOM, a division of American Management Association,
1601 Broadway, New York, NY 10019.

This publication is designed to provide accurate and authoritative information in regard to the subject matter covered. It is sold with the
understanding that the publisher is not engaged in rendering legal,
accounting, or other professional service. If legal advice or other expert assistance is required, the services of a competent professional
person should be sought.

Library of Congress Cataloging-in-Publication Data

Stanat, Ruth.
    Global gold : panning for prorifts in foreign markets / Ruth
Stanat.
        p.   cm.
    Included index.
    ISBN 0-8144-0410-3 (alk. paper)
    1. Exports—United States—Management.   2. Export
marketing—United States—Management.   3. United States—
Commerce.   4. International trade.   I. Title.
HF1416.5.S73   1998
658.8′48′0973—dc21   97-53275
                                                         CIP

Printing number

10 9 8 7 6 5 4 3 2 1

*This book is dedicated to
my three children, Scott, Christine, and Michael, my
mother, Ellen Corrigan, and especially to my husband, Bill*

CONTENTS

PREFACE

The world will be approaching a global marketplace in the next millennium. Just about every aspect of our lives, from the food we eat, to transportation, energy, clothing, financial services, household goods and entertainment, is either sourced from or exported to other countries. While the large multinational firms have made direct investment in other regions of the world during the past decade, smaller to mid size firms are currently facing the issue of how to expand their business in the global marketplace. Unlike the large multinationals, these firms have limited financial and human resources and cannot afford to take significant risks in the global marketplace. The large firms generally have hefty research budgets for international market research which is critical to market entry in foreign markets.

Most business development efforts by small to mid size firms are a result of a "knee jerk reaction" to the press or media on "hot countries" or a response to your competition going global. Global Gold is intended to provide you with a tool or a resource book to avoid expensive trips which yield poor results or to avoid costly international business development failures. As such, the book is a culmination of the contribution of over 50 experts throughout the world to give you the "tools" to avoid these costly mistakes.

For the past decade and a half, my firm, SIS International Research, has been active in providing global market research and market feasibility studies for firms seeking international expansion. What I have found is that while firms know that they should be evaluating and entering foreign markets, there is a major "void or gap" that exists in identifying the optimum worldwide regions or countries, adaptation of their products to the local culture countries, and most importantly, knowledge of "how to actually do business in the country." The scope of this book attempts to cover these three obstacles to going global.

Global Gold will not only give you the inside track on how to research these markets, it will also provide you with the marketing success and failure stories on a country by country basis in addition to giving you valuable source lists of organizations to contact by country. *Essentially, the book contains valuable research secrets which typically can only be afforded by large, multinational firms. The total estimated value of global research and experience contained in this book exceeds $1 million USD.* Essentially, the book is organized on a regional basis: the Asia Pacific region, Western Europe, Central and Eastern Europe, Latin America, the Middle East and Africa, and the United States. Within each region, I have provided a regional overview which discusses the culture of the region, the market opportunities, barriers/pitfalls to market entry and a recommended approach to market entry into the region.

Within each region, we have selected "experts" from these countries who are in the business of assisting businesses with market entry into their country. Many of these individuals are prominent heads of local business development or market research firms, in addition to key officials involved with business development in the country. Most of the contributing country authors have been affiliated with SIS International Research during the past decade and have years of experience in this field. In my opinion, the country sections are the "gold nuggets" in the book as they describe the marketing successes and failures in their country and the reasons why. This type of information is not contained in the press, nor will you hear about it in the press or in the media. This market insight into over 40 countries which "tells it like it is" saves valuable time and money in terms of foreign travel and research expenses.

As a result of over 15 years in the business and my travels throughout the world, I have included a section of my "**Stanat Notes**" in each country or region, which add insight into the cultural and business nuances of the country or the region. Through doing business in over 80+ countries, I have (painfully) learned what works and what does not. In spite of my international background, as a *businesswoman* I established our worldwide research affiliate by traveling to over 80+ countries during the 80s and early 90s. These notes are a result of not only building a worldwide organization and making the contacts, but actively doing business in these countries during the past decade. *Most importantly, these cultural and business notes were important to my keeping these relationships over a long period of time.*

The **Source Book Section** of the book contains two parts: (1) brief country fact sheets and (2) a source section which contains valuable research sources (demographic, manufacturing, trade data, company data, databases), listing of research and consultancy firms, governmental sources and business development firms and brokers. These sources were generated from the local country authors and cannot be found in any other source book (in one volume). Thus, the value of these sources is significant in terms of saving you time and money searching for these sources. More importantly, use these sources to make contacts in the countries before you spend expensive travel funds for a trip. Clearly, it is easy to make initial contacts via fax and letter prior to spending thousands of dollars on a trip.

For small to mid size firms, much of the globalization process starts with developing a "mind set" for going global. While this sounds simple, this can be overwhelming to you and your executive management. Chapter 1 of this book outlines the scope of the current and future global marketplace. More importantly, it segments the global markets into three categories, the "I," "We," and "They" economies which are driven by the cultural values of our worldwide regions. This chapter also asks and answers critical questions such as, *Why Go Global? What Are the Risks of Going Global? Are You Ready to Be a Global Player?* Chapter 1 also gives you a step by step approach as to "how to organize your efforts to go global."

Chapter 2 outlines what it takes to be a successful player in the global markets. The chapter outlines numerous case studies of mid size firms that have successfully entered international markets. In addition, it gives you step-by-step critical success factors to launch a successful globalization effort. This chapter should enable you to determine what worked for the size and culture of these companies and what factors can work for your firm.

Chapter 3 contains the Asia Pacific region, which we define as "The Engine of the Next Millennium." This chapter contains valuable insight into not only the market and cultural dynamics of the region, but also the "Americanization of Japan," the continued growth of the "Tiger economies," e.g., South Korea, Thailand, Taiwan, Singapore, etc. China, Hong Kong and Taiwan are addressed as the Chinese Economic Area. We have outlined in detail the opportunities and pitfalls of market entry into China. Lastly, the "second wave" of emerging countries, such as Indonesia, India, Malaysia, Vietnam, Cambodia, and Laos are presented. From reading the Asia chapter, you should be able to answer the following questions: *Does my firm have opportunities in Asia? If so, what countries? Who should I contact in these countries? Do I need a local representative to represent my products? If so, what is the best country to serve as a springboard into the region? Should I go directly into China or through Hong Kong? What about the lower labor cost of emerging countries such as Indonesia, Malaysia, Vietnam?*

Chapter 4 outlines Western Europe in the future; the forces uniting Europe, the process of change, the European customer and the market opportunities in the next millennium. The chapter also outlines the changing market dynamics in France, Germany, Italy, the United Kingdom, Belgium, the Netherlands, Scandinavia and Spain. While most of us have had some experience in Europe, there are forces which still separate the countries in light of the issue of unification or segmentation. Gold still exists in this market through target research.

Chapter 5 provides a comprehensive overview of Central and Eastern Europe, as "The Last Frontier." These markets offer market opportunities in telecommunications, utilities and energy, tourism, and technology. You must do your research in these markets as the risks are higher than in Western Europe. The country section provides detail on the Czech Republic, Hungary, Poland and Russia. Particular emphasis is given to the current economic, political, crime and corruption issues in Russia.

Chapter 6 gives you a comprehensive overview of Latin America yesterday, today and tomorrow. The chapter advises that "you must have the stomach to enter and stay in Latin America." The chapter outlines the emergence of several powerful trade pacts in the region and the market opportunities that are emerging in Argentina, Brazil, Chile, Colombia, Mexico, Peru and Venezuela. More importantly, the chapter gives you insight into the Latin American consumer and how to reach these people.

Chapter 7 puts the Middle East into perspective with the need for peace and stability in the region. It is important to view the "new face" of the Middle East, with a perspective given to the past. Market opportunities are discussed in detail for the major countries in the Middle East and Africa. Particular attention is given to South Africa since the abolition of apartheid.

Chapter 8 is an "eye opener" for countries planning to enter the U.S. market. The chapter candidly tells of the size and complexity of the market. The cultural or ethnic diversities that exist in the United States, coupled with the regional segments of the market are not to be ignored. Yet, the chapter will explain that you can find "gold" in this large market if you have a targeted, "niche" product or service.

Chapter 9 discusses globalization issues—what you need to know. Specifically, the chapter outlines the issue of bribery and patent and copyright infringement. The chapter also gives you a comprehensive and detailed guideline on the importance of and how to formulate strategic alliances. The chapter also includes a section on how to locate strategic alliances through the Internet.

Global Gold contains a wealth of information—which in itself is a "pot of gold." If used to the fullest, this book will give you information that can enable you to get a head start in the race for global markets. The step-by-step approach in Chapter 1, plus the critical success factors and the "golden rules of international business" in Chapter 2 are clear and simple to follow. The book should become your guide to your international expansion efforts.

Global Gold is the culmination of nearly two decades of experience for both myself and the contributing authors to the book. I wish to acknowledge David Follmer, Diana Gillooly, Doug Bukowski from Lyceum Books for their superb editing of the book, and Julie Klink and Alyson Hoffman for their hard work in coordinating the communications and in compiling the fact sheet and source section of the book. I also wish to acknowledge the excellent work from the contributing authors to the book: Akin Alyanak, Cindy Allgaier, Jan Bauer, Babette Bensoussan, Gale Dinces, Niranjan Ganjawalla, Jorge Gonzalez, Shashi Halve, Makoto Hori, Yelena Kisseleva, Chuck Klein, Dr. Lily Lai, Carlos Lemoine, Gustavo Mendez-Kuhn, Jan Nawrocki, Dr. Hyan Doo Park, Peter Redden, Pedro Ribeiro, Orlando Riebman, Igor Shevchuk, Ola Svennson, Timm Sweeney, Alfredo Torres, Katalin Vajda, B. N. Weaver, Chris West, Pawel Wojcik and Paul Woodward. I also wish to acknowledge my understanding family and friends during the authoring of this book.

Ruth Stanat
New York
September 1997

PART I

HOW TO DO BUSINESS GLOBALLY:

Regional Overviews

Chapter 1

GLOBAL EXPANSION:

Is Your Business a Candidate?

THERE IS A GOLD RUSH OUT THERE

If you haven't begun to expand your business outside your local country, you are missing *"the global gold rush."* Many firms, such as yours, have reached their maturity in their local markets and are aggressively seeking expansion into foreign markets. You read and hear that business is booming in countries such as China, India, Korea, Saudi Arabia, Thailand— yet, how do you capitalize on these market opportunities in developed, developing, and emerging-growth countries? You are hearing that millions of companies and entrepreneurs are transforming traditional countries into economic powerhouses. You are hearing stories that both industrial and consumer markets need your products . . . and they need them now.

While this thought is exciting, optimistic, and exhilarating, it is overwhelming when you consider the size, complexity, and risk of expanding into global markets. Certainly, when you consider all of the barriers to entry into foreign markets, you become overwhelmed by the thought: *While "there may be gold in them there hills," is it worth the risk for panning for gold in these foreign markets?* The following are common excuses for avoiding the risk:

- We have limited resources; we can barely handle our domestic business.

- It's too risky. We are not making enough money at home in our local market.
- How can we make a profit in foreign markets?
- It will take years for international business to pay back.
- We have never exported any of our products. How do we go about this?
- Who in our company can/will handle this effort?

Within your firm, the biggest problem that you will face is internal: the global mindset of your management and staff.

MAINSTREET WORLD: THE NEW GLOBAL MARKETPLACE

Today, the opportunity for companies to enter international markets is greater than at any time in history. According to a study by Peat Marwick, corporations spent a record $284 billion on acquisitions, joint ventures, and minority investments, shattering the quarter-trillion-dollar barrier for the first time. The average value of cross-border deals (deals in which the purchaser and the target are based in different countries) rose 37 percent worldwide, from $38 million to $51 million, while the actual number of such deals declined in 1996.

According to a survey conducted by *Inc. Magazine* of 463 private companies that reported a five-year growth rate of 713 percent or higher since 1985, only 5 percent did business in the international markets when they first started the business. During the past five years, however, this percentage grew to 21 percent of their total sales.

Companies with the highest rates of success have cultivated "global mindsets" from the beginning. What do I mean by this? Well, the meaning of "national mindset" is pretty clear. Most firms already have one: It would be a rare New Jersey firm, for example, that decided Pennsylvania (or even California) consumers were none of its business. We all know to look for our markets where we can find them. We ship *water* from California to Maine!

Why, then, does this kind of thinking so often stop at the national border? There were reasons in the past, of course: the walls of trade barriers around most foreign countries and the high risk of economic or political upheaval. But, today, all this has changed.

"I" GLOBAL MARKETS

Countries like the United States are consumer driven, have mature markets and infrastructure, and have products that are designed for the comfort, safety, and intellect of the consumer. These cultures are very *individualistic,* and as a result, the products and services of the society are geared to the consumer. Decision making is also very individualistic. These economies and societies can thus be classified as "I" countries or markets. Products that are designed or targeted for export to these markets should include individualistic features, product uniqueness, product options, and unique designs and should be able to create a "niche" market within a mass consumer market. Remember, individualistic consumers (both male and female) drive these markets.

"WE" GLOBAL MARKETS

Asian countries or markets have a strong sense of group decision making in business and family matters. Products and services designed for these cultures will have a "we" orientation. The elders of the society still carry the power and respect of the family and society. Products that are exported to this region should take into consideration the strong Asian or "we" culture that still exists within the different countries. Remember, decisions are still made by consensus in groups within companies and in the family.

"THEY" GLOBAL MARKETS

Countries with a longstanding heritage and sense of nationalism are among the "they" global markets. The countries within the European Union (EU) and Latin America are examples of these types of international markets. While these countries are seeking to form economic unions for trade purposes, they still refer to the other countries or cultures as the "they" culture—"the French," "the Germans," "the British," "the Brazilians," "the Mexicans," and so forth. Products developed for or exported to these markets must be adapted to the traditional cultures and heritage of these countries. Decisions are made within the context of the country heritage. Remember, it is difficult to market one product or brand to a "they" market—for example, to all of Europe or to all of Latin America at once.

Why Should *You* Go Global?

Getting a global mindset does *not* mean panicking and jumping on the next bandwagon across the Pacific. It means understanding what your company needs and giving yourself the best chance of finding it, even if you end up looking in the Scottish Highlands or along the Yangtze River.

Don't approach global expansion as an alternative or sideline to your domestic business. Having a global mindset means realizing that the need to go global lies at the heart of your business.

So, what are some reasons to go global?

. . . To Grow Your Business

One of the most basic reasons for taking your firm global is to grow your business. International markets, particularly developing and emerging growth countries, have high rates of growth. We define a *mature market* as one with a forecast GDP growth rate of 1 to 3 percent per year. These economies typically have well-developed infrastructure: government; health care; education; highways; water system; telecommunications system; and industrial, retail, and consumer product sectors. Most of the economy is private, and capitalism (or a mixture of capitalism and varying degrees of socialism) and competition are the dominant economic ideologies.

The majority of the world's mature economies—the United States, the countries of Western Europe, Australia—underwent significant industrialization in the nineteenth and early twentieth centuries. At present, most of these countries have well-developed, mature, industrial and consumer economies and have now become technology- and information-based economies. Because their domestic markets are mature, they are now forced to market their products and services throughout the world to achieve growth.

A *developing market* is one with a forecast GDP growth rate of 4 to 6 percent per year. Consumers in these economies are beginning to have high enough average disposable income that they start to develop brand preferences. Markets for automobiles, various food brands, and health and beauty aids are beginning to emerge. The government is beginning to privatize sectors such as telecommunications and is investing capital in infrastructure improvements. Most developing countries have achieved political stability and are democracies; examples include Chile, Korea, Brazil, Thailand, and Mexico.

An *emerging market* is one whose government has only recently stabilized. While most organizations or companies are publicly held, there is significant demand for industrial development. These countries have been known historically for their cheap labor pool. Typically, these countries are attractive to three types of investors or exporters:

- Manufacturers of products in mature and developing countries that seek lower manufacturing costs and intend to reexport their products throughout the region
- Developers of infrastructure projects
- Exporters of basic consumer goods that will meet the demand of young, growing populations

The Phoenix Rises Abroad

Phoenix Metal Fabricating rose from the ashes of a bankrupt firm and was born anew under the ownership of Harold Andersen, president and CEO. About four years ago, Andersen realized that the domestic market for his products in the United States was limited. He met with his local congressman, who arranged a trade mission to Monterrey and Mexico City in the summer of 1994. Phoenix now exports about 30 percent of its products. Phoenix has subsequently expanded into Sweden, and Andersen is looking into other international markets.

Similarly, Justice Brothers Car Care Products in Duarte, California, was a successful family business that produced high-quality car care products engineered to prolong the life of the vehicle. About twenty-five years ago, the family decided to tackle the Japanese market. They mapped out a marketing plan and took the plunge. They expanded into the Asian marketplace and developed a number of solid relationships that continue to strengthen today. They then set up a network in Europe, Africa, and Central and South America.

... TO IMPROVE YOUR PROFITABILITY

For the most part, your products can command higher prices in foreign markets. This is often surprising to small businesses, who believe that they will have to export their products for reduced margins. Most often, however, foreign markets do not have the expertise, technology, or resources to produce the things that you can. This is where market research and product testing prior to market expansion can point to profits.

Sometimes Opportunity Comes Out of Disaster

Both Ray Ciliv and Robin Hillyard, cofounders of a software start-up outside of Boston, pledged their homes for seed capital for their software firm, NovaSoft Systems. Although they had a good product, the latest technology in computer-based engineering-document management systems, their dream started badly. Because of the intense competition in the U.S. software market, they soon found themselves down to their last $250. Then the 1987 stock market crash and subsequent panic hit the U.S. economy and reduced their chances of attracting venture capital to nothing. Ciliv and Hillyard knew they had to generate some sales, but they also knew it was impossible to market their software in the United States without any resources.

They had to find *some* market. So, as novice owners of a nearly broke company, they took their last few dollars and bought a plane ticket to Europe, where they believed they would find demand for their technology. The Turkish-born Ciliv planned to begin selling in Italy because he believed that the Italians would be open minded and spontaneous about adopting a new product. His instincts were right. After two months, Ciliv closed a deal with Italcad, a large Italian distributor of computer-aided-design and computer-aided-manufacturing equipment. According to Ciliv, it wasn't a hard sell. The Italian firm was supplying similar software and could see the appeal of NovaSoft's product within its customer base. Italcad gave NovaSoft $100,000 up front and, within weeks, had placed NovaSoft products with Fiat. Within two years, NovaSoft had established distributor relations in Italy, Belgium, and Germany.

NovaSoft then moved on to the Pacific. Having no idea whom to approach as a strategic partner in Japan, Ciliv phoned the Japanese consulate in Boston, asked for a list of companies servicing the engineering market, and wrote to the president of the firm that seemed most promising. On the basis of the cold call, Tokyo-based Mutih-Kogyo sent a team of planners to Boston. The Japanese firm signed a three-year contract with NovaSoft and arranged for NovaSoft to modify the product for the Japanese market at Mutih-Kogyo's expense.

While Ciliv didn't return home for three years, NovaSoft's bank account was filled with foreign revenues. By 1992, the firm had forged strategic alliances in fifteen countries that spanned South America, Australia, Europe, and the Far, Middle, and Near East. As NovaSoft added partners overseas, its credibility grew at home, and in late 1992, venture capitalists began calling. By this time, Ciliv and Hillyard could afford to hire a seasoned marketer and sales force for their home market (Robert A. Mamis, "Not So Innocent Abroad," *Inc. Magazine* archives, http://www.inc.com).

While companies usually develop their domestic markets first and then expand internationally, here is a situation where overseas sales financed a firm that didn't yet have the resources to compete at home. A weak market at home is not a reason to avoid global expansion. In this situation, what looked like hamburger in the crowded U.S. market won recognition as steak abroad.

... TO COUNTERACT YOUR DOMESTIC AND INTERNATIONAL COMPETITION

We are now competing in a global marketplace. If you do not capitalize on market opportunities in global markets, your competition will. In developing and emerging growth markets, early market entry often commands dominant market share. Once the government has signed large infrastructure projects with your competitors and once consumers have switched their brand preferences from local brands to those of your competitors, you will have a difficult time not only entering the market but also meeting the additional challenge of facing your competitors in global markets, in addition to your domestic market. Alternatively, this is your opportunity to compete against your international competitors on their "turf." This experience will give you additional insight into adaptation of your products to other international markets.

... TO CONTINUE TO ATTRACT HIGH-QUALITY PERSONNEL

Today's youth is educated in a global economy. Firms that can offer international experience are very attractive to young university graduates. As our economy becomes more global—with global financial markets, telecommunications, transportation systems—firms that lack a global presence will be at a strategic disadvantage in the next millennium. With these reasons for going global, it is important to focus your efforts as follows.

... TO STAY ABREAST OF YOUR CUSTOMERS ... AND YOUR SUPPLIERS

When your customers go global, you should follow them. In this day and age, your customers are more likely to be exporting their products or seeking sourcing for their products from international markets.

Taking Your Suppliers Abroad

Wink Fasteners is a distributor of corrosion-resistant fasteners, nuts, bolts, and screws based in Richmond, Virginia. Only five years old, the company is active, not only domestically, but also internationally, sourcing products from overseas markets and selling them in the United States, Europe, Latin America, and the Middle East. According to Janet Winkelman, president of Wink, about 7 percent of the firm's business is sourced from Taiwan, Malaysia, and Canada; her goal is to increase this volume to 40 percent. Winkelman doesn't view global expansion as an alternative to domestic business but as a means of strengthening her relationships with the suppliers she deals with domestically. As a distributor, when she increases her foreign sales volume to 40 percent, she will be guaranteeing her suppliers a significant amount of overseas business that would be difficult for them to develop directly ("Doing It Your Way in the Global Market," *Industrial Distribution*, September 1996).

... TO CAPITALIZE ON THE CHANCE TO JOIN FORCES

You can gain a competitive edge by cultivating international contacts with scientists, researchers, marketers, and so forth. GenPharm International indicates that their company will have a competitive edge over others in the young field of transgenic animal technology as a result of their twenty people working in Mountain View, California, and twenty-five working in Leiden, in the Netherlands, and $10.7 million in U.S. and European venture capital (copyright 1996, 1997 Goldhirsh Group, Inc.). Polymer Solutions, a joint venture between GE Plastics, a manufacturer of engineered plastics, and Fitch Richardson Smith, an international product design company, represents what could be the wave of the future for small start-ups; joining forces with an international company to capitalize on people, offices, equipment, and contacts that are already in place (copyright 1996, 1997 Goldhirsh Group, Inc.).

... TO BALANCE OUT SWINGS IN YOUR DOMESTIC MARKET

International markets may offer a way to counterbalance the swings and cycles in your local economy. When it's winter in your market, it may be summer in another, thus evening out the sales cycle for some products. For example, a manufacturer and distributor of a foldable fabric-and-metal shade for car windshields chose to expand its product marketing to Europe, Japan, and Australia for this reason. They were able to capitalize on the summer buying cycle by retailers in the United States (June–August) and also in Australia (December–January).

Entering international markets is like learning to walk on two legs. Firms that depend only on their domestic markets cede a certain amount of control over their business to the vagaries of the domestic economy. Your domestic market may turn sour. And if your sales at home are strong, so much the better; they should be a springboard, not a straitjacket.

Your Domestic Market May Go Sour

The Hiller Group, in Tampa, Florida, originally sold specifically treated coal for ferro-alloy smelting to America's leading metal producers. At the end of the 1980s, world metal prices dropped and Hiller's domestic customers cut production. To survive, Hiller had to look abroad. Last year, exports made up half of its $25 million in sales. Nevertheless, when Hiller sought financing to cover the 180-day credit terms of its export sales, it was turned down repeatedly by domestic banks and government agencies. Eventually, it got the support it needed from Mitsubishi Trading in New York, which agreed to provide trade credit and to arrange for all shipping ("America's Little Fellows Surge Ahead," *Business Week,* May 13, 1993, p. 60).

WHAT'S THE UPSHOT?

If you look at the reasons to go global listed above, you'll note that each one addresses a basic need of every business:

- To find customers
- To protect market share
- To attract the best employees
- To keep customers
- To upgrade technology and practices
- To survive market swings

If your firm faces any of these challenges, global expansion is an option that you may want to consider. This realization brings you to the first step.

How Do You Go Global?

Step 1: Develop a Global Mindset

The first barrier that you and your firm will face is *making the decision* to market your products globally. This step is very real and is all the bigger for being psychological. You can't hire a consultant to do it for you. You can't accomplish it by forming a task force to study the matter. You just have to do it. Once that decision is made, the rest will fall into place.

During 1989, I made the decision to take my business global. From that point on, I traveled to nearly eighty countries to set up affiliate production and sales or distribution offices. While I didn't have all the answers to every technical question about doing business in each of these countries, and while I didn't speak all the different languages, *I had the courage to make the decision—and just do it.* If you try to think of all the complexities of marketing your products and services throughout the world, you'll never do it. You'll become so overwhelmed with the technicalities of the situation that you will delay or even not bother to sell your products into foreign markets.

More particularly, your global mindset should consist of the following:

1. A decision (and commitment) to sell your products in international markets
2. A choice of one or two product lines that you believe have potential overseas
3. A choice of "international champion" within your company
4. A mental time frame for your first export sales
5. A mental picture of how you will service this business

Step 2: Determine Whether Your Products Have Global Potential

I have two pieces of advice in this area:

1. Do your homework.
2. Conduct cost-efficient market research.

There are two phases of market research: phase 1, preliminary market research; and phase 2, in-depth market research.

Phase 1: Preliminary Market Research

Preliminary market research is necessary to accomplish the following:

1. Determine which regions and countries have the potential for your products
2. Identify the local competition—their products, prices, and so forth
3. Determine the distribution channels
4. Determine whether you can profitably export and distribute your products in the countries you are targeting

Phase 1 market research is a relatively low cost way to minimize your risk in international markets. The more comprehensive the research you perform in this phase, the fewer costly mistakes you will make and the greater the dividends you will reap, particularly in emerging markets. The following are some of the critical questions you should answer and some suggestions for obtaining the data.

1. What is the market potential (size) for your products?

   - Does this country need your product(s)?
   - Is that need currently being met?

2. Who and where are the customers; for example, what is the country's demographic profile?
3. What are the competing products—price, technology level, packaging, and so forth.

   - Is there room for your products?

4. What are the distribution channels?

   - Can you get your products sold and delivered?

5. What are the risk factors?
6. What are the local tariffs and trade regulations?

   - Can you get your products in at a reasonable cost?

How to obtain phase 1 data.—Most of the data in phase 1, or preliminary, research can be obtained through public information sources. We have included a source list section at the end of this book to assist you in this effort. Much of the information can be obtained from the local embassy in your country, in addition to your local chamber of commerce, trade groups, outside consultants, and your state government. The Internet is also a source of information. We have also included an Internet section with web site locations in the source list section of this book.

Having been in the business of gathering this type of information for over a decade and a half, I have found that while public information provides a good snapshot of the market opportunity in a particular country, it only takes you so far. The next step is getting out and determining for yourself what the market opportunity is. You may wish to exhibit at a local trade show in the country or attend a trade mission sponsored by one of the state trade organizations or the commerce department of your country. These are cost-effective ways to test customer reactions to your products as well as good ways to make business contacts that can be valuable for future sales.

Phase 2: In-Depth (Field) Market Research

Having determined that there is a strong possibility that there is significant market demand and potential for your products and services in a country or a series of countries (a region), your next step is to conduct in-depth research that will provide you with the following information:

1. Customer attitudes and preferences toward your products or services
2. Accurate market sizing data—rural-urban breakdown demographics, distribution channels, and so forth
3. Product tests (feasibility studies) in the field
4. Pricing studies
5. Generation of a potential customer list
6. Identification of distributors, joint venture partners, strategic alliances, and so forth
7. Generation of a list of potential local representatives
8. Local site-location studies

How to obtain phase 2 data.—Phase 2 data are obtained purely through field research. This type of data is generated by feasibility studies or field market research studies. Clearly, this type of international field research is best conducted by a firm that has wholly owned or affiliate offices across the globe, in addition to *at least a decade of experience in these countries* (particularly the developing and emerging growth countries). Because this type of research is costly, it is important to first determine an approach to your global expansion efforts.

STEP 3: SELECT YOUR GLOBAL APPROACH

Clearly, you wish to select high potential markets for your products, identify your competitors, develop a sound market entry strategy, and establish profitable operations in these countries. Your phase 1 research should generate a list of high potential countries for your products and services. Essentially, there are two different approaches to globalization.

Approach 1: Ready, Aim, Shoot

Based on your preliminary research, select one country and send a team of personnel to the country to initiate the following effort:

1. Make customer contacts
2. Develop distribution contacts
3. Meet with governmental and local trade representatives
4. Select representatives
5. Negotiate agreements

This is a very focused, targeted approach. The advantages to this approach are that you will concentrate your efforts on one country and that you can use the country as a test market for similar countries in the same region—for example, within Asia, Latin America, Europe, or the Middle East. But remember: Each country is different, and you should avoid drawing conclusions between countries within a region. Just because your products either succeeded or failed in one country within a region does not translate to other countries within that region.

On the other hand, most medium-size and small firms have limited time and resources (both human and capital). Their concentration of efforts on one country can tie up resources that could be used to explore market opportunities in other countries. As a result, some firms opt for the "shotgun" approach.

Approach 2: The "Shotgun"

For this approach, identify an *international general* within your company, and send him or her out to determine your product's potential in various regions and countries throughout the world. For cost-efficiency purposes, we recommend that your phase 1 research identify the market potential on a regional basis and then identify high-potential countries within these regions.

This type of "shoot, ready, aim" approach requires grueling travel by one person (or a limited team of people) to several countries within a region. They should spend one to two weeks in a country and should be prepared to spend twelve- to sixteen-hour days in discussions with potential customers, distributors, or affiliates. In short, they will attempt in a brief period of time to determine the market feasibility for your products in a country and then will move on to other countries in the region. At the end of this type of regional trip, your international general should be able to determine which country offers the best location for a regional headquarters. Equally important, he or she should be able to determine whether you even need a regional headquarters.

The advantages of this approach are the following:

- It accelerates your globalization effort.
- It enables you to gain the perspective of the market opportunity in several countries on a global basis.
- It maximizes your resources on a regional basis.

The disadvantages are the lack of an in-depth understanding of a local market and the potential risk of rushing into a country and obtaining sales orders before you are ready to service these orders.

The decision between the ready, aim, shoot approach and the shotgun approach depends on the mindset of your CEO, the culture of your company, and the types of products and services that you will be exporting.

STEP 4: SELECT AN INTERNATIONAL CHAMPION

After you have selected your approach to globalization, you should identify someone, either yourself or your top sales or marketing person, to be your *international champion*. This person should be your champion for international growth. This is the person who should be sent to the initial country or series of countries to meet with potential customers, representatives, agents, affiliates, and partners. This person should plan on spending at least one to two weeks in a country to immerse himself or herself with the total market potential for your products and services in the country.

The only way to determine whether select countries are hot markets for your products or services is to get yourself over there and to sell the product. You can maximize your travel budget if you plan trips on a regional basis. However, do not assume that the countries within the region have similar markets, customers, preferences, or demand for your product. Also, be careful when granting an agent or distributor exclusive rights for a region. You can miss significant market opportunities on a country-by-country basis.

Your international champion should be able to standardize your sales presentation, yet adjust the sales pitch to the cultural nuances of each country. Some countries will require more time to digest the sales presentation of your products. While your products and services in your domestic market may be almost a commodity product, they may have significant uniqueness in some countries. Moreover, you may be able to command premium prices for these products in developing and emerging growth countries. In some countries where high prices are expected (for example, Japan), your lower prices may even scare potential buyers off!

STEP 5: KEEP YOUR MARKET ENTRY COSTS LOW

Your initial costs should consist of your travel expenses, communications, literature and promotion materials, and so forth. You should initially avoid the expense of leasing an office, hiring staff, or negotiating formal joint ventures. Your customers should have the expertise to handle your exports. They have been doing this for years. They should be able to instruct you how to handle letters of credit, customers, and freight forwarders. In your home country, you should locate a banker who has expertise in handling international letters of credit. There are several international freight forwarders and shipping facilitators who will be able to assist you in the shipping of your products.

You should not have to hire a staff of people to service your international orders until you cannot possibly handle the volume yourself. Typically, most firms start with one person dedicated to the effort, plus a telephone, a fax machine, and a travel budget.

STEP 6: MAINTAIN YOUR PRODUCT QUALITY AND SERVICE, SERVICE, SERVICE YOUR INTERNATIONAL ACCOUNTS

In many respects, once established, international accounts are more loyal to your brands and have more longer term relationships with suppliers than your domestic market. It is important to service your international distributors, customers, and affiliates. When you are competing in global markets, all you have is your reputation. While the world is a large place, your reputation for your products and services (either good or bad) can spill over into other countries within or outside of the region.

In addition, when you are competing on a global basis, you can learn not only from other cultures but from global competitors selling in that country or local market. You may find better ways of manufacturing, selling, distributing, and servicing your products from other cultures. This is a great opportunity to take these methods and export them back to your domestic operation.

STEP 7: STAFFING IN FOREIGN MARKETS

After you have developed sufficient sales volume in select countries, you may have a need to staff with a local manager to run the operation. All of the experience in this area points toward staffing with a local national from the country or a person who has lived and has done business in the country for at least fifteen to twenty years. This person should know all of the ins and outs of the country, the culture, the industry, and the products. Most important, this person should be highly motivated and provided with ample incentive to grow your business in that country or region.

AND . . . SHOULD YOU BE CONTACTED BY A FOREIGN FIRM, CAPITALIZE ON THE OPPORTUNITY

Should your firm be contacted by a foreign customer, distributor, or supplier, capitalize on this opportunity. They have obviously done their research and selected your firm for various geographical, technology, or product attributes that you may have. These opportunities often enable small firms to leverage their research and development activities with European and Asian firms.

WHAT ARE THE RISKS OF GOING GLOBAL?

Clearly, the risks of going global entail the expenditure of the precious, and probably limited, resources (human and capital) of your firm. Aside from the risk of the loss of capital, many firms are concerned over the risk of having their ideas, products, and patents stolen or copied, with no legal recourse. This is a risk not only in foreign countries, but also in your domestic country. Imports continue to erode domestic market share throughout the world.

There is no such thing anymore as a captive domestic market—not in this day and age of global competition. The race for global markets and for global competitiveness will only continue into the next millennium. While there is the risk that your foreign distributors may not be able to reach their sales targets, the opposite is also a risk: that they will exceed their sales targets and you will have a situation that you may not be able to fulfill their demand for your product!

Realistically, international expansion failures can impact a company in three critical areas:

- *Finances*—Setting up an international operation can cost millions
- *Focus*—International expansion can take the focus off of the domestic market
- *Time*—International expansion is a long-term investment and takes time

Our research indicates that the three most common mistakes made by companies going international are:

- Failure to develop a good international marketing plan before starting an export business
- Insufficient commitment by top management to overcome the initial difficulties and financial requirements of exporting
- Insufficient selection of overseas distributors of your products or services

Quaker Oats, for example, lost millions when it withdrew its Snapple soft drink from the Japanese market. After investing heavily in the market, the company found consumers there would not buy the product for several simple reasons: the glass bottles were twice the size Japanese consumers were used to, the product was too sweet for the Japanese palate, and Japanese consumers did not feel comfortable with the sediment that collected at the bottom of the bottle (*World Trade Magazine*, June 1997, p. 92).

Chapter 2 will look at some small- and medium-size firms that went global, where they succeeded, and where they failed. Nothing is a better teacher than experience, and by examining the experiences of these pioneers, you can learn valuable lessons about minimizing your risk of failure in international markets.

ARE YOU READY TO BE A GLOBAL PLAYER?

DO YOU WANT TO BE?

The first step is to decide that you want to be a global player. Once you've made that decision, the next step is to just do it. You can come up with hundreds of excuses to avoid researching a market, selecting an international champion . . . you can resist every step of the way.

Of course, expanding globally is risky—expanding domestically is risky! Expanding your business into international markets involves having the courage to risk the precious resources of your firm. Along with courage, you must develop the stomach for international political risk and long-term results. In my experience, there are no quick hits in this global gold rush. Panning for gold in global markets entails research, planning, and taking action at the right time.

ARE YOU READY TO STAY?

Remember, once you enter a foreign market with your products or services, you have to stay there. Companies that have entered a market, withdrawn, and then tried to enter again have had a very hard time regaining any market position. International markets are like elephants: They do not forget anything. The Mexican market will remember that your firm abandoned the country when the peso dropped in value. If you are not ready to make the kind of commitment necessary, you should rethink your globalization efforts.

WHERE ARE YOU GOING?

Perhaps you are overwhelmed at the thought of globalizing your firm. This is understandable as we live in a complex and fast-paced world. With some cost-efficient preliminary market research, you should be able to develop a strategic opportunity grid. This type of analysis will enable you to synthesize your market research and to develop a framework from which to evaluate the market opportunity for your products on a country-by-country basis. Preliminary market research should yield the following information for your firm:

- Total sales of your product by country and by market sector
- Market penetration (estimated share of potential market already captured)
- Projected growth of your product sales (over the next five years)
- Factors driving your sales growth in select regions and differences between countries within these regions
- Current competitors and their shares of the market
- Competitive environment and basis on which vendors compete—value-added sales, system support, price competition, product quality
- Political and economic risk per country

With this information, you can then weight, rank, and score the importance of the data into a strategic opportunity grid (table 1). From this type of analysis, you will be able to determine the most attractive countries for exportation of your product.

HOW'S YOUR TIMING?

Timing and commitment to globalization are critical. Similar to a family's decision to have another child, there is never an optimum time. You have to make the plans to expand your business and follow through. On the other hand, should political and economic conditions of select countries change dramatically, of course it is prudent to delay your expansion efforts.

ARE YOU SURE?

If you still have doubts, stay domestic until you're sure going global is a good decision. When you expand globally, you will do it because it is best for your company. If your firm is just getting started or just becoming a regional company, you may need to concentrate your resources and capital. International expansion can fuel rapid growth that your firm cannot yet handle. Furthermore, you must consider all aspects of international expansion. International markets may not have the unique demand or niche for your product that exists in your own country. For example, convenience is a way of life in the United States, but many cultures see no advantage in fast foods or convenience stores. *Again, you must do your homework and research not only on other markets and cultures but on the driving forces of these markets and cultures.*

In spite of the risks of going global, opportunities abound for small-

Table I
Strategic Opportunity Grid

Countries (Europe)	Market Size			Market Growth			Market Penetration			Number of Competitors			Strength of Competition			Risk Factors						Total Score		
																Economic			Political					
	W	R	S	W	R	S	W	R	S	W	R	S	W	R	S	W	R	S	W	R	S	W	R	S
Austria																								
Belgium–Luxembourg																								
Denmark																								
Finland																								
France																								
Germany																								
Greece																								
Italy																								
The Netherlands																								
Norway																								
Portugal																								
Spain																								
Sweden																								
Switzerland																								
United Kingdom																								

W (Weighting):   The importance of the factor
R (Rating):   The rating of each country on the factor
S (Score):   The weighting multiplied by the rating

and medium-size firms seeking global expansion. While this book will not give you all the answers, it should give you snapshots of select countries and the market opportunities that may exist there. Use it as a guide for your global business expansion efforts. *Remember . . . information is power.* As you pan for profits in international markets, information on these markets can yield gold.

Chapter 2

HOW TO FIND GOLD IN FOREIGN MARKETS

The question that you now face is not whether to go global but how to maximize your success and minimize your risk in these markets. This chapter will look at some success stories—small and medium-size firms that went global—and draw general lessons from the experiences of these forerunners.

These lessons are applicable to companies of any size (one involves a one-woman operation) and to almost any country regardless of culture or location. Keep in mind, however, that when you start making specific plans, culture and location matter a lot. You will need to have market information for each individual country you hope to enter, and you will have to know how to adapt your products and services to each market you choose to enter. Underlying all of the lessons in this chapter, you should hear a steady drumbeat:

Do your homework . . . Do your research . . .

LESSON 1: DON'T LET THE SIZE OF YOUR COMPANY SCARE YOU OFF

While most small and medium-size firms recognize the attractiveness of foreign markets, many feel they don't have the size or scale to go global. In fact, the most important qualifications for global expansion are the willingness to do research and the patience to build solid relationships. There's no reason a small company can't succeed, and even excel, at these tasks. Don't let the size of your firm or the volume of your product sales deter you from expanding into global markets.

SMALL COMPANY GOES TO BIG CHINA

Conveyant Systems is tiny, but it's gobbled a 3 percent slice of the enormous Chinese market for digital private-branch-exchange (PBX) products, thanks to its 60 percent ownership position in Tianchi Telecommunications in Tianjin, China. With only sixteen employees, Conveyant Systems, based in Irvine, California, seems an unlikely match for China's immense market. Nonetheless, the small distributor of PC-based telecommunications is stealing some thunder from its larger, better known competitors such as Northern Telecom, Alcatel, Siemens, and AT&T.

According to Joe Leonardi, founder and president of Conveyant Systems, his willingness to cut a generous deal over licensing rights back in 1986 was the key to cutting out the big guys. He was able to put together a complicated joint venture—Tianchi—with Tianjin's local municipal government, the state-owned postal and telecommunications authority, and a local economic development group. During its first year, Tianchi's sales fell far short of the target. Leonardi responded with a proposed commission structure for the Chinese sales force, in addition to incentives to the factory workers. Sales of PBXs soon took off. Now, Tianchi sales offices stretch from Heilongjiang province in the northeast of China to Guangdong province in the south (*Inc. Magazine* archives, http://www.inc.com).

This is an example of not only a small firm with a big vision but of a firm that did its homework. Most businesses have been swept away by the enormous size of the Chinese market. Conveyant Systems wasn't because its research revealed a specific opportunity to participate in one of many government-driven development plans designed to build up China's infrastructure. This combination of small size, global mindset, and thorough research can be a winner. One caveat: even with all this going for him, it was Leonardi's creative approach (commissions and incentive plans) that finally pushed the joint venture to success.

GLOBAL MARKETS FOR A COOKIE COMPANY

For a very small U.S. company with a perishable food product to export around the world, it takes determination, commitment, and much hard work, as well as informed use of the trade services the U.S. government offers. This is how Diana's California Cookies succeeded in reaching an agreement to have its product made in Ireland and marketed throughout the European Union.

Diana Todaro, the one-person operation, developed the recipes for her gourmet, all-natural cookies in her own kitchen. Diana's cookies have been very successful in their native California market, selling over one million cookies in the first three months in 1991 and growing ever since.

For little or no cost, Todaro took advantage of U.S. Commerce Department services, developing a close rapport with the U.S. Export Assistance Center staff in California and participating in President Clinton's Conference on Investing in Ireland last year. Diana's California Cookies became the first company involved in the White House conference to achieve a joint-venture marketing agreement in Ireland, and Todaro credits the conference and the contacts she made with the Irish Food Board during a trade mission with bringing her together with Braycot Foods, the Irish bakery that will produce and sell her cookies in Ireland.

Braycot had been looking for an American cookie to sell in the Irish and European markets, and it believes that Diana's California Cookies are a very strong product whose health consciousness and palm tree/sun logo are instantly identifiable as American. Todaro is currently exploring exporting her cookies to the Middle and Far East and to South America (U.S. Commerce Department).

For Diana's California Cookies, success lay in Diana Todaro's ability to obtain international export information at virtually no cost in spite of the small size of her company and its limited resources.

LESSON 2: LEARN HOW TO (PROFITABLY) EXPORT YOUR PRODUCTS

Two of the biggest barriers to exporting are finding financing and getting paid. It's a challenge to line up enough financing to enable you to get through the export process. Exporting your products involves assuming the risk of currency fluctuations, collecting payments, and running the risk of political upheavals in foreign countries. Generally, it takes overseas customers longer to pay their bills. As a result, you will have to arrange for lines of credit, loan guarantees, and insurance programs. Organizations such as the Export-Import Bank in the United States have been criticized for being a banker for multinationals. In recent years, however, they have been increasing their share of business with small businesses.

As an exporter, you must be educated and gain experience in the process. The most common method of securing credit (in the United States) is the typical "letter of credit" (LOC), which can cost between $200 and

$300. These are best obtained through regional or money center banks. An alternative to the LOC may be to secure a certain percentage of the total bill paid up-front prior to executing any work against foreign contracts. This is particularly useful for firms in the service sector ("So You Think the World Is Your Oyster?" *Business Week Enterprise,* June 9, 1997, p. 1). Another problem is the fragmentation of the U.S. banking industry. Most of the international trade expertise is concentrated in the big banks, not the local banks that most small companies use. Typically the largest banks focus on the most profitable deals.

Other firms seek the assistance of an agent or broker who can assist them in the export process. Here, you must be sure that you are aligned with someone who is reputable and that you can trust. Trading companies typically conduct their own market research and generally keep customers' lists a secret. They generally have numerous contacts, and they can be quite helpful. However, you must develop trust in these agents as pricing is generally "out of your hands." If you can locate a trading company that you can trust and can also help you with pursuing sales in select regions of the world, with minimal financial risk, you can have a "win-win" situation.

There are also several governmental organizations in your country that can assist in this effort. In the United States, there is an alliance among the Small Business Administration (SBA), the Commerce Department, and the Federal Bar Association, where new exporters can receive a free consultation with an international attorney drawn from the Export Legal Assistance Network (ELAN).

Given the relatively sad state of export financing, the following are some options to consider:

- Locate someone in your bank's international department, or find a bank that has one.
- Try the U.S. branches of foreign banks.
- Get Foreign Credit Insurance Association insurance (the FCIA is backed by Ex-Im Bank and administered by private insurance companies).
- Sell your product to an export trading company (while it will assume the hassles, you will realize lower margins).
- Check out your state's programs—or those of Ex-Im Bank's (some states such as California have aggressive and favorable export programs for smaller businesses).

- Look into alternative financing sources.
- Use another nation's program (some firms are reported to be trying Japan's new import promotion programs which are designed to reduce political tension by helping finance U.S. exports to Japan (Martha E. P. Mangelsdorf, "Unfair Trade," *Inc. Magazine,* April 1991, p. 28, *Inc. Magazine* archives, Inc. Online, ref. no. 04910281).
- Consider alternative financing mechanisms that have recently evolved from the private sector. Trading Alliance Corp., or TAC, is a New York trade finance merchant bank founded in 1988 from people who left Manufacturer's Hanover's nondefunct export trading company.

EXPORTING DOES PAY OFF

Lamb-Gray's Harbor Co., a manufacturer of equipment for paper mills, exports their products extensively. They report that as the dollar declined, the company's sales have soared from $27 million in 1987 to a record high of $120 million in 1990. While they initially used Ex-Im Bank, they eventually required outside financing from Canada, from their Export Development Corporation to help them with their growth in exports.

Quintiles Transnational Corporation, in Morrisville, North Carolina, analyzes drug-testing studies that pharmaceutical companies prepare for government agencies. The firm has grown rapidly as a result of their venture into international markets, as 35 percent of its business is now done outside of the United States. The firm has now evolved from a small U.S. professional service business to a multinational growth company. In 1986, the firm entered the European market by opening up an office in London. While the expansion cost more than $200,000 in fourteen months, it paid off. The firm has subsequently expanded to Dublin and to Frankfurt. Despite the difficulties they faced, they are further along than most young companies on the path to global business success (Martha E. P. Mangelsdorf, "Building a Transnational Company," *Inc. Magazine* archives, *Inc. Magazine* Online, March 1993, p. 92, ref. no. 03930921).

Gaining skill at exporting your products' profitability in global markets is a matter of experience. Unfortunately, both large and small companies had to start somewhere, at some point in time. Do not forget that everyone has to go through the same process. The only difference is the increased difficulty of smaller firms to obtain financing. After a while, it becomes the same process as processing your domestic orders. Persistence and patience are the key words to exports beginners.

LESSON 3: KNOW THE LAY OF THE LAND

Firms are often carried away by the magic of a foreign country. Several firms have sought global expansion as a "follow the leader" or "follow the competitor" syndrome or have "jumped on the bandwagon" to enter hot or highly publicized markets. My words of advice, particularly in developing and emerging markets are: *Look before you leap.*

Did you know, for example, that while the dynamic young executive in your organization may be a rising star, you should never, *ever* send this youngster to handle things in China? The Chinese respect older, seasoned professionals; this is part of their culture. When doing business anywhere, you need to blend in culturally.

Your products and services must also be adapted to blend in with the local culture.

A classic—and very serious—mistake is to staff foreign operations with your domestic personnel. Should you plan to hire staff, you should hire local nationals to work within the management ranks of your company.

However, you need to mind the labor laws. Many countries have strict severance provisions that require employers to compensate certain terminated employees for three months or more. If possible, you should hire temporary personnel and sign them on full-time after a probation period. Consider conducting background investigations. In Europe, it is easy to do a quick criminal check on potential hires at both the local and the national levels.

Trust plays a very large role in any overseas employment relationship. To ensure that trust, give the local operator a minority ownership take or reward tied to performance (Donna Fen, "International: Opening Up an Overseas Operation," *Inc. Magazine* archives, *Inc. Magazine* Online, June 1995, p. 89, ref. no. 06950892).

And don't ignore the real estate considerations of a country. Small to mid-size firms, in particular, often neglect to include the country's real estate as part of their global expansion plan. To achieve a competitive advantage, they should include the impact of the local real estate market in the operations of their business.

LOCATION, LOCATION, LOCATION

A Benelux company wished to establish a presence in New York to market and distribute its chocolates, in addition to the marketing of their products in other states in the U.S. market. Because they had been importing to various locations in the United States, including New York, they felt confident in their knowledge of the market and to find a site and negotiate for a U.S. headquarters sales office and distribution center. As a result, they did not seek the advice of a local real estate consultant.

Through a Chamber of Commerce and Industry seminar, they met a consultant with inside knowledge about the local market. A plan was drawn up by the consultant that addressed the local business practices, economic incentives, access both physical and electronic, appropriate skilled workforce, lifestyle issues, and transportation. Sites were then identified to meet the predetermined criteria.

The result was an easier and quicker decision process with a lease obligation that saved the company 50 percent of their original cost estimate. These local productivity factors enabled the operation to quickly build a reputation for cost efficiency and fast order turnaround in the United States. As a result, the first year sales growth target was achieved in six months. The U.S. local manager credited this performance in part to access by transportation and the work ethic of the labor force. Costs were minimized. Municipal incentives and tax advantages were an additional bonus (Gale I. Dinces).

International real estate decisions must be made cautiously to avoid costly errors. Although substantially lower prices and values may be attractive, you may not be able to achieve your business goals from the wrong side of the tracks. The trade-off for lower prices may be poor or no access to mass transit systems as at the United Kingdom's Canary Wharf. You should also consider whether the local workforce has a skill set appropriate to the needs of your particular operation. To make an informed decision, you need to assess the key drivers of your business and apply that knowledge to the local business environment in the target country.

LESSON 4: ADJUST YOUR EXPECTATIONS FOR PROFITS

Many firms take a short-term view with international expansion. Your expectations for sales, profits, market share and penetration, and global branding should be lengthened to allow for a long-term perspective in these markets.

LESSON 5: BUILD YOUR OWN SUPPORT NETWORK

When you are beginning and continuing to go global it is important to cultivate contacts at home to help you build your international business.

A HELPING HAND

Pavion Cosmetics, founded in 1980 (Nyack on the Hudson, New York), is a medium-sized manufacturer of color cosmetics for women. With 500 employees, Pavion is a major employer in Rockland County, New York. Exports account for 10–15 percent of their revenues and their international group has been recently charged with doubling their exports.

According to Karen Acker, President of Pavion's International Operations since 1990, "Pavion exported right from the beginning to the Middle East, South America, Europe, and Asia. We've sold to over 125 countries and we're currently active in about sixty to sixty-five countries." The company sells primarily through distributorships, and Ms. Acker does a lot of travel and trade shows to ensure that the export goals are met.

One of the keys to their exporting success is their relationship with the U.S. Department of Commerce's International Trade Administration (ITA) in the local Westchester (New York) district office. In their early years of exporting, the ITA office was a big help in identifying distributors and prospective overseas customers. Ms. Acker credits the ITA with "actively being in place to support in terms of education, contracts, and networking, in addition to Ex-Im Bank and export management companies." They were also there in problem times such as Mexico's peso devaluation and resolving a problem with labeling one day before a product was to be exported.

YOU MAY HAVE TO TEAM UP WITH YOUR COMPETITORS

Denmark is a model of this system. In 1989, Denmark's small businesses started to form into teams of three or more companies working together to create new brands, expand product lines, and conquer the export market. Within eighteen months, 3,500 businesses—from textile and furniture manufacturers to lawyers and landscaping companies—were operating in those networks. The results were impressive. For the first time in thirty-two years, Denmark reversed its negative trade balance with Germany. Even more remarkable, it was the only European country to do so, enabling it to claim title to the world's highest per capita trade balance in 1992 (J. Lipnack and J. Stamps, "The Best of Both Worlds," *Inc. Magazine* archives, March 1994, p. 33, ref. no. 03940331).

Another successful example of this kind of cooperation is Tri-State Manufacturers' Association of Minnesota. In the association's buying cooperative, companies that are competitors team up and jointly purchase manufacturing supplies and sophisticated training. If each company were to do ISO 9000 training alone, it would cost $900 per employee plus travel costs. By jointly importing a trainer, the cooperative cut per employee costs to $300, with minimal travel costs (J. Lipnack and J. Stamps, "The Best of Both Worlds," *Inc. Magazine* archives, March 1994, p. 33, ref. no. 03940331).

In addition to your home network, you should be continually building your international network of suppliers, distributors, export agency companies, international partners, etc. This global or international network of people "*will be there for you in the long term*" if you cultivate and nurture these relationships through continued communications, correspondence, and mailings.

LESSON 6: LEARN THE GOLDEN RULES OF INTERNATIONAL BUSINESS

RULE 1: KEEP IT SIMPLE

Make sure that people at all levels of your company know your global strategy. It should not be a surprise to them when they have to ship product to Mexico or Thailand. If you can't explain your global strategy in simple terms to the troops, then it is probably not a good one.

RULE 2: LEVERAGE THE VALUE OF YOUR PRODUCTS IN THE GLOBAL MARKETPLACE

While your product may be a commodity back home (in the domestic market), it may be the latest technology in another country. In addition to different time zones throughout the world, there are also different "decade zones" of economic development between regions and countries.

RULE 3: PAY ATTENTION TO THE LANGUAGE

You must research and find out what is appropriate in a particular country. When Pepsi first went to Germany with the advertisement "Come

Alive with Pepsi" it was translated as "Come out of the Grave with Pepsi." In addition, Schweppes was not happy when their tonic water was translated into Italian as *Il Water*, "the bathroom."

RULE 4: REMEMBER, IT'S A SMALL WORLD WITH A LONG MEMORY

Countries in Latin America have long-term memories. If you have a problem and pull out of a Latin American market, it will be hard to recover and reenter later. This "disease" can also spread to other countries in the region, as many of the countries are connected through trade pacts (Mercosur, NAFTA, etc.). This underscores the need for thorough market research to avoid marketing disasters since the recovery period can often take decades.

Chapters 3 to 8 are organized by region and by country. Each chapter gives a detailed overview of the region, followed by separate country profiles written by marketing and business development experts from each country.

The overviews will direct you to the market opportunities for your products and services within the particular region under discussion—Asia Pacific, Western Europe, Central and Eastern Europe, Latin America, the Middle East and Africa, and the United States—and the country profiles will give you advice from local experts on the various countries. In these firsthand accounts, you will read about many more successes—and not a few failures—as companies have faced the global marketing challenge.

ABOUT THE CONTRIBUTING AUTHOR

Gale I. Dinces
Commercial Real Estate Ltd.
74 Rye Ridge Road
Harrison, New York 10528
Phone: 1 800 GDINCES
Fax: 914-967-1045

Gale I. Dinces is a real estate advisor nationally and worldwide. She aids companies in change. For the operation, she develops a competitive advantage through her methodology combining strategic planning, strategic information intelligence, and creative real estate expertise. Her training includes an MBA from the Stern School of Business of New York University. During that time, she consulted to General Electric Company, providing competitive analysis and strategic intelligence information. She held strategic planning, new business development, and turnaround positions at American Can Company/Primerica/TravelersGroup, James River Corporation, and Metropolitan Insurance Company. She established **Commercial Real Estate Ltd.** in 1993 after six years of experience at a privately held New York City major owner/manager tenant representation real estate brokerage firm, and also a national real estate investment and corporate services firm.

Chapter 3

ASIA PACIFIC

The Engine of the Next Millennium

THE FASTEST GROWING MARKET IN THE WORLD

The Asia Pacific region is the fastest growing market in the world. By the year 2000, it will account for one-quarter of the world's GNP. As per capita income follows the growth of GNP in these countries, sizable and fast-paced consumer and industrial markets are emerging—with unlimited potential as we enter the next millennium.

During the postwar period, we thought of the "West" or the "Western" economies of the United States and Western Europe as being the premier industrialized, high-technology, consumer economies. During this period, the "East" was defined as developing and emerging-growth economies. Clearly, Japan led the way in developing.

It was not until the late 1970s and early 1980s, however, that Western firms realized the region's market potential. Japanese high-quality products coupled with their successful penetration of established U.S. and Western European markets gave the Western world a loud wake-up call.

The West was particularly surprised to find that rapid economic and social change was not confined to one country. Japan was soon followed by "the four tigers of Asia": South Korea, Singapore, Hong Kong, and Tai-

---

Many of the countries in the Asia Pacific region are tied to the "we" culture. Much of the decision making in these countries is based on group consensus. Businesses, distribution channels, policy decisions, consumer attitudes, and preferences are all affected. Keep this in mind when expanding your business to the region. Understanding the culture should be a part of your strategic marketing plan for the region and for specific countries within the region.

wan. These economies have consistently grown at annual rates in excess of 6 to 7 percent during the 1980s and well into the 1990s. They have developed reputations as centers for technology, distribution, consumption, and growth. Health care, highways, water systems, and energy are just some of the areas where the Asia Pacific nations have developed, or plan to.

During the early 1990s, countries such as China, India, Thailand, Malaysia, and Indonesia experienced similar rapid growth rates. Political stability, privatization, and infrastructure investment have fueled the growth of these economies. Specifically, these nations have experienced annual growth rates between 7 and 12 percent during the decade.

Combined, China and India represent a potential consumer market in excess of two billion people. Thailand, Malaysia, and Indonesia have now become the next set of "tigers." The dynamic growth in the region led to the founding of the Association of Southeast Asian Nations (ASEAN) to focus on intra- and interregional trade issues. The group consists of Singapore, Thailand, Indonesia, Malaysia, the Philippines, and Brunei. ASEAN is the United States' fourth largest trading partner.

The much larger Asia Pacific Economic Cooperation (APEC) was formed in 1989. This organization began as an informal forum for twelve trading partners in the Asia Pacific region to discuss trade and economic issues. In time it grew to eighteen members on both sides of the Pacific: Australia, Brunei, Canada, Chile, China, Darussalam, Hong Kong, Indonesia, Japan, Malaysia, Mexico, New Zealand, Papua New Guinea, the Philippines, Singapore, South Korea, Taiwan, and the United States. Its members account for about 38 percent of the world's population, half the world's GNP, and about 46 percent of the world's total import-export trade ("Strengthening Diversity," *International Business,* November 1996, p. 18).

The two richest members, Japan and the United States, have per capita GNPs ranging from 30 to 65 times those of China and Indonesia, the two poorest member economies. Approximately 70 to 80 percent of the total APEC exports are traded within the region. APEC can be expected to have several effects on business.

First, trade liberalization within APEC will reduce tariffs and nontariff barriers. As a result, companies will have better access to Asian markets for products and services. In addition, the organization wants to increase business mobility between countries, institute common product testing procedures, and harmonize customs procedures. These actions are designed to cut costs, decrease cycle time, and improve the efficiency of business ("Strengthening Diversity," *International Business*, November 1996, p. 18).

During the early 1990s, the Chinese Economic Area (CEA) emerged as one of the largest as well as most important and dynamic organizations in the region. The CEA consists of China, Taiwan, and Hong Kong. Taiwan and Hong Kong are two of the biggest trading partners and investors in China. The CEA is the largest trading partner of the United States. Most spending in these countries is for infrastructure projects. Competition is intense for this market as the United States, the European Union, and Japan compete for market share.

THE GOLD RUSH IN THE ASIA PACIFIC

The CEA is somewhat similar to the "gold rush" in the United States during the nineteenth century. China has a vast land and human resource base. Both Taiwan and Hong Kong have poured significant sums of investment capital into China to develop manufacturing facilities and capitalize on the country's lower labor costs. Clearly, firms in both Taiwan and Hong Kong have the capital, technology, and expertise to invest, manage, and grow these businesses for exporting their products throughout the world. Success is the product of the strong capital and technology base that Taiwan and Hong Kong have together with the ethnic homogeneity of all three members.

China should become the economic engine for the region. Its economy will benefit from worldwide investment coupled with increased imports. While India has recently lowered its tariffs and increased the rate of privatization, development may be slower because of perceived cultural barriers. The future may see the rapid growth of other Asia Pacific countries that have a lower labor-cost base. Countries such as Vietnam, Laos, and Cambodia will become the manufacturing backyard of the more affluent Asia Pacific countries. This assumes political stability as a prerequisite for economic growth.

It is interesting to view the strategy of the two mature economies in the Asia Pacific region—Japan and Australia. Japan continues to invest in the region and to pursue a strategy of regional market dominance (from an investment and product/market standpoint). The strategic issue remains one of definition: Will Japan identify itself with the West as a mature, developed, and industrialized economy, or will it continue to seek leadership of the Asia Pacific region?

Australia has made the strategic commitment to identify with the region and position itself as an attractive regional headquarters location for management of U.S. and Western European businesses. However, while firms have historically selected Singapore, Hong Kong, and Australia for their Asia Pacific headquarters or as springboards into Asia, many firms are now jumping in and setting up facilities directly in countries like China and Thailand.

MARKET OPPORTUNITIES IN THE ASIA PACIFIC

Market opportunities abound in the Asia Pacific region. With the exception of the developed economies of Japan, Singapore, Hong Kong, and Australia, the Asia Pacific compares in economic growth to the post–World War II era for the United States and Western Europe. From the 1950s to the early 1970s, these economies stressed infrastructure development. This included investment in highways, medical and health care systems, energy projects, waste management systems, business and residential construction, telecommunications, and transportation systems.

It should be noted that as per capita income rises above the level needed for food, housing, and transportation systems, a consumer economy develops. This means a strong demand for consumer goods (durable and nondurable), food products, health and beauty aids, apparel, entertainment, tourism, and related goods and services. At the same time, a service sector develops to meet the strong demand for financial services, medical services, legal services, business consulting, etc.

The same is happening with the Asia Pacific countries. They are demonstrating a relatively strong demand in nearly all these areas: infrastructure, consumer goods, and services. While this presents an opportunity for the firm with plans to expand into the region, opportunity also presents challenges:

- What are the best market opportunities for my products by country? . . . Today? . . . Five years from now?
- Do I have to establish a regional headquarters for distribution to several countries, or should I set up distributors in each country?

- Can my products be marketed across borders in this region, given the significant cultural differences between the countries?
- Can I leverage brands across the region?
- How do I service my customers in this fast-paced region?
- How do I monitor the changing competitive situation in the region (on a country-by-country basis)?
- Given the high cost of doing business in the region, how do I minimize my market entry costs?

Given sufficient preliminary and in-depth market research, firms should be able to answer these questions before committing sizable resources. And just as important, these questions should be addressed within the context of the following challenges and potential problems.

Barriers and Pitfalls to Market Entry Within the Asia Pacific

These are the most common mistakes made by firms seeking market entry into the Asia Pacific region:

1. Assuming That the Asia Pacific Countries Have Similar Cultures

The cultures of the countries in the Asia Pacific region are significantly different from one another. Even within a single country such as China, there are vast ethnic differences in the people throughout the country—e.g., between provinces or urban and rural populations—coupled with hundreds of different dialects. Clearly, while the three members of CEA essentially have a "Chinese" population, they also have vastly different cultures.

For openers there are obvious differences in political structures. China is communistic and Taiwan capitalist while Hong Kong is unique unto itself. Further, the "Chinese" consumer or businessperson in each of these markets has significantly different preferences, a different socioeconomic frame of reference, and even different value systems.

Not only do the countries of the Asia Pacific have vastly different cultures, they also have a long history of wars, economic struggles, and even hatred between cultures. Do not assume that because your product sells well in Japan, it will do the same in South Korea, Hong Kong, or Thailand.

While many of these countries have joined together in APEC, they nevertheless still compete with each other on economic, ethnic, and cultural issues. Failure to research and recognize these differences can result in market entry failure.

2. *Assuming That You Can Package and Advertise as If Beijing Were Peoria*

Prior to formal market entry, you need to test your product for local advertising, product usage, packaging, and so forth. For example, homes are very small in Japan, China, and other Asian societies. Household durable goods suitable for use in the United States are likely to be too big for homes in the Asia Pacific. This holds true for other consumer goods and food products.

3. *Failure to Research the Demographics of Each Country*

With the exceptions of Japan and Australia, Asian countries have relatively young populations, which translates into emerging, large consumer economies in the immediate future. This factor should have a major bearing on household formation, telecommunications, health care, consumer goods, financial services, transportation, education, and just about every facet of life in a modern society. Your country market research should detail both current and future market potential.

4. *Lacking an Efficient Distribution System in the Country and in the Region*

Distribution is very complex in the Asia Pacific region. Many of the firms are family owned. As such, distributors will distribute not just a line of goods—say, consumer electronics—but they will distribute consumer goods, industrial goods, and a mixture of different products. Moreover, markets such as Hong Kong are known as places where goods enjoy limited patent protection. Independent dealers have been known to disappear with products.

As a result, you must establish a distribution network with great care. It is important to invest the time, money, and effort in establishing distribution channels that you can monitor, evaluate, and trust.

For example, the Chinese rely on the system of *guanxi* ("relationships"). In 1987, Xerox entered China as a sales organization and developed a successful dealer network based on friendships. Xerox was reported to have captured a significant share of this market as a result of careful monitoring of its distribution system. Other firms such as Bausch & Lomb, Revlon, Max Factor, Heinz, and Maxwell House have reported successful distribution in China.

5. Ignoring the Local Competition

Many firms thoroughly research and monitor their local and global competitors in their domestic markets and in the Asia Pacific countries. What they neglect to research are their local competitors. In many respects, Asian firms have caught up with the West in terms of technology and are rapidly developing products for their own cultures. You ignore this fact at your own risk. It is easier for a local firm to develop a product for its own culture than for a firm to adapt its product for another country. You should either contract out research in this regard or have your local staff monitor the local competitive products.

6. Failing to Adapt Products to the Asia Pacific Countries

Depending on the product or service provided, you most probably will have to adapt your business to the local culture. Again, market research and product testing are critical prior to expensive advertising and distribution campaigns.

7. Assuming That One Country Is One Market

A country like China is incredibly diverse by region and lifestyle. In short, what sells in the city won't necessarily in the countryside, and what's popular in the north may cause barely a ripple in the south or east. On top of that, the economy is still run by bureaucrats, and there are thousands of underdeveloped distribution channels. Your market research should take these factors into consideration.

8. Operating on Trade Stereotypes

The literature has been rampant with the difficulties of market entry into the Japanese market. Clearly, while Japanese consumers have distinct preferences, their tastes have become more Westernized. To enter the Japanese market, you must thoroughly understand (1) the culture and society, (2) business practices, and (3) the market and distribution system. While the Japanese are a tough sell, you must make a long-term commitment and modify your products to the culture. For example, Japanese youths are eager for brands like Levi Strauss and Marlboro. You must also stay abreast of the trade situation with Japan. The government appears ready to start relaxing restrictions.

9. Entering the Market Without Prior Research on Governmental, Trade, and Legal Issues

Within the Asia Pacific region, trade regulations can change daily. One good example is South Korea, which has significantly altered its trade policies. During the 1980s, the country initiated a five-year economic plan that included economic deregulation. The country has the potential for a dynamic consumer market, and its current per capita income has fueled the hunger of its middle class for household items and leisure products. South Korea also has launched a new anticorruption campaign and increased its liberalization of domestic and international trade.

10. Depending on Advertising Campaigns That Worked in the West

Comparative or competitive advertising (comparing your brands to those of your competitors) does not work in the Asia Pacific region. In fact, such advertising is shunned in China, Hong Kong, Taiwan, Japan, and the Philippines. Also, ads that brag or that imply "we do everything better" are likely to fail in Asian countries. Additionally, you should check the translation of Western humor into Asian advertisements. For example, telecommunication ads that tell you to "move before your phone bill arrives" would be translated as dishonorable in most Asian countries.

A Recommended Approach to Market Entry Into the Asia Pacific

Success in the Asia Pacific depends in large part on preparation done prior to expensive travel, business negotiations, and investment in new markets. My experience is that companies must first do the necessary groundwork.

This entails reading and researching as much as possible regarding the country, the competitors, the business and trade environment, etc. Attending to the following recommendations will help minimize the chances of failure:

1. Change your mindset. Do not view the Asia Pacific market as a pan-Asian market.
2. Conduct market research country by country. Specifically focus on the marketing message and packaging concepts.
3. Thoroughly assess the cultural differences between and within Asia Pacific countries.
4. Thoroughly research distribution channels so you understand the problems and opportunities they pose within and between countries.
5. Continue to monitor changing trade regulations and changing per capita income (the barometer for growth of consumer product demand) in each of the countries you do business in.
6. Do as much research as possible and try to set up appointments before making a trip. Travel to and from, and within, the Asia Pacific region is very expensive. Allow for at least an extra week or two to extend your trip to negotiate with distributors.
7. Do not feel pressured to make any decisions on the first trip. When in Asia, you will feel the fast pace of business negotiations and economic activity. It can be very disconcerting at first.
8. Take time with your negotiations. The businesspeople of the Asia Pacific pride themselves on long-term relationships. Plan to make at least two trips a year for the first three years to demonstrate continued support for the region and your distributors.
9. Always pay your bills on time. This is a region which moves quickly, and honor drives business decision and relationships. Timely payment will make or break the business relationship.
10. Closely monitor the distribution and patent protection of your products. In the Asia Pacific region, copyright, patent, and other legal product protection mechanisms have not been developed or enforced at the same level as in the West.
11. Plan to run a training program in many of these countries. Since the Asia Pacific region has a relatively young population, it is short of experienced managers in many fields.
12. Check to ensure that all advertising and communications regarding your products and services adhere to the cultural values of the specific countries.

AUSTRALIA
AUSTRALIA NO LONGER LIVES OFF THE SHEEP'S BACK

Similar in some ways to the United States, Australia is often mistakenly assumed to be a clone of the United States. After all, both are lands of diverse regions, ethnicity, climates, and markets. And yet . . . Melbourne has the second largest population of Greeks in the world after Athens, and Chinese has overtaken Italian, Greek, and Arabic to become Sydney's second largest language after English. Better to consider Australia on its own terms.

The Australian government's foreign investment policy is framed and administered with a view to encouraging foreign investment and ensuring that such investment is consistent with the needs of Australia. The basic condition underlying the shaping and conduct of Australia's foreign policy is that Australia is a significant middle-level power with a strong Asia-Pacific orientation.

So here we are, a vast land, a small population, and numerous multinationals fighting for market share. Why market to Australia?

Australia is a country rich in natural resources and is a major exporter of agricultural commodities, fuels, and minerals. It is also a good base for entering the Asian marketplace, where more than 73 percent of merchandise exports from Australia went to Asia Pacific economies. In fact, organizations seeking to establish manufacturing operations in Australia have sought export markets to use excess production capacity, and what better markets to serve than Asia?

Further, Australians have a high adaptation of new technology. In 1996, 56 percent of Australian homes had computers, 18 percent modems, 20 percent Internet access, and 10 percent pay TV, which was launched only the year before (David Keig, "It's about to Explode," *Ad News*, February 28, 1997, p. 32). In fact, Australia has the second highest number of computers per capita in the world, after the United States, and the third highest level of mobile phone subscribers per one hundred people. But don't jump to conclusions: Australia's high technology adaptation operates only if Australians see that there is a benefit. Adaptation of new technology for the sake of new technology will not operate here.

Australians also buy more magazines per capita than any other country—twelve million copies of the biggest selling magazines are bought every month by a population of only eighteen million. And sales are still increasing—up 17 percent in four years. Perhaps that (and the vora-

AUSTRALIA NOTES

- Business appointments are relatively easy to schedule as the people are friendly. Because of the travel distance to Australia, however, book appointments at least one month in advance, either by fax or by phone.

- Begin meetings with small talk about the weather, your travels, and so forth.

- Australians are direct. They do not find it difficult to say no. Don't be offended if they argue a point at a meeting or at dinner.

- Do not make exaggerated claims for your products or services. Australians appreciate modesty.

- Because Australia has a classless society, don't emphasize your academic credentials (if you do, you may be ridiculed). The individual, rather than the credentials, wins the business or trust of select distributors.

- Australians like responsiveness in business matters. On the other hand, it is offensive to continually fax a firm if you have not heard from them in days. Sometimes a call gets better results.

- Do not dictate timetables. This may offend an Australian firm forever. *Collaborate* on developing timetables for business deals and so forth.

- If you are invited for drinks or cocktails, it is customary for each individual to pay for a round of drinks. Don't miss your turn.

- Full names are used for initial greetings, but Australians are quick to use first names.

- While dress is generally informal, business dress is conservative, as in the United States.

- Australians are private. They will not discuss their families or invite you into their homes right away.

---

cious appetite for books, the Internet, and all things media) stems from Australia's geography and the apparent need to keep in touch with what's going on.

So how have companies succeeded and where have some failed in marketing in Australia?

MARKETING

Small Market in a Vast Land

The typical industry structure in Australia is two or three large firms competing on a national basis with local, regional, and niche players. As such, there are a number of marketing principles that need to be understood within this context.

First, because of Australia's relatively small market size, many marketing strategies, like market segmentation, should *in some cases* be applied only sparingly in Australia. Foreign car manufacturers have learned this lesson. In the car industry, while there is a need to offer a range of models to accommodate different types of buyers, applying total market segmentation simply does not work in Australia because of its population size. In fact, the more you segment, the smaller the production runs become and the higher the costs per unit. This became quite evident for Japanese car manufacturers and the local automotive industry.

Then there is retail. Foreign companies have overlooked some crucial differences between the markets of Australia and those of the United States and Europe. This is particularly evident in the new phenomenon of the superstore, which is certainly making its mark here (M. Houghton, "Invasion of the Category Killer," *Marketing Magazine,* November 1996). The cornerstone of the superstore concept is large population access.

Although Australians are concentrated in the major cities, these cities are far more spread out than most cities in the United States and Europe.

(For example, Sydney is the world's third largest city *in land area* after Tokyo and New York, yet it has a population of only four million.) As a result, Australians are being asked to travel farther to shop at superstores than, say, U.S. consumers. The problem is compounded by the Australian tendency to shop locally and a disinclination to travel to shop. Research has shown that Australian consumers do more local shopping, shop more often, and resist traveling more than ten minutes or seven kilometers to do their shopping (M. Houghton, "Invasion of the Category Killer," *Marketing Magazine*, November 1996).

The disparity between size and population in Australia is something foreigners must never forget but that they often ignore to their loss.

Understanding Consumer Taste

From superstores to fast foods, the problems can be similar. Not only is there the need for locality, but in foods there is the need to clearly understand consumer tastes.

The retail food business is an industry that is quite easy to enter or exit. Everyone eats; consequently, the consumer base is wide. With outlets ranging from top-of-the-range, high-class restaurants to cheap eateries, operations are also quite diverse. Large chains and national franchises compete against local independent outlets. One of the key elements of success in this highly competitive yet lucrative market is having strong customer identification and understanding consumer tastes.

A couple of years ago, a large U.S. fast-food chain decided to enter the Australian market. Fast-food sales were growing, as was the idea of franchising. McDonald's, Kentucky Fried Chicken, and others operated successfully and were well established in the marketplace. Now this U.S. fast-food chain was offering Mexican. Everyone likes Mexican. Yes? No.

Well there was a "slight" problem, the result of poor market research: Australian tastes are oriented toward Asian foods. As mentioned before, Australia's proximity to Asia is not just geographic. Many Asians have immigrated to Australia, and many Australians have traveled to Asia, developing a taste for Asian cuisines. This U.S. firm ignored the basic concept of international marketing— understanding the consumers' tastes. Result: it no longer operates in Australia. An expensive exercise when you consider the distance traveled and the funds spent to enter the market.

It is critical, as with any market anywhere in the world, that organizations do their research and gather as much intelligence as possible to enable them to enter the market with a strong sustainable advantage and a good strategy. And there is nothing smarter than using local expertise.

Direct Marketing: Meeting the Challenge

According to one of the largest direct marketing firms in Australia, K&D Bond Direct, Australians are very direct marketing responsive. In fact, Australians are often two or three times as responsive as their counterparts in the Northern Hemisphere. The only countries that appear to be as responsive as Australia are New Zealand and South Africa (I. Kennedy, "Tell the Media Where to Stick It!" *Best of Marketing II,* June 1991).

However, many internationally successful direct marketing organizations have assumed that in coming to the Australian market, they could build their databases in the same way they have done in other countries. In Australia, because the quality and supply of data are low (although improving), alternative strategies have to be used in order to build quality data from scratch. This has not prevented a number of companies from succeeding.

For example, Cellarmasters is the single largest wine outlet in the country. As a $50 million per annum business built out of direct marketing in eight years, it is one of the great success stories in marketing wine around the world.

Making Your Mark

Over the years, Australian companies have been very good at building images that are embedded in the culture, images that are difficult for foreign companies to move. In fact, there is no way that an overseas player can enter this "brand" market without an acquisition. Many large multinationals have learned this lesson the hard way. Although their brands may be strong in their own countries, they forget that it is consumer loyalty—built up over many years—that makes the brand.

We all know that you cannot compete head to head with a brand that has top market share—in Australia, for example, Speedo (swimwear), King Gee (work gear), Bonds (undergarments), and Arnotts (biscuits). Yet some international companies have tried just this, as in the classic case of Hanes versus Bonds. Hanes (an international company also involved in the undergarments market) tried to compete head-on with a campaign that attempted to identify it with Australians and the country. Good advertisements, good jingle, good campaign—but poor results. Average Australians were tied to their Bonds. They have been for generations.

Others have been smarter, purchasing the icon, as Campbell's did with Arnotts. However, this strategy, too, must be handled with care. Campbell's acquisition of Arnotts was seen by locals as a hostile takeover and was not well regarded. Australians, not surprisingly, love their icons. Beware the foreign invader who takes on a strong and successful home brand! This is the case in most countries.

FIND A CULTURAL FIT

To state the obvious, marketing is an important factor in doing business in any country. But what about some of the cultural issues that also highlight whether a company will succeed or fail in the Australian market? Read on.

Service or Servitude?

In general, Australian managers are tired of foreign management arriving in Australia and, based only on experience elsewhere, saying this model worked very well and that model made a lot of money; yet, when it comes to implementation, the foreign model is useless because of differences in work styles, labor costs . . . anything and everything.

For example, the American model of customer service is less successful when exported to Australia. Australians interpret customer service as servitude, and servitude is associated with the history of the convicts who first populated the country. So, whereas the United States is known for its high standards of customer service, getting Australians to accept and deliver this kind of service is a long battle. Australian workers don't like the idea of being cheerful servants!

The Age of Colonialism Is Over

Then there is the story of a large multinational that wanted all deals to be cleared with the head office back in the home country. It did not take long for the local businesspeople to realize that the company's people in Australia were not in charge and did not have full authority and autonomy. What kind of message did that give to the Australian business community?

What Does It All Add up To?

The important issue is cultural fit. *You need to think globally but act locally.* Localization is the cornerstone for doing business successfully in any country, and Australia is no exception.

Australians need to develop personal relationships with their contacts and counterparts. They like to know the "mettle of the man" they are dealing with. They need to develop a sense of respect in relationships, and this is in fact quite important culturally. It's all about "mateship" between colleagues and friends. Not being the actual person responsible for decisions, not allowing someone to share a drink, being needlessly strict on numerous issues—all these stand in the way of developing closeness and—with the Australian laid-back attitude—respect.

S<small>OME</small> S<small>IMPLE</small> R<small>ULES</small>

The rules of doing business in Australia can be summed up as follows:

1. Do your homework.
2. Market hard, sell soft.
3. Arrogant posturing does not go down well. In fact, it repels the buyer.
4. Selling needs to be laid back. An aggressive approach won't work.
5. Beware of cultural icons.
6. Use local expertise and knowledge.
7. Think globally, but act locally.

And always remember that Australians are a nation of sports people: They love the outdoors and look forward to welcoming overseas guests to its vast expanse. We will even put "a shrimp on the barbie for you!"

A<small>BOUT THE</small> A<small>UTHOR</small>

Babette Bensoussan
MindShifts
Level 2, North Tower
1–5 Railway Street
Chatswood NSW 2067
Sydney, Australia

Phone: 61 2 9411 3636
Fax: 61 2 9411 3900

Babette Bensoussan, B.A., M.B.A., is a director and the founder of the MindShifts Group, an organization specializing in business and marketing projects in the Asia Pacific. She has undertaken major studies in strategic marketing and planning, business intelligence, business planning, and strategic analysis in such fields as microelectronics, personal computers, real estate, travel, pharmaceuticals, information management, mining, small manufacturing operations, transport, water and wastewater, and financial services. Before founding MindShifts in 1990, Ms. Bensoussan worked for over fifteen years in marketing management positions for such companies as Apple Computer and Levi Strauss. She is vice president of the Society of Competitive Intelligence Professionals in Australia, secretary of the Global Business Development Alliance based in Geneva, and an associate fellow and past councillor of the Australian Marketing Institute.

CHINA
POVERTY IS NOT SOCIALISM

Like a tiger strolling down a garden path, China and its emerging markets are impossible to ignore; any nation with a population of 1.2 billion and an economy growing by as much as 10 percent a year commands respect. But size also begets fantasy: If people could train a tiger to play football or sell a pair of shoes to every man, woman, and child in China, how rich they would be. If only life were that simple.

Tigers have yet to throw a touchdown pass, but businesses do thrive in China, provided they understand the environment. Gaining a competitive edge in this tempting if at times unfathomable market requires tapping into the Chinese system of relationships (*guanxi*). The right relationships open doors and make possible deals necessary for doing business in China. And few relationships will be as important as the one a company establishes with the government, local and national.

Chinese officials want foreign companies to invest in their country, train their people, and transfer technology. Although China no longer has a planned economy, the government continues to play an important role in economic activities. A wise market entrant will figure out how to benefit from this reality.

GOOD GUANXI OR BAD BUSINESS

In sectors dominated by the government, it is best to make a virtue of a necessity: Avoid conflict by finding a way to work with the government. For example, a European digital switching system manufacturer, already a leader in the international telecommunications market, wanted to enter China. After careful analysis, it launched a program for market expansion that took into account government control of the telecommunications business (through the designated operators China Telecom and China Unicom). The European company negotiated an equity joint venture agreement with the government—in particular, with the Telecommunications Administration Department—thus making its customer a shareholder in the endeavor.

The initial plan was for the European company to sell equipment to the joint venture company, which would then sell to the end user, the Telecommunications Administration Department. Sales to the joint venture company triggered instant payment whereas sales to the end user were subject to deferred payment. Therefore, the joint venture company was soon short of working capital at a time when market share was exploding. The situation was remedied by returning profits to the joint venture and raising loans from Chinese banks. At the same time, many local users, with the approval of the government, imported equipment directly from the European company to fill out the supply from the joint venture company.

So, the company not only avoided confrontation with the government, it gave the government an interest in the firm's success. This decision allowed the firm to introduce its products to the market in a cost-effective manner. Further, those products currently have a good image among Chinese end users.

If encounters with the government are not carefully managed, they can lead to disaster. For example, provinces create their own rules and regulations and can change them at any time. Horror stories abound.

In general, a company should plan on building a network of relationships at the national, provincial, and municipal levels of government. (Several firms have located suitable partners through the Internet; many provincial Chinese governments now maintain Web sites.) It is also important to revitalize these relationships constantly and to monitor partners carefully as they may be establishing relationships with competitors.

CHINA NOTES

- If you are serious about doing business in China, you will have to schedule at least one or two trips a year to develop the business. The Chinese are sensitive to protocol; send a senior representative from your firm.

- Conduct research before your trip to ensure that you are not meeting with competitive firms or with firms that may have signed agreements with your competitors.

- If you travel with your PC, bring the appropriate power transformer and adapter plug to avoid frying your computer. You will also need adapters for foreign telephone jacks. Check with your modem manufacturer to see if you will be breaking some rules with the use of specific modems in the country.

- At present, no rental car market exists in China. Taxis are reasonable and safe. In cities like Shanghai, the subway is an efficient way to travel in terms of time and cost. The system, however, is not yet fully developed.

- Book meetings well in advance. Confirm appointments at least one week ahead of time.

- Book meetings either at your contact's firm or at a good hotel. Meetings can be held in hotel conference rooms, lobbies, coffee shops, or restaurants.

- Follow-up to all meetings is essential, not only to show your commitment but because of the fast-paced business environment. E-mail is becoming as popular, if not more popular, than faxes.

- Mandarin is the written language throughout China, but there are many mutually unintelligible spoken dialects. Have an interpreter attend meetings.

- If possible, bring business cards with a translation in Mandarin on the reverse side. When receiving a business card, always place it on the table (not in your pocket or wallet) and never write on it.

- While business lunches are common, you may be treated to dinner or a banquet. Always arrive on time and never begin to eat or drink before your host does.

- Attempt to use chopsticks at all meals. You will be presented with several courses on serving dishes, which will not be passed around. While you can reach in front of others to get the dishes, do not reach for the food with the end of the chopsticks that you put in your mouth.

- Generally, you should not discuss business at a meal.

- Buying Chinese currency is easier than selling it. The Chinese government discourages the repatriation of profits by limiting the amount of hard currency available through the currency-swap exchanges. Sellers of renminbi (RMB, "people's currency") recoup roughly half of their original hard currency cost.

- Dress conservatively—dark conservative suits for both men and women—even for casual events.

- While handshakes are common, some Chinese may simply nod or bow slightly.

- Do not use exaggerated gestures or facial expressions when speaking. The Chinese do not like to be touched by people they do not know.

- The Chinese pay attention to names, status, and titles. Chinese names consist of a family name, a generational name, and a given name. Some people may have adopted an English first name if they conduct a lot of business with English-speaking people.

- Because gift giving is sensitive in China, give a gift from your whole company to the whole Chinese group, and present it to their leader. Gifts that represent your firm or a region of your country are appropriate. Do not wrap gifts in white, which is the color associated with funerals.

TO MARKET, TO MARKET . . . WHICH MARKET WILL IT BE?

One strategy when entering China is to follow the advice of John F. Kennedy: "If you want to make money, go where the money is." In other words, find out where state loans are going. Recently, loans have gone to key energy, transportation, telecommunications, and raw materials projects. In particular, prospects look good for suppliers of heavy machinery to the railway, petroleum, petrochemical, and stone production industries.

In the longer term, China will direct loans to the improvement of the less developed central and western regions of the country, funding key industries and projects. Priority will be given to agriculture, large and medium-size state enterprises, technical renovation, housing, machinery and electronic exports, and environmental protection.

Fast growth in other sectors of the Chinese economy are a reflection of the improved living standards in urban areas; these include computer hardware and software and telecommunications.

The current "hot" exports to China are aircraft and replacement parts, computers, power generation equipment, telecommunications equipment, and electric machinery. In addition, powerful consumer demand is emerging for consumer durables, apparel, personal care products, and food products. For example, Chinese demand for frozen food is expected to triple by 2000 as consumers follow trends in developed countries.

MAGIC SPELLS AND REALITY CHECKS

Market Research: Knowing a Silk Purse From a Pig's Ear

A potential market of 1.2 billion people can easily cast a spell on eager foreign businesses. Distracted by the "magic" of China, foreign firms often rush in while ignoring the good business practices that are second nature back home. The pressure is to act fast and avoid falling behind in a rapidly developing market. This is a recipe for failure, or worse. Because the China market is both large and complicated, the first step should always be careful market research.

A well-known German motor manufacturer decided to enter China at a time of greatly increased demand for electric motors. As part of their preparation, the company's senior management traveled to the major cities in China and visited key state enterprises. They concluded that the potential market was sizable; most motors would have to be replaced within the next three years. They also determined what adjustments to voltage range and operational stability would be needed for the local markets they would target.

Instead of direct sales to end users, the company decided to donate 300 motors to Capital Iron and Steel Group Corporation, one of the largest iron and steel plants in China. After the motors had been installed, the firm hired a commission agent to do promotion.

The motors operated perfectly, so the agent's first step was to launch an advertising campaign. The feedback was overwhelming. Taking aim at a larger Chinese market than initially planned, the company developed a product series of motors that could stand extreme conditions. Sales volume rose remarkably.

Cultural Issues: "You Aren't in Kansas Anymore"

To cultivate the business relationships that are so important in China, a market entrant must understand and bridge cultural differences.

Consider the case of a United States food company looking to hire a sales manager for its Beijing branch. After a careful search, the company found a qualified candidate and offered him the position. After several months, he was fired. Because he had ties to the government, the United States company suspected that he was a government spy or monitor. However, most Chinese believe that good relations with the government are essential for success. A cultural difference caused this misunderstanding and may have led to losses for the firm.

Foreign companies also must keep in mind the importance of hosting Chinese visitors and delegations in their home countries. The host's duties include taking the delegates out to dinner and arranging programs for the weekend. Often the impression that visitors get from a company's hospitality and the quality of its arrangements will be more important than the project and product itself. When the delegates return to China, they most likely will remember how good—or bad—the company's hospitality was and act accordingly.

It can be demanding and sometimes frustrating to receive delegations. Cultural differences have a way of complicating matters, like the Chinese delegation visiting Europe: Members had been instructed to finish all the food on their plates, as this was the European custom. Conversely, their European host had been taught that the Chinese, out of politeness, always wish to leave some food on their plates.

Political Issues: It Isn't Textbook Civics Yet

The Chinese government is beginning to emphasize decentralization and reliance on market mechanisms, but its efforts in this direction can be inconsistent or ineffectual. And when it comes to big issues, the government may make decisions based primarily on political considerations. The problem for a foreign business is that it can't know in advance how the government will react.

The challenge is to avoid the kind of experience Jardine Pacific, a British consulting and trading company, went through. The firm was shocked when all of its clients suddenly terminated all contracts with them. After a careful consultation with various sources, the company learned that in the course of business, it had collected information the Chinese government regarded as confidential.

In retaliation, the government issued a secret order to all Chinese companies to cancel all contracts signed with Jardine Pacific. The company found a copy of the order and lodged an official protest. The government, however, denied issuing the order, and the matter went unresolved for years. The company suffered greatly.

In general, the government still plays a very important role in trading activities. Further, the approval of the State Planning Commission is needed for a company to participate in any project financed by the government. This approval is often given or denied based on the state of political relations between China and a company's home country.

The Challenge of Distribution: A Marathon Times Ten

Distribution is the major challenge in China. Before economic reform, China, like most communist countries, relied on a fixed distribution system. Suppliers produced goods under government supervision and sold the goods to wholesalers, who then resold them to retailers and specialized trading units. Now, after reform, domestic suppliers no longer rely on the traditional method of reaching retailers through wholesalers.

China currently has a two-tier distribution system: Tier 1 involves distribution to major cities (for example, Beijing and Shanghai); tier 2 involves a loose network of local dealers. This system is a function of relationships. A company must build its dealer network with care and understand the particular problems of distribution. Independent dealers can "disappear" with products. Products must be packaged better than in the company's home country because they undergo greater product abuse.

A number of companies have learned how to make the system work for them. Xerox entered the market and built a dealer network based on friendships. It has captured significant shares of select markets by cultivating these relationships. Other successful brands include Bausch & Lomb contact lenses and Avon, Revlon, Max Factor, and Christian Dior cosmetics. Cosmetic producers have worked hard to establish good relations with major department stores and beauty salons, hoping to increase brand awareness by having their products prominently displayed. By and large, they have been successful.

Protecting the Rights of a Business: "You Aren't in Kansas . . ."

Consider the story dating to 1962, when Rado, a Swiss company, introduced the first wear-resistant watch in the world. In 1979, the company entered China, running advertisements in leading newspapers and sponsoring popular television programs. As part of its expansion plans, the company registered its watch patent in countries around the world. Although the company attached great importance to the Chinese market, it had already made a serious mistake. Under Chinese law, a company must obtain a patent *before* entering the Chinese market; otherwise, it cannot assert patent rights.

A Chinese company began producing the watch with an imitative design and registered *its* patent with the China Patent Office. Unfortunately, Rado did not become aware of this until the two watches were being displayed together, separated "only" by a fivefold price difference.

The Swiss company pointed out that it had advertised in China before the Chinese company was even formed. Asserting that it had priority in the matter, the firm requested the patent office cancel the Chinese patent. While the Swiss won the case, the Chinese company was given the right to continue to produce and sell its watches. Formally, they compete on even ground.

However, the tariff on imported watches can run as high as 180 percent; even if China accedes to the World Trade Organization, the tariff will not drop below 100 percent. So a price difference is inevitable. Moreover, the Chinese company could set up many distribution outlets and obtain quick market feedback. The Swiss company, by contrast, must try to reach consumers through Chinese trade companies and distribution units. It has lost any advantage its early entry might have provided. The Swiss company's market has now shrunk to a few cities such as Beijing, Shanghai, and Guangzhou.

The Great Wall of Trade Barriers

Apart from a few sectors monopolized by the state, China is open to foreign companies, although import licenses are sometimes needed. In addition, China has applied for membership in the World Trade Organization. When it joins, tariffs will have to conform to international standards.

ABOUT THE AUTHOR

Ola Svensson
  East Net (China) Ltd.
  24 Jianguomenwai Avenue
  2-1502 Beijing 100022 China
  Phone: 86 1 5159328
  Fax: 86 1 5158916

Sten Ola Erik Svensson, B.A., M.S., runs his own consultancy firm, East Net (China) Ltd., specializing in developing China-related business in the information industry. Trained as an engineer, Mr. Svensson has extensive experience in telecommunications and electronic information systems. He has worked for Ericsson, the Royal Academy of Engineering Sciences in Stockholm, the science and technology office of the Swedish embassy in Beijing, and Svenska Handelsbanken in Beijing. He is currently chief representative in Beijing for Elekta Instrument AB, manufacturers of high-tech surgical equipment.

HONG KONG
THE GATEWAY TO CHINA

There will probably be endless speculation about the political and economic future of Hong Kong after its 1997 transfer from British to Chinese sovereignty. China has promised to allow Hong Kong to keep its system intact for a 50-year period, until 2047, but who knows?

In the midst of such uncertainty, it's worth remembering what the Danish physicist Niels Bohr reputedly said: "Prediction is difficult, especially about the future." With that qualifier in mind, the prediction here is that Hong Kong will be fundamentally different by 2047 and the changes are far more likely to be driven by a rapidly changing business environment than by the dictates of the government in Beijing. This vision is born of Hong Kong's proven capacity to reinvent itself time after time, often in the face of serious adversity.

Hong Kong's long-term success will likely be a product of the following: Hong Kong has a strong service economy (83 percent of the GDP) that is growing faster than the service economy of other advanced countries.

The manufacturing sector continues to expand rapidly. This should ensure Hong Kong a leadership position as a world leader in garments, watches, toys, and consumer electronic products.

Hong Kong's strong entrepreneurial culture based on small, family-owned businesses is not likely to change in the near future. It is the engine of the economy.

The unusually strong business skills of small to mid-size Hong Kong companies in conducting business through cross-border manufacturing is unique.

Hong Kong's position as a regional headquarters for multinational firms is expected to continue. Its large international community of expatriates should continue to expand international trade and investment opportunities.

Hong Kong serves a variety of purposes, including a testing ground to launch new products on mainland China; Campbell Soups is one company that has done precisely that. Similarly, Polaroid, Avon, Bausch & Lomb, Carrier, Gillette, and McDonnell Douglas have enjoyed success in Hong Kong. The testing ground is also a regional headquarters for 782 firms. Of these, 198 are American, 116 Japanese, and 94 British.

Hong Kong's competitive advantage clearly lies in its ability to adapt to

HONG KONG

NOTES

- The best way to do business in Hong Kong is to *actually do business there.* If you're serious about having a firm distribute or sell your products, try to negotiate a deal and do it.

- Always do research before meetings. Know who the firm's competitors are and understand the complex channels of distribution in Hong Kong (and the related areas of product distribution in mainland China). Remember patents and copyrights have been violated in this area in the past. You should use your resources to avoid any future problems of this sort.

- Some Chinese firms close during the Chinese New Year. You should plan for this.

- Taxis from the airport are relatively inexpensive. However, Hong Kong has traffic problems. The ferry is a quick, inexpensive method of travel between Hong Kong and Kowloon. Always check the addresses of meetings well in advance and allow enough travel time.

- Hong Kong's two official languages are Chinese (Cantonese) and English. You can expect meetings to be conducted in English. Most signs are in English, and buildings are easy to find.

- Because time is money in Hong Kong, meetings are hard to schedule. Book meetings at least one to two months in advance. Don't expect meetings to last more than an hour. Always confirm the meeting date, time, and place at least one week in advance by fax or e-mail.

- A good way to maximize your time in Hong Kong is to "stack" meetings one after another at a good hotel (in the lobby or coffee shop). Always leave at least a half-hour between meetings to avoid the embarrassment of having meetings run together.

- Lunch is a popular time for meetings. Also, don't turn down dinner meetings if invited.

- Hong Kong is a very competitive country. Don't schedule meetings with competitors consecutively, or, if you can avoid it, on the same day. They will appreciate your letting them know, however, that you are meeting with their competitor(s).

- The Chinese will typically bring a "negotiating team," which may consist of a senior person and one or two operation team members. Often, one of the members will translate for the rest of the team.

- Follow-up is important. If you promise the Chinese a proposal or contract, fax or send it no more than one week after the meeting.

- Remember, the Chinese are interested in *doing business.* If you don't do business within six months or a year, you should continue to communicate with the firm to let them know that you are still interested in a potential relationship.

- Pay your bills promptly. The Chinese are very aware of delayed payment.

- The Chinese are reserved. Avoid aggressive or loud behavior. While the Chinese may stand physically close to you, don't initiate any physical contact. Meetings have a serious tone to them.

- Hong Kong is extremely hot in the summer. If you make a trip in the summer, dress in a conservative

lightweight business suit (both men and women).
Short sleeves are acceptable.

■ Always try to leave an afternoon open for shopping!

---

quickly changing market conditions. That ability includes a manufacturing force of more than five million people in mainland China. In short, the "one country, two systems" concept may enable Hong Kong to continue as a capitalist economy.

After the British leave in 1997, Hong Kong will continue as a free port and separate customs territory. It will also continue to operate under its existing legal system, viz, British Common Law, and maintain independent finances. Moreover, travel to and from should remain the same.

Gateway—and Neighbor—to Mass Markets

Of course, even in Hong Kong some things remain constant. Frank Martin, the highly respected president of the American Chamber of Commerce in Hong Kong, noted, "The major attraction of Hong Kong as a regional headquarters is the location, equidistant to north and south Asia. That was true twenty years ago, and it certainly isn't going to change" (Asia Inc.). Not only is Hong Kong five hours' flying time from 40 percent of the world's population, it is actually on the doorstep of 20 percent of the total in China.

Hong Kong's role as the gateway to China is widely recognized. In their book, *The Hong Kong Advantage* (Oxford University Press, 1997), Michael Enright, Edith Scott, and David Dodwell point out that Hong Kong "is a uniquely convenient location for doing business with the mainland, in terms of its geographic proximity, unrivaled transport and communications linkages, and, in addition, the high concentration of mainland entities physically present. For overseas firms that need to plug into world-class infrastructure, services, and professional skills, Hong Kong is likely to remain unsurpassed as a foothold onto mainland China."

Enright and his coauthors go deeper, however, with an exceptional insight into the Hong Kong economy. They debunk the idea that Hong Kong acts simply as a gateway to China or merely as a financier of business operations. (That "merely" needs to be taken in perspective, of course; in 1996 Hong Kong was the world's fourth largest source of foreign direct investment.)

No, the skills of Hong Kong (and therefore the opportunity it represents to foreign companies) go well beyond providing access to China or putting up money. Hong Kong excels at integrating manufacturing capacity (roughly 10 percent in Hong Kong, 60 percent in China, and 30 percent in the rest of the world), manufacturing management expertise, design talent, marketing and packaging skills, and financing. This sort of integration is increasingly a critical advantage for Hong Kong companies and something that all businesses in the territory need to pursue in some way to remain competitive.

For example, one important aspect of the gateway has not yet been fully exploited: It works in both directions. Most companies have only one-way traffic with China. Major U.S. retailers typically maintain a base in Hong Kong to source products for their U.S. stores; none has yet found a really effective route into the Chinese market. Even Wal-Mart's much vaunted entry has been tentative.

Other companies, particularly those outside the "fast-moving consumption goods" sector, continue to use Hong Kong solely as a primary base for sales in China. Admittedly, for medium-size companies or those with highly specialized product lines (especially those with a high level of new technology, which would be at risk in the hands of mainland factory managers), this approach makes sense.

But all the one-way traffic misses the opportunity to leverage expertise built up in one direction for other business activities. One company, like others from around the world, established very successful garment factories in several parts of China during the 1980s. Eventually, it was able to develop its own Chinese market. In the broadest terms, this company did little that was unusual or special by way of marketing and product management. Rather, success came from understanding the value of Hong Kong as a place to integrate the skills and know-how needed to transform the firm's China operation from a one-way assembly business into a two-way flow. The same results could not have been directed from the home office, and the task would have been far more difficult attempted solely within China.

MOVING THROUGH THE GATEWAY WITHOUT GETTING STUCK

The Costs of Doing Business

In general, Hong Kong is ideal for business. There are, however, a number of ways in which Hong Kong needs improvement. High on the lists of most people is cost: Prices and rents in Hong Kong for both commercial and residential property are among the highest in the world. Otherwise, the general cost of living is reasonable, although salary inflation in the past 10 years (particularly among local managers) has been substantial. Hong Kong also is no longer a cheap place to hire staff.

These cost issues are to some extent ameliorated by Hong Kong's extremely favorable tax structure. Personal income tax is capped at 15 percent and operates at levels that exclude a large portion of the working population. Corporate profits tax is 16.5 percent and is charged only against Hong Kong earned income. There are no capital gains taxes, and there are no duties, except on tobacco, alcohol, and petroleum products.

The flip side is the government's policy of "positive nonintervention" in business, which means that many of the tax incentives to investment that exist elsewhere are absent in Hong Kong. For this reason, Hong Kong's tax advantage over such places as Singapore and China's "special economic zones" is not always as high as it might seem.

Language Problems and Business Opportunities

The skill base of the population is not always appropriate for an economy that is now 83 percent service-based, and a number of studies suggest that much needs to be done to adapt the educational system to Hong Kong's new needs. This is particularly true with respect to English language standards.

A substantial portion of the population who would once have worked in factories are now being called upon to take jobs that require foreign language skills. Many simply do not have such skills, and this puts Hong Kong at a clear disadvantage to Singapore, Malaysia, and the Philippines, and even China, where only a tiny proportion of the population speaks English.

Still, language is not a barrier to doing business. The U.S. Department of Commerce has identified some of the most attractive sectors for U.S. companies in Hong Kong. These range from telecommunications equipment, pollution control equipment, and insurance services to cosmetics and toiletries, drugs and pharmaceuticals, and architecture, construction, and engineering services. Almost all of the sectors represent products that support Hong Kong's current version of itself as a high value-added service economy. Insurance, travel, financial services and telecommunications equipment also rank high on the list, along with high-quality consumer products. Sales supporting Hong Kong's ongoing boom in construction, property, and infrastructure also promise to be large.

A significant feature of demand in Hong Kong is the imbalance between domestic market size and imports. Except in a few specialized service sectors, Hong Kong statistics show the almost unheard-of characteristic of a significant surplus of imports over domestic consumption. In the most extreme case, more than six times as much medical equipment was imported into Hong Kong as was consumed.

There is no great mystery about where most of this surplus is going: China. A detailed account of the ins and outs of importing Western finished products into China is beyond the scope of this discussion. Suffice it to say that getting products from ship to shop is a challenge.

The problem results from continuing high tariffs together with complex local distribution systems and venal customs officials. So, beware. Even companies that have become intimately involved in the marketing and selling of their products in China don't want to go it alone; they seem to prefer having experienced Hong Kong traders get their products into China. Only the largest multinationals appear interested in exploring more direct alternatives.

Your Company and Hong Kong: Making the Fit

Given all this rapid change, how can a company seize the opportunity presented by the growing promise of regional trade in Greater China and Asia? Newcomers to the region can decide from several strategies. The decision should take into account the resources of the company, the product line it wishes to promote, and the scale of its ambitions.

For some companies, it makes the most sense to use Hong Kong as a convenient occasional base for "parachuting" in management teams. Hong Kong is a ready destination for most major airlines, and, more important, the business and trade services needed to develop business are readily accessible to occasional visitors.

This approach, however, represents a minimal level of commitment. The next step would be to work with a local Hong Kong firm to develop a business in the region. This is the standard, recommended route but not one without problems. Outside firms will basically have to choose from two distinct classes of Hong Kong companies. This might be called the Goldilocks dilemma.

One possibility would be the large, well-established corporate organizations. They are well funded and professionally managed and tend to represent the world's great brands. Unfortunately, it is often difficult for companies with relatively small potential sales to get their attention in any serious way.

The alternative is to work with a small, local company. Often family managed, with no more than ten to twenty staff members, these companies generally represent a limited range of principals and often specialize in a particular type of industry. This kind of attention is attractive to many principals, in contrast to the more impersonal attitude of the larger companies, assuming they are even interested in the first place.

But small may be *too* small, when a company finds its potential customer base is both large and widely scattered. This is often the case when the target region is Asia, where flying distances are substantial and travel is expensive. Or products may need very sophisticated marketing and promotion techniques. In such cases, the small Hong Kong companies could lack the resources to service their principals effectively.

Many companies find a happy medium by using a Hong Kong trading company representative; this remains far and away the most common market entry strategy for foreign companies. It also avoids those nasty complications Goldilocks encountered in looking for the right fit.

Once they have secured a foothold, many companies move on to establishing their own regional presence. Hong Kong more often than not serves as the best location for such a presence. Niels Bohr to the contrary notwithstanding, it is likely to do so into the indefinite future.

ABOUT THE AUTHOR

Paul Woodward
Asian Strategies Ltd.
4401 China Resources Building
26 Harbour Road, Wanchai
Hong Kong
Phone: 852 2827 4627
Fax: 852 2827 6097

Paul Woodward, B.A., is managing director of Asian Strategies Ltd. (ASL), a division of Miller Freeman Asia, a United News & Media company. ASL is a management consultancy and information services operation focused on the Asia Pacific, with special interests in greater China, information technology, telecommunications, travel, and health care. Mr.

Woodward is responsible for ASL's activities in various aspects of China business and supervises its regional strategic consulting assignments. Recently completed assignments include summaries of the cosmetics business in fifteen Asian countries, the prospects in China for foreign retailers, the opportunities in China for producers of high-quality leather goods, and network marketing in Hong Kong with a particular focus on health products.

INDIA
THE ELEPHANT RISES

India's history has given it a very strong sense of national identity (and businesses should take care not to express an attitude that could be construed as hostile to the Indian people). Decades of struggle against British rule led to independence on August 15, 1947. British India was partitioned into primarily Hindu India and mostly Muslim East and West Pakistan. Since independence, war has broken out between the two neighbors three times, the result of a centuries-old antagonism between Hindus and Muslims.

But the tumult of Indian life should not be confused with paralysis. Indeed, the elephant is stirring. The current leadership of India is implementing sweeping changes—including privatization and liberalization of trade—to attract international business to India. For the first time, these changes have broad-based support. It is not just economists and financiers who recognize the need for economic reform and privatization in India. All major parties now accept the overall necessity of these reforms, and a recent survey revealed that 43 percent of urban Indians perceive the economic reforms as "mostly good."

The current multiparty United Front government is implementing sweeping changes to attract international business. That policy includes deregulating and privatizing such government-owned activities as power generation, airlines, and telecommunications. According to official press releases, the government's goal "is to make foreign investment structures within India 'as transparent, investor friendly and attractive' as those in other emerging economies. Infrastructure, agribusiness, and export-oriented businesses are among the new sectors allowing automatic approval of foreign investment up to 51 percent." Prior to this, the emphasis was on heavier import or capital goods industries (*International Business,* December 1996–January 1997, p. 20).

INDIA NOTES

- Personal relationships drive business. Be prepared to phone, phone, and fax. Continued contact shows that you are interested in developing a personal as well as a business relationship. Try to make contacts at the top of the company.

- If you receive a call from India, return it promptly. In many cases, a phone call is more efficient than a fax.

- Because of the difficulty in communications at times, always acknowledge receipt of faxes, phone calls, reports, and so forth.

- Conduct research before your trip. Talk to business colleagues who have been to India.

- Plan your trip well in advance. Keep your schedule flexible. Find out whether your government requires you to have any vaccinations.

- Indians have several religious holidays. Check with your local Indian consulate or embassy before your trip.

- Book meetings at least two months in advance. Because faxes can be unreliable, confirm by phone.

- Schedule most meetings in the late morning or early afternoon. Try to schedule meetings between September and March.

- Be on time for your meetings. You may still experience delays or even cancellations. Be prepared to reschedule.

- Much of the business culture is tied to India's religious traditions. Time is not a source of anxiety and passivity is a virtue.

- Meetings are highly personal in India. Expect to talk about family and to have refreshments (sweet, milky tea).

- Most business meals are at lunch time. Eat only with your right hand. Hindus do not eat beef, and Muslims do not eat pork. Never offer anyone food from your plate.

- Dress conservatively for business. Women should wear pant suits for casual wear.

- While handshaking is common in large Indian cities, Western women should not initiate a handshake with Indian men. This is particularly important with Indian Muslim men.

- Always use formal titles such as Dr., Mr., or Mrs.; they are very important to Indians. Hindus do not have family surnames.

- Indians are typically too polite to say no. You must build relationships by discussing friends and family. Remember, friendships are more important than expertise.

- The American nod (up and down) to mean "yes" means "no" in India.

- While there is equality under law, the caste system prevails. Women have few privileges.

- Tipping (or baksheesh) is often necessary to get things done.

- Never touch someone's head or point your feet at another person.

The government has recently taken the initiative to sell stakes of up to 74 percent in publicly owned industries in the "noncore" and "nonstrategic" sectors. There is speculation that hotel and tourism-related industries will be part of the offering (*International Business,* December 1996– January 1997, p. 20) and even that the government is willing to sell 49 percent stakes in certain core industries.

In addition to increasing privatization, the government is addressing the fundamentals, including a budget deficit generally in the range of 6 to 7 percent. To get the deficit under control, the government has announced austerity measures to stem the growth of public spending. And the idea of fiscal control does not come easy to Indian politicians.

However, the results of the May 1996 elections reflected a change in thinking by the Indian electorate. Indian politics typically focuses on the poor and is concerned with social development. But world events of the last decade have led many voters to believe that only significant and sustained economic growth can improve the lives of the poor in India.

MARKET OPPORTUNITIES

India functions on the regional level. Its states have been taking economic matters into their own hands, even during the reign of the Congress-led central government in Delhi. Attempts to manage large regional projects from the center rarely work out.

Small and medium-size infrastructure projects tend to fare much better. These projects are not big enough to gain national attention or political notoriety, and companies that work on them face fewer problems. Until recently, for example, if a power company was involved with a project producing less than 250 megawatts of power, it did not have to apply to the federal government for clearance.

Such has been the experience of AGRA Industries of Toronto, Canada, a medium-size firm with sales of approximately $850 million. AGRA specializes in technologies relating to power, process industries, and infrastructure, including environmental technologies, and it has constructed two hydroelectric and one nuclear plant in India.

Its engineering subsidiary, AGRA Monenco, recently formed a joint venture with Indian industrial giant RPG-RR Power Engineering Pvt. Ltd. and is bidding for several medium-size regional power projects at a reported cost of about $100 million for a 100 megawatt plant. Such a facility could serve a single large industrial client, an industrial park, a smaller city of about one million people, or a suburb or section of a large city.

Clearly, bypassing the Indian central government is a critical factor. Ease of entry and relatively fast project start-ups are major advantages in dealing with local Indian governments; a whole level of bureaucracy is eliminated. Everybody within a state, from the state and city governments down to the local industry, is eager to welcome such smaller scale, privately financed power projects (*International Business*, December 1996–January 1997, pp. 22–23).

India's goal is to make infrastructure a mostly private-sector activity. The main challenge is to find ways to make projects suitable for private financing. Many of the plans by the new government for infrastructure privatization and open foreign consumer project marketing into the country are certainly ambitious. If successful, they will signal a real break from the old days of slow-moving bureaucracy (*International Business*, December 1996–January 1997, p. 23).

Some of the best prospects for the sale of goods and services to India are as follows:

- Seafood processing and preservation
- Hazardous waste and handling equipment
- Port construction
- Oil and gas field equipment and supplies
- Computer software services
- Food processing and packaging equipment
- Electronic components
- Biotechnology
- Refinery and petrochemical equipment
- Pumps, valves and compressors
- Machine tools and metalworking equipment
- Drugs and pharmaceuticals
- Mining technology and equipment
- Railway modernization

In general, the consumer market is wide open. But given the range in socioeconomic levels and cultural norms and preferences, success will in large part reflect the quality of the market research done.

HOW TO BE PEACEABLE AND HAPPY IN INDIA

Entering the Megamarket: These Four Areas First

Companies new to India should first introduce their products and services to the four metropolitan areas—Mumbai (Bombay), Chennai (Madras), Delhi, and Calcutta, *strictly* in that order—because these cities together with their satellite townships and rural areas have well-organized markets. These areas have modern infrastructure and generally respond to adequate marketing efforts. The consumers have tremendous buying power and are extremely knowledgeable about foreign products.

Later, sales can be extended to other, smaller cities. These small urban markets are opening up as never before. They now tend to be served by radio, TV, and cable networks. The consumers have good purchasing power and are well educated and enlightened. They are open to information about new products.

Finally, sales can be extended to rural regions. These markets have only recently become accessible and therefore represent virtually untapped sales potential.

Location, Location . . .

An important decision will be where to locate a company in India. Land prices play a key role in this decision. Real estate is prohibitively expensive in the four major urban areas. Nonetheless, they are the best locations for company headquarters and for the central office of commercial and trading operations. However, costs—especially for land—make them unattractive sites for manufacturing.

India's real estate market has been known to chasten the mighty. A top international fast-food chain found itself with only one outlet in the suburbs of Mumbai. Likewise, a top international ice cream company had to be content franchising to small outlets in Mumbai and medium-size outlets in the suburbs.

Local Help: Know It, Use It

A company can enter the Indian market by selling a franchise, cooperating with a local company, or organizing a subsidiary. Whatever the strategy chosen, a new entrant should maximize the use of local personnel for day-to-day administration and marketing. This will help to comply with local laws and statutes, maintain good public relations, and develop a market strategy suited to local market conditions.

Consumers: They Spell Success or Failure

Indian consumers traditionally are known to prefer products that have a reputation for durability and quality. They also prefer products with a proven record for providing service and honoring guarantees. Once satisfied, Indian consumers will demonstrate strong brand loyalty.

If India's consumer market is big, it is also different. Missteps can be costly. For example, food companies must fully understand that the majority of Indians are vegetarians. This means they will avoid ice cream suspected of containing egg whites or cakes, pastries, and jellies based on nonvegetarian ingredients. However, such preferences can sometimes be changed. The National Egg Coordination Committee, through the use of audiovisual media, was able to increase the consumption of eggs from seventeen eggs per person to thirty. But don't expect a little Madison Avenue–type public relations to erase centuries or more of tradition.

When in doubt, do market research to understand the Indian consumer. Some products, like microwave ovens, will do far better in Denver than Delhi. Indians prefer fried food to baked food and like food to be served hot immediately upon cooking. They do not like reheated food. Microwave ovens simulate baking and are especially suited to reheating, but they can't be used for frying. Such an appliance held little appeal for Indian housewives. Success depended on some product modification to suit the particular market, as was later demonstrated by a manufacturer of electric ovens.

Beyond adjusting to the *different* tastes of Indian consumers, foreign companies must also adjust to the *tastes of many different* Indian consumers. India is not a single market but a conglomerate of many geoclimatic, ethnic, linguistic, and caste segments where consumers have widely varying product perceptions.

Successful marketing must take into account these market characteristics. Even domestic companies planning to expand nationally must adapt their products as necessary. For example, a South Indian pickle manufacturer, on deciding to go national, had to introduce pickle varieties suited to the North Indian palate.

Each product and service must have a customized marketing program. Everything should be coordinated from start to finish. This will be easier if (1) the company has a local collaborator, (2) the firm is able to sustain itself for six months, (3) it promises to replace defective parts or goods and to buy back unsold product, and (4) it mounts a good advertising campaign, using popular local media, to develop brand and company image well before the product's introduction.

India is characterized by a large number of dialects and regional languages. For effective promotion of new products and optimum market penetration, the use of regional languages and dialects is essential. Special emphasis should be given to audiovisual material that can reach illiterate segments of the sizable rural population.

Products That Sell

Product differentiation and brand positioning are crucial factors for market entry. When products are regarded as status symbols, consumers prefer foreign goods, which have snob appeal (for example, Mercedes and BMW cars, French perfumes, imported wine and liquor, and foreign publications). However, foreign producers must work harder when products lack any inherent status value. Indian consumers can be very practical and make purchases based on availability, suitability, price, and after-sales service.

Straightforward competition is one way to enter the market. There are others, like the Japanese preference for expanding into a market slowly. The Japanese tend to be cautious and start small. They increase participation, gain insight and confidence, and then enter the market in a big way. They focus on the consumer's ability and willingness to pay and then produce and price the product accordingly. This approach has paid rich dividends, as witness the large number of Japanese companies present in Indian markets. The Maruti-Suzuki collaboration is a case in point.

Whatever strategy it selects, a business should do the research necessary for understanding the Indian market. Cutting corners here can mean failure later on.

Bigger Is Not Better

Small and medium-size companies will not be at a disadvantage when entering the Indian market. In fact, it is the international giants that face special problems. Indians have high expectations of what might be called the glamour firms. If these companies fall short, they lose both goodwill and market access. Some top international giants have abandoned a high profile in India and are now trying to operate in relative obscurity!

Indians have not always had happy experiences with giant foreign companies. Foreign refineries, for example, were nationalized because they were thought to be pursuing anti-Indian policies. And a major American corporation was asked to leave the country because it was not ready to share technical knowledge with its Indian subsidiary. The Indian government is sensitive to perceived slights and will not hesitate to respond. It is a risk in doing business in India that must be kept in mind.

Similarly, foreign entrants are better off dealing with small and medium-size Indian companies. Big corporations, in India as elsewhere, are often inflexible in approach and dilatory in tactics, traits that can make for a frustrating experience. Ironically, medium-size foreign companies tend to seek out large Indian companies, only to regret the decision.

Keeping the Government Happy

Although the government pursues a policy of "Be Indian; buy Indian," this is basically an expression of support for domestic industries rather than of hostility toward foreign companies.

Once in the Indian market, companies should pursue policies that will endear them to the government and people of India. In particular, they must ensure that their activities reflect the development goals of the country. They must also participate in and support such socially desirable activities as family planning and environmental protection.

The government will allow a foreign company to have a 100 percent stake in an operation, as long as an agreement exists for the foreign owner to divest itself of 49 percent equity over a stipulated period. Normally, though, participation of up to 49 percent is preferred.

ABOUT THE AUTHOR

Niranjan R. Ganjawalla
ITVASLINE
New Ganjawalla Building
510 Arthur Road
Tardeo
Bombay, India
Phone: 91 22 495 4718
Fax: 91 22 262 4027 or 91 22 262 4064

Niranjan R. Ganjawalla is founder and managing partner of Online Searchers and Accessors, a pioneer in India in the field of on-line information access, retrieval, dissemination, and related value-added services. He is also president of ITVASLINE, a firm specializing in formulating market entry and business development strategies for foreign companies in India. Mr. Ganjawalla has considerable experience and expertise in telecommunications, information and related value-added services, strategic planning, and publicity, publications, and public relations. For over two decades he has served at high levels of the Congress Party, holding among other offices those of advisor to the chairman of the Foreign Affairs Department and national coordinator of the Foreign Affairs Department.

INDONESIA
THE SPICE ISLANDS PROGRESS
INTO THE NEXT MILLENNIUM

Many foreign companies can readily see the sales and business potential of a nation with 200 million people. But they also need to understand the ripple effects of history on the Indonesian economy and the citizens, from heads of state and their families, who dominate the large corporations, right on down to the parking attendants in the streets of Jakarta.

The essence of Indonesia's business order places control of major business in the hands of high-ranking officials and their extended families. The arrangement allows for a slow, trickle-down effect to increase the standard of living of Indonesia's many other citizens. It helps that Indonesia's very large population benefits from a very strong agricultural base. Farming keeps unemployment quite low. However, many employed people are making bare subsistence incomes.

This is beginning to change as a larger middle class emerges and carves out a place for itself. But even as these social changes transpire (slowly), the fact remains that President Suharto, his children, and his extended family have the real power. This influences almost all major business projects in Indonesia today.

The huge disparity in wealth and power between the ruling families and common Indonesians could fit a scenario of general unrest. However, Suharto has maintained enough steady economic growth to allow average Indonesians to be part of the rising tide. This prosperity comes with strings attached: Indonesians are not supposed to care about political opposition parties or the unrest in East Timor.

Although Indonesia's minimum wage and average salaries are not the highest of emerging countries, Indonesia continues to show steady improvement. This has been a major factor in maintaining the people's general confidence in President Suharto. Combine this with a political, military, and economic power base built up over thirty years, and another reason for his longevity becomes clear: It's very difficult to change a strong government in control of the economy and military. Although there has been some political opposition and unrest, for the most part Indonesia is a country of long-term potential for the foreign company.

Indonesia is opening up to more foreign products and investment and is trying to comply with international trade initiatives encouraged by the World Trade Organization (WTO) and other international bodies. So, there are more opportunities for foreign companies that have quality products and wish to enter this large and growing market. Political issues aside, President Suharto's government and its strategies are helping the Indonesian GDP, which eventually benefits the quality of life for all Indonesians.

The government's economic goal is for Indonesia to become a modern industrial nation by the year 2020, with an improved quality of life and business environment. Part of the strategy is to shift costly infrastructure projects to entrepreneurs and private businesses. The effect of this will be increased infrastructure and more business opportunities for Indonesia and foreign businesses, although the question remains: How much of that opportunity will actually be available to foreign-owned companies or those less wealthy Indonesians who need it the most?

Among the many opportunities in Indonesia, several industries have recently emerged as high-potential areas. One of these is transportation: automobile, train, and—especially important for an island nation—ship. These have directly or through secondary markets opened up new outlets for small and medium-size companies with the necessary products or services.

Telecommunications is another sector where there is a growing market. Although this sector will be dominated by major players and institutional joint ventures, there will nonetheless be countless opportunities for businesses providing peripheral technologies and superior service support. As in other countries, Indonesian telecommunications has received a great deal of governmental focus and aid.

INDONESIA NOTES

- Be careful in scheduling trips and meetings. There are numerous holidays in observance of the Islam, Hindu, and Christian religions.

- You can schedule meetings one week in advance. You have a high chance of meeting with the CEO of an Indonesian firm.

- While the traditional Muslim weekend is Thursday and Friday, Indonesians follow only the Friday observance. Thus, their work week is four full days, Monday through Thursday, and two half days in the morning on Friday and Saturday.

- Status and rank are very important in Indonesia. While you should be prompt for all meetings, it is not unusual for your party to be late. Indonesians will make someone of a lesser status wait for them; however, they will not be late for someone of a higher status.

- It is essential to be polite in all business dealings (this will not weaken your negotiating position). Because status is so important, don't be offended if Indonesians ask you personal questions (about your marital status, salary, etc.) to determine your status.

- In the Bahasa Indonesia, it is important to have an interpreter. Because politeness drives society, Indonesians have many ways to say yes and no. There are many subtleties, and you will have to learn to determine when they are saying yes but really mean no.

- Do not show anger in meetings or anywhere else. This will be interpreted as your losing face, known as *malu*.

- It may be difficult to obtain a status report on your business operations in the country because Indonesians will tell you (the boss) "what you will want to hear." Develop a network of colleagues (of your own nationality) in Indonesia as a source of independent information about the management of your business.

- Expect long negotiation periods and some amount of bureaucracy in the signing of contracts. Don't expect to negotiate deals in one business trip.

- When receiving an Indonesian's business card, place it on the table until the end of the meeting. Do not write on it or immediately put it in your pocket or wallet.

Energy is yet another field of opportunity. This includes petroleum, coal, natural gas, and all refined fuel products from the Pertimina (national oil company) oil refinery. Remember that Indonesia has an established oil industry and a productive economy seeking efficient energy sources. It is a mix that promises opportunity.

Other industrial sectors where opportunities may exist are the cement and pulp and paper industries, as Indonesia has emerged as a major player in the paper production business. Indonesian textile and garment factories also employ many capable Indonesians while continuing to supply foreign companies with high-quality goods; this industry will also continue to grow.

Mining and ore processing are also industry sectors where potential exists, as a result of the rich natural resources of Indonesia. Within the mining industry, there will likely be instituted a new set of investment legislation resulting from recent incidents in which foreign companies used illegal mining practices and many local investors suffered. Although these problems do occur occasionally, they are not widespread.

Agriculture and forestry are also major businesses in Indonesia and will continue to be so as long as the West continues to demand hardwoods. Although many rainforest areas are protected and clear cutting has been outlawed in most areas, there still exists a great deal of illegal activity. Forestry, however, is an important issue for the government and hopefully a sector that will remain heavily controlled.

Finally, tourism is a major growth area for Indonesia. It has many isolated and unspoiled areas, both islands and sea, where the seasoned traveler can discover one of the remotest places on earth and its many beauties. And "eco-tourism" seems to be catching on.

ISSUES AND CAVEATS

Ethics and Reality

When your company does go into an emerging market, you will inevitably deal with the issue of some type of "alternative business practice." You could be faced with a difficult choice to make between achieving business objectives and staying within international law. When wrestling with the many facets of the market entrance decision process, do not ignore the prevalence of reimbursement practice awareness.

Like it or not, these invisible frameworks of payments and expected business advantages exist. This presents problems for a company that, first, knows nothing about how, why, where, and how much money is involved and, second, understands nothing about the historical system that is in place. For this reason, it is strongly recommended that you conduct your business, at least initially, through a reputable and qualified dealer.

The correct entrance strategy should allow your company to set up business guidelines that adhere strictly to your corporate policies, both legally and morally. Select an Indonesian partner or dealer representative in an established position and support customer needs. As you begin working with this local dealer, the legal and moral issues effectively go away.

The dealer actually conducts business in Indonesia, and you provide support according to actual country and international law. That is the reality of business, unless you and your company desire to attempt to change an entire economic framework, instead of merely participating in the current business environment and prospering along with it while adhering to your high integrity. The dealer acts as a shield in this foreign maze of complicated favors and requirements, allowing your business to grow and, hopefully, blossom.

This does not illustrate the entire system of alternative business practices nor is it intended to jade the reader into thinking less of Indonesia or any of the emerging markets worldwide. It is simply intended to make the small to medium-size corporate management aware that these issues exist. This knowledge alone should reinforce the belief that the local approach regarding partners or dealers is without a doubt the best initial approach to these diverse markets.

Staying With a Good Thing

Some companies, now well established in Indonesia for some time, still maintain their local partners because of the long-term business benefits and continued insurance that whatever the issue, with the help of their local partners or agents, the wrinkles can be ironed out in the most cost-efficient manner. One company that has maintained its solid relationships in Indonesia is the oil field service and product supply business Hot-Hed.

Hot-Hed is a small, truly international company based in Venezuela, with support offices throughout the world. Their main product is sold to the oil field drilling market. This product was designed many years ago by Louis J. Wardlaw, the president and founder of the company. He took his idea and provided a better solution to a major drilling problem and founded his company on the sales and manufacture of that product.

As the need was realized and sales increased worldwide, Hot-Hed began setting up offices in many oil-producing areas. Mr. Wardlaw has run a successful business by taking Hot-Hed from concept to international success. The relevance here, however, is the approach Hot-Hed took in the often difficult Indonesian oil market. He learned a great deal about the market and then, through diligence, selected a successful partner in this field who would also stand to prosper.

This partner company then began doing efficient business selling to the oil drilling companies to the benefit of all parties. Hot-Hed gained several advantages in the process. One was rapid entrance into the market: Their partner had been in the industry for many years, had established contacts, and was therefore able to jump-start their entry. This partner was already accepted in the local Indonesian oil industry (noted by international oil businesses as a rather slow and often difficult business location). This greatly enhanced Hot-Hed's position, brought the product to market more quickly, and sidestepped any cultural problems that could have become an issue.

Trade Barriers

Barriers in Indonesia have been in place in several sectors, including agriculture and certain industrial sectors, with clear focus being put on financial areas. Of late, in compliance with WTO dictates and the many initiatives within the ASEAN countries, those barriers have been coming down and will continue to do so. The business community and its monopolistic nature regarding most of the domestic economy continue to be a hindrance or at least a slight, unofficial barrier.

The simple official average duty on goods is 7.25 percent, but this is in no way indicative of true assessments. Here, too, a local dealer, agent, or partner is the ideal solution, since that Indonesian company can help find the most efficient way to import goods. Some of these methods are quite ingenious and would never occur to a foreign company entering the market for the first time.

ABOUT THE AUTHOR

Peter W. Redden
  Tangling P.O. Box 0142
  Singapore 912405
  Phone: 65 738 9942
  Fax: 65 738 9945
  E-mail: redden@singnet.com.sg

Peter Redden, B.A., is the managing director of Pacific Marketing Company (PMC), Ltd., an independent commercialization company incorporated in Labuan, Malaysia, with regional coverage extending to Singapore and other Southeast Asian countries. PMC was established to assist international medical manufacturers with the introduction of their products into the dynamic Asian market. PMC's services include in-depth market research, regional product introduction, dealer selection, and sales management. Clients include Johnson & Johnson; Interspec, Inc.; Advanced Technology Laboratories; Siemens Medical Devices; Lufthansa Technik; and Moberg Medical Corporation. Mr. Redden is a skilled professional sales manager with exceptional experience in the Asia Pacific. He has successfully built and supported profitable sales and service organizations from their initial phases through mature product cycles.

Japan
The Fruits of Americanization

While Japan is roughly the size of Montana and shares its rugged terrain, their economies could not be more different. The Big Sky State is home to agriculture and ranching while Japan is one of the most industrialized societies in the world. The Japanese workforce is educated and highly skilled. Entry into the Japanese market depends on an understanding of culture and society, business practices, and the market and distribution system. Businesses should expect to modify their products to Japanese standards and preferences. This is where market research becomes vital to success.

Americanization: The Quest for Convenience

The major factors leading to Japan's incredible postwar recovery and boom have been thoroughly analyzed and discussed by economists and business experts around the world. It will be more useful for our purposes to discuss the backbone of Japan's economic success: put simply, the Japanese preference for an Americanized lifestyle.

"Americanized" here means the pursuit of convenience and the amenities of life, sometimes in conflict with traditional values. Some people may prefer the term "Westernized," arguing that European ways of thought, lifestyles, and products have also had important effects on Japan. However, the concept of Americanization more accurately describes the significant economic developments in postwar Japan.

Hollywood movies, Coca Cola, automobiles, radios, televisions, refrigerators and other home appliances, computers ranging from mainframes to PCs, fast-food chains such as McDonald's, convenience stores—almost all originated in the United States and came to Japan after 1945. These products and businesses have contributed much to the nation's economic growth by way of convenience and comfort. The high regard that Japanese consumers hold for things American is key to understanding Japan's economic success over the past four decades. Without it, the major growth factors so dear to economists and business analysts simply cannot explain Japan's extraordinary growth.

JAPAN NOTES

- The bus is the most efficient way to get from the airport to downtown Tokyo. Within Tokyo, the subway is the most efficient mode of travel.

- Obtain directions to meetings before your trip (both in English and in Japanese characters). If you get lost, you can show a cab driver or someone else the Japanese characters.

- Book meetings in good hotels.

- Never arrive late for a meeting.

- Most Japanese companies will have two or three people attend a meeting: a senior staff person and two others, one of whom will speak English.

- The Japanese deal with formalities first. They usually establish the ranking order of their staff, and it is important that you establish the ranking order of your staff.

- Always present and receive business cards with both hands and lay them on the table during meetings. Never write on Japanese business cards.

- Speak clearly and concisely. The Japanese value factual information. Never denigrate competitors or their products or services.

- Establish a long-term commitment. Outline the history of your company.

- While more Japanese are drinking coffee, plan to be served tea or soft drinks during meetings.

- Allow time for evening entertainment along with business dinners. Deals are clinched by personal relationships. Guard your behavior during these hours, however, as information can be gathered.

- Answer faxes and phone calls within 24 hours.

- Pay your bills promptly to Japanese suppliers (within twenty to thirty days—if not sooner).

- Expect to exchange favors with the Japanese. The regular exchange of information is important.

- Women should wear dark, well-tailored suits to meetings.

- While you are not expected to initiate a bow, you should reciprocate a bow.

- Always show respect. Avoid talking loudly, using slang, or making jokes during meetings.

Nevertheless, there are Japanese cultural values that come in conflict with and sometimes lead to the rejection of Americanization. One is the Japanese aesthetic sense; this will be discussed in detail below. Another is an ethical predisposition influenced by Confucianism. This set of beliefs came from China long ago and maintains a strong hold on the Japanese moral sense.

Aesthetic value or a sense of the aesthetic in the Japanese people often conflicts with Western world notions, especially American. This includes both physical (e.g., product style, silhouette, or color) and emotional dimensions, such as human behavior, way of thinking, way of life, management style of organization, etc. Business people who ignore these differences do so at their own peril.

Japanese consumers readily accept American products (including such services as fast-food franchise chains, convenience stores, etc.) that can improve convenience and quality of life. But the behavior of consumer tastes changes for products that are more aesthetic than functional. In such cases as jewelry, apparel, or other fashionable goods the market will be smaller because people tend to rank American products behind those of other Western nations.

The Japanese auto market is one where aesthetics dominate. United States automakers could succeed by introducing a revolutionary next-generation vehicle ahead of Japanese or European manufacturers. For example, a zero-emission vehicle with both reasonable price and greatly improved fuel efficiency might do well. Another possibility could be an ultrasafe vehicle with a reasonable price. The problem doesn't apply to European cars, which are widely accepted on functional and aesthetic grounds.

Americanization is expected to continue in Japan for the foreseeable future because consumers want convenience and amenity. Probably nothing outside of a combination of environmental factors would change that trend. And, if that happened, it would likely be a global phenomenon.

RIDING THE MEGATRENDS

There are a number of societal and historical waves that can be regarded as megatrends that will greatly affect Japan's economy and business climate. They can be broken down into five major categories as follows:

1. Aging society
2. Women's growing power
3. Information society
4. Deregulation and globalization
5. Conflicts between ecology and economy

Nothing is hard and fast here, though. Following a megatrend may be smart business, but it does not ensure success. And, success may be possible independent of the trends. Since almost everyone will try to follow or ride one of these waves, there will be tough competition and hard-to-earn profits. Given these conditions, you may find success in those areas where the megatrends don't affect your idea as much.

Aging Society

Japan's population is aging two to four times faster than populations of industrial nations in the West. According to the Ministry of Welfare, people over 65 will account for 17 percent of the total population by the year 2000 and 25.5 percent by 2020. In 1950 the figure was only 5 percent, which was less than half of the present ratio of 13 percent. This is due to the greatly decreased birthrate and the reduced mortality rate after World War II.

As a result, Japan's social needs as a whole will shift to what seniors require, for example, health care and pensions or related medical products and systems. Conditions, then, should translate into considerable opportunity for manufacturers of pharmaceutical products, insurance companies, and medical equipment industries as well as peripheral services like catering, linen suppliers, and cleaning.

These will also be a big challenge—and opportunity—as businesses adapt to the needs of a different generation. Consider just one example, how sporting goods will need to be made senior-friendly. Remember that bigger tennis rackets were initially developed with older players in mind.

Women's Growing Power

Japanese women have always been strong in the family. However, they had little chance to work actively outside the home until 1986. That date marks the implementation of the Law of Equal Opportunity and Treatment Between Men and Women in Employment.

Progress has been fitful, but sooner or later the situation will improve when society demands it. One major factor is the long-term decline in the number of younger workers as society ages. Another factor is globalization. Foreign businesses in particular will be relatively free of prejudice and find it easier to employ more intelligent women than less trained and incompetent men. Perhaps most important, women workers will be a valuable asset in a society where intellectual work has become more important than physical labor.

The changing status of Japanese women will, in turn, affect consumer markets. For example, the bridal industry will have to target a broader spectrum of women to promote its goods and services, and the women's apparel industry will need to develop the office apparel market.

Americanization can have a particular impact on Japanese women as they find convenience and amenity ever more important in their lives. Such fields as fast-food, convenience stores, direct marketing, and mail-order shopping will have a chance to capture more customers as Japanese women become part of the modern world.

Information Society

The changes here apply to Japan just as they do to industrially advanced societies like the United States and Western Europe. In essence, people at home and at work are connected to the so-called information superhighway. Computers and the Internet allow them to access information sources and interact with one another in new ways. The growth of an information society will accelerate the globalization of Japan, although it will also lead to conflict. The traditional style of Japanese management organization stresses that employees work as a group doing routine operations. The Web is anything but a group operation.

Computer software and hardware industries will of course have plenty of business opportunities. Growth of computer networking in turn will affect at least some of the traditional ways business has been done in Japan. Specifically, the distribution of merchandise will be greatly affected because it is highly controlled by such information as product specifications and where, when, and to whom products should be delivered. This system may soon face a revolution that will benefit foreign players in Japan.

Deregulation and Globalization

Japan has long operated a protective trade system. It began as a way to develop and nurture industries destroyed by the war. But, now established and guarded by a multitude of laws and regulations, the system is hard to dismantle even when everyone admits it is necessary. Unfortunately, the sheltered industries adamantly oppose change. To do so much longer, however, may hurt Japanese industry as a whole. Protection has left business ill equipped to face the fierce competition of international markets.

As to globalization, remember that over 15 million Japanese travel abroad annually either on business or for pleasure, and forecasts predict that the number of travelers overseas will exceed 20 million by the year 2000. Their per capita expenditure is more than double that of Americans or Europeans. Foreign companies need not enter the Japanese market to profit from this trend.

Instead, they can focus on preparing programs or accommodations that are so appealing that Japanese nationals will be happy to spend their money. The majority of Japanese travelers are not familiar with foreign languages, including English, so it is important to travel industries to provide Japanese-language brochures, menus, catalogs, and guidebooks. It's also important to use intermediary services through travel agencies, which can provide comprehensive information on your services, activities, or programs. Also consider that advanced telecommunication networking like the Internet will soon begin to play an important role in providing travel and destination information to potential customers.

Conflicts Between Ecology and Economy

Last, but not least, is the global trend of paying greater attention to environmental issues. This trend often conflicts with industrial and new business development, but it can also create opportunities for business in some areas. Two good examples would be the waste management and cleaning industries that serve offices, factories, and households. Yet another would involve pollution control technology, which has become central to environmental protection.

Another promising area is merchandise or products that can be shown to improve the environment or human health. These would include nonpolluting detergents, non-CFC refrigerants, zero-emission vehicles, agricultural products grown without chemical fertilizers, and so forth.

DOING AS THE ROMANS DO

Invisible Barriers Still Exist

Many foreign businesspeople believe they face too many trade barriers in Japan. For example, government approval to do business may depend on complicated administrative procedures along with a long period for examination. For what it's worth, though, misery loves company, and barriers can snag a Japanese business just as it can foreign ones.

Edmund J. Reilly, president of Digital Equipment Corporation, Japan, says: "I think people don't realize the change that has gone on in Japan. When I look back at the '70s and in most industries, certainly within the computer industry, it was a relatively closed market. In computer products at that time, the duty rate was around 15 to 20 percent on most products, there was a quota system in place, you were not allowed to sell to large corporations. In the '80s, all that has changed. The market is opening. All of the real substantive trading barriers have disappeared (*Look Japan,* December 1989, p. 13).

And now the complaints of domestic corporations' excessively complicated administrative procedures (including lengthy examination periods) seem to be bearing fruit. The government policy of deregulation is expected to end or drastically reduce the worst of the problems.

Even so, some invisible barriers will remain. The problems posed by language, history, and social customs exist in any foreign country, but they may be harder to overcome in Japan. As E. J. Reilly added, "I think that simply stated, it's a lot more difficult for an American company to do business in Japan than it is for a Japanese company to do business in America. A lot of it relates to culture . . . That's the structural thing that's so difficult. The answer to that is really time. As long as these realities exist, the trade barriers will never really come down. That's a problem today. It's hard for the governments to sit down and discuss that sort of thing; it's not tangible."

One explanation may be that the Japanese people are largely comfortable with a system that, up until now, has worked extraordinarily well. This success has produced great confidence in the methods by which it was achieved. The Japanese, therefore, see little reason to accept the exotic business practices of foreign firms.

Even Coca Cola Supplies Canned Japanese Green Tea

The smart foreign business knows to market products and services to local tastes. Nowadays, even Coca Cola supplies canned Japanese green tea to meet Japanese consumer preferences. Understanding culture also helps in coping with the invisible barriers mentioned above.

Always remember that many social customs are completely different from those in Western countries. Consider some of these typical examples. In Japan, the family name is written or said first. The Japanese greet one another by bowing, not shaking hands. When entering a house, they take their shoes off. They eat their noodles rather loudly by Western standards, and they pour another person's alcoholic beverage first. These are just some of the good manners in a society where tipping is not customary.

The simple act of working a saw provides a good metaphor for the difference between the Japanese and Western approaches to business: The Japanese pull a saw, Westerners push it. So too the Japanese use a collective work style while Westerners work individually. Decision making comes from the bottom up. Their way of speaking may appear indirect or oblique, but only from a Western perspective. Where Westerners will simply sign an agreement, the Japanese both sign it and use a seal. When in Rome, or Tokyo, ...

Distribution: The Dark Continent in Japan

One of the major business issues in Japan is the inefficient and complicated distribution system that drives up costs for customer delivery of products. In the United States, most manufacturers deal directly with retailers. In Japan, that kind of relationship is rare. A more popular method is to sell via wholesalers. Producers generally believe it to be less risky because domestic outlets are often too small and scattered for manufacturers to approach directly. This is also true for the so-called *Sogo-sosha*, or Japanese big trading companies that dominate exports and imports. At one time, it was thought they would soon disappear or lose considerable power because manufacturers would want to avoid the associated costs of doing business with them. In fact, the very opposite happened.

So what is the most effective way of doing business in Japan? Is it better to use a trading company or deal directly with retailers and manufacturers as the primary customers? Or does it make more sense to deal directly with end-users, viz., general consumers, via direct mails, telemarketing, or the Internet? Export only? Be more aggressive and establish joint ventures with some Japanese partners? Take a step further by having a wholly owned subsidiary in Japan? Like all interesting questions, these have no set answers.

ABOUT THE AUTHOR

Makoto Hori
  Nikkei Research, Inc.
  Park Side 1, Building 2-2-7
  Kanda Tsukasa-cho
  Chiyoda-ku
  Tokyo 101, Japan
  Phone: 813 5296 5155
  Fax: 813 5296 5228

Makoto Hori is director of the International Division of Nikkei Research, Inc., the preeminent Japanese economic and marketing research firm. He has extensive experience in marketing and marketing research. A specialist in consumer behavior, he developed the application of unidimensional psychographic scales to consumer behavior patterns. In addition, he has conducted many successful studies for overseas clients seeking to enter the Japanese market. A graduate of Tokyo University, Mr. Hori has been a member of ESOMAR since 1992 and is a member of the Marketing Development Committee of the Japan Marketing Association.

MALAYSIA
ECONOMIC VISION BUILT ON A COLORFUL HISTORY

Malaysia is a diverse tropical country, which until independence served colonial powers as a storehouse for such raw materials as palm oil, tin, copper, and rubber. All of that is changing as Malaysia's leaders implement an economic development plan geared to the twenty-first century.

Malaysia has a gross domestic product of approximately $81.3 billion; a low inflation rate is the result of some very prudent economic policies. The chief economic goals are to upgrade the country's technology sectors while increasing everyone's standard of living. Opportunities for foreign businesses should come as the government implements various incentive plans to achieve its goals. Success will belong to those business people who understand the market and have a cohesive plan to address its needs.

Building an Independent Future on a Colonial Past

Foreign companies wishing to take advantage of this dynamic and growing market must understand the foundation of Malaysian society, which happens to be Islam. The majority of Malaysians are Moslems and thus adhere to Islamic doctrine as dictated by the Koran and religious elders. However, Malaysia also has maintained steadfast campaigns against fundamentalist Moslem extremism of the type often witnessed in the Middle East.

Another characteristic of Malaysian business is the government's active involvement through legislation, regulation, and planning. Any business that thinks it can enter the Malaysian market while ignoring the government does so at its own peril.

Government controls have been enacted to promote Malaysian business while attracting the necessary foreign investment. But activist government does not mean hostility to business, by any means. The government wants foreign businesses and their products to succeed, as long as the Malaysian people and business sector do as well.

Malaysia is one country that has not forgotten its colonial past, when resources were developed to benefit foreigners. Malaysians have cast off the weight of colonialism and replaced it with a vision of Malaysia as a developed country by the year 2020. It is an objective that they are on track to complete.

OPPORTUNITIES: THEY HAVE PLANS, YOU PROVIDE THE KNOW-HOW

Malaysia has outlined the phases of its economic growth through a series of economic plans; they allow for step-by-step development of infrastructure and businesses necessary to support modernization. The current Vision 2020 Plan outlines what must be accomplished to achieve developed-country status by the year 2020. It even states expectations for Malaysian growth into the next millennium.

Rapid economic growth will depend on Malaysia's ability to stay focused and generate projects that will attract high technology and foreign capital. One such major undertaking of Mahathir's administration is the Multimedia Super Corridor (MSC) project. This project alone will generate many opportunities for foreign companies that provide products or services used in the information technology (IT) sector. Malaysia is hoping to convince the world's foremost multimedia corporations to locate business units and R&D facilities in the MSC, an area of 600 square kilometers encompassing Kuala Lumpur City Center over to Putrajaya and the new Kuala Lumpur International Airport. Participants would then act as catalysts in Malaysia's transformation into multimedia supplier to the region and—in the not too distant future—the world. The MSC is designed to be the center for advanced technical products such as teleservices, gateway services, resale and refile, remote data services, and Islamic banking (facilities organized by and operated for Islamic people and companies). The MSC also proposes to attract companies that can manufacture, enter into a joint venture, or sell computer components.

The corridor project is already generating opportunities for large companies. Microsoft has committed to locating its regional office in Kuala Lumpur and assisting with the creation of the MSC. Netscape also is considering participation in the plan. As these larger companies join up, opportunities should arise for small and medium-size companies with products and services that support the multimedia and IT industries.

Growth demands infrastructure, which in Malaysia will translate into such projects as the new Kuala Lumpur International Airport, the mass rapid transit system, and the new hotels, factories, and offices that will

MALAYSIA NOTES

- Malaysians will do business with people they've gotten to know, like, and respect. You must build personal relationships to succeed.

- It is difficult to form any relationships by fax. You must schedule a trip to Malaysia to develop business relationships. Try to avoid the monsoon season.

- Chinese Malaysians are very hardworking and are prompt to meetings. It may be hard to schedule meetings with these people as they are very busy.

- While English is the predominant language, there are many dialects.

- Malaysia is a Moslem state. Liquor will not be served at meals.

- Women should cover their arms and legs, preferably with pant suits, in deference to Moslem customs.

---

house the multimedia companies coming to take advantage of the MSC. And with public works comes more opportunities.

Big construction companies like Bechtel may get huge contracts, but this will also create many niche opportunities for smaller firms. Those in turn can mean new markets for food, Western medical equipment, Western and European financial services, Japanese electronics, and Asian manufactured goods and services. The MSC alone will open up markets across the board, resulting in many great opportunities for companies with solid plans and an understanding of the market.

Malaysia also aspires to become the regional hub for medical treatment and research. It hopes to do this by attracting experienced doctors and technologies, expanding the existing number of hospitals and improving their quality, and using government support to connect state-of-the-art medical technology and hospital centers via telemedicine. Telemedicine will utilize multimedia products as it improves health care for the Malaysian populace. Malaysia is therefore looking to create joint ventures with companies that can facilitate new technologies such as teleconferencing, telecommerce, and teleservices via the MSC.

Opportunities also exist for businesses that provide products and services for the petroleum business sector. Malaysia has substantial production capacity in its many refineries, both on the Malaysian peninsula and in East Malaysia. Joint ventures have been set up between the state-owned oil company Petronas and other groups, including Shell Oil and CONOCO.

SPECIFICS: SUCCESS IS IN THE DETAILS

Patterns of Race and Ethnicity

As foreign companies contemplate entering this growing market, clear plans and objectives should be developed. These plans should include specifically an understanding of Malaysians and their needs.

Malaysia is the product of its history, and, as in the United States, race has played a significant role. In particular, the *bumiputra* laws are a tangible expression of racial tensions in Malaysia's population between ethnic Malays and the prosperous Chinese Malays. These laws mandate preferred treatment of the ethnic Malay people, called the *bumiputra*. There are extensive laws that require *bumiputra* ownership of at least 30 percent of certain companies. Quotas also exist for the number of ethnic Malay students attending universities and on *bumiputra* employment levels in companies.

These laws resulted from race riots in 1969 and have been successfully implemented to ensure ethnic Malay participation in business; their existence has played a crucial role in making possible Malaysia's prosperity. But even though a peaceful coexistence has evolved, the Chinese Malays still control large pieces of the Malaysian economy. There are, however, large, successful *bumiputra* businesses that will flourish and grow even more successful as the Vision 2020 Plan and the MSC become realities.

If you spend time in the country and work with the local people, you will come away impressed. Cultural and ethnic diversity have not torn Malaysia apart. Rather, the Malaysian government has succeeded in linking material progress to cultural tolerance. It's a lesson that many developed countries could appreciate.

Governmental Incentives: Vitamins for Growth and Profit

Prime Minister Mahathir has stated he will repeal the *bumiputra* laws for companies that establish their offices in the MSC and for foreign companies that list their stocks on the Mesdaq (the Malaysian stock exchange). Changing the *bumiputra* laws is intended as part of the effort to benefit Malaysian business, especially in the MSC where companies will enjoy the least governmental interference.

On the whole, Malaysia has very few trade barriers, but it does have import duties ranging from zero to 300 percent. Most of the heaviest duties are levied on automobiles and luxury goods that compete with major Malaysian government-supported industries such as the auto industry. Such duties are relatively few, however. For companies operating within special economic zones, tax burdens are very favorable, especially for those companies that reexport the majority of their manufactured goods.

Whatever the incentive program, it is based on the government's awareness that low trade barriers, tax incentives, and protection of intellectual property rights must be embraced—and upheld—if Malaysia is to win the confidence and with it the business of foreign markets.

Long-Term Planning for Long-Term Growth:
Forget the Quarterly Approach

The horizon for Malaysia's development plans stretches to the year 2020 at a minimum. So contractors, medical supply companies, multimedia software companies, aerospace producers, and other foreign businesspeople anticipating future business in Malaysia should not be thinking short term, especially if the government isn't.

For proof, look at Sony, Mitsui Trading, or the large numbers of peripheral Japanese ventures that have taken hold and become successful. The Japanese, much more than their Western counterparts, believe in taking the time to establish business relationships and lay the groundwork for long-term success. Such a strategy meshes well with Malaysia's economic plans as it benefits the country and the foreign business both. The opportunities in Malaysia are long term; this fact alone should make a long-term financial commitment more practical with more substantial returns to be won through those investments. Corporate headquarters will have to follow through on this commitment, recognizing that although Malaysian investments may not run on the same clock as the U.S. accounting system, they represent considerable potential.

Local Partners Help Avoid Local Problems

Although the Malaysian government is creating many new opportunities for foreign firms, business in Malaysia—especially big business—often operates more smoothly when a company forms a joint venture or takes a local partner. In years previous, there was a greater need for *bumiputra* relationships. While the laws have been modified, *bumiputra* businesspeople remain powerful and well established in the business community. As in any international market, a powerful local partner can greatly assist business growth. Moreover, with a local partner, a business can better identify and react to the specifics of the Malaysian marketplace as it avoids major cultural errors.

Remember, though, that Malaysians are not likely to defer to foreign partners just because they're from developed countries. Malaysia's variegated resources, long-term plans, and substantial business achievements are all for the Malaysian people first; the goal is to make Malaysia an equal. With that understood and a clear awareness of the long-term opportunities that Malaysia can provide to foreign business, Malaysia is certainly one of the best opportunities within the emerging markets.

Distribution: Another Piece of the Puzzle

This dynamic economy has a substantial distribution network led by local sales companies and agents who know the market and can play a key role in helping you expand.

ABOUT THE AUTHOR

Peter W. Redden
Tangling P.O. Box 0142
Singapore 912405
Phone: 65 738 9942
Fax: 65 738 9945
E-mail: redden@singnet.com.sg

SINGAPORE
SPRINGBOARD TO ASIA

Since Singapore won independence from Malaysia thirty years ago, it has enjoyed constant growth in economic stability and sophistication; this, in turn, has translated into a growing influence. Singapore is now one of the world's principal financial centers and, as such, offers enormous opportunities to financial service companies, both large and small. And while not a large consumer market, Singapore enjoys the stability and good relations with neighbors that can make it an ideal springboard to the rapidly expanding markets in this region in Asia. To paraphrase Frank Sinatra, if you can make it in Singapore, you can make it anywhere in Southeast Asia.

Singapore has become the model city for other Asian countries. The infrastructure and educational system have made it the choice of many multinational firms for their headquarters in that part of the world. The governments of China and India, for example, are actually creating cities after the Singapore model.

Singapore's success is a product of its long-term commitment to order, stability, and family (not to mention the elimination of welfare). In terms of strategy, you can use Singapore as your "market entry" point or as a test market for your products or services in Asia. You may also wish to consider it as the hub for reexporting your products to such developing countries as Thailand, Indonesia, and Malaysia. Whatever your decision, Singapore makes an excellent location for doing further market research on your products and services in a new and exciting market.

USING THE SPRINGBOARD

An efficient port facility together with local infrastructure and good relations with neighboring countries have combined to give Singapore a substantial regional trade capability. This in turn offers excellent opportunities for foreign businesses that wish to enter the Asian markets. Given Singapore's history and long-term relationships with its neighbors along with the huge influx of capital investments and international sales/marketing interest in the region, it is easy to understand the growth of at least one related industry: the *financial and business services* sector.

Information technology and related demands should continue to increase along with the general volume of regional business. This is good news for both foreign and local companies with the technologies or services to enhance the efficiencies of the financial sector. Those firms will find a great deal of opportunity in Singapore and from there, other points in Southeast Asia.

The government's economic policies have succeeded in encouraging local businesses to expand activities overseas. Given the solid relationship between Singapore, the People's Republic of China (PRC), and other Asian countries, a good number of opportunities exist for foreign business.

As Singapore follows its long-term business blueprint, small to medium-size foreign companies will find it a good market or a springboard to other markets in Southeast Asia. Companies should take the time to determine exactly what their objectives are within the region; set realistic time frames; and decide on the best approach to any market. Opportunities are not limited to business and financial services; manufacturing; petroleum; or basic commerce and trading. Incredibly, there is more. As this dynamic region continues to mature and grow there will be opportunities for almost any product or service which is required by the marketplace.

Success, of course, depends on such factors as quality, price, and product support. If your company and products meet those requirements, Singapore could offer great prosperity and growth for your company in Southeast Asia and possibly beyond.

DIVING IN GRACEFULLY

After deciding to enter the Asian market, a company must address several factors regarding *how* to take those first steps efficiently and correctly.

Upon arriving in Singapore, you will experience a modern airport and garden-lined roads as well as streets and highways filled with luxury cars. Singapore is a country that is serious about "quality of life" issues. But this is not Los Angeles or New York.

As your plane is landing, you will be asked to sign the standard custom forms and something else—statements as to whether you are transporting drugs or other illegal substances. Do not take this issue lightly because the forms will instruct you that these are criminal activities *punishable by death*. Singapore is deadly serious about keeping illegal drugs out and protecting its quality of life.

SINGAPORE NOTES

- Always answer faxes promptly—this is a fast-paced environment.

- Book meetings in good hotels if you don't have a local office.

- Follow-up to all meetings is important.

- At business meals, ask your host to order the local food.

- Before signing business documents, consult your business advisor.

Setting up Shop: Registration and Licensing Requirements

In Singapore there are several methods of registering your company with the government; they range from the basic representative office through the formation of the full private limited entity. There are very specific stipulations and requirements for each type of registration, as well as filing and tax responsibilities. For companies wishing to set up a presence in regional sales support, it would be practical to start with a representative office. This will allow your foreign personnel to get work permits, your company to set up marketing support, and families to become legally involved in schools, clubs, or social activities in Singapore.

To form an office in Singapore, representative or otherwise, the company must register with the Singapore Registry of Companies. Upon approval, the Certificate of Registration will be valid for one year, when it must be renewed. For companies wishing to incorporate, the process is a little more involved but remains fairly straightforward. Local companies can be hired to assist in forming your entity should there be any questions or concerns.

A basic difference between the representative office and a full corporate organization is the fact that a representative office is not allowed to sell directly in Singapore. It cannot collect moneys owed the company resulting from direct sales in Singapore and cannot inventory or import goods. However, the representative office is clearly an excellent way to support a sales or marketing effort in Singapore and the region, with the Singapore sales being handled by a local sales agent.

Certain businesses are required by law to apply for special licenses to operate in Singapore. Examples include banks, financial institutions, insurance companies, stockbroking firms, commodities trading companies, and money changers. Other companies such as electrical contractors, housing developers, shipping firms with foreign interests, broadcasting and publishing companies, travel agents, massage and health centers, hotels, restaurants, and entertainment companies all have to apply for relevant operating licenses.

Taxes: The Cost of Doing Business

The Inland Revenue Authority of Singapore is responsible for assessing, collecting, and enforcing payment of taxes, duties, and/or levies under the various revenue acts. The income tax is levied on all persons who earn their living in Singapore and are paid from Singapore or persons who earn their income in Singapore but are paid outside of Singapore for those services. Singapore also has a double taxation agreement with thirty-four countries.

Singapore is officially termed an "open and free-market structure," which for the most part is correct. The government also has instituted a 3 percent general services tax (GST) placed upon all goods and services in Singapore and the government places a 4 percent tax along with a 10 percent service charge on all hotel and restaurant bills.

No import duties are imposed on a vast majority of products including electronic equipment, computers, software, medical equipment, and other consumer and industrial items. Singapore belongs to many regional trade-and-development associations and has been a major player in initiating free-trade discussions through these organizations. And, thanks to modern infrastructure together with strong historical and cultural ties with neighbors, Singapore makes an excellent choice for the reexport of goods throughout the region.

Choosing a Regional "Face"

Success depends on preparation. Along with an understanding of the registration requirements and different organization possibilities, a company also will have to make certain decisions about business structure and management. Let's say your company is looking to introduce a product and maintain regional support for it. Then the most effective methods would be to sell through carefully selected dealers. They should have an established track record, good relationships with your target market, and the capital necessary to run their businesses properly.

This selection must be made with care as these dealers will be your "face" in the region. Their sales force will have your company name somewhere on their business cards, and what they tell the customer in sales meetings will shape *your* customer's beliefs about your company and products. In other words, those dealers will make your name synonymous with success or failure. So it is essential to do research, speak to your customers, or hire knowledgeable people within the region who can assist with the selection process.

Day-to-Day Business Management: Staying on the Learning Curve

Typically, companies choose their best salespeople from New York or Chicago and promote them to an international managerial position in Asia or some other emerging market. They are then told to "go get as much sales revenue as you possibly can, as fast as you can!" This "standard" approach fails for several reasons.

First, it will take a competent American executive at least two years to gain enough cultural understanding, basic language skills, and sensitivity to get a real grasp on the Singapore market. Second, a company that sends out its best sales or managerial employees from the region they know best takes a double risk: Talented people are pulled away from one market and sent to new postings in Singapore, where they probably won't have a clue how extensive the variation in business practices can be.

To make the most successful market entry possible, I often suggest hiring a consultant who knows Western or U.S. business pressures and requirements yet understands Singapore and Asia. This is a good way to develop a solid strategy for doing business in Singapore or the surrounding region. This person can work as a direct employee or consultant, helping your staff to organize day-to-day business or assisting your new regional manager during the introduction phase. You and your new manager will benefit immeasurably from a consultant who can help you both focus on learning the ropes of the new market rather than having to recover from mistakes already made.

Remember Culture or Forget About Making Money

Singapore has a long history and close affiliation with the United Kingdom; so do Malaysia, Hong Kong, and others. As a result, English is spoken widely in business circles, and a basic understanding of Western business increases with the ever-growing number of students studying abroad in Australia, England, Europe, and the United States. This close affiliation does *not* mean, however, that all Asian business companies and customers care about the U.S. quarterly financial system.

In fact, this system is often the butt of sarcastic comments in Asia. While they recognize that it allows investors to maintain current investment information, Asian businesspeople believe such a system inherently breeds short-term thinking and a hurried sales approach. So it is essential that you regularly make your dealers aware of your company's financial calendar and give them plenty of time to close their sales deals so those purchase orders can be processed on time.

Companies also must understand Asian culture. From our perspective, Asian businesspeople may seem overly sensitive to "real time" issues. They do not want to have to wait for answers to their questions to come from London or New York; subconsciously, the delay may signal that they are still part of someone's empire. Avoid giving that impression by setting up a regional office to support the local activities of your sales force. That way, problems and questions can be answered immediately, in real time.

Otherwise, your customers are always days behind in getting necessary communications or support, a situation they are likely to find intolerable. Deliver support on time and you gain another advantage. Your customers and agents will gain confidence in a company that has the foresight to open a regional office. That confidence will translate into more sales.

Service and trust are, possibly, the two most crucial elements for newcomers to understand about the Asian market. When two competing products are roughly equal in quality and price, the company able to provide the best service will always win. And remember that the challenge does not end at the time of sale. You need to *maintain* the trust of your customers. If you let them down, your company may never regain that trust—or that business. In other words, don't expect much by way of damage control.

Distribution Means Competition

The distribution system in Singapore and Southeast Asia is facilitated by Singapore's excellent port, the very small size of the country, its proximity to other Asian markets, and its superior infrastructure and transportation systems. These factors all combine to make this small but dynamic port a focal point for regional business.

As a springboard to Asia, Singapore is one of the most competitive markets in the world. Many companies entering Asia sell their products in Singapore at the cheapest prices, on the best terms and with the most support in order to establish a foothold from which to build substantial regional sales. Any plan to enter the Singapore market alone should be considered carefully and, in most cases, adapted to allow a two-tier approach: first, introducing the product to Singapore, then expanding to the surrounding regional market. Selling in Singapore alone incurs maximum cost and minimum benefit.

Conversely, any plan for successful sales in Indonesia, Malaysia, Brunei, the Philippines, Thailand, and the emerging markets of Vietnam, Cambodia, and Myanmar must exploit Singapore's regional role. These nations all look to Singapore with respect and trust. If you can establish your products in tiny Singapore, the other Asian markets are likely to feel an immediate confidence in your company and your products. Without that Singapore presence, customers will invariably ask you why Singapore hasn't had enough confidence in your product or technology to use it.

About the Author

Peter W. Redden
  Tangling P.O. Box 0142
  Singapore 912405
  Phone: 65 738 9942
  Fax: 65 738 9945
  E-mail: redden@singnet.com.sg

SOUTH KOREA
A NEW ASIAN TIGER

South Korea has become an industrial giant capable of undertaking practically all aspects of high-technology production. Over the past thirty years, its economic growth has been among the fastest in the world. Korea has overcome many obstacles to transform itself from a subsistence agrarian economy into an industrializing nation. Considering the devastation wrought by the Korean War, these achievements are all the more impressive.

MARKET STRATEGIES

Korea's economy is one that survives on a thriving middle class, which makes up a majority of the population. Korea is closing in on the status of being highly developed. It has been able to export some high-tech equipment to North America and Western Europe.

Technology is the key to determining substantial economical growth in Korea. The export market for such products as semiconductors, computers, and other such technology-intensive products keeps the economy thriving. In order for Korean products to continue to succeed worldwide, Korea must open up its domestic economy by allowing import competition.

Inside Korea, the foreign investor will want to consider a number of things. To begin with, a skilled labor force with rising incomes will demand a better quality of life, so a variety of consumer goods will do quite well. And new residential developments are needed to keep pace with demand.

The government has responded by investing in the construction of super high-speed railways, roads, ports, and airport facilities, but this has done little to answer the call by the private sector for the construction of large-scale offices, factories, and private housing. For example, timber-frame housing systems, computer science, telecommunications, biotechnology, multimedia products, automobile parts, and pharmaceuticals are all good examples of products and services sure to do well in Korea.

It is also very important for foreign investors to remember that everything has its price. Korea's rapid economic growth was obtained at a high social cost, a deteriorating environment. Many environmentalists claim that because Korea is an example of rapid industrialization emulated by other Asian countries, the nation needs to show that it can create an economy that is environmentally safe (Yoon Suh Kyung, "World-Renowned Environmentalists Prod Korea to Become Model for Developing Nations," *Korea Times*, June 3, 1997, p. C3). Foreign investors should realize that Korea is becoming increasingly concerned about its environment. Businesses will need to promote environmentalism and do something to help Korea's suffering environment recover.

SOUTH KOREA

NOTES

- Unlike meetings in Japan, which usually involve a group of people, meetings in South Korea will most likely be with one person.

- Do not book meetings during July and August, which are the peak vacation months.

- Most meetings can be conducted in English (the most widely used foreign language in South Korea).

- Expect to be entertained, most likely over dinner. Use chopsticks, and expect the dinner to be a fun affair.

- Do not be misled by Koreans' extreme Western orientation; their cultural values are very strong. Don't rush into negotiations. Take your time and build a business relationship at the first meeting.

- Do not forcefully say no. Find a tactful way to make your point understood.

- Trustworthiness and character are very important to Koreans. They will sometimes be silent in a meeting to examine your credibility.

- Pay attention to age and rank, as they are very important. Be humble in your approach. Don't boast about your or your company's status or achievements.

- If problems arise in your business dealings with South Koreans, don't expect an immediate answer. They will take time to carefully explain the problem to their boss and position the situation to him.

■ Never sign any documents in red ink—it is a symbol of bad luck or death. Never give a handkerchief as a gift; it symbolizes suffering.

■ Women are not generally active in business in South Korea. They are, however, powerful in the home and in the family.

Korea offers many incentives to foreign investors. It is a growing country and is quickly making its presence known in the world market. Korea is also one of the fastest expanding markets in the world. The level of consumption by Koreans will rise with growing incomes and changing social structures. As purchases of automobiles, electronics, and furniture increase, the local consumer market is likely to keep pace (Digital KOTRA, http://KOTRA.or.kr/emain/e2/e21/economy/economy. html, *Foreign Direct Investment Climate in Korea*, p.11). In general, the outlook for the foreign consumer goods and the foreign business market is bright.

The Government

The Korean government has built its base on democratic principles and a free market economy. For example, the number of antigovernment protests and labor disputes has dropped sharply in the past eight years. Since 1993, the civilian government under the leadership of President Kim Young Sam has implemented plans to improve foreign investment through liberalization, simplification, the expansion of tax benefits and financial assistance, and by creating industrial parks for enterprises with foreign investment. Prospective investors should take a closer look at these four areas of special government measures.

International investors during the 1980s were put off by the limitations imposed on foreign business operations. As of March 1997, 97.6 percent of all Korean business lines have been opened up to foreign investment; some of the most recent include newspaper publishing, leasing of residential buildings, and insurance appraisals. By the year 2000, all but sixteen business areas will be open to foreign investment; those exempted include medical insurance, television broadcasting, and gambling. Foreign investment is now possible in all sectors, including restricted businesses, simply by submitting an application for investment along with an investment plan to the main office of any domestic bank or the branch office of any foreign bank in Korea.

Foreign investors may qualify for tax benefits and financial assistance when they choose Korea. The government offers an array of tax breaks and incentives. Most of the tax breaks are associated with particular industries or particular locations—for example, the free export zones, Masan and Iksan. Financial aid comes in the form of commercial loans and rent-free or reduced-rent factory sites.

The creation of industrial parks is another incentive for foreign investors. For example, Kwangju City and Chonan City offer land at reduced cost along with a plentiful labor supply to businesses specializing in high-technology and general manufacturing. And the two cities are both increasing their performance and benefits in an attempt to attract foreign investment.

In a related area, electricity rates for industrial use are much cheaper in Korea than in other Asian countries. Korean industries pay about one-third of the Japanese rate and three-fourths of the Taiwanese rate. There are eleven atomic power units in operation and five more units are due to be built by 1999 (Digital KOTRA, *Foreign Direct Investment Climate in Korea*, p. 8).

The telecommunications industry is growing rapidly in Korea. The government has indicated it will expand its level of investment in information and telecommunications. The Information Super Highway is scheduled for completion by 2015; this is a promising sign that Korea will continue to be receptive to new technology.

Some investors may fear that Korea's location could be a problem, but transportation infrastructure projects should indicate otherwise. There are approximately 70,000 kilometers of railways in Korea, and the Seoul-Pusan High-Speed Railway is scheduled to be completed by 2000. It will reduce the transport time between the capital and the largest port city to less than two hours. There are fourteen airports in Korea and three international airports in Seoul. By 2020, the construction of Inchon International Airport is scheduled for completion.

Current Economic Conditions

There are a few glitches in the economy that may cause a foreign investor to be wary of beginning a financial venture. The budget deficit widened to $23 billion last year even though the economy grew at an annual rate of 7.1 percent and inflation was contained at 4.5 percent. Public concern grew over the state of the economy, even though Korea's performance was much better than the world's average. The cyclical downturn of the economy, some deterioration in trade, and structural problems are contributing to Korea's suffering economy.

Korea's economy tends to run in a 50-month cycle. It remains high for thirty-one months, then declines during the last nineteen. The economy peaked in the third quarter of 1995 and has yet to bounce back. The prices for memory chips, automobiles, steel, and petro-chemicals fell this year, and trade levels deteriorated. Declining export prices are not reflected in consumer prices and only hit corporate profits. Consumers rarely realize what is occurring when export prices decline, and they fail to adjust their economic activities so that they can successfully respond to the situation.

Structural difficulties present another problem. International competitiveness has eroded in the last few years. Korean wages have increased faster than those of the competition and have caused products to lose some of their edge. Major business conglomerates are finding themselves burdened with rising debt ratios, increasing costs on factory-site leases, and inadequate social overhead capital. Korean products suffered further with the devaluation of the Japanese yen; Japanese goods suddenly became more cost competitive. Nor did regulations on corporate activity help to boost Korea's flagging economy (Seung-Soo Han, "The Challenges and Choices Facing the Korean Economy," *Korean Economic Update* 8.2 [1997]:1–4).

A series of reform measures have been put into place. They aim to stabilize prices, balance trade, strengthen market mechanics by deregulation, reform the labor and financial markets, establish a more open economic system, and continue reforming those government institutions that find it difficult to adapt to rapidly changing domestic and international economies. It appears that progress is being made thanks to Korea's willingness to attack the problem head on.

Foreign businesses should remember that not all Asians are alike—Koreans, Japanese, and Chinese are not interchangeable. A strategy for one market is not guaranteed to fit another. The differences between Korea and Japan in particular are vast. Historically, the nations have been adversaries, and it would be wise to remember this point.

This translates into the way you approach business opportunities. The Japanese tend to be reserved; by comparison you will be surprised at how assertive and outspoken Koreans are. In some respects, they are eager to prove to the West that they, not the Japanese, are the preferred business partner in Asia. This eagerness may make it difficult for a Korean business partner to admit to any difficulties at hand. Remember this in your business negotiations.

Also stay current with the political situation. Business and politics are closely tied in South Korea, with the government having significant influence in the private sector. Business conditions can change dramatically if a high-ranking government official is replaced. As a result, it is wise to know what kind of relationship your South Korean business partner has with key government officials.

As in most cultures, relationship building is crucial to successful business relationships. Along those ends, it is important to keep visiting. You may have more business in other Asia Pacific nations, but you should not neglect continued trips back to South Korea. Your continued presence will solidify business relationships, especially if they come under strain.

ABOUT THE AUTHOR

Hyun-Doo Park
Pacific Consultants Corporation
Korea World Trade Center, 35th floor
159 Samsung-dong
Gamnang-gu
Seoul 135-729
Phone: 02 551 3351 9
Fax: 02 551 3360

Hyun-Doo Park, B.S., M.C.P., M.P.A., Ph.D., is president of Pacific Consultants Corporation (PCC), which provides full consulting services in research, public affairs, public relations, executive training, and corporate strategic planning. Recent clients include the U.S. Departments of Agriculture and Commerce, the Canadian embassy, the Australian Meat and Livestock Corporation, and Brown and Williamson Tobacco. Dr. Park has wide experience in international affairs and development economics, gained in both the private and the public sectors. Before becoming president of PCC in 1985, he was managing director for overseas business development at the Ssangyong Construction Company. Before that, he established extensive connections in the public sector as director of international development exchange at the Korea Development Institute (KDI). Prior to joining KDI, Dr. Park was director of economic affairs at the Korean embassy in (then) West Germany.

TAIWAN
AN ASIA PACIFIC REGIONAL OPERATIONS CENTER

In the past forty years, the government and people of Taiwan have created an economic miracle and brought about a democratic society. The next step is laying the groundwork for developing Taiwan into an Asia Pacific regional operations center for multinational corporations.

THE ECONOMIC MIRACLE

Taiwan is not rich in natural resources. Almost all of the raw materials needed for manufacturing and energy generation must come from abroad. In light of these drawbacks, Taiwan's economic growth has been remarkable. Per capita income has increased from $145 in 1950 to $12,396 in 1995, an 86-fold increase over forty-five years. Moreover, unofficial estimates suggest that real per capita income is closer to $20,000 because of a large underground economy.

In the past twenty years, the average real GDP growth rate has been around 8.5 percent. Other indicators of economic vitality are just as impressive. Although the unemployment rate topped 2.6 percent in June 1996, the highest in a decade, it is still remarkably low for a maturing economy. Taiwan's household saving rate, still high at 29.5 percent, is decreasing annually—a sure sign that domestic demand and private sector consumption are increasing.

Most recently, the ROC government has committed itself to a series of changes that should transform Taiwan into a fully developed nation by the year 2000. These changes include infrastructure improvement projects, tightened environmental regulations, new trade and industrial policies to establish Taiwan as an Asia Pacific regional operations center, and furthered democratization. Taiwan enjoys a strategic location together with an ample supply of talented and diligent professionals. These factors coupled with economic strength, sophisticated financial institutions, solid industrial networks, and substantial foreign exchange reserves give Taiwan the potential to become a regional hub for multinational corporations.

OPPORTUNITIES IN THE ASIA PACIFIC REGIONAL OPERATIONS CENTER

On January 5, 1995, the government approved the plan to develop Taiwan into an Asia Pacific regional operations center (APROC). The goals of the plan are two-fold: to speed up the opening and internationalizing of the

TAIWAN NOTES

- Do not book meetings during Chinese New Year. Most locals return to both paternal and maternal homes, and most expatriates leave for non-Chinese countries. Most offices, supermarkets, and restaurants are closed, with the exception of international hotels. During this period, firecrackers are a 24-hour experience. Be ready for the noise.

- Allow at least one-half hour extra for traffic in Taipei. Most street signs are written in Chinese characters. It's best to go by cab with written directions to the company.

- Develop a personal network to be able to gather and check market and financial information on Taiwanese companies. You will need to have several sources for your research.

- Find a good local representative who speaks Mandarin. However, don't assume that this one person will have all of the answers to your questions.

- Have your business cards printed both in English and in Chinese, and bring plenty of them. When receiving business cards, leave them out on the table during the meeting rather than putting them in your pocket.

- Always be polite. Don't show anger or displeasure with anything as this will upset the harmonious relationship necessary for business.

- Do not discuss business at meals unless your host brings it up first. Learn to eat with chopsticks.

- Do not discuss Taiwan's political situation with mainland China.

---

economy while making the island a base for both domestic and foreign enterprises targeting Asian markets, especially in Southeast Asia and mainland China.

In addition, APROC also hopes to turn Taiwan into a base for developing comprehensive economic and trade relations with countries of the Asia Pacific region. The specific measures can be divided into two parts: macroeconomic adjustments and the development of six specific operations centers. Among the macroeconomic adjustments are liberalizing trade and investment, reducing entry and exit restrictions on personnel, easing restrictions on capital movement, and creating a modern legal system.

As noted, the plan also calls for establishing six specific operations centers. These will support manufacturing, sea transportation, air transportation, financial services, telecommunications and information services, and media.

In a related area, Taiwan has planned its National Information Infrastructure (NII) development since 1994. The government has established four goals for NII development:

1. Promoting the use of the Internet.—The goal is to reach three million Internet users in three years.
2. Putting all schools on the Internet (all colleges and universities already are connected).—All senior high and senior vocational schools are to be connected within three years, and all junior middle schools and primary schools within five years.
3. Developing Taiwan as an Internet hub in the Asia Pacific region.— By completely liberalizing the telecommunications and information services market, the government hopes to attract international Internet service providers and major Internet/Intranet technology companies to use Taiwan as a base for delivery of Internet services in the Asia Pacific region.
4. Establishing a "global Chinese network information center."—One-

fifth of the world population speaks Chinese. Taiwan inherited a deep-rooted Chinese culture, and the government plans to turn Taiwan into the global Chinese network information center.

In addition, the government is developing an intranet for all levels of government. Pooling resources from the private sector (including foreign companies), the government will install public information kiosks in every village, town, city, county, airport, and train or bus station in order to promote the utilization of its information network. Laws and regulations are being revised to pave the way for Internet-based electronic banking, trades, and transactions.

The APROC plan also calls for major legislative and regulatory reforms together with massive economic reform. Such an ambitious undertaking may leave some foreigners skeptical about the feasibility of APROC. Fortunately, the government has a successful track record in implementing massive reforms and major economic programs.

Taiwan is already making headway in the first phase of its APROC plan: liberalizing financial markets, establishing and upgrading transshipment facilities, and introducing competition into the telecommunications market. The Asia Pacific region promises to be one of the most dynamic and high-growth areas in the twenty-first century, and the success of APROC will make Taiwan the best gateway to the Asia Pacific region.

CULTURAL CHALLENGES

While the government is removing legal and other obstacles for foreign companies to do business in Taiwan, there are still many cultural barriers that foreigners have to overcome. It is simply impossible to bring together Western and Chinese business cultures without an occasional glitch. There is one shortcut, however: finding out how others have done it right or wrong.

Misconceptions

The first step to success in Taiwan, long-time expatriates say, is casting aside misconceptions. Many Westerners have gotten off to a bad start by underestimating local business or government. An American lawyer who has worked in Taiwan for more than twenty years said, "Westerners have to recognize that the Taiwanese people, working with a very small island and very limited resources, have created the richest nation in the world."

Foreigners should keep in mind that the talent level of the local people is extremely high. They are smart, well-educated, and hard-working. Unfortunately, it usually takes a long time for foreigners, especially Westerners, to appreciate fully the ability of their Taiwanese clients, partners, and employees.

Another common mistake is to rely on the person who speaks the best English in the office. There are many Taiwanese who are smart, hard-working, and have good ideas, but they do not speak good English. It is important for foreigners to judge people based on all of their qualifications, not just language skills.

Finally, Westerners tend to make the mistake of assuming either that the Taiwanese think and work like Westerners or that they are completely different. The fact is that some business operations are conducted in the usual Western mode while some are not. Sometimes Taiwanese think like Westerners, and sometimes they do not.

The Facts About Face

One of the most popular pieces of advice from old Taiwan hands is to learn the importance of face. No matter how mundane the topic of a conversation, the exchange could cause someone to lose or gain face. It's up to you to manipulate the outcome.

What exactly is face? An American who leads cross-cultural training sessions for foreign and local businesses defines face as a complicated psycho-sociological structure. Each time one person makes a move that gives or depletes face, other people are forced to react. Consider the story of a Western boss who offered a Taiwanese employee a promotion. When she refused, merely out of politeness, he took her seriously and promoted someone else. This loss of face forced the woman to quit the company. The employer meant to promote her, but without knowing it, he fired her.

Learning to avoid such disasters is likely to be one of the toughest challenges for Westerners. Face is something that foreigners always talk about with reference to the Chinese, but it is too complex, too culturally bound, too language-linked for foreigners to understand it fully. When confused about some aspect of face, seek local expertise.

One face-related caveat for foreigners: Hold your temper. Blowing up in the office inevitably causes someone to lose face. Unlike back home, an outburst is not easily forgiven or forgotten. If a Taiwanese colleague does get angry, it really is a serious problem. It won't be fine tomorrow. That person might quit tomorrow.

And what if you do get angry at work? If a Western manager blows up at the staff over missing a deadline, for example, the tension can later be eased with an office lunch, perhaps when the project is completed. Check the appropriate expense, timing, and setting with a local confidante.

However, the importance of face can sometimes be overblown. One long-time expatriate has observed, "Taiwanese do not care about face when it comes to money. They will not let face stand in the way of making money." As a Taiwanese herself, the author agrees.

The Importance of Guanxi

Another crucial ingredient for success in Taiwan is understanding and respecting *guanxi,* the Chinese version of networking. "If you don't understand the importance of *guanxi,* you're going to find yourself very lonely and ineffective," one seasoned expatriate says. Simply put, life in Taiwan gets a lot easier after a person cultivates friendly relationships with colleagues and clients and does a few favors for them. At the same time, newcomers must realize that no matter how good their product or how low their rates, they often cannot compete against well-connected insiders.

Learning to understand Chinese-style diplomacy, in which polite talk should not be taken literally, is another key consideration. Taiwanese education since childhood emphasizes the importance of being polite. For example, "Do you think . . ." may actually mean "I think . . ." or even "I want . . . ." Or "No problem" may actually mean "I can't say 'no' to your face, but . . . ." Put another way, the Taiwanese would not say a woman is ugly. They wouldn't even say she is not pretty. They would just say she is smart. But such roundabout comments are often lost on Westerners.

Local executives also advise Westerners to adopt the Taiwanese soft touch at times. One complaint often raised by the Taiwanese is that foreigners come on too strong. They come in and say: "This is the way it's gonna be." Such an approach disregards Taiwanese culture.

Negotiation With the Taiwanese

The Taiwanese are good business partners. They are fair and willing to compromise. A U.S. expatriate who had lived in Korea for ten years before coming to Taiwan fifteen years ago said, "The difference between Taiwanese and Koreans is that Taiwanese are willing to compromise because they believe that the sum of two plus two equals five while Koreans believe in the zero-sum game and will take three when there are only four on the table." Many joint ventures in Taiwan work out very well.

When Westerners lay out every request right off the bat, they look rude and foolish to the Taiwanese. Such a heavy-handed approach may even force a Taiwanese to counter the Westerner in order to save face. It is wise for foreigners to listen more at the beginning of negotiations. Take a little time to understand the Taiwanese plan, and let them show their opinions first. The Taiwanese will appreciate your politeness and repay you in kind.

At the negotiation table, Americans tend to show every emotion through body language, facial expressions, and tone of voice, whereas the Taiwanese are able to smile at you and still say "No." It would be advantageous for Americans to learn the Chinese skill of concealing emotions while negotiating.

Many Taiwanese are particularly critical of the American view of contracts. The Taiwanese believe that if you have a good relationship, you don't need a contract, and if you don't have a good relationship, the contract isn't worth the paper it's printed on. Moreover, some local executives view a contract as the beginning of negotiations, not the end. But to Westerners, a contract represents the final—and legally binding—form of an agreement.

Bargaining can cause another type of misunderstanding. In general, Western companies bargain far less frequently than Taiwanese companies do. For example, American companies are used to attracting customers by offering the lowest price possible rather than offering an initial price that they expect to bring down during negotiations.

Oftentimes, Taiwanese companies expect the American companies they do business with to drop their prices. But because the Americans came in with the lowest price, they have nothing to give away. By the same token, Westerners may not be expecting a Taiwanese company to bargain. They may expect the first price quoted to be the actual price.

When to Adapt to Local Business Customs

Perhaps the toughest challenge is determining when to adapt to local business customs and when not to. At one end of the spectrum are people who have come to Taiwan and said, "I am who I am. People have to understand that they work for me. If changes are going to be made, they are going to make them." Such people develop an "us against them" mentality that makes for an unproductive stay.

On the other end of the spectrum are Westerners who get into ethical or even legal trouble by adopting what they perceive to be "anything goes" Taiwanese business practices. As a U.S. expatriate said, "Taiwanese have a healthy disrespect for the law," which is difficult for foreigners to imitate. The best approach is to be willing to change some aspects of your business style (spending more time and money entertaining clients, paying Chinese New Year bonuses) but to go slow on some others and to educate yourself about the laws that pertain to your business.

Then too, there may be instances in which success means changing local practices to meld with Western ones. It is important to strike a balance between local and foreign practices and customs. If you feel strongly about changing a specific problem within the office, you have to be persistent and really follow through.

ABOUT THE AUTHOR

Lily K. Lai
Vision 21 International, Inc.
310 South Street, 2nd floor
Morristown, NJ 07960
Phone: 201-292-0212
Fax: 201-292-0258
E-mail: 1stad,lklai@worldnet.att.net

Lily K. Lai, B.S., M.S., M.A., M.B.A., Ph.D., is president and CEO of First American Development Corporation, a global business development company. At First American, she works with senior corporate executives to identify growth opportunities, formulate and implement growth strategies, and implement business process changes to improve management efficiency. Dr. Lai has over twenty-five years of broad-based global business experience. She has opened up new markets in Asia, Europe, and North America for Fortune 500 companies and has completed more than 40 global startups, acquisitions, joint ventures, and strategic alliances. Her prior business experience includes heading global business development, corporate strategy and development, corporate finance, and international operations for AT&T, Pitney Bowes, and U.S. West International.

THAILAND
THE LAND OF SMILES AND OPPORTUNITY

Although the "boom years" of the late 1980s and early 1990s have receded, Thailand's economy can yield substantial revenues for those foreign companies that offer the necessary products or services which are required, have done their homework and developed a solid business plan, and have a clear understanding of the financial and time requirements necessary to make that plan succeed.

Companies must understand that in Thailand time moves a bit more slowly, the weather is very hot and humid, and the U.S. quarterly reporting system may not take top priority in people's day-to-day business activities. Success will come in part from understanding these and many other cultural nuances. Failure may be the result of ignoring them.

Thailand is not one of the easiest markets in the world, but, if approached properly, the benefits will far exceed the shortcomings. The key to Thailand is *corporate patience*—things will not happen overnight and the pace of movement may seem slow, especially when you're eager to introduce your product or service. But take heart. Patience is a rite of passage.

ADDING VALUE, GETTING VALUE BACK

Companies entering Thailand or other developing markets need to understand the importance of "value added"; like the monarchy, it is something Thais take seriously. The more value a firm brings to the economy, the warmer will be its welcome. Conversely, a company interested merely in taking capital out of the economy will find a less enthusiastic market.

There are many ways that foreign companies can add value without hurting business. Training "in country" workers and paying an honest wage for work performed is a good start, but lateral and practical approaches will yield many specific value-added situations that will create the necessary win-win model. Those will allow your business to continue growing toward its market potential.

Toyota is one company with outstanding business achievement in Thailand. Their vehicles look to be everywhere. Of course, there are many other automobile companies in Thailand today, but Toyota worked hard from the start to ensure a solid market.

As an Asian firm, Toyota knew the importance of developing a long-

THAILAND NOTES

- The best time to visit Thailand is between November and April.

- Always be prompt for meetings, although your contact may not be. Hold meetings at your contact's office or in a business hotel lobby or restaurant.

- Always allow at least one to one-and-a-half hours for traffic in Bangkok. The traffic is among the worst in the world. Always confirm meetings at least one day in advance; cancellations are common.

- You can entertain at a Western hotel. It is considered an honor to have the last bite of food. When offered the last bite of food refuse it, and when offered it again, accept it.

- Dress conservatively, although short sleeves are acceptable (Thailand is *hot* in the summer).

- A Western handshake is acceptable between men. Thai businesspeople will be impressed even if you know only a few words in Thai.

- Never lose control of your emotions during negotiations. Thais will always avoid confrontation. While they will never say no, they may pretend that they don't understand and that they have to check with other people.

- Address people by titles like Mr., Mrs., and so forth. Titles are very important to Thais. Many Thai businesspeople are Chinese. Chinese names consist of a family name, a generational name, and a given name.

- Be very careful of gesture taboos. These include touching or passing an object over another person's head. Don't point the sole of your foot at another person, stamp your feet, or touch a person with your foot. Don't cross your legs while seated or place your arm over the back of a chair in which another person is seated. When seated on the floor, men should sit cross-legged and women should tuck their legs to the side. Remove your shoes if you enter a home or a Buddhist temple, and avoid stepping on the temple doorsill when entering.

- Never criticize the monarchy, even in private.

term relationship with the businesspeople of Thailand. Toyota took considerable time to plan how this business could benefit all interested parties, including the Thai government. This lengthy planning stage allowed all sides to learn more about each other. It costs money, but in the Asian context, it's money well spent.

The plan called for a significant Japanese investment in Thai production facilities. These would employ Thai engineers, managers, and factory workers, thus giving back to the local economy. Further, the Thai workforce would gain experience in a variety of industrial occupations. The Toyotas produced would be "Made in Thailand," sold by Thai businesspeople, insured by Thai insurers, and maintained by Thai mechanics. This was made possible with Japanese money, management techniques, and business strategies, all to the benefit of many workers in the Thai economy.

The obvious benefit for Toyota was a substantial sales increase in an otherwise difficult market, low-cost labor able to perform high-quality work, and the use of that low-cost, high-quality production to supply demands in other international markets. Toyota did its homework, invested funds in a specific and carefully conceived business strategy, and achieved its objectives. Who could ask for anything more?

MARKET OPPORTUNITIES

Thailand is no longer a rice, teak, and rubber only economy. Economic activity has expanded into the manufacture of textile products, computers and related parts, footwear, processed foods of all kinds, plastics, and rubber products. Moreover, Thailand is a leading producer worldwide of cements, ceramic tiles, sanitary wares, bearings, printed circuit boards and computer assemblies, hard drives, and varied agro-industrial products. It has become a world leader in gem trading and the cutting of gem stones. It also has a sizable service industry sector and a growing tourist trade.

Free enterprise is the essence of the economy. During the past decade, Thailand has grown at a rapid growth rate. Thailand is a member of ASEAN, a regional economic organization consisting of Singapore, Thailand, Indonesia, Malaysia, the Philippines, and Brunei. This is one of the fastest growing markets in the world with an average growth rate in excess of 5 percent, a total population over 350 million and a combined GDP of over $400 billion.

This trading bloc is the United States' fourth largest trading partner. The World Bank predicts that Thailand alone will have a larger economy than Taiwan, Brazil, Britain, France, or Italy by the year 2020. Thais expect their economy to double from 1996 to the end of the decade and be the leading economy in the ASEAN organization.

And the economic climate is lively in other ways. According to the Economic and Social Development Board, large-scale investments will occur in infrastructure over the next four years. These will bring ample opportunity to companies whose goods and services can compete in energy projects ($35 billion), communications ($24 billion), and transportation ($56 billion). If your company services these niche markets, then Thailand should be on your agenda. Infrastructure projects not only allow great opportunity for major companies such as Bechtel, who provide direct technology, products, or expertise, but they also open the doors for a huge number of secondary suppliers. Any time you pump over $115 billion dollars into an economy within a relatively short period of time, markets will appear for companies that can recognize them.

Thailand also is a ready market for exports of medical products and instrumentation, information technology products, infrastructure products and services, telecommunications, and consumer goods. The economy is expected to remain strong during the next several years.

Technology

Thailand has made a significant investment in information, computer, and communications technology. The academic and business communities are highly educated and are very involved in promoting domestic and international trade. Thais have been open to information on most issues. Their consumer market is opening up, and they are very interested in purchasing Western goods.

Opportunities abound for companies whose products or services meet the needs of the computer and/or electronics industries. This includes everything from end-product manufacturing to software and all products or services falling between the two. There is a corresponding push in the systems. Government data suggest that more and more companies are seeking and receiving the International Standards Organization (ISO) certification by adhering to the many strict standards such as management, quality systems, documentation, customer supply systems, inspection and testing, storage, contract review, reliability, quality controls for nonconforming products, packaging, process controls, etc. These investments in quality and efficiency will indeed guide Thailand on its path of growth and success.

Food Industry

The food industry in general remains a solid exporting industry for Thailand. It maintains a varied agricultural foundation with tropical areas and more temperate areas that allow for growing many assorted food products. These can be locally manufactured into finished food products ready for export or local consumption.

Another advantage for Thailand is familiarity with the local Asian markets. Thais understand the customary foods and tastes of the region's peoples. This knowledge allows local producers to expand into an international market with new types of foods while relying on the local tastes of the region to generate core revenue. This concept also leaves the doors open for foreign providers of niche foods or food processing equipment to enter and generate substantial market gains.

Textiles and Garments

Textiles have long been an established industry in Thailand. They continue to flourish, even though their percentage of national GDP has dipped slightly, because they are producing more European, western-type fabrics that are competitively priced and of excellent quality. For any foreign company involved in the manufacture of garments, materials, and/or designs, Thailand will offer a solid opportunity. That opportunity will again need to be clearly defined, planned, and supported within the reality of business conditions. In other words, it won't happen overnight, but with perseverance the rewards are potentially great.

DOING BUSINESS IN THAILAND

As in many of the countries of Asia, it's almost impossible for a foreigner to understand all the many nuances in Thai business, unless that person was raised in Thailand or has spent a great deal of time studying the language, culture, and market. For most companies, Thailand will be just one of many Asian markets under consideration.

The model for a sales organization entering this intriguing market will fall into one of a few general categories. The large company with substantial revenue or major in country business will most likely organize some variation of a private limited corporation. There are several laws in Thailand that allow certain businesses to be owned 100 percent by foreign businesses or investors while other businesses are required to have 51 percent Thai ownership.

The most common organizational form for the small to medium-size businesses is the dealer or agency relationship. This is not the only option, but unless the home office projects considerable revenue and appropriates substantial funds to make it happen, there are certain advantages in working with an established Thai company to get your product to market.

Cultural Issues

Thai culture is based on Theryada Buddhism, which involves the remembrance and recognition of ancestors. Thais respect unselfishness and people who lead virtuous lives. While Thai men have traditionally been expected to become Buddhist monks for at least three months of their lives, the practice is no longer strictly enforced. Traditionally, wealth has not been considered a reflection of virtue.

There are many cultural issues that pertain both to Thai business and to the general behavior of the Thai people. It is a frequent occurrence for the foreign businessperson or tourist to offend the Thai cultural belief system without having any idea why. Such would be the case in showing anger. No matter the reason (and I would venture to say that anyone who tries to organize business in Thailand will have his or her patience tested), *do not* appear angry. Thais interpret the expression of anger as a lack of self-control, and it could seriously affect any personal or business relationship.

Keep your cool and understand that displaying anger will only make a frustrating situation worse. It is far wiser to practice "polite persistence" to make your point understood. This accepted method of dealing with disagreement will also allow more fruitful discussions in the future.

Other customs worth knowing include not touching the head of a person, especially a child, and not pointing your feet at someone else or showing anyone the bottoms of your feet. Thais consider the head to be the most sacred place on the body, the feet the least sacred. Remarks critical of the royal couple are not appreciated, and neither are displays of affection (e.g., holding hands or kissing) in public between the sexes.

So a touch here and a comment there (or putting your feet up on the furniture) could get in the way of doing business.

Distribution Issues

The distribution system in Thailand is well organized, but depending on the goods in question, it can involve any form of transportation imaginable. This system ranges from delivery of local goods via motorcycle or small truck to international corporations guaranteeing same-day delivery or, in light of Bangkok's notorious traffic, as soon as possible.

The standard import and export of goods via the ports or the air cargo areas is up to date. Another advantage of working through local dealers is their thorough knowledge and experience with Thai customs and the paperwork that accompanies your goods as they enter or exit the country. This process is fairly straightforward for those who have gone through it many times, but without a knowledge of the Thai language or experience with Thai documentation or customs procedures, the exercise can be frustrating and can end up costing more money than originally thought. And you don't want to be seen getting angry, right?

All important documentation and customs clearance should be handled by your local representative. To import and distribute goods efficiently, the dealer will initially require your documentation and factory paperwork. Once the goods have been registered with Thai customs and documents accepted, the subsequent importation of goods will be a simple customs filing procedure.

Trade Barriers or Governmental Issues

The Thai government with its current development strategy tends to label itself a "free market" economy, but it's common knowledge that a great deal more needs to be done to reach that point. Protectionist policies persist. However, the government is opening up specific business sectors more than in the past, when a firm import substitution policy was used to contain capital outflow.

One area where the liberalization process continues to lag is the financial sector. It is, nevertheless, slowly opening up to international competition, and the government has included liberalization in its plans. And even though the current trade regulations make Thailand slightly less accessible than other regional neighbors such as Singapore or Hong Kong, the government's macroeconomic strategy is laying the foundation for future "defined open trade" and more international cooperative exchange.

ABOUT THE AUTHOR

Peter W. Redden
Tangling P.O. Box 0142
Singapore 912405
Phone: 65 738 9942
Fax: 65 738 9945
E-mail: redden@singnet.com.sg

VIETNAM, LAOS, AND CAMBODIA
GROWTH AND POTENTIAL FOR THE PERSISTENT
AND WELL INFORMED

The neighboring countries of Vietnam, Cambodia, and Laos hold great promise, Vietnam in particular. Whether you choose to expand your business there or in all three countries simultaneously, you need to understand that this exercise will take time, patience, money, and due diligence. Nothing will happen overnight. But those who study the market, plan well, and implement their plans systematically stand to gain an early foothold in these dynamic and growing markets.

LOOKING TO THE FUTURE

In many ways, the past has taught the Vietnamese that they can endure the harshest of situations and eventually succeed. So why wouldn't they feel confident of ultimate economic success? Most long-term analysts believe it's only a matter of time.

Conflict in Vietnam has also affected Cambodia and Laos. War and its aftermath, including the Khmer Rouge, have devastated both nations. The process of rebuilding has created some opportunities in Cambodia and Laos, though to a lesser degree than in Vietnam. Both countries have less money to buy imported goods, and (at least in Cambodia) a less than stable political foundation on which to build a strong economy. It is hoped that these predominantly agricultural economies (in Cambodia 45 percent of GDP is derived from agriculture, in Laos 56 percent) will find international investment to upgrade their infrastructure, modernize industry, and accelerate the rebuilding process. These growing economies may have great potential but generally lack opportunities at the present for small to medium-size companies. Nevertheless, certain niche-product opportunities may exist.

OPPORTUNITIES

Singapore already has identified Vietnam as a good investment. This ASEAN member has followed a consistent strategy of investing in large joint ventures where it can organize and control the entire operation. Such a method allows Singapore's proven business practices to take firm hold. It allows for very accurate business plans to be followed with little discrepancy, thus ensuring success. The Singapore model also calls for precise monitoring of investment dollars; this ensures that an investment is accomplishing all that it is supposed to achieve. Singapore has just been granted a license for an urban development project outside Hanoi. This project is Singapore's largest investment, worth $2.1 billion.

The capital city of Hanoi with its population of 3 million people has attracted over 270 projects with potential capital investments exceeding $6.7 billion. Many of the opportunities in this northern area of the country are geared toward high-tech industries such as electronics, industrial and export processing zones, aviation, road and water transportation, food processing, tourism, finance and banking, property development in office building, service-apartment, rental complexes, entertainment facilities, and educational facilities. There are even hopes for a stock exchange in the not-too-distant future.

In all, there are over 400 new major projects underway in the four main industrial zones outlined by the government. The process, for all the at-

VIETNAM, LAOS, AND CAMBODIA

- Unfortunately, the only way to validate your market research is to travel to the country yourself before you invest or attempt to do business. Don't rely solely on research reports.

- Contact other firms that have successfully entered these markets before making any type of investment (e.g., exports or foreign direct investment).

- The infrastructure of these countries is poor. Don't expect telephones, faxes, and the like to work all of the time. Vietnam, Cambodia, and Laos *do not* have legal systems to protect your patents, copyrights, or technology. Don't expect to have any legal recourse against copyright and patent infringements in these countries for a long time.

- Do not talk about the past war; the Vietnamese are very sensitive about this topic.

- While the Vietnamese economy continues to grow at a very rapid rate, don't forget that Americans, particularly those aged 45–55, may have strong emotions about the country.

tention it receives, has nevertheless turned out to be a challenging proposition for even the most culturally aware and seasoned international businesses. The words patience and persistence must be used again and again to help explain a company's success in Vietnam.

One result of the war with the United States was the decentralization of the Vietnamese industrial base. This began as a way to protect industries from frequent U.S. air strikes. The main consequence has been a focus on specific industries of particular goods within certain areas. The village that was ordered to begin developing light industry sectors such as silk farming, porcelain manufacture, or furniture making now has strong abilities in those fields and a history of doing these types of work. These light industries can offer exporters quality goods at a very fair price. The Vietnamese have been slowly building and growing their business in other areas at the same time.

The state of Vietnam's distribution system presents opportunities for foreign entrants. Generally, the distribution system—encompassing water, train, truck, motorcycle, and bicycle transportation, not to mention warehousing—needs a great deal of work: Roads are for the most part poorly maintained, transport equipment is often old, and reliability of service often questionable. Even as Vietnam modernizes, water transportation is still the most popular method of moving people and goods from point A to point B. This intricate system is still efficient and allows goods to move very cheaply.

Unfortunately, domestic airlines are not yet efficient or cost effective enough to make much of a difference in mass transportation or the large-scale shipment of goods. The national airline, Vietnam Airlines, has few newer makes of aircraft and has been functioning at less than optimum safety levels. But the situation is changing. Companies such as the German airline maintenance company, Lufthansa Technik, are entering the market to provide aircraft service, repair, and overhaul services.

The telecommunications sector is looking for solid growth as it attempts to improve usage from one phone for every seventy people in 1995 to four or five telephone units per one hundred people by the year 2000. This is a very ambitious goal, but tangible results can already be seen. Much of the telecom growth has been facilitated by a consortium of regional and international players who have invested and offered their particular expertise.

In 1987 the Australian company Overseas Telecommunications International (OTCI), now Telstra, was instrumental in installing a new link via the Intelsat system. Telecom in Vietnam has a long way to go, and therefore many opportunities will exist into the distant future. Still, it is difficult to ignore how far the country has come in such a short time.

The energy sector is an example of a large industry still tightly controlled by the government. Although there are large potential business opportunities to be gained, the process often moves slowly and with interruption.

In basic terms, the market delineation between Vietnam, Cambodia, and Laos is the result of many factors. The most important is population size, which translates into market potential. Vietnam has a population of over 74 million people while Cambodia has an estimated population of approximately 10.3 million and Laos 4.6 million people. Combining these numbers, the agricultural percentages, and the state of the various industrial sectors, it is obvious that Cambodia and Laos may indeed yield excellent returns on investments, but not for some time to come.

Things are different in the larger business or service sectors, where large infrastructure projects in telecommunications, energy, or manufacturing could yield opportunities for international business. So, you may find the larger Vietnamese market will lead you to Laos. But it depends on the right partner and the market niche your company services. It is far less likely that a presence in Vietnam will translate into one in Cambodia. The two nations have had a less than cordial relationship in recent decades.

Issues and Caveats

Don't Go It Alone

The current business situation in Vietnam, although improving, is still very deceptive and difficult compared to the other countries of Southeast Asia. Unresolved emotional issues over U.S. actions in the 1960s and 1970s, poverty, and the centralized planning model of the past years make this potentially lucrative market a challenge for even the best-equipped companies. For the smaller company, Vietnam will present many obstacles that are not an issue in the other well-established economies of the region.

The same holds true for Cambodia and Laos. For example, Laos has one of the few actual communist governments still functioning in the world. Ideology combined with an undercapitalized agrarian society will substantially reduce the need for many foreign products, although certain niche services or products could find great opportunity.

These would be in electrical power generation via hydroelectric dams; construction; and agricultural fertilizers, pesticides, and equipment. Any undertaking will require a partner company in the Laotian capital of Vientiane, and most business would likely be facilitated, at least initially, via Thailand or Vietnam.

Cambodia, given its present political situation, also remains a challenging market, and most product or service companies should think long and hard about whether the return on investment will justify the time, effort, and expense. This is not meant to discourage foreign companies from entering but to highlight the need for approaching with eyes wide open and a reliable partner to show the way.

Have Your Dealers Go by the Book

The typical method used by small to medium-size companies will often be the dealer representative. Very high tech products, which require a certain amount of service and support, will take more effort (and money). Alleviating some of that added cost will be the lower cost of service labor—once the dealer's Vietnamese employees have been thoroughly trained. Vietnamese employees are likely to be very hard working and capable but in most cases will require complete training. Don't waste time thinking the perfect dealer will come with an already-trained workforce. That simply isn't Vietnam, at least not yet.

Once the right company has been selected, employees must be thoroughly trained regarding both sales and service of your products. This will allow the new personnel to understand completely whom they represent and the intended market, and how you expect them to sell the product. As these training classes are organized, it would be wise for them to follow a comprehensive training manual that covers virtually every aspect of your product. The manual itself should be translated into Vietnamese for local use. This way, everyone involved will understand the product and their role in selling and/or servicing it.

The manual should include such items as product descriptions, price lists, service warranty information, correct and consistent information about the principal's company (with a corporate history), accessing customers, do's and don'ts of selling the product, a clear outline of an actual sales presentation (to be modified, of course, for local use), and information on competitors. In addition, I always suggest the inclusion in the manual or elsewhere of a comprehensive list of accounting requirements and procedures.

Be Ready to Barter

Starting up business in Vietnam, Cambodia, or Laos will be a challenge, even if everything goes smoothly. A creative approach to often unpredictable conditions would include the age-old practice of bartering. While it may not be an activity small and medium-size companies are accustomed to, bartering can work to your advantage.

The barter system gives a company with connections in the commodities business the chance of making money through the sales of its goods as well as the resale of that traded commodity. Barter transactions are not for the faint of heart, but they are a creative way to facilitate business in certain situations.

The basic idea is for a foreign company to trade for compensation instead of taking currency out of a country where capital is in high demand. Bartering can allow your company to negotiate excellent terms while giving customers a way to purchase a product they otherwise would not have. This approach is currently being used in varying degrees by companies that trade coffee, rubber, tea, and sugar, to name a few.

However, a new market entrant should be very careful and gain the advice and expertise of a reputable commodity trading company. It is best to begin the business slowly enough so that your experience won't come at the loss of all your investment. Again, this method is only one of many possible market approaches that will allow both parties a favorable outcome. Other creative approaches might include special financing arrangements, locking down exchange rates, or facilitating affiliated business opportunities both inside and outside of Vietnam for the partner companies.

Distribution

Legal distribution in Vietnam entails three basic methods. The first involves a local distributor, as discussed. This offers many advantages unless your business requires large inventory levels, but even this can be negotiated for the benefit of both parties. Local dealers can be either state-owned companies or firms in the private sector. State-owned dealers offer several advantages because they have access to more capital and will have a much easier time remitting funds overseas. The downside of these state-owned enterprises is they often lack motivation and are relatively inflexible.

The second method is to set up a representative office. This has certain advantages for the expatriate employee who would be working in country, but there are many regulations as to exactly what duties such a person can perform. This method is often costly—an expatriate would command a salary in the $200,000–300,000 range depending on family and seniority compensation package. It does, however, allow for direct establishment of the business and day-to-day guidance and understanding that is not otherwise possible.

A variation on this approach would be the negotiated usage of another company's established representative office for your employee. Your firm would have to negotiate compensation with the already-established company to cover all obvious costs and registering documentation with the government for the added services that would now be provided. All told, it is not overly difficult to organize and could afford savings for a company entering the Vietnamese market.

The third method of organization, called WOFEs, or foreign agents, is intended for foreign entities that have goods manufactured locally and need an organization to facilitate their export. This type of organization cannot, without special documentation, import goods for local sale in Vietnam.

Dealer agreements should touch on several points, particularly for private dealers who most likely cannot import goods. The contract should have a clear definition of time and clear stipulations for termination. It is not wise to offer exclusive agreements not based on a longstanding relationship. Do not transfer proprietary technologies and information to this company unless needed for manufacturing or assembly of goods. It is highly recommended that the payment be by 100 percent letter of credit at sight; this should be validated by a well-known international bank.

Do not scheme with the local dealer to undervalue the worth of imported goods. The penalty for this is very severe and could place future business operations in jeopardy. Finally, remember that if a dispute does occur, the local judiciary system will most likely support the Vietnamese company.

Trade Barriers

Put simply, import-export duties and trade barriers have gone through and will continue to go through many changes. The ASEAN directives for the opening of regional markets, with very specific duty rates and streamlined trade systems, will do a great deal to move Vietnam, Cambodia, and Laos toward opening their markets; that in turn will improve their economic growth. Presently, various products are categorized and then assigned a particular duty.

But trade barriers are not the real challenge here. More important are the ever-changing terms of import licenses, poor infrastructure that hinders distribution, and a slow-moving bureaucracy. When these are resolved, Vietnam, Cambodia, and Laos will be well on their way to joining the race for global gold.

ABOUT THE AUTHOR

Peter W. Redden
Tangling P.O. Box 0142
Singapore 912405
Phone: 65 738 9942
Fax: 65 738 9945
E-mail: redden@singnet.com.sg

Chapter 4

WESTERN EUROPE

However you analyze it, Europe is a major part of the global market and will remain so for the foreseeable future. A place with 390 million customers with a combined GDP of $24 trillion cannot be ignored. Although the population and income growth does not match that of the Asian Tigers or offer the potential of Latin America, the Old World markets are large, mature, and sophisticated, and they should be included on any global marketer's target list.

Despite their importance—or maybe because of it—European customers do not make it easy for the foreign seller. The problems of marketing in Europe reflect those faced by companies marketing globally: European countries exhibit a number of characteristics that, if unrecognized, will trap the unwary. The history of foreign assaults on the European customer base is littered with failures, some of them spectacular. Would-be conquerors, large and small, have retreated to their home shores wondering what went wrong and vowing not to return. Those who feel that there is a cunning plot on the part of the Europeans to keep their markets to themselves may well be right—at least to an extent.

Major global marketers have had a longstanding strategy in Europe that is based on the precept "if you can't beat them, join them." For many years a combination of acquisitions, green-field developments, and joint ventures have provided the world majors with strong local bases from which to assault European markets. Some of the implants and acquisitions proudly proclaim their origin and ownership and treat it as part of their assets; others do not.

Small- and medium-size companies are less likely to have the resources to set up in Europe and must therefore rely on exports to achieve market penetration. This does not make things any easier. These firms will encounter the full weight of local competition and suffer from a shortage of local contacts and resources that would otherwise ease their entrance. They must also bear the full brunt of the common external tariff.

If this sounds like a message to middle-market companies to stay away, don't give up, at least not yet. There is still hope thanks to the changes occurring in Europe. Over time, the markets will be reshaped.

THE NATURE OF THE EUROPEAN MARKET

Panning for gold in the European market is one of the most difficult exercises in any global marketing program, particularly for companies with limited resources. The overriding problem is that, despite the extensive reduction of differences among European countries, Europe is not a single market. Nor will it become one for some time.

Depending on where you draw the line between east and west and how you treat tiny states such as Monaco and Liechtenstein, "Europe" consists of at least fifteen separate markets, each with its own distinctive characteristics, systems, and requirements. Most of them do not even speak the same languages. To liken these European "states" to New York or California is symptomatic of the kind of naïveté that precedes the demise of even the most energetic export marketing strategy.

That's the bad news. The good news is that the Europeans are equally foreign in each others' markets and proximity does not generate affection. Indeed, some 2,000 years of warfare and rivalry among the European nations ensures that a supplier from outside the region might easily be welcomed more readily than one based in a neighboring country. Conflicts stretching far back into history have left scars that can subconsciously influence supplier acceptability.

But change is most definitely in the air, and the extent to which the current fragmentation will persist depends on the effect of a number of forces. Many of these are pulling in opposite directions.

UNIFICATION OR SEGMENTATION

While the dreamers look forward to a full political and economic union created by European legislation, the realists see something else: progress held back by periodic pitched battles to defend particular areas of sovereignty. So, the pace of change is almost impossible to gauge. In some countries the desire for unity is quite strong, but, in others, less so. And there is no evidence that the weight of public opinion in Europe is fully behind complete integration, either.

At the level of products and service demand, there has already been some major convergence of requirements brought about by the global marketing efforts of suppliers and retailers. But for every can of Coca Cola, every Benetton sweater, and every Toyota, there are still a multitude of locally originated products that have no recognition outside their own regional boundaries.

It seems clear that the forces separating countries are still stronger than those seeking to unite them. To determine how the situation will evolve, it is necessary to identify the opposing pressures and assess the likely changes in their strength.

THE FORCES THAT SEPARATE COUNTRIES

The European countries are separated by forces deeply resistant to change. From a marketing standpoint, the most potent of these are

- Culture
- Language
- Politics
- Currency
- Banking systems
- Distribution channels
- Marketing and selling methods
- Product preferences
- Regulatory systems
- Standards
- Government procurement policies
- Legal systems

Collectively, these forces still divide Europe into relatively watertight compartments.

Culture and language are obvious and highly effective barriers to any pan-European marketing program. Packaging, labeling, and promotion are of necessity organized on national lines simply to ensure that messages are understood. The translation business has benefitted considerably from the requirements of international marketers, but sometimes the nuances of marketing descriptions have defeated even the most able practitioners. Fortunately, not all translation problems have been as disastrous as the rendering of "Body by Fisher" into Flemish as "Corpse by Fisher" or "Come Alive with Pepsi" into German as "Come out of the Grave with Pepsi."

More common are the product names that are innocent or even evocative in their own languages but have an unfortunate meaning in another. For example, the General Motors model Nova was a disaster in Spain, where "no va" means "does not go." The mighty Rolls Royce Silver Mist ran afoul(!) of the German meaning of "mist," which is "dung." Mitsubishi had a close call when it realized the vehicle name for its about-to-be-introduced four-wheel-drive model would translate into Spanish as "sodomite" (to put it politely).

Distribution systems are also organized on national lines. The various attempts to superimpose a European distribution system have generally met with disaster. Pan-European logistics systems are being established, and, at a local level, distributors perform similar tasks. Still, the actual structure of distribution can vary significantly, along with the requirements placed on suppliers.

Consider: The major supermarket chains that control food distribution in the United Kingdom contrast strongly with the independent retailers and street markets favored in Italy. U.S.-style office product warehouses are common in the United Kingdom but are unknown in the Mediterranean countries. The free distribution of liquor found in the southern European countries is unheard of in Scandinavia, where the sale of alcohol is subject to strong government controls. The national idiosyncrasies of distribution mean that suppliers need a country-by-country distribution strategy that reflects differences in local conditions.

What works well in one country can be totally ineffective in another, and pan-European advertising campaigns are still the exception. This explains the mixed reaction to a recent Benetton poster campaign using emotionally charged images depicting a newborn child, an AIDS sufferer, Bosnian wounded, a priest and a nun, and black and white horses. There were howls of protest in some countries and complete indifference in others.

Some product preferences are unlikely to generate a discernible demand outside their countries of origin. Swedish blueberry soup; Norwegian goat's cheese; and brovada, a strange concoction of turnips and wine lees produced in Trieste, have all failed to attract an enthusiastic following outside their respective countries and regions.

This is not to say that it cannot happen if correctly handled. Fisherman's Friend is a cough lozenge produced in Hull, the English fishing port; the product's taste helps make it a true local niche product if ever there was one. And yet it struck a chord with hardy Scandinavians visiting the area and is now exported in substantial volumes.

For the time being markets are regulated nationally and operate under the respective national legal systems. There is a superstructure of European law, but the harmonization of legal and regulatory conditions that govern markets and marketing is a long way off. This results in a situation in which actions that are feasible and legal in one country are completely unacceptable in another.

Government procurement policies have traditionally favored national suppliers. EU rules now stipulate that contracts over a specified size have to be published in the *European Journal* and open to competition from (at least) all EU countries, but the chances of this happening at a grass-roots level in the foreseeable future are small. Although there have been exceptions, most governments faced with the choice of awarding a job-creating contract to a domestic or a foreign company will find some way of keeping it at home.

FORCES UNITING EUROPE

Now, for the other side. The forces that blur the differences between European markets are powerful in their own right. However, their impact tends to be concentrated in specific market segments. The key unifiers are

- Population mobility
- International trade
- Communications technology
- Activities of regional and global marketing companies
- Mergers and acquisitions
- Privatization and deregulation
- European Union

Over the centuries, population mobility has exposed national cultures to products and services that, although at first alien, often become popular. This mobility helps explain the growth of the ethnic food business. Indian food in Britain; Indonesian food in Holland; and Chinese, Italian, and French food everywhere have been supported by substantial immigrant communities of Indians, Indonesians, Chinese, Italians, and French. Eventually, someone else tastes the food and. . . .

Instant international communications is another force that has greatly facilitated international trading. First written, then voice, data, and visual communications have exposed Europeans to activities and events on a scale certain to influence their product preferences. The ability to communicate quickly with any part of Europe also facilitates trade and enables companies to harmonize and centralize the control of their activities in all countries.

One of the most potent forces for change is the activities of global marketing companies. The big international names have changed consumer and business expenditure patterns, sometimes to a major extent. They are driven by the need to expand demand for their products to a level at which production costs can be slashed and heavy R&D expenditures can be recovered quickly. As such, the global companies are a major force in harmonizing the demand for products and services and driving out local competition.

The global companies also have received a boost from international mergers and acquisitions. Europe long has been a happy hunting ground for the acquisitive, and the normal consequence of a foreign takeover is the introduction of new products, new management, and new systems that parallel activities in the parent company.

In addition, privatization and the deregulation that often accompanies it are major forces in most European markets, noticeably in telecommunications, energy, and air transport. The plethora of state-owned and -operated companies that proliferated throughout Europe following World War II are gradually being privatized as governments look for ways to make money.

A major effect of privatization has been to open up markets to the full blast of international competition. The privatization and deregulation of European telecommunications markets has attracted all the major North American international carriers and some from the Far East. These changes have even encouraged European national companies to go international.

To compete, suppliers have enlarged the scope of the services they offer, improved performance, and reduced prices. Those decisions have transformed telecommunications Europe-wide to the point that the industry is converging on a single standard of service. International competition can be expected to do the same to whatever markets and marketing practices it encounters.

But the European Union should be the biggest unifying force of them all. The European Single Market launched in 1992 was designed to open up a market of 320 million customers to all suppliers within the Community, and the obstacles to marketing throughout Europe were to be dismantled. In terms of trade and tariff barriers this has largely happened. Marketing is another story.

The idealists in Brussels overlooked the fact that taking down walls facilitates movement but does not necessarily cause it. The obstacles discussed above are still effective in maintaining separate markets, and the much-discussed Euromarketing is yet to happen.

THE PROCESS OF CHANGE

The forces that divide markets are considerably stronger than those that unite them, and suppliers panning for gold in Europe must prepare a program that treats each nation as a separate market. The prevailing attitude should be: Think Europe-wide in terms of opportunities and overall coordination, but act locally in terms of marketing implementation. Failure to do so will result in major problems.

THE EUROPEAN CUSTOMER

There is no one way to describe the European customer because no such creature exists. The reality is a menagerie of different customers conditioned by the local and international influences described above. However, there are a number of basic customer requirements when it comes to doing business in Europe. They are more or less common to all countries and must be factored into all European marketing programs. These cover

- Technology
- Customer service
- Information flows
- Origins
- Pricing
- Competition

In general, Europe should be regarded as a high-technology market. Europeans seek technology that either cannot be provided by local sources or is superior to their own. And they want technology that provides real benefits. For example, industrial users are interested in higher productivity levels, higher quality output, higher levels of manufacturing flexibility, greater reliability, and lower cost.

High standards of customer service are expected throughout Europe by both corporate and individual buyers. In the past European companies suffered from a reputation for providing poor service. However, the recession of the early 1990s taught them that good service is a prerequisite for survival.

Especially important are delivery speed and reliability, technical support, customizing of products, and after-sales service—all items that can make the life of the customer easier and reduce customer costs. In many cases European industrial customers have adopted practices, such as "just in time" delivery, that make high service standards from suppliers mandatory.

Individual consumers have also been educated to expect high levels of service. The "take it or leave it" attitude that used to be meted out in retail establishments is no more. It has been replaced by a recognition that customers have a choice and can take their business elsewhere if service levels are unacceptable.

The increasing pressures on business and personal lives and the high cost of failure have made European customers more choosy about whom they deal with. They want plenty of information on potential suppliers before choosing. Access to European markets has always depended as much on who you know as on what you know. If anything, this characteristic has only grown in importance.

The 1990s recession has made Europe quite a price-sensitive culture. There are many examples of stiff price competition in retailing, service businesses, and manufactured products. And the heavy policy emphasis on achieving low inflation in all countries has reinforced the perception that the era of annual double-digit price hikes is over. Suppliers are responding by cutting costs. In this environment, suppliers will find it difficult to launch premium-priced products unless there is a strong justification.

INTELLIGENCE GATHERING METHODS IN EUROPE

Prospecting for gold in any form means knowing where to look. Fortunately, data on European markets are generally as available as in the United States and most other developed countries, so the development of a statistical and qualitative map is far from difficult. All European countries have sophisticated statistical sources and a choice of research companies. These will be capable of generating primary data that range from sales, market segmentation, and demand forecasts to qualitative assessments of customer expectations, customer satisfaction, and decision-making processes.

PUBLISHED STATISTICAL SOURCES

The search for published data on European markets takes place in large data mines that sometimes contain rich seams. Each country has its own statistical sources, and there are a number of important international sources of data covering Europe as a whole.

The main sources of data in each of the European countries are

- Government statistical bureaus
- Government departments
- Company registrars
- Trade, industry, and research associations
- Trade press
- National press
- Data collectors and distributors
- Report publishers
- Equity analysts
- Publishers of business directories and buyer's guides
- Exhibition organizers

All countries have a government-run statistical service that publishes data on the performance of their economies and a variety of activity-specific information. This can range from the structure and growth of the population to lifestyles and expenditure on products and services. An overview of this information is generally available in each country's annual statistical yearbook, but more detailed data can be found in the publications of the various government ministries (such as finance, health, social affairs, and trade).

Company data are more freely available in Europe than in the rest of the world. In the major countries private as well as public companies have to publish their accounts and lodge them in national or state registrar services or with local courts. The documents can be obtained from the organizations holding them. The process is greatly facilitated because in most cases the information can be called up on national databases.

Trade, industry, and research organizations abound in Europe either as pressure groups, meeting grounds, or jointly sponsored research services. Their value as information sources for nonmembers varies considerably. While some publish statistical series on their businesses, others provide a service only to member organizations.

The trade press is somewhat more accessible. All industries are covered by a lively trade press in most European countries, and the depth and quality of information provided is on a par with trade magazines in most parts of the world. It is generally strong on new product introductions, new technologies, major industry events, and the activities of key people in the business and relatively weak on hard market information. The major weakness is that the information is rarely published in English. Although abstracts are on the on-line databases, the full article must either be translated or read in the original.

PRIMARY INFORMATION

In Europe, market research generally means survey research that focuses on the analysis of customers. There are over 400 market research companies active in the United Kingdom alone, and across Europe there are probably well in excess of 1,000. They range from small qualitative research companies specializing in the collection of detailed information on customer requirements, preferences, and attitudes to larger organizations that can carry out market quantifications.

MARKET OPPORTUNITIES

European countries are highly receptive to new developments that improve efficiency and reduce costs. While it is not an appropriate dumping ground for old technology, Europe will absorb innovations. Companies seeking to establish or expand a beachhead in Europe are advised to focus their activities on new products.

There are two key types of opportunities to look for. The first includes products—or services—born out of a *technological breakthrough*. These either permit a longstanding need to be filled, spawn a new generation of existing products, or permit existing products to be offered at lower cost.

Such breakthroughs are as likely to occur within Europe as outside it, but those responsible for developments should certainly determine whether their breakthrough has unlocked an exportable opportunity. The only significant risk is that a product developed for customers outside

Europe may be totally unacceptable to Europeans. This risk is minimized in the case of products or services that address a fundamental need not likely to be influenced by cultural or linguistic differences.

Such was the case with Dentalogic, a Cincinnati-based developer of dental equipment. The firm was established to exploit the brainchild of Greg Verderber, a young dentist. He had been working on a solution to a problem confronting all dentists: directing enough light into the human mouth to see well enough to carry out treatment. Dentists obviously manage, but they are always seeking more light.

Verderber hit on the idea of a dental mirror that projected a beam into the patient's mouth. This approach had been tried before with light bulbs mounted on the mirror, but it didn't work. Verderber's breakthrough was to use an optical plastic shaft to transmit the light to the mirror, where it was then directed up into the patient's mouth.

The level of illumination was stunning compared to traditional external light sources. The product was developed in the United States, where a ready market awaited it, and considered for use in Europe. The market research found an overwhelmingly favorable reaction, to the extent that European dentists using the test products were willing to buy them there and then.

It was clear the product would sell in Europe as in the United States, and at the same price levels. This was amazing since some markets were state-controlled and a good number of European dentists made less than their U.S. counterparts. But the basic concept of the product was a winner, and working methods of dentists in Europe were identical to those in the United States.

New technology in Europe has to come with a kind of built-in credibility. Most buyers, for example, would be suspicious of microchips manufactured in Uganda. Obviously, that wasn't a problem for Dr. Verderber, but there are a number of areas where European manufacturers consider themselves to be the technological leaders rather than followers.

Electrotechnical products (equipment for power generation, transmission, and distribution), telecommunications, and railroad equipment are three prime examples. In each case European manufacturers have developed a system they consider to be superior to anything from the United States or Asia. Equally important, they have convinced their customers of the same. So, non-European suppliers have struggled to gain market acceptance and market share.

The second type of opportunity for the global player arises out of *needs not currently recognized or acknowledged* by European customers. These are often examples of supply creating demand and include a wide range of foodstuffs and appliances: Coke, McDonald's, Levi Strauss, bread-making machines. Exploiting such opportunities may require a high level of customer education or a lucky chance.

Whatever the specifics, Europe represents an additional geographical market for product developments that have worked elsewhere. As such, the risks normally associated with new product development are considerably reduced although not eliminated.

PAN EUROPEAN MARKETING

By now, it should be clear that pan-European marketing is still in its infancy. But the advantages of a marketing program that is common to all countries are so great that companies are continuously seeking ways of circumventing problems. Some high-profile and highly publicized successful campaigns may convince the unwary that the problems are well on the way to being solved. Unfortunately, these successes are the exception, and their common characteristics serve only to highlight the difficulties of establishing a pan-European program.

The problems are all at the grass-roots level. Take advertising as a prime example. It is extraordinarily difficult to run the same campaign in different countries using national media. The languages, advertising standards, and laws that apply to the media differ to such an extent that very few campaigns can be run without extensive modifications for each country. The alternative is to use pan-European media, but the options are very limited in a world still dominated by natural media.

Even if suitable media were available, it is incredibly difficult to select messages and brand values common to all countries. Personality-driven advertising depends on the personalities' being as well known and respected in all countries. There are some people like this, just not enough to suit all products.

Advertising based on humor runs afoul of the age-old problem of different people laughing at different things. As to a simple common message, good luck. British advertising can be highly emotional and suggestive while German advertising needs to be factual and rational. So, where's the common ground?

And while a car may be a car may be a car, it better have a promotional campaign that recognizes the differences of each possible European market. Advertising for the Ford Mondeo, designed for the world market, uses three different messages for European consumers in 1997. Ads for Germany are aimed at establishing the Ford brand (previously the Taunus brand was promoted over that of the parent company); a second general campaign for Europe as a whole highlights driving pleasure; and a third campaign for the United Kingdom uses a complex message about the driver's senses being in tune with the car.

COUNTRY MARKETING

If pan-European marketing is the exception, the rule is a separate program aimed at each country. To be effective, such campaigns must both treat a country as a separate market and take account of local business conditions and trading practices rather than assume they conform to some general European norm. The challenge of working in Europe is to not be overwhelmed by the number and complexity of national markets.

FRANCE

France is the second largest of the European economies with a forecast GDP of $1,620 billion in 1997. In terms of income per head, France is seventh in the European league at $27,600. This position was achieved following a period of rapid growth, restructuring, and modernization during the 1970s and 1980s.

The French are regarded as the most difficult business partners of the major European nationalities. The French view themselves as clever, artistic, intelligent, and articulate. Actually, everyone is right.

While the French can be direct in their opinions, somewhat explosive during meetings, and less likely than most to disguise their true feelings, they are sound business partners and extremely generous to those they know and trust. Establishing that level of trust has to be the first objective of those seeking to do business there.

In terms of business relationships and business problems, the French will commonly favor complex and elegant solutions. The failure of other nations to do the same leads the French to wonder why.

RESOURCES

France offers the full range of marketing resources in terms of import facilitation, distribution, advertising, and other marketing services.

FRANCE

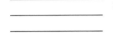

- Book meetings by e-mail or fax at least one month in advance.

- Most of July and all of August are French vacation months. Don't schedule meetings or market research during this period.

- Always allow for traffic in Paris. Don't be late for meetings.

- If you do not speak French, hire a translator. While many French businesspeople speak English, they prefer to conduct business in French.

- Do not expect the French to quote figures in U.S. dollars. Expect them to quote prices in French francs.

- Make sure that you call French people by their proper titles. Don't use first names unless they ask you to. Call French women "Madame."

- When invited to lunch, relax and enjoy—don't overload the lunch with facts and figures.

LANGUAGE

The French come in second only to the British in their determination to do business in their own language. Although an increasing percentage of French businesspeople speak English, and in some regions German and Spanish as well, it is difficult, and certainly impolite, to initiate a business relationship in any language other than French.

Once a relationship has been established communication may gravitate to English, but those seeking to do business in France need to ensure that initial correspondence is translated and that early meetings are held in French. French businesspeople will often permit potential partners to struggle in schoolroom French before revealing they speak perfect English. They will also applaud the fact that some effort has been made.

ETIQUETTE

French business practices have gradually merged with those of the rest of Europe, but there are still some that differentiate the country and can trap the unwary foreigner. French business organization remains hierarchical, and gradations between management and staff are more rigidly observed than elsewhere. Direct access to the top of any organization is difficult unless there is a formal introduction from a contact of similar status. The normal route to senior management is upward referral from lower layers.

Business relationships are also very formal. The use of Christian names, other than between close colleagues, is uncommon and any attempt at familiarity will be given a frosty reception. Even between the French, progression from the formal "vous" in addressing colleagues to the familiar "tu" is a slow ritual. The French also tend to keep their business and private lives separate. So, family and personal matters are not regarded as acceptable subjects during business meetings, even as a means of getting acquainted.

HOLIDAYS

The French concentrate their annual holidays in the month of August. Although less so today, much of the populace still decamps to the beaches for the entire month. The major cities are depleted of inhabitants except for tourists bewildered at the fact that the national treasures are left for their sole enjoyment.

GERMANY

Germany is by far the largest of the European countries with an expected total GDP of $2,340 billion in 1997. GDP jumped significantly following the absorption of the German Democratic Republic into the Federal Republic, although average incomes per head were diluted. German average per capita income is currently fifth in the European league, behind only Switzerland and three of the Scandinavian countries.

GERMANY
NOTES

- Formal, written correspondence is best in introducing yourself and your company to a potential German customer, distributor, and so forth.

- Always be on time for meetings (if you can, be early). *Never be late.*

- Most meetings last one hour. Organize yourself and do not waste time in presenting your company or proposal.

- While most German businesspeople speak English, it is wise to have someone with your firm who speaks and writes fluent German.

- Never call German businesspeople by first name. Always address them by their proper titles.

- Germans appreciate technical discussions. Don't gloss over data and facts that could interest them in your products.

- If you are using a German supplier to bid on a project for you, and you do not get the project, always let them know why you were not awarded the job.

Unlike France and Britain, Germany has retained a powerful industrial base, and the strength of German companies in the world market has been maintained by high levels of manufacturing technology and a highly trained and sophisticated workforce.

It is worth noting that heavy social demands and business restrictions make Germany's employment costs among the highest in Europe. The net effect is two-fold: Germany has not been a popular destination for foreign investors in Europe, and major German companies are seeking to relocate more of their own activities outside Germany.

Business organization in Germany is more concentrated and controlled than in most European countries, despite the relative absence of state-owned companies. The Federation of German Industry and the quasi-governmental local chambers of commerce are powerful organizations that coordinate the voices of industrialists in influencing government and public opinion. Concentration is also enhanced by trusts and cartels active in the steel, coal, chemical, and other basic industries and that have a tacitly approved legal position.

The reunification of Germany has cost the former West Germans dearly. Resources (paid for by a "solidarity" income tax surcharge) have been poured into renewing the infrastructure in the east, creating demand for a wide range of basic products and services, particularly construction, telecommunications, and health care. But the gap between east and west remains large.

Unemployment and wage inflation are higher in the east, and despite the investment in state-of-the-art production plants, productivity is lower. The best estimates are that it will take the eastern states another fifteen to twenty years to catch up.

LANGUAGE

The Germans are more likely to speak English, and to a lesser extent French, than the other continental nations. They are also less likely to be insulted by the fact that foreigners cannot speak their language and will do all they can to aid communications. The German education system teaches languages at a very early age.

ETIQUETTE

German businesses are hierarchical in structure, with a strong tendency to be secretive rather than open. Letters from German companies are commonly signed by two staff members (the writer and his or her superior), suggesting that the content is closely checked before dispatch.

Inquiries about German companies will often be rebuffed on the grounds that answering them infringes on data protection laws. Business decisions can be delayed for days because subordinates need to confer with their bosses before agreeing to any meetings or providing information over the telephone.

Business relationships are very formal. The use of first names is uncommon even between colleagues, unless they are the same age. It can take a very long time before someone will be invited to address colleagues with the informal "Du" instead of the formal "Sie," and remember that only the elder person can initiate the use of "Du."

HOSPITALITY

Important business decisions are usually made in the meeting room, not at lunch and very rarely on the golf course. Lunch will rarely be more elaborate than a three-course meal in the executive area of the staff canteen. It is quite common to consume alcohol at lunches, although in moderate amounts.

HOLIDAYS

Germans do have a very generous holiday entitlement, an average of thirty days per year. It is quite common for even senior businesspeople to leave for a three-week period. As in France, there is the tendency to take Friday or Monday off as an additional holiday when a national holiday falls on a Thursday or Tuesday.

ITALY

With a forecast GNP of $1,310 billion in 1997 Italy is the third largest of the European economies. In terms of income per head it lies eleventh in the European pecking order at $22,942. In politics and business, Italy provides the most mercurial of all the European environments. If you don't like the current situation in Italy, stick around, it is sure to change.

A series of corruption scandals came to a head in the early 1990s and led to the downfall of a prime minister amid threats of incarceration for large numbers of Italian business leaders and politicians. Although the resulting anticorruption measures may have been more spoken about than acted upon, the crisis did initiate a period of political and economic reform. This was marked by budget austerity, privatization, and rationalization, all of which are much needed but will take a considerable time to achieve.

LANGUAGE

Italians, like the occupants of other Mediterranean countries, are less likely to speak English than the northern Europeans. French is spoken as a second language in the northwest, and German in the area south of the Austrian border (often referred to as the South Tyrol). Elsewhere in Italy there are strong local dialects that can prove incomprehensible even to good Italian speakers.

Unlike the French, the Italians are not offended if visitors do not speak Italian but are inordinately impressed if they do. Business meetings always are expected to be in Italian, but the host will do everything possible to ensure that visitors understand what is taking place even down to speaking some rusty English to clarify a specific point.

ETIQUETTE

Italian companies are intensely hierarchical, and the general business environment is relatively formal. As in France, senior staff are difficult to reach, and junior staff rarely have the authority to conclude important deals. As a result, networking—having good contacts and using them to open doors and gain introductions—is an essential part of business life. Having a good client list will be a major asset in attracting new buyers who will be interested in seeing a supplier's other customers.

In many other ways, business in Italy is quite casual. Dress tends to be smart/casual rather than formal, with the accent on style rather than tradition. The Italians are not themselves obsessively punctual and will not find it strange or unwelcome in others. In many organizations, particularly government departments and state-owned companies, patience is an essential characteristic for the would-be supplier.

In other European markets, entertainment and hospitality create a bond between buyer and supplier. In Italy the deal "sweetener" may still be cash-related, and nepotism is still an important method of career advancement. The recent scandals have heightened awareness of these practices and may have gone some way to reducing their incidence.

UNITED KINGDOM

The United Kingdom is the fourth largest of the European countries, with a projected 1997 GNP of $1,230 billion. Income per head is $20,883, which places it twelfth in the European league. The overall business envi-

ITALY NOTES

- Dress well for meetings in Italy.

- Have someone from your firm who speaks Italian at your meeting to ensure that there are no misunderstandings.

- Italians are very warm and expressive people. Let them talk and finish their sales presentations at their pace.

- Even if business doesn't develop immediately, keep up your personal contacts and relationships in Italy for when the market timing is right.

- Word of mouth is a good way to determine the reliability of an Italian supplier.

- Check on methods of payment from Italian companies. Payment can take up to six months.

---

ronment in the United Kingdom closely parallels that of the United States. This follows a long period of adjustment during which the balance of economic activity switched from manufacturing to service businesses.

Such traditional British businesses as textiles, steel, and heavy engineering have succumbed to foreign competition while the financial, professional, and business services sectors have boomed. Aided by legislation during the 1980s and 1990s, the restructuring has been accompanied by a switch to a liberal-operating environment where old vested interests like labor unions have been neutered and a stronger enterprise culture has been fostered.

The British reputation for being reserved, superior, disdainful, quietly competent, and pompous is well earned since these were characteristics that enabled them to build an empire and survive two world wars. However, the fall of the moneyed classes and the rise of the meritocracy has brought a leveling downward in attitudes and personal characteristics.

A senior businessman is as likely to have a London or northern accent as one honed in the Oxbridge schools. His contacts will be drawn from university, the golf club, or business rather than the military, a gentleman's club, or the society set. He is altogether a much easier person to do business with than his forebears.

RESOURCES

Marketing is one of the service businesses that has flourished in Britain. As a consequence, the country enjoys a substantial reservoir of research, advertising, public relations, and promotional agencies. Many of these are internationally renowned and operate throughout Europe either directly or through subsidiaries. For companies whose first, or first foreign, language is English, the United Kingdom is an attractive launching pad for any European marketing effort.

LANGUAGE

While English makes Britain attractive as a market and as a base for international operations, fluency in foreign languages is not a key British skill. This may seem strange for the country that once controlled a quarter of the globe and is a major trading nation. Then again, the standard approach to the native peoples was either to ignore them or teach them English.

ETIQUETTE

The rigid social hierarchy that once prevailed in Britain has been virtually swept away. Informality now rules, and even government ministers have been instructed to address each other by their first names. In business there is still some deference to age and seniority, but it is also common for contacts to be on first-name terms, even on first telephone contact.

HOSPITALITY

What were once the prime social events in the summer social calendar are now dominated by corporate hospitality tents in which business contacts are forged and honed. Everything from Ascot and Wimbledon to Henley

UNITED KINGDOM

- Answer faxes and business correspondence promptly. Don't assume that just because they speak English, you can delay getting back to them.

- Most business will be conducted either at your contact's office or over lunch. Don't expect an elaborate lunch.

- The British usually schedule one-hour meetings and run on tight schedules.

- If you want the British to quote in U.S. dollars, rather than pounds sterling, tell them so.

- Do not drag out payment to a British supplier.

- Like Americans, the British use first names in business. Do not call someone by first name, however, until asked to do so.

and the Derby provides an opportunity for corporate entertainment designed to create a bond and an obligation to do business.

SPAIN

Spain is physically a large country, but in terms of income it is roughly half the size of the leading European markets. GDP in 1997 will be an estimated $611 million. In terms of income per capita, Spain's average of $15,500 is also significantly lower than those of the major countries. Until recently, Spain existed as a kind of appendage to Europe, more interested in Latin America than its more immediate neighbors.

Like Italy, Spain recently has gone through a series of scandals that stem from traditional political and business practices. Having the right contacts is still important while the giving and repayment of favors remains part of the interface between government and business. This suggests that success will go to foreign organizations with strong local partners who can introduce them into the business environment.

LANGUAGE

The primary language in Spain is Castillian Spanish. There are, however, significant minorities speaking Catalan (17 percent), Galician (7 percent), and Basque (2 percent). Businesspeople in the areas where minority languages are spoken will commonly speak Castillian Spanish as well, but a nod of understanding that there is a local language will generate considerable goodwill.

ETIQUETTE AND HOSPITALITY

Businesses in Spain are run on rather formal lines. Age and experience are deferred to, and initial contacts with foreigners will be somewhat stiff rather than overtly friendly. Without some form of introduction, business contacts are harder to initiate than elsewhere in Europe. Once the barriers are penetrated, the Spanish are hospitable, but they will maintain a certain distance, not to say aloofness, for some time.

As in all Mediterranean countries, much business contact revolves around meals. Lunch is a long affair, even though the traditional siesta has been rendered irrelevant by air conditioning. Long lunches mean that working hours stretch until well into the evening, and a visitor should not be surprised at meetings starting at 8 p.m. and dinner dates commencing at 10 p.m.

BELGIUM

Even though one of the smallest European countries, Belgium is the home of the European Commission and is closely associated with the integration of Europe. Its international outlook has developed over many years, which may explain why Belgium has been the host country for so many multinational corporations.

However, cosmopolitanism gives way to ethnicity in the matters of everyday life. Belgians are oriented either toward France (the Walloons in the south of the country) or the Netherlands (the Flemish in the north of

SPAIN NOTES

- Book meetings at least one month in advance. Bring a Spanish-speaking colleague to meetings with you.

- Research the market and your potential Spanish partners thoroughly before meeting.

- While many businesses in Madrid and Barcelona have a 9:00 a.m. to 5:00 p.m. work day, the norm for Spain is 9:00 a.m. to 1:30 or 2:00 p.m. and then 3:00 p.m. to 6:30 p.m.

- If you are invited to dinner, don't expect to be served until 9:00 or 10:00 p.m. Don't discuss business until the end of the meal.

- As in other Latin countries, business negotiations will not be direct. They will take time.

- Spaniards love to talk about sports. Brush up on local sports as well as some worldwide sports.

---

the country). The ethnic tensions that divided the country in the 1960s and 1970s appear to have subsided and been replaced by a prosperous coexistence.

Meeting the demands of the international community in Belgium has given Belgians an unusual diversity of products and services and created a highly sophisticated market. Like most small European countries, Belgium has thrived on trade, and it is now seeking to promote itself as a logistical center for European operations.

THE NETHERLANDS

Although relatively small physically and economically, the Netherlands is the most international of all European countries. Sitting at the head of the Rhine river, Holland long has traded with Europe and the world. Combined exports and imports account for 60 percent of GDP.

The Netherlands is one of the easiest countries to do business in. It is completely open to foreign suppliers, who receive the same treatment as domestic companies. Foreign firms account for a quarter of Dutch output and employment.

The Dutch population is relatively young, highly educated, and multilingual. It is unusual to encounter a person who does not speak fluent English or German. The business environment is quite informal. Dress tends to be casual, and contacts are easy to make. A full range of sophisticated marketing resources is available.

SCANDINAVIA

The Scandinavian markets (Sweden, Norway, Denmark, and Finland) are among the smallest in Europe—and the wealthiest. Their wealth is based on natural resources (forestry, fishing, oil, and minerals) in addition to a longstanding investment in high-quality, highly innovative manufacturing.

Relative to their size, Scandinavian countries contribute a surprising number of household names to the listings of major international companies. Companies like Volvo, Saab, Electrolux, Lego, and Norsk Hydro were forced into global marketing at an early stage of their development; their domestic markets were too small to fulfill their ambitions. Even mid-size Scandinavian companies are leading players in a wide range of high-technology niche markets.

Many Scandinavians have lived and worked abroad, and most speak fluent English. In the past, working overseas was an acceptable escape from punitive personal tax burdens, high levels of state intervention, and a rather severe culture.

The international outlook makes Scandinavians highly receptive to foreign products, but even the most ardent supporters of Scandinavia would have to admit that the region is boring to outsiders. That impression is bolstered by the long and severe winters that affect all of the region north of Denmark. The northern parts see no daylight in midwinter, and to compensate, a high proportion of Scandinavians spend the summer months on the beaches of southern Europe. The months of June and July are virtually dead for business.

Scandinavians are formal in their business relationships, but as might be expected in an egalitarian society, business structures are simple and senior staff are easily accessible.

ABOUT THE AUTHOR

Chris West
Marketing Intelligence Services Ltd
109 Uxbridge Road, Ealing
London W5 5TL
Phone: 441 81 579 9400
Fax: 441 81 566 4931

Chris West is managing director of Marketing Intelligence Services (MIS) Ltd. He has extensive market research experience in a broad range of business sectors, including industrial markets, consumer sectors, energy, chemicals, and the pharmaceutical and health care industries. Before founding MIS in 1984, Mr. West worked for the Supply and Planning Department of Shell International, for Eurofinance, and for the market analysis firm Industrial Market Research Ltd., where he was named managing director in 1978. A graduate of the London School of Economics, Mr. West is a member of the Market Research Society in the United Kingdom and of the Society for Competitive Intelligence Professionals. Macmillan will publish his book *Marketing Research* in 1998.

Chapter 5

CENTRAL AND EASTERN EUROPE

The Last Frontier

THE "BACKYARD" OF EUROPE

Having emerged from communism in the early 1990s, the Central and Eastern European economies have become the "backyard" of Western Europe. Lacking the "entrepreneurial momentum" and economic vibrancy of Asia, the Central and Eastern European economies have been relatively slow to recover from communism. During the past five years, their challenge has been to make the transformation from state-controlled to market-driven economies. Their challenge is also extended to attain political stability, control inflation, attract foreign investment, control unemployment, and rebuild the infrastructure of their economies.

For the purposes of this book, we will regard Central Europe as comprising Hungary, the Czech Republic, Poland, Slovakia, and Slovenia. These are the economies geographically close to Western Europe and that have made relatively smooth transitions to a market economy. Most of these countries have a moderate level of infrastructure development. As such, while their transition to a market economy has been met with some problems (e.g., inflation, unemployment, etc.), they are well on their way to attaining a stable economy, attracting foreign investment and exports, and developing a consumer economy.

Again, for purposes of this book, we will regard Eastern Europe as consisting of those countries that are still in the process of their transition to a market economy and that are still struggling with internal political and economic problems. As such, their infrastructure is in need of investment, including basic services such as transportation systems, utility systems, medical care, education, etc. We will define Eastern European countries such as Russia, Albania, Bulgaria, Romania, Serbia, Croatia, the Ukraine, Estonia, Latvia, Lithuania, etc. We would also include many of the former USSR states (e.g., Afghanistan, Belarus, Georgia, Armenia, Azerbaijan, Uzbekistan, Turkmenistan, and Kazakhstan, etc.) in this group.

Within this section of the book, we have separately profiled Hungary, Poland, the Czech Republic, and Russia, as they are currently the most active countries in terms of attracting foreign investment and exports. While these countries are the leading economies in this decade, the lesser developed, or emerging economies should emerge as "economic opportunities" in the next millennium.

YOU MUST HAVE THE PATIENCE TO ENTER CENTRAL AND EASTERN EUROPE AND STAY IN THE MARKET

As a result of over forty years of communism in these countries, there is a significant backlog of much needed infrastructure development in transportation, telecommunications, housing, and road construction. A major characteristic of the transformation in Central and Eastern Europe is that investment is concentrated in the region's more advanced countries. The ratio of foreign capital in Hungary, the Czech Republic, and in Poland is significant. Many of these countries are aggressively seeking foreign partners to finance the rising costs of research and development and modernization in these countries. In the long term, integration into the European Union would be of benefit for these economies. Hungary, Poland, and the Czech Republic appear the three most attractive economies (in the region) to the European Union. Membership would provide advantages for these three countries on three levels; those of the market, the currency, and uniform security and regulation. It is forecast that these three countries should achieve European Union membership by the end of the decade.

While competitive manufacturing, raw materials, and labor costs (less than the United States and Western Europe) still make Eastern and Central Europe a very attractive investment prospect, western managers should not make the mistake that the costs of setting up a country office are lower in Eastern Europe than in the West. The cost of establishing offices, joint venture partners, and strategic alliances are similar to those in Europe and in Asia. While privatization has continued at a rapid pace in Russia, the Czech Republic, Hungary, and in Poland, it is now thought that foreign owners should exercise control, rather than company management, and supervise the latter.

MARKET OPPORTUNITIES IN CENTRAL AND EASTERN EUROPE

Central and Eastern Europe have attracted a wide range of investment and imports into their economies. Many of the successful companies that either have invested or exported their products and services are in the field of electronics, biotechnology, environmental technology, automotive, chemicals, packaging, information systems, advanced materials, lasers and sensors, financial services, retailing, and entertainment. Some of the successful firms include: General Motors, Daewoo, Sony, Ericsson-Schrack, Chrysler, IBM, Siemens, and Philips.

THE "HOT" INDUSTRIES

Telecommunications

Catching the wave of investment opportunities in telecommunications infrastructure, a group of U.S. telephone companies gained a foothold in Hungary. Through a joint venture with Hungarian municipalities, Denver & Ephrata Telephone & Telegraph in Pennsylvania, and Consolidated Cos. and Huntel Systems in Nebraska, along with United International Holdings, Inc., in Colorado, are now providing telephone and cable TV service to thousands of Hungarians southeast of Budapest. What is significant is the investment costs less than if the group had bought a telephone company in the United States. Investment in telecommunications companies in Central and Eastern Europe is like a "gold rush." Under communism, most Hungarians had to wait up to twenty years for telephone installation.

Utilities and Energy

Utilities and energy are also "hot" areas for investment. During 1990, General Electric Lighting acquired Hungarian-owned Tungsram after it became the first major Central European privatization. GE used the transaction to gain a foothold on Europe's lamp business, an industry dominated by Philips and Osram. While GE had a tough time making a profit during the first several years, the effort has paid off. Today, it has moved into third position in the European lampmakers' market.

Tourism

Tourism is a vital industry in Central and Eastern Europe. Since the democratic revolutions in these countries, the number of tourists visiting these countries has been significant. Hungary receives over 3 million visitors, Poland attracts 57 million, and the Czech Republic receives over 64 million tourists annually. Many of these tourists are reported to be seeking the exotic and authentic sights in these countries, in addition to the culture prior to communism in the countries. Many of these tourists are from countries where "the customer is the king." This presents both challenges and opportunities for the developers of tourism in these countries. It should be cautioned, however, that tourism developers must undertake market and consumer research in order to determine the expectations and needs of tourists visiting their region.

Energy

Lack of capital has historically been the main limiting factor in the further development of Eastern European energy resources. Mining equipment in the state-run operations is antiquated and unreliable, with replacement parts difficult to obtain. Coal preparation is limited to coal destined for export or for home heating uses. Electric utilities and industrial consumers receive coal as well as the tailings from export and home heating coal. The region suffers from significant air pollution and ash disposal problems in high coal use areas.

Within the coal utilization area, there is a need for additional coal preparation facilities and technology. The region suffers from air pollution along with a strong need to upgrade existing power plants, as well as transmission and distribution systems. Overall, the region's energy infrastructure will require considerable attention. Significant opportunities for energy firms lie in the areas of electrification and distribution, plant repair, upgrading, and environmental cleanup, and also in the construction of refineries and pipeline distribution systems.

In the longer term, as domestic coal production is phased down and replaced by natural gas imported via pipeline from Russia and other "newly independent states" of the former Soviet Union, opportunities will exist in the marketing of gas turbines and licensing of related technologies, especially of a size suitable for smaller combined cycle and district heating plants. Increased petroleum imports from these countries will also create increased demand for equipment used with liquid fuels.

Technology

In spite of the slow movement to a market economy, the labor force of Russia, Poland, Hungary, and the Czech Republic are educated and "crave technology." For example, ATM technology has already become an accepted technology in the Czech Republic and in Russia, with Poland, Hungary, and Slovenia not far behind. Many of these economies have talented engineers who have taken to the hardware and software markets. Moreover, these countries are aggressively trying to upgrade and update their computer networks. Specifically, market opportunity exists for value added resellers (VARs). These organizations generally boast the best combination of street smarts, technical savvy, and customer responsiveness. They know how to work with the local bureaucracies to get leased lines provisioned or cabling pulled. Some of the VARs that boast of success in Eastern Europe are Bay Networks, Inc. (Santa Clara, California), Cisco Systems Inc. (San Jose, California), Novell, Inc. (Orem, Utah), Microsoft Corp. (Redmond, Washington), and 3Com Corp. (Santa Clara, California).

One of the most impressive points about Eastern European VARs is how fast they have come up to speed on complex networking technology. During the early 1990s, information technology in Eastern Europe meant "running some Eastern European mainframe knockoff." As such, the Eastern European networking market is still new for most major integrators (e.g., IBM, Digital Equipment Corp.), so corporate networkers generally subcontract the regional jobs to VARs. In short, you must thoroughly research the market distribution channels for technology products and services in these Central and Eastern European economies. You can find gold—however, you will have to pan "segment by segment," country by country.

COUNTRIES OF THE REGION

Similar to Western Europe, Asia, Latin America, the Middle East, and the United States, you cannot assume that Central and Eastern Europe are a homogeneous or a "pan market." *If anything, the market opportunities are*

very diverse. This factor, coupled with the recent movement to market econo-
mies, compounds the risk factor of investment in this region. In this region,
it is particularly important to have market research conducted by a firm
that has global and local field capabilities (in each of the countries). These
firms *must* have knowledge of the local customs, changing political environment, local trade regulations, and the changing consumer in the
country.

We recommend that preliminary (phase I) market research be conducted to determine if select countries meet your market potential and/or
investment criteria. Second, personal contacts in addition to local agents
or representatives are necessary in this region. Because the legal framework is not developed in these countries, you will need local assistance
with business contract negotiations, importation laws, the local tax and
tariff structures, etc. In most of these countries, you will be able to locate
branch offices of your international accounting and consulting firms to
assist you in this process.

Bulgaria

The transition to a market economy has been a "rough one" for Bulgaria.
Aside from the poverty and deteriorating infrastructure of the country,
the overall pace of privatization has been unsatisfactory to the general
public in the country. The Bulgarian Socialist Party (BSP), which took
office in January 1995, has declared mass privatization one of the priorities
of the country. Even so, many Bulgarians are skeptical about the government's ability to manage the process in a way that is free from "inside
deals" or corruption. While Bulgaria offers low-cost labor, the population
is not as educated as that of Russia, Poland, and the Czech Republic. Given
the current risk factors, Bulgaria is often considered for investment at a
later phase.

Czech Republic

The Czech Republic is a healthy economy in spite of its small population
of ten million. Even prior to the demise of communism, the country has
been known for its highly educated society, strong manufacturing sector,
and large population of scientists and engineers. While Western European
and U.S. firms have invested heavily in the Czech Republic as a means for
lower labor costs and to capitalize on their educated technical work force,
a consumer economy is beginning to surface. Because Prague is a high

cost center, firms have sought investment in Brno, Olomouc, and Plzen, which have established industrial zones and have the necessary infrastructure for manufacturing facilities. Unlike Hungary and Poland, which offer tax incentives on a city-by-city, case-by-case basis, the Czech Republic has a strict "no incentives" policy. Despite the heavy predominance of manufacturing in the country, a consumer economy is emerging in the retail sectors.

Estonia

In spite of its small size, Estonia represents considerable market potential. Given its proximity to the Nordic countries, the European Union, and Eastern Europe, their trade conditions and tax provisions are the best of any of the states that were formerly occupied by the Soviet Union. Foreign firms are free to compete in virtually all industries in Estonia, such as pharmaceuticals, consumer durables, computers, telecommunications equipment, and software.

Western companies have found Estonia a prime location to set up shop. They are concerned about corruption, crime, and political instability in Russia, but Estonia is strategically located both geographically and economically to allow them close proximity to Russia and yet be prepared to enter the CIS markets without the concern of the changing legal environment, official corruption, and the personal danger to their staff.

Estonia business infrastructure is among the best in Central and Eastern Europe and is expected to equal, if not rival that of Western Europe in the future. Estonia has a well-developed transportation and distribution system. Goods can be warehoused in Estonia for up to one year tax-free. Estonia's free ports offer both the combination of low crime and low cost. Estonia boasts of regular ferry lines and good airlines in addition to their railway network, which offers superb entry into the other Baltic states and Russia.

Estonia offers both digital and mobile telephone systems. A fiber-optic cable connection between Tallinn and Helsinki is already in operation and will later be extended to St. Petersburg and Riga. Access to banking services is easy, and Estonian banks can handle a wide variety of international payments. More important, there are numerous legal firms and business consultants from which to get *reliable advice*. Firms such as KPMG Peat Marwick, Coopers & Lybrand, Price Waterhouse and Ernst & Young have set up in the country.

Estonia is well positioned as a "gateway" into Eastern Europe. Foreign businesses are treated favorably in Estonia, and after-tax profits are guaranteed 100 percent repatriation. The country's knowledge of English is one of the highest in Eastern Europe. Most Estonians also have full command of Russian and Finnish, and they also speak German and Swedish as well. The society is well educated and reports a large number of scientists and engineers, which is attractive for high-technology projects.

Moreover, the Estonians have adapted to market principals that are difficult to find in the rest of the formerly socialist world: honesty and integrity, balanced budgets, and a stable currency. This, coupled with their low labor costs (in relation to the Nordic countries and Western Europe), underscores the country's attractiveness. Countries that have established subsidiaries in Estonia include: Svenska Tobacco, Pepsico, Apple Computer, ABB, Shell Oil, Nestle, the Coca-Cola Company, Upjohn Pharmaceuticals, and Auto Radiator Sales.

Hungary

The Hungarian economy has made a relatively smooth transition to a market economy. Hungary still offers lower labor costs, an educated and cultured society, and, with the prospect of potential membership into the EU by the year 2002–2003, the country continues to be an attractive market for investment and exportation of goods. The retail sector is beginning to emerge with demand for shopping malls, entertainment, and computer products. Overall, while there are some problems in their pension system and reported corruption in their banking system, it is thought that Hungary has already paid the price for market reform. The growth of imports and the improvement of corporate profitability make it likely that growth is to continue through the end of this decade.

Poland

While Poland got off to a "rocky start" on its road to a market economy, the country could end the decade as one of the strongest. The country's population, strong work ethic, and its sheer will to become a successful Westernized economy have carried it through periods of political instability and high inflation in the early 1990s. In addition to its attractiveness for low cost of labor and educated work force, a consumer economy with a strong middle class is emerging. Significant opportunities exist in the development of infrastructure of the country (e.g., telecommunications, transportation, energy, health care, etc.). On the other hand, all business contracts must go through the bureaucratic channels of the government and related agencies. It is wise to hire a local agent or contract out the local office of a multinational consulting or accounting firm. You may also encounter dealing with management and government officials with some of the "old beliefs" of distrust of Western businessmen. Aside from these nuances of the country, Poland remains an attractive market—if you do your research.

Russia

In spite of its political instability, crime, and pervasive corruption, one very encouraging sign has appeared in Russia: the emergence of a well-educated, energetic, "under 40 generation" that is quickly adapting to a "free marketplace" and showing energy unheard of in the days of the Soviet economy. While Russia offers the largest market in terms of labor force (150 million), the country has experienced dramatic changes in the past decade. Political and economic uncertainty, challenging distribution networks, changing tax and legal structures, and security issues are just some elements that pose difficulty in the burgeoning Russian market.

Clearly, the infrastructure of the Russian economy was in shambles after the demise of communism. The transition from a military state to a market economy has been equated to a "roller coaster ride." On the other hand, President Boris Yeltsin has stabilized the economy to the point where firms are willing to take the risk of exporting and investing in the country. The country is in significant need of investment in communications, transportation, distribution systems, health and medical care, and the retail sectors. Moscow, having developed rapidly, is competitive, costly, and becoming saturated while St. Petersburg, in contrast, has been slower to develop.

The most significant issues facing investors or companies doing business in Russia are as follows:

- Corruption (the price of corporate and personal protection in the markets)
- Crime (and personal safety)
- Political and economic stability
- Potential ethnic uprisings
- Instability of the banking systems
- Distribution systems

Aside from these *major issues*, companies continue to invest and import and export from the country. The new breed of "young Russians" have a vision for the "New Russia" for the country to evolve into a dynamic market economy. Because a legal system does not exist that can control market pricing, product distribution, copyrights, patents, etc., the "mob" or other organizations have evolved to control what may appear to be "the wild West." There exists a strong need for control of these market conditions; however, it may take some time for the legal system to "catch up" with the economic force of the economy.

Slovakia

In spite of the small economy, the Slovakia market offers low-cost labor and an educated economy. However, as of late, Slovakia has stabilized and attracted foreign investment, retail sales are up, and GOP is expected to grow around 5–7 percent over the next five years. Most of the investment to date has been in the infrastructure and manufacturing area. Slovakia's retail market has been slow to develop, stifled by political instability, slow economic growth, and a small population (5.3 million; the largest city, Bratislava, has under 500,000 inhabitants). In summary, look to Slovakia for their low cost of labor and "will" of their work force.

RETAIL OPPORTUNITIES EMERGING IN CENTRAL AND EASTERN EUROPE

After decades of economic stagnation and political regression, consumer economies are beginning to emerge in Central and Eastern Europe. Although some countries have been slow to reform their economies, consumer markets are beginning to emerge in some of these countries. While Mexican retailers remain focused on a saturated U.S. market, European retailers have begun to carve up these emerging markets.

According to a study by Coopers & Lybrand, Russia offers the largest long-term potential with its population of 150 million people and its underdeveloped urban areas. To date, few Western retailers have entered the market, and the leading retailers in Russia are GUM and TsUM, from the Soviet era.

In Hungary, many Western European retail chains were quick to enter the market, but have since slowed their expansion activities. Consumers are still feeling the heavy tax burden and a large deficit. In spite of this, approximately twenty malls are scheduled to be open through 1998. With the increase in home ownership, the home improvement sector has grown to $1.7 billion.

Poland's retail market is at a very early stage of development, but a large population and growing middle class are promising. While a number of foreign retailers have entered the market (e.g., Bills of Austria, Auchun of France, Makro of Holland, and Plus of Germany), none have a major presence in the country. The home electronics segment is close to $1 billion in Poland and is expected to grow at a rate of 10 percent per annum, despite a strong black market presence.

Retailing has always been a healthy sector in the Czech market as retail sales account for about 10 percent of their GDP. While the market is small, two-thirds of the population consider themselves middle class. Much of the growth is projects in the provinces rather than in Prague, which is considered too competitive and too expensive. The drugstore segment has grown to over $600 million in sales and offers opportunities in the sectors such as pharmacies, drugstores, and outlets selling cosmetics and toiletries. The Slovakia retail market has been slow to develop because of its small population and political instability.

The Coopers & Lybrand Consulting study advises retailers who are interested in expanding into Central and Eastern Europe to:

- Engage local market specialists who can provide research on local customer needs.
- Choose target markets by creating risk provides that take into account economic, investment, and political risks.
- Consider alternative entry methods to wholly-owned subsidiaries, such as joint venture or franchise arrangements, where retailers can control costs and minimize risks. Search for local partners to offset your weaknesses in the markets.
- Adapt a format that is compatible with the cultural conditions of your target market. (1)

BARRIERS AND PITFALLS TO MARKET ENTRY WITHIN CENTRAL AND EASTERN EUROPE

Given the slow and "rocky" transition to market economies in this region, there are several risk factors you may wish to consider or some reasons why *not* to go to this region, such as follows:

- Economic risk factors of international trade balance, government debt, inflation, and exchange rate risks
- Political risk factors of the transition process to a market economy and present political structure of the government
- The legal system in these former communist countries have not kept up with the evolving economic environment fostered by their governments
- Corruption that exists in terms of privatization, legal contracts, bribery, etc.
- Deteriorating infrastructure in several of the countries can make for "slow going" of business ventures and startups
- Lack of "trust" of former Central and Eastern European organizations of Westerners (this is particularly prevalent in Eastern European executives over the age of 40)
- The threat of your personal safety in some of the countries (e.g., Russia)
- The issue of management of local operations that do not have an "entrepreneurial work ethic"

Clearly, in the republics of Central Asia—Uzbekistan, Tadjikistan, Kirgizia, and Turkmenistan—there exists a dangerous mixture of Islamic fundamentalism and autocratic communism. Moldavia will probably continue to integrate with Romania on the basis of their common origin and geographic proximity. A problematic country in this region is Kazakhstan, where more than 30 percent of the population is of Russian origin. The question remains as to what will happen in the future with the multiple "autonomous republics" and "autonomous provinces." Many of them are located in the old Russian Federation, some of which have claimed independence and sole authority over their national resources. In spite of this situation, the political climate in Russia appears to be stabilizing.

In spite of these reasons "not to enter" these countries, you will definitely "miss the boat" on market opportunities in select countries and their markets. The Japanese and several countries from the European Union (e.g., Germany, Sweden, France, the United Kingdom, etc.) have made significant investments in this region. Their early market entry, if successful, will give them a "foothold" in the region. Our recommendation is to evaluate the regional and countries' opportunities in lieu of your local and global competitive situation, vis-à-vis select market opportunities.

AN ALTERNATIVE

Rather than run the risk of directly investing in Central and Eastern European countries, some firms have chosen Western European cities or countries such as Austria to be their "business gateway" to this region. During the past decade, Austria has become a "hub" or a "gateway" to Central and Eastern Europe. They can offer available expertise in management, legal, and financial services in addition to the business amenities and support of a modern Western economy. It is reported that over 2,000 foreign enterprises (300 of which are American) operate in Austria. Over 800 research companies and organizations were located in Vienna, which has become a center for research and innovation. Specifically, Vienna's International Airport is a top distribution asset, which serves as the first mega hub for cargo and travelers.

A RECOMMENDED APPROACH TO MARKET ENTRY INTO CENTRAL AND EASTERN EUROPE

Because of the diversity of the markets in Central and Eastern Europe, several companies have taken a "geographic market segmentation approach" to the region. Very often companies will group Poland, Hungary, and the Czech Republic together; Bulgaria and Romania together; Slovenia, Croatia, and Bosnia together; the Baltic Republics together; Russia and the Ukraine together; and Romania and Serbia together, as they are still ruled by their former communistic governments. Rather than this traditional geographical segmentation, which leads to "market entry myopia," we recommend the following approach:

STEP 1: CONDUCT YOUR RESEARCH BASED ON THE MARKET POTENTIAL FOR YOUR INDUSTRY, PRODUCTS, AND SERVICES IN EACH OF THESE COUNTRIES; START WITH THE INDUSTRY FIRST.

With market research, you can determine the aggregate market potential for your products into logical country segments.

STEP 2: DO NOT ASSUME THAT THERE IS A HOMOGENEOUS EASTERN BLOC FOR YOUR PRODUCTS.

The markets and their cultures are very diverse in this region. You must conduct your research and develop your market entry strategy, country by country.

STEP 3: WHILE SOME COUNTRIES MAY OFFER POTENTIAL IN TERMS OF SIZE (E.G., RUSSIA), YOU MUST CONSIDER THE RISK FACTORS IN THESE COUNTRIES (E.G., CORRUPTION, CRIME, BRIBERY, ETC.).

It is clear that the "cost of market entry" into countries such as Russia entails the cost of personal safety, protection for key executives, etc. You must be willing to accept these costs and methods of doing business.

STEP 4: EXAMINE GOVERNMENT INCENTIVES BEING OFFERED TO INDUCE ENTREPRENEURS TO DO BUSINESS WITHIN EACH COUNTRY.

Firms do not thoroughly research the incentives being offered directly by these governments. Countries such as Estonia, Poland, and the Czech Republic are offering attractive incentives for investment in their countries.

STEP 5: DO NOT ASSUME THAT THE EASTERN OR CENTRAL EUROPEAN CONSUMER HAS THE SAME PREFERENCES, NEEDS, OR REQUIREMENTS FOR YOUR PRODUCTS IN YOUR DOMESTIC MARKET.

There are numerous examples of product marketing failures in Eastern and Central Europe. For example, products that were introduced with environmental information which boasted that they were ecologically "good" because they were free of certain chemicals, met with minimal success. Most of the consumers not only did not understand the labels on the products but did not understand the need for the products.

STEP 6: FIRST CONSIDER THE "IMPORT/EXPORT" MODE OF ENTRY AS THE LOWEST COST AND INITIALLY, REDUCED RISK OPTION.

You may wish to consider directly exporting your products to these countries, which means that you assume the risk of market entry or indirectly importing your goods, and locating a local Eastern European market specialist to assist you in the export/import business. There are a wide variety of firms, such as (1) export management companies (EMCs), which serve as the international marketing specialist for manufacturers in noncompetitive lines, (2) agents, brokers and commission houses, which represent manufacturers in the international marketplace, and (3) complementary exporters, which contract for private labeled products from a variety of manufacturers.

This mode of entry gives you the time to further assess the potential of these markets. It also increases your knowledge and experience in this region, which does have risks.

STEP 7: CONSIDER FOREIGN LICENSING AS MODE OF ENTRY.

Companies that are involved in the transfer of technology to these countries, and that wish to counteract counterfeiters and avoid the high involvement and the risk of joint ventures and foreign-owned subsidiaries, may opt for this method of market entry in this region. This method of market entry has not been successful in Eastern Europe because of the lack of management skills, the reputation and the brand name of the licenser, and the existence of "gray markets," where licenser's products are sold by other unlicensed merchants without permission and without paying the appropriate royalties and fees.

It is reported that Sony experienced negative results in Poland in 1991. Despite increased demand for their products by Pewex, the local company licensed to distribute them in Poland, private dealers began selling Sony products to the gray market supplied by "parallel" imports, independent of Pewex. Sony considered a number of options to deal with the situation, but concluded that opening its own subsidiary would be the best solution because this would give the company control over sales and service, enhance its local image, and fit the corporate philosophy of "global localization."

STEP 8: CONSIDER JOINT VENTURES AS MODE OF ENTRY.

Joint ventures have been a traditional method of entering foreign markets, which allow more rapid market access than exports and have lower costs than joint investments. However, the legal contract that binds the parties with different cultural and political backgrounds can be perilous. Because the legal systems in many of these countries are undeveloped, and enforcement methods of these contracts are practically nonexistent, few joint ventures have been successful. Of the 5,000+ joint ventures registered in the former Soviet Union in 1991, only 250 were operational at the end of 1992.

Other disadvantages of a joint venture in Eastern or Central Europe could include:

- Lack of full control over the company (this is exacerbated when one of the partners lacks basic management skills)
- Serious problems in dispute resolution (particularly when the local partner has a different attitude toward management and workers relations)
- Possibility of corruption (particularly when one of the local directors are government employees)

In spite of these pitfalls, joint ventures will probably continue to be preferred in countries that are adverse to foreign private property (e.g., Russia and the former Soviet Republics). This trend will also continue where the risk-sharing incentives are high (e.g., telecommunications, extraction, energy, and other specific large-scale infrastructure projects). This mode is particularly useful for oil and gas extraction in Russia and the republics, where there is still a tendency to regard foreign investors as "nasty capitalist robbers." One such joint venture, "White Nights," is a three-way partnership between Phibro Energy of Connecticut, Anglo-Swiss of Texas, and Varyegannyeftegas (a Siberian oil association). White Nights drills for new oil in leased fields. So far, the oil goes to the Russian government and the revenues are split.

STEP 9: LAST, CONSIDER WHOLLY OWNED SUBSIDIARIES AS THE MODE OF ENTRY.

Larger firms consider Eastern and Central Europe as an extension of Western Europe. As such, they have adopted a long-term strategy of investment in this region for the long term. While the investment in local production facilities may not yield profits in the short term, they have decided to become serious, long-term players in these markets. These companies include Daimler-Benz, Samsung, Daewoo, Matsushita, Siemens (electronics), Proctor & Gamble, Unilever (food), Ericsson, and AT&T. Even in retailing, the conglomerate Austrian food retailer Jiulius Meinl formed Czech and Slovak subsidiaries with food stores in Prague and Bratislava. BSN, the French food giant, which signed deals in the Czech Republic and Poland to produce its Dannon brand yogurt, plans to run its own trucks and warehouses to ensure fresh delivery.

On the other hand, parent companies should be prepared for a long adjustment and modernization process in their East European subsidiaries before profits accrue to the company. GE, which purchased the Tungaram lighting company in Hungary in 1989, still lost $14 million in 1991, even after cutting staff by 28 percent and increasing volume by 30 percent. On a smaller scale, Coinmach Industries, a company in Roslyn, New York, invested in Hungary. They anticipate that the project will take twice as long to be implemented and become less profitable than initial estimates.

STEP 10: RESEARCH THE BANKING AUTHORITIES IN THE COUNTRY.

In countries, such as Russia, banks have proliferated. On the other hand, there has been rampant corruption reported in the system. On the other hand, several multinational banks have expanded in this region, and you may be able to extend your domestic banking relationships to this region.

PUBLISHED SOURCES

(1) Source: Coopers & Lybrand Consulting study: "Global Retailing: Assignment Eastern Europe," Susan Nocilla (212) 259–2145.

CZECH REPUBLIC
THE RIGHT PLACE AT THE RIGHT TIME

When the Czech people overthrew their communist rulers in the remarkably peaceful "velvet revolution" of 1989, 10 million people started an energetic march toward a free market economy. Experts now consider the Czech Republic among the most stable and promising of the world's emerging markets. An incredible amount of structural change has taken place in just eight years. The Czech Republic is trying to accomplish quickly what the United States was able to do over decades.

IN THE MIDST OF THINGS

Companies seeking to do business in Central and Eastern Europe may find the Czech Republic an ideal point of entry, both because of its central location and its stage of economic development. The Czech Republic is in the heart of Europe, at the intersection of east-west and north-south trade routes. The country has long benefitted from its location. Prague in particular was one of the leading cities of the Austrian Empire until Czechoslovakia became independent in 1918.

The Czech Republic (which separated peacefully from Slovakia in 1993) continues to benefit from its proximity to Germany, Austria, and Poland.

CZECH REPUBLIC

NOTES

- Most meetings are held at company offices. Meetings usually start in the morning and continue through lunch. Don't discuss business during lunch.

- While many executives may speak English, have a local translator. For serious negotiations, hire a local lawyer and accountant to represent you.

- Always research potential partners thoroughly.

- With a business culture similar to Germany's, the Czechs are very methodical in their thinking. Don't expect them to make rapid decisions.

- Describe your firm and its products and services fully. Bring ample promotional material and product demonstrations.

- Do not make remarks about the former communist regime, the Slovak government, and so forth.

- Over lunch or dinner, you may be offered several different types of beers, drinks, and liquors. If possible, join your hosts in a drink on this social occasion.

For example, Coca-Cola Amatil recently established one of the world's largest Coca-Cola bottling plants in the Czech Republic. It's hard to imagine that the 10 million Czechs would drink it dry. Rather, the Czech Republic provides an ideal launchpad for regional soft-drink distribution.

Recent events mark a return to the nation's pre-1939 democratic roots. The republic also has a centuries-old tradition of education (Charles University in Prague is one of the oldest in Europe), and foreign business-people will find a highly educated population. Now that the interruption of Communist rule is over, the Czech Republic is eagerly returning to its natural place as a typical European country.

The republic is well into its transition from a centrally planned to a free market economy. The country has already privatized most state-owned industries and services, liberalized foreign trade, established currency convertibility, and lifted wage regulations. The process of price liberalization continues apace. Similarly, the adjustment of legal standards and regulations to EU standards is advancing. In fact, the overall situation in the Czech Republic is so positive that foreign businesses need little encouragement. As such, the Czech government offers no subsidies or supports to foreign investors beyond what is available to domestic companies as well.

This did not keep Matsushita, the Japanese consumer electronics manufacturer, from selecting the Czech Republic as the location for its new assembly facility to help boost its European sales. The selection process took months, and despite a lack of Czech subsidies, the Japanese company preferred the Czech Republic over other Eastern and Western European countries. The choice is sure to benefit both the manufacturer and its host.

The well-educated Czech workforce was crucial for the American manufacturer Motorola. At the beginning of this decade, the company established a relationship with a local computer chip manufacturer. Not surprisingly, the local company was unable to meet Motorola's quality standards at first. However, with Motorola support, quality went up at a pace exceeding both original expectation and previous experience.

Consequently, Motorola established a design center next to the production facility to utilize the talents of local designers. It was the first design center of its kind established in one of the former communist countries. Technology and the people behind it can mean success in the Czech Republic.

OPPORTUNITIES

Since the end of communist rule in 1989, the fastest growth in the Czech Republic has come from upgrading and expanding the infrastructure. Everyone who visited the country at the beginning of this decade would recognize the dramatic change that has occurred. Building up the infrastructure will contribute to economic growth for many years ahead. Right now, it provides rich business opportunities for foreign suppliers.

Closely Watched Trains . . . and Planes

The Czech Republic has no direct access to the sea, but goods do not travel by water alone. The economy is well served by air, rail, and highway links.

The major airport is located in the vicinity of the capital, Prague, and welcomes the majority of business visitors to the country. The need for airport expansion became obvious with the increase of travelers. A foreign construction company took the opportunity, doubled the airport terminals, and implemented up-to-date logistics technology. There are at least three or four other airports serving industrial and trade centers that anticipate similar upgrades.

Borders can be reached by car in a maximum of four hours from any point inside the Czech Republic. The highway system, however, connects just the major cities. The extension of the existing system is either under construction or planned for the near future. Construction requires both financial resources and building know-how. This is an obvious source of opportunity.

The Czech Republic has one of the most extensive railway networks in the world. Traditionally, railways were the most cost-effective means of transportation. Unfortunately, state ownership eroded much of that advantage.

Communication

"Without communication there is no command," say the military people. The Czech Republic was dependent on a monopoly telecommunications-services provider for decades. While the stories about waiting seven to ten years for a phone may be an exaggeration, the system was in fact inferior.

The political and economic changes of 1989 brought a new dynamics into play. Building new lines and digital switchboards, establishing high-quality lines for data transfer, and focusing on customer satisfaction made Czech telecommunications more like those of Western Europe.

Czech Manufacturing

The Czech Republic has a strong industrial base; Czechoslovakian industry was a cornerstone of the Soviet Bloc for decades. It is difficult to find a country the size of the republic with the concentration of expertise and skills in so many industries. Newly privatized Czech industry is going through restructuring to sharpen its competitive edge and enter the global market. The new generation of managers, now accustomed to competition, is beginning to succeed. What exactly are the opportunities here?

For openers, German companies have increased their competitiveness by relocating operations to the Czech Republic. Both joint and independent ventures utilize the high quality of Czech labor and the short-term advantage of costs dramatically lower than in Germany.

Riding the Coattails of Privatization

The big multinationals have had a ripple effect on Czech industry. Large companies have pushed local suppliers to deliver products on time and up to standards, and they do not back down from their requirements. The situation has forced local companies to change dramatically. Some have done it on their own while others have sought out partners; still others were forced out of business entirely.

After winning a stake in Skoda, a Czech passenger car manufacturer, Volkswagen began marketing Skodas internationally. The joint Skoda-VW effort gave birth to a new car for Volkswagen and up-to-date production facilities for Skoda. But the benefits spread further, since the venture attracted many of Volkswagen's first-tier suppliers, which began to sell to Skoda-VW from newly established or acquired production facilities or through joint ventures with local producers.

Retail Opportunities

The Czech Republic represents a market of about 10 million consumers with an average gross per capita income of $350 per month. This market could support a variety of local industries and services already common in the West.

The consumer market went through substantial changes since its opening to competition, which in turn introduced massive advertising to the republic. Advertising became a new phenomena for Czechs, and it started to influence their behavior, to the benefit especially of foreign brands. These were generally perceived as better value products. Although the populace has grown more accustomed to advertising, it as well as other marketing tools may influence the behavior of local customers considerably more than in developed markets.

Knowledge of local conditions is obviously important for gaining strong market share. And good customer service is another essential tool.

The Czech Republic was for decades dominated by monopolistic, state-owned retail chains. In the early 1990s, a large number of small, independent outlets opened up. These businesses gradually built up a distribution system with manufacturers. But the entry of multinational chains with deep pockets has altered conditions dramatically. Chains bring both higher standards and lower prices. As such, they represent a serious threat to local entrepreneurs and manufacturers.

The adjustment has come in various ways, like the owner of a small drugstore in the main square of an historic city. He discovered that a drugstore belonging to a multinational company was opening on the opposite side of the square. The independent could not keep his customers in the face of lower prices for identical products, so he decided to rent his drugstore to another multinational company.

Local Dealers for Your Products

Specialized products and services are mainly provided by local dealers and branch offices of bigger companies. These have replaced state-owned importing companies that disappeared during privatization. The newcomers are now fully accepted.

The country's strong educational and scientific base provides foreign manufacturers with a pool of capable experts who can introduce their products and build ties with customers. Due to the concentration of specific expertise in particular geographic region(s), selecting the right dealer can mean tapping into already-existing personal relationships with important contacts.

Not everyone should open a branch office in the Czech Republic. The size of the local market may not make it a worthwhile investment. In these cases, the local dealer is a natural way of starting in the market. With the improved infrastructure in the Czech Republic, dealerships can work throughout the country.

ABOUT THE AUTHOR

Jan Bauer
  Gamex, a.s.
  Průmyslová 2
  České Budějovice
  370 21
  Phone/fax: 420 38 57354

Jan Bauer, M.B.A., an independent consultant, is currently deputy managing director of Gamex, a 400-employee production facility of the Spanish Viscofan Group. His team oversaw the transformation of an old-fashioned, state-owned stationery factory into the most successful facility of Viscofan worldwide in terms of quality and productivity. Before joining Gamex, Mr. Bauer worked with Czechinvest, the division of the Czech Ministry of Industry and Trade handling foreign direct investment. While at Czechinvest, he provided support at the governmental level for the manufacturing projects of Motorola, Panasonic, ITT, Philips, Canstar, and Arrow, among others.

HUNGARY
RICH IN HISTORY AND POTENTIAL

With a national history that goes back some eleven hundred years, Hungary is rich in history, culture, life, and market potential. After forty-five years of occupation, the first truly free elections since the end of the Second World War were held in 1990. Hungary became an associate member of the European Union in 1993 and applied for full membership in 1994. As one of the most prosperous members of the Warsaw Pact, the country is undergoing a relatively smooth transition from one-party communist rule to democracy.

The new freedom in Hungary has given rise to great optimism, even though traces of Hungary's communist past remain. Most mature businesspeople (aged 40 to 55) were educated and trained under the communist regime. Nevertheless, during the recent opening of the economy, many of these managers and executives have risen to the occasion. In some cases, their work ethic and entrepreneurial spirit have surpassed that common in Western economies.

This drive is particularly true of Hungarians who have invested money in the privatization movement. In addition, a remarkable small- and medium-size company sector has emerged in recent years. There are approximately 1 million entrepreneurs (in handicrafts, trading, and so forth) and 200,000 business organizations in this country of 10 million inhabitants.

But this new openness, risk taking, and optimism do not mean that Hungary has chosen capitalism over some form of socialism as its economic model. That decision will depend largely on the economy's performance in the years ahead. Under communism, workers were guaranteed

HUNGARY NOTES

- Choose a representative to help you with negotiations and interpretation and, in general, to facilitate the business development process. You may want to make two trips: a preliminary one to evaluate potential representatives and a second during which your chosen representative assists you.

- Schedule meetings by fax, phone, or letter at least one month in advance. Budapest has a wide range of first-class hotels where you can stay and hold meetings.

- Allow enough time between meetings. Travel by taxi or trolley is efficient. If you don't have an interpreter with you, be sure to have addresses written in Magyar and, if possible, a map.

- Negotiations nearly always entail a lot of wining, dining, and entertainment. Most entertaining is done in hotels or at the Hungarian company's office because there is a housing shortage in Budapest.

- While some business may be discussed over lunch, business should not be discussed at dinner because there is often entertainment and it can last late into the evening.

- Try to arrange your trip so that you can spend a weekend in Budapest. Not only are there wonderful sights to see and cultural events to attend, but this is an excellent opportunity to strengthen business relationships.

- Be prepared to be taken to the opera or invited to cultural events over the weekend.

- In Hungary, surnames are listed before given names. You are safe, however, in using formal titles in business situations.

---

a job, living quarters, and enough food to support a family. Now, people throughout Central Europe, Hungary included, want to know if the new system will perform as well. Of particular concern for many Hungarians is the fate of the pension system, now under debate.

OPPORTUNITIES

Hungary has become an attractive target for foreign direct investment. Almost half of all working foreign capital invested in Central Europe has gone to Hungary. Some 25,000 Hungarian companies have attracted foreign participation. The major investors are Germany, the United States, Austria, France, and Italy. Among the major corporate investors are General Electric, General Motors, Audi, IBM, Philips, Nokia, Deutsche Telecom, Electrolux, and Siemens. They provide jobs for about 20 percent of the employed population.

Hungary offers excellent conditions for foreign investors who want to start a business. Regulations governing the establishment of companies and other business organizations have been liberalized. In addition, the free transfer of profits and capital is guaranteed, and no prior licenses are necessary from the government to set up a business in Hungary.

Unlike other parts of the world, foreign companies are treated the same in Hungary as domestic firms. Hungary also has concluded agreements with most developed countries for the protection of investments and the avoidance of double taxation. Laws on accountancy, bankruptcy, and financial institutions are compatible with Western standards.

The workforce is well trained and highly motivated. Labor in Hungary—especially skilled labor—is cheap by international comparison. Moreover, the presence of many large international companies offers additional possibilities for economic cooperation, subcontracting, and so forth.

Several production sectors merit particular attention from investors: computer parts and components (software and hardware), tourism (including hotel construction), food products (fruits and vegetables, beverages, sugar), and health care products and toiletries (pharmaceuticals, medical equipment, cosmetics). For example, Glaxo Wellcome, the London-based pharmaceutical giant, has made a long-term commitment to Hungary. The firm has built facilities, signed a cooperation agreement with the Ministry of Welfare, and begun production of the antibiotic Zinacef.

Opportunities also exist in the retail sector. Although Hungary has a somewhat small consumer base (10 million people), its people know how to live and enjoy life. They like to eat out, listen to music, attend cultural events—and they love to shop. This is the stuff of a consumer economy, one that could serve as a model for other Central and Eastern European countries.

For local producers and wholesalers, the entry of the international chains offers the potential for unprecedented export sales through the cross-border supply networks of global retailers. According to some Western experts, Central Europe will be Europe's new (retail) battleground.

In November 1996, the Polus Center opened its doors in a Budapest suburb. It was the first in a chain of seventeen shopping mall/theme parks to be developed in the region by the Canadian-Hungarian TriGranit Corporation. Many mall developers believe the Polus Center represents the first stage of a retail revolution in Central and Eastern Europe.

According to the media relations director for investor TrizecHahn Corporation, "We feel very confident there is a need in the [Eastern European] markets for convenience and excitement in shopping. The Polus will satisfy these needs." The excitement at Polus comes in the form of a 500-meter skating rink, a cowboy theme park, a six-screen multiplex theater operated by Canada's Cineplex Odeon, the Magic City games area run by Canada's International Leisure System, and the theme restaurant Cafe Hollywood.

Critics argue that malls like Polus could devastate the small shops in downtown Budapest. Budapest, however, is rich in cultural and tourist attractions as well as hotels. Rather than killing the city center, large, suburban-style malls should only make for a more vibrant retail environment.

Of course, at some point a consumer economy depends on infrastructure. Hungary's could be characterized as "building." The rail and highway networks focus on Budapest. Highway construction has increased, with the hope of linking the capital to surrounding countries. All important rail lines are now electrified. The telecommunications system is also undergoing modernization, including the partial privatization of MATAV, the Hungarian telecom utility. In most parts of Budapest, dialing is available with excellent digital exchanges, although the per-capita number of telephones remains low.

ISSUES AND CAVEAT

Taxes and Laws, Oh My

The Hungarian government promotes foreign direct investment through various incentives, including those embodied in the corporate tax system. To encourage companies to reinvest their earnings in business activities, the government levies only an 18 percent corporate tax on profits retained in the firm; this rate is considered low by international standards. Offshore companies registered in and having their headquarters in Hungary and held exclusively by nonresidents enjoy an 85 percent tax break applicable to both the 18 percent corporate tax and the 23 percent supplementary tax on dividends.

Hungary also tries to channel investment to particular regions and particular sectors. If a company invests capital in a crisis-stricken region or an entrepreneurial zone, it can be given a 100 percent tax exemption for five years, with the option of another 50 percent allowance for the following five years.

Another incentive applies to companies investing more than 1 billion forint ($6.7 million) in businesses anywhere in Hungary. To qualify, the firms must also must produce physical goods and increase export sales originating from the investment by at least 25 percent, but by not less than 600 million forint, compared to the previous year. Firms meeting these requirements are automatically eligible for a 50 percent tax allowance.

All companies must submit an application for registration to the Court of Registration in order to commence operation.

Not Yet a Franchiser's Paradise

With 5 percent of Hungary's nascent retail market owned by chain stores, the country must look like easy pickings to U.S. franchisers. Since they control some 35 percent of the U.S. retail market, franchisers no doubt assume they can do the same overseas. But Hungary is likely to present something of a challenge. Entrepreneurs lack capital, credit is tighter, and business regulations are strict.

Nonetheless, some franchisers have done well in Hungary. The American triumvirate of fast food—McDonald's, Wendy's, and Burger King—is present, although two of the companies have had to change their way of doing business. Burger King, for example, does not have a single traditionally operated franchise in Hungary. All twelve of Budapest's Burger Kings and the single location outside the capital city, in Szeged, are owned by a group of American investors.

Rather than search fruitlessly for well-heeled entrepreneurs, the investors bought the stores themselves and rely on Hungarians only as employees. In contrast, McDonald's has expanded to fifty-five franchises in Hungary through a variety of means, including corporate ownership of about half of its locations and various levels of joint ownership of the rest. Either way, it appears that a little creativity goes a long way in establishing a market presence.

An Old Story: Don't Mess With the Phone Company

Significant opportunities exist in the telecommunications sector, but they must be treated with caution. Hungary is home to a monopoly with pretensions to Tyrannosaurus rex. Dealing with the Hungarian Telephone Company (MATAV) can kill small telephone firms.

An Anglo-American company providing 06-90 service, similar to 1-900 service in the United States, has gone bankrupt because of its dealings with MATAV. The original agreement called for the small firm to use MATAV lines, with MATAV keeping half of the proceeds from the phone traffic generated as payment. Eventually, MATAV grew suspicious that too much of the measured traffic on the 06-90 lines was illegally generated, and it assumed that the clients who used these numbers were accessing without paying. So MATAV suspended payment to the company.

MATAV has proceeded in the same way with other small phone service providers. Some of them were able to make an agreement with MATAV; others went bankrupt. The Anglo-American 06-90 company started with 10,000 phone numbers and ended up with 4,000. The illegal traffic was made by subcontractors, according to someone who knew the situation.

Always Forecast the Market

Whatever the cost in time and money, thorough market analysis is always a good bet. Consider it insurance against the unexpected.

Take the example of Hungary's second biggest producer of the aluminum ingredient alumina, which may halt production. At present, world alumina prices are very depressed, and production is uneconomical. The only hope is a new investor or owner who can guarantee a well-paying market for the company's products. The current owners, Germany's Alfer and Britain's Russian Alucan, are trying to attract financial investors.

The company was part of the giant Hungarian Aluminum, Inc. After its collapse in 1991, the firm was divided into smaller companies. At the time, demand from Russian smelters seemed reliable, but now these smelters cannot pay enough to make continued production profitable. Switching some capacity to the production of non–smelter-grade alumina, which is used in industries from construction to pharmaceuticals, may be an option.

Non–smelter-grade alumina is more lucrative than smelter-grade alumina. But the market is smaller and more difficult to enter, which means non–smelter-grade alumina sellers must spend heavily on marketing. In any case, ÁPV RT is unlikely to allow this important company to be shut down.

ABOUT THE AUTHOR

Katalin Vajda
  BMC Ltd.
  H-1137 Budapest
  Szent Istvan Park 22
  Phone: 361 131 0222
  Fax: 361 132 3964

Katalin Vajda, an independent consultant, works for the Legal Information Department of the Hungarian Ministry of Justice. A graduate of the Academy of Finance and Accounting, she has 25 years of experience in information technology, systems analysis, systems design, strategic planning, macroeconomic projects, and statistical analysis of trend effects. Before joining the Ministry of Justice, Ms. Vajda has held positions with the Hungarian Chamber of Commerce, the Ministry of Finance, and the Ministry of Food.

POLAND
THE CAKE THAT CONTINUES TO RISE

When Western businessmen land at the airport in Warsaw, they will no doubt look around in amazement and say: "But this is a new airport. Why

POLAND NOTES

- Book meetings either at your contact's office or at a good hotel.

- Poles are eager to do business. Their workday starts as early as 8:00 a.m. Business lunches are the norm, and they may be held later in the day and last as long as two hours.

- Have a Polish translator at meetings.

- Use formal titles (Mr., Mrs., etc.) for business introductions. Poles have a ceremony that celebrates the decision to go to a first-name basis.

- You may have some trouble getting faxes through. Often it is better to call directly. Always confirm receipt of faxes, letters, documents, and so forth.

- Always confirm pricing and terms of business deals. If you have an interpreter, have these terms translated into Polish.

- If you are negotiating for distribution of your products, do your homework. Be aware of the pitfalls of several distribution channels.

- Expect to be taken on a small sightseeing tour. Poles are proud of their country.

- Poles entertain late into the evening. Be prepared to drink vodka rather than beer.

- Avoid loud behavior as Poles are quiet people.

- Do not discuss cultural heritage issues with respect to Germans, Hungarians, or Russians. Don't discuss anti-Semitism.

- Remember that Poland is still a male-dominated society. If you are a woman, ask directions from another woman, as it could be interpreted as flirting with a man.

---

is it so crowded? Why isn't it three times larger?!" That's how it is with everything here—what seemed to be cutting edge only three or four years ago, what was supposed to serve for decades to come, is now virtually obsolete. Poland is learning the value of getting it right the first time.

UNDERSTANDING AN EXPANDING—AND DISTINCTLY POLISH—MARKET

Poland is the product of its history. In the late eighteenth century, it was divided among Austria, Prussia, and Russia; independence would not return until the end of World War I. Then came the devastation of another war, followed by Soviet domination. The move toward liberalization began in the 1980s with the Solidarity labor movement and culminated in 1990 with the election of Solidarity leader Lech Walesa as leader of the Polish Republic.

The republic is a multiparty democracy. The president serves as chief of state, and the prime minister acts as head of government. While Poles in and out of government want to be part of the West, it has not been an easy transition. The relationship with the European Union is, at times, strained, possibly because Poland is not yet a full member. Such are the growing pains of a society undergoing Westernization in the 1990s.

There are few restrictions on foreign trade, with these exceptions: some types of high-proof spirits; cars more than ten years old; and commercial vehicles and farm machinery over three years old. Export licenses are required for the following: petroleum products, metals, soil products, plastics, polyvinyl chloride, synthetic rubber and synthetic fiber, chipboards, preserved and half-tanned hides, munitions, and internationally controlled strategic goods.

U.S. exports to Poland face a real challenge because of Poland's association agreement with the European Union; tariff preferences go to members of the union. Some American products have also encountered barriers in the form of surprisingly stringent labeling and certification regulations. However, the government is trying to work these problems out. One area already seeing improvement in this regard is pharmaceuticals.

But statistics only tell part of the story. There are no markets without people. So the real question is: What are Polish consumers like? Well, consider the following. Several years ago, new car ads were a source of irritation to Poles. Sure, everyone dreamed of owning a Western car, but who could afford one? The best most Poles could hope for was a used car, often on its last legs, and even that would stretch their purchasing power to the limit.

Those days are gone. Today, readers snap up automotive magazines chock full of ads, sales are down at used car lots, and dealerships are selling new cars hand over fist. In fact, Poland has experienced the fastest growth in car sales in all Europe.

What changed to put so many Poles in the driver's seat? In a word, credit. That, and confidence. Poles believe enough in the new system to go into debt. This confidence is particularly strong in the emerging middle class, whose purchasing power has soared over the last few years and continues to climb at a dizzying rate.

The auto boom is just one of many examples of pent-up demand. This explains the fantastic success of large supermarkets in Poland: They give Polish consumers the opportunity to pick and choose between dozens of brands in every product category and blow off steam after years spent in long lines just to get toilet paper. Shopping has become the latest national passion.

As everywhere, though, there are pitfalls to snare the unwary. Missteps made by Western companies in Poland usually stem from:

- *A lack of knowledge about specific consumer needs and habits.* This was the case when the first shampoo with conditioner was launched in conjunction with a large and expensive advertising campaign. The product flopped because at the time Poles didn't use conditioners! The producer failed to do the necessary research, skipped the educational phase in introducing a new product in the Polish market, and ended up paying dearly for it.

- *Ignorance of specifics when planning promotional campaigns.* People in many countries like to receive free product samples, provided they don't feel their privacy is being violated, and Poles are no different. A few years back, problems arose when a cosmetics firm mailed samples to thousands of Poles around the country: Mail boxes were broken into, samples were stolen, and the victims turned their ire against the company that was trying to win their favor. The promotion did more harm than good.

  The same holds for advertising. For example, Western television commercials are regularly used in Poland with no changes except dubbing, and not always the best dubbing at that. The effect is often the opposite of that intended. Such commercials annoy Polish consumers by showing surroundings and lifestyles totally unrelated to their own experiences and making viewers feel slighted by the poor quality of the dubbing.

- *Ignorance about the Polish distribution system.* We saved one Western client from losing a good deal of money on a mail-order business because our research indicated the need for using a more efficient delivery system than the postal service was able to provide at the time.

One of the less obvious pitfalls from the standpoint of Western investors is the complex yet subtle differentiation of the market here. Let's take a look at some of the problems in this area.

First, a considerably higher percentage of the Polish population lives in the countryside than in Western countries. Moreover, product and media consumption patterns vary widely between urban and rural areas. The same holds for purchasing power, which is much lower in the countryside.

Second, consumption patterns vary substantially by region. If you don't understand some Polish history, you'll be in for trouble. For example, beer is consumed differently in Silesia, which was under German influence, than it is in central Poland, which was ruled by Russia for over a century. And linguistic differences, while generally smaller in Poland than in major Western European countries, nonetheless can have a large impact on marketing efforts.

Third, Poland is clearly divided into a more affluent western and central section and a poorer eastern section. It is crucial for producers and advertisers to understand this difference. Billboards advertising the most expensive brand-name computers along the dusty roads of the poorest region in eastern Poland is just one mistake that could have easily been avoided.

Fourth, consumer differentiation according to age is sharper in Poland than it is in the West. Younger Poles were not adults under the communist system, and so they are more open than their elders to almost everything associated with the free-market. In fact, it is the young people of Poland who accept the Western, consumer lifestyle to an unusually high degree—a very important factor that Western businessmen need to take into account when launching new products here.

Finally, a problem from our own backyard: research methodology. Many Western companies doing research in Poland rely on tools (questionnaires, focus group guidelines, etc.) that have worked well in Western countries and are meant to be used in comparative studies of various markets. Unfortunately, these ready-made materials often prove difficult to adapt to Polish circumstances. Put simply, you can't measure for apples when you're looking at oranges. When Western companies refuse to adapt their methodology, they obtain data that can be readily plugged into their comparative studies. But convenience comes at the cost of losing information that is truly useful because of its local relevance. Who in the United States would pass up information about how product and packaging are perceived and the consumer's motives for purchasing it? So, why make that mistake in Poland?

OPPORTUNITIES
Advantages and Challenges of Manufacturing

Given its recent dynamic growth, Poland is a market offering an enormous number of investment opportunities. In practically every sector of the economy, there are areas promising handsome returns on relatively modest investments.

After making the decision to invest in Poland, the question becomes: What should I invest in? We could, of course, point to dozens of industries that mid-level investors would find rewarding, but which ones are the real money makers? Let's start by taking a look at manufacturing.

There are good reasons to invest in manufacturing. Many former state enterprises—despite highly trained employees and surprisingly good facilities—are on the verge of bankruptcy and can be bought for very little money. Why, then, are they going broke? The answer is simple: No one ever showed management or employees how a business should function in a free Market economy. They have no idea what modern marketing is about. But there is no doubt they want to learn and can offer something in return. Who better to provide the ins and outs of doing business in Poland than Poles?

Investors are entitled to various, often substantial, tax incentives for creating jobs; the specifics depend on the number and location of jobs provided. But whatever the motivation for investing, we must point out the manufacturing sector in Poland is not free of risk. Labor unions are strong, enterprises must often be totally restructured at great expense, and competition in certain industries is increasing rapidly.

The Service Sector: Needing to Pump up

Now let's take a look at services. This is the soft spot of the Polish economy; years of overinvestment in heavy industry led to their woeful neglect. The consequences of this neglect can be observed even now, almost eight years after shock therapy first introduced the free market into Poland.

Sectors in the best shape—although not yet fully developed by Western standards—are banking, insurance, and telecommunications. Many commercial banks are currently operating in Poland, but most of them are Polish; over the next few years, the entrance of large Western banks is expected. Some of the leading players on the insurance market are the Polish firm PZU, the Dutch firm Nationale Nederlanden, and the British firm Commercial Union.

These companies offer a wide selection of policies more or less on a par with those offered by major insurance companies in Western Europe. As to telecommunications, the situation has been improving steadily. While it's still difficult to install a regular telephone line, users can obtain cellular telephone numbers quickly and easily. This contrast is the result of most telecommunications services remaining in the hands of the national phone company while the cellular market is open to competition. Such firms as Era Gsm, Plus Gsm and Centertel are constantly improving their cellular services and lowering prices. It should be noted that the national phone company is in the process of being privatized.

Consumer services remain the most poorly developed. Anything from medical services to laundries, hairdressers, and restaurants can be a real challenge, especially outside major cities. While private enterprise was permitted in these areas under the communist regime, it was so restricted and treated with such contempt by the state that it never developed beyond a very primitive level.

As a result, there aren't enough qualified people and businesses to provide the necessary services. Although constantly growing, the service sector has yet to match the rising demand for high-quality services. Thus, consumer services would seem to be an excellent bet for mid-size investors.

Perhaps the most promising area in the service sector is tourism. Poland could be a very popular destination for tourists with its Alpine-like mountains along the southern border to beckon skiers and hikers; a gorgeous lake district in the northeast; and the long coastline along the Baltic with sandy beaches relatively free of the kind of development seen along the coastal areas of many West European countries.

BARRIERS OTHER THAN AN IRON CURTAIN

Get It in Writing

Western firms are likely to find that Polish culture can have an effect on business dealings. To avoid difficulties, follow these three rules: All contracts must be written, declarations and promises made by Polish partners should be taken with a grain of salt, and the old-fashioned gallantry shown women should not give offense.

Contracts in Poland must—let's repeat that *must*—be concluded in detailed, written form. All too often, oral agreements are disregarded, misrepresented, or interpreted in whatever manner best suits the Polish party. Written contracts, of course, can also suffer that same fate, but rarely do. In general, agreements committed to paper and signed by both parties are treated as irrevocable.

The declarations of Polish businesspeople should be treated with healthy skepticism for two reasons. For openers, many of them, especially small- and medium-size entrepreneurs, have not yet fully realized that honesty pays in the long run. Instead, these people are only interested in getting rich quick. Second, Polish businessmen suffer from an inferiority complex toward their Western partners, whom they assume to be more experienced and professional and to have far greater resources and capabilities. As a result, some Polish businessmen exaggerate their own business skills and resources.

Prejudices and Biases

Women in Poland—at least in public—are treated with a level of gallantry that may seem very old-fashioned to Westerners. Kissing a woman's hand when greeting and saying good-bye, letting women through doors first, helping women into their coats or into chairs, lighting their cigarettes—all these gestures are part of the normal code of male conduct toward women, even in business situations. Western women should not feel offended or belittled, nor should they interpret such behavior as a sign of amorous interest.

However, while this behavior may not be a manifestation of male chauvinism, sexism does exist. Problems could arise at the decision-making level, when women engaged in direct negotiations with Poles may sometimes feel that they are not taken as seriously as their male colleagues would be.

Besides gender, racial-ethnic issues may also affect business dealings in Poland. Although the country is nearly homogeneous in terms of ethnicity (98 percent Polish), race (virtually 100 percent white), and religion (95 percent Roman Catholic), there is no shortage of prejudice toward others. This was clearly evident in a recent survey of attitudes toward foreigners and their influence on the economy. When asked what nationalities they would not wish to have as employers, 42 percent said they would not work for Germans and 53 percent for Jews ("Stosunek do inwstycji zagranicznych: kwestie narodowoœciowe," Raport z badan'nr 1446/95, CBOS, s. 3 ["Attitude to Foreign Investments: Nationalistic Questions," Report No. 1446/95, CBOS, p. 3]).

In business you are unlikely to have a direct encounter with such prejudices as distrust of Jews, fear combined with a sense of superiority toward Russians, and ambivalence toward Germans. However, in some cases these attitudes may underlie what would otherwise appear to be inexplicable behavior on someone's part. Unfriendly attitudes toward foreigners is more likely to stem from a desire to knock Western businessmen down a peg or two, since they are often perceived as arrogant and unfriendly. Poles value nothing so highly as the knowledge that they are being treated seriously and respectfully, as equals and colleagues.

Distribution

The retail trade network in Poland is divided for the most part among very numerous and very small operators. A study conducted by Company Assistance Ltd. in 1994 found that there are approximately 500,000 retail sales points (including open-air markets and catering firms) in Poland. Most of these are small stores with less than 300 square meters of floor area.

Supermarkets—by definition, stores in excess of 300 square meters—accounted for less than 0.5 percent of all retail sales points. But this situation is gradually changing in favor of supermarkets, as Western chains like Billa, Macro Cash & Carry, Auchan, Hit, Leclerc, and Tesco enter the Polish market.

The highly dispersed nature of the retail sales network means producers often have difficulty bringing their products to consumers; distributing these products just to a simple majority of the countless small vendors in Poland is a formidable task. Of course, fast-moving consumer goods are the most problematic in this regard. It should also be noted that the wholesale distribution network is still underdeveloped and varies a great deal from region to region. Thus, one of the keys to successful marketing in Poland is getting the goods to market.

The Law, Such as It Is

There is one major problem that all foreign businessmen will encounter in Poland: the law, or to be more precise, its many shortcomings and vagaries. These can be attributed to the tendency to enact temporary solutions, the susceptibility of the legal system to pressure from the government and the needs of the national budget, and the ongoing effort to adapt the country's many outdated laws to the needs of a modern, free-market economy.

Because of frequent changes in taxes, tariffs, import regulations, tax documentation requirements, and so forth, success goes to the businesses most able to adjust rapidly to changing legal conditions. Fortunately, the need for this kind of agility will diminish as the Polish legal code is put into order and adapted to meet the requirements of the European Union.

ABOUT THE AUTHOR

Jan Nawrocki
Institute for Qualitative Studies
Lekarska 7, 00-610
Warszawa
Phone: 48 22 25 09 33; 48 22 25 98 81; 48 22 25 75 86-88
Fax: 48 22 25 48 70; 48 22 25 06 09

Jan Nawrocki, M.A., is president of the Institute for Qualitative Studies (IQS). Since 1989, he has conducted or coordinated market research projects for Allied Domecq, Ammiratti Puris Lintas, Colgate-Palmolive,

Don Trading, Hewlett-Packard, Kraft Jacobs Suchard, L'Oreal, McCann-Erickson, Philips, Reynolds Tobacco, Sara Lee, Skandinavisk Press AB, Unilever, Westland, and Young and Rubicam, among others. Before joining IQS, Mr. Nawrocki was lecturer in sociology at Warsaw University and director of social research and qualitative research for SMG/KRC Poland. He is a member of ESOMAR.

RUSSIA

Russia is like California or Alaska during the gold rush. No other comparison will work, really. With the demise of communism, Russia has moved, haltingly, toward a market economy similar to that in many of the Eastern Bloc countries. However, the mighty bear is more complex and is a country both of high risk and high reward.

Since the demise of communism, Russians have had a taste of the West; as a result, they are not likely to vote for communism again. Russians crave the goods and lifestyle of their old foes. The challenge is to find a way of affording their dreams. One good sign is that more private property exists in Russia than in any of the other former Eastern Bloc countries.

There are some basics about the country that must be understood. First, Russia is immense. While it took Americans three or four generations to settle the western part of the United States, it has taken Russia at least four hundred years to settle Siberia. While Russia is twice the size of Canada, over 60 percent of the people live west of the Ural mountains, or in European Russia. The remaining 40 percent of the population is scattered across vast stretches of territory.

Communism failed because it could not live up to its promise. However, the adoption of a market economy has been anything but easy. Under the old regime, nobody worried about budget deficits or monetary policy. Now, everyone is discovering that they must.

As the foundation of the Soviet Union, Russia used much of its steel, aluminum, uranium, oil, and many other basic materials for its command economy. When domestic demand for these products fell in the early 1990s, Russia began exporting them to the West, to a less than enthusiastic response. As a result, Russia fell behind many of its Eastern European counterparts in the race to enter the European Union (EU). Clearly, Russia needs foreign trade and foreign investment if it is to become a major player in global markets.

President Boris Yeltsin has taken several bold steps in aligning Russia

RUSSIA NOTES

- Most meetings will be scheduled at your contact's office or at a good hotel.

- Be on time for meetings. However, you may have to wait.

- Allow plenty of time for meetings; they can last more than two hours.

- The Russians are known for their endurance and patience in negotiations. They don't believe in compromises. They also get emotional during negotiations and will, on occasion, get angry and walk out; they expect you to do the same.

- Usually, the longer you hold out in the negotiations, the more attractive the offer you will get.

- Culturally, Russians have a tendency to say no to everything. Only recently have Russians said yes to keep their business contacts with the West and promote their businesses.

- Do your homework. Many Russian firms try to make themselves look prosperous and full of market potential. Appearances can be deceiving.

- *Be careful* when traveling in Russia. Crime and corruption are pervasive. Do not flash jewelry. Do not wander off to places away from your business contacts.

- If your Russian representative tells you that you need "protection" money, reevaluate your business proposition. You may not know who you're dealing with, which is dangerous given the current corruption in the country.

- You can bring items that are in short supply to meetings as gifts.

---

with the West and in seeking their help. While his actions have been controversial and even unpopular at home, they have positioned Russia to become "one of the Western club." This was essential in repositioning Russia both politically and economically.

OVERVIEW

The Economy

It is important that Russia prosper both as an outlet for Western exports and capital and as a "peaceful neighbor" of the East as well as the West. In spite of the odds, the prospects for Russia look good. Why?

First, Russia is a country with more human capital relative to income, and these types of countries tend to grow faster than others. Second, Russian workers are better educated than workers in other countries at the same income level, except for the nations of Eastern Europe. Third, Russia is rich with natural resources and farmland. Fourth, Russia has privatized faster than any of the rest of Eastern Europe.

The privatization of factories began in 1992; within eighteen months over 80 percent of Russian industry had been privatized. The sectors which remain to be privatized include fuel and energy, telecommunications, air transport, and banking.

Much of the foreign investment flowing into Russia is drawn to Moscow. Capital has come from such Western nations as the United States, Germany, Holland, Switzerland, and the United Kingdom. The focal points include industry and the remunerative, albeit risky, financial markets.

With the nation's incredible natural resources, Russian industry can be a worthwhile investment; a well-trained and, from an employer's standpoint, affordable workforce is a definite plus in this regard. Joint ventures also represent a promising opportunity.

Now, for some specifics. Three major obstacles stand in the way of opening a new business in Russia: the bureaucracy, the lack of a real estate market, and organized crime. Russia still suffers from a poor communications and distribution system. In addition, the communist economy went from essentially one bank to a series of new independent banks.

As such, banking has become the elite profession in Russia. Even so, the current banking system has little expertise in lending and has recently shown itself to be corrupt. While Russia was a net exporter of capital from 1992 to 1994, the country has not been investing in itself. If nothing else, this underscores the mobility of capital between Russia and the West.

The Legal System, Organized Crime, Corruption

Compared to western standards, the legal system is "nonexistent" in Russia. Organized crime, or organized criminal groups (OCGs), and corruption are serious impediments to new business development in Russia. In 1994, more than 32,000 people were murdered in Russia. This equates to 21.8 murders per 100,000 people.

While crime in America appears most common in particular areas, crime in Russia is everywhere and anywhere. Much of it is street and domestic crime; 14,000 of the 32,000 murders were domestic cases, largely alcohol related.

There are three types of OCGs in Russia. The first is the traditional mafia, which collects protection money, runs prostitution rings, peddles drugs, etc. The second type consists of small businessmen who own shops and typically know or pay gangs to "protect" them.

The third type are "businessmen" whose methods are questionable, to say the least. They avoid paying taxes, use bribery, sell licenses to import or export at controlled prices. Yet their businesses are usually legal. While they are not responsible for crimes of violence, they are mainly responsible for the corruption that pervades Russia. Some critics estimate that between one-third and one-half of all "hot money" in Russia went through the hands of corrupt officials in 1994.

Clearly, crime and corruption have seriously hurt the Russian economy. According to a report commissioned by President Yeltsin, three-quarters of all private enterprises were being forced to pay between 10 and 20 percent of earnings to criminal gangs. This "cost of protection" is not only a drain on the economy but scares off potential investors, importers, and exporters. Many firms ask themselves the questions: Who needs this? Why risk the capital or my life?

Opportunities

One of the features in a market as gigantic as Russia is that it has not yet been developed in full. There are niches for both large international investors and small businesses. Real competition is actually absent in most sectors.

Since the inflation level is still high and the reliability of Russian financial institutions causes some doubts, Russians prefer to invest money by purchasing U.S. dollars and imported consumer goods. Such purchases have been considered a good investment. In the first quarter of 1997, the money spent for foreign currency conversion totaled 21.7 percent of all expenditures available to the population. This constituted about $14 billion and ranked second on the list of their general expenditures.

Viewed from another perspective, that figure represents an unmet demand for goods in any category: cheap, moderately priced, and expensive. There are many Russians willing to buy quality goods at a high price. The lack of such goods leads to a situation where West European shops are literally packed by Russian customers.

Western products obviously sell well in Russia. A good illustration is Crocus International Company. In 1992 with a staff of just two people, the firm started operations by supplying inexpensive clothes purchased by weight in the United States and sold on consignment in Moscow. In 1997, the company had a network of ready-made clothes shops in the capital, and its operations extended far into surrounding regions.

While Moscow and some other large cities are to a considerable degree saturated with Western products, the regional markets are not. In fact, they lack goods and services of all kinds. As a result, a great number of goods are purchased in small batches by individual traders in the capital and shipped and sold elsewhere in Russia and other CIS countries; thus, Moscow has grown into a sort of transshipment point for such goods.

There is also a great demand for all types of services in Russia. Even in Moscow and some other large cities, the saturation of the service market stands at less than 20 percent. This helps explain the phenomenal success of such a simple undertaking as a network of Kodak and Fuji photo labs developed by Rostix International.

Until 1995, there were no modern dry cleaners in Moscow, a situation which prevented many Russians from having high-quality clothing cleaned well. Once launched in 1996, the California Cleaners network proved a tremendous success. Here is one firm that truly found its niche.

BARRIERS, PITFALLS, CAVEATS

Political Risks

The frequent change in Russian government (policies) means an uncertain course for economic reform. Investors may suddenly find government restrictions affecting the course of business operations.

The political history of post-communist Russia can be divided into two main phases: (1) 1991 to mid-1996 and (2) mid-1996 to the present. During the initial phase, changes in the cabinet of ministers were basically contingent on considerations related to a specific political situation. Through these appointments, the president could counterbalance the interests of various political representatives around him.

By mid-1996, a few influential financial and industrial groups emerged in Russia, and they started to lobby the government actively through their representatives, who then held key governmental posts. This means that starting in mid-1996 those who have come to power in Russia represent specific financial and industrial groups that have distinct economic rather than political interests. In Russia it has been a tradition to grant power along a group or clan basis.

On the one hand, this makes the position of a Western investor easy since a change in government does not bring about sharp changes in the economic policy or jeopardize business itself. On the other hand, one should make a thorough analysis of key government figures and understand who is behind them and what the interests of their group or clan are. This would allow an investor to know precisely what kind of policy a person is going to pursue as part of the government and how this policy is likely to influence one's specific business interests in Russia.

Threats from Criminal Structures

For our purposes, threats from crime can be divided into two types: (1) threats to personal safety and (2) threats from OCGs. Counter to assertions by many journalists, TV programs, and public opinion that threats to the personal safety of Russian citizens are growing, Moscow is not filled with places too unsafe for people to visit without some type of security. In fact, the number of murders in Moscow is one-third that of New York City.

Common sense rules of conduct in large Russian cities do not differ substantially from those in large American cities. Some Russian regions have their own specific features in terms of security, and you can learn about them from special reports that can be prepared by major Russian and Western security companies as ordered by their clients. Such companies can be contacted when you plan to stay long in the host country, move around in it, and/or open your office there. In addition, valuable information can be obtained from special bulletins disseminated by the many embassies in Moscow. Otherwise, common sense goes a long way in avoiding a threat to your personal safety.

Threats to business on the part of Russian OCGs are quite real. They are the result of the collapse of the old system and the struggle in building a replacement. There are many well-equipped and perfectly organized criminal groups with their own intelligence and counterintelligence, contacts in law enforcement agencies, and experts in finance and banking.

Large-scale OCGs operate globally and coordinate their operations with national OCGs elsewhere. One well-known Russian OCG is called Solntsevo, for the district in Moscow where most of its members used to live. The recent arrest of the leader, nicknamed Mikhas, in Switzerland did not affect activities.

OCG representatives never approach your office without cause. Reasons for a visit would include a company's involvement in illegal operations in Russia, tax dodging, regular business relations with OCG-associated or -controlled partners, or attempts to interfere in the sphere of OCG interests in a particular area. Otherwise, they are unlikely to pay a visit to someone's office.

Let us assume that they have visited you. What should you do? There is no sense in applying to the militia or any other law enforcement agencies. The militia is, as a rule, corrupt and unqualified and in any case cannot respond to your request fast enough. Besides, information can leak from the militia to the OCG seeking to control you.

If worse comes to worst, you should apply immediately to one of the security firms manned by former employees of KGB antiterrorist units; they have regular ties in the law enforcement agencies and a good record of operations. The firms are staffed by ex-officers of such KGB special units as the Alfa and Vympel Groups. Following a thorough analysis of the situation, they can tell you what to do next, establish contact with the law enforcement bodies, and provide your personal security should you perceive the need for protection.

Unless you are short of funds, you are recommended, upon arriving in Russia, to establish contact with such a security company in order to avoid problems. However, these firms normally cannot investigate your partners for possible ties to OCGs. To avoid extra expenditures, you should contact a firm specializing in providing business information support that can also recommend a reputable security company.

Corruption

Corruption in high places is much discussed in Russia. Every new government promises that it will stop official extortion. Still, corruption is expected to affect the Russian business situation for a long time.

It is unlikely that the widely hailed anticorruption campaign the government launched in early 1997 will make a noticeable difference. Given that fact, we would like to pose the following questions and answers based on five years' experience as a business consultant in Russia:

1. Should you offer bribes or not? Our understanding is that you should never hand over bribes to officials or anyone else, and here's why. First, it's unlikely to matter because foreign investors don't know whether a particular official can actually settle the problem. Second, offering a bribe directly places both parties in a criminal position.

2. Who is to be paid? Suppose that you want to settle a problem with an official who, for some reason, blocks your project. You should apply to those professionals or organizations that are engaged in lobbying and know precisely how to solve your problem. But this is not a simple choice.

   In more than one instance the so-called facilitators were paid in excess of $50,000 to help settle a problem without actually doing so. Yet, on the other hand, some distinguished Western consulting companies received fees just as high for producing the same result.

   It is our belief that there is no blanket response in cases like this.

Remember that in Russia there are various large associations designed to lobby government on behalf of their members.

3. How can you do it and not lose money? First of all, you should find a business-intelligence or competitive-intelligence company that can identify precisely the association or organization to settle your problem. Such research should be assigned to more than one company to rule out the possibility of favoritism. It is best to handle the situation immediately rather than ignore it or let it drag on. That is how you will lose time and money.

Imperfect Investor's Rights

One of the greatest shortcomings of government in Russia is that things change so often. Frequent changes together with inconsistencies in laws and regulations leave potential investors confused, and sometimes an investor has to follow rules that are far worse than those which were in effect when he or she signed the investment agreement. Unfortunately, the laws do not protect an investor's rights.

Any "business" in Russia may be defined so broadly as to be borderline. While not strictly illegal, authorities may not believe it merits protection. In 1992–1993, cheating was common in the area of securities circulation, while in 1995–1997 many securities transactions involving Russian enterprises have been based on insider information. However, there is a growing tendency to take measures on protecting investors' rights, and that has been observed since the end of 1996.

Underdeveloped Infrastructure

Russia's underdeveloped infrastructure is improving gradually. Many companies based in large cities offer cellular communication services, including immediate long-distance telephone calls. Service companies now exist to handle personal and product transportation around the country.

A number of medical centers are organized by Western companies in Moscow and St. Petersburg, and they offer qualified medical assistance, including emergency evacuation of patients from Russia. There are sufficient recruiting agencies both in Moscow and elsewhere to handle your personal needs.

ABOUT THE AUTHOR

Igor V. Shevchuk
Business Intelligence Consultancy
Offices 50, 57–60
8/7 Bolshoy Zlatoustinsky Lane
Moscow
Phone: 7095 733 9278
Fax: 7095 597490

Igor V. Shevchuk is founder and principal of Business Intelligence Consultancy (BIC), a company specializing in research on companies, industries, and individual entrepreneurs in the computer information systems area. BIC provides support to domestic and international companies seeking to enter emerging CIS markets. Mr. Shevchuk has over ten years of experience in government and commercial intelligence. He is a member of the Society of Competitive Intelligence Professionals.

Yelena V. Kisseleva
Phone: 7095 943 9127
E-mail: kisel@newsbox.msk.su

Yelena V. Kisseleva is an expert with *Kommersant Rating* magazine, a new publication from the major Russian publisher Kommersant. Her areas of expertise are Russian banking and the market for precious stones and metals.

Chapter 6

LATIN AMERICA

If You Stick It Out, You Can Find Gold in Latin America

YOU MUST HAVE "THE STOMACH" TO ENTER LATIN AMERICA AND STAY IN THE MARKET

Companies that have done business in Latin America most likely possess not-too-distant memories of high inflation, debt-ridden economies, political instability, currency devaluations, and impossible distribution and payment situations. But that was then, and this is now, the 1990s. So, let's put Latin America in perspective.

Clearly, the integration of Europe mostly came from a central authority (the European Union), while the integration of Asia was purely market

Do not make the mistake in thinking that the Latin American countries and economies are "connected" or "linked" to each other. Similar to the countries within Western Europe or the European Union, the Latin American countries have different cultures as a result of their heritage, different consumer markets, different infrastructures and different markets. If we assume that Latin America begins with Mexico and continues through Central America into South America, even the geography, resources, and landscape of the countries are quite diverse. Because the per capita income is not at the level as in North America, the economies are not "consumer" economies or as individual driven as the "I" economy of the United States. In some respect, Latin America is a checkerboard of mixed Latin cultures who currently have a desire to become connected with the rest of the world economy.

driven. The integration of Latin America, however, will likely be a hybrid as a result of the following:

- Important regional and hemispheric organizations and trade pacts
- Businesses formulating working ties with other businesses in the region
- Transferring technologies
- The formulation of strategic alliances that drive the convergence of Latin American companies

Specifically, we are referring to the integration of Mexico, Central America, and South America. For the first time in history, most of the Latin American economies are democracies with elected leaders. Most of the countries also have tariffs under 14 percent. And while Latin America has typically imported European products during the past forty years, they are currently "hungry" for U.S. products.

The region consists of approximately 600 million people, represents an $890 billion market, and has an average per capita income of $8,000. However, while the U.S. and Western European markets are maturing, the Latin American market is still "young." About 54 percent of the population is under the age of twenty-five.

This demographic factor is fueling demand for such products as apparel, sporting goods, entertainment and cable TV, electronics, and computer equipment and software. A young population coupled with increasing literacy rates has increased the awareness of U.S. products through newspaper and magazine readership and direct marketing.

By the year 2010, more U.S. exports in dollar value are expected to go to Latin America than to Europe and Japan. Latin America has become the "land of promise" for American companies such as Apple Computer, Federal Express, Philip Morris, and Uniroyal. This gold rush is expected to continue for the next several years.

But the streets won't be paved with precious metal. In comparison to marketing to the United States, Western Europe, and Asian markets, you will need the patience to market your products and invest in Latin America over time. While most of the "political, financial, and economic ills of the past" have waned, you may still have to lengthen your strategic or marketing plans for returns on your investments and market share expectations.

More important, a firm courts disaster when it makes a commitment to a young country but then doesn't stay if the economy becomes weak—those left behind are not likely to forget. Once you make this decision, you will pay the price on market reentry at a later date, when the currency or the government stabilizes. This was underscored by the recent peso crisis (or devaluation) in Mexico and its "tequila effect" on the economies of other Latin American countries (for example, Argentina).

LATIN AMERICA—A SECOND UNITED STATES?

Some observers believe Latin America will become a "second United States" as we enter the next millennium. Perhaps, but doing business there is not yet risk-free due to:

- Poor distribution channels and services
- Corruption and crime
- Currency fluctuations and devaluations
- Inflation
- Bureaucratic procedures

Most important, don't make the mistake of thinking that the Latin American countries and economies are connected or "linked" to each other. Just like the members of the European Union, Latin American countries have different cultures, which makes for different markets.

If we assume that Latin America begins with Mexico and continues through Central America into South America, even the geography, resources, and landscape of the countries are quite diverse. Because per capita income is not at the level of the United States or Canada, the economies are not as consumer (or individual) driven as the United States. In some respects, Latin America is a checkerboard of mixed Latin cultures with a desire to become connected with the rest of the world economy.

The region cannot be considered pan-Latin. Expert target marketing within the region and individual countries is necessary due to the disparity between the rich and poor. While several trade pacts and organizations are striving to facilitate trade between countries, Latin America will not reach the marketing homogeneity of the United States until at least the year 2020 or beyond. However, in the interim, numerous dynamic markets offer both exporters and investors significant market opportunities.

THE BUSINESS CLIMATE IN LATIN AMERICA

A company should understand the business climate in Latin America as the first step in identifying market opportunities. It will be (or should be) clear that the markets are very diverse. While most of the economies are improving and privatization is creating opportunities throughout Latin America—e.g., in telecommunications, energy, utilities, infrastructure, health care, and environmental services—*marketers who rush in before laying a solid foundation are likely to fail.*

Businesses also must understand the political environment in each Latin American country. Your company or local representative needs to have a close relationship with the current and dominant political parties. Further, you and your company will need to understand the dynamics of other political parties.

When marketing industrial, health care, or communications products or services in Latin America, it is important to conduct business-to-business research on a country-by-country basis. This type of market or industry research should involve interviews with the following parties:

- Manufacturers or suppliers of raw materials
- Suppliers and distributors
- Key government organizations or officials
- Potential customers
- Competitors

This type of "market feasibility" research is critical in evaluating market size, potential, pricing, distribution channels, and the "optimum method of market entry."

THE LATIN AMERICAN CONSUMER

Doing business in Latin America means understanding consumers (in the rational, emotional, and cultural senses) along with the product. Market research must be conducted on a country-by-country basis. Do not assume that research findings in one country will apply to another. And always remember that the family is central to most Latin cultures, so products must appeal to the emotional and family side of the individual.

A study by Market Development Inc. (a San Diego–based market research company) categorizes Latin American buyers into five distinct psychographic groups as follows:

1. *Cosmopolitan climbers* are young, trendy, upscale consumers, open to new, expensive, and imported products.
2. *Hopeful homebodies* cling to "the old ways;" they are least likely to buy new or imported goods.
3. *Relaxed realists,* primarily from the emerging middle class, have an unhurried attitude and will spend money on imported goods as long as they are a good value.
4. *Hurried handlers,* who are mostly women, live fast-paced, tightly scheduled lives; their primary purchasing concerns are value and convenience.
5. *Careful shoppers* are price-conscious and cautious. They generally stick with products they know and trust, which often means domestic rather than imported goods.(1)

In short, savvy marketing of products to the Latin American consumers takes into consideration the culture of individuals, their preferences, their emotional position, and how a particular product fits into the world of the Latin American consumer. Clearly, marketing to the Latin American consumer requires sophisticated market research in every country.

MARKET OPPORTUNITIES IN LATIN AMERICA

THE TRADE PACTS

Many of the current market opportunities in Latin America have been created by trade pacts and organizations whose purpose is to further trade within the region, along with increasing the attractiveness of the region for foreign investment and exports.

The Andean Pact

This pact (established in 1969) consists of Peru, Ecuador, Colombia, Venezuela, and Bolivia. It does not include Brazil and lacks a common tariff scheme between the countries. As such, it is losing strength to Mercosur.

Mercosur

This customs union began with the economies of Argentina and Brazil uniting with those of Paraguay and Uruguay to create a market of 200 million people with a combined GDP of about $1 trillion. Total trade reached approximately $45 billion in 1997. Chile joined the pact in 1996, and Bolivia was named an associate member.

Mercosur accounts for about 43 percent of the Latin American population, 50 percent of it GDP, and about one-third of its total foreign trade. Brazil accounts for 80 percent of Mercosur's GDP. More important, the Brazilian and Argentine economies are working together, which indicates a "letting go" of their strife-ridden past. (2)

As much as 95 percent of Mercosur's trade is duty free today, and other countries are expected to join. Mercosur has added a measure of political and economic stability in Latin America and has been the foundation for the Free Trade Areas of the Americas (FTAA). Latin American countries are beginning to trade with each other, rather than with Europe or the United States.

NAFTA (North American Free Trade Agreement)

NAFTA was signed by the United States, Mexico, and Canada in 1993, and it has led to a "stampede" of U.S. firms investing in and exporting to Mexico. Despite the activity, it is not yet clear what NAFTA has achieved.

Several firms were disappointed to find that the hoped-for market was constrained by traditional distribution channels and ways of doing business. In most cases, U.S. business methods did not translate well. This disappointment, coupled with the subsequent peso crisis, has forced many U.S. firms to reevaluate and reformulate their strategy in Mexico.

COUNTRIES IN THE REGION

Overall, market opportunities in Latin America lie in the areas of technology products, automotive supplies, food, and communications. Because the population is young, products that involve "family formation" or appeal to the Latin American "baby boomer" will be in demand. By the year 2000, telephone subscribership will increase from 10 percent of the population to 25 percent of the population.

The PC market is expected to grow 20 percent annually, and sales should double to $4 billion in the next few years. Sales in Brazil are particularly strong. The client-server market is reported to be more advanced in Latin America than in the United States.

Advances in education are making for both more sophisticated consumers and new channels of distribution—e.g., the Price Club in Mexico,

Chile, and Brazil. The retail industry is expanding rapidly in Latin America, including "value-added market," similar to the United States. Because the markets are so diverse, the following will give a brief overview of some of them and the opportunities that exist. There has never been a better time for small and medium-size firms to enter the Latin American markets.

Argentina

Argentina has been often called "the door to Latin America" because of its political stability; relatively high per capita income; large, educated middle class; high literacy rate; rich cultural infrastructure; and very European, cosmopolitan influence. Both European and U.S. firms find it easy to do business in Argentina. The inflation rate is currently one of the lowest in the world (at approximately 1 percent).

Market opportunities exist for value-added industries and services, technology-based products and services, fast food, and insurance and financial services. Unlike other Latin American countries, Argentina has good distribution and transportation systems. Its consumers are sophisticated and report the highest cable TV subscription rate in Latin America (about 60 percent of households).

Argentina suffered from the "tequila effect" of the Mexican peso crisis in 1995, as the economy went into a recession from investors and exporters "pulling out of the Latin American market." The economy has recovered and opportunity exists in travel services, telecommunications equipment, electrical power, and computers. Privatization continues in the local economy. Companies such as Wal-Mart and 3M have reported successful ventures and marketing efforts there.

Brazil

Brazil is the largest of the Latin American countries and the most complex, with diverse market segments concentrated in thirteen major cities. Brazil's dominance of the Mercosur market has strengthened its regional leadership position. With the introduction of the Real, or the currency stabilization program, and its aggressive privatization program, Brazil is attracting significant imports and investment.

Prosperity has meant the increased purchasing power of the lower income class for both consumer nondurables (e.g., clothing, videos, entertainment, and computer products) and durables (refrigerators and so forth). Deregulation has created market opportunities in the development and improvement of the infrastructure and in such sectors as telecommunications, power, and engineering. Careful research must be taken to ensure distribution of products in this geographically diverse country.

Chile

Chile is increasingly referred to as "the Singapore of Latin America." Since the early 1990s, Chile's economy has demonstrated steady growth in both the industrial and consumer sectors. Most important, it is perceived as politically stable. Chile's per capita income is just reaching the level to demand imported food products, upscale apparel, convenience stores, and computer and entertainment products. The country wants to improve the delivery of health care, education, transportation, and telecommunications.

Of all of the Latin American countries, Chile currently offers the least risk for investment. Most of the economy is privatized, and Chilean companies are flush with cash as they received $6 billion in foreign investment in 1995. Chile's recent entry into the Mercosur trade group will accelerate its trade within South America and could have as much, if not more, impact than its potential acceptance into NAFTA. To achieve its goal of obtaining "First World" status, the government is making a significant investment in education throughout the country.

Colombia

Colombia is a country with nearly one-third of the population below the poverty line while a surprisingly high percentage has graduate degrees in economics and business. While the country has been associated with such problems as violence and drug trafficking, Colombia has developed its infrastructure and initiated programs to accelerate trade.

During the past decade, Colombia has attracted businesses in fast foods, snacks, clothing, electric power, mining, and financial services. While safety and literacy (average 7.5 years) remain problems, the country is strategically located as the center of the five members comprising the Andean Pact, whose objective is to establish a common market within South America. Opportunities exist in the environmental sectors and in waste management.

Mexico

Mexico is beginning to recover from the devaluation of its peso in 1995, which hit both the consumer and the business sectors hard. At the same time, the country continues to strengthen its privatization and investment efforts in such infrastructure areas as telecommunications, utilities, waste management, water systems, construction, and transportation (highways). In the consumer sector, demand is strong for computer products and music and entertainment products.

The higher income groups also are beginning to demand upscale products. Manufacturers and marketers who do their homework (conduct local market research) and who stay in the market (and don't retrench in times of trouble, like the peso crisis) will find their "gold" in the long term in the form of market share along with brand and customer loyalty.

Peru

Peru is a nation rich in resources. Despite a young and oftentimes impoverished population (about 50 percent are below the age of twenty-five and/ or classified in the lower socioeconomic group) with a high illiteracy rate, market opportunities exist in agriculture, mining (e.g., copper, silver, and zinc), fisheries, and tourism. In the early 1990s, the government essentially declared bankruptcy. However, since then, it has begun an aggressive privatization program to attract trade and investment. Because of the young population, market opportunities exist at the retail level in supermarkets and in the cable TV market.

Venezuela

Venezuela's economy has been affected by periodic changes in government. Despite these "roller-coaster" political years coupled with high inflation, firms continue to take advantage of market opportunities. U.S. firms find it relatively easy to enter the Venezuelan market thanks to lessons learned from investing in the oil industry.

Opportunities exist in infrastructure, e.g., telecommuncations, health care, transportation, water treatment systems, and computer equipment and peripherals. Firms must do their research in this country in view of possible political and economic changes.

Central America

Central America is defined here as those countries south of Mexico and connecting Mexico to South America. They include El Salvador, Costa Rica, Nicaragua, Honduras, Guatemala, Panama, Haiti, Trinidad, the Dominican Republic and, perhaps by extension, Puerto Rico, the Bahamas, and the Cayman Islands. While this geographic area seems to be skipped or passed over by the "mega" trade pacts—NAFTA, Mercosur, the Andean Pact—the market should not be overlooked in the long term.

Most of these countries are small, with periodic political problems and a significant percentage of the population living below the poverty line. While local consumer economies exist in each of them, only a few like Puerto Rico and Costa Rica have the purchasing power for imported goods and services.

Several economies in this region have suffered as a consequence of political unrest. For example, El Salvador was once known as the "Taiwan of Central America" because of its industrialized economy and relatively high standard of living. The country's civil war, however, changed all this. By the time it ended in 1992, some 75,000 people were dead and El Salvador's infrastructure lay in ruins. But with peace, El Salvador has had growth rates of 5 to 7 percent a year.(3)

Many firms look to Central America as a source of cheap labor close to the United States. In 1996, Honduras climbed to the world's number nine position as a source of apparel exports to the United States. In the past five years, the Honduran government has attracted several garment makers with the passage of new laws facilitating investment. The decision to locate in Honduras is the result of political stability, plentiful and qualified labor, and favorable tariff policies.

While these countries offer relatively cheap labor, they are not without problems. Many local unions have filed complaints regarding working conditions at apparel firms. You should personally and extensively research these markets (with a representative who speaks Spanish) to the point you can determine the risks/rewards of doing business in a particular country.(3)

Barriers and Pitfalls to Market Entry Within Latin America

Aside from the marketing opportunities, you may be asking yourself, Why go to Latin America? Here are some of the reasons *not* to go:

- Runaway inflation
- Military takeovers
- Crime and border corruption
- Underdeveloped infrastructure
- Distribution and logistics problems
- Frequent strikes in many ports

Despite such problems, companies continue to invest and export goods here. For example, it costs a Latin American farmer forty-five cents to get one dollar's worth of goods to market; in the United States, it costs the farmer five cents on the dollar. Yet companies such as General Motors continue to invest in the region to the tune of $2 billion for a recent four-year project.

It is essential for you to research each country separately and not generalize about market potential throughout the region. While Mercosur and NAFTA have made strides in creating common trade zones, exporters should not forget the differences in culture and geography between the countries.

A Recommended Approach to Market Entry Into Latin America

Step 1: In general, recognize and respect these basic tenets of Latin American culture.

1. Strong respect for family values
2. Respect for age and the role of the elderly in society
3. Appreciation for U.S. products.
4. Absence of individual empowerment (as in the United States)
5. Extensive community involvement
6. A "live-and-let-live" attitude
7. A general conservatism reflecting the pervasiveness of the Catholic faith

Understanding the culture takes many forms. For example, advertising and promotions should not use colloquialisms or slang. And Latin Americans do not identify with the U.S. notion of being "constantly on the go." A case in point is Federal Express's introduction of its "next-day delivery" service in Latin America. After extensive market research, Fed Ex discovered that Argentina, Mexico, Venezuela, Brazil, Uruguay, and Chile would be the most receptive to the concept of next-day delivery.

To advertise the concept, they hired local advertising agencies in each market. By initially increasing local awareness, Federal Express achieved more of an impact with its pan-regional advertising.(4)

And again, never use slang. For example, the seemingly innocent phrase "throw me a pen" has sexual connotations in Venezuela. Braniff Airlines' ad campaign "We will fly you in leather," when translated into Spanish read, "We will fly you nude."(4)

STEP 2: CONDUCT LOCAL MARKET RESEARCH (COUNTRY BY COUNTRY) TO ENSURE THAT YOU UNDERSTAND THE MARKET AND CONSUMER PREFERENCES.

Your market research should also take into consideration market segmentation within a country—by city, urban versus rural, socioeconomic stratum, age, and so forth. While most Latin American countries have young economies (with the bulk of the population under the age of twenty-five years of age), there are significant cultural differences in this "youth" society from country to country—even within the geographical regions of a country.

Be careful not to draw conclusions across market segments. Additionally, you should select a market research firm that has considerable experience with the country and the culture and that has sophisticated analytical and statistical projection techniques.

STEP 3: PERSONAL RELATIONSHIPS AND FACE-TO-FACE MEETINGS (VERSUS TELEPHONE AND FAX) ARE ESSENTIAL AND CRITICAL IN LATIN AMERICA.

You will have to invest considerable time meeting the key people and going to dinner, to lunch, and so forth. Personal relationships are the basis for doing business in Latin America. Remember that local contacts are critical. You must "nurture" your contacts over the long term to be successful here.

The following case study shows how a company failed to follow this point. L. M. Ericsson Telephone Company was noted for the highest quality products in the market. As such, it tried to win the contract for switching products in the Brazilian telecommunications market. However, Ericsson made one big mistake: It brought in a "hot-shot" Swedish lawyer to make a formal presentation before the Brazilian Advisory Board. The lawyer had no personal connections there. Ericsson lost the contract.

STEP 4: KEEP YOUR MARKET ENTRY STRATEGY SIMPLE AND YOUR MARKET ENTRY COSTS LOW.

Dell Computer proved that you can enter Mexico without crossing the border. In the early 1990s, Dell placed ads in local Mexican computer magazines that asked potential customers to call Dell's Austin, Texas, office, which was staffed with Spanish-speaking operators. The test proved quite successful. Dell now has a workforce of over sixty people in Mexico City and has opened a production plant in Mexico.

Also remember to market your brands or products locally . . .

STEP 5: WHEN YOU ENTER THE MARKET, DEVELOP AND KEEP A "LONG-TERM" PERSPECTIVE ON YOUR LATIN AMERICAN BUSINESS.

To succeed in Latin America, you must nurture and expand your contacts, build your credibility, and show your commitment to the country by remaining for the long term. This means in good times and bad.

Coopers & Lybrand made a significant commitment to the region years ago. Today, it maintains over forty offices in sixteen Latin American countries. As such, Coopers & Lybrand handles most of the accounting work in the region's ongoing privatization programs. The company has even launched a newsletter to advise all of their worldwide partners of the business opportunities in Latin America.

PUBLISHED SOURCES

(1) Market Development, Inc., 1643 Sixth Avenue, San Diego, CA 92101, USA, 1997 entrepreneur, All rights reserved.

(2) *International Business,* September 1996, pp. 41–42

(3) Source: *Expansion Management,* January/February 1997, "Peace Dividend in Central America," pp. 68–69.

(4) *International Business,* "Beg to Differ," November 1996, p. 28.

ARGENTINA
YOUR DOOR TO LATIN AMERICA

Argentina has one of the fastest growing markets in the developing world—bringing together a stable democracy, an expanding economy, low inflation, and well-educated consumers looking for quality products. It presents opportunities not only for Fortune 500 companies but for many small and medium-size firms as well. Furthermore, many foreign companies are based in Argentina as the door to the Mercosur common market, which includes Brazil, Paraguay, and Uruguay.

In the past Argentina displayed many characteristics of the "typical" Latin American country: political turmoil, economic instability, high budget deficits, and high inflation. Although the Argentine Republic was formed in 1853 with a constitution patterned on that of the United States, its democracy has been interrupted several times by military coups.

Today, however, after fourteen years of democratic government and six years of economic reform—including the introduction of free-market principles, the deregulation of the economy, and a massive privatization program—the contrast between past and present could hardly be more dramatic. For example, in July 1989 inflation was 204 percent a *month;* prices changed five times a day. Argentina's inflation rate is now one of the lowest in the world: in 1996, it was 1 percent for the *year.*

In the past, the government owned and operated (often very poorly) all key services. Under recent reforms, privatization has included the national airline, petroleum, gas, electricity, water, sewage, railways, subways, highways, waste management, and mining. Even parking enforcement and driver licensing have been privatized. The changes have not only reduced the government deficit but improved the quality of service as well.

The differences can be extraordinary: The local petroleum company, YPF, when government owned had a payroll of over 70,000 and lost money. Today, it has a payroll of 7,770, is quite profitable, and has expanded internationally.

MARKET OPPORTUNITIES

Argentina is one of the most promising markets in Latin America. Enjoying the highest per capita income in the region, with a large well-educated middle class, it is an ideal market for high value-added products (durables and technology-based products) and services. A further advantage is the extreme concentration of Argentine consumers: For many sectors, Buenos Aires alone constitutes 50 percent of the potential market.

The retail sector reflects Argentina's growing sophistication. Although "mom and pop" stores traditionally were the major channels for household goods, now over 65 percent of sales are generated by self-service outlets, particularly supermarkets and hypermarkets. Several international chains are very active: Carrefour, Wal-Mart, C&A, and Makro, among others. This domination of the market in turn has led many retail chains to pressure suppliers to offer better deals.

Private labels, although not yet common, will surely show important growth in many product categories. For example, Carrefour, expects to carry over 130 product categories with its own labels—everything from fast-moving consumer goods (FMCG) to household electronics and durables. FMCG manufacturers actively marketing in Argentina include Lever, Clorox, Colgate, Danone, Nabisco, Parmalat, Nestle, CPC, Reckitt & Colman, and Kimberly-Clark.

Shopping centers feature a large proportion of the non-FMCG products, such as clothes, books, and household electronics. While high-quality cafes and restaurants are widespread, fast-food chains also have been growing. McDonald's and Pizza Hut were among the first to enter; they have now been followed by Wendy's.

Argentina's appetite for media is just as impressive. Newspapers, magazines, TV, radio, and cinemas are everywhere. Cable penetration is the highest in Latin America—over 60 percent of households are cable subscribers, and cable viewing accounts for over 40 percent of total viewing. Argentine cable subscribers receive a wide range of programming from U.S., European, and Latin American feeds. And the business continues to boom. TCI[2] bought one of the largest cable operators for several hundred million dollars. In addition, DTH recently launched a satellite system, even though satellite dishes are not yet widely used.

The population has embraced telecommunications, too. Some of the enthusiasm may, of course, reflect people's new ability to *get* phone service. In the past, people sometimes were forced to wait 20 years or more to have a phone line installed; today, installation happens in one or two days. Cellular phone ownership is extensive (with 1 million subscribers), and in 1997 the government will auction the rights to two bands of the PCS digital system, which will compete against cellular operators. The pager market has been growing steadily, as well.

ARGENTINA NOTES

- Do not expect your faxes or phone calls to be returned promptly. Argentines work at their own pace.

- Remember not to book meetings during Carnival, which always precedes Ash Wednesday, the beginning of Lent.

- Be punctual for business meetings. Nevertheless, you may have to wait for your contact.

- Fluency or conversancy in Spanish is necessary for negotiations in Argentina. Hire a translator if you aren't fluent in the language.

- As in other Latin American countries, personal relationships drive business deals in Argentina.

- Do not discuss business during lunch or dinner. Only at the end of the meal is it appropriate to discuss business. (Dinner can start as late as 10:00 p.m.)

- Be cautious of your money in cities such as Buenos Aires. Count your money and watch your wallet and briefcase.

One of the many benefits of controlling inflation has been the growth of the financial sector. Until recently, the life insurance business was nonexistent because high inflation levels made such long-term financial commitments impossible. In the past few years, however, economic stability has allowed companies such as Metropolitan Life, CIGNA, and Eagle to operate with great success. In addition, the privatization of pension funds has created a large and growing domestic capital market.

ISSUES AND CAVEATS

It's Only an Advantage if People Want It

Like some wines, product attributes and features don't necessarily travel well. This can affect advertising and product positioning. In particular, if you plan to sell a product by touting its advantages, make sure that Argentines actually regard these features as such.

A leading European toiletries company decided to launch a new product that was doing well in the United States, Canada, and Australia: a toothpaste with mouthwash. The product allowed the user to perform two steps in one (brushing one's teeth and using mouthwash), and where the product had succeeded, this feature gave it a major advantage over the competition. In Argentina, however, hardly anyone uses, or wants to use, mouthwash. The "two in one" advantage made no sense, since only "one" was desired.

Renault's Twingo had a different problem. It was positioned as a luxury car and, therefore, sold at a very high price. When shopping for cars, however, most Argentines want value for their money rather than luxury. The Twingo has now been relaunched at a lower price.

Even cultures that seem similar to an outsider are different in ways that can have serious implications for marketing and sales. Some years ago, a car manufacturer imported large cars into Argentina based on their sales in Brazil, Colombia, and Venezuela. But the preference in Argentina is for small cars, even at the top end of the market, where you would find Fiats, Peugeots, Renaults, and Volkswagens selling well. To Argentines, size does not imply quality.

Only Uncle Sam Eats Peanut Butter

The marketing of food provides many examples of what can go wrong when a company launches products without careful consideration of the local market. In extreme cases, consumers may reject the product outright.

A U.S. peanut butter manufacturer launched its product as a bread spread to be used at breakfast and tea time. Argentines, however, overwhelmingly prefer preserves or "dulce de leche" (a local milk-based product). Peanut butter had to be pulled from the market entirely.

In more typical cases, the mistakes are more subtle. For example, a few years ago a leading U.S. pizza retail chain opened a franchise operation to market "pan" pizzas. Although Argentines certainly like pizza, the new venture was a major failure because local consumers love flat "pizza a la piedra," which is available everywhere.

Even when there is nothing intrinsically wrong with the product, bad positioning can kill its market opportunities. For example, Argentines love beef—it is part of their history, and they have access to some of the world's best meat at moderate prices. They consume on average 90 pounds of beef per person per year. Seeking to capture this market, a large chain of fast-food restaurants specializing in hamburgers positioned itself as the best "food" provider. But because Argentines can eat a high-quality steak for the price of a Big Mac, they regard hamburgers as a convenience choice, not a food choice.

Inflation Isn't Always the Problem

Mail-order catalogs have failed as a business for different reasons at different times. First, when inflation was high, mail-order suppliers listed their products at prohibitively high prices; they did this to protect themselves from exchange rate exposure. Later, with inflation finally brought under control and mail-order goods competitively priced, it was the unreliability of the postal system that discouraged potential customers from ordering.

However, the situation is changing. Several new private courier services now make for quicker delivery, and post office performance is expected to improve with its privatization. In addition, telemarketing has in some areas replaced catalogs as the basic sales medium.

More Room for Improvement

One consequence of the massive reduction of government involvement in the economy and the private sector's new competitiveness and efficiency has been unemployment. It has reached a record high of 17 percent. This is one of the major problems facing Argentina today. Although the government is sponsoring retraining and other educational programs, unemployment is not expected to fall by much. A reform that might make a difference—government action on high labor costs—is being discussed in Parliament, but major reform is not expected.

The legal system, based on the Napoleonic Code, tends to be slow and bureaucratic, as in other Latin American countries. For example, a simple labor claim can take over ten years to wind its way through court. So, it is sometimes necessary to hire a local legal advisor to help in navigating through the system.

ABOUT THE AUTHOR

Jorge Garćia-González
ASECOM S.A.
Av. Cordoba 1345
Piso 8
1050 Buenos Aires
Phone: 54 1 815 1499
Fax: 54 1 812 8213; 54 1 812 1662

Jorge Garćia-González, M.B.A., is president of ASECOM S.A., a leading marketing research and consulting company specializing in the Latin American region. His clients include Cadbury, Coca-Cola, Clorox, Exxon, HBO, Iberia Airlines, J. P. Morgan, NTT/Itochu, Ralston Purina, Shell, Sony, and Wella, among many others. For the past twenty-seven years, Mr. Garćia-González has been professor of marketing and marketing research at UCA University and the business school of the Argentine Chamber of Commerce. Before founding ASECOM in 1978, Mr. Garćia-González worked in marketing for John Deere and spent many years in advertising with McCann-Erickson, Ogilvy and Mather, and Lintas (Unilever). He is a member of the American Marketing Association, the American Management Association, and ESOMAR.

BRAZIL
REVISIT BRAZIL TODAY

Modern Brazil's history dates to 1500, when the region was colonized by Portugal; it soon became one of Portugal's most important colonies. Three centuries later, with Portugal occupied by Napoleon, Rio de Janeiro became the seat of the entire Portuguese empire. So, Brazil's history is anything but ordinary. Fifty percent of the population is a first-, second-, or third-generation immigrant. Portuguese and African influences are more evident in the north while German, Italian, and Japanese influences are found further south.

Brazilians' friendliness is reflected in their business conversations,

BRAZIL NOTES

- Do not schedule any business transactions around Carnival, which always precedes Ash Wednesday, the beginning of Lent.

- Always make business appointments three to four weeks in advance. Allow time for faxes to be received, circulated to the right person, and responded to.

- Try to reach the decision maker for a meeting in the late morning or late afternoon. Business lunches take at least two hours.

- Hold meetings and entertain at first-class hotels. Don't discuss business until the end of meals.

- Business dinners start late (7:00 to 10:00 p.m.) and often end late.

- Business in Brazil is based on personal relationships and personal connections. Try to hire a Brazilian in your industry to help you meet the right people. Also, hire a local Brazilian accountant rather than one from your own country.

- Brazilians can be offended by direct, "get to the point" business behavior. You may have to make several trips to Brazil to complete contract negotiations.

- Brazilians are friendly and outgoing. They will gesture and may engage in physical contact.

- Do not use the American "OK" sign. It is considered offensive.

- Conservative dress—for example, a dark blue suit—is particularly important for women. Don't wear green and yellow dresses; these are the colors of the Brazilian flag.

- Brazilians are avid soccer enthusiasts. It is better to discuss sports than politics.

- Safeguard your briefcase, jewelry, and handbag in Rio de Janeiro. Foreigners are often targets for crime, particularly if they are wearing expensive watches or jewelry. Lock all valuables in a safe in your hotel room.

---

which can take place with the participants five to twelves inches apart. That intimacy may be uncomfortable for business executives from other cultures, just as Brazilians might feel uncomfortable talking business the way people do in the U.S., at a distance of two feet. This seemingly small detail can prove very stressful and distracting during a business conversation if the foreign executive is not prepared for it. The same holds true for greetings, which can be effusive. Even a first business meeting can involve extended handshakes and back-thumping.

Family will also play an important role in business dealings. Family-owned businesses will prefer to do business with people they like, and that relationship may take some time to build. Family-owned businesses also want to make sure that a decision makes "family sense" as well as business sense. The "hard sell" will not work in this environment; if anything, it will be considered aggressive.

Another characteristic of Brazilian culture is its flexibility with time. Be prepared if you're coming from a time-based culture.

SEEING MARKETS AND INFORMATION FROM A DIFFERENT PERSPECTIVE

Measuring Brazil with a generic statistic like per capita income ($4,345) paints the picture of a developing, not developed, economy. But different pictures tell different stories, especially if Brazil is divided into markets by specific category or region. This second approach helps explain why international companies are showing ever more interest in Brazil.

From computers to potato chips, many Brazilian subsidiaries of multinational corporations have demonstrated exceptional growth in sales. For example, in 1996 sales for Elma Chips in Brazil grew 25 percent as compared to global sales growth of 4.6 percent. For Philip Morris, the comparison is 18 percent versus 1.47 percent; for the Italian automotive company Fiat, 6.5 versus 3 percent; and for Coca-Cola, 10 versus 3 percent. Also, Microsoft's sales in Brazil grew from $30 million in 1993 to $160 million in 1996.

OPPORTUNITIES IN A CHANGING COMPETITIVE LANDSCAPE

After 15 years of little or no growth and ruinous inflation, the government in 1994 implemented the Real Plan to stabilize the currency. The plan introduced a new currency, the Real, as it restrained Brazil's high inflation rate. As a result, Brazilians now enjoy a marked increase in their purchasing power. The gross domestic product stood at $677 billion in 1995. Agriculture represented 10 percent of GDP, industry 35 percent, and services 55 percent.

The most dramatic increases have occurred among low-income Brazilians, although salaried workers have benefitted as well. This group has realized a 15 to 30 percent gain in purchasing power. A stable currency should also fuel demand for capital goods. Conditions should remain promising as long as the government continues the course and pursues other necessary fiscal and administrative reforms.

With inflation under control, the government has moved to embrace privatization, deregulation, and the removal of barriers to competition. The economy has been opened to foreign entrants, and industry has restructured itself impressively. Exporters now can expand their activities and participate in new business opportunities. With these changes and the government's commitment to continued reform and increased privatization, Brazil is entering a new era of business opportunities and growth for domestic and international investors.

Promising sectors of the economy for exports include telecommunications, pay TV, computer hardware and peripherals, medical equipment and supplies, electric power supplies, oil and gas-field machinery and services, pollution control equipment, computer software, processed food, and transportation equipment. It is an impressive list for a not-yet fully developed economy.

ISSUES AND CAVEATS

Applying Local Knowledge

Companies planning to enter the country should leverage local knowledge as much as possible in adapting processes to local conditions. Even a company as widely known as Coca-Cola understood the importance of adapting to a particular market.

Coca-Cola adapted by establishing strong partnerships with local bottlers. These bottlers translate Coke's global objectives into practice by making wise use of their own expertise. This is how Coca-Cola is distributed in the challenging regions of northern and northeastern Brazil.

The product literally travels up and down the Amazon River on barges. In Maraba, "a sun-blasted outpost in Brazil's remote northeast," a distributor known as "Chico da Coca," Francisco Bezerra da Silva, scrambles Indiana Jones–style along roads, rivers, and mountains to deliver Coke to the miners of the Pelada mine, the world's largest open-pit gold mine. Knowing the local terrain, weather conditions, and consumption patterns, Bezerra da Silva delivers Coca-Cola to a different kind of paying customer (Coca-Cola Company, *Journey* 3, no. 1).

Realizing That What Works at Home Doesn't Work Everywhere Else

Failing to recognize the realities of a different competitive environment can be a costly mistake even for a Fortune 500 giant like Wal-Mart. The company's tried-and-true formula for success in the United States could not be duplicated in Brazil.

Entering the market in a joint venture, Wal-Mart started a price war by selling all products at least 5 percent below the competitor's lowest price. Almost one thousand key products were sold at prices 15 percent lower than competitors, regardless of profit margins. Enraged at the start of a price war that could damage long-established interests and local business relationships, many suppliers rebelled. They suspended product sales and changed negotiation conditions. One supplier even took the step of walking into a store and buying all the company's products off the shelves!

With few stores in Brazil, Wal-Mart could not act as a major distribution force as it can in the United States. As a result, the retailer had to call off the price war. The increased prices had at least one nasty side effect—

they left customers wondering what had happened to all the bargains. And even though it achieved almost twice the sales volume of equivalent stores in the USA, Wal-Mart suffered losses of US$16 million on the first 40 days of operations, and US$33 million for all of 1996.

Wal-Mart opened a second São Paulo store in May. Shelves were stocked with a large quantity of seasonal products for spring, which was fine for United States but not Brazil, where the seasons are reversed; imagine the surprise of customers looking for autumn merchandise. After these initial missteps, Wal-Mart had the good sense to go back to the drawing board and refine its approach to the Brazilian market.

The lesson here is clear. The size, power, and knowledge a company displays in its home market do not automatically transfer to Brazil as if by magic. Preparation is essential.

Emerging Consumer Markets

Brazil's inflation rate dropped sharply in 1995. Prior to the Real Plan, inflation stood at about 50 percent *monthly*. The inflation rate now is less than 10 percent *annually*. This change has meant a noticeable increase in the purchasing power among salaried workers and low-income groups. Suddenly, there appeared a new group of Brazilian consumers, people who spent on the average of US$1,850 per year.

This may not sound like much, but remember, figures can mean something different in Brazil than they do in the United States or Western Europe. Low-income Brazilians, although without much disposable income, account for almost half of the population. In a country of more than 160 million inhabitants, that translates into a market of close to US$150 billion a year.

The decisions made concerning a market this size can make or break even large companies. The increased purchasing power was felt in such areas as food, house cleaning, clothing, refrigerators, freezers, video rentals, construction materials, and even language courses. In 1995 for example, food consumption increased 30 percent while the sales of refrigerators jumped by 27 percent; color TVs, 23 percent; stoves, 28 percent; and automobiles, 12 percent.

Small and medium-size firms looking for opportunities should consider finding a niche that is part of one of the high-growth markets. Possibilities include telecommunications, computer software, retailing, automotive, machine tools, pollution control equipment, security and safety equipment, chemicals, and construction. One way or another, large firms may have to depend on smaller firms if they want to succeed.

Looking for Gold in Soap

Many products marketed by international companies in Brazil are designed for the typical middle-class family in a developed country. Gessy Lever used an entirely different approach. The firm produced a laundry soap for a target market of 35 million low-income people with a monthly income under $200. This income group does not have washing machines; members do their laundry in rivers and backyards.

Using experience gained in India, Gessy Lever talked to low-income families to understand their needs and the firm proceeded accordingly. The company marketed a no-frills product at a very low price—no fancy or expensive packaging here—and made sure distribution met customers' buying habits (at small and/or out-of-the-way stores). The new soap captured 30 percent of the target market in just six months, and it is now being considered as the first step in a new line of products specifically tailored to low-income groups.

Chasing Opportunities While Avoiding the Web of Bureaucracy

Despite the government's continuous efforts to simplify regulations for businesses in Brazil, the bureaucracy remains an obstacle. Documentation requirements on relatively minor items and confusing administrative procedures can create unbelievable amounts of red tape and impose high costs in terms of time and money. Be prepared.

The Brazilian solution to bureaucracy is the expediter, or "*despachante.*" This is a firm or person who has extensive knowledge of governmental administrative procedures and can expedite the bureaucratic process by using knowledge and contacts. There are many sizes and shapes of *despachantes* in Brazil, from small firms to full-fledged law firms, depending on the size of the task at hand.

Before even attempting to confront the Brazilian bureaucracy, a newcomer should consult the sources described below. Trivial as it may at first seem, bureaucracy can do in the best-laid plans.

Setting Up Shop

Starting a business in Brazil is basically the same as in other parts of the world. The government does not favor native Brazilians over foreign residents regarding such basic rights as liberty, personal security, and property ownership. With the exception of some security-related sectors where the federal constitution places restrictions on foreign capital, international investors can easily establish subsidiaries; associate with Brazilian or foreign investors; have representatives; or transfer its trademark or technology to a local company.

Brazilian law provides for legal structures that are broadly similar to those found in the United States or Great Britain. However, because of the complexity of the law, investors are strongly advised to seek professional advice before making any commitment.

Although most investors or businesses will have some idea of how they want to operate, it will be important for them to keep an open mind while doing market research, establishing first contacts and becoming acquainted with local practices and options. The simplest way of testing the Brazilian market is via exports. The format is easier to set up and does not require much investment.

A company can start small and grow with demand. The downside is losing touch with emerging Brazilian opportunities. A company selling through a distributor only has little direct control over such matters as product handling and full market penetration.

One alternative is finding a local representative; this allows a firm to make a serious commitment to the Brazilian market without having to establish a formal presence. Given Brazil's size, a company would do well to find a representative for the largest market in the largest city in South America, São Paulo. If everything goes well, a firm can then decide to expand, either to other Brazilian markets or elsewhere in South America.

Most smaller and some larger companies interested in Brazil enter into joint ventures with domestic firms. A joint venture allows the newcomer to complement existing strengths in technology, product development, and know-how with the practical experience of its Brazilian partners. The joint venture also offers a handle on local market conditions and business practices as well as greater speed in launching products and reducing the amount of capital needed for starting up.

Alliances of all sizes and shapes, even between multinationals and state companies undergoing privatization, are possible in Brazil. For example, Embratel, the Brazilian state telecommunications company expected to be privatized in 1997, worked out an agreement with IBM to offer EDI and services based on Lotus Notes software for workgroups using Embratel's large infrastructure. IBM has structured similar alliances in Canada, Germany, Italy, and Australia. The objective of the newly formed alliance is to achieve 35 to 40 percent participation in a $1.7 billion-a-year market.

Yet another possibility is establishing a wholly owned subsidiary. This offers total control and avoids the potential of conflict with a joint venture participant, but it also increases the risk of failure due to unfamiliarity with local conditions. The continuous monitoring of changing market conditions is crucial to success here.

Franchising is another popular way of doing business in Brazil, which has the fourth highest number of franchising points (or points of sale) in the world. With 60,000 points of sale and 932 names, Brazil lags behind only the United States, Japan, and Canada in this category. Any foreign franchiser may choose to enter Brazil, either via a wholly owned subsidiary or a joint venture, and use this company to franchise to local operators or utilize cross-border franchising. Some potential franchisers have opted to test the market by opening a limited number of wholly owned outlets. Such was the case with 7-Eleven.

Successful franchisers know to adapt their fare to local tastes and consumption habits. For example, Dunkin' Donuts added tropical fruit fillings to its flavors. Based on local research, McDonald's created the McBacon, a sandwich that was added to its worldwide menu. Arby's changed its traditional emphasis on roast beef to chicken, which now accounts for 45 percent of Arby's sales in Brazil.

The Brazilian franchising market has annual sales of $60 billion, so it attracts them all, from big names like Blockbuster (planning to open 170 franchised stores by the end of the decade) and McDonald's (planning to invest $500 million to double its presence in Brazil in the next four years) to small companies like American Leak Detectors, which has world sales of $40 million and local sales of $1 million. It would appear that the developing economy of Brazil has some very developed tastes, indeed.

Special Incentives for U.S. Companies

The U.S. government offers special incentives to help U.S. companies establish stronger bilateral commercial relations with Brazil. One example is the U.S.-Brazil Business Development Council, a mixed private-public forum. The council is developing a program of activities to facilitate commerce and investment.

The Export-Import Bank also offers short-, medium-, and long-term programs to support U.S. exports to Brazilian private sector entities. The export of consumer goods, spare parts, and raw materials (on terms up to 180 days) and bulk agricultural commodities and quasi-capital goods (on terms up to 360 days) also can be supported under Ex-Im short-term credit insurance policies.

ABOUT THE AUTHOR

Pedro C. Ribeiro
Synthesis Ltd.
R. Oscar Freire 953–195
São Paulo, SP 01426–001 Brazil
Phone/Fax: 55 11 534 9122

Pedro Ribeiro, B.A., M.B.A., is founder and president of Synthesis Ltd., a firm specializing in providing management teams with instruments for competitive decisions. Before founding Synthesis, he held strategic planning and competitive intelligence management positions with major corporations in Brazil such as Chase Manhattan, Exxon, and Hanna Mining/MBR.

CHILE
THE SINGAPORE OF LATIN AMERICA

A stable economy coupled with democratic government has transformed Chile into the showcase of Latin America. With a financial profile similar in many respects to an Asian "tiger," Chile is the Singapore of Latin America. While most of the investment opportunities so far have been in infrastructure, Chile's consumer economy is expanding thanks to increased disposable income. Even with a small population of 14 million people, Chile offers rich opportunities as a regional springboard.

OVERVIEW

Chile's economy has expanded for the past thirteen years. This growth is largely due to a boom in exports of primary products and processed natural resources, e.g., copper, fresh fruit, and forestry and fisheries products. Chile's exports are becoming increasingly diversified; the era of copper dependency is definitely on the decline. Chilean goods are finding a market in Latin America as well as the United States, Asia, and the European Union.

Vigorous economic growth has meant an increase in real wages of approximately 35 percent; at the same time inflation has declined since 1990. Chile's credit rating is the best in Latin America with total debt around 30 percent of annual GDP. (The diminished international investor confidence in Latin America following the December 1994 Mexican devaluation had little effect on Chile.) The high domestic savings rate is fostered in part by mandatory retirement contributions. These are administered by private pension fund management firms.

The principal growth sectors are likely to be mining, telecommunications, manufacturing, forestry, and financial services. Businesses in Chile are predominantly owned and controlled by private interests. Prices, except those of regulated utilities, are set by competition. Although the military and democratic governments have privatized many public corporations in the last twenty years, the state retains holdings in several industries.

The most important public corporation is CODELCO, the world's largest copper company and, for the present time at least, an asset that is not for sale. However, the government is in the process of privatizing passenger rail service and a major electric utility. There are also discussions underway concerning ports, airports, and water/sewage facilities. Major new highway projects will be built under a concession arrangement.

OPPORTUNITIES

To date, most of the investment has involved infrastructure. Chile is a particularly promising market for high technology and products that lend themselves to infrastructure projects. There are also excellent opportunities in consumer products and services such as tourism and franchising.

The Chilean consumer economy is yet another developing market. During the past few years, consumers have been interested in imported food products, apparel, entertainment, and software products. Note, however, that there is an 18 percent value-added tax (VAT) which applies to all sales transactions and accounts for 43 percent of total tax revenue in the country.

Most manufacturing, trade, and service activities are located in the capital city of Santiago. Although the government hopes to spread development throughout the country, Santiago remains the best place for establishing businesses. The city is near two major ports, Valparaiso and San Antonio. In addition, Santiago is served by the nation's largest airport, Comodoro Arturo Merino Benitez.

CHILE NOTES

- Stay at one of the better hotels in Chile and book your meetings there. This creates a favorable impression.

- Spanish is necessary for all business negotiations.

- While senior executives usually make the decisions, the next level of management, or *gerente,* will be the one that does most of the work and negotiating.

- Personal contacts and relationships are central to doing business.

- Because of the country's location, Chileans feel isolated from south America and the rest of the world. Make every effort to service your accounts in Chile in a way that will overcome this feeling.

- A "hard sell" doesn't work well. You should be polite and show respect.

- It is illegal to sell anything without issuing a receipt. Make sure you obtain receipts for any goods you buy in the country.

In the Chilean capital it is common for importers and manufacturers dealing in mass distribution items to deal directly with large wholesalers or retail stores. Sales outlets are mainly the traditional store fronts, but large department stores and supermarkets are making their presence felt.

Well-designed shopping malls have recently been a booming business both in Santiago and other large cities throughout Chile. These malls are anchored by one or two large department stores surrounded by attractive specialty stores or boutiques. This is a suitable way to display and market textile products, electronic appliances and devices, sporting goods, cosmetics, office supplies, kitchen utensils, etc.

There are no discount general merchandisers currently operating in Chile. Only one general merchandiser operates, and it is neither discount nor very comprehensive. This means that most products found in U.S.-style stores (e.g. Wal-Mart, K-mart, Caldor, etc.) are still sold through more specialized retailers.

Franchises have developed rapidly in Chile since 1990. Presently, there are about 65 franchises operating in Chile with over 200 franchisees. The successful economy along with access to credit make franchising a good opportunity. It also helps that the fast pace of daily life has created a market for fast food and other franchise offerings.

Most franchises in Chile focus on fast food: McDonald's, Au Bon Pain, Domino's Pizza, Pizza Hut, Taco Bell, Kentucky Fried Chicken, and Burger King. However, there is still a good and largely unexplored market for franchising companies in the fields of automotive services, cosmetics, repair and rental services, cleaning (home and industrial), clothes, fitness centers, real estate business, hotels/motels, and supermarkets.

Marketing is well established in the services sector, mainly in banking and financial institutions, seminar organizers, telecommunication services, etc. Direct marketing or catalog sales are not yet common. So far, Chilean consumers have not been won over by warranty claims and promises of after-sales services.

Another problem is that database listings are not easily acquired and commercial firms are cautious in keeping their customers' privacy. However, firms such as DICOM and Puketing provides prospects listings and up-dating upon request.

Chilean consumers prefer to window-shop. They walk and browse in shopping malls or shopping districts and personally choose the goods rather than purchase through catalogs. Less enjoyable is the matter of returns and exchanges. These are complicated for vendors due to the complexity of VAT.

CHALLENGES

While there are solid opportunities for your products in Chile, it is a very competitive market. The United States is Chile's largest single supplier (about 25 percent of the import market), but European and Asian competitors are also strong in Chile. Many foreign companies have subsidiaries or branch offices in Chile while others utilize distributors or representatives. Most important, incoming businesses should not forget that personal contacts and relationships are the key to success in Chile.

Distribution Channels

Establishing a local subsidiary or branch office is the best way for exporters to receive efficient service and appropriate promotion of their products. Any corporation legally constituted abroad may form, under its own name, an authorized branch (Agencia) in Chile. This method of market penetration may involve a considerable investment but sales volume, service, support, and/or inventory needs may dictate it.

In general, though, foreign suppliers go with an agent, distributor or wholesaler with technical expertise and access to relevant markets. This is important because of the distance between regions and the differences in their respective economies. Larger firms usually have branch offices in the various regions. Also, large end-users such as mining and forestry enterprises demand quick service and specialized technical support.

To be effective, the local representative must be aggressive, knowledgeable about your products; and well-connected with decision makers at end-user firms. The representative will need to promote your products through newspapers and specialized magazines as well as radio and TV commercials. Agent/representative commissions normally range from 5 to 10 percent depending on the product. For contract negotiations, you will need a local attorney.

Joint ventures and licensing arrangements are another way to enter the market. These are especially attractive for products that need local manufacturing or finishing and where shipping costs are a factor. Joint ventures also give manufacturers entry into such sectors as consumer goods and clothing.

Chilean industry has increased its technology and productivity to the point that it can be an attractive partner. One example is the significant increase in the production and export of denim wear for various brands. Other foreign apparel, cosmetics, and perfume companies also are producing good quality, lower cost goods.

Regulatory Systems

Chile has one of the simplest regulatory systems in the region for trade and business activities. Careful review of applicable regulations and full compliance with them will guarantee more successful and trouble-free operations. Chile does maintain import and export licensing requirements, but they are more for statistical purposes than control. For all but a few sensitive items, virtually anyone is free to import anything.

Intellectual Property Protection

Chile's intellectual property laws are generally compatible with international norms, with a few exceptions. Industrial designs and models are protected for a nonrenewable period of 10 years. The registration of trademarks is also valid for renewable 10-year periods.

In 1992, the Chilean Congress approved legislation to extend the term of copyright protection from 30 to 50 years. Despite such efforts, however, industry sources estimate that copyright infringement in Chile cost U.S. firms $24 million in 1991, with $15 million coming from computer-software piracy. An estimated 60 percent of all software installed in Chile is pirated. Software piracy should decline as local suppliers adopt more vigorous legal strategies to protect their rights.

A common problem faced by foreign companies is that foreign trademarks may already be registered by other individuals or companies. Chilean courts have been supportive in cases where the trademark has been stockpiled but gone unused, but less so in cases where investments were made in use of the trademark. Either way, proceedings can be lengthy and expensive. Foreign firms should make a business decision whether to take legal action or negotiate with the party who registered the trademark.

A trademark should be registered as soon as the exporter/investor has any intention of doing business in Chile. Ownership of the trademark is not prejudiced by lack of use in cases where the registered party makes use of it in other countries, and trademarks may be perpetually registered for ten-year periods.

Get a Local Attorney

Contracts with Chilean firms must abide by Chilean laws, so companies entering the Chilean market should have all legal documents drawn up or checked by a qualified local attorney. Suppliers can establish their legal relationship with a local representative in one of two ways: (1) an ordinary work contract regulated by Labor Law 19.010, for which some legal guidance is advisable, or (2) the more customary commercial or commission contract, where the parties establish their own terms and conditions and are not bound by the requirements of LL 19.010, especially its severance conditions.

To avoid legal expenses under a commission contract, the supplier should (a) establish specific performance conditions for the representative; (b) decide on ground rules for termination; (c) determine territory to be covered by the representative, as the supplier may later wish to appoint additional agent(s) elsewhere in Chile; and (d) have local counsel review the text to ensure its consistency with Chilean legal standards. In establishing a contractual relationship with a local representative, the U.S. supplier should also ascertain its contractual liability vis-á-vis the representative under Chile's labor law.

This may seem a burden, but only if you forget what Chile represents. Being prepared to do business in the Singapore of Latin America is the best way to guarantee success.

Adapted from *Chile: Country Commercial Guide, Fiscal Year 1997* (Springfield, VA: U.S. Department of Commerce, National Technical Information Service, 1997).

COLOMBIA
THE BEST CORNER OF SOUTH AMERICA

The Colombian writer Gabriel Garcia Márquez has noted that the two basic characteristics of Colombians are creativity and a firm determination to achieve personal growth. These are assisted by a drive ever strengthened through adversity. It has been so since the Spaniards arrived centuries ago.

Latin America is a market of approximately 400 million people, with an average per capita income of around $8,000. Colombia enjoys the advantage of a strategic location in the middle of the continent and in the center of the five countries that comprise the Andean Group: Panama, Venezuela, Ecuador, Colombia, and Bolivia. Colombia also belongs to the Group of the Three with Brazil and Mexico.

Colombia makes the perfect springboard for the foreign business interested in operating throughout the region or continent. Spanish banks use a similar approach throughout Latin America. They begin in one country, which in turn becomes the center of regional operations.

Likewise, several chemical laboratories use Colombia as a center of production to distribute their products to such countries as Ecuador and Venezuela. Automobile manufacturers frequently use one location as a production point to supply the Andean Group countries. Central location makes Colombia one such production point.

The governments of Venezuela, Colombia, and Ecuador in particular have shown a longstanding interest in de-emphasizing frontiers and establishing a common market. A free trade zone between Colombia and Venezuela has resulted in commerce totaling US$3 billion in 1997, up from $300 million in 1988. Trade between Colombia and Ecuador has seen a similar expansion.

OPPORTUNITIES

The modernization of Colombia's distribution system is about half completed, and there are wide opportunities for companies that wish to participate in the process. But don't postpone doing business in Colombia until everything is up-to-date. The old ways, including traveling salesmen and street trading, can lead to success. These informal channels have contributed greatly to the success in the national market of Chilean fruits, Marlboro cigarettes, and many other products from abroad.

Free Zones to Spur Growth and Profits

Colombia is well aware of the need to create incentives to attract technology and investment. Since it cannot create these opportunities for the entire country, the government has set up special economic zones that will be particularly attractive to foreigners and nationals. These are the free zones. They are exempt from import and export taxes, are operated by private companies, and represent ideal locations for firms interested in the export trade.

The Promise of Mining and Energy

Recent energy discoveries in Colombia are a reminder that the country is rich in important natural resources. Shell Oil and British Petroleum have been impressed to the extent of investing in oil and gas extraction.

These negotiations have opened the way to a series of reforms intended to encourage investment and exploration in this area. The government is very much aware of the need to intensify oil exploration. Current trends indicate a shortage within two to three years, a situation that would have

COLOMBIA NOTES

- Research the market for your industry and products thoroughly before your trip. Less information may be available in Colombia than in other Latin American countries. A good local contact is valuable.

- Schedule meetings at least one month in advance, and confirm them by telephone or fax one week in advance.

- If you are concerned about crime or your safety, arrange for your flight to arrive in the daytime, and travel with a partner.

- Stay at first-class international hotels. Business meetings can be held there.

- Be aware of the current exchange rate and try to change your money at a bank.

- If you have a meeting scheduled in Bogota, arrive a day early to adjust to the altitude (8,600 feet).

- Be on time for meetings, although your contact may arrive late. On social occasions, it is acceptable to arrive 15 to 30 minutes late.

- While Spanish is the official language, many businesspeople understand English. Nevertheless, hire an interpreter if you are not fluent in Spanish.

- It is important to develop personal relationships to negotiate business successfully. Colombians like to have long and warm greetings. In addition to a handshake (and perhaps a hug), they may ask you a series of personal questions before business discussions.

- Most Hispanics have two surnames: one from the father and one from the mother. Never address a Colombian by first name and use the father's surname.

- Colombians are generally more formal than other South Americans. They use fewer gestures. Don't use the American "OK" sign.

- Do not compare your country with Colombia. Colombians are very proud of their country.

- Avoid discussing crime, terrorism, or illegal drugs.

serious consequences for the economy should Colombia be forced to import oil. So, the government is willing to offer investment possibilities under conditions fully competitive with those of other countries.

Experience in International Business

In Colombia there are very important business groups that have functioned for some time. They include the Syndicate of Antioquia, the Santo Domingo Group, the Cafetero Group, the Ardila Lule Group, the Luis Carlos Sarmiento Group, the Bolivar Group, the Lloreda Group, the Social Group, Gillinsky, San Ford, Carvajal, Olimpica, Espinosa, Coca-Cola, Mundial, Corona, Superior, Aime, and Mayaguez among others.

These groups operate in practically any business area and have wide experience in international strategic alliances. They seek to perform a two-way globalization by facilitating entry into the Colombian market in exchange for help expanding into new markets abroad. Their interest is mainly, but not exclusively, in Latin American countries.

In addition, there is a varied number of companies in a similar situation. They control an area and are anxious to go into business with companies that will allow them to handle new technologies.

Mass Media

Marketing in Colombia is becoming more and more modern. Currently there are six TV channels, with the appearance of private channels set for next year. In addition, there are close to 600 radio stations in Colombia.

There are three national newspapers and three important regional newspapers. As to magazines, there are three with nationwide coverage and at least three more dealing with business; these are an excellent means for promoting a business. In other words, it is easy to advertise in the country.

The Environment

People asked to list the five greatest problems facing Colombia typically list unemployment, violence, and environment as the top three. If nothing else, this shows a general awareness that something needs to be done to solve growing environmental problems. Businesses can make use of that general sentiment by offering detailed plans for the proper use of the forests; conservation of water sources; handling of waste from basic industries like coffee; threshing waste disposal in large cities; development of energy sources in rural areas to replace wood; and mass education programs on the proper use of the environment. Most recently, companies from Chile and Argentina have done quite well by improving the collection of waste in Colombia's cities.

Precautions: An Ounce of Prevention

"Not Very Strict Planning"

With respect to planning, the habits of European and Asian societies are considerably stricter than in Colombian culture. However, attitudes are changing.

It has not been easy, and projects continue to take longer than anticipated. A typical example is Medellin's metro, which took builders twice the time they thought it would to finish. Needless to say, time is money, and the metro ended up costing more.

Colombia, then, will require reserves of patience and more for those wishing to invest in its future. Engineering firms and any other business that utilizes the planning process are encouraged to teach the process and the philosophy behind it. Such lessons would be well worth the effort, however.

Expectations of the Good Corporate Citizen

Colombians believe it is necessary to strengthen the ties that make the country a viable and compassionate community. This implies certain expectations of every person and every institution in civic life. Be advised that the popular company is one that seeks constructive relations with more than just its own workers (although that is a start). In Colombia, companies are expected to have a public personality sensitive toward the social problems of the country. Decisions based on the bottom line may be harder to defend here than in the United States.

The population is receptive to a business that shows concern in such areas as education, children's rights, and the environment. For example, McDonald's has demonstrated its interest in protecting children's rights and identifying work that will improve children's quality of life. Also, BP and Mazda have done well by promoting the environment.

The Government

The government has not yet established a consistent policy on the tariff for luxury items. Therefore, businesses dealing in luxury items should be aware that the tariff tends to swing back and forth and plan accordingly.

A related concern is the exchange rate; an inflation rate of 20 percent can be expected to have an effect. Anyone who obtains a loan in U.S. dollars learns this the hard way. Conversely, the opposite business is very attractive for foreign capitals, viz, invest in pesos and recover dollars. Either way, be careful about the money exchanges.

Another word of caution on investments: Although the tendency is to streamline the paperwork for foreign investments, there is a need in some cases to register the investments before the National Planning Department.

With the government committed to combat unemployment, it will favor companies that can produce jobs. Colombia's government will also be interested in any proposal from a business to improve the efficiency of social services or other aspects of state administration; the management of environment; the battle against drug trafficking and violence; and the development of the infrastructure. In Colombia, the government is an important market that must be taken into account.

The government also has fairly strict immigration regulations that may affect business operations. Patience is needed when the companies require foreign technicians who must work permanently in the country.

Safety: Don't Leave Home Without Planning It

Areas of Colombia are under the control of guerrillas. Therefore, when you leave the cities, consult knowledgeable people regarding the safety of your destination; it is better to be safe than sorry, or worse. Colombia does have very high kidnapping and murder rates.

ABOUT THE AUTHOR

Carlos Lemoine
Diagonal 34 No. 5–27
Santa Fe de Bogota
Colombia
Phone: 57 1 2883100
Fax: 57 1 2872670

Carlos Lemoine, Ph.D., is president of Centro Nacional de Consultoria, a leading Colombian market research firm. He is president of Consorcio Iberoamericano de Empresas de Investigacion de Mercados and is a member of ESOMAR.

MEXICO
THE SLEEPING GIANT

According to an ancient myth, Iztlazihuatl—one of the volcanoes seen from Mexico City—is a giant sleeping woman. Popocatepetl, another volcano in the area, has been active for the past few years. On a clear day the two volcanoes can be seen side by side, one active, the other dormant. In its own way this vista captures the history of Mexico, its economy, and its politics. The sleeping economy is now awakening as an emerging market. The active "fires" in Mexico's social and political life are turning a developing country into an outstanding potential market.

AN IN-DEPTH LOOK AT THE ECONOMY

The Peso Crisis of December 1994

During December 1994, the Mexican peso declined 50 percent in value, an event which was followed by an inflation rate of 50 percent and interest rates of almost 60 percent. Thousands of businesses shut down and an estimated 1.8 million jobs were lost during 1995. Purchases of consumer durables fell 47 percent while in some cities 10 percent of the businesses closed during the first two months of the year. More important, the peso crisis touched the rest of Latin America with the so-called tequila effect, in terms of foreign investment levels and exports to the region.

Fortunately, the country largely recovered by 1996. The economy is more open and competitive. While the consumer sector has been slow to recover, inflation has been curbed, and Mexican exports have grown as a result of the peso's devaluation.

U.S. companies are the leading investors in Mexico, followed by Asian firms. Hot areas for investment include telecommunications, the automotive industry, electric and electronic plants, chemical and petrochemical sites, and agriculture projects. While privatization is continuing, particularly in the transportation infrastructure (airports, railroad systems, etc.), Mexico has yet to privatize its oil and energy sectors.

The Long-Term Picture

The long-term picture is certainly improving. Cumulative direct foreign investment is now an estimated $56 billion compared to $43 billion at the end of 1995. Analysts agree that further deregulation and trade liberalizations will improve conditions further. Right now, the biggest challenge may be for domestic companies to produce for the domestic market. (1)

While privatizing the oil industry may make economic sense, the Mexican government is reluctant to move in that direction. Petroleos Mexicanos (Pemex) believes that the oil concern will attract $63 billion in foreign investment in petrochemicals, power plants, and natural gas companies. However, investment restrictions on upstream exploration of oil production and refining may have put off many potential investors. (1)

Mexico has managed to keep up with its debt payments, sending over $700 million in interest and fees to the United States. At the same time, the government has attacked inflation through an austerity program and continued its participation in NAFTA. (1)

Infrastructure Privatization

Mexican officials are focusing on their country's transportation infrastructure, specifically its seaports, airports, and railroads. They are attempting to modernize by selling-off the state-owned enterprises to private investors, usually European or American companies joint venturing with Mexican partners. (2) First to go on the auction block last year was the port of Ensenada in Baja, California.

More than 45 million travelers passed through Mexico's airports in 1996, and more than a dozen private European, American, and Mexican firms already have expressed an interest in buying one or more of the country's thirty-five more profitable facilities. In addition, the country's

MEXICO
NOTES

- Make appointments at least one month in advance. However, when in Mexico, be prepared for changes in your contacts' schedules.

- Be on time for meetings, but expect to wait up to an hour for your contact.

- If you are not fluent in Spanish, have a representative on your team who is. Arrange for simultaneous translation of all presentations. Have your company literature translated into Spanish if you are serious about doing business in Mexico.

- Long proposals written in "legalese" will scare your Mexican contact away from the deal. Negotiations may not proceed in an orderly fashion.

- In Mexico, the decision maker is usually one person. Find out who the decision maker is before entering negotiations. Remember many Mexican businesses are family owned.

- Mexicans are very concerned about status. Make sure the person negotiating for your company is of "equal status" with the Mexican on the other side—similar age, education, rank in the company, and so forth.

- Personal relationships are vital to business relationships. Spend time building long-term relationships based on mutual trust and reliability or *personalismo*.

- Mexicans are very serious about trust in business relationships. Although the country is three times the size of Texas, the business community is small. Once you lose their trust, you'll find it hard to recover. For example, they will never forget if you flee the country because of a peso crisis.

- Do not show weakness during negotiations by over-compromising. Emphasize your integrity and long-term commitment, both to your contact and to Mexico.

- Mexicans may say yes out of politeness when in fact they mean no. When negotiating, use the same approach.

- Be aware of your Mexican partners' continual struggle to finance their goods and services. The cost of money is as high as 20 percent, so they will not only demand but *need* payment for their services as soon as possible. You cannot let your Mexican suppliers or distributors wait more than thirty days. On the other hand, you should expect to wait at least four to six months for payment from Mexican customers. This is just the way it is.

- Do not discuss business during dinner. Wait until the very end, if then.

- Gift giving is common in Mexico. Never give gifts of yellow flowers (which represent death), gifts made of silver (which are associated with the trinkets sold to tourists), or knives (which symbolize the severing of a friendship). Gifts with company logos or liquor are acceptable.

railroads are also being put on the market. However, bidders on rail projects will have to prove that they have at least $250 million in the bank.

BUSINESS AND CULTURAL ISSUES

Mexicans Don't Say "No"

To fully understand business in Mexico, it's essential to grasp some general cultural facts. Although Mexicans have assimilated many American consumer ideas, they still hold very traditional values. In Mexico it's common for people to live at home until they get married. Even then, many lower income couples continue to live with one set of parents.

Mexicans also have a peculiar way of expressing themselves. Their culture has taught them that it's not polite to say "No." Many people would rather say "Yes" and not follow through than refuse something and feel guilty about it. For example, it is a normal practice for domestic companies to cancel a business meeting at the last minute. Saying "Yes" to appointments or other situations many times doesn't necessarily mean a commitment. Foreign companies sometimes have a hard time interpreting those nuances; sometimes they can't tell whether a person really means "Yes" or "Maybe yes" or "I'll think about it", or even "Definitely 'no,' but I'm afraid to say 'no.'" Knowing a real "Yes" from all the others comes only through experience.

In doing business, Mexicans also tend to feel that they are being taken advantage of. As a result, it may take longer to initiate a business relationship with them than expected. Younger people who are part of the information and entertainment age are less likely to be suspicious. However, there are still many poor and uneducated young people who think others want to take advantage of them.

Business Intelligence

Mexico borders but does not mirror the United States, at least in terms of desk research sources. For one thing, Mexico has few publications and sources. Moreover, there is an entrenched bureaucracy—only now starting to change—that makes it very hard to obtain information.

This is frustrating for some companies because they don't know whom to contact for necessary information. Many times chambers of commerce, corporations, and government offices don't have enough information, or they have it but lack a good network to communicate it. They can also possess information they don't wish to share.

Luckily, there are some exceptions. The Instituto del Consumidor publishes periodical magazines with outstanding sources and information essential for business intelligence. Also, thanks to the Internet, research is starting to become an easier process.

Tips for Doing Business in Mexico

There are two main different types of business deals. The first is for companies that want to establish a product or service in Mexico, and the second is for companies looking to export products to Mexico and needing only a distribution network.

For businesses intending to launch a product or service in Mexico, it's best to find a local who already knows the market, the rules, and the regulations. Forming a joint venture will considerably reduce start-up costs and the time it would take to learn the market by trial and error. Businesses looking for partners can get good advice from two sources: Instituto Nacional de Comercio Exterior and Nacional Financiera. Private consultants can also help.

For businesses looking to distribute a product, the smartest way to start is by doing market research to choose the best distribution channel for the particular product. Many people want to avoid this step because they don't see it as a worthwhile investment. The reality is that without market research, the chances of choosing the right distribution channel are very slim.

Mexico has many wholesalers who utilize extremely efficient methods, including distribution to mom-and-pop retailers, drug stores, and specialized stores. Another way to distribute a particular product is to make a deal with a company that carries products that complement yours.

Conducting Successful Market Research in Mexico

There are different points to consider when conducting market research in Mexico. The most important in selecting a marketing agency is to choose one that can work with foreign businesses and adapt foreign products or services to the Mexican market. Always keep in mind that Mexicans "can't say 'No.'" A marketing agency without the experience of adapting international products or services may not admit it if even they know they can't complete the work successfully.

There are several good marketing agencies. However, be aware that a marketing agency franchise does not necessarily mean uniform quality.

Although many international companies keep very good standards at their franchises, others don't; so a good name doesn't necessarily equal the good service a client would get in another country with the same company.

Also, don't choose a marketing agency based solely on the price quoted for the study. A very low cost estimate may be a warning sign the company won't meet its deadline and/or will supply poor quality information.

The right agency will know how to obtain meaningful data. Since Mexicans are reluctant to say "No," market research has to use different scales to ensure an accurate answer from customers. For example, if you ask Mexicans whether they would buy the product or service, in most cases they'll say "Yes" because they want to be polite. So, there has to be a scale of answers: (1) Definitely "Yes," I would buy it; (2) "Yes," I'm interested in buying it; (3) "Yes;" (4) Maybe yes, maybe no; (5) I would not buy it, or (6) I would definitely not buy it.

Another good approach would be to disassociate the respondent from responsibility. This is done by asking, "Would your close friends or relatives buy this product or service?" and then giving the scale. In this way, a person doesn't feel obligated to be polite and say, "Yes."

The success of a product or service will be determined at least in part by price, so information to guide pricing strategy needs to be collected with care. A marketing agency that doesn't follow certain guidelines to ensure accuracy in its tests will deliver greatly misleading information to its client. For example, when asked "Would you buy this product or service for $1, $5, $10, $15, or $20?" Mexican people in most cases have a hard time choosing, or, if they do choose, may simply say "Yes" to any price.

The marketing agency must have some way to insure that the answers are useful. One good way to overcome the price-question problem is by having a random sequence of prices and then doing careful analysis to verify that the prices chosen by the respondent are consistent.

Finally, the marketing agency may need to conduct a pilot test to determine what questions consumers are willing to answer candidly. A good example of where this applies is income. Many multinational firms insist that marketing agencies ask respondents for yearly income. We try to explain that in most cases that question will be useless because Mexicans generally don't like to answer it correctly.

Mexico's culture is different, and its economy is not yet on a par with its neighbor to the north. But with the necessary commitment and attention to detail, businesses will find a giant asleep no more.

PUBLISHED SOURCES

(1) "The Peso's Crash in 1994 Shattered Mexico's Economy but Has Caused Many Changes and Boosted Exports to Record Highs," *International Business,* June 1996.
(2) "Whatever Can go Wrong, Will," *World Trade,* June 1997, pp. 52–56.

ABOUT THE AUTHOR

Gustavo Méndez-Kuhn
Improdir   Rio Lerma 78 Col. Cuauhtemoc
U.S. Phone: 1 512 261 8497   06500 DF
U.S. Fax: 1 512 261 8220   MEXICO
E-mail: improdir@compuserve.com.mx; gusmenkuhn@aol.com

Gustavo Méndez-Kuhn, M.B.A., is president of Improdir, a marketing research and consulting firm. He has twenty-eight years of experience in marketing research and strategic planning. Mr. Méndez-Kuhn has worked as marketing research and strategic planning director for Coca-Cola (Mexico), as managing director for Burke Marketing Research (Mexico) and Louis Harris Indemerc (Mexico), and as director of analysis of economic growth for the Mexican government.

PERU
LAND OF OPPORTUNITIES

Peru is marked by a vast territory, amazing environmental diversity, varied geography, and enormous cultural and social complexity. As such, the nation is a unique tourist destination offering a range of options to lovers of archeology, adventure and environmental sports, and other activities. The potential for development is clear. Moreover, Peru's location makes it a strategic hub for transport, business, and travel in South America. Finally, a plentiful labor pool and the traditional handicraft skills shown by Peruvian workers along with abundant natural resources mean extraordinary opportunities for the development of manufacturing.

A population of some 24 million is spread over three regions: the western, Pacific seaboard, where the main cities are found; the highlands, which are predominantly rural; and the vast though sparsely populated jungle areas. With 28 percent of the total population, Lima is the largest city and the capital of Peru; 23 percent of the population lives on the rest of the coastal plain, 36 percent in the highlands or Sierra, and 13 percent

PERU NOTES

- Book business meetings by fax or telephone one month in advance.

- Stay at a first-class hotel. You can use it as a base for meetings or for lunches.

- Have a Spanish translator present at all meetings. Have your company literature available in English and in Spanish.

- If you are invited for dinner, it will be served at 9:00 to 10:00 p.m. Don't discuss business over dinner.

- Cover small details in business negotiations to avoid any misunderstanding. Expect these negotiations to go slowly. After the deal has been made, always allow for a 20 percent increase in price or time frame as a "contingency factor."

- Peruvians are very loyal. Once you have established solid personal relationship, you can expect 100 percent effort from them.

- Always pay your bills on time; the cost of money is high for your Latin American affiliate or partner.

in the Amazon jungle known as the Selva or Montaña. Most people (72 percent) live in cities and the remaining 28 percent in the countryside. Young people make up the majority of the population, with 51 percent of the total under the age of twenty-five.

Census figures for 1993 show that the labor force (economically active population) of fifteen years and older comprises 51.2 percent of the working-age people. Of this total, 92.9 percent work while the remaining 7.1 percent are jobless. However, most of the working, economically active population—or EAP—are underemployed and make low wages from peddling wares in the streets or from an occasional job. Remarkably, 73.4 percent of the active population is male while only 29.7 percent is female.

Human resources are complemented by natural resources. Peru's coastal region is considered one of the richest in the world as natural conditions have made it home to an amazing variety of marine species. Peruvian vessels sail to capture open-sea fish from ports dotting the country's coastline of more than 2,500 kilometers (1,600 miles), which includes ideal spots for fish farming. Peruvian agriculture is likewise capable of offering a gamut of agro-industrial products year-round. Farming opportunities reflect the high quality of the soil and the variety of climates found at varying altitudes.

Peru ranks among the top ten nations of the world in the production of copper, zinc, lead, and silver. It ranks second for its phosphate reserves and possesses vast gold, iron, molybdenum, tungsten, tin, and other mineral reserves. Also worthy of notice is Peru's huge fuel potential. Eighteen sedentary basins with oil-bearing potential spread over 84 million hectares. Proven natural gas reserves of some 2.2 billion barrel equivalents in the Camisea fields are among the world's most important.

STABILIZING FOR PROSPERITY

Political turmoil and instability characterized much of Peru's recent past, including several military juntas and political regimes of various shades. Oftentimes, interventionist policies did little to bring about hoped-for economic development.

In 1990, Peru experienced the second longest period of hyperinflation recorded anywhere in this century: In the five years preceding 1990, prices rose 20,000 times over. By 1990, per capita GDP had fallen back to where it was on average in the 1960s. The government was bankrupt and the central reserve bank had depleted its foreign currency reserves. Private banks and industry resorted to using only U.S. currency for transactions.

In July 1990, the administration led by President Alberto Fujimori launched a program of structural reforms and stabilization. The intent was to bring Peru back into the fold of the international financial system while implementing education, health, and infrastructure programs necessary for economic development.

The stabilization program managed to bring inflation rates to normal levels by enforcing strict fiscal policies and severe monetary discipline. Several structural reforms helped revive the economy.

By promoting private investment in state-owned companies, the government made possible the modernization and growth of economic sectors formerly dominated by state-owned companies. Almost all 181 state-owned companies were or are being sold or closed. These include power utilities, telephone companies, and infrastructure works.

Peru also regularized its relations with the international financial community. Financial isolation was a consequence of the former administration's foreign debt moratorium; this move downgraded Peru's relations with the financial community and made it ineligible for more loans from multilateral and international government agencies. Normalization began when an agreement was reached with the IMF to reschedule old debt. Then, a support group of friendly nations was established to broker the successful negotiation of Peru's commercial debt.

A final set of reforms comprises the farming, fisheries, mining, and oil industries, all crucial to Peru's economy. The measures removed all restrictions to competition, banned monopolistic practices, and struck down concessions awarded by government.

The measures enforced in the 1990–1995 period created a favorable climate for the return of foreign investment and the recovery of internal and foreign confidence in Peru. Additionally, internal stability contributed to a more dynamic flow of capital to Peru. Economic reform has come a long way.

Structural reforms and a stabilization plan—together with deregulated prices and free competition—have done their work. Peru now enjoys a healthy economic climate. The commitment to produce more efficiently and ensure sustainable economic growth can only benefit the economy in the long run.

OPPORTUNITIES
The Cornucopia of Agriculture

Peru's diverse regions offer top-grade soils and a variety of altitudes and climates that make it possible to grow a wide range of fruit and vegetable crops. For instance, mangoes, oranges, and asparagus are grown on the northern coastal plain. Strawberries, broccoli, and tomatoes thrive on the central coast, while legumes are produced on the south coast.

Climate in the highlands varies by altitude, with rich farmland in temperate valleys tucked in the Andes mountains. On the eastern slopes of the Andes, coffee and cocoa plantations dominate while Brazil nuts and other crops grow in the Amazon plain.

Mining Nature's Resources

Peru is one of the most important mining countries in the world thanks to the great wealth of minerals and metals buried in the Andes. There are large reserves of copper, silver, and zinc. Mining and energy are the two most likely Peruvian industries to offer foreign investors the best opportunities. Peru's current administration has so far sold twenty mines to private companies for a total of $1 billion.

In 1996, mining output grew 4.9 percent compared to the year before as a consequence of investment programs in the Yanacocha mine, the commissioning of the Yscaycruz zinc mine, increased tin output from Minsur, and the expanded copper leaching plant at the Southern Peru Copper Corporation mine in southern Peru. Metallic mining is bound to become one of the most dynamic industries in the near future.

Imminent privatization of nine mining compounds should bring more revenues to government coffers and substantial investment commitments from the new owners.

Fishing in All the Right Places

Seas rich in marine plankton make Peru's marine resources some of the most productive in the world. Changing water temperatures during the course of the year help sustain an amazingly diverse and peculiar marine life. At least thirty types of mammals and 700 fish species have been identified in Peruvian waters, ranked among the most diverse marine environments on Earth.

Investments are planned for fish meal factory expansion, new compounds, and environmental projects. Investments in frozen and canned fish capacity should result in substantially increased production capabilities.

Tourism: More Than Just Another Trip

Three distinct regions—the arid coastal plains, the valleys nestling in the Andean mountain ranges, and the wild plant and animal life of the Amazon jungle—make Peru a prime tourist destination.

Archeological remains found in practically every corner of the country are among the most important in the world. World-renowned ruins include the Sacred Citadel of Machu Picchu in Cusco, the Royal Tombs of the Lord of Sipán, and the Lines of Nazca. Public buildings, monasteries, churches, convents, and aristocratic residences built during Spanish colonial times are another part of Peru's rich cultural and historical heritage. Intriguing sights can be found in the cities of Ayacucho, Cusco, Arequipa, Trujillo, and Lima.

In the Andean region, snowcapped mountains offer ideal conditions for mountaineering while rivers like the Colca in Arequipa and Urubamba in Cusco have carved deep canyons ideally suited for white-water rafting and other adventure and nature sports. A still largely virgin territory, the Amazon jungle shelters magnificent animal and plant life whose survival is ensured by vast national reserves, in particular the Manu Reserve in southeastern Peru.

Tourism has grown thanks to better land transportation and roads, greater disposable income, and more widely available credit. Growth is expected to continue.

Santa Isabel Supermarkets: To Market, to Market, in New Ways . . .

In the 1990s Chile began making sizable investments in Peru. The supermarket retail business offered an attractive opportunity, with only 6 percent of retail shopping done at supermarkets. However, such a low figure reflected both an opportunity and a challenge: Middle-class customers were not in the habit of shopping in supermarkets rather than at the traditional open-stall street market. Santa Isabel, a Chilean supermarket operator, met the challenge by opening five stores in September 1993.

Santa Isabel places a premium on customer service. Nevertheless, earnings are based on continually increasing sales volume, inventory turnover, and consumer loyalty rather than on fat margins. Additionally, the stores are pleasant to shop at, the aisles are ample, parking space abundant, checkouts numerous, and personnel are trained to perform various functions. A pricing strategy based on sales volume rather than high margins is aimed at competing with traditional open-stall street markets and vendors and so to increase supermarket penetration.

Additionally, Santa Isabel introduced its Panda credit card to increase consumer loyalty. With over 10,000 members, the charge-free card carries a financial cost for Santa Isabel by giving cardholders the option to pay their bills in the first ten days of the month after their purchases.

Santa Isabel increased its sales by 153 percent in 1994 and by 38 percent again in 1995. In 1996, sales rose another 15 percent compared to a year before. In the first two months of 1997, sales are estimated to have grown by 5 percent compared to the same period a year ago.

Telefónica del Perú: Answering the Call

The Peruvian Telephone Company Ltd. (Compañia Peruana de Teléfonos Limitada), or CPTSA, was first established in 1920 to supply local and long-distance telephone services in the city of Lima. In 1969, the state-owned Empresa de Telecomunicaciones (ENTEL) del Perú started supplying national and international long-distance service. Both companies remained under state control until 1994. The Peruvian government's privatization program launched in the 1990s included the 1994 sale of stock in both companies. The company's name was then changed to Telefónica del Perú. In 1996, the company registered its shares on the New York Stock Exchange.

An additional capital contribution to CPTSA gave the business 35 percent control over both companies, now valued at $2.002 billion. Investments were made in each of the new company's business lines: For basic service, $493.1 million was invested to create 500,000 new access lines, 18,000 pay phones, and 170 new central stations, and to connect 350 rural towns to the grid; in mobile service, cable television, and business communications, investments totaled $146.9 million to increase network capacity and expand service supplies.

Large investments in the telecommunications industry have led to substantial transformations in recent years. Telefónica has played a dramatic role in expanding the telephone network to previously unattended areas, bringing modern technology to replace old equipment, expanding the range of services, and enhancing quality standards. Telecommunications is expected to continue growing in 1997, with increased earnings in the various industry segments.

A Blockbuster of an Idea

Before 1995, Peru's home video market was characteristically informal, with no single distributor legally established. This created an opportunity for investors, although it presented a daunting challenge in the need to dismantle the informal market and educate consumers. With the help of the National Police, the Consumer Defense Institute (INDECOPI) visited informal video rental businesses and gave them a period to purchase authorized copies.

Meanwhile, authorized distributors and formal video rental businesses started a campaign to educate consumers in requesting original, quality copies from authorized dealers. Thanks to these changes, formal distributors were persuaded to enter the business. In December 1995, a group of Colombian and Peruvian entrepreneurs opened a franchise of Blockbuster, the U.S. video rental chain.

The same consumer behavior changes that are favoring supermarkets are likely to help Blockbuster. Results for 1996 were satisfactory with actual revenue at 92 percent of projections and 118 percent of estimated customer recruitment. Activity levels reached 42 percent compared to the planned 35 percent, and seven more stores started operating in mid- and high-income level Lima neighborhoods. Blockbuster thus carved a solid market position with an 80 percent market share.

Blockbuster's sales strategy was to ensure excellent customer service and give clients a one-stop solution to their video entertainment needs; this was to be done in an agreeable environment where customers are served by highly trained personnel who looked after every detail to provide maximum satisfaction. High-quality service and product were essential in the face of rental prices four times higher than those charged in the gray market.

A LARGE CAVEAT: TERRORISM

Peru was under siege from terrorists in the 1980s and early 1990s. At one point, terrorist groups seemed to have the upper hand in their fight against Peru's government, institutions, business class, and general population. Government figures have put the number of terrorist victims for the period 1990–1995 at about 25,000 casualties, with damage to property and the economy at an estimated $25 billion.

The current administration has made substantial progress in ridding the nation of the terrorist scourge; among those arrested have been the leaders of the two terrorist groups. The leader of the Sendero Luminoso organization was captured in September 1992 while some 2,000 members of his organization and the MRTA—the other terrorist organization—have since been arrested. Meanwhile, another 6,000 have pleaded to cooperate with the State under the protection of a "repentance" law.

Nevertheless, isolated incidents have continued. One such incident was the capture of hostages at the Japanese ambassador's residency by MRTA terrorists in December 1996. However, Peru's military forces rescued the seventy-two prisoners and garnered broad-based support for President Fujimori.

ABOUT THE AUTHOR

Alfredo Torres
  APOYO Opinion y Mercado S.A.
  Av. Republica de Panama 6380
  Lima 18
  Peru
  Phone: 511 445 2846
  Fax: 511 447 9556

Alfredo Torres, B.B.A., M.A., is managing director of APOYO Opinion y Mercado, a member of the APOYO Institute Board of Directors, and professor of market research at Pacific University. The author of numerous articles and papers on public opinion research, Mr. Torres is an international consultant on public opinion and corporate image studies and acts as technical advisor to the Ministry of Labor and Social Promotion.

VENEZUELA
A PROMISING FUTURE, IN THE MAKING

Venezuela is a highly urbanized society. Over eight of every ten households dwell in urban concentrations of over 20,000 inhabitants, and over 45 percent of the population lives in the seven major urban markets. Nevertheless, the character of the population is not simply urban. In the past thirty years, most large cities have been the recipients of a great rural migration. Thus, most low-income sectors in urban areas tend to reflect rural values. This is reflected in the typical *telenovela* (Spanish for soap opera), one of Venezuela's key exports. Typically, the poor country girl lives as a maid in an upper-class household and falls in love with the master's son.

The Venezuelan people are also quite cosmopolitan thanks to several waves of migration over the past fifty years. From the 1940s to the early 1960s, a strong European immigration affected habits as different as food and travel. Then, in the 1970s, came a great influx of Latin American immigrants. An estimated 19 percent of Venezuela's population is of Colombian origin; many of these newcomers work in the manual trades. This has

VENEZUELA NOTES

- When traveling to and from the airport, guard your personal belongs.

- Have all your literature printed in Spanish. If you don't speak fluent Spanish, make sure you have the assistance of a translator.

- Personal relationships drive business. For initial meetings, it is better to develop one-to-one relationships rather than sending a team of people.

- Trust is important to Venezuelan companies. This may take time to develop and may occur only after several business dealings.

- Given recent economic developments in the country, pay your Venezuelan suppliers promptly.

- After Venezuelans get to know you, they may greet you with an embrace or kiss on the cheek.

- Businesswomen should dress conservatively and should not give gifts to Venezuelan businessmen.

become a major opening for the Andean Regional Market, with Venezuela becoming a prime market for Colombian goods.

These new demographics have made Venezuelans from every walk of life open to the outside world, be it in the adoption of new technology, customs, or points of view. Venezuelans now look to Miami as their standard of reference for buying anything from state-of-the-art technology to bargain clothes, to the point that there are probably as many daily flights from Caracas to Miami as to Maracaibo.

Venezuela is a young market. More than half of the population is under twenty-one years old: Trendy products and services, especially those supported by well-known brand names, represent good opportunities. Which is not to say the adult segment should be ignored. Here, too, is a sizable market to tap into.

Venezuelan consumers also tend to be less sophisticated in terms of product expectations. Thus, a consumer-satisfaction survey may garner results far different from those in the United States, possibly because of a narrower scope of product options. And yet the Venezuelan consumer may be just as uncompromising on quality as people in more developed markets.

And now a caveat. Although the Venezuelan market is relatively small, it is by no means homogeneous. Venezuela shows clear regional idiosyncracies in a population no larger than California's. State-of-the-art technology and image-leader consumer product may test quite well in the capital city of Caracas but not in Maracaibo. Venezuela's second largest city consistently reflects a more conservative nature.

WHERE DO THE OPPORTUNITIES LIE?

An important 20 percent of the population still takes its economic and social cues from the global economy. These are generally well educated individuals. They are well aware of the latest technology, willing to take advantage of the opening of the economy, and considering opportunities within and outside of Venezuela's economy.

The remainder of the population will be open to all sorts of basic goods and services in light of the expected economic upturn. Evidence of changing times can be seen in the recent opening of Construcentro, a Home Depot–like store, in Caracas. After just one month in operation, management expects to more than double its initial projection for first-year sales revenue.

Purchasing power allowing, Venezuelan consumers tend to have a positive regard for imported quality goods. This can be seen with the high penetration of brand-name consumer goods, even among the poor. For example, cellular phones are probably the highest growth market this side of Hong Kong. Cellular phones are so "mainstream" that there are 800,000 owners out of a population of 21 million. This is probably one of the highest penetrations worldwide and certainly impressive for a developing country.

In contrast to other markets in the region, Venezuela is just opening up to competition, and local product offerings are perhaps not as ample as in other markets. So imports, especially those perceived as of more than average quality, are now quite appealing. Here are some of the more promising markets:

- Consumer products and services
- Transport
- Telecommunications
- Educational services
- Health services
- Financial services
- Computer systems
- Distribution

CAVEATS

Large foreign multinationals can afford a long-term strategy of "looking over the waves" of economic change as they establish their products. Smaller firms are not quite so lucky. To succeed in Venezuela, they will have to do some detailed study, lest they get swamped by those waves.

Don't Kick the Underdog

Do not compare yourself to your competitor through advertising. It is simply not done and may give your product a negative image. Venezuelans love to support an underdog. Telecommunications and consumer electronics firms have found this out through competitive advertising. This type of competitive advertising lost Venezuelan consumers to the competitor.

In other ways, though, Venezuelan consumers may be ready for some new marketing approaches. Promotional activities of the sort used in the United States are just now being introduced. They represent another opportunity.

Overall, be cautious about generalizing from successful or unsuccessful marketing experiences elsewhere in the region. Venezuela, although a definite part of the region, may not reflect consistent behavior with other markets.

Distribution

The market, although open to new entries, is in many cases bound by complex and antiquated distribution systems. Opening up your own distribution system may be extremely expensive. Thus, every effort should be made to identify the appropriate wholesaler and make your business his business.

Be Ready to Adjust to Shortcomings

Dealing with the public sector can be a challenge. Look for assistance from reputable local law offices since the government can pose a major barrier in starting new ventures. Opening businesses may involve government paperwork that will prove time consuming.

Bits and Pieces of Information

Most of Venezuela's economy is tied to the production and exportation of oil. After twenty years of nationalizing its oil industry, Venezuela has reversed course and is pushing to establish "strategic alliances" with foreign oil companies. The country is well positioned over the long term with abundant natural resources, its pool of skilled labor, low energy costs, and geographic location.

The United States has traditionally been Venezuela's most important trading partner. The country's strongest markets are in petroleum technologies and infrastructure, particularly telecommunications, followed by computer hardware and software, vehicles, environmental products, security, and medical equipment and engineering services.

The key sector for foreign investment is petroleum. Some government-owned aluminum companies may be opened to private investment. Most foreign and domestic companies operating in Venezuela have learned to live with delays and added paperwork brought by new government controls. Product entry, however, is still relatively simple in most cases. Import duties remain at a maximum of 20 percent in almost all categories, although a 12.5 percent tax on the CIF value and other luxury taxes are now also applied.

The state continues to control key sectors of the economy, including oil, gas, iron ore, and much of the coal and petrochemical industries, steel, and aluminum. Foreign investment continues to be restricted in the petroleum sector. Foreign equity participation is limited to 19.9 percent in enterprises engaged in television, radio, Spanish language press, and professional services subject to national licensing legislation.

At present, the consumer market is somewhat limited, reflecting a per capita gross domestic product of about $3,200. As the economy and education levels of the country improve, the consumer economy should evolve too. But relatively high tariffs on consumer goods could dampen the prospects for a vibrant consumer economy.

From a marketing standpoint, franchises will probably succeed in Venezuela only if they bring technology, services or systems which are not generally available. Marketing through TV commercials, newspaper inserts, house visits, or street vendors is common. Mail orders are impossible because of the low reliability of the postal system.

Placing orders by phone with delivery by messenger is becoming popular, and several such companies have been successful by placing their catalogs in newspapers as weekend inserts. As the telephone system continues to improve, direct marketing by phone will become more common. Almost all businesses use fax machines in their day-to-day business.

Sales at the retail level are different in Venezuela. Price bargaining is not common, and, while special offers are frequent, they are often seasonal in nature. There are numerous malls but few department stores.

Companies often make the mistake of providing sales literature in English when selling to their agents or distributors. While many businessmen speak English, much of their staff and customers do not. Failure to prepare materials in Spanish eliminates a key selling tool. In most cases, you will have to provide new agents or distributors with technical support, or training and information if the product is new or entails new technology.

When selling to the Venezuelan government, all official business must be done in Spanish. Any correspondence sent in English is unlikely to get a response. There is no specific Venezuelan agency to handle government procurement or provide guidance to foreign bidders or sellers. However, anyone wanting to sell to a Venezuelan governmental agency must be registered in the National Register of Contractors, which is maintained by the Central Office of Statistics and Informatics.

Venezuela's average tariff rate is approximately 10 percent. Venezuela and its Andean Pact partners established a common external tariff (CET) that took effect on February 1, 1995. The CET has a four-tier structure with levels of 5, 10, 15, and 20 percent for most products. In accordance with the Andean Pact CET, Venezuela is harmonizing its tariff schedule with Colombia and Ecuador, with some exceptions taken by each country. Venezuela has continued its efforts to conclude trade arrangements with other countries in Latin America and the Caribbean.

While Venezuela has made progress in protecting intellectual property rights, it does not yet appear to provide adequate and effective protection. As a result of its laws and practices, Venezuela was placed on the "watch list" under the Special 301 provision of the 1988 Trade Act. On the other hand, Venezuela belongs to the Andean Pact, which provides a 20-year term of protection for patents and a reversal of the burden of proof in cases of alleged patent infringement.

Companies should familiarize themselves with the following when doing business with Venezuela:

- Foreign exchange procedures; how to maximize assurance of payment or repatriation of profits
- Price controls; consumer protection laws, intellectual property protection, "quality standards" and other product restrictions
- Multitiered taxes, which are applied over and above tariff rates, sometimes adding more than 30 percent to the landed cost of a product
- Labor laws which can add significant costs to establishing offices or retaining representation

You should consider contracting a reputable local law firm which can assist you with establishing a presence in Venezuela; this will facilitate joint ventures, registering a trademark or entering into any type of business relationship. A good law firm will also provide essential start-up information on labor laws, tax regulations, etc. A list of Venezuelan law firms which specialize in various aspects of commercial and investment law can be requested from the U.S. Embassy in Caracas.

ABOUT THE AUTHOR

Orlando Riebman
StatMark S.A.
Avenida Francisco de Miranda
Torre Bazar Bolivar, Pizo 2 Boleita Sur.
Apartado 68196
Caracas
Phone: 582 235 0702
Fax: 582 235 0796
E-mail: 73050.3022@compuserv.com

Orlando Riebman, B.S., M.B.A., is founding partner and managing director of StatMark S.A., one of the leading market research firms in Venezuela. StatMark is networked with reputable research agencies across Latin America. Mr. Riebman has served as product manager for both Warner Lambert and Philip Morris. He has also been professor of market research at the Universitario de Tecnologia in Caracas. He is a member of ESOMAR.

Chapter 7

THE MIDDLE EAST AND AFRICA

Markets in Need of Peace

Because of a history of political unrest and war, this region is not well understood, nor has it been sought after by companies seeking global expansion. With the recent peace accords signed in the past few years, many have hoped for political stability in the region. As such, this region has lagged behind the other global regions in terms of market expansion and investment. The region, however, is not to be ignored as it offers potential well into the next millennium, if long-term peace can be achieved.

With regard to Africa and specifically, South Africa, these markets are also in "need of peace and stability." With the abolishment of apartheid in South Africa, the situation looks promising. The economy has since attracted foreign investment again along with importers and exporters. Here again, the challenge is to obtain stability in the country over the long term.

Because of the Islamic and Jewish religions that dominate the area and because of the racial differences in Africa, the countries in this region could be termed the "they" global markets. They are not driven by individualism, as in the United States, nor do they have the "we" ideology of the Asian culture. Similarly, they can also be called "the other" global markets as their cultures are the least understood throughout the world. With regard to global market expansion, companies should view and analyze this region in the context of the present and future political situation.

YOU MUST EVALUATE THE MARKET POTENTIAL OF EACH COUNTRY IN THE CONTEXT OF ITS POLITICAL STABILITY

We must remember that this region of the world is symbolic of "the holy land" for many religions and cultures. As a result, the region does not exude the entrepreneurialism and vibrancy of Asia, and individualistic/consumer-driven economy of the United States, the cultured heritage of Western Europe, the Catholic/family-oriented societies of Latin America, or the reformed/post-communistic societies of Central and Eastern Europe.

It must be remembered that these economies must first achieve political stability and *"harmony"* in the region before large and small to mid-size firms will invest and export into the region. In spite of the continued strife in the region, there are "pockets of gold" that can be currently found in the region. Countries such as Turkey, Saudi Arabia, the United Arab Emirates (U.A.E.), Israel, Morocco, and Egypt have demonstrated relatively stable economies and as such, have attracted investment and imports into their markets.

Unfortunately, when war (the Gulf War or the Civil War in Lebanon) or violence (between Israel and Palestine) strikes in this region, the region experiences the domino effect. Companies are reticent or reluctant to invest or explore market opportunities in this region. Moreover, the strengthening of the fundamentalist Islamic movement in Iran and Iraq during the past decade has precluded Western investment in the region. Continued acts of terrorism (e.g., the bombing of the World Trade Center in New York) also have not enhanced the marketing image of the region. In spite of the abolishment of apartheid in South Africa, the country is still plagued with crime. Again, long-term stability and peace in the region will do much to support investor and marketing confidence in the region. Market opportunities, however, can be found in doing business with those countries that have demonstrated a commitment to their regional and to world peace.

THE CHANGING FACE OF THE MIDDLE EAST

The recent round of peace talks could easily transform the Middle Eastern economy. The signing of a Palestine Liberation Organization (PLO)–Israeli peace accord and future pacts with the front-line Arab states, such as Jordan, Syria, and Lebanon, will reshape the business terrain of the

Middle East. It is hoped that these peace accords will reduce the risk for multinational corporations (MNC), put an end to the Arab League boycott of Israel, and attract financial aid to rebuild the occupied territories. It is anticipated that much of the investment would flow into Saudi Arabia and the Gulf States, where investments have been deferred.

As a result, the Arab countries would no longer have an excuse for their lagging global economies. It remains as to whether Syria will embrace this new kind of peace in the region and as to whether the hostility surrounding Israel will cease. This last round of peace making, however, seems positive. Should this establish long-term peace in the region, the Middle Eastern countries can then concentrate on other issues that inhibit their growth. Some of these include:

- Poor infrastructure
- Potential water crisis
- Relatively low rates of foreign investment
- Expensive terms of financing investment and imports and exports
- Poor trading experiences with other economic regions of the world

Countries and companies have been reticent to lend or invest in the Middle East because of the difficult peace process. It is expected that this situation will continue until peace is secured with Syria. In spite of the peace situation, many multinational companies are now expanding their operations in the area because of the market potential and the educated populations at relatively lower costs.(1)

POTENTIAL TRADE WITHIN THE MIDDLE EASTERN REGION

While the peace process is proceeding within the Middle East, there are still many barriers to trade within the region. If you consider the statistics, the Arab region is potentially a high-potential consumer market with over 250 million people and an average per capita income of almost $9,000 a year. In spite of these attractive numbers, extensive import barriers exist between the Arab states, as the focus of each country has been to "keep out cheap imports." With the use of high tariffs to outright sanctions, countries such as Egypt, Saudi Arabia, the U.A.E., Kuwait, Iran, Iraq, Jordan, Lebanon, Syria, and others, have limited regional trade at the expense of developing their own economies. Some of these trade limitations have also been due to political decisions (e.g., Jordan siding with Iraq during the Gulf War, etc.), which have "fueled" the interregional trade situation.(2)

THE "OLD FACE" OF THE MIDDLE EAST

While the total Arab region represents a $140 billion import market, inter-Arab trade accounts for only $1 billion of the total. Many of these countries produce the same types of products and most of them export oil. Saudi Arabia, in particular, has protected its domestic economy with stiff trade barriers. For example, they imposed a 12 percent customs tax on imported jewelry. As a result, this strengthened their domestic jewelry market, and they are now expected to be the producer of the largest gold market in the Middle East. Not only do the Saudis report a healthy export market, they also are active importers for certain luxury goods. It should be noted that Saudi Arabia still perceives itself as "the keeper of Islam." Open trading with Israel is still "an enforced taboo" until the Arab states have reached an agreement about the final status of the holy sites in Jerusalem.(2)

In addition to the imposition of import taxes to increase government revenue and protect local industries, many of these countries have perpetuated "long-term hostilities" toward each other. Iraq and Iran have been long-term arch enemies. Saudi Arabia and Jordan have virtually no communication between each other. Israel faces trade barriers throughout the entire region. Egypt has imposed significant bureaucracy (along with reported bribery costs for post officials) in getting imported goods released from their ports. To increase trade in the region, these Arab countries must be willing to reduce their trade barriers and "open their doors" to the regional and international markets.(2)

Even though Jordan was the second Arab country to make peace with Israel, and they signed a range of joint projects in the area of energy and transportation infrastructure and tourism, none of these have come to fruition. Moreover, Jordan has imposed import taxes as high as 200 percent on imported goods. While the Arab world has historically united against Israel for fear that it will become an economic superpower, they are now beginning to realize that they must open their doors to the rest of the world for trade. While this fear of Israel is beginning to wane, they must take proactive steps to become part of the global economy in the next millennium.(2)

THE "NEW FACE" OF AFRICA

When most companies think of sub-Saharan Africa, they think of civil wars, starvation, high political risks, and low rates of return. For many firms, Africa is the lowest priority business region for global expansion. According to the late U.S. Commerce Secretary Ronald H. Brown, while Asia and Latin America are viewed as potential trading partners, businesses often view Africa as "potential aid" recipients. Although sub-Saharan Africa cannot match the booming Asian economies, it is a region that should not be ignored.

Africa has a poorer image than usual in the West these days—an image that is dominated by news coverage of violence in the streets of Monrovia, or endless ethnic violence in Rwanda and Burundi, or relentless dictatorship in Nigeria, or chaos in Zaire and Somalia and of spreading disease throughout many African countries. The brightest shining light in the midst of this is South Africa, which is becoming the role model for the rest of the continent.

While investment in Africa still carries a high degree of risk, a significant amount of investment has gone into South Africa, Nigeria, Cameroon, Liberia, Kenya, Ghana, and Zimbabwe. This area is attracting an increasing amount of investment in transportation, telecommunications, and energy. One of the largest problems U.S. firms face in wanting to trade with sub-Saharan countries is obtaining credit and risk protection because of the overhang of debt that several of these countries have with the United States. Almost everything is done with letters of credit and is short term. The Ex-Im Bank, however, does not support several countries on the continent. While many companies talk of investing in Africa, most of them refer to investing in South Africa.

While Africa still continues to be on the perimeter or margins of the global economy, early market entry enables firms to gain a foothold in the region. According to an African proverb, "only one digs the well, but many will come drink out of it." Africa is clearly one of the last emerging markets. While countries such as Nigeria still pose significant political risks, African countries such as Botswana and Ghana are improving their economies as a result of assistance from the World Bank. The retail banking sector in Morocco appears to have taken hold.(3)

Several industrial companies are expected to benefit from Nelson Mandela's reconstruction and development program in South Africa, which should build millions of houses and supply electricity to them. South Africa also shows promise for tourism and for consumer businesses that will service the growth of the middle class in Africa.(3)

Retail chains have reported growth in Kenya (Akimbo Supermarkets), Zimbabwe (Delta Corporation), and in Morocco (the ON conglomerate). Mining of platinum is expected to grow in South Africa. Additionally, cellular providers, such as Teljoy, in South Africa are reporting high rates of growth. In summary, the middle-class market should drive the South African economy. This would include products and services in the health care, light manufacturing, telecommunications, tourism, and basic service businesses.(3)

MARKET OPPORTUNITIES IN THE MIDDLE EAST AND AFRICA

According to the World Bank, the Middle East region attracted a minimal 3 percent of private capital flows to the developing world in the 1989–1993 period, compared to 40 percent attracted by East Asia, 30 percent given to Latin and Central America, and 22 percent invested in Europe and Central Asia. Sub-Sahara Africa reported only 1 percent. Most global marketers and manufacturers complain that the region is "closed" as a result of the royal families and the "old boy network" of the six countries of the Gulf Cooperation Council.(4)

Additionally, these countries are known for being overreliant on their local government as the main engine of growth, in addition to historically being suspicious of the private sector. Egypt is a prime example and has been criticized for its slowness in opening up its market. In order to attract foreign investment, most of these countries will have to dramatically reform their economies. It is reported that the Middle Eastern region, as a whole, will have to attract approximately $60 billion just in the development of electrical power generation over the next decade.(4)

There is, however, some evidence that this is happening in some countries. For example, Tunisia has implemented an economic stabilization and trade liberalization program. As a result of the success of its stock exchange and direct foreign investment program, Tunisia became the first Arab country to be assigned a country credit rating, provided by the Japan Bond Research Institute. They were followed by Jordan. Moreover, Moody's Investors Service (in the United States) has recently opened up an office in Cyprus, which suggests that other countries may follow.(4)

Morocco is another Arab country where continuing economic reform is taking place. Morocco is reported to have the Arab world's most advanced privatization program in addition to reduced taxes on imports and a trade agreement with the the European Union. Jordan has recently passed a wide range of legislation that includes strengthening intellectual property protection. At present, non-Arab investors are limited to a 49 percent stake in Jordanian enterprises.(4)

In the Gulf region, the six countries of the Gulf Cooperation Council have traditionally depended on oil revenues to finance domestic development. Because these countries embrace the concept that all property is "royal," there have been few successful attempts at privatization in Saudi Arabia. At present, only Bahrain and Oman permit foreign portfolio investment in their local stock market. Dubai appears to be well positioned to host the potential pan-Gulf stock exchange as it has looked to the fast-growing Asian markets for investment.(4)

MARKETING SUCCESSES IN THE MIDDLE EAST

Nivea, a manufacturer and marketer of skin care products, has successfully marketed their product, "Nivea Visage" in the Middle East. The product enjoyed the number one position in the face care category in Europe. As a result, the product was launched in the Middle East in 1995 and was targeted to a population of over 21 million consumers, who not only have high disposable incomes, but who are also young (50 percent of the population are under the age of thirty).

In the restaurant sector, T.G.I. Friday's, the original American Bistro, entered the U.A.E. with the opening of its first restaurant in Dubai. Other openings are scheduled for Egypt, Kuwait, and Lebanon. In the United States, the restaurant is known as a "casual dining" restaurant with alcoholic beverages. This is interesting as Arabic states do not foster alcoholic beverages as part of their culture.

Smaller to mid-size companies have also successfully entered the Middle Eastern and African markets. Cardiac Control Systems, Inc., in Palm Coast, Florida, has signed a deal with Spanish distributor Madrid-based Grupo, Taper S.A. This three-year agreement is expected to distribute a minimum of 6,000 pacers for these markets for cardiac implants. This is an example of the need for medical equipment and products in this region.

Culligan Water Technologies, Inc., a water products and water technology company, successfully signed a joint venture agreement to build a bottled water plant in Jericho in October 1995. As such, it holds a 40 percent share of the joint venture to construct a plant to process and bottle water in the region and sell it in the West Bank and Gaza region. This is an example of a company that has been selling its products in the Middle East for more than thirty years, largely through its network of licensees. The firm has sold equipment for water purification and desalination as well as bottled drinking water in several countries in the region: Saudi

Arabia, Egypt, Israel, Jordan, etc. Here is an example of a company that has been willing to venture into new territories on solid ground where the political stability is reasonably assured and the laws and regulations are clear.

MARKET SUCCESSES IN AFRICA

Most of the investment and marketing successes in Africa have been made by large multinational firms. Because of the political and economic risks of this area, smaller to mid-size firms must be very cautious in their efforts to these countries. On the other hand, they should continue to monitor the growth of the region and the successes and failures of the larger firms.

Some firms, however, have ventured into this region. One company, United Meridian Corporation (UMC), a small- to mid-size firm in the field, joined some of the large oil companies such as Mobil, Shell Oil, Occidental Petroleum, Marathon, Agip, and Elf Aquitaine in their search for energy reserves beneath the coastal waters of Cote d'Ivoire and Equatorial Guinea. This is an example of a search by a smaller, independent oil company (with approximately 300 employees and a market capitalization of about $800 million) for global expansion. Following the discovery of two oil fields, UMC began daily production from those fields in 1995. By the end of the year, their daily output had reached 19,000 barrels of oil and 60 million cubic feet of gas as they recorded their first year of profitability. What is significant is that the country of Cote d'Ivoire, in 1990, initiated a recovery plan focused on increasing foreign investment and on privatization.(5)

COUNTRIES IN THE REGION

Bahrain

Bahrain has a small population of around a half a million, and it is more important as a trade thoroughfare than a final export destination. Traditionally, Bahrain served as a way station for companies looking to export products to other countries in the region. It also hosts large trade fairs and serves as a showcase for many Middle Eastern handicrafts.

Egypt

Egypt offers high trade potential with its large population of approximately 60 million people, and represents an attractive consumer market for producers of staple goods such as rice, flour, building materials, etc. Their oil industry, is still, however, the key to the economy, accounting for more than 10 percent of the country's GDP. Business organizations in Egypt are generally in the form of incorporated companies, partnerships, and sole proprietorships. In spite of its trade potential, import taxes, alleged bribery costs for port officials, and the difficulty in obtaining import licenses in order to release goods from customs limit the country's potential as an attractive export destination. In addition, there are many choices for distributors, dealers, and agents in Egypt; however, you much search for a firm with good management.

In 1991, the country initiated a comprehensive economic reform and stabilization program; however, this program slowed down in 1994. In 1993, the government ended the import ban list for all products except textiles, apparel, and poultry. During the past several years, the government continues to improve its position on privatization and trade liberalization. The challenges of trying to do business with Egypt include their bureaucracy in masking the decision-making process and the relative poverty of the majority of the population, which limits the consumer market and requires localizing of product characteristics (e.g., smaller than normal size of goods to "fit" within the "smaller than normal" consumer budgets).

On the other hand, Amoco reports one of the success stories in Egypt. As such, they capitalized on Egypt's pace-setting use of its abundant natural gas as a transportation fuel. They formed a joint stock company with Egypt Gas and introduced this alternative transportation fuel, called CNG. The joint venture is reported to be a success because it is a "win-win" situation for both parties.

Iran

Despite the damper that Moslem rule has put on the country's economy, the carpet industry is thriving in Iran. Carpets are reported to be illegally being smuggled out to Iraq and food and other staples are also rumored to be crossing the border illegally.(6)

Iraq

The Gulf War during the early part of this decade did much to dampen trade with Iraq. At present, Jordan remains Iraq's largest trading partner, having backed them during the war. Jordan continues to send food and medicine to Iraq, while Iraq, in turn, exports oil to Jordan. It is reported that other smuggled goods are coming in from other Middle East countries.(6)

Israel

For half a century, Israel has been isolated from her regional environment, forging her economic alliances primarily on the European and American continents. The main goal of Israel's foreign trade policies are:

1. Promotion and expansion of Israeli exportation to all foreign markets
2. Expansion of business and industrial alliances with actual trade partners while forming new alliances with potential trade partners.

Through its signature of several trade pacts with North America, Western and Eastern Europe, South America, Asia and Oceania, and Africa, Israel has successfully achieved the status of a dynamic export global economy. The economy, however, faces four challenges:

1. *Maintaining national security.* Israel spends some 10 percent of its GDP on defense.
2. *Absorbing large numbers of immigrants.* This is the "core rationale" for the state. Since its inception, Israel has absorbed over 2.5 million immigrants.
3. *Establishing a modern economic infrastructure.* While the basic networks of roads, transportation and port facilities, water, electricity, and communications exist, they still require additional development and expansion.
4. *Providing a high level of public service.* While Israel is committed to ensuring the well-being of its population, the people have special concern for the weaker elements in the society and are committed to meet these obligations.

In recent years, the economy has experienced a drop in unemployment and the approach to almost full utilization of its labor force. Yet, the political situation with its Arab neighbors continues to threaten the state, as experienced during the Gulf War. In spite of the recent peace accord, it remains to be seen as to whether the other Arab states will open up trade to Israel. Israel continues, however, to expand its markets globally through aggressively exporting their products throughout the world.

Companies looking to expand their business in Israel should research the local competitive situation. The ecologically correct cosmetics chain of the Body Shop International Plc. had stopped doing business in Israel after it failed to prevent a local copycat chain from using its name and a look-alike logo. While this meant that the Body Shop lost its trademark in the country (one of seventy-two where the names are registered around the world—the company determined that it was not worth the additional litigation). While this can happen in any country, it underscores the need for research on the competitive market in a target country.

Jordan

Because Jordan was the second Arab country to make peace with Israel, some assume that they are more open to change than some of their Arab neighbors when it comes to promoting free trade. While a number of joint projects between Israel and Jordan have been proposed in the area of tourism, electricity, road infrastructure, and water and energy development, none have yet started. Jordan still has very high import taxes, which range from 5 to 200 percent. Since this often makes the price of imported items too costly for local consumers, Jordan has virtually erected trade barriers via taxation. This helps to protect Jordanian producers from cheaper imports and brings in ongoing revenue into the government. Jordan exports fruit and vegetables to some of the Gulf states and a small amount of pharmaceuticals to its Mideast neighbors.(6)

Kenya

Kenya has one of the most prosperous economies in all of Africa. It is the center of East African economic growth and the principal point of export for many countries in the region. Kenya is one of the most open countries for investors in the region, and the government has encouraged privatization and foreign investment and partnerships. The following are some of the reasons to invest or export your products to Kenya:

- Resources and infrastructure
- Political stability
- Liberal economic policies and incentive packages

- Abundant supply of educated, trainable, mobile, skilled, and inexpensive labor
- Large and growing domestic consumer market of approximately 24 million people
- Good living conditions

Some of the larger, multinational firms who have successfully invested in the country include KLM Royal Dutch Airlines, Del Monte, Mobil, IBM, GUI Plc., and Bridgestone. Smaller to mid-size firms should be aware that Kenya is a member of the PTA (Preferential Trade Area), Organization of African Unity, the United National Organization, and the British Commonwealth.

Kuwait

In spite of its small size, Kuwait buys large quantities of American products and services and is likely to continue to do so. Kuwait is beginning to emerge from the devastating economic hardships that resulted from the 1990 Iraqi invasion. Kuwait is a potentially large consumer of luxury goods, especially gold and jewelry. The population of the country, however, is only two million. Because there are high taxes on luxury imports, much of the trade in this market is carried out in the black market.

Kuwait is a highly priced competitive market and because of its low tariffs (only about 4 percent) there are few import barriers. Foreign firms generally need to work through a local agent or distributor and should monitor the agent's performance and potential conflicts of interest. Because of Kuwait's oil wealth and affluent and young population, exporters will find opportunities in building materials, household formation items, furniture, appliances, home furnishings, clothing, jewelry, cosmetics, fast food, automobiles, giftwares, and foodstuffs. Because Kuwait does not have an agricultural base, this presents opportunities for restaurant franchisers.

English is widely spoken in the country, and many Kuwaitis have been educated abroad. Again, the culture bans pork and alcohol and requires Arabic labeling on all products. There are also reinvestment requirements and restrictive immigration laws along with the lack of patent and copyright protection.

Lebanon

This is a country that I know well. As a child, I grew up in Beirut, Lebanon. In the 1950s through the 1960s, the country was called "the Paris of the Middle East" and was clearly the financial center of the region. However, the civil war in the 1970s destroyed the city and country. It is estimated that the bill for Lebanon's devastation came to $25 billion and cost more than 150,000 lives. Having experienced over two decades of war, the infrastructure of the country was destroyed.

Lebanon's new prime minister, Rafic Hariri, a billionaire businessman, is rapidly rebuilding the country in terms of its infrastructure and is attempting to make it, once again, a financial and tourism center of the region. The rebuilding of Beirut's city center is one of the boldest undertakings of its kind since Europe and Japan resurrected their cities after World War II. Beirut may serve as a model for similar cities, such as Sarajevo. Beirut will also serve as a city of the future, as no other city in the Middle East will have such modern infrastructure. In spite of the building boom, imports did not exceed $9 million in 1996.

Lebanon still remains a tiny country with no more than four million people and with seventeen different Christian and Muslim religious sects. While the country is now Muslim, the country is expected to once again, have a strong European influence after the rebuilding of Beirut. Only the future will tell whether the country can remain peaceful and attract foreign marketers and manufacturers.

Morocco

Morocco is a Southern Mediterranean nation that is proud to report ten years of continued privatization and continued economic development in the country. One of the selling points of the country is its relative economic and political stability. Morocco has always been closely identified with Europe as most of its trade has been with members of the European Union. On the other hand, dissatisfaction is growing in the country as half of the population is under twenty years of age, unemployment is high, and there are few jobs for graduates. Morocco remains an Arab/African country and cannot go on "chanting Europe."

It is reported that authorities have responded harshly to Morocco's thirteen known Islamic groups. It is reported that torture is used to contain militant Islamic groups in the country and the prisons are believed to hold several hundred prisoners as a result of this issue. On the other hand, business development success stories are reported by NCR in the region. So far, it has been mainly large multinationals like NCR that have set up offices in the still underdeveloped economies of the southern Mediterranean, such as Morocco.

But since the European Union started reaching out to its southern neighbors, providing links and strengthening ties in order to form a Mediterranean free trade zone by early next century, the entire Mediterranean region has started to become a focal point of interest for foreign investors. During 1996, the European Union and twelve Mediterranean Basin states (Cyprus, Malta, Morocco, Tunisia, Algeria, Egypt, Israel, Jordan, the Palestinian Authority, Lebanon, Syria, and Turkey) all signed a Declaration at the Barcelona Conference, which called for the establishment of a free trade area in industrial goods, along with the progressive liberalization of trade in agricultural goods and trade in services with due regard to GATT by 2010.(7)

Morocco has taken steps to liberalize its economy by privatizing its state enterprises and opening foreign exchange regimes and capital markets. In 1995, the United States and Morocco signed the Trade and Investment Framework Act, an agreement that calls for lowering barriers and expanding trade between the two countries. As a result of this agreement, trade with the United States has increased significantly. The local market of Morocco has a large and growing consumer class that has been relying on European products. As a result, U.S. companies now have the opportunity to compete in this market. 3M opened an office in Morocco in July of 1995, and they report that they will be expanding slowly there in the next few years. Other companies are expected to follow this example in the next decade.

Nigeria

Nigeria is about four times the size of the United Kingdom, with a population of over 88 million people, and is primarily an agricultural economy. Nigeria currently has a military government headed by the Head of State and Commander in Chief of the Armed Forces. Oil dominates Nigeria's economy and foreign trade. In addition, the country is principally noted for exports of agricultural products such as cocoa, cotton, groundnuts, oil palm products, natural rubber, tea, coffee, gum arabic, shea butter, soya beans, cashew nuts, kola nuts, ginger, and benne (sesame). The country is also rich in petroleum oil, natural gas, coal, iron ore, tin, zinc, and tropical timber. The government, however, has launched a sustained effort to diversify the economy. Opportunities exist in the areas of construction and manufacturing.

Nigeria has recently come into the "eye" of the international business community as a result of fraud in the country. There have been many celebrated cases of Nigerian businessmen who allegedly attempted to defraud the Central Bank of Nigeria to the sum of $18 million. In some sense, these fraud cases are similar to stories of the "gold rush" of previous centuries. In any case, you should be aware of these alleged cases of fraud in the country. The U.S. Department of State warns U.S. citizens of the dangers of travel to Nigeria. Tourists have experienced violent crimes. Additionally, they are also warned of the poor conditions of air travel to the country. The roads are in poor condition, and the medical facilities are limited.

Oman

There are only 2 million people living in Oman, which makes this country less of a mass consumer export market. On the other hand, taxation is low and like Qatar, it has been a relatively open market since the early 1970s.

Qatar

Less than 500,000 people live in Qatar and this affects the country's manufacturing and import policies. Most of the country's goods and services are imported. Local per capita income in the country is high, estimated at $15,000 a year. Import taxes are reported to be relatively low in the country.(6) Qatar launched its own news led satellite channel during early 1997, broadcasting in Arabic across Europe and the Middle East.

Saudi Arabia

Saudi Arabia has an open, developing economy with a large government sector. Oil dominates the Saudi economy, comprising an estimated 37 percent of its GDP. Even much of the nonoil GDP is tied to oil, as consumption and investment are dependent on oil receipts and services, and supplies are sold to the oil sector. While the United States is the largest exporter to Saudi Arabia, foreigners may not invest in joint ventures engaged solely in advertising, trading, distribution, or marketing. Real estate ownership is restricted to wholly-owned Saudi entities or citizens of the Gulf Cooperative Council (GCC).

Saudi Arabia is often called "the protectors of Islam." While Saudis are large importers of Western goods, they cannot normalize relations with Israel until an agreement with Syria and Lebanon is worked out and a decision is made on what to do with Jerusalem. Saudi Arabia has high import taxes on cars, textiles, jewelry, and other luxury items. It is reported that companies with operations in Saudi Arabia prefer not to hire nationals because they usually demand higher wages, are less manageable, and few have the skills to handle the job. To counteract this, the Saudi authorities have banned recruitment ads aimed at non-Saudis as the Saudi law requires that firms give preference to nationals.

Before you do business in Saudi Arabia, you should be familiar with their holy documents (*Aur'an, Sunah, Hdith, and Shari'ah*) as the entire Saudi life is based on them. You should be aware that because of their religious beliefs, Muslims donate at least 2.5 percent of their capital, do not drink alcoholic beverages, and do not eat pork. It is illegal or forbidden to drink alcohol; carry weapons or ammunition; have homosexual encounters; engage in public dancing, pornography, music, the movies, or betting. Narcotics trafficking is punishable by death.

In Saudi Arabia, businesses are open Sunday through Wednesday. Thursday and Friday are days of rest and worship. Private businesses are open 8:00–noon and 3:00–6:00 p.m. Muslims will stop to pray at dawn, noon, mid-afternoon, sunset, and nightfall. For one lunar month out of the year, which may fall either in the summer or winter, most Muslims will fast. This is called Ramadan. Business will be conducted only during the morning hours of this period. Muslims will also make their annual pilgrimage to Makkah. This is called "Haj." Women should not travel alone, should wear ankle-length dresses with long sleeves—and in many places wear a long black cover (nabaya) over their heads—and may not drive a car or ride a bicycle on public roads.(8)

South Africa

With a population of nearly 50 million people, South Africa is the most advanced, broadly based, and productive economy in Africa, with a GDP nearly four times that of Egypt, its nearest competitor on the continent. It provides a modern infrastructure supporting an efficient distribution of goods to major urban centers throughout the region and well-developed financial, legal, communication, energy, and transportation sectors. South Africa boasts a stock exchange that ranks eleventh in the world.

With the abolition of apartheid, South Africa offers excellent potential in its long-term reconstruction and development efforts to distribute economic benefits, traditionally enjoyed by only 5–6 million South Africans to 35 million people disenfranchised by apartheid. In order to deliver what it promises, the government seeks substantial investment in areas such as project management, financial services, electrification, consulting, construction, housing, and telecommunications. Opportunities in the consumer market are also expanding with the emergence and growth of a nonwhite middle class with disposable income.

The following are the advantages of investing and/or doing business with South Africa:

- An infrastructure with considerable capacity (e.g., low-cost electrical supply, efficient railway systems, two world-class deep water harbors, etc.)
- Highly specialized medical services
- Supply of raw material
- A market-oriented, long-established business sector
- The largest digitally based cellular communications networks in the world outside of Germany
- Sophisticated technological-based banking and financial services
- Availability of skilled and unlimited unskilled labor
- A supply of raw materials land minerals that position South Africa as a world leader
- An industrial capacity that is capable of meeting the demand for local manufactured goods

Syria

With a population of just under 14 million people, Syria represents a medium-size import market. The GDP is rising, indicating that the country is moving forward economically. Syria exports a small amount of textiles and oil to the Arab world, but its local infrastructure needs development and is sadly lacking (e.g., the telecommunications system and the transportation system, etc.). In spite of the infrastructure, prospects for Syrian private sector investment and imports continue to improve, supported by economic reforms, including an investment encouragement law.

It should not be forgotten that the United States imposed trade controls in 1979 on Syria, as a response to Syria's involvement with terrorism.

While the recent peace accord has gone a long way to further the "feeling of peace" in the region, it remains to be seen as to whether Israel, Syria, and Lebanon can work out their problems. Most companies will continue to evaluate the political and economic stability of the country prior to investment and/or export into the country.

Tunisia

Similar to Morocco, Tunisia has positioned itself strategically as an attractive investment in the Mediterranean. While it has "piggy-backed" off of much of Morocco's reforms, the country has attracted significant investment in the past few years from Europe and North America. By September 1996, the country had completed the privatization of fourteen companies, and it intended to privatize another fifteen companies by the end of 1996. To date, privatization has been concentrated in the hotel industry. The Ministry of Trade and Industry in Morocco is expecting the local pharmaceutical industry to grow significantly in the coming years. According to estimates within the Ministry, an investment of $150 million in this industry is expected by domestic and foreign companies.

Turkey

Turkey has been the center of trade and enterprise in the region for centuries, and its location between the continents of Europe and Asia remains the crossroads between the East and the West. As such, Turkey can be defined as both a European and a Middle Eastern country. For purposes of this book, we have classified it as a Middle Eastern country because of the current Muslim influence in the country. In fact, it is listed as one of the world's ten big emerging markets.

With a population of close to 60 million people, Turkey has one of the largest single markets in the region. It is rich in human resources, its business community has developed a very strong entrepreneurial spirit and experience about the market-oriented approach, and it possesses a good mix of skilled, semiskilled, and highly qualified and productive work force. While the official language is Turkish, English is the dominant language for international business. While the infrastructure of the country is good for business development (e.g., telecommunications, transportation, energy, medical care, etc.), the economy has undergone some significant changes in the past few years and appears on the road to recovery.

While Turkey may appear to be a Westernized and a European society, it is largely a Muslim or Islamic society today. *You should note that Turkey has strict antibribery laws—never give a valuable gift or cash to a government official. This could be construed as a bribe and you can be punished by the law. If you recognize an obligation, exchange favors rather than cash.*

Most of the opportunities for investment or exportation are in the development of the infrastructure of the country. Some opportunities exist for consumer goods (e.g., tobacco products, foodstuffs, etc.).

The United Arab Emirates (U.A.E.)

The U.A.E. is a federation of family-ruled states on the southern shore of the Persian Gulf. Following full independence from Britain in 1971, Abu Dhabi, Dubai, Sharjah, Unal-Qiwwan, Ajman, Fujairah, and Rasal al Khaimah united under parliamentary Federal National Council and a representative Council of Ministers. Out of all the countries that make up the U.A.E., Dubai, Abu Dhabi, and Sharjah are the three leading centers in economic terms.

The government is stable and the currency (the U.A.E. dirham) is linked to the U.S. dollar. The U.A.E. is an active member of the United Nations, the IMF, the World Bank, OPEC, and the Arab League. Although the population of the Emirates is approaching 2 million, fewer than 20 percent are U.A.E. nationals. The remaining 80 percent consists of large expatriate communities of workers from other Arab countries, the Indian subcontinent, Europe, and North America.

Dubai: "Gateway on the Gulf"

Specifically, Dubai has become the fastest growing and most attractive business center in the Middle East. Dubai is often called "the Hong Kong of the Middle East," as it offers a modern export processing zone that is located at Jebel Ali port, 35 kilometers from the city center. Created in 1985 to attract international investment, the Free Zone offers the perfect manufacturing, trade, and distribution location, combined with government incentives unavailable anywhere else in the region.

The Jebel Ali Free Zone (JAFZ) boasts the world's largest man-made harbor, easy access to air cargo facilities, and continuous expansion in order to meet demand from foreign companies. The zone permits complete foreign ownership and unrestricted repatriation of capital and profits, and it offers exemption from all import duties and a renewable fifteen-year guarantee of freedom from all taxation. Businesses wanting to locate in the U.A.E. normally require either a local partner or sponsor that ensures that a company operates within the country's norms. However, in the JAFZ, no agent or sponsor is required. If a company is based in an area just outside of Dubai, they are treated as "offshore" firms or outside the U.A.E. for legal purposes.

The Jebel Ali Free Zone offers the following incentives:

- A business friendly environment
- A stepping stone for many firms into Saudi Arabia and other Gulf markets
- Access to a market of over 1.5 billion consumers in the surrounding markets of Iran, GCC, CIS, South Africa and the Indian subcontinent
- 100 percent foreign ownership
- No import duties and 100 percent repatriation of capital and profits
- No personal taxation
- Well-developed infrastructure (e.g., telecommunications, energy, and road, sea, and air links)
- Highly skilled, inexpensive work force
- Computer interfaces with all local ports and government departments

Some of the companies that are operating in this region are AT&T, Nissan, Honda, Hyundai, Compaq, Daewoo, Casio, Estée Lauder, Nokia, and Star TV. On the other hand, the most common problems with the region are:

1. *Market access.* It is necessary to do your local market research and homework.
2. *Financial and management costs.* Financial arrangements are often complex. If you are seeking cheap, unskilled labor, look elsewhere. The cost of living is high, especially for food, housing, and schooling in this area. You will also be out of touch with your home office with a nine-hour time difference and Friday not being a work day.
3. *Language and culture.* Arabic is still the official language, although English is the common language of business in the area.
4. *Local management.* Finding a high-quality local manager will be difficult.

BARRIERS AND PITFALLS TO MARKET ENTRY
WITHIN THE MIDDLE EAST AND AFRICA

The following are some of the barriers or pitfalls in doing business in the Middle East:

- Many of these countries have local labor laws that require the hiring of nationals.
- Because they are Muslin countries, pork, alcohol, and several Western activities are banned from these countries. Expatriates often have a difficult time adjusting to the culture.
- You will most likely have to use a local agent or distributor in the Middle East. It is often difficult to monitor their performance.
- You will have to adhere to the Muslim holidays, work week, and traditions.
- Timewise, you may be "disconnected" from the West in terms of communications. Oftentimes, it is difficult to fax or call these countries.
- You may have difficulty obtaining the medical attention (or specialists) you may need in these countries.
- Arabic is the main language. You should attempt to learn the language to conduct business in the country.
- Hiring a good and qualified local manager may be a challenge.
- The Muslim societies are not favorable toward women. Your family may have major personal adjustments.
- In some countries, the political risk is high and your personal safety may be at stake.

The following are some of the barriers or pitfalls to doing business in Africa or South Africa:

- It is difficult to obtain quality market research on some of the African countries due to lack of quality data.
- Several of these countries report ethnic division and are still undergoing civil wars. Your personal safety could be threatened.
- The economics of many of these countries have not yet stabilized, thus increasing your business risk.
- Crime and corruption are pervasive in many of these countries.

- With the exception of South Africa, the infrastructure (e.g., transportation, telecommunications, energy, medical care, etc.) is poor for doing business.
- The medical and health care conditions of many of these countries is not up to the standards of other regions of the world (except for South Africa).
- The government is not fully stabilized in many of these countries.
- Telecommunications can be a problem in some of these countries.

A RECOMMENDED APPROACH TO MARKET ENTRY INTO THE MIDDLE EAST AND AFRICA

STEP 1: BECAUSE OF THE TRADE RESTRICTIONS IN THESE COUNTRIES, OBTAIN AS MUCH DETAILED INFORMATION ABOUT THE COUNTRY AS POSSIBLE.

This type of country-specific trade information can be obtained from your local embassies, the Internet, and local and global market research firms, in addition to publications. For example, Country Commercial Guides (CCGs) are available that contain trade regulations, the country's economic and political environment, and business travel information. In the United States, these reports can be purchased through the U.S. Department of Commerce.

STEP 2: IF YOU ARE SERIOUS ABOUT DOING BUSINESS IN THE MIDDLE EAST, LEARN THE ISLAMIC CULTURE.

This is absolutely necessary in this region of the world. You could get into serious trouble for violation of the rules of these societies.

STEP 3: EXPAND YOUR PERSONAL NETWORK OF ARABIC PERSONAL AND BUSINESS CONTACTS.

One way to do this is to consider becoming a member of the local Arab Business Council or other organizations in your country. You will definitely need business contacts in this region of the world. They can provide tremendous support and assistance on business trips to these countries.

STEP 4: UTILIZE GLOBAL MARKET RESEARCH FIRMS WITH "LOCAL FIELD OFFICES" WHO KNOW THE CULTURE AND WHO HAVE MANY YEARS OF EXPERIENCE IN THE REGION.

This is not a region of the world to leave to "marketing or business development" novices. It is better to spend more money on a high-quality firm to conduct your research. If possible, you should take a trip to the country to "observe" the market research being done. If you are a woman, you will have to "send a man" to some of these countries as you will be restricted from countries such as Saudi Arabia.

STEP 5: MAKE CERTAIN THAT MARKET ENTRY INTO THE MIDDLE EAST AND AFRICA FITS INTO YOUR GLOBAL EXPANSION PLAN.

Surprisingly enough, many companies enter the Middle East and Africa without a rationale for entering the region. You should make sure that investment in this region fits with your plans for expansion into other regions of the world.

STEP 6: TARGET THE MORE "DEVELOPED" OR WESTERNIZED ECONOMIES IN THE REGION FIRST TO REDUCE YOUR RISK.

Countries such as Israel, the U.A.E., Saudi Arabia, Kuwait, Turkey, and South Africa offer the lowest business risk and the most potential.

STEP 7: EVALUATE YOUR INVESTMENT BASED ON THE LONG-TERM RETURN ON YOUR INVESTMENT IN THIS REGION. IT IS BETTER TO BE ON THE CONSERVATIVE SIDE, GIVEN THE POLITICAL AND ECONOMIC RISKS OF THE REGION.

Because political and economic events can change rapidly in this region, we recommend to proceed slowly and evaluate your investment based on the long-term potential in the region. Again, it is more conservative to begin exporting than to make a foreign direct investment in the region.

STEP 8: ALWAYS FOLLOW THE FOLLOWING CULTURAL RULES THROUGHOUT THE REGION.

- Always allow time throughout the day for Moslems "time out" to pray
- Never refer to a Moslem as "Mohammedan"

- Never use your left hand when greeting, dining, or passing documents
- Do not allow the sole of your shoe to be exposed to someone (for example, when sitting)
- Avoid touching the head (a holy area) of even little children
- Always remember that Arab countries require respect for observing aspects of Islamic life
- Do not drink alcohol or plan to eat pork in these countries
- Research the laws of these countries prior to traveling to them. You could seriously violate a law in these countries without knowing it.

PUBLISHED SOURCES

(1) 1996 Global LINK Ltd. All Rights Reserved.
(2) "The Middle East: Keep Out," *LINK Magazine,* March 1996.
(3) "Into Africa," *Time* Inc., copyright 1996.
(4) "The Middle East: Keep Out," *LINK Magazine,* March 1996.
(5) "Black Gold off the Ivory Coast," *International Business,* November 1996, p. 43.
(6) *LINK Magazine,* 1996.
(7) "Mediterranean Sunshine," *International Business,* March 1996, p. 45.
(8) "A Shortlist of Inter-Arab Trade Problems," *LINK Magazine,* March 1996.

SOUTH AFRICA
IS THERE GOLD AT THE END OF THE RAINBOW?

South Africa is the largest, most diverse, and most advanced economy in Africa, with a GDP more than three times that of Nigeria or Egypt. The region was a colony first exploited by the Dutch in the seventeenth century and the British in the nineteenth century. As such, South Africa's development was molded by "remittance children" sent by their Victorian parents to seek fortune in a distant colony. These were soldiers, adventurers, and entrepreneurs, all of whom recognized an opportunity to exploit the country's resources, both mineral and human. South Africa's twenty-first century economy will be considerably different.

The republic's largest source of foreign exchange was always the mining sector. Since the election and with the liberalization of exchange control regulations, the financial services and manufacturing sectors now represent a larger portion of GDP by economic activity.

South Africa has a modern financial and industrial sector with an infrastructure that is the envy of the African continent. The trains, albeit slow, run on time; extensive paved national roads link the major urban areas; and domestic flights provide rapid and efficient air communication between the major centers. Industrial policy encourages export growth, with lower tariffs prompting increased competitiveness.

The view among current investors is that social problems will decrease with prosperity, and it is a prosperity that will largely be funded by Asian investment. Although separated by color and creed, many Asian investors have recognized similarities between their own countries and the multiracial demographics and income disparities of South Africa.

It is their optimism and pragmatic approach to the uncertainties of life that may give Asian investors the advantage in exploiting business opportunities in South Africa ahead of their Western counterparts. Perhaps Western companies should look to the Asian experience in South Africa as the best indicator of their own chances for success when investing in the richest country on the continent. There is gold at the end of South Africa's rainbow, but you must look for it.

The government has helped by unveiling its macroeconomic policy framework. This plan outlines what the government needs to do to move the economy to higher levels of growth, development, and employment, to the benefit of all South Africans. The idea is to introduce privatization of state assets through strategic equity partnerships, generate 10 percent annual growth in nongold exports, and induce large-scale public and private financial investment to boost economic growth to 6 percent and create 400,000 new jobs by the year 2000.

For its part, South Africa's Department of Trade and Industry has drafted a new investment code to remove all restrictions on foreign direct investment, remove import/export controls, give foreign investors the same constitutional protection enjoyed by local companies, and reduce corporate tax levels. In addition, the government is offering investment incentives, including depreciation allowances, loans, and double-taxation avoidance agreements.

Some of the best opportunities for investment are aircraft and parts, industrial chemicals, telecommunications equipment, computers and software, medical equipment and pharmaceuticals, franchising, environmental technologies, and tourism. The South African economy is also in

SOUTH AFRICA

- Be responsive to faxes and literature from South African firms. Most are very serious about doing business because the economy has just reopened.

- Book meetings three to four weeks in advance. Research the political climate of the region you will be visiting.

- Try to have your contacts pick you up at the airport and escort you to meetings. They will know which areas and routes are relatively safe.

- Although English is widely spoken, don't assume that everyone speaks fluent English. Afrikaans is spoken throughout the country, as are numerous tribal dialects.

- Most countries have lifted their embargoes and restrictions on trade with South Africa, but research thoroughly your country's trade policies with respect to South Africa with regard to specific products.

- When assessing market size or potential, segment the market according to urban or rural residence. Distribution and labor may not be available in rural areas.

- South African businesspeople are very genuine and forthright. Let them discuss their views on the country's local political situation and future.

- Try not to leave the country without a trip to the desert to see the wildlife or to the spectacular countryside.

need of project management, financial services, electrification, consulting, and building designs and technology for low-cost housing units. "Gold" can be spelled in any of a variety of ways.

THE MARKETING ENVIRONMENT

Before investing in this Rainbow Nation, foreign companies should consider the cultural and economic factors that clamor for attention in a newly independent country. South Africa is a land of extremes, from weather to wealth and poverty. In addition, the South African market has changed dramatically over the past five years and will be transformed further over the next decade.

The doyen of scenario planning in South Africa is Clem Sunter. His "high-road/low-road" forecasts constitute the framework around which many businesspeople predict economic and political changes in South Africa. Using the high road, Sunter anticipates an optimistic future of growth, employment, and prosperity. The low road is an alternative "too ghastly to contemplate." Whichever road South Africa takes, marketing will become increasingly important.

The high-road scenario requires marketing in a steadily growing economy with stiff competition from global players. Marketing will therefore make it possible for more people to improve their standard of living. On the other hand, a low-road scenario will require marketing expertise to prevent a drastic lowering of existing lifestyles.

Inflation

A review of the South African economy over the past ten years clearly indicates that inflation is increasing steadily, despite attempts to curb it. Inflation has become a threat to South African society, causing a rise in the price of consumer products and increased wage demands. These in turn have reduced the competitiveness of South African manufactured goods in the global marketplace. Between 1960 and 1987, the percentage price increase for all consumer products was 882 percent. The low-road scenario would forecast South Africa's current inflation rate of 13 percent following the examples of Israel, Argentina, and Brazil and reaching 100 percent.

Population Growth

The growing population, whatever its size, represents an enormous marketing opportunity for foreign companies. While global attention is focused on China, the South African market should not be ignored. Within this market, too, the black population is expanding at an accelerating pace.

The black population sector already constitutes the largest market for ordinary consumer products such as beer, tea, snacks, and toiletries. As the purchasing power of many black consumers increases as a result of the Reconstruction and Development Program (RDP), affirmative action, and foreign investment, so the market will increase for luxury products and labor-saving appliances.

An article in the Afrikaans financial journal *Finansies en Tegniek* indicated that by the year 2000, 75 percent of the economically active South African population will be black and their personal income will be more than three times the 1980 level. Indeed, these projections may be too conservative given the earning potential of an increasingly liberalized workforce.

As the lifestyles of the South African population change, it is likely that the growing market of black consumers will become more Westernized and consumption oriented. Consequently, new and different distribution channels will have to be developed to supply the demand for food, clothing, furniture, appliances, luxury products, recreation facilities, and vehicles. Already, one international accounting firm has studied the feasibility of introducing holiday camps in South Africa, catering to the "average worker."

The disparity between rich and poor in South Africa has resulted in a mix of consumers. Some are receptive to informative advertising messages and the wide range of products and services available within the existing economy. Other consumers, living in a subsistence economy with an average income of less than $250 a year, do not have the purchasing power to satisfy even their basic needs. Poverty is a very real issue in South Africa, and marketers need to develop programs that will benefit and uplift less fortunate people.

Educational Demand

Part of South Africa's poverty trap has been caused by poor educational facilities and the lack of proper schooling for a growing number of black scholars. Since the election, and with the introduction of the RDP program, politicians and the general public have realized that education is central to achieving the "African Dream."

CASES AND CAVEATS

Building Corporate Image: The Personal Touch

Marketing strategies that have been successful for local companies can also work for foreign market entrants. Consider the following example.

The HDL Jewellery Fashion House was established in March 1977 on a farm in Bloemfontein by a woman who knew little about jewelry but much about her own abilities. Delores Laubsher built her business by the personal approach. The jewelry fashion house soon decided to incorporate, extra personnel were hired, and turnover quadrupled. By the mid-1980s, the original store and factory were combined, and HDL Jewellery focused on designing and fabricating exclusive jewelry according to customer preferences.

HDL Jewellery is successful because of the special relationship between the customers and the company. Consumers must regard a jeweler as absolutely reliable, with good-quality products and ample stock. To reinforce this market perception, the company creates publicity opportunities to build on its image. Receptions are held for various groups including businesswomen, housewives, and women's organizations. During these events, new designs are introduced and general information provided on the purchasing and care of jewels.

Talks and demonstrations are often held for organizations, and interviews are broadcast on radio and television. Laubsher is invited to speak at business seminars, where she presents information on jewelry but also discusses other topics such as entrepreneurship and the role of businesswomen in the South African economy.

HDL Jewellery advocates personal selling as the most direct and effective means of communication. All sales staff are well trained in both product knowledge and selling techniques. Potential customers are invited to private exhibitions and shows. When Laubsher planned to show jewelry at a small-town agricultural show, for example, she sourced lists of householders and sent invitations to attend a special viewing.

The success of the company can be attributed to the personal touch Delores Laubsher maintains with the community she serves. The company maintains high ethical standards in business, has good products, and continually disseminates information to its customers and prospective customers. These three factors allowed the company to secure a strong market presence in the jewelry trade.

Building Brands: The Analytic Approach

Another luxury consumer market in South Africa is wine. Here, Paarl's Douglas Green has shown that a less personal, more analytic approach can be equally successful if it is built on the same solid foundation of responsiveness to the customer.

The wine sector constitutes about 15 percent of the total market for alcoholic drinks in South Africa. The other major players in this market are malt beer (46 percent), sorghum beer (20 percent), and spirits (20 percent). Flavored wines, which form part of the wine cooler market, have also been introduced. However, like flavored water, the wine cooler category is a very small niche market with little obvious growth potential in the short term.

Although South Africa's per capita wine consumption of 8.82 litres is low compared to France (63.5 litres) and Italy (60.0 litres), the local market for wine is expanding as exports have encouraged wider publicity of wine's benefits. Douglas Green has positioned itself within the industry to provide wine with a value-for-money appeal. The company's growth has been attributed to this careful positioning.

Douglas Green conducts extensive market research and, based on its findings, spends a considerable amount of time and money ensuring that its promotional strategies are a success. The promotions are geared toward original point-of-sale material that create an instant impact. Sports sponsorship is also conducted but only if it is specifically related to a market: Red Heart Rum, for example, sponsors darts and fishing competitions.

Traditional media such as TV, radio, and print are also used. Television advertising by the company tends to concentrate on establishing a certain mood or ambience and so relate the advertised products to consumers' aspirations. The company made a strategic decision to build brands rather than corporate image; and for many years its in-store promotions and major wine promotions have sustained this brand growth.

Security: Personal and Corporate

The international media and the local press have focused on the crime rate in South Africa: Cape Town is the murder capital of the world, a total of R10 billion in commercial crime is currently being investigated by the police and the Office of Serious Economic Offenses, and rapes and assaults occur approximately once every two minutes. Such statistics should alert foreign investors to the need for security.

South African citizens have been victimized for so long that they have taken to publicizing their plight. Commuters in both Johannesburg and Cape Town created massive traffic jams by stopping their vehicles in a massed protest against crime. And more than 150,000 postcards depicting three bullet holes through the national flag have been posted to President Mandela to make the point about popular dissatisfaction with the government's response to crime.

The judicial and penal systems are unable to cope with the influx of criminals. It has also been reported that only 4 percent of people charged are actually convicted and jailed. The judiciary itself could be a problem. In many European countries, the powers of investigation and prosecution rest with independent magistrates who are appointed by the courts and are able to commandeer police resources. Spanish magistrates led the fight against Basque terrorists while Italian magistrates have successfully prosecuted organized crime. In South Africa, until the police are properly trained and deployed, the criminal situation in South Africa is not likely to improve.

The prospects for corporate security are somewhat brighter. Currently, legislation is being drafted to give increased protection to technological developments, information resources, trademarks, and copyrights. Owing to the years of international sanctions and the resultant protectionist economy, South African laws relating to intellectual property have been somewhat biased. Reverse engineering was commonplace and prompted many of South Africa's technological developments until the 1990s.

With the passing of the South African Copyright Act, it is now possible to register the copyright of cinematographic films. Protection of computer programs as a category of work eligible for copyright was passed as an amendment to the act in April 1992. Therefore, should foreign investors be signatories to the Bern Convention, they will be afforded protection under the various acts relating to copyright in South Africa.

Trademarks, too, have been protected with the introduction in August 1993 of the Trademark Act. Indeed, the high-profile case of McDonald's indicates the success of this law, which allows the owner of a well-known trademark to restrain the use in South Africa of reproductions or imitations of that trademark. The legal point with regards to this law is not only to protect well-known trademarks but also to ensure that the abuse thereof does not cause confusion by deception.

As happened in the McDonald's case, the South African courts have now determined that for a trademark to be well known in South Africa, it must be shown that the trademark is well known to persons interested in the goods or services to which the trademark applies. This law has assisted brand-conscious companies such as Coca-Cola, Levi's, Nike, and Adidas to compete successfully in South Africa and to ensure the integrity of their brands within a local and global context.

Finally, counterfeit goods legislation, when passed, will assist copyright and trademark owners by preventing others from dealing in counterfeit goods. Inherent in this legislation is the right to have counterfeit goods seized by the Department of Customs and Excise, with the assistance of the South African Police Services (SAPS). Recently, investigations conducted against foreign textile companies have resulted in the successful prosecution of several companies that were importing substandard and counterfeit garments to sell at South African markets.

ABOUT THE AUTHOR

Benedict N. Weaver
Zero Foundation
10 Tindale Road, Diep River
Cape Town 7945, South Africa
Phone: 27 21 72 3024
Fax: 27 21 72 6897
E-mail: zero@aztec.co.za
Web: http://www.zerofoundation.com

Benedict N. Weaver, M.A. (Oxon), is chairman of Zero Foundation, a corporate intelligence agency specializing in sourcing critical intelligence about private companies and individuals both in domestic and international markets. Before founding the agency, he worked for a security consultancy in the City of London, conducting due diligence investigations and competitive analyses for a varied client base. Since 1990 Zero Foundation has worked for a variety of companies, ranging from small businesses to international conglomerates. It was the first company in South Africa to join the Society of Competitive Intelligence Professionals. Mr. Weaver is a former chapter chairman of the American Society of Industrial Security.

THE GULF COOPERATION COUNCIL NATIONS
POINT OF ENTRY INTO THE MIDDLE EAST

The Gulf countries, which hold among the world's largest reserves of oil, consist of six nations: the Kingdom of Saudi Arabia (K.S.A.), Kuwait, United Arab Emirates (U.A.E.), Bahrain, Oman, and Qatar. The kingdoms share a common language (Arabic), religion (Islam), and origin (Bedouin). This common ancestry and faith have forged a bond—a shared vision for the future—and brought about regional unification and economic cooperation in the form of the Gulf Cooperation Council (GCC).

Oil obviously contributes to a large portion of the wealth of these kingdoms. But over the past decade there has been significant progress in diversifying their economies. This has meant investing in the development of infrastructure to help attract business to the region.

Besides setting up manufacturing bases in key industries, the region has also seen a boom as a trading center with the establishment of free trade zones, especially in the U.A.E., and reexports to neighboring nations such as India, Iran, Pakistan, Egypt, Lebanon, and Jordan. These business policies have helped make the region an attractive site for foreign investment and technology.

When planning to enter the region, it is imperative for management to be sensitive to religious, social, cultural, and demographic issues that are important determinants of success. Working environments in the Gulf are different from other regions in the world but, once understood and appreciated on their own terms, provide considerable rewards.

Conducting business in the GCC goes hand-in-hand with a deep understanding of Islam and Arabic culture. The secret of Islam's powerful appeal lies in the fact that it is not only a religion regulating spiritual behavior but also an all-embracing way of life governing the totality of the Moslem's being. Understanding this is the first step in understanding Arab consumers and the Middle East market they represent.

The GCC countries are serious in their pursuit of progress. An examination of the current environment reveals a modern infrastructure that coexists with highly traditional lifestyles and beliefs. For example, we see:

- A proliferation of satellite dishes and censorship of the media.
- A thrust toward providing the best education for young nationals and a society that accepts the secondary status of women. Young people

GULF COOPERATION COUNCIL (GCC)

NOTES

- These Islamic, or Arabic, nations have very strict laws regarding the possession of illegal substances, alcohol, pornography, pork, and so forth. You must adhere to these rules.

- Non-Muslims may not enter Saudi Arabia without an invitation. Generally, you must be sponsored by a prominent Saudi. Once you enter the country, you are subject to Saudi Islamic law; you are not protected by your government.

- You must have an exit visa to leave Saudi Arabia.

- You can be arrested if you dress immodestly (by Saudi standards). If a woman's dress is too short, her legs can be whipped by the police. Even with a visa, there are strict limits on what businesswomen can do.

- The work week is Saturday through Wednesday, although some businesses and banks may be open on Thursday mornings.

- Locate a local Saudi representative to assist you in negotiations. Choose carefully. Once you've made a choice, you will not be allowed to switch.

- Negotiations are conducted at a slow pace.

- When conducting market research in Saudi Arabia or other GCC countries, don't expect all respondents to show up at focus groups or for interviews(even if they agreed to attend). Because they are usually busy people and pray during the day, other activities take precedence over research projects. Women can be interviewed only through personal introductions in their homes.

- Do not ask a Saudi about his wife or daughter.

- The left hand is considered unclean in Islamic countries. Do not eat with your left hand.

- Never show the bottom of your foot to an Arab; this is considered offensive. Keep both feet on the floor.

---

have also been slow to explore the opportunities afforded by higher education.
- High-technology products in communication and transportation and a traditional lifestyle and beliefs.

Successful marketing in the region is the product of a carefully studied understanding of the balance between the aspirations (as encouraged by Western influences) and the cultural-religious heritage of the populations and their rulers. A business perspective on the GCC tends to focus on two countries: the K.S.A., whose population represents the largest consumer base, and the U.A.E., whose progressive outlook presents the most conducive environment for business activity.

In addition, the U.A.E. has a population that is about 70 percent expatriate and so has needed to be more liberal and tolerant in its outlook toward other cultures and nationalities. Living conditions for expatriate families are extremely comfortable and compare well with some of the more developed world economies. These factors make the U.A.E. the first choice for most corporations looking for a regional base.

For logistical reasons, the large population and geographical spread of the K.S.A. make it a suitable base for manufacturing operations. Thus, in a typical setup, the manufacturing base of a company tends to be in the K.S.A. and the marketing office in the U.A.E., which hosts most of the advertising agencies in the region. Sales and distribution depots are set up in other countries, as needed.

Distribution channels in these countries are dominated by the traditional trade, e.g., small and medium-size groceries in the food sector;

modern supermarkets contribute to only about a third of all supply in the chain. Business managers tend to travel a great deal across the region in their conduct of business.

NATIONAL PRIORITIES AND OPPORTUNITIES

The GCC countries have been making a concerted effort to develop such industries as tourism, banking and finance, agriculture and dairy products, food processing, aluminum, stainless steel, electricity cables, pharmaceuticals, water resource management, and plastics. Further, the GCC imports 40 percent of the world's arms, and local regulations require that arms manufacturers invest a certain proportion of the value of their sales in some form of industrial development.

Of the GCC countries, the U.A.E. and especially Dubai have generated considerable nonoil income over the past five years. Oil revenues have been wisely reinvested into the economy to develop a free-market environment with sound infrastructure in the form of modern telecommunications, readily available power and water supply, and an extensive sewage system to attract manufacturing and marketing bases. For example, the U.A.E. can boast of sophisticated communications technology; fully developed sea and air transport systems; low-interest bank loans; and government agencies to facilitate industry and economic development.

While corporate taxes tend to be minimal to nonexistent, companies looking to set up and obtain licenses must have local partners (usually inactive sleeping-partner arrangements; the proportion of holding varies from country to country). The labor ministries of the various states provide the requisite number of visas to enable the hiring of expatriate labor and management. This is strictly regulated to protect the interests of both employers and employees.

Under GCC development programs, water, electricity, and telecommunications have been heavily subsidized by government (for example, there are no local call charges in the U.A.E.!). Rapid growth has led to an explosion in the demand for these utilities, however, and costs have increased enormously. The U.A.E. and K.S.A. have been moving increasingly toward privatization of public services, starting with the telecom sector.

More recently, water and electricity have also been offered to the private sector to further improve efficiencies. The privatization of these utilities would be one of the largest in the Gulf and could encourage other governments to follow suit.

UNDERSTANDING THE POPULATION DYNAMICS

The total GCC population is estimated at 25 million people: the K.S.A. accounts for 17 million; the U.A.E. and Oman about 2 million each; and Bahrain, Qatar, and Kuwait make up the balance. About 70 percent of this population is urban. Given the small total population, economies of scale depend on the best regional strategies. Further, population distribution makes the K.S.A. virtually the sole consideration in the planning of any regional marketing strategy.

The national population of the GCC nations is very young—56 percent are nineteen years old or younger and 21 percent are between twenty and twenty-nine years old. Product and brand strategies targeting the youth market would seem a wise choice. For example, Pepsi Cola's international strategy to present itself as a youthful brand has seen great success. The company commands a regional market share exceeding 75 percent for its brands. Products (including media) geared to sport and leisure activities see high demand for the same reason.

The GCC nations are highly dependent on expatriates to provide both skilled and unskilled labor. The expatriate workforce ranges from 70 percent in the U.A.E. to 26 percent in Oman. Of this workforce, the largest group are of Asian origin, from India, Pakistan, Bangladesh, Sri Lanka, the Philippines, etc. This is followed by such Arab societies as Egypt, Lebanon, Syria, Jordan, etc.; there is also a small number of Europeans and Americans.

These varied nationalities bring with them their own cultures, languages, and preferences. The challenge to most marketers is to appeal to this diverse consumer population without resorting to fragmented and uneconomical strategies. And since the expatriate consumer population is in a constant state of flux, there are challenges to any long-term brand-building strategies. For example, about 210,000 workers (roughly 10 percent of the entire U.A.E. population) were repatriated from the U.A.E. in 1996, which caused instability in the labor market and also affected the demand for many products.

The constant issue faced by any marketer is: Should the focus be on the stable but small national population or the transient but large expatriate population? Over time, the larger companies have tended to focus their messages on the stable national populations without alienating or ignoring the expatriates. However, this dilemma will remain for some time the main challenge to companies operating in the region.

The national populations of the GCC possess some of the highest per capita incomes in the world. Further, the favorable tax structures of the countries increases the disposable income of their resident populations. Given the young age of the national populations, recent exposure to Western culture, and high disposable incomes, there is tremendous demand for luxury goods.

This would include high-end luxury cars, electronics, jewelry, designer clothes and accessories, cosmetics and perfumes, and sports and leisure products. For example, it is estimated that the GCC is one of the largest markets in the world for high-end cosmetics and perfumes. The middle and lower end of the economy tends to be supported by the expatriate workforce. This suggests the coexistence of mid-range and luxury products.

UNDERSTANDING RELIGIOUS AND CULTURAL ISSUES

The societies of the GCC nations are regulated by strong Islamic beliefs. The extent of these regulations and their impact on individual conduct vary greatly, from the extremely conservative K.S.A. to the relatively more liberal U.A.E. and Bahrain. The largest religion in these nations among both nationals and expatriates is Islam; there is also a scattering of other religions. In Islam, the state, judiciary, and religion are intertwined, and religion governs all aspects of an individual's daily regimen—prayers, clothing, personal hygiene, the conduct of business, family life, food and drink, social conduct, leisure activities, the status of men and women in society, and so on.

Moreover, Islamic law is applicable to all residents regardless of religious belief. Strict adherence to the moral code—in particular, the death penalty for all drug offenders and murderers—has attracted international attention in recent times. This is especially true when foreign nationals have been involved.

Setting up a base in the region requires an understanding and, better yet, a great degree of respect for these social and cultural beliefs. Here are some examples of how they have a direct impact on the day-to-day work environment:

- A fair amount of time is spent before beginning a business meeting in establishing social rapport. The well-being of both parties is leisurely discussed (but it is rude to inquire about the well-being of wives), and business is treated almost as a secondary issue, although in reality it is not. Only when this technique has been mastered can an expatriate manager truly belong and conduct business successfully. To the Arab businessman, personal and professional conduct and trust are completely interlinked, and respect has to be gained on both fronts.

- There are no women in the workforce in countries such as the K.S.A. (Other GCC nations are more liberal and allow women to work.) In other countries gender segregation is very apparent and encouraged.
- The working day in many countries is broken into two parts with a long afternoon break for lunch and siesta.
- All companies have to adhere to reduced working hours during the holy month of Ramadan. Public consumption of meals, smoking, and drinking are banned during this fasting period.
- Friday is observed as the weekly day of rest. All commercial activity stops on Friday mornings until the afternoon prayers are completed.
- All companies must allow Moslem employees to conduct their prayers. Of the five calls to daily prayer, two to three may occur during work hours. Frequently, large companies provide prayer rooms for their employees.
- Dress codes are strict, especially the use of the veil or scarf and abaya for Muslim women.

All corporate communication needs to be sensitive to religious and social norms (language, symbols, references of a sexual nature, etc.) Religious beliefs determine the regulatory guidelines for business. Lack of sensitivity to this can sometimes result in severe consequences to companies. Corporations embracing a global approach in their marketing practices frequently need to deviate from the prescribed global norm to accommodate local regulations in planning, product development, communication development, packaging, etc. A few examples are provided below:

- In the banking sector, Islam prohibits the individual from accruing rewards in the form of interest, and Islam also prohibits profiting from means that are not a direct result of some form of effort, labor, or risk. Foreign banks need to offer competitive advantages to their customers through nonfiscal, innovative means. This regulation has resulted in the development of Arabic banks, whose business ethics are built around Islamic principles of commerce.

- In the food industry, all meat products must be *halal* (in Islam, animals must be slaughtered and cleaned in a prescribed manner), and pork products cannot be sold to Moslems. That information must be clearly stated on the packaging and advertising. Drinking alcohol is banned in the K.S.A. and is a severely punishable offense. In other GCC countries, Moslems are not allowed to drink, although those of other faiths are permitted to do so after acquiring the required permits. No sale of alcohol is permitted through supermarkets or groceries.

- The change in eating habits during Ramadan (the month of fasting) results in a slow season for the food and beverage industry. This must be planned for in company projections. Ramadan also influences people's TV-viewing habits, shopping behavior, and working patterns.

- All advertising must first be cleared by a censorship board that monitors mass media. Advertising and communication (visuals, language, symbols, and logos) must not make any sexual references, however oblique, express any anti-Islamic sentiments, make any Semitic references, or conduct any critical review of the ruling families. For example, even the Swiss Air logo (in the form of a cross) might not find acceptance in Saudi air space. A critical review made by the BBC on its Arabic channel in 1996 had the channel being temporarily banned across the GCC. Competitive advertising in the form of direct reference of the competition is banned. For example, Pepsi cannot run its Pepsi versus Coke challenge in these markets.

- In the K.S.A., product promotions that involve a game of chance (lucky prices, raffles, etc.) are forbidden as they are deemed to be gambling. However, promotions that involve price-offs, collect-and-win, and pack-on-pack offers are permitted as these are not deemed matters of chance.

ABOUT THE AUTHOR

Shashi Halve
AMER World Research
P. O. Box 22525
Sharjah
United Arab Emirates
Phone: 9716 391086; 9716 598324
Fax: 9716 31271; 9716 597490

Shashi Halve is director of consumer research for the AMER World Research Group in the U.A.E. She has over thirteen years of experience in marketing research, working with leading research and advertising agencies in India and the U.A.E. and, on the client side, with Brooke Bond Oxo in the United Kingdom and Pepsi Cola International in the U.A.E. Ms. Halve has presented numerous papers on advertising research, marketing to women in the Middle East, and tracking and managing secondary data sources.

ISRAEL
THE NEXT SILICON VALLEY

With a population of under 6 million people living in an area about the size of New Jersey, Israel is a westernized, highly developed, technology-oriented country undergoing dramatic changes in its business environment. In fact, Israel has been called the next Silicon Valley (or "Silicon Wadi") by leading business publications, primarily because of the number of high technology companies and start-ups that have attracted international attention. Technology innovators such as Scitex, Tadiran, ECI Telecom, RAD, Checkpoint, and Indigo have become known worldwide, with unprecedented numbers of high-tech start-ups sprouting every month.

The entrepreneurial wave has carried over to almost all fields of business. Many small import- and export-oriented firms have sprung up in consumer products, industrial supplies, medical goods and services, and almost all other types of products. The Israeli high-tech/entrepreneur spirit is the product (at least in part) of young army veterans utilizing talents they acquired in the military combined with the influence of such multinationals as IBM, Digital, Intel, and Motorola. All have been operating in Israel for many years.

The government recognized this potential and expanded their offering of business assistance programs. Qualified companies can receive public funding for R&D, manufacturing facilities, marketing, sales promotion, and consulting services. Overseas companies entering into joint ventures with Israeli firms can participate in these benefits as well.

ISRAEL  NOTES

- Israelis may be slow in responding to faxes and telephone calls.

- Business is conducted Sunday through Thursday. Don't expect business to be conducted on Fridays, although some firms may be open Friday mornings.

- Price is a key issue when doing business in Israel. The Israeli economy has experienced several swings in the past decade. As a result, many firms have learned to price their products and gauge their production accordingly.

- The Israeli business community is casual and informal. Nevertheless, you should address people by their formal titles. Once you know them well, you can call them by their first names.

- Because Israeli Jews come from all over the world, their behavior may differ according to their cultural heritage.

- Most international businesspeople from Israel are secular and do not strictly observe traditional Jewish rituals.

KEY FACTORS IN UNDERSTANDING THE BUSINESS ENVIRONMENT

While the changes in the Israeli business environment are numerous, five trends in particular stand out. Exporters should make an effort to understand them prior to exploring market opportunities. They are:

- Westernized society and the rise in the standard of living
- Technology

- Immigration
- International trade agreements
- Media and market segmentation

Westernized Society and the Rise in the Standard of Living

Western influence, especially American, is everywhere. While many people support this "Americanization" of Israel and seek opportunities to be "more American than the Americans," others are concerned that these trends will dilute the special character of Israel. Regardless of one's views, the changes are here and keep coming at a rapid pace.

The increasing American—or Western—influence is evident, for example, on supermarket shelves. Just a few years ago only a small portion of Israelis ate breakfast cereals, and there was a correspondingly small cereal section in supermarkets. Today, entire aisles are devoted to this food category, with extensive offerings from Post, Kellogg's, Quaker, and General Mills alongside newly developed local brands.

And the changes in Israeli business extend beyond retail. For example, such American investment banking firms as Lehman Brothers, Smith Barney, and Alex Brown have opened offices for the purpose of bringing Israeli high-tech companies to Wall Street. Top U.S. accounting giants such as Arthur Andersen and Price Waterhouse have acquired Israeli firms, and hotel chains including Hyatt, Hilton, and Holiday Inn have either opened or expanded their properties. Financial services corporations including American Express have established a presence as well.

The overall attitude toward imports is very positive and open among Israeli consumers. While the government and some trade associations periodically try to run a "Buy Blue and White" (the colors of the Israeli flag) campaign, most consumers are not deterred from seeking out the latest imported product. On the other hand, the quality, variety, and packaging of Israeli-made products have improved greatly over the last few years, with many producers exporting their products throughout the world. Locally made products are often less expensive as well, providing them with an advantage over comparable imports.

Exporters to Israel should be encouraged by the fact that the use of the English language is widespread. English is taught in the schools from an early age; American TV shows, movies, computer software, and the Internet provide extensive exposure to the language; and a significant percentage of Israelis, especially in the business sector, have spent extended periods abroad, often in the United States.

In the high-tech sector, knowledge of English is even more prevalent, with some companies conducting all of their business, including internal communications, in English. The small but growing number of immigrants to Israel from English-speaking countries provides an additional pool of English speakers. Many people from this well-educated population are employed in key international trade and technical positions in leading Israeli corporations.

It is not uncommon for Israelis to know three, four, or more languages. Exporters from around the world can easily find companies in Israel that speak their language.

Technology

Quite simply, Israelis like technology and adapt quickly to new technological products. When fax machines were first imported in the mid-1980s, unprecedented numbers were sold and newspapers reported that per capita, the use of fax machines was higher and increasing faster than in the United States or Europe. The story is much the same with personal computers. Israel is among the top ten markets worldwide on a per capita basis.

When the Internet opened to the general public, both business and consumers greeted it with open arms. Sales of imported modems skyrocketed, and subscriptions continue to grow both for the leading Internet provider Netvision and others. According to a recent survey conducted by the World Economic Forum and published in Newsweek, Israel is fifth on the list of the ten most Internet-connected countries (as a percentage of population), coming in after Finland, Iceland, Norway, and Australia, and way ahead of Canada and the United States.

Israel currently has 51,000 Internet users per million people. Local companies have been aggressive in setting up commercial sites on the World Wide Web, providing marketers interested in Israel with easy access to preliminary company information through this medium.

Cellular phones are another example of technology adoption. While the first cell phone company, Pelephone, targeted business executives and charged high prices, the second company, Cellcom, quickly signed up hundreds of thousands of customers in both the consumer and business markets, charging low rates for initial penetration.

Cellular telephone use in Israel is extremely high compared to other countries. According to a recent BBC report, Israel is second worldwide in per capita cellular telephone use, behind Finland. However, while the world average of minutes used per cell phone per month is 300, Israel leads the world with an average of 600 minutes per month per person. Visitors from abroad are often amazed at how many people—including teenagers—can be seen walking down the street using these telephones. The government recently published a bid for a third cellular carrier, which will fuel penetration even further.

As mentioned before, large numbers of technology-oriented businesses have been launched, many funded in part by overseas venture capital firms as well as the government. Key industries include communications, Internet and intranet technology, medical products, wide-ranging software applications, security systems, agricultural technology, and educational products. The growth in these industries has created a manpower shortage for technical personnel, with some companies hiring overseas subcontractors to help with product development. These shortages are expected to continue for the foreseeable future.

Immigration

Israel's population is made up of immigrants from around the world. In the past several years, most immigration has been from Russia and other locations in the former Soviet Union. Because so many immigrants needed to be absorbed (more than 700,000 into a population base of about 5 million in 1989), significant government and private investment was made in areas such as home construction, job retraining, and language-skills training, as well as infrastructure improvements such as telecommunications and roads. These investments benefited both domestic and international suppliers of products and services.

International Trade Agreements

Israel has free-trade agreements with numerous countries and regions, providing a reduction or elimination of tariffs on trade between the respective countries or regions. These agreements have generated opportunities for exporters selling to Israel or to other regions via Israel.

The most important agreements are with the United States and the European Community. The U.S.-Israel Free Trade Area agreement went into effect in 1986 and has provided for the gradual elimination of tariffs on goods shipped between the two countries. This agreement has been at least partly responsible for the large influx of American goods of all kinds into Israel in recent years. Israel's agreement with the European Community provides comparable benefits.

Israel has many additional free trade agreements, which include the following partners: European Free Trade Agreement (Austria, Norway, Finland, Sweden, Switzerland, Iceland, and Liechtenstein), Canada, Turkey, and the Slovak and Czech Republics. Others are being discussed or negotiated. All in all, these agreements provide direct benefits to exporters from countries with free-trade agreements with Israel. They provide indirect benefits by using Israel as a bridge between two countries that do not have agreements of their own.

Media and Market Segmentation

Government statistics indicate that Israel's population comprised 81 percent Jews and 19 percent non-Jews. But that 81 percent figure is far from homogenous. It includes Ashkenazim (Jews of European descent), Sephardim (Jews of Northern African descent), Orthodox, Ultra-Orthodox, kibbutz members, immigrants, and so on.

In addition to traditional media, opportunities for reaching customers via electronic media have grown in recent years. The government-owned Channel 1 still does not run advertisements beyond program sponsorship messages. However, since Channel 2 television began accepting advertisements at the end of 1993, more than 1,000 firms have taken advantage of this relatively new and effective advertising medium.

In addition, cable television is very popular in Israel, although stations are not allowed to accept paid advertising. Even with the advertising restrictions, cable stations provide public relations opportunities for companies with products or services that are unique or newsworthy.

Radio advertising options have increased substantially in recent years. Along with stations that reach listeners nationwide, regional radio stations are now broadcasting to a wide range of audiences, each in a specific area. Some broadcasts are simply oriented to the location (such as Haifa and the northern region of the country or metropolitan Jerusalem), while others have an ideological, religious, or business focus. All combined, regional radio stations are a relatively low-cost advertising option for businesses seeking to target their message to local rather than national markets.

Interestingly, billboard advertising is still extremely popular, with most major campaigns investing significant resources on outdoor advertising. High-tech is seen here as well, with various types of electronic billboards displaying commercial messages in the main cities.

OPPORTUNITIES

Consumer Products

With the reduction in import duties, quality consumer products can now be exported more easily to Israel. Exporters are advised to work with an experienced local partner, often a manufacturer of complementary products. Numerous manufacturers in Israel now market the products of non-Israeli manufacturers as well, taking a "if you can't beat them, join them" attitude.

Mail order is still underdeveloped in Israel, although it is growing. Because of the small population, the types of test marketing popular in the United States are not practical here. However, as customs and foreign currency barriers are reduced or eliminated, sales of consumer products via non-Israeli mail-order catalogs to Israelis may become a reality. Direct sales via the Internet may also become attractive, helping Israeli consumers find lower prices than those available locally. In certain categories such as books (where consumers can import directly without paying duties), Israelis are already buying directly from overseas suppliers at a substantial savings.

Business to Business

Technology products—as throughout the world—represent a dynamic, fast-changing market. The continuous growth of Israeli high-tech offers many niches for suppliers to these industries. Exporters of products for the growing small-business sector—for example, the small office/home office market may find growth opportunities as well.

Services

The growth and increased sophistication of Israeli industry has opened the doors to consultants and experts offering the skills and expertise domestic workers need, e.g., hardware and software engineering, human resources, management, finance, and marketing. These same consultants can offer training seminars and courses in cooperation with local associates and training institutes. "Off the shelf" training materials, offered to local trainers and consultants, could find a market in Israel as well.

CULTURAL BARRIERS AND CAVEATS

Ethnic and Cultural Issues

Unintentional cultural clashes are not uncommon between businesspeople in Israel and the West. While such misunderstandings are not as obvious in Israel as elsewhere, exporters are well advised to visit the country and meet casually with Israeli business people before attempting to do business. If needed, local help is readily available in conducting preliminary market research, learning the structure of the market, determining a marketing strategy, and finding Israeli marketing partners or manpower.

Israel is a very informal country, although changes have occurred here as well. While it is no longer uncommon to see people in suits and ties, most managers still dress relatively informally at work—no jackets or ties, and even wearing sandals during the warmer weather. When meeting with business associates, almost everyone is addressed by first name.

Personal relationships are very important, and in fact substantial business is conducted based on contacts from the army, school, political party affiliations, and so forth. Understanding and tapping into this network is a key to success in Israeli business. Personal and business relationships in Israel can be closely intertwined. Asking associates whether they are married and have children could appear intrusive to some Westerners; in Israel such questions are completely normal. Israeli managers will invite overseas guests to their homes as well—it is all part of developing a personal relationship. The importance of this kind of relationship cannot be overemphasized.

Exporters interested in selling to the government should determine whether their associates in Israel are connected with the political party currently in office (national elections are held approximately once every four years). Doors are not closed to others, but the right contacts help enormously. Also keep in mind that many people have very strong political opinions. Discussing local politics and taking the opposite view of your potential customer could harm a relationship—and the deal.

Distribution and Marketing

Because Israel is a small country, exporters tend to work exclusively with one local agent, although there are numerous exceptions, like Hewlett-Packard's computer printer division. It works with two local distributors under the supervision of a corporate-owned Israeli office. In general, exclusivity is important to agents in Israel, and most will ask for it prior to promoting an imported product.

While strong in almost every other area of business, overall Israeli expertise in marketing is considered weak compared to Western countries. Investment in market research, availability of consumer demographic information and mailing lists, the use of coupons, database marketing, and cause marketing are all less advanced than in the United States. This may be due in part to the small, relationship-oriented nature of the country.

In the past, companies may not have needed sophisticated marketing tools in order to compete. This is changing rapidly with the entry of multinational competitors as well as the availability of marketing assistance from local experts trained in the United States and Europe.

RECOMMENDATIONS

Exporters planning to sell in Israel should keep in mind the following points:

- Despite attention from the world media, Israel is a very small country.
- The business sector is becoming increasingly sophisticated as a result of growing competition and greater exposure to world markets.
- As the "Silicon Valley" of the Middle East, Israel's high-tech industry base offers many opportunities for suppliers of products and management services. Many of these firms are interested in joint ventures with companies throughout the world.
- The Americanization of Israel is felt everywhere. From Burger King to Toys R Us, Israeli consumers buy American products, see American television, and root for the Chicago Bulls. American investment bankers have set up shop in record numbers in order to find high-tech investment opportunities and bring companies to Wall Street.
- Israel's population adopts new technology enthusiastically and quickly. Technology exporters will find consumers and companies willing to accept technological changes and improvements.

- Led by the high-tech sector, there is a growing entrepreneurial spirit in all product areas. Opportunities for direct sales and joint ventures abound. Sales of products and services to entrepreneurs in all sectors is a growth area.
- The population is very segmented. Despite the small size of the country, there is no one "Israeli consumer," and exporters to Israel should conduct research to determine their market potential, strategy, and positioning.
- Israel has numerous free trade agreements with foreign governments. Exporters are advised to check the trade status of their home country with Israel.
- Personal relationships are critical to successful marketing in Israel, and exporters should strive to forge such relationships with their Israeli marketing partners. They should also seek out Israelis with the appropriate business and political connections for their product or service.

Overall, Israel is open to exports and developing relationships with foreign companies and their marketing representatives. Businesses are encouraged to do their homework by obtaining marketing feedback, evaluating opportunities, and determining obstacles. With that accomplished, they can begin the actual process of marketing in Israel. Shalom!

ABOUT THE AUTHOR

Charles Klein
Amcon Marketing Strategy International
11 Hasadna Street, Suite 205
P. O. Box 2233
Industrial Center
Ra'anana 43654
Israel
Phone: 9729 743 1986
Fax: 9729 743 1982
E-mail: amcon@ibm.net

Charles Klein, B.S., M.B.A., is managing partner of Amcon Marketing Strategy International, an international consulting firm with offices in Tel Aviv and Chicago that specializes in business intelligence, market research, business strategy, and the forging of strategic partnerships. Amcon's wide range of experience includes computer software, technological products, industrial machinery and components, chemicals, law enforcement services, industrial security services, retail consumer products, and financial services. Having managed hundreds of competitive intelligence and market research projects, Mr. Klein is a leading authority on international business and export development. Before forming Amcon, he worked in marketing research and management for General Electric.

Chapter 8

COMING TO
AMERICA

*Foreign Firms Marketing
in the United States*

"FOR THE FOREIGN NATIONAL, THE U.S. MARKET CAN OFTEN BECOME THE TAIL THAT WAGS THE DOG."

Anyone wanting to do business here must know the terrain. The United States has a culture based on *individualism*. Citizens value freedom of expression and embrace competition as a rule of life. Quick, decisive responses are almost always preferred to a more studied, collective approach. And anything that looks to be "men-only" in composition or benefit will not go over well in a society where women continue to fight for equality.

The United States has the largest single national economy in the world, as vast in its own way as the Grand Canyon. As such, it represents a premier consumption market for world manufacturers and service companies, especially those offering high value-added products and services.

Obviously, the large European and Japanese multinationals have the capital resources and experience needed to exploit potential U.S. demand for their exports. For smaller firms looking to world markets for expansion (especially those from developing countries), however, the U.S. market can be daunting. After all, the Grand Canyon looks awfully big.

BEWARE! TERRA INCOGNITA

Old European maps labeled the land to the west *terra incognita,* or land unknown, and warned sailors to beware its waters. Indeed, even today the United States can appear to be bewildering, uncharted territory to many foreign marketers.

For openers, there are rule makers and rule makers. In addition to the federal or national government of the United States, each of the fifty states that make up the union has wide-ranging legal and regulatory powers. Therefore, marketing in the United States often calls for local and regional, as well as national, strategies. In fact, the most useful way to visualize the U.S. market is as a diverse quilt of many (often smaller) markets rather than as one great blanket.

For small and medium-size firms, this can be a blessing. Foreign firms can focus on one part of the American economic quilt and thereby avoid the enormous cost of national marketing and distribution. But this diversity is also a danger. Snow shovels do not sell well in Florida. Success depends on thorough research and careful preparation.

FINDING A MARKET THAT FITS

HOW A SMALL FISH CAN THRIVE IN A BIG POND

Most firms attempt to enter the U.S. market through trade shows in their home country. This is all well and good insofar as it provides industry contacts. But the easy optimism generated on a trade show floor can be deceiving. Dreams won't come true unless you have a firm understanding of such matters as the U.S. distribution system and product legislation. Do you want to ship it by air or rail? Does the law say your product is dangerous or even illegal? You have to know if you want to play smart.

You must also understand the United States is an extremely litigious society when compared to other nations. Consumers have ready access to the legal system to pursue claims of product defects and harm. Food,

UNITED STATES

NOTES

- Most travel is done by air or car. The rental car market is well developed, and rental locations can be found in urban, suburban, and rural areas. You will need a driver's license and a credit card to rent a car.

- Always book appointments well in advance. Always find out who will be attending meetings. Be prepared for last-minute cancellations.

- Business is often discussed with meals. Meetings sometimes carry over into lunch or dinner, and breakfast meetings are becoming very popular.

- Meetings are expected to last no more than one hour; lunch or dinner, no more than two hours. Americans talk freely about their families, vacations, and so forth over meals.

- In meetings, a firm handshake is the rule. Women can either smile or offer their hands.

- In comparison with other countries, the United States is by far the most informal. Use the title Mr., Mrs., or Ms. when meeting someone for the first time. After the initial introduction, first names are the norm.

- Americans get to the point quickly. After they give you a brief overview of their industry, products, and services, they will expect you to outline your company and will expect to receive your literature. They will then expect you to get to the point—your sales proposition or business development proposition.

- Remember that many firms underwent significant downsizing (staff reduction) during the early 1990s. The decision maker you meet with may not have a staff and may be handling several functional areas.

- U.S. businesses expect short-term results and have shorter planning horizons than is usual in other countries. Keep this in mind during negotiations.

- Americans expect direct eye contact—but not intense staring.

- Americans use gestures to make points. Do not be offended by these gestures or by jokes. Americans often use humor in meetings.

- It is important that you follow up with Americans after meetings. This will remind them of your interest and will encourage them.

- Business styles and practices differ by region. The Northeast style is fast paced, quick to the point, may not ever respond to you; the Southeast, polite, slower paced, relationships are important. Midwesterners are friendly, moderately paced, engage in honest discussions, will let you know "yes" or "no," or at least which way they're leaning, and want long-term relationships. The Southwest is friendly, slower paced; the people want stable relationships. Those from West Coast are relaxed, easy-going, and like new and innovative products and technology.

- Americans are very conscious of competitors. Avoid negotiating deals with competitive companies.

- The United States is information rich. You will have access to more information about U.S. firms than they will about your company. Any information that you can provide about the market in your country will be appreciated.

- U.S. small and middle-market companies are very interested in developing "strategic alliances" and joint ventures with international firms. However, they don't want to waste time. Your presentation of what you can do for them and what they can do for you will get results sooner.

- Americans may not be aware of political and economic events in your country. Your update will be appreciated.

- Americans love to hear success and failure stories about other firms in the same industry or business.

- Business dress is conservative in cities and can be more casual in suburban and rural areas.

- Be well prepared for meetings. Americans may have a casual attitude, but they strive to achieve profits, quick action, and global competitiveness.

---

consumer, automotive, and medical products are among the areas most likely to draw such litigation. If you intend to expand to the United States, you would be wise to consider product liability as a key factor. You must ensure that your products pass all industry and government specifications.

The Food and Drug Administration (FDA) of the federal government is the most important agency that regulates the import of food and ingredients, consumer products, drugs, and health devices. The FDA has entered into agreements with foreign governments to ensure that their products are manufactured under sanitary conditions, meet U.S. standards for quality, and are sampled in a specific way before shipping. The FDA clamps down both on imports and importers, so consider yourself warned.

If you are seeking FDA approval, you should contact the FDA office in the United States (refer to the U.S. source section) for detailed specifications for your products and make sure that you follow these guidelines: Determine before shipment that your product is legal, have private laboratories examine samples of foods to be imported and certify their findings, acquaint yourself with the FDA's legal requirements before contracting for a shipment, request assistance from the FDA district office responsible for your port of entry, and know the food-importing procedure as published by the FDA.

To cut it down to size, the American economy is often divided into segments and regions. The regional markets are, of course, a function of geography: Northeast, North Central, Southeast, Southwest, Midwest, Rocky Mountain, West Coast, and Pacific Northwest. There are distinct urban, suburban, and rural divisions within these markets. Following World War II, many American cities went into decline as the middle and upper-middle classes flocked to suburbs. Recently, however, cities have attempted to restore their image through investment in education, crime prevention, and infrastructure, to the extent that major retailers are rediscovering urban markets.

Per capita wealth and the desire of consumers to express their individuality make the United States a marketer's dream or, if a marketing plan goes awry, nightmare. The challenge is to understand the American consumer—and there are 255 million who are pretty willing to tell you what they like and dislike.

Here are some key ways to research the American consumer: by region, including state, city and ZIP code; ethnic, racial, and religious background; age, income and occupation; education; family status; and home ownership. If it seems overwhelming, take heart. Most Americans willingly take part in market research. To them, it is a form of free speech.

Research may consume time and money, but the cost will be less than having to pull out of the market. Good market research identifies potential barriers for a product or service. These can include a difficult-to-identify mass consumer base; high-technology that has yet to gain the attention of consumers; a highly competitive market, such as automotive, consumer electronics, and photography; significant government red tape on the state and/or federal levels; and media (print and television) reaction. Ignoring just one of these can sink a project.

AMERICA BLOWS HOT AND COLD

In some cases, research reveals that *no* market exists. Obviously, this is a good thing to learn *before* inventory and staff start making their way across the ocean. Nobody wants to be emperor if it means trying on embarrassing new "clothes."

While "blowing hot and cold" is a phrase Americans use to refer to inconsistency, it quite literally describes the country's climate. In addition to covering five time zones from New York to Honolulu, the United States consists of climate zones that range from arctic to tropical. Even discounting the states of Alaska and Hawaii (which marketers often do given their small populations and distance from the "mainland"), the range of environmental conditions in the United States is dramatic, not only from region to region but within regions.

For example, the annual temperature range in the high plains of the upper west region (e.g., the Dakotas, Montana, Wyoming) can be from $-40°C$ in the winter to $+36°C$ in summer. Even a temperate zone city like New York can range from single-digit winter temperatures and snowfall measured in meters to high humidity and temperatures in excess of $+30°C$ in the late summer.

Such dramatic differences within and across regions can affect both product design and product marketing. For example, manufacturers of automobile antifreeze must manufacture and credibly advertise products that work equally well in both extremes, and processed food and beverage products must be formulated to withstand wide variations in temperature during shipping and storage.

The varied climate in the United States may affect the fortunes of overseas manufacturers who are used to serving markets with less extreme weather. For example, a successful manufacturer of prefabricated steel-frame houses (sold to builders as a kit) decided to expand to the United States. The firm was located in Australia, which has both tropical and temperate zones, but no real cold.

Market research for this new business (i.e., the company was a franchiser of the fabrication plants) soon showed that steel-frame homes were impractical in many northern regions of the United States, since a steel superstructure did not retain heat nearly as well as a wood frame. So, hope for a national market gave way to a focus on southern regions, where wood is either inexpensive (in the Southeast) or little used (brick and stucco in the Southwest).

There were still other problems. While promoted as a more labor cost-effective alternative to wood frame construction, the steel-frame home still depended on the skills and knowledge of craft workers, and there were relatively few of them in the South. The shortage of local skilled labor in turn limited the market and inflated construction prices to the point where steel-frame homes lost their cost advantage.

In addition, the "kits" had to be assembled from raw materials shipped long distances to a central factory for fabrication and then sent to a distant building site for final construction. While such centralization was cost effective for preassembled homes (which basically only have to be trucked to a site and placed on a foundation), it did not hold for homes needing on-site assembly. It ended being more cost effective to build a wood-frame home from locally available materials.

The climate range in the United States reduced the company's initial "national" market to a much smaller regional one. This, plus local market conditions, turned what seemed a large and promising market opportunity into a situation that did not make business sense for local franchise investors nor for the company.

FITTING YOURSELF TO CONSUMERS

THE "AMERICAN PEOPLE" DON'T EXIST

The Latin phrase *E pluribus unum* is stamped on American coins; it is a motto meaning "Out of many, one." This should serve as a warning that few countries are as racially and ethnically diverse as the United States. At one point or another in its history, people have immigrated to America from virtually every region of the world. So when a foreign firm plans to enter the U.S. market, it may find that products with broad appeal back home need extensive alteration.

Consider the experience of an Asian manufacturer of skin care and beauty products. The firm had developed technology that essentially analyzed skin conditions and then recommended specific products based on the results. This was to be used to further sales in retail shops.

The company decided to modify the machine for "American" skin types. The problem, of course, is that no such thing exists in this multiethnic and multiracial society. So what began as a simple project to recalibrate turned into a complex process of recruiting women from a wide variety of ethnic and racial groups. While the resulting technology only had settings for three broad, racial-group skin types (i.e., "Caucasian," "Black," and "Asian"), the calibrations themselves required taking measurements from a wide variety of women from different racial and ethnic groups.

The company might have done better to be sensitive to the fact that the United States, unlike its home country, is not populated with a single "people." The golfer Tiger Woods illustrates this point perfectly. Of mixed parentage, Woods refuses to categorize himself as African, Caucasian or Asian; he insists on being all three. What kind of machine could measure that?

ATTITUDES ABOUT FOREIGNERS IN AN IMMIGRANT NATION

An initial question foreign marketers interested in entering the U.S. market is, Do they want to make reference to the product's country of origin? In some cases (e.g., French wine, German beer), the home country contributes greatly to a brand's appeal. But it can also present problems. For example, sales of Stolichnaya Russian vodka dropped dramatically when the Soviet Union invaded Afghanistan and anything Russian became unpopular. So, early on determine the "import status" of your product or service relative to the brand positioning.

Do this by identifying the prevailing perceptions and attitudes about the country or region of origin. For example, an Indian manufacturer of over-the-counter pharmaceuticals wished to enter the U.S. market with an analgesic balm. But U.S. consumers thought it was "old fashioned" (i.e., the successful products on the market had what was regarded as a "new" type of formulation offering meaningful product benefits), and they were unimpressed that it came from India.

The American perception of India is of a "dirty" and unsanitary country, and this dampened the appeal of a health product to be used on the body. However, a more appealing position was to say it came "from the East" and has been an effective remedy for "thousands of years." The phrasing made the product pleasantly exotic while avoiding the negative association to a particular country.

Sometimes, however, negative stereotypes aren't so easy to dissolve. For example, a European airline was so closely associated with its country of origin that it could not be positioned better unless it changed its name and national ownership! In fact, such a move was recommended. It made economic sense given conditions in the industry worldwide, and it would have avoided identifying the company with a negative national stereotype held by Americans in the target market. In general, companies should realize that success in the United States may come at the cost of modifying or rejecting national identity.

TWO COUNTRIES SEPARATED BY A COMMON LANGUAGE

Marketers from English- or Spanish-speaking countries (e.g., the United Kingdom or Spain) may be tempted to think they will have an easier time in America because of a common language. However, the Queen's English—or Spanish—is not much spoken or always understood in the United States.

For example, British Airways was introducing a new frequent-flyer's incentive program. Such programs had long been in place in the United States, and British Airways was coming late to the market. In addition, competing airlines also offered a premium service for valued customers, for which one pays a fee.

A problem surfaced when it was found that the British were using a word for their nonpremium service that American customers thought referred to the premium service. Thus, many Americans were surprised to find that they were being denied the premium service which they thought they had decided on. When the client asked Americans why they thought they were getting the premium service at no charge, the Americans said they assumed it was a promotion to attract business. The response caught the British by surprise. So, the Executive Club became the Executive Club Frequent Flyer Programme.

A company and its customers were ostensibly speaking the same language, but in fact found that the same words carried different meanings. The problem was compounded by different cultural expectations of normal business practice, which led to a near-disastrous public relations debacle.

A related problem here involved the value of the nonpremium service, even after the language problem was corrected. The company felt it was offering a loyalty program with very valuable incentives. But from the American perspective, the rewards were useless because they could only be used outside the country. Had the client looked at the offer from the local customer's perspective, it would have crafted a far different program. When doing business in New York, think as New Yorkers would.

A ROSE BY ANY OTHER NAME MAY NOT SMELL AS SWEET

Fine wine has been a growth category in the United States, with domestic product (notably from California) achieving a level of respectability traditionally reserved for European wines, especially French. But American vintners and marketers do not use the European system of referring to a wine by region, district, or property. Instead, they use grape variety as the primary identifier. This means American consumers tend to seek out a "Chardonnay," a "Merlot," or a "Cabernet Sauvignon."

The more successful shippers of foreign wine have adjusted to the market by labeling wines with the grape variety, rather than the region name. American consumers can now find French wines labeled "Merlot" rather than "Bordeaux." They buy accordingly. The implication here is that while American consumers may evolve to demand "foreign" products, they may nonetheless want them to have an American identity.

TECHNOLOGY PRODUCTS SHOULD BE MARKET DRIVEN

Manufacturers of telecommunications equipment are constantly investigating the U.S. market potential for ever more advanced and exotic personal telecommunications devices. The focus tends to be on technology and sales rather than in meeting customer needs. These technology firms (like computer manufacturers) tend to be more "product driven" in their business strategy than "market driven."

Another problem with the United States is that consumer choice (whether for individuals or companies) is skewed by economic factors beyond the control of manufacturers. In particular, devices are usually offered by service providers (e.g., telephone companies) as part of an overall service contract and oftentimes carry their name rather than that of the manufacturer.

These service contracts are highly promoted, with select models offered "free" or "for a penny" depending on the terms of the contract. While the true cost of the unit is in fact amortized over the course of the contract, the low cost of entry (and the perception among many consumers that they have a free device) make an unpromoted item (usually the latest technology) uncompetitive. It does not matter that service pricing is quite high or "number cloning" (in effect, stealing a phone's data signal and putting it in a copy or "clone") is a major theft problem.

High-tech manufacturers wanting a piece of the American market should take heed of a popular American saying, Keep It Simple. Product features intended to promote interest beyond the most basic transmission needs tend to be rejected, and rejection is as bad for business as it is for love. Products must be geared to local market conditions, especially when your product is used as part of someone else's system. Don't get fancy unless a particular market calls for it. Keeping it simple allows you to follow some very wise business advice: sell globally and market locally.

CONTROL DISTRIBUTION: AVOID THE OUTHOUSE

The U.S. distribution system is one of the most efficient in the world. However, significant research is necessary to understand the distribution channels by industry, market, and product. While the United States has excellent air, rail, truck, cargo, and postal systems, each is governed by its own set of regulations. In addition, each system has its own leaders and ways of doing business. Therefore, product distribution can become a real exercise in linear programming.

European manufacturers of premium products run the risk of damaging the brand's image if they fail to control product distribution. For example, two European manufacturers (one of cookware, the other of beauty products) assumed their products enjoyed the same high status and exclusive distribution in the United States as they did elsewhere. But research showed the exact opposite.

When the products failed to sell in the original retail outlets, jobbers took the stock and it wound up in discount stores, close-out catalogs and other down-market outlets. By not doing their homework and buying back the unsold goods, these firms took their brand's reputation from the penthouse to the outhouse.

Imagine the shock of finding that all the effort spent on crafting an exclusive brand image was wasted because you did not control the distribution chain. Understanding that system can mean the difference between success and failure.

CONCLUSION

As everything above suggests, entry into the United States involves legwork, legwork, and more legwork. The good news is that if you can target a market niche, research the regulatory and legal environment, sustain a significant advertising and promotion budget, and continue to track your competition, you will reap the benefits of one of the largest and most lucrative markets in the world.

But you had better like to exercise if you want to keep making money in the United States. The market is driven by competition, the essence of the American economy. Even when a company has a successful product or service in the United States, competitors will appear to offer the same or better product at a lower price. The only effective way to protect yourself is by continually monitoring the competition.

ABOUT THE AUTHOR

Timm R. Sweeney
SIL Worldwide Marketing
7601 North Federal Highway, Suite 205B
Boca Raton, Florida 33487
Phone: 561 997 7270
Fax: 561 997 5844

Timm R. Sweeney is founder and president of SIL Worldwide Marketing, an international marketing and research consulting firm with offices in Miami, New York, Chicago, and Brussels. Before founding SIL in 1983, Mr. Sweeney held client service and executive positions with several marketing research firms and advertising agencies, including J. Walter Thompson. He has experience working with foreign firms marketing a wide variety of business, industrial, and consumer products and services in North America and has published papers on subjects ranging from international research methodologies to positioning brands for global markets.

Chapter 9

BUSINESS DEVELOPMENT ISSUES

BRIBERY

Each region of the world has different ways of doing business. Do not expect to change—or ignore—deeply entrenched practices; it's not possible in the short term. One of the by-products in the race for global markets during the past decade has been the realization that "business ethics" may not be defined the same way in Kansas, Kashmir, and Kiev.

And don't expect any global business police to monitor each and every business transaction on a daily basis. In the real world, companies have to act in accordance with the legal structure of their domestic country. If the rules of the game are different abroad, a firm has two options: Choose not to do business in a particular country, or try to do business under their domestic regulations, even at the risk of losing the contract. Some firms have taken a very risky third option: trying to adhere to the regulations of the home market while local representatives use local methods to secure business for the firm.

While we all do not like to use the "B" word, bribery nonetheless exists. In some cultures, it is the standard method of doing business, both legally accepted and expected. Conversely, companies and individuals can face severe penalties (including prison terms) for engaging in such activities in a foreign country. So, unless you like prison food, do your homework. And make sure your research includes the local partners, suppliers, distributors, customers, and so forth, for these countries you plan to do business in. They will prove indispensable in helping you find out exactly what is required and expected of your firm.

Exporters, trading companies, and consulting firms are other excellent sources. The Source Book section of this book lists experts who should be able to give you accurate information on the local business situation in the respective countries. These sources belong to long-established and reputable firms that have been doing business with international companies for years and know the ropes.

Penalties for Bribery in the United States

The Foreign Corruption Practices Act (FCPA) was established in 1977 after the Securities and Exchange Commission (SEC) found that more than 400 U.S. companies admitted having made questionable or illegal payments in excess of $300 million to foreign officials and political entities. The law prohibits giving anything of value to any foreign official, candidate for political office, or political party for the purpose of influencing government officials regarding commercial activities, either directly or indirectly. This act covers U.S. citizens, businesses, or residents, as well as any company regulated by the SEC (Skip Kaltenheuser, "The Real Cost of Doing Business," *World Trade Magazine,* June 1997, pp. 80–83).

Violation of this law can result in individuals paying up to $500,000 and spending five years in a federal prison. Companies can be charged with as much as $2 million in penalties, or if the Alternative Fines Act kicks in, twice the value of their gain or others' loss. Lockheed, a US aerospace firm, was charged $24 million for their efforts to influence an Egyptian official, and General Electric was charged $70 million for improper political activity in Israel. (1)

Now, consider this hypothetical situation: A joint venture organized in Indonesia may not be directly subject to the FCPA. But if the senior officials are U.S. citizens or a U.S. entity controls the joint venture, compliance with FCPA is mandatory. All foreign officials, political parties, or candidates for political office are covered foreign persons and as such cannot be offered bribes. While certain payments for routine governmental action are exempted, payment to induce a favorable decision to award business or obtain discretionary permits and concessions is not protected.

Indirect payments (through intermediaries) are also proscribed if the person making the payment is aware of a high probability that the payment will end up in the hands of a covered foreign person. Joint venture agreements should have provisions binding the participants to compliance with the FCPA. Even more important, you should establish an on-the-ground compliance program to avoid the criminal penalties imposed by this far-reaching law. (Copyright 1995, Luce, Forward, Hamilton, & Scripps. All rights reserved.)

Bottom line: U.S. firms need to ensure that their overseas managers know the high cost of FCPA violations and ensure that foreign projects incorporate FCPA compliance guidelines (Copyright 1995, Luce, Forward, Hamilton, & Scripps. All rights reserved.)

Violators of the law can be barred from doing business with the federal government, with indictment causing suspension. If any government agency bars a company, all of the other agencies are obligated to follow, under the Office of Management and Budget guidelines. Potential penalties accumulate and export licenses can be put at risk.

A domino effect can occur with SEC penalties and disciplinary actions by the Overseas Private Investment Corporation. Under the Racketeer Influenced and Corrupt Organizations Act, competitors may bring a private suit for triple damages, as well as legal actions under other federal or state laws (Skip Kaltenheuser, "The Real Cost of Doing Business," *World Trade Magazine,* June 1997, pp. 80–83).

Competing on the Basis of Quality and Service Only

Given the above regulations, American exporters and manufacturers trying to expand their businesses globally may feel they are being held to higher standards than other regions of the world. According to Frank Vogl of Vogl Communications, Washington, DC, the single biggest factor for companies that believe strongly in the bottom line is to make sure your overseas managers know the high cost of violating the FCPA. Rather than engage in risky short cuts, they need to build the credibility and reputation that will make possible new business opportunities worldwide.

Vogl is also a vice president of Transparency International, a Berlin-based nonprofit organization seeking worldwide legal reforms to fight corruption. He stresses that U.S. companies, unable to fall back on bribery, have placed greater emphasis on getting business the right way, through innovation and smarter operation. (Skip Kaltenheuser, "The Real Cost of Doing Business," *World Trade Magazine,* June 1997, pp. 80–83).

The antibribery laws have not prevented U.S. firms from reporting staggering growth in exports and foreign direct investment throughout the world. Bribes total approximately $35 billion a year worldwide, with German companies paying about 10 percent of the total. And when the German mark gets stronger and makes exports expensive, pressure will build for higher bribes.

Transparency can boast of a growing list of corporate supporters throughout the world. It is particularly sad that bribery hits the developing nations particularly hard as public officials usually misallocate funds originally intended for schools, hospitals, and the needy (Skip Kaltenheuser, "The Real Cost of Doing Business," World Trade Magazine, June 1997, pp. 80–83).

Bribery scandals have also affected governments in Japan, Italy, Brazil, and Venezuela and have caused the resignation of important political figures in Germany, France, and Spain. The heads of NATO and French television lost their positions to bribery scandals, and rumors continue to plague the former president of Mexico. In addition, two former presidents of South Korea were touched by scandal (Skip Kaltenheuser, "The Real Cost of Doing Business," World Trade Magazine, June 1997, pp. 80–83). Given the increasing sensitivity to this issue, both China and Russia—two countries which have reported corruption and scandals along these lines—have to recognize this is a serious global issue.

An exporter in any of the fifty United States should know that payments to a foreign official, political party, or candidate by intermediaries to obtain or retain business can put a company in jeopardy if the company knows what the intermediary is up to. "Knowing" includes the concept of conscious disregard or willful blindness. Ignorance will not save you.

Payments need not even change hands. A mere offer, promise, or authorization of payment, or an offer of anything of value will suffice. Additionally, the business sought need not be with a foreign government: The purpose of directing business to any person also is prohibited (Skip Kaltenheuser, "The Real Cost of Doing Business," World Trade Magazine, June 1997, pp. 80–83).

Because speed is often critical in international transactions, the FCPA was amended in 1988 to allow businesses to grease the slow-grinding gears of bureaucracies and willful incompetents. The bribery prohibition has the explicit exception of facilitating or expediting payment to a foreign official, political party, or party official for the purpose of expediting or securing the performance of a routine governmental action by a foreign official, political party, or party official. These actions include obtaining

permits, licenses, or other qualifying documents, and processing government paperwork (Skip Kalthenheuser, "The Real Cost of Doing Business,"
World Trade Magazine, June 1997, pp. 80–83).

Companies have become quite creative in providing substitutes for
bribery. Companies that can provide educational or medical assistance
or legal systems training may find that these measures go further than
traditional bribes. All in all, firms need to research this situation thoroughly and know the lay of the land before finding themselves in an embarrassing situation.

COPYRIGHT AND PATENT PROTECTION IN FOREIGN MARKETS

With the race for global markets, most Westernized firms have in some
way or another faced the issue of protecting products, and/or technology
(patents, copyrights, and so forth) in overseas markets. The good news
is that North America, Western Europe (the EU), and Japan have well-
established regulations and regulatory authorities in this area. The bad
news is that, while these laws and regulatory authorities are being developed in Latin America, Asia, Eastern Europe, and the Middle East, companies are at risk in these markets. But remember your products are also at
risk in your domestic markets.

A PERSPECTIVE

From the minute you develop a product or service, a technology, a logo,
a package, or anything, you are at risk from someone copying it domestically or internationally. In international markets, you must do the research
to determine exactly what risks exist in a particular country. This type of
information is contained in Country Global Reports published by the
United States Department of Commerce and is also available from the
embassies of the countries in question.

Exporting goods includes the possibility of a product being copied (or
distributed in channels you do not want to use). One recourse is to stop
exporting your goods to that country. But a joint venture agreement to
co-produce a product locally means your risks are much higher. When a
joint venture goes awry, both parties are often unhappy, and provisions
which are not self-executing don't tend to get executed.

If you assigned your technology, you may find that it has been forfeited to your foreign partner under a law or regulation you were not told about. What works in the United States (or your country) may not work overseas, even if you have a provision in the agreement providing for U.S. (or domestic) law to apply. (Copyright 1995, Luce, Forward, Hamilton, & Scripps. All rights reserved.)

Bottom line: Don't enter an agreement that fails to protect you from laws and policies of other countries. (Copyright 1995, Luce, Forward, Hamilton, & Scripps. All rights reserved.)

STRATEGIC ALLIANCE PARTNERSHIPS

Now, are you ready to go global? "Going global" is a business mind set, says Max Downham, former vice president of business development for sweetener giant NutraSweet. If you think only in terms of your domestic market, you're not ready. And, even if you are ready, you need to consider how to go global.

We recognize that foreign direct investment is primarily for large multinational firms. Joint ventures involve complicated legal arrangements with local firms. In most cases, both parties have to invest either capital, technology, human resources, and so forth. Strategic alliances are much simpler and less costly.

In the simplest form, you can develop an alliance with a partner in another country over the Internet or via fax or phone. Still, face-to-face meetings are essential. In some regions of the world, Asia, for example, people will not consider doing business with someone unless they meet first, and it may still take several meetings afterwards to form an alliance.

Strategic alliances are relationships to benefit both parties. These include supplier-distributor relationships, manufacturer-supplier or distributor relationships, subcontractor relationships, and even cross-border competitive relationships. But they work only when both parties benefit. Internationally, these alliances can be formed as follows:

- With an oral agreement between parties and, if culturally appropriate, a handshake
- In the form of a letter
- With legal documents signed by both parties
- Over a period of time, based on each party's experience with the situation

In other words, these are loosely structured, flexible relationships that are low cost and low risk for both sides. If they work, they work, and, if they don't, they don't, and that's it. This section will discuss how to make strategic alliances work and offer case studies of companies that have done so.

BUILDING A LANDMARK

Some companies start out global, or at least international. For example, consider Landmark Systems Corporation, a performance management software firm based in Vienna, Virginia. The company is now fourteen years old with 1996 revenues of $50 million.

Co-founder and CEO Kathy Clark worked as a systems programmer with Blue Cross Blue Shield before founding the company. Clark and co-founder Pat McGettigan developed a software product to help them do their work more effectively at Blue Cross. Initially, they both saw their product as a part-time venture that might earn them money on the side.

Not long after developing the product, Clark attended a Blue Cross meeting, where she met some international distributors. She took the opportunity to ask them questions about launching products. Although not initially encouraging, each agreed to show her brochures to some of their customers for feedback. Within a week, she received a call from one of the distributors—who at first had been the most discouraging—asking her to come and meet some of his Benelux customers who were very excited about the product's potential.

Knowing nothing about international business, Clark and McGettigan found an expert who gave them an intensive, one-day course on the fundamentals of business development, and off they went. The trip was obviously a success. They installed the product on several customer sites and formed a partnership with the distributor to market the product throughout Europe. The relationship worked so well that U.S. revenues did not equal Landmark's Europe figures for two years.

What were Landmark's early partnering criteria? It looked for partners who were capable of doing the job, trustworthy, and a good fit with the team. These attributes are fundamental to any good partnering relationship, no matter how complex.

What were the key factors in Landmark's early market success? First, the product solved a real problem, which demonstrated the potential of real demand. Often distributors are approached with market concepts rather than fully developed and ready-to-go products. Second, the product was supportable from the United States.

Third, Landmark offered a very generous deal to partners. Recognizing that it was asking them to make a commitment to an unknown product from an unknown company, Landmark kept only 30 percent rather than the standard 50 percent of revenue. Last, Clark and McGettigan understood the all-important intangibles of trust and communication in business. Landmark treated its strategic allies as partners and recognized the importance of having constant, open, and honest communication. Each was committed to the success of the other.

There are many ways to enter a new foreign market. Landmark was a start-up firm that launched itself from a solid product base. The company benefitted from a willing partner capable of selling the product, thus creating revenue. Landmark had different evaluation and success criteria than a company in another growth phase, where the perception of risk might differ.

Because the criteria for success can differ with many variables, it is difficult to outline the "right" business development or partnering activities in a neat package. In general, entry strategies come from your company's business strategy. Business development activities are instruments of strategy implementation. Effective strategies are often underpinned by ongoing research and business intelligence to maintain a relevant market focus and enhance competitiveness.

Business development initiatives are defined by criteria such as capital investment objectives, the need for control, hurdle rates and margins, time-to-market, corporate culture, and other important elements to your company's business. As these issues are understood in context with country-specific investment requirements, the venture objectives, terms, resources, implementation and exit strategy are articulated in a business plan. Each business development venture, deal, or relationship merits its own specific business plan.

THE CHALLENGE OF STRATEGIC ALLIANCES

Global can be good, points out Manos Fourakis, a consultant in international business development and principle with AEF Group, Inc., but it is not for everybody. You have to understand your company and the exact nature of the opportunities out there.

Kim Mackay, executive director of business development for the Seattle-based telecommunications company MOSAIX, notes that business development investments require patient money. Companies should not expect immediate returns and must realize it often takes a little longer to get their payback. It is critical for companies to maintain realistic expectations for what they can achieve, what it will cost, and when they can expect the reward.

John Cebrowski is the former CEO of Solerex, a Maryland-based solar energy company. Cebrowski has found that success in global business development requires a commitment to long(er) term investment. This is especially difficult for small and medium-size businesses with significant revenue and margin pressure and limited ability to sustain slow start-ups or intermittent problems. He suggests that such companies go after markets the big guys ignore.

Jim Carruthers, CEO of Norpak, a developer and manufacturer of TV-based VBI data broadcasting systems, agrees and suggests that successful ventures require a significant amount of up-front money to establish legitimacy. Sometimes the country next door provides the best opportunity to try international investment and test if your company is ready for it. A market close by allows for easy travel, lessens the unknowns, and helps a business to manage the risk of early investment forays.

Max Downham adds that global business development initiatives are inherently risky because they often involve doing something completely new in areas you have never worked in before. A key objective in planning for global expansion is to approach it in such a way as to minimize inherent risks. One tried and true way is to engage in as much up-front preparation as possible to create a comfort level for the proposed venture before any sizable investment is actually made. Preparation means thoroughly investigating and evaluating market conditions, opportunities, and players before acting.

Your company's internal research and business intelligence teams can provide significant support during this phase of planning. If your company has little if any research resources on staff, it's money well spent to bring in a consultant who will assess the opportunity. This allows you to cover your company's evaluative bases, so to speak.

Tom Eckersly is vice president of business development for Virginia-based Comsearch, a wireless telecommunications company in the early stages of going global. Eckersly sees another major globalization challenge: enthusiasm. Companies need to balance the excitement for the venture with their actual ability to capture business, Eckersly says. It is important not to let enthusiasm blind you to warning signs on the fast road to global prosperity.

It is also important to avoid the "brain drain" that may accompany business development initiatives. Many people will be intrigued by the notion of capturing new markets, particularly in far-away and seemingly exotic lands. While a company should be sensitive to the interests of employees who may want to go, it is equally important that all of the best and brightest not be stripped from domestic operations. That would only lead to poor performance on the home front.

PARTNERING FOR BUSINESS DEVELOPMENT SUCCESS

How, then, to address emerging opportunities with minimized investment risk as well as tempered enthusiasm? As noted, the specific answer to that question stems primarily from your business objectives. By utilizing strategic alliance partnerships to achieve business development goals, a company can leverage risk and cost as well as it meets time-critical business needs by enabling faster and more intelligent market entry. Jim Carruthers, for one, believes that in-country partners are very important for successful business development activities.

Finding a partner is a good method of entry into other countries, notes Robert Guillaumot, Chairman of Paris-based Inforama, a software developer and systems integrator. One approach Guillaumot's company uses is to find partners who are also interested in expanding to Europe.

While partnering works for large, medium, and small companies alike, it gives the latter two in particular a boost that helps them compete more effectively in markets where large players already enjoy scale and resource advantages. Nonetheless, smaller companies must realize they have to be focused, perhaps more so than the big guys who have the resources to absorb mistakes and downturns.

UNDERSTANDING WHAT IT TAKES TO BE SUCCESSFUL

While partnering accomplishes much, it takes a significant level of due diligence and commitment to implement. Handshakes on a golf course can be fine for starters, but for smaller companies especially (although certainly companies of all sizes are not immune), it can herald a significant cash drain.

Evaluative rigor realistically defining needed resource commitments and investment requirements is fundamental to the business development as well as partnering process. It is important not to be so carried away with the investment potential that you, your company, or both lose sight of what it might take to get those envisioned rewards.

Kim Mackay seconds the point made by Tom Eckersly, that strategic alliance partnerships can be difficult, and often, Mackay adds, the euphoria of getting the deal obscures the postagreement work required. This can lead to inertia and, possibly, the ultimate failure of the partnership.

Mackay further notes that careful planning, monitoring, and communication (at all levels) of these initiatives is of the utmost importance if a company is to achieve its objectives. The agreement cannot be entered into with follow-up work thrust onto company personnel. The partnership needs commitment and buy-in early on and the empowerment of individuals charged with making the postagreement phase work.

Realistic goals and expectations are critical to global partnering efforts. Partnerships can help companies experience revenue growth quickly, attain enhanced geographic reach, access an existing customer base, aid in the skills transfer between partners, and develop and enhance a company's overall portfolio. Such relationships can enable companies to hit the ground running while leveraging someone else's capabilities. But as our partnering experts can attest, it is critical not to underestimate the task

WHAT IS STRATEGIC ALLIANCE PARTNERING?

Simply put, strategic alliance partnering is a business arrangement, that is, licensing agreements or joint marketing initiatives. These focused and bounded partnering relationships offer lower risk than more complex, integrated relationships. In such cases, the arrangements generally form tactical (short-term or with a narrow objective) rather than the more long-term strategic relationships, although they are often referred to as strategic. "Strategic" is often a misnomer in these situations.

Partnering relationships such as fully resourced joint ventures or mergers and acquisitions can meet objectives on strategic or tactical (or both) levels. In some cases, organizations can function as a strategic bridge to draw other companies together in pursuit of a specific objective. But like everything else in the business world, forming an alliance is not risk-free. Luckily, diminishing those risks is what this book is all about.

Partnering benefits are not always easy to achieve. Business newspapers and magazines regularly carry stories of woe and waste. It is because the more complex relationships carry a high potential for failure that our experts stress the critical need for realism and rigor in evaluating what approach is the best for your company.

Alliances can be resource intensive. Therefore, it is always wise to pay attention to detail to help ensure that they provide a good way of reducing cost and making effective use of resources. Experience underscores the importance of doing your homework and having realistic expectations as to what and when the relationship can achieve the benefits desired.

The key to any successful business relationship is its ability to offer a win/win opportunity for both partners. Capturing the interest and commitment of a desired partner requires demonstrated business sense. Gemplex, a French company with 85 percent of its business outside France, specializes in software development and the manufacture of "smart cards." Co-founder and senior vice president Philippe Maes is intent on developing Gemplex's worldwide presence and enhancing its marketing power. Maes's partnering strategy concentrates on creating competitive advantage for its partners through Gemplex services.

For example, traditional pay phone suppliers in a specific country were experiencing increased competition from a new entrant that offered the same basic products they did; in addition, this newcomer utilized technology the others could not offer. Gemplex was able to enter this market by partnering with these traditional suppliers, thereby creating a new market opportunity for itself and competitive advantage for its partners through their use of Gemplex's technologies to even the competitive playing field. The relationship brought significant value to both parties.

Opportunities can vary significantly from country to country and even from region to region within a country. Cookie cutter approaches aren't likely to yield much. Remember to think globally and act locally. Companies can't convince people to buy something they don't like or need. Each venture must be evaluated in light of a country's social and cultural framework.

For example, Maes tells of a social issue that affected adoption of an electronic payment system in Asia. For special celebrations, clean—never used—money is given to a bride as a sign of respect. Old bills are given to a widow at a funeral, also as a sign of respect. Electronic payment systems disburse money that is put into the machine without regard for such social customs. Sensitivity to cultural issues has a real bearing on market success.

CRITICAL SUCCESS FACTORS

Before we begin looking at the steps involved in strategic alliance partnering, let's summarize some of the critical success factors required to achieve full value from your company's alliance efforts:

- A clear understanding of your company's own vision, goals, and objectives to help determine what the partnering venture is to achieve.
- Before investment begins, significant homework, e.g., research and market intelligence assessments, evaluation of the reality of market opportunities and conditions as well as existing and potential competition.
- Development of a localized, country-by-country strategy.
- A clearly articulated business plan outlining success requirements, including financial resources and exit strategies.
- The organization's adoption of both a global and investment mind set along with the commitment to think "outside the box."
- Early and ongoing top management involvement, commitment, and support.
- A rigorous and objective partner selection process.
- Realistic venture expectations.
- Good cultural, business, and personality fit between partners.
- Recognition that partnerships are fundamental business relationships and, like all good relationships, are built on open communication, trust, and respect.
- No assumptions that people in other countries or cultures will think or do business as you do. No attempts to impose your will on them.

THINKING IT THROUGH

Before your company can evaluate appropriate alliances, it must first do the strategic planning. This process identifies company goals and objectives and outlines ways to achieve them. The clearer the vision and goals, the better to direct investment activities. From there, the process requires in-depth research—the up-front homework Max Downham talked about—to identify business conditions and potential partners to support development of a country-specific entry strategy and business plan.

Conducting business intelligence is a cornerstone of the homework or due diligence process. In the context of business development, this process helps to provide the information critical to making the right investment or partnering decision.

ORGANIC GROWTH

Even though partnering is a well regarded tactic in today's business world, your company's entry strategy should always consider the option of organic growth, viz., building it yourself. Even if your company decides not to enter a market in this manner, understanding the approach helps to further identify the criteria your company will want from an intended partner.

When going "organic," be sure to weigh the following: legal, regulatory, and certification processes; environmental considerations; political and economic stability; the availability of facilities; land costs; transportation; communications infrastructure; raw materials; labor laws and labor costs; and available skills and workforce, just to mention a few. In addition, the intended product has to be localized to the specific country.

Language and the four P's (product, price, position and promotion) must all be revisited. Product localization is a common global business development theme. All of these are issues in partnering as well and can form the basis for a checklist to identify desirable partner attributes.

You may find it useful to array these and other relevant issues in a matrix; this can be used to capture and evaluate what it would it will take for your company to enter a new market directly. Since these issues pertain to doing business in a particular market, they are also relevant to partnering as well and could be used to form the foundation of identifying and understanding desirable attributes in a potential partner.

DETERMINING ALLIANCE OBJECTIVES

Before your company begins the partnering process, it must first determine alliance objectives consistent with the strategic plan to guide partner selection. The following matrix, figure 9.1, can help you focus on the goals and issues that need to be considered in your evaluative stages.

CLASSES OF PARTNERS

Not surprisingly, all partnering objectives do not strive to achieve the same end. As you begin to think through your partnering approach, identify the basic type of partnering relationship(s) that best achieve your company's

Figure 9.1
DETERMINING ALLIANCE OBJECTIVES

Determine Goals by	Product	Reach	Customers	Revenue
Each product segment or line of business Each country What capabilities do we need to be successful and enhance our competitive position?	Does it fit the region? Is there a market for this product/ service in this country? What competition exists or may enter? What advantage do we have in this market?	Can this country be supported? What will it take to get in? In what country vs. another can our product/service create the most business benefit to our partner?	Existing channel opportunities I. Direct II. Indirect New channel opportunities III. Partners own channels IV. Expand my company channels	Can we make money in this market? What is the expected strategic investment from the partner? How long will it take to achieve a return?

goal(s). The type of partnership you seek will help determine the interactive role the partners will play to make the relationship succeed.

There are three basic partner categories:

1. Mission critical alliances that provide key capabilities currently unachievable in the company (as in the Gemplex example). Such partnerships are sometimes referred to as *elevators*.
2. Partners who can provide enhancing elements to your company's portfolio, or solutions to better position it for solid revenue growth. Because these relationships provide only a piece of your company's offering, there is often limited participation in joint customer activity and access to partner customer channels in this type of relationship. Such partners are sometimes referred to as *stairs*.
3. Relationships that generally result in little direct revenue and are characterized primarily by talk and little or no real activity. They encompass such areas as interconnected agreements in the telecommunications industry or announcement of product compatibility, as in the computer and software industry. Such relationships are often

good for public relations value and may enhance the attractiveness of your company's product and cost little to maintain. These relationships are sometimes called *ground level.*

THE HUMAN ELEMENT

Through all these steps and business processes, it is easy to forget that partnering relationships are forged by people and that personal relationship building is a key to achieving successful alliances.

Each partnering process has three distinct personality variables: the individual, corporation, and project. These need to be understood and integrated into the venture. Understanding individual managerial personalities is a critical component of successful strategic relationships.

For example, on the corporate side, companies often display personalities that reflect their life or growth cycle. Start-ups are often freewheeling and have little structure, as we saw in the Landmark example. Everybody pitches in to help where they can with little apparent concern for how lowly the task at hand may be. People here thrive on making their personal, hard-working contribution to the cause.

The project personality tends to be a function of how important the venture is to the company or its overall strategic role. Where the partnership is mission critical, it is no doubt integral to the future viability of the corporation. It fits into the company's broader strategy, is well financed, and enjoys top management involvement. The project personality is a suitable fit for a similarly minded ally.

Projects that primarily extend the market take on different characteristics. Those projects tend to be important but are secondary to a major element. They are often part of the business strategy with respect to implementation, but represent only some aspects of the macro strategic elements. There is usually some top management involvement at the inception of these deals, but it often wanes over time. Such a partner would be frustrating to one with mission critical objectives.

Another project personality type develops around relationships that are more experimental. These projects tend to have limited importance to top management, but yet are vital to particular segments of the organization. Resource commitment is made, but generally limited by time and results. Conflict resolution mechanisms in these types of deals do not tend to be well designed.

The other important personality element not to be overlooked is that of the individual managers. Aggressive risk takers are likely to be frustrated and less productive when partnered with a risk-averse partner unless they can reach a comfortable compromise to balance each other's more extreme tendencies.

It doesn't matter what the particular personality traits are per se. More important is that personality traits for all three elements (corporate, project, and individual) be recognized as critical elements of ultimate deal success and are factored into your company's search for an appropriate partner.

IMPACT OF THE INTERNET

One recent—and on-going—sea change in business has the potential to alter at least certain aspects of development and the partnering process. We are talking about the Internet, a business development tool so new that it's difficult to assess the ramifications of its use and evolution over the next few years.

In many ways, the Internet has the promise of becoming the ultimate tool for making connections. For openers, it can expand your company's ability to identify potential partners. These may be businesses just emerging or not part of the traditional networks often used for locating partnering prospects.

And it can make you seem big when you really are small. The Internet levels the playing field with respect to company size, at least in terms of perception. All companies, no matter how great or humble, appear the size of a computer screen, one page at a time.

The Internet also has the potential to let you reach your customers in a fundamentally different way. The beauty of the Internet, says Tom Patterson, IBM's chief strategist for electronic commerce, is that when someone needs your service, they can find it and pay for it.

Data security and language issues, ways to make using the Internet easier, and the ability to transact secure payments all will determine Internet acceptance and utilization as a business tool. Those issues, coupled with other operational and regulatory questions, may be tempering some of the enthusiasm the Internet has garnered since its inception.

As the problems diminish, however, the Internet will play an increasing role in breaking down borders and enabling communication and information accessibility as never before; it already offers access to ideas and new ways of thinking. Hilary Thomas, a pioneer in interactive services, has seen that people from different cultures and countries think differently. The challenge for a global business player is not to assume all people think alike. The Internet should be of great help in that regard. Thomas also suggests that the Internet is just beginning to influence some of the cultural and sociological factors that affect successful global business.

As companies develop private intranets and extranets to achieve specific goals, such technology will have an increasingly pervasive effect on how business is conducted. Firms will get ever closer to their customers, thanks to the new approaches made possible by the Internet's developing capabilities.

CONTRIBUTING AUTHOR TO THE STRATEGIC ALLIANCE AND INTERNET SECTIONS:

Cyndi Allgaier
  The Pine Ridge Group
  3324 Highland Lane
  Fairfax, Virginia 22031
  Phone: 703 280 0933
  Fax: 703 280 2259

Cyndi Allgaier, M.A., M.S., is managing director of the Pine Ridge Group (PRG). She is a recognized expert in understanding global market dynamics and translating market knowledge and insight into innovative strategies and marketing programs to improve corporate performance, marketing, and business development with MCI, Bell Atlantic, New York Times Corporation, and Marriott Corporation. She is past president and fellow of the Society of Competitive Intelligence Professionals.

Those who contributed to this chapter are gratefully acknowledged:

Ken and Judith Allen (Washington, DC)
Jim Carruthers, CEO, Norpak Corporation (Canada)
John Cebrowski, President, Sales Builders, Inc. (Virginia)
Kathy Clark, CEO, Landmark Inc. (Vienna, Virginia)
Max Downham (Chicago, Illinois)
Tom Eckersly, Vice President, Comsearch (Reston, Virginia)
Jon Fichthorn, Vice President, Pine Ridge Group, Inc. (Fairfax, Virginia)
Manos Fourakis, Principle, AEF Group, Inc.
Judy Gray, President, Fairfax Chamber of Commerce (Fairfax, Virginia)

Robert Guillaumot, Chairman, Inforama (Paris, France)
Ellen Lamagna, Manager, Comsearch (Reston, Virginia)
Kim Mackay, Executive Director, Mosaix (Redmond, Washington)
Philippe Maes, Co-Founder and Senior Vice President, Gemplex,
   (Gemenos, France)
Bruno Martinet, Vice President, Ciments Francais (Paris, France)
Tim McCarthy, Senior Vice President, Crestar Bank (Washington, DC)
Tom Patterson, Chief Strategist for IBM Electronic Commerce and
   Director of GlobalLink (Fairfax, Virginia)
Spish Rurak, Principle, Rurak & Associates (Washington, DC)
Jim Seering, Principle, Kirkman and Seering (Vienna, Virginia)
Katarina Svensson, University of Lund (Sweden)
Hilary B. Thomas, President, Telecommunication Services Inc. (Denville,
   New Jersey)
Kirk Tyson, CEO, Kirk Tyson International (Chicago, Illinois)

PART II

AN
INTERNATIONAL
SOURCE BOOK

ARGENTINA

GEOGRAPHY
Area:
Total Area: 2,766,890 sq km
Land Area: 2,736,690 sq km
Comparative Area: slightly less than three-tenths the size of the US
Natural Resources: fertile plains of the pampas, lead, zinc, tin, copper, iron ore, manganese, petroleum, uranium

PEOPLE
Population: 34,672,997 (July 1996 est.)
Age Structure:
0–14 years: 28% (female 4,707,293; male 4,904,380)
15–64 years: 63% (female 10,834,593; male 10,851,004)
65 years and over: 9% (female 1,961,315; male 1,414,412) (July 1996 est.)
Population Growth Rate: 1.1% (1996 est.)
Ethnic Divisions: white 85%, mestizo, Indian, or other nonwhite groups 15%
Religions: nominally Roman Catholic 90% (less than 20% practicing), Protestant 2%, Jewish 2%, other 6%
Languages: Spanish (official), English, Italian, German, French
Labor Force: 10.9 million

GOVERNMENT
Type: Republic
Capital: Buenos Aires

ECONOMY
National Product: GDP—purchasing power parity—$278.5 billion (1995 est.)
National Product Per Capita: $8,100 (1995 est.)
Exports: $20.7 billion (f.o.b., 1995)
Commodities: meat, wheat, corn, oilseed, manufactures
Partners: US 9%, Brazil, Italy, Japan, Netherlands
Imports: $19.5 billion (c.i.f., 1995)
Commodities: machinery and equipment, chemicals, metals, fuels and lubricants, agricultural products
Partners: US 21%, Brazil, Germany, Bolivia, Japan, Italy, Netherlands
Industries: food processing, motor vehicles, consumer durables, textiles, chemicals and petrochemicals, printing, metallurgy, steel

TRANSPORTATION
Railroas: Total of 37,910 km
Highways: Total of 215,578 km
Merchant Marine: Total of 37 ships
Airports: Total of 1,253

COMMUNICATIONS
Telephone System: 2.7 million (1983 est.); 12,000 public telephones; extensive modern system but many families do not have telephones; despite extensive use of microwave radio relay, the telephone system frequently grounds out during rainstorms, even in Buenos Aires

DEFENSE FORCES
Branches: Argentine Army, Navy of the Argentine Republic, Argentine Air Force, National Gendarmerie, Argentine Naval Prefecture (Coast Guard only), National Aeronautical Police Force

ARGENTINA SOURCES

RESEARCH SOURCES

Demographic Data Sources

National Census Bureau
Instituto Nac. De Estadistica y
Censos
Dir. Nac. de Estadisticas de la
Produccion y el Comercio
Julio Roca 609
Buenos Aires
Argentina
Tel: (541) 349 9372

Manufacturing Data Sources

Argentine Industrial Union
(UIA)
Union Industrial Arg.
Av. Alem 1067
Buenos Aires
Argentina
Tel: (541) 311 9499

Car Manufacturers Association
(ADEFA)
M.T. de Alvear 636—5°
Buenos Aires
Argentina
Tel: (541) 312 3483
Fax: (541) 315 2990

Industry & Production
Chamber
Florida 1
Buenos Aires
Argentina
Tel: (541) 331 0813
Fax: (541) 331 9116

Building Industry Chamber
Camera Argentina de la Con-
struccion
Paseo Colon 823
Buenos Aires
Argentina
Tel: (541) 300 1813

Trade Data Sources and Trade Associates

National Office for External
Trade
Direccion Nacional de Com-
ercio Exterior
Buenos Aires
Argentina
Tel: (541) 331 1881
Tel: (541) 331 3758

Argentine Chamber of
Exporters
Camara de Exportadores de la
Republica Argentina
Av. R.S. Pena 740
Buenos Aires
Argentina
Tel: (541) 328 9583
Tel: (541) 328 8658
Tel: (541) 328 5944
Fax: (541) 328 1003

Argentine Chamber of
Importers
Camara de Importadores de la
Republica Argentina
Belgrano 427
Buenos Aires
Argentina
Tel: (541) 342 1101

Baker & McKenzie
Av. L.N. Alem 1110
Buenos Aires
Argentina
Tel: (541) 311 5412

Korsky & Co.
Maipu 42
cpo. 2
Buenos Aires
Argentina
Tel: (541) 342 3161
Tel: (541) 342 6153
Fax: (541) 343 5869

Breuer
25 de Mayo 460
Buenos Aires
Argentina
Tel: (541) 312 5678
Fax: (541) 311 4199

RESEARCH AND CONSULTANCY FIRMS

Basic Market Information
Bureau
SIMA (Servicio de Informacion
del Mercado Arg.)
Bolivar 226 - 4°
Buenos Aires
Argentina
Tel: (541) 393 9953
Tel: (541) 825 3467

Price Waterhouse
Cerrito 268
Buenos Aires

Argentina
Tel: (541) 381 8181
Fax: (541) 383 6339

Horwarth Consulting
Cerrito 146
Buenos Aires
Argentina
Tel: (541) 381 8091
Tel: (541) 381 8093
Fax: (541) 383 0226

ASECOM—Market Analysis
Audits & Surveys Latin
America
Av. Cordoba 1345, 8th Floor
Buenos Aires
Argentina
Tel: (541) 815 1499
Fax: (541) 812 1662

A.C. Nielsen
Rivadavia 620, 5th Floor
Buenos Aires
Argentina
Tel: (541) 334 5410
Fax: (541) 334 7938

Research International
V. del Pino 2458
Buenos Aires
Argentina
Tel: (541) 785 6451
Fax: (541) 785 6467

O'Farrell
Av. de Mayo 645
Buenos Aires
Argentina
Tel: (541) 331 0501
Tel: (541) 331 0502
Fax: (541) 331 1659

Estudio Barreira Delfino
Sulpacha 576, 4th Floor
Buenos Aires
Argentina
Tel: (541) 322 8658
Tel: (541) 326 1550

Brons & Salas
M.T. de Alvear 624
Buenos Aires
Argentina
Tel: (541) 311 9271

Young & Rubicam
Paseo Colon 275
Buenos Aires

Argentina
Tel: (541) 331 8491
Tel: (541) 331 8495
Fax: (541) 331 8023

McCann-Erickson
Tucuman 512
Buenos Aires
Argentina
Tel: (541) 325 7145
Fax: (541) 322 4257

Graffiti/DMBB
Uruguay 1112
Buenos Aires
Argentina
Tel: (541) 815 0533
Fax: (541) 811 1629

Vincit
Maipu 859
Buenos Aires
Argentina
Tel: (541) 314 6201
Fax: (541) 314 7730

GOVERNMENTAL SOURCES

Local IRS (DGI)
Hopolito Yrigoyen 370
Buenos Aires
Argentina
Tel: (541) 347 2000

Industry & Commerce Sec-
retary
Secretaria de Industria y Com-
ercio
Av. J. Roca 651
Buenos Aires
Argentina
Tel: (541) 343 7241
Tel: (541) 343 7269

Market & Price Analysis Office
Direccion de Analisis de Pre-
cios y Evaluacion de
Mercado
Buenos Aires
Argentina
Tel: (541) 349 4046
Tel: (541) 349 4054
Tel: (541) 349 4056
Fax: (541) 349 4064

Dir. de Estadisticas del Com-
ercio Exterior
Buenos Aires
Argentina
Tel: (541) 349 9436

Argentine Chamber of Com-
merce
Camara Arg. de Comercio
Av. L.N. Alem 36
Buenos Aires
Argentina
Tel: (541) 331 8051
Tel: (541) 331 8055
Tel: (541) 342 6371
Fax: (541) 343 9423

American Chamber of Com-
merce
Viamonte 1133 - 8°
Buenos Aires
Argentina
Tel: (541) 371 4500
Fax: (541) 371 8400

Japanese Chamber
Libertad 976
Buenos Aires
Argentina
Tel: (541) 816 1025

Small & Medium Business
Chamber

Camara de la Pequena y Medi-
ana Industria
L.N. Alem 1067
Buenos Aires
Argentina
Tel: (541) 311 0190

US Embassy
Cervino 4320
Buenos Aires
Argentina
Tel: (541) 777 0681
Tel: (541) 777 0197

**BUSINESS DEVELOPMENT
FIRMS AND BROKERS**

Federal Investment Council
Consejo Federal de Inversiones
San Martin 871
Buenos Aires
Argentina
Tel: (541) 313 2034
Tel: (541) 313 2471

Argentine Banks Association
Asociacion de Bancos Argen-
tinos
San Martin 229
Buenos Aires
Argentina
Tel: (541) 394 1836
Tel: (541) 394 1430
Tel: (541) 394 1538
Fax: (541) 394 1998
Fax: (541) 393 9764

Stock Exchange Operators
Camara de Agentes de Bolsa
Sarmiento 299
Buenos Aires
Argentina
Tel: (541) 315 3188

AUSTRALIA

GEOGRAPHY
Area:
Total Area: 7,686,850 sq km
Land Area: 7,617,930 sq km
Comparative Area: slightly smaller than the US
Natural Resources: bauxite, coal, iron ore, copper, tin, silver, uranium, nickel, tungsten, mineral sands, lead, zinc, diamonds, natural gas, petroleum

PEOPLE
Population: 18,260,863 (July 1996 est.)
Age Structure:
0–14 years: 21% (female 1,912,605; male 2,009,915)
15–64 years: 66% (female 5,980,315; male 6,129,285)
65 years and over: 13% (female 1,261,452; male 967,291) (July 1996 est.)
Population Growth Rate: 0.99% (1996 est.)
Ethnic Divisions: Caucasian 95%, Asian 4%, aboriginal and other 1%
Religions: Anglican 26.1%, Roman Catholic 26%, other Christian 24.3%
Languages: English, native languages
Labor Force: 8.63 million (September 1991)

GOVERNMENT
Type: Federal parliamentary state
Capital: Canberra

ECONOMY
National Product: GDP—purchasing power parity—$405.4 billion (1995 est.)
National Product Per Capita: $22,100 (1995 est.)
Exports: $51.57 billion (f.o.b., 1995)
Commodities: coal, gold, meat, wool, alumina, wheat, machinery and transport equipment
Partners: Japan 25%, US 11%, South Korea 6%, NZ 5.7%, UK, Taiwan, Singapore, Hong Kong (1992)
Imports: $57.41 billion (f.o.b., 1995)
Commodities: machinery and transport equipment, computers and office machines, crude oil and petroleum products
Partners: US 23%, Japan 18%, UK 6%, Germany 5.7%, NZ 4% (1992)
Industries: mining, industrial and transportation equipment, food processing, chemicals, steel

TRANSPORTATION
Railroads: Total of 38,563 km
Highways: Total of 810,264 km
Merchant Marine: Total of 76 ships
Airports: Total of 442

COMMUNICATIONS
Telephone System: 8.7 million telephones (1987 est.); good domestic and international service

DEFENSE FORCES
Branches: Australian Army, Royal Australian Navy, Royal Australian Air Force

AUSTRALIA SOURCES

RESEARCH SOURCES

Demographic Data Sources

Year Book Australia
Australian Bureau of Statistics
P.O. Box 10
Belconnen ACT 2616
Australia
Tel: (616) 252 5000
Fax: (616) 251 6009

Trade Data Sources and Trade Associations

Foreign Investment Review
Board
The Treasury Building, Parkes
Place
Parkes ACT 2600
Australia
Tel: (616) 263 3755
Fax: (616) 263 3868

World Trade Centre, Sydney
c/- State Chamber of Commerce (NSW)
Level 12, 83 Clarence Street
Sydney NSW 2000
Australia
Tel: (612) 9350 8100
Fax: (612) 9350 8199

Australian Commodity Statistics
Australian Bureau of Agricultural & Resource Economics
G.P.O. Box 1563
Canberra ACT 2601
Australia
Tel: (616) 272 2000
Fax: (616) 272 2001

Regional Headquarters Group
Dept. of Industry, Science & Tourism
Central Office
Canberra City ACT 2600
Australia
Tel: (616) 213 6000
Fax: (616) 213 7336

Company Data Sources

State Chamber of Commerce
G.P.O. Box 4280
Sydney NSW 2001
Australia

Tel: (612) 9350 8100
Fax: (612) 9350 8199

Business Who's Who—Australian Business Rankings
Riddell Information Services
19 Havilah Street
Chatswood NSW 2067
Australia
Tel: (612) 9935 2700
Fax: (612) 9935 2777

Kompass APN
46 Porter Street
Prahran VIC 3181
Australia
Tel: (613) 9245 7777
Fax: (613) 9245 7848

Dun & Bradstreet
19 Havilah Street
Chatswood NSW 2067
Australia
Tel: (612) 9935 2700
Fax: (612) 9935 2666

RESEARCH AND CONSULTANCY FIRMS

AGB McNair
168 Walker Street
North Sydney NSW 2060
Australia
Tel: (612) 9911 7200
Fax: (612) 9959 4947

Roy Morgan Research Centre
232 Sussex Street
Sydney NSW 2000
Australia
Tel: (612) 9261 8233
Fax: (612) 9261 8512

Frank Small & Associates
(Aust.) Pty. Ltd.
144 Riley Street
East Sydney NSW 2000
Australia
Tel: (612) 9334 4200
Fax: (612) 9331 7973

The MindShifts Group Pty.
Ltd.
Level 2, North Tower
1–5 Railway Street
Chatswood NSW 2067
Australia
Tel: (612) 9411 3900
Fax: (612) 9411 3636

GOVERNMENTAL SOURCES

Australian Bureau of Statistics
G.P.O. Box K881
Perth, Western Australia 6001
Australia
Tel: (619) 360 5140
Fax: (619) 360 5955

Australian Trade Commission
Level 23, 201 Kent Street
Sydney NSW 2000
Australia
Tel: (612) 9390 2000
Fax: (612) 9290 2024

Foreign Investment Review
Board
The Treasury
Canberra ACT 2600
Australia
Tel: (612) 263 3795
Fax: (612) 263 2940

Australian Industrial Property
Organization
Level 6, 189 Kent Street
Sydney NSW 2000
Australia
Tel: (612) 9262 6304
Fax: (612) 9262 6309

Australian Customs Service
477 Pitt Street
Sydney NSW 2000
Australia
Tel: (612) 9213 2000
Fax: (612) 9213 4034

Australian Securities Commission
Level 8, City Centre
55 Market Street
Sydney NSW 2000
Australia
Tel: (612) 9911 2500
Fax: (612) 9911 2550

Australian Stock Exchange
20 Bond Street
Australia Square NSW 2000
Australia
Tel: (612) 9227 0000
Fax: (612) 9227 0885

Dept. of Employment, Education and Training
16–18 Mort Street
Braddon ACT 2601

Australia
Tel: (616) 240 8111
Fax: (616) 240 7735

BUSINESS DEVELOPMENT FIRMS AND BROKERS

Austrade's Investment Australia
Sydney
Australia
Tel: (612) 9390 2712
Fax: (612) 9390 2713

Australian Chamber of Manufactures
7/157 Liverpool Street
Sydney NSW 2000
Australia
Tel: (612) 9372 0444
Fax: (612) 9372 0400

Australian Employers' Federation Ltd.
313 Sussex Street
Sydney NSW 2000
Australia
Tel: (612) 9264 2000
Fax: (612) 9261 1968

Australian Franchise Association Ltd.
G.P.O. Box 512
Brisbane QLD 4001
Australia
Tel: (617) 3221 9444
Fax: (617) 3221 8447

Australian Institute of Company Directors
71 York Street
Sydney NSW 2000
Australia
Tel: (612) 9299 8788
Fax: (612) 9299 1006

Australian Government Trade Agency

Web site: http:// www. austrade.gov.au
Australian Institute of Management Ltd.
181 Fitzroy Street
St. Kilda VIC 3182
Australia
Tel: (613) 9534 8181
Fax: (613) 9534 5050

Australian Marketing Institute
Level 2, 464 St. Kilda Road
Melbourne VIC 3004
Australia
Tel: (613) 9820 8788
Fax: (613) 9820 8650

Business Council of Australia
P.O. Box 7225
Melbourne VIC 3004
Australia
Tel: (613) 9274 7777
Fax: (613) 9274 7744

Committee for Economic Development of Australia
G.P.O. Box 2117T
Melbourne VIC 3001
Australia
Tel: (613) 9662 3544
Fax: (613) 9663 7271

Franchise Association of Australia and New Zealand
Unit 9, 2–6 Hunger Street
Parramatta NSW 2150
Australia
Tel: (612) 9891 4933
Fax: (612) 9891 4474

Franchise Systems Franchising Consultants
P.O. Box 654
South Perth, Western Australia 6951
Australia
Tel: (619) 367 2863

Public Health Association of Australia
G.P.O. Box 2204
Canberra ACT 2601
Australia
Tel: (616) 285 2373
Fax: (616) 282 5438

QED (Australia) Pty. Ltd.
11 Henderson Drive
Kallaroo, Western Australia 6025
Australia
Tel: (619) 401 1299

Retailers Council of Australia
Level 2, 20 York Street
Sydney NSW 2000
Australia
Tel: (612) 9290 3766
Fax: (612) 9262 1464

Small Business Development Corporation
553 Hay Street
Perth, Western Australia 6001
Australia
Tel: (619) 220 0222
Fax: (619) 221 1132
e-mail: sbdc@vianet.net.au
web site: http://www. wa.gov.au/gov/sbdc

Therapeutic Goods Administration
P.O. Box 100
Woden ACT 2606
Australia
Tel: (616) 232 8664
Fax: (616) 232 8659

BAHRAIN

GEOGRAPHY
Area:
Total Area: 620 sq km
Land Area: 620 sq km
Comparative Area: 3.5 times the size of Washington, D.C.
Natural Resources: oil, associated and nonassociated natural gas, fish

PEOPLE
Population: 590,042 (July 1996 est.)
Age Structure:
0–14 years: 31% (female 89,554; male 92,455)
15–64 years: 67% (female 156,556; male 236,048)
65 years and over: 2% (female 7,473; male 7,956) (July 1996 est.)
Population Growth Rate: 2.27% (1996 est.)
Ethnic Divisions: Bahraini 63%, Asian 13%, other Arab 10%, Iranian 8%, other 6%
Religions: Shi'a Muslim 75%, Sunni Muslim 25%
Languages: Arabic, English, Farsi, Urdu
Labor Force: 140,000

GOVERNMENT
Type: Traditional Monarchy
Capital: Manama

ECONOMY
National Product: GDP—purchasing power parity—$7.3 billion (1995 est.)
National Product Per Capita: $12,000 (1995 est.)
Exports: $3.2 billion (f.o.b., 1995 est.)
Commodities: petroleum and petroleum products 80%, aluminum 7%
Partners: India 20%, Japan 14%, Saudi Arabia 7%, US 6%, UAE 5% (1994)
Imports: $3.29 billion (c.i.f., 1995 est.)
Commodities: nonoil 59%, crude oil 41%
Partners: Saudi Arabia 37%, US 12%, UK 6%, Japan 5%, Germany 4% (1994)
Industries: petroleum processing and refining, aluminum smelting, offshore banking, ship repairing

TRANSPORTATION
Railroads: N/A
Highways: Total of 2,671 km
Merchant Marine: Total of 6 ships
Airports: Total of 3

COMMUNICATIONS
Telephone System: 73,552 telephones (1987 est.); modern system; good domestic services and excellent international connections

DEFENSE FORCES
Branches: Ground Force, Navy, Air Force, Air Defense, Coast Guard, Police Force

BAHRAIN SOURCES

RESEARCH AND CONSULTANCY FIRMS

Amer Research
Apt. 23, 2nd Floor
463 Exhibition Road
Manama
Bahrain
Tel: (973) 293 448
Tel: (973) 292 199
Fax: (973) 293 448

Arthur Andersen
P.O. Box 20323
Manama
Bahrain
Tel: (973) 530 400
Fax: (973) 530 321

Coopers & Lybrand / Jawad
Habib & Co.
P.O. Box 30520
Manama
Bahrain
Tel: (973) 530 077
Fax: (973) 530 088

International Consultancy
Center
P.O. Box 11116
Manama

Bahrain
Tel: (973) 716 066
Fax: (973) 712 633

International Information
Technology
P.O. Box 31030
Manama, Sehla
Bahrain
Tel: (973) 404 766
Fax: (973) 404 686

Gulf Business Development
Co.
P.O. Box 31188 Diraz
Manama Centre
Bahrain
Tel: (973) 214 714
Fax: (973) 214 914

GOVERNMENTAL SOURCES

Bahrain Chamber of Commerce & Industry
P.O. Box 248
King Faisal Highway
Manama
Bahrain
Tel: (973) 229 555
Fax: (973) 224 985

Ministry of Commerce
P.O. Box 5479
Manama
Bahrain
Tel: (973) 531 531
Fax: (973) 530 455

Ministry of Finance & National
Economy
P.O. Box 333
Manama
Bahrain
Tel: (973) 530 800
Fax: (973) 532 853

Ministry of Information
P.O. Box 253
Manama
Bahrain
Tel: (973) 781 888
Fax: (973) 534 115

Ministry of Labour & Social
Affairs
P.O. Box 32333
Manama
Bahrain
Tel: (973) 687 800
Fax: (973) 686 954

BELGIUM

GEOGRAPHY
Area:
Total Area: 30,510 sq km
Land Area: 30,230 sq km
Comparative Area: slightly larger than Maryland
Natural Resources: coal, natural gas

PEOPLE
Population: 10,170,241 (July 1996 est.)
Age Structure:
0–14 years: 18% (female 886,632; male 930,919)
15–64 years: 66% (female 3,326,853; male 3,380,105)
65 years and over: 16% (female 981,972; male 663,760) (July 1996 est.)
Population Growth Rate: 0.33% (1996 est.)
Ethnic Divisions: Fleming 55%, Walloon 33%, mixed or other 12%
Religions: Roman Catholic 75%, Protestant or other 25%
Languages: Dutch 56%, French 32%, German 1%, legally bilingual 11% (divided along ethnic lines)
Labor Force: 4.126 million

GOVERNMENT
Type: Constitutional Monarchy
Capital: Brussels

ECONOMY
National Product: GDP—purchasing power parity—$197 billion (1995 est.)
National Product Per Capita: $19,500 (1995 est.)
Exports: $108 billion (f.o.b., 1994) Belgium-Luxembourg Economic Union (BLEU)
Commodities: iron and steel, transportation equipment, tractors, diamonds, petroleum products
Partners: EU 67.2% (Germany 19%), US 5.8%, former Communist countries 1.4% (1994)
Imports: $140 billion (c.i.f., 1994) Belgium-Luxembourg Economic Union
Commodities: fuels, grains, chemicals, foodstuffs
Partners: EU 68% (Germany 22.1%), US 8.8%, former Communist countries 0.8% (1994)
Industries: engineering and metal products, motor vehicle assembly, processed food and beverages, chemicals, basic metals, textiles, glass, petroleum, coal

TRANSPORTATION
Railroads: Total of 3,396 km
Highways: Total of 137,876 km
Merchant Marine: Total of 23 ships
Airports: Total of 42

COMMUNICATIONS
Telephone System: 5.691 million telephones (1992 est.); highly developed technologically advanced, and completely automated domestic and international telephone and telegraph facilities

DEFENSE FORCES
Branches: Army, Navy, Air Force, National Gendarmerie

BELGIUM SOURCES

RESEARCH SOURCES

Demographic Data Sources

Institut de Statisque
20, Voie du Roman Pays
1348 Louvain-la-Neuve
Belgium
Tel: (3210) 47 4314
Fax: (3210) 47 3032

Manufacturing Data Sources

Belgian Standards Institute
Avenue de la Braban onne 29
1000 Brussels
Belgium
Tel: (322) 734 9205
Fax: (322) 733 4264

Confederation Europeene d'Organismes de Controle
(CEOC)
rue de Commerce 20–22
B-1040 Brussels
Belgium
Tel: (322) 511 5065
Fax: (322) 502 5047

Cellule Interfacultaire de Technology Assessment
The University of Namur
Rue Grandgagnage, 21
5000 Namur
Belgium
Tel: (3281) 72 49 61
Fax: (3281) 72 49 67

Trade Data Sources and Trade Associates

Belgian Foreign Trade Office
Boulevard Emile Jacqmain, 162
1210 Brussels
Belgium
Tel: (322) 209 3511
Fax: (322) 217 6123

Office of Quotas and Licenses
(OCCL/CDCV)
Rue de Mot 24/26
1040 Brussels
Belgium
Tel: (322) 233 6111
Fax: (322) 233 8322

World Trade Center Association Brussels A.S.B.L.
162/52 Boulevard Emile Jacqmain
B-1210, Brussels

Belgium
Tel: (322) 219 4400
Fax: (322) 217 2820

Belgian Foreign Trade Board
(BFTB)
Blvd Emile Jacqmain,
162/36
B-1000 Brussels
Belgium
Tel: (322) 206 3511
Fax: (322) 203 1812

International Club of Flanders
Sint-Pietersplein, 11
B-900 Ghent
Belgium
Tel: (329) 222 9668
Fax: (322) 221 7943

Company Data Sources

Hoppenstedt—BNLU
ABC voor Handel en Industrie
C.V.
Konigin Wilhelminalaan 16 -
Postbus 190
NL-2012 JK Haarlem
Netherlands
BECO-Infotrade
Infortrade
A. Grossetlaan 32A
B-1702 Groot-Bygaarden
Belgium
Tel: (322) 466 6480
Fax: (322) 466 6970

Le NCMV
Spastraat 8
1000 Bruxelles
Belgium
Tel: (322) 238 0424
Fax: (322) 230 9354

Banque nationale de Belgique
Bibliotheque scientifique
Boul. De Berlaimont 14
1000 Bruxelles
Belgium
Tel: (322) 221 2410
Fax: (322) 221 3163

Databases

Datastream International, Ltd.
Clos du Parnasse, 1F
1040 Brussels
Belgium
INSEA

Excelsiorlaan 91
B-1930 Zaventem
Belgium
Tel: (322) 720 9806
Fax: (322) 720 8023

RESEARCH AND CONSULTANCY FIRMS

IRIS—International Research
Institute
Rue Kolonel Bourgstraat 28
B-1040 Brussels
Belgium
Tel: (322) 732 6515
Fax: (322) 736 9238

ITC Management Consultants
Sneeuwbeslaan 20
2610 Antwerpen-Wilrijk
Belgium
Tel: (323) 829 2526
Fax: (323) 830 4372

NV Gates Marketing Research
Rue Kolonel Bourgstraat 28
B-1040 Brussels
Belgium
Tel: (322) 736 9030
Fax: (322) 736 9238

PMSI Belgium
Rue De Stalle
63 Bte 4–1180 Bruxelles
Stallestraat 63 Bus
4–1180 Brussels
Belgium
Tel: (322) 332 1757
Fax: (322) 332 1567

Sobemap
Avenue Louise, 250
Boite 103
B-1050 Brussels
Tel: (322) 627 0200
Fax: (322) 627 0201

GOVERNMENTAL SOURCES

Office de la Propriete Industrielle
154, bd E, Jacquemain
1000 Bruxelles
Belgium
Tel: (322) 206 4111
Fax: (322) 206 5750

Ministerie van Economische
Zaken
General Lemanstraat, 60

B-1040 Brussels
Belgium
Tel: (322) 230 99043
Fax: (322) 230 8322

Federal Office for Scientific,
   Technical and Cultural
   Affairs (O.S.T.C.)
rue de la Science 8
B-1000 Brussels
Belgium
Tel: (322) 238 3411
Fax: (322) 230 5912

**BUSINESS DEVELOPMENT
FIRMS AND BROKERS**

DIMARSO-GALLUP Belgium
57 Boulevard Lambermont

1030 Brussels
Belgium
Tel: (322) 215 1930
Fax: (322) 216 1396

Dedicated Research
Avenue des Sept Bonniers 198
1190 Brussels
Belgium
Tel: (322) 344 0088
Fax: (322) 344 3013

OR Belgium S.A.
Avenue Delleur, 8
1170 Brussels
Belgium
Tel: 32/2/343 4780

Economisch Studiebureau voor
   de Provincie Antwerpen
Lange Lozanastraat 223
B-2018 Antwerp
Belgium
Tel: (3223) 240 6800
Fax: (3223) 240 6868

G.O.M Limburg
Kunstlaan 18
B-3500 Hasselt, Belgium
Tel: (32211) 300 100
Fax: (32211) 22 1706

BRAZIL

GEOGRAPHY
Area:
Total Area: 8,511,965 sq km
Land Area: 8,456,510 sq km
Comparative Area: slightly smaller than the US
Natural Resources: bauxite, gold, iron ore, manganese, nickel, phosphates, platinum, tin, uranium, petroleum, hydropower, timber

PEOPLE
Population: 162,661,214 (July 1996 est.)
Age Structure:
0–14 years: 31% (female 24,422,897; male 25,286,278)
15–64 years: 65% (female 53,094,724; male 52,232,435)
65 years and over: 4% (female 4,552,160; male 3,072,720) (July 1996 est.)
Population Growth Rate: 1.16% (1996 est.)
Ethnic Divisions: white (includes Portuguese, German, Italian, Spanish, Polish) 55%, mixed white and African 38%, African 6%, other (includes Japanese, Arab, Amerindian) 1%
Religions: Roman Catholic (nominal) 70%
Languages: Portuguese (official), Spanish, English, French
Labor Force: 57 million (1989 est.)

GOVERNMENT
Type: Federal Republic
Capital: Brasilia

ECONOMY
National Product: GDP—purchasing power parity—$976.8 billion (1995 est.)
National Product Per Capita: $6,100 (1995 est.)
Exports: $46.5 billion (f.o.b., 1995)
Commodities: iron ore, soybean bran, orange juice, footwear, coffee, motor vehicle parts
Partners: EU 27.6%, Latin America 21.8%, US 17.4%, Japan 6.3% (1993)
Imports: $49.7 billion (f.ob., 1995)
Commodities: crude oil, capital goods, chemical products, foodstuffs, coal
Partners: US 23.3%, EU 22.5%, Middle East 13.0%, Latin America 11.8%, Japan 6.5% (1993)
Industries: textiles, shoes, chemicals, cement, lumber, iron ore, tin, steel, aircraft, motor vehicles and parts, other machinery and equipment

TRANSPORTATION
Railroas: Total of 27,418 km
Highways: Total of 1,661,850 km
Merchant Marine: Total of 207 ships
Airports: Total of 2,950

COMMUNICATIONS
Telephone System: 14,426,673 (1992 est.); good working system

DEFENSE FORCES
Branches: Brazilian Army, Brazilian Navy (includes Marines), Brazilian Air Force, Federal Police (paramilitary)

BRAZIL SOURCES

RESEARCH SOURCES

Demographic Data Sources

Instituto Brasileiro de Geografia e Estatistica (IBGE)
Brazilian Geography and Statistics Institute
R. General Cana Barro 706
Rio de Janeiro, RJ 20271–201
Brazil
Tel: (5521) 284 1109
Fax: (5521) 284 1109

Manufacturing Data Sources

Confederacao Nacional das Industrias—CNI
National Industry Confederation
Av Nilo Pecanha 50 sl 2509
Rio de Janeiro, RJ 20044–900
Brazil
Tel: (5521) 534 8000
Fax: (5521) 262 1465

Federacao das Industrias do Estado de Sao Paulo—FIESP
Sao Paulo Industry Federation
Av. Paulista 1313—5 andar
Sao Paulo, SP 01311–923
Brazil
Tel: (5511) 252 4464
Fax: (5511) 252 4633

Federacao das Industria do Rio de Janeiro—FIRJAN
Rio de Janeiro Industry Federation
Rua Graca Aranha 1—10 andar
Rio de Janeiro, RJ 20030–002
Brazil
Tel: (5521) 292 3939
Fax: (5521)226 6705

Trade Data Sources and Trade Associations

American Chamber of Commerce—Sao Paulo
Rua da Paz, 1431
Sao Paulo, SP 04713–001
Brazil
Tel: (5511) 246 9199
Fax: (5511) 246 9080

Associacao Brasileira de Franchising—ABF
Brazilian Franchising Association

Rua da Balsa 559
Sao Paulo, SP 04027–000
Brazil
Tel: (5511) 875 0002
Fax: (5511) 876 6988

Associacao Brasileira de Supermercados—ABRAS
Brazilian Supermarkets Association
Av. Diogenes Ribeiro de Lima, 2872
Sao Paulo, SP 05083–010
Brazil
Tel: (5511) 837 9922
Fax: (5511) 837 9933

Federação do Comércio do Estado de São Paulo
Sao Paulo Commerce Federation
Rua Mituto Misumoto 320
Sao Paulo, SP 01513–010
Brazil
Tel: (5511) 278 6833
Fax: (5511) 278 6833

Company Data Sources

Associacao Brasileira da Industria Quimica e de Produtos Derivados—ABIQUIM
Brazilian Association of Chemical Industries
Rua Santo Antonio, 184 17/18 andar
Sao Paulo, SP 01314–900
Brazil
Tel: (5511) 232 1144
Fax: (5511) 232 0919

Associacão Brasileira da Indústria Eletroeletrônica—ABINEE
Brazilian Electric and Eletronic Industry Association
Av. Paulista 1313—7 andar
Sao Paulo, SP 01311–923
Brazil
Tel: (5511) 251 1577
Fax: (5511) 285 0607

Associacao Brasileira da Industria de Ferramentas—ABF
Brazilian Association of Machine Tools Industry
Av. Paulista, 1313—9 andar
sala 905

Sapo Paulo, SP 01311–923
Brazil
Tel: (5511) 251 5411
Fax: (5511) 251 5192

Associacao Brasileira das Industrias de Alimentacao—ABIA
Brazilian Food Industries Association
Av Brigadeiro Faria Lima
2003 -11 andar cj 11004
Sao Paulo, SP 01451–001
Brazil
Tel: (5511) 816 5733
Fax: (5511) 814 6688

Associaçao Brasileira da Industria de Máquinas e Equipamentos - ABIMAQ
Brazilian Machinery and Equipment Industry Association
Av. Jabaquara, 2925
Sao Paulo, SP 04045–902
Brazil
Tel: (5511) 5582 6311
Fax: (5511) 5582 6312

Associacao Brasileira da Industria de Plastico—ABIPLAST
Brazilian Association of Plastic Industry
Av. Paulista 2439—8 andar
Sao Paulo, SP 011311–936
Brazil
Tel: (5511) 282 8288
Fax: (5511) 282 8042

Associaçao Nacional dos Fabricantes de Veiculos Automotores—ANFAVEA
National Association of the Motor Vehicles Industry
Av. Indianopolis 496
Sao Paulo, SP 04062–000
Brazil
Tel: (5511) 549 4044
Fax: (5511) 549 4044 Ext 225

Databases

Fundação Getulio Vargas—FGV
Praia de Botafogo 190
Rio de Janeiro, RJ 22253–900
Brazil

http:www.fgvrj.br/
conjuntura.htm

Suma Economica
Rua São Manuel, 36
Rio de Janeiro, RJ 22290–010
Brazil
Tel: (5521) 275 9796
Fax: (5521) 295 2292

**RESEARCH AND
CONSULTANCY FIRMS**
Instituto Brasilieiro de Opinião
Pública e Estatística—
IBOPE
R. Uruguaiana 174–10 andar
Rio de Janeiro, RJ 20050–092
Brazil

Tel: (5521) 291 2121
Fax: (5521) 221 3251

Instituto Gallup
Av. Aclimação 225
São Paulo, SP 01531–001
Brazil
Tel: (5511) 279 5333
Fax: (5511) 270 8459

GOVERNMENTAL SOURCES
The Embassy of the Federative
Republic of Brazil
3006 Massachusetts Ave. N.W.
Washington, D.C. 20008
USA
Tel: (202) 745 2700
Fax: (202) 745 2827

Brazilian Consulate New York
Brazilian Government Trade
Bureau
551 Fifth Avenue—Suite 210
New York, NY 10176
USA
Tel: (212) 916 3200
Fax: (212) 573 9406

Ministerio da Relações Exte-
riores
Departamento de Promoção
Comercial
Anexo I—Salas 518 e 528
Brasília, DF 70170–900
Brazil
Tel: (5561) 211 6392
Fax: (5561) 223 2392

CAMBODIA

GEOGRAPHY
Area:
Total Area: 181,040 sq km
Land Area: 176,520 sq km
Comparative Area: slightly smaller than Oklahoma
Natural Resources: timber, gemstones, some iron ore, manganese, phosphates, hydropower potential

PEOPLE
Population: 10,861,218 (July 1996 est.)
Age Structure:
0–14 years: 45% (female 2,432,620; male 2,505,998)
15–64 years: 51% (female 3,007,838; male 2,579,986)
65 years and over: 4% (female 191,017; male 143,759) (July 1996 est.)
Population Growth Rate: 2.77% (1996 est.)
Ethnic Divisions: Khmer 90%, Vietnamese 5%, Chinese 1%, other 4%
Religions: Theravada Buddhism 95%. other 5%
Languages: Khmer (official), French
Labor Force: 2.5 to 3 million

GOVERNMENT
Type: Multiparty Liberal Democracy under a Constitutional Monarchy established in September 1993
Capital: Phnom Penh

ECONOMY
National Product: GDP—purchasing power parity—$7 billion (1995 est.)
National Product Per Capita: $660 (1995 est.)
Exports: $240.7 billion (1995 est.)
Commodities: timber, rubber, soybeans, sesame
Partners: Singapore, Japan, Thailand, Hong Kong, Indonesia, Malaysia
Imports: $630.5 billion (1995 est.)
Commodities: cigarettes, construction materials, petroleum products, machinery, motor vehicles
Partners: Singapore, Vietnam, Japan, Australia, Hong Kong, Indonesia
Industries: rice milling, fishing, wood and wood products, rubber, cement, gem mining

TRANSPORTATION
Railroads: Total of 603 km
Highways: Total of 34,100 km
Merchant Marine: Total of 5 cargo ships
Airports: Total of 14

COMMUNICATIONS
Telephone System: 7,000 telephones (1981 est.); service barely adequate for government requirements and virtually nonexistent for general public

DEFENSE FORCES
Branches: Khmer Royal Armed Forces (KRAF/Royal Cambodian Armed Forces (RCAF)) created in 1993 by the merger of the Cambodian People's Armed Forces and the two noncommunist resistance armies; National Army of Democratic Kampuchea (Khmer Rouge) created as a resistant force

CHILE

GEOGRAPHY
Area:
Total Area: 756,950 sq km
Land Area: 748,800 sq km
Comparative Area: slightly smaller than twice the size of Montana
Natural Resources: copper, timber, iron ore, nitrates, precious metals, molybdenum

PEOPLE
Population: 14,333,258 (July 1996 est.)
Age Structure:
0–14 years: 29% (female 2,041,417; male 2,071,816)
15–64 years: 65% (female 4,651,030; male 4,599,173)
65 years and over: 6% (female 566,803; male 403,019) (July 1996 est.)
Population Growth Rate: 1.24% (1996 est.)
Ethnic Divisions: European and European-Indian 95%, Indian 3%, other 2%
Religions: Roman Catholic 89%, Protestant 11%, Jewish
Languages: Spanish
Labor Force: 4.728 million

GOVERNMENT
Type: Republic
Capital: Santiago

ECONOMY
National Product: GDP—purchasing power parity—$113.2 billion (1995 est.)
National Product Per Capita: $8,000 (1995 est.)
Exports: $15.9 billion (f.o.b., 1995)
Commodities: copper 41%, other metals and minerals 8.7%, wood products 7.1%, fish and fishmeal 9.8%, fruits 8.4% (1991)
Partners: EU 25%, US 15%, Asia 34%, Latin America 20% (1995 est)
Imports: $14.3 billion (f.o.b., 1995 est)
Commodities: capital goods 25.2%, spare parts 24.8%, raw materials 15.4%, petroleum 10%, foodstuffs 5.7%
Partners: EU 18%, US 25%, Asia 16%, Latin America 26% (1995 est.)
Industries: copper, other minerals, foodstuffs, fish processing, iron and steel, wood and wood products, transport equipment, cement, textiles

TRANSPORTATION
Railroads: Total of 6,782 km
Highways: Total of 79,593 km
Merchant Marine: Total of 37 ships
Airports: Total of 344

COMMUNICATIONS
Telephone System: 1.5 million (1994 est.); modern system based on extensive microwave radio relay facilities

DEFENSE FORCES
Branches: Army of the Nation, National Navy (includes Naval Air, Coast Guard, and Marines), Air Force of the Nation, Carabineros of Chile (National Police), Investigations Police

CHILE SOURCES

RESEARCH SOURCES

Demographic Data Sources

INE—Instituto Nacional De
Eestadisticas
Avda. Bulines 418
Santiago
Chili
Tel: (562) 699 1441
Fax: (562) 671 2169

Trade Data Sources and Trade Associates

Banco Central De Chili
Agustinas 1180, Casilla 967
Santiago
Chili
Tel: (562) 670 2000
Fax: (562) 698 4847

Camara De Comercia De San-
tiago
Santa Lucia 302
Piso 3, Casilla 1297
Santiago
Chili
Tel/Fax: (562) 632 1232

Centro De Documentacion
Direccion De Promocion De
Exprotaciones

Prochile
P.O. Box 14087, Correo 21
Santiago
Chili
Tel: (562) 696 0043
Fax: (562) 696 0639

Company Data Sources

Gui Silber
Directorio De Instituciones De
Chili
Silver Editores Limitada
Perez Valenzuela, 1551, Of. 35
Providencia, Santiago
Chili
Tel: (562) 235 0661
Tel/Fax: (562) 235 0662

Asesoria Y Comercio Internaci-
onal Ltda.
Nueva Amunategui 30, Of. 701
Santiago
Chili
Tel: (562) 696 4677

Dahlma Comercio Exterior
Paseo Las Palmas 2230
Santiago
Chili

Nivel 4 Local C-51
Tel: (562) 233 5925
Fax: (562) 251 5736

R. Rodriguez & Asociados S.A.
Estado 359 Piso 8
Santiago
Chili
Tel: (562) 337 145
Fax: (562) 337 135

Databases

GOVERNMENTAL SOURCES

Congreso Nacional—Biblioteca
Compania 1175 Piso 2
Santiago
Chili
Tel/Fax: (562) 230 065
Tel/Fax: (562) 230 995

Banco Central De Chili—Bibli-
oteca
Agustinas 1180, Casilla 967
Santiago
Chili
Tel: (562) 670 2000
Fax: (562) 698 4847

CHINA

GEOGRAPHY
Area:
Total Area: 9,596,960 sq km
Land Area: 9,326,410 sq km
Comparative Area: slightly larger than the US
Natural Resources: coal, iron ore, petroleum, mercury, tin, tungsten, antimony, manganese, molybdenum, vanadium, magnetite, aluminum, lead, zinc, uranium, hydropower potential (world's largest)

PEOPLE
Population: 1,210,004,956 (July 1996 est.)
Age Structure:
0–14 years: 26% (female 151,601,650; male 167,448,148)
15–64 years: 67% (female 393,913,510; male 421,455,418)
65 years and over: 7% (female 40,529,821; male 35,056,409) (July 1996 est.)
Population Growth Rate: 0.98% (1996 est.)
Ethnic Divisions: Han Chinese 91.9%, Zhuang, Uygur, Hui, Yi, Tibetan, Miao, Manchu, Mongol, Buyi, Korean, and other nationalities 8.1%.
Religions: Daoism (Taoism), Buddhism, Muslim 2%–3%, Christian 1% (est.)
Languages: Standard Chinese or Mandarin (Putonghua, based on the Beihing dialect), Yue (Cantonese), Wu (Shanghaiese), Mingei (Fuzhou), Minnan
(Hokkien-Taiwanese), Xiang, Gan, Hakka dialects, minority languages (see Ethnic divisions entry)
Labor Force: 583.6 million (1991)

GOVERNMENT
Type: Communist state
Capital: Beijing

ECONOMY
National Product: GDP—purchasing power parity—$3.5 trillion (1995 estimate as extrapolated from World Bank estimate with use of official Chinese growth figures for 1993–95; the result may overstate China's GDP by as much as 25%)
National Product Per Capita: $2,900 (1995 est.)
Exports: $148.8 billion (f.o.b., 1995)
Commodities: garments, textiles, footwear, toys, machinery and equipment (1994)
Partners: Hong Kong, Japan, US, Germany, South Korea, Singapore (1994)
Imports: $132.1 billion (c.i.f. 1995)
Commodities: industrial machinery, textiles, plastics, telecommunications equipment, steel bars, aircraft (1994)
Partners: Japan, Taiwan, US, Hong Kong, South Korea, Germany (1994)
Industries: iron and steel, coal, machine building, armaments, textiles and apparel, petroleum, cement, chemical fertilizers, consumer durables, food processing, autos, consumer electronics, telecommunications

TRANSPORTATION
Railroads: Total of 58,399 km
Highways: Total of 1.029 km
Merchant Marine: Total of 1,700 ships
Airports: Total of 204

COMMUNICATIONS
Telephone System: 20 million (1994 est.); domestic and international services are increasingly available for private use; unevenly distributed domestic system serves principal cities, industrial centers, and most townships

DEFENSE FORCES
Branches: People's Liberation Army (PLA), which includes the Ground Forces, Navy (includes Marines and Naval Aviation), Air Force, Second Artillery Corps (the strategic missile force), People's Armed Police (internal security troops, nominally subordinate to Ministry of Public Security, but included by the Chinese as part of the "armed forces" and considered to be an adjunct to the PLA in wartime)

371

CHINA SOURCES

RESEARCH SOURCES

Demographic Data Sources

Beijing Statistical Bureau
2 Huaibaishu Street
Beijing 100053
PRC
Tel: (8610) 630 11133 ext. 2518
Fax: (8610) 630 11166

Tianjin Statistical Bureau
244 Nanjing Road
Heping District
Tianjin 300020
PRC
Tel: (8622) 734 6694

Statistical Department of Shiji-
azhuang in Hebei Province
12 Changan East Road
Shijiazhuang City
Hebei Province 050031
PRC
Tel: (86311) 505 2932
Fax: (86311) 505 4079

Shanxi Statistical Bureau
21 Donghuoxiaohe
Taiyuan
Shanxi Province 03002
PRC
Tel: (86351) 304 6580

Inner Mongolia Statistical
Bureau
1 Xinhua Street
Huhehaote
Inner Mongolia 010055
PRC
Tel: (86471) 696 2858
Tel: (86471) 696 3826

Shenyang Statistical Bureau in
Liaoning Province
260 Shifu Road
Shenyand
Liaoning Province 110013
PRC
Tel: (8624) 272 2024
Tel: (8624) 272 3214

Jilin Statistical Bureau
32 Xinmin Road
Changchun City
Jilin Province 130000
PRC
Tel: (86431) 892 4333
Tel: (86431) 892 9105

Heilongjiang Statistical Bureau
202 Zhongshan Road
Harbin City
Heilongjiang Province 150001
PRC
Tel: (86451) 634 0850

Shanghai Statistical Bureau
1008 Changzhi Road
Shanghai 200000
PRC
Tel: (8621) 654 55100

Jiangsu Statistical Bureau
70 Beijing West Road
Nanjing
Jiangsu Province 210013
PRC
Tel: (8625) 663 4366
Tel: (8625) 663 1764
Fax: (8625) 330 7297

Zhejiang Statistical Bureau
Xingzheng Center,
  Building 2
Hangzhou
Zhejiang Province 310025
PRC
Tel: (86571) 705 2743
Tel: (86571) 705 2789

Anhui Statistical Bureau
3 Shucheng Road
Hefei City
Anhui Province 310025
PRC
Tel: (86551) 265 3382
Tel: (86551) 265 7155

Fujian Statistical Bureau
Guping Road
Fuzhou City
Fujian Province 350000
PRC
Tel: (86591) 782 1946

Jiangxi Statistical Bureau
Nanchang Governmental Com-
  pound
Jiangxi Province 330000
PRC
Tel: (86791) 626 6113

Shandong Statistical Bureau
Jinan City
Shandong Province 250000
PRC
Tel: (86531) 692 3951
Fax: (86531) 691 5414

Henan Statistical Bureau
Weier Road
Zhengzhou City
Henan Province 450003
PRC
Tel: (86371) 595 1571

Hubei Statistical Bureau
13–2 Shuiguohu Dongyi Road
Wuhan City
Hubei Province 430071
PRC
Tel: (8627) 782 2112

Hunan Statistical Bureau
Wuyizhong Road
Changsha
Hunan Province 410011
PRC
Tel: (86731) 221 4131
Tel: (86731) 221 2567

Guangdong Statistical Bureau
129 Qianjin Road
Guangzhou
Guangdong Province 510220
PRC
Tel: (8620) 440 0113

Guangxi Statistical Bureau
Xinhu Road
Nanning City
Guangxi 530022
PRC
Tel: (86771) 585 4356

Haikou Statistical Bureau
Longkun North Road
Haikou City
Hainan Province 570005
PRC
Tel: (86898) 679 7637
Tel: (86898) 679 7640
Fax: (86898) 671 6440

Sichuan Statistical Bureau
3 Xiyu Street
Chengdu City
Sichuan Province 610041
PRC
Tel: (8628) 664 3683
Tel: (8628) 664 4143

Guizhou Statistical Bureau
53 Yananzhong Road
Guiyang City
Guizhou Province 550004
PRC
Tel: (86851) 582 3504

Tel: (86851) 582 2862
Fax: (86851) 582 3543

Yunnan Statistical Bureau
155 Dongfeng East Road
Kunming City
Yunnan Province 650051
PRC
Tel: (86871) 313 8324
Tel: (86871) 313 5510

Gansu Statistical Bureau
Gaolan Road
Lanzhou City
Gansu Province 730000
PRC
Tel: (86931) 888 6466

Qinghai Statistical Bureau
West Street of Xining City
Qinghai Province 810000
PRC
Tel: (86971) 823 9490
Tel: (86971) 823 7615

Ningxia Statistical Bureau
Jiefang West Street
Yinchuan City
Ningxia Region 750001
PRC
Tel: (86951) 504 337

Xinjiang Statistical Bureau
Wulumuqi City
Xinjiang Region 830000
PRC
Tel: (86991) 286 1421
Tel: (86991) 282 7010

Manufacturing Data Sources

China Software Industrial Association
31 Xue Yuan Road
Beijing 100083
PRC
Tel: (8610) 620 12233

China Jade Industrial Association
64 Xisi Funei Street
Beijing 100812
PRC
Tel: (8610) 665 85613 ext. 821
Fax: (8610) 660 24523

China Casting Industrial Association
277 Wangfujing Street
Beijing 100740

PRC
Tel: (8610) 651 26679
Fax: (8610) 651 26675

China Hydro-Electrical Enterprise Management Association
2nd Lane of Bai Guang Road, Building 1
Beijing 100761
PRC
Tel: (8610) 632 73322 ext. 4323

China Commercial Enterprise Administration Association
45 Fuxingmennei Street
Beijing 100081
PRC
Tel: (8610) 660 38583 ext. 2557

China Building Material Enterprise Administration Association
State Building Material Bureau
Baiwnzhuang
Beijing 100831
PRC
Tel: (8610) 683 11144 ext. 851

China Industrial Economy Association
9 Huangchenggen South Street
Beijing 100032
PRC
Tel: (8610) 660 34061
Tel: (8610) 660 21306

China Advertisement Association
8 Sanlihe East Road
Beijing 100820
PRC
Tel: (8610) 685 11918
Tel: (8610) 685 11925

China Internal-Combustion Engine Industrial Association
26 Yuetian South Street
Beijing 100825
PRC
Tel: (8610) 680 32003

China Chemical Reagent Industrial Association
Dongjiao Huagong Road
Beijing 100022
PRC
Tel: (8610) 677 13678

China Measuring and Testing Industrial Association
27 Xisanhuan North Road
Beijing 100081
PRC
Tel: (8610) 684 19657

China Milk Association
56 Xixi Zhuanta Lane
Beijing 100034
PRC
Tel: (8610) 660 18095

China Machine Tool Industrial Association
26 Yuantian South Street
Beijing 100825
PRC
Tel: (8610) 685 23767
Tel: (8610) 680 31649

Fax: (8610) 680 32517

China Machinery Enterprise Administration Association
26 Yuantian South Street
Beijing 100825
PRC
Tel: (8610) 680 33551

China General Machinery Accessory Industrial Association
16 Fuxingmenwai Street
Beijing 100045
PRC
Tel: (8610) 632 73924

China Enterprise Administration Association
17 Zizhuyuan South Road
Beijing 100044
PRC
Tel: (8610) 684 16622

China Transportation Association
31 East Changan Street, Building 2
Beijing 100005
PRC
Tel: (8610) 651 25071
Tel: (8610) 652 40875

China Agricultural Machinery Industrial Association
26 Yuetan South Road
Beijing 100825
PRC
Tel: (8610) 680 34356

China Antiseptic Association
5 Xinei Dongguang Lane
Beijing 100035
PRC
Tel: (8610) 660 20517

Testing Association of China
Import and Export Com-
modity
12 Jianwai Street
Beijing 100022
PRC
Tel: (8610) 650 65990
Fax: (8610) 650 65990

China Textile Machinery Indus-
trial Association
14 7th Lane of Hujialou Xili
Beijing 100026
PRC
Tel: (8610) 650 02953
Tel: (8610) 650 60251
Fax: (8610) 650 60250

China Air Conditioning Indus-
trial Association
2 Beifengwuo Fuxingmenwai
Beijing 100038
PRC
Tel: (8610) 632 66379

China Quality Administration
Association
12 Zhongjingji Road
Beijing 100032
PRC
Tel: (8610) 660 37131

China Real Estate Association
Ministry of Construction, Bai-
wanzhuang
Beijing 100835
PRC
Tel: (8610) 683 93906

China Machinery Association
of Construction Industry
10 Changwai Luliqiao South
District
Beijing 100039
PRC
Tel: (8610) 632 62915

China Building Material Associ-
ation
7 Fengtailu Qingta East District
Beijing 100039
PRC
Tel: (8610) 682 15814

China Urban Gas Association
30 Middle Road of Dong-
sanhuan
Beijing 100020
PRC
Tel: (8610) 650 26213

China Standardization Associ-
ation
2 Yuetan Beixiao Street
Beijing 100837
PRC
Tel: (8610) 683 58392

China Bearing Industrial Asso-
ciation
16 Fuwai Street
Beijing 100045
PRC
Tel: (8610) 632 73925

China Scientific Technology
Association
86 Weigongcun
Beijing 100081
PRC
Tel: (8610) 683 18877
Tel: (8610) 683 17924

China Cosmetic Industrial
Association
101 Laochenggen
Beijing 100038
PRC

China Food Industrial Associ-
ation
5 Taiping Qiao Dongli
Beijing 100073
PRC
Tel: (8610) 632 69354

China Survey and Drawing
Instrument Association
9 Sanlihe Road
Beijing 100830
PRC
Tel: (8610) 683 22214

China Adhesive Industrial
Association
20 Xinyuan Street, Suite A
Beijing 100027
PRC
Tel: (8610) 646 64618

China Casting and Forging
Association
277 Wangfujing Street

Beijing 100740
PRC
Tel: (8610) 651 26679

China Coal Processing and Uti-
lization Association
13 Xueyuan Road
Beijing 100086
PRC
Tel: (8610) 620 24012

China Matrix Industrial Associ-
ation
16 Fuxingmenwai Street
Beijing 100045
PRC
Tel: (8610) 632 73923

China Scale and Balance Indus-
trial Association
14 Dongxie Street
Beijing 100032
PRC
Tel: (8610) 660 31522

China Construction Welding
Association
Fangshan District
Beijing 102500
PRC
Tel: (8610) 693 52481

China Starch Industrial Associ-
ation
5 Middle Road of Heping
Shijiazhuang City
Hebei Province 050011
PRC
Tel: (86311) 505 2820

Chemical Industry Association
of China International Trade
Promotion Committee
7th District of Hepingli, Build-
ing 16
Beijing 100031
PRC
Tel: (8610) 642 25384
Tel: (8610) 642 29317

Electronic Industry Association
of China International Trade
Promotion Committee
46 Sanlihe Road
Beijing 100823
PRC
Tel: (8610) 632 94976
Tel: (8610) 632 94978
Fax: (8610) 685 13867

China Health Care and Nutrition Association
17 Changzhi Road
Taiyuan City
Shaanxi Province 030012
PRC
Tel: (86351) 404 8684

China General Ventilation Equipment Industrial Association
36 Yunfeng North Street,
Shenyang
Liaoning Province 110021
PRC
Tel: (8624) 580 1590

China Rubber Industrial Association
9 Beisan East Road, Shenyang
Liaoning Province 110025
PRC
Tel: (8624) 587 6270

China Machinery Welding Industrial Association
65 Hexing Road
Harbin City
Helongjiang Province 150080
PRC
Tel: (86451) 634 0850

China Fashionable Color Association
35 Yongjia Road
Shanghai 200020
PRC
Tel: (8621) 647 10214

China Industrial Boiler Association
84 Shiqiao Road
Hangzhou City
Zhejiang Province 310000
PRC
Tel: (86571) 814 3062

China General Equipment Components Association
Santan Lane, Building 4
Zhejiang Province 310005
PRC
Tel: (86571) 806 6418

China Household Appliance Association
202 Zhuque Street
Xian City
Shaanxi Province 710061

PRC
Tel: (8629) 526 8264

China Electrical Transformation Equipment Association
29 Daqing Road
Xian City
Shaanxi Province 710082
PRC
Tel: (8629) 426 1137

Trade Data Sources and Trade Associates

China Statistical Information and Consultancy
Service Center, State Statistical Bureau
75. Yuctan Nanjie
Sanlihe
Beijing 100826
PRC
Tel: (8610) 685 29225
Tel: (8610) 685 29223
Fax: (8610) 685 71739
e-mail: csicc@public3.bta.net.cn

Company Data Sources

The China Phone Book Company Ltd.
24th Floor, Citicorp Center,
18 Whitfield Road, Hong Kong
G.P.O. Box 11581, Hong Kong
Tel: (852) 250 84448
Fax: (852) 250 31526

Shanghai Telephone Directory Corp.
333 Jiang Xi North Road
Shanghai 200085
China
Tel: (8621) 632 40554
Fax: (8621) 632 48118

China Yellow Pages Directories Company
4/F., Stanhope House, 734 King's Road
North Point, Hong Kong
Tel: (852) 280 76868
Fax: (852) 250 32601

Dun & Bradstreet Information Services
3rd Floor, Champion Building
363 Chang Ping Road
Shanghai 200041

China
Tel: (8621) 621 88103
Fax: (8621) 621 88183

Databases

Suns Information Services
Beijing Fuxing Rd. No 15, 10038
China Science and Technology Information Institute
Beijing
China
Tel: (8610) 685 76949
Tel: (8610) 685 15544
Tel: (8610) 685 13389
Fax: (8610) 685 76949

Kompass (China) International Information Service Co., Ltd.
28 DongHouXiang
Andingmenwai
Beijing 10001
China
Tel: (8610) 642 48799
Tel: (8610) 642 48801
Fax: (8610) 642 11497
e-mail: kompass@mail.chinapro.net.cn

RESEARCH AND CONSULTANCY FIRMS

East Net (China) Limited, Beijing Office
24 Jianguomenwai Street, Suite 2–1502
Beijing 100022
PRC
Tel: (8610) 651 59328
Fax: (8610) 651 58916

China Guoxin Information Corporation
26 Yuetan South Street
Beijing 100825
PRC
Tel: (8610) 685 96067
Fax: (8610) 685 96062

Infomedia of Institute of Scientific and Technological Information of China
15 Fuxing Road
Beijing 100038
PRC
Tel: (8610) 685 11818
Fax: (8610) 685 11838

SINO TIME MARKETING
Room 304 Dingheng Office
Building No 5
Changwa Street Haidian Dis-
trict
Beijing 100081
Tel: (8610) 684 59096
Fax: (8610) 684 59121

ISIS Research
Beijing Representative Office
773, Office Tower, Poly Plaza
Ltd.
14, Dongzhimen Nandajie
Dong Cheng District 100027
PRC
Tel: (8610) 650 11317
Beijing 100080
PRC
Tel: (8610) 625 68693
Fax: (8610) 625 66871

Consulting Department of
China Guoxin Information
Corporation
26 Yuetan South Street
Beijing 100825
PRC
Tel: (8610) 685 66065
Fax: (8610) 685 96062

Beijing Jingfang Consultants
Corporation
8 Beichen East Road
Beijing 100101
PRC
Tel: (8610) 649 16233
Fax: (8610) 649 16168

Nomura-Citic Economic Con-
sultants Co., Ltd.
1705 Beijing Fortune Building,
5 Dongsanhuan North Road
Beijing 100004
PRC
Tel: (8610) 650 87470
Fax: (8610) 650 16666

SINOTRUST Business Risk
Management Ltd.
Credit Reporting Services,
makes Company Credit
Reports
31 Beisanhuan Zhong Lu
Beijing 100088
PRC
Tel: (8610) 623 83786
Tel: (8610) 623 83789

Fax: (8610) 623 83790
Fax: (8610) 623 83791

Beijing Jinyu Consulting Co.,
Ltd.
Beijing University's East
Resource Building
Jinyu Report Weekly
Beijing P.O. Box 8763
Beijing 100080
PRC
Tel: (8610) 626 24017
Tel: (8610) 625 36794
Tel: (8610) 626 26258
Fax: (8610) 626 25956
e-mail: jinxinda@public3.-
bta.net.cn

Information Consulting Center
of China Scientific Academy
Zhongguancun, Building 18
Beijing 100080
PRC
Tel: (8610) 640 12233

China Road Engineering Con-
sulting Corporation
33 Dongsi Qianchaomian Lane
Beijing 100010
PRC
Tel: (8610) 651 22387

Consulting Corporation of
Bank of China
17 Xijiaomin Lane
Beijing 100031
PRC
Tel: (8610) 683 13388 ext.
11015
Fax: (8610) 683 22344

China Utilities Construction
Engineering Consultants
Corporation
65 Ande Road
Beijing 100011
PRC
Tel: (8610) 640 13674
Fax: (8610) 640 13828

China Hydro-Power Electricity
Construction Engineering
Consulting Corporation
Liupukang
Beijing 100011
PRC
Tel: (8610) 640 14192
Fax: (8610) 640 14192

China Investment Consultants
Corporation
9 Fuxing Road
Beijing 100038
PRC
Tel: (8610) 685 13834
Tel: (8610) 685 14894
Fax: (8610) 680 14353

China International Technol-
ogy and Economy Coopera-
tion Consulting Corporation
1 Fuxingmenwai Street
Beijing 100860
PRC
Tel: (8610) 685 11156
Fax: (8610) 680 11370

China International Economic
Consulting Corporation
2/F CITIC Building, 19 Jiangu-
omenwai Streeet
Beijing 100004
PRC
Tel: (8610) 650 03422

China Foreign Trade Con-
sulting Corporation
13–12 Guanghua Road
Beijing 100020
PRC
Tel: (8610) 650 52255
Fax: (8610) 650 51571

China Petroleum Chemistry
Consulting Corporation
3 Xitucheng Road, North
Building
Beijing 100088
PRC
Tel: (8610) 620 32211
Fax: (8610) 620 29616

China Automobile Industry
Engineering Consulting Cor-
poration
16 Fuxingmenwai Street
Beijing 100860
PRC
Tel: (8610) 632 66594
Fax: (8610) 632 67058

East Net (China) Ltd. China
Office
24 Jianguomenwai Street, Suite
2–1502
Beijing 100022
PRC

Tel: (8610) 651 59328
Fax: (8610) 651 58916
e-mail: eastnet@public.bta.-
net.cn

Scientific and Technological
Consulting Corporation of
China Space Industry
1 Binhe Road
Hepingli
Beijing 100031
PRC
Tel: (8610) 642 13714
Tel: (8610) 683 72655
Fax: (8610) 642 13714

Trade Consulting Company of
China National Technical
Import and Export Corpo-
ration
55 Chegongzhuang Beili, Zhan-
lan Road
Beijing 100044
PRC
Tel: (8610) 683 55723
Tel: (8610) 683 55847

Tianjin Electrical Technology
Information Center
1 Beiyingmen
Hongqiao District
Tianjin 300123
PRC
Tel: (8622) 331 5484

Tianjin International Engi-
neering Consulting Corpo-
ration
3 Xikanglu Biyunli
Heping District
Tianjin 300201
PRC
Tel: (8622) 328 6768
Fax: (8622) 328 6769

Tianjin International Scientific
and Technological Con-
sulting Corporation
25 Friendship Road
Hexi District
Tianjin 300201
PRC
Tel: (8622) 235 8222
Fax: (8622) 235 9329

Tianjin Huaxia Construction
Budget Consulting Corpo-
ration

118 Chongqing Road
Hexi District
Tianjin 300050
PRC
Tel: (8622) 331 5456

Tianjin International Economic
Cooperation Consulting
Corporation
333 Nanjing Road
Tianjin 300073
PRC
Tel: (8622) 737 3646

Tianjin Urban Construction
Engineering Consulting Cor-
poration
16 Lechangli
Heping District
Tianjin 300070
PRC
Tel: (8622) 337 4597

Hebei International Economic
and Technological Con-
sulting Corporation
54 Qingyuan Street
Shijiazhuang
Hebei Province 050011
PRC
Tel: (86311) 602 1740

Hebei Engineering Consulting
Corporation
52 Zinqiang Road
Shijiazhuang
Hebei Province 050051
PRC
Tel: (86311) 702 7755

Information Exchange Center
of Shanxi Province
18 Wenyuan Lane
Taiyuan City
Shanxi Province 030001
PRC
Tel: (86311) 202 9103

Scientific and Technological
Exploration Information
Center of Shanxi Province
8 Yingze West Street
Taiyuan City
Shanxi Province 030024
PRC
Tel: (86351) 606 3497

Shanxi Engineering Consulting
Corporation

388 Yingze Street
Taiyuan City
Shanxi 030001
PRC
Tel: (86351) 403 1551

Shanxi Economic and Techno-
logical Exploration Con-
sulting Corporation
41 Shuixiguang Street
Tiayuan City
Shanxi Province 030002
PRC
Tel: (86351) 404 2801

Huhehaote Textile Technologi-
cal Consulting Corporation
Hulun South Road
Huhehaote
Inner Mongolia 010020
PRC
Tel: (86471) 696 5404

Liaoning International Engi-
neering Consulting Center
103 Shisanwei Road
Shenhe District
Shenyang 110025
PRC
Tel: (8624) 282 3997
Fax: (8624) 282 4018

Liaoning Real Estate Con-
sulting Centre
1–1 Xinxin Guang, Ning-
shan East Road
Shenyang 110032
PRC
Tel: (8624) 622 7576

Liaoning Foreign Economic
and Trade Information
Center
2 Zhongshan Guangchang,
Dalian
Liaoning 116001
PRC
Tel: (860411) 263 5309
Tel: (860411) 264 4581

Liaoning Electronic Informa-
tion Center
4 Liuzhou Sreet, Heping Dis-
trict
Shenyang
Liaoning 110002
PRC
Tel: (8624) 282 5077

Shenyang International Economic and Technological Consulting Corporation
92 Shashan Street, Heping District
Shenyang
Liaoning 110002
PRC
Tel: (8624) 270 8041

Liaoning Trade Information Corporation
165 Huigong Street
Shenyang City
Liaoning 110013
PRC
Tel: (8624) 272 2323
Tel: (8624) 274 0569

Shanghai Knitting Technology Consulting Center
24 Zhongshan Dongyi Road, Suite 327
Shanghai 200002
PRC
Tel: (8621) 632 31969

Shanghai Industrial Development Consulting Center
69 Jiujiang Road
Shanghai 200002
PRC
Tel: (8621) 632 88860
Tel: (8624) 632 38116
Fax: (8621) 632 32166

Shanghai Automobile Technological Consulting Corporation
665 Weihai Road, Suite 40
Shanghai 200041
PRC
Tel: (8621) 625 68686

Shanghai Chemical Industrial Consulting Corporation
126 Xingzha Road, Suite 406
Shanghai 200003
PRC
Tel: (8621) 632 75706
Tel: (8621) 632 76969

Information Center of Guangdong Petroleum Refinery Institute
48 Shamian Street
Guangzhou
Guangdong Province 510130

PRC
Tel: (8620) 440 0113

Guangzhou Economic Development Consulting Corporation
49 Xiatang West Road
Guangzhou
Guangdong Province 510000
PRC
Tel: (8620) 332 7789
Tel: (8620) 331 8689

Zhuhai South Engineering Consulting Corporation
Shihua West Road
Zhuhai
Guangdong Province 519015
PRC
Tel: (86756) 333 2397

Guangdong International Engineering Consulting Corporation
405 Dezhen North Road
Guangzhou
Guangdong Province 510055
PRC
Tel: (8620) 333 0577

Guangdong Machinery Engineering Consulting Corporation
143 Wanfu Road
Guangzhou
Guangdong Province 510110
PRC
Tel: (8620) 332 4515

Guangdong Food Industrial Information Corporation
85 Binjiang East Road
Guangzhou
Guangdong Province 510000
PRC
Tel: (8620) 443 2149

Shenzhen Telecommunication Information Center
30 Shenanzhong Road
Shenzhen
Guangdong Province 518042
PRC
Tel: (86755) 336 0961
Fax : (86755) 335 0221

Shantou Construction Engineering Consulting Corporation

29 Shilouyuan, Jinyuan District
Shantou
Guangdong Province 515041
PRC
Tel: (86754) 832 7492

Shenzhen Liyuan Water-Supply Statistical and Consulting Corporation
Shennanzhong Road, Hongling Building
Futian District, Shenzhen City
Guangdong Province 515041
PRC
Tel: (86755) 227 2045

Shenzhen Zhongshen International Economic Consulting Corporation
13 Phenox Street
Shenzhen
Guangdong Province 550003
PRC
Tel: (86851) 550 3255
Fax: (86251) 554 1106

Shenzhen Engineering Consulting Corporation
Shennanzhong Road
Shenzhen
Guangdong Province 518000
PRC
Tel: (86755) 224 0640
Tel: (86755) 224 0613

China Architecture Designing Consulting Corporation—Shenzhen Branch
Haiyunge, Haibin Garden, Shekou District
Shenzhen
Guangdong Province 518000
PRC
Tel: (86755) 667 3768

GOVERNMENTAL SOURCES

1997 Customs Tariffs of China
Beijing CDS Information Consulting Co. Ltd.
6/F. China Daily Center, 15 Huixindongjie
Chaoyang District
Beijing 100029
China
Tel: (8610) 649 18210
Tel: (8610) 649 40199
Fax: (8610) 649 18211

e-mail: CDs@public3.bta.-
net.cn

China Statistical Yearbook 1996
People's Republic of China Year
Book
N.C.N. LIMITED
2/F., Xinhua News Agency
Building,
5 Sharp Street West
Wanchai
Hong Kong
Tel: (852) 283 39001
Fax: (852) 283 81177

China Patent Office
Xueyuan Road
Beijing 100088
PRC
Tel: (8610) 620 19307
Tel: (8610) 620 19570
Fax: (8610) 620 1903

Ministry of Foreign Affairs
225, Chaonei Street
Beijing 100701
China
Tel: (8610) 651 35566
Tel: (8610) 651 35980
Fax: (8610) 652 55110

Ministry of Foreign Trade and
Economic Cooperation
2, Dongchangan Street
Beijing 100731
China
Tel: (8610) 651 98114
Tel: (8610) 651 98203
Fax: (8610) 651 29568

General Administration of
Customs
6, Jiangguomennei Street
Beijing 100730
PRC
Tel: (8610) 651 94114
Tel: (8610) 651 95215
Fax: (8610) 651 95170
Fax: (8610) 651 26020

State Administration for the
Inspection of Import and
Export Commodities
15, Fangcaodixi Street, Chaoy-
ang District
Beijing 100020
PRC
Tel: (8610) 650 07744

Tel: (8610) 650 04042
Fax: (8610) 650 02387

The Administration of Animals
and Plants Quarantine of
China
11, Nongzhanguannanli
Beijing 100026
PRC
Tel: (8610) 659 36560
Tel: (8610) 650 25087
Fax: (8610) 650 25273

Peoples Bank of China
32, Changfang Street
Beijing 100800
PRC
Tel: (8610) 660 15522
Tel: (8610) 660 16710
Fax: (8610) 650 16724

State Administration of For-
eign Exchange Control
8, Beichendong Road
Beijing 100101
PRC
Tel: (8610) 649 15738
Fax: (8610) 649 14783

State Planning Commision
38, Yuetannan Street, Beijing
100824
PRC
Tel: (8610) 685 01240
Tel: (8610) 685 02114
Fax: (8610) 685 01920

State Economic and Trade
Commision
26, Xuanwumenxi Street
Beijing 100053
PRC
Tel: (8610) 639 45531
Fax: (8610) 630 45326

State Administration for Indus-
try and Commerce
8, Sanlihedong Road
Beijing 100820
PRC
Tel: (8610) 685 22771
Fax: (8610) 685 70848

State Administration of Taxation
68, Zaoinqian Street
Beijing 100053
PRC

Tel: (8610) 635 43388
Fax: (8610) 632 69664

National Tourism Adminis-
tration
A9, Jiangoumennei Street
Beijing 100740
PRC
Tel: (8610) 651 38866
Fax: (8610) 651 22096

Civil Aviation Admistration of
China
155, Dongsixi Street
Beijing 100710
PRC
Tel: (8610) 640 18328
Tel: (8610) 640 12233
Fax: (8610) 640 30986

Ministry of Public Security
Administrative Bureau for
Exit and Entry
14, Dongchangan Street
Beijing 100741
PRC
Tel: (8610) 651 21176
Tel: (8610) 651 22831
Tel: (8610) 651 21476
Fax: (8610) 651 22779
Fax: (8610) 652 41596

Embassy of the United States of
America
U.S. Department of Com-
merce, The Commercial
Service
No. 3 Xiu Shui Bei Jie
Beijing 100600
PRC
Tel: (8610) 653 26925
Fax: (8610) 653 23297
http://www.redfish.com/
USEmbassy-China/fcs/
fcs.htm

U.S. Consulates in China
http://www.redfish.com/
USEmbassy-China/
consulmap.htm

Offices of Organizations of the
UN System
Chancery 2, Dongqijie, San-
litun
Beijing
PRC

Tels: (8610) 653 23730 through
(8610) 653 23739

Food and Agriculture Organi-
zation of the UN (FAO)
Chancery: 4-2-151
Jianguomenwai
Beijing
PRC
Tel: (8610) 653 22835
Tel: (8610) 653 22836
Tel: (8610) 653 22837
Tel: (8610) 653 21345

UN Childrens Fund (UNICEF)
Chancery: 12, Sanlitun
Beijing
PRC
Tels: (8610) 653 23131 through
(8610) 653 23138

World Health Organization
(WHO)
Chancery: 9-2-151. Tayuan
Diplomatic
Compound, 1, Xindong Road
Beijing
PRC
Tel: (8610) 653 25633
Tel: (8610) 653 25634
Fax: (8610) 653 22359

UN Educational, Scientific and
Cultural Organization
(UNESCO)
Chancery: 5-153
Jianguomenwai
Beijing
PRC
Tel: (8610) 653 21725
Tel: (8610) 653 22828
Tel: (8610) 653 26469
Fax: (8610) 653 24854

International Labour Organiza-
tion (ILO)
Chancery: 1-11-2, Tayuan
Office Building
Tels: (8610) 653 25091
Tels: (8610) 653 25092
Tels: (8610) 653 25093

World Bank Resident Mission
in China (RMC)
Chancery: Bldg 5, Diaoyutai
State
Guesthouse, 2, Fucheng Road

Tel: (8610) 685 12227
Fax: (8610) 685 24140

UNIDO Center for Interna-
tional Industrial Coopera-
tion, Beijing
Chancery: 5-1-41, Tayuan Dip-
lomatic
Apartment, 1, Xindong Road
Beijing
PRC
Tels: (8610) 653 26140 through
(8610) 653 26143
Fax: (8610) 653 26145

International Monetary Fund
Chancery: 11/F, Hongkong-
Macao
Center
Beijing
PRC
Tel: (8610) 650 12551
Fax: (8610) 650 11565

International Finance Corpo-
ration
Chancery: 37/F, Jingguang
Center,
Hujjalou
Beijing
PRC
Tel: (8610) 650 15171
Tel: (8610) 650 15172
Fax: (8610) 650 15176

**DEVELOPMENT FIRMS
AND BROKERS**

China Daily
No. 15 Huixin Dongjie, Chaoy-
ang District
Beijing 100029
PRC
Tel: (8610) 649 24488
Fax: (8610) 649 18377

North American Edition:
China Daily Distribution Corp.
One World Trade Center, Suite
3369
New York, NY 10048
USA
Tel: (212) 488 9677
Fax: (212) 488 9493

China Daily also has a Web
Page with search facility:
http://www.chinadaily.com

Far Eastern Economic Review
25/F, Citicorp Centre, 18 Whit-
field Road
Causeway Bay
Hong Kong
Tel: (852) 250 84300
Fax: (852) 250 31537

Window Publisher:
Asian Regional Projects Ltd.
Unit A-2, 22/F, Chaiwan Indus-
trial Centre
20 Lee Chung Street
Chai Wan
Hong Kong
Tel: (862) 255 66242
Fax: (862) 288 93144

Marathon Communications
Group
2001 North Second Street
Wausau, Wisconsin 54401
USA
Tel: (715) 845 4231
Fax: (715) 845 9276

The China Business Review
1818 North Street, NW Suite
200
Washington, DC 20036–5559
USA
Tel: (202) 429 0340
Fax: (202) 833 9027
Fax: (202) 775 2476

China Economic Review
(monthly)
The China International Trade
Journal
Alan Charles Publishing, 27
Wilfred Street
London, SW1E 6PR
United Kingdom
Tel: (44171) 834 7676
Fax: (44171) 973 0076

China Council for Promotion
of International Trade
CCPIT Building, No. 1
Fu Xing Men Wai Street
Beijing 100860
PRC
Tel: (8610) 685
13344(operator)
Cabel: COMTRADE BEIJING
Telex: 22315 CCPIT CN
Fax: (8610) 685 11370

Web Page: http://
www.ccpit.com/

CCPIT—China Council for
the Promotion of International Trade
Representative Office in U.S.A.
4301 Connecticut Avenue,
N.W.
Suite 136
Washington, DC 20008
USA
Tel: (202) 244 3244
Fax: (202) 244 0478
Email: ccpitweb@public.-
bta.net.cn

Information Department of
Tianjin Foreign Economic
and Trading Committee
279 Jiefang South Road
Tianjin 300042
PRC
Tel: (8622) 331 0431
Fax: (8622) 331 7342

Tianjin Foreign Economic and
Trading Committee
Chongqing Road
Tianjin 300050
PRC
Tel: (8622) 330 6551
Tel: (8622) 331 4828

China International Trade Promotion Council—Hebei
Branch
Shijiazhuang City
Hebei Province 050000
PRC
Tel: (86311) 704 5932

China International Trade Promotion Council—Shanxi
Branch
388 Yingzhe Street
Taiyuan City
Shaxi Province 030001
PRC
Tel: (86351) 404 0594

China International Trade Promotion Council—Liaoning
Branch
56 Beiling Street
Shenyang City
Liaoning Province 110032
PRC

Tel: (8624) 686 4774
Tel: (8624) 689 923

China International Trade Promotion Council—Harbin
Branch
281 Daxin Street
Harbin City
Heilongjiang Province 150020
PRC
Tel: (86451) 468 1700
Tel: (86451) 468 1758

China International Trade Promotion Council—Shanghai
Branch
55 Loushanguan Road
Shanghai 200335
PRC
Tel: (8621) 627 50700

China International Trade Promotion Council—Jiangsu
Province Branch
29 Beijing East Road
Nanjing
Jiangsu Province 210008
PRC
Tel: (8625) 771 3240
Tel: (8625) 771 3560

China International Trade Promotion Council—Zhejiang
Branch
470 Yanan Road
Hangzhou City
Zhejiang Province 310006
PRC
Tel: (86571) 515 0017
Tel: (86571) 515 0098

China International Trade Promotion Council—Anhui
Branch
135 Hongxing Road
Hefei City
Anhui Province 230001
PRC
Tel: (86551) 267 5626

China International Trade Promotion Council—
Fujian Branch
Hualin road
Fuzhou City
Fujiang Province 350000
PRC
Tel: (86591) 784 1878

China International Trade Promotion Council—Jiangxi
Branch
60 Zhanqian Road
Nanchang
Jianxi 330002
PRC
Tel: (86791) 621 7029

China International Trade Promotion Council—Shandong
Province
187 Jinger Road
Jinan City
Shandong Province 250001
PRC
Tel: (86531) 693 0924

China International Trade Promotion Council—Hubei
Branch
8 Jianghan North Road
Wuhan
Hubei Province 430022
PRC
Tel: (8627) 577 5177
Tel: (8627) 579 7573

China International Trade Promotion Council—Hunan
Branch
4 Wuyi East Road
Changsha
Hunan Province 510250
PRC
Tel: (86731) 442 9419
Tel: (86731) 228 96998

China International Trade Promotion Council—Guangdong Branch
829 Huayuan Building
Guangzhou
Guangdong Province 510000
PRC
Tel: (8620) 334 8056
Tel: (8620) 778 7068

China International Trade Promotion Council—Nanning
Branch
Jiangbin Road
Nanning City
Guangxi 530012
PRC
Tel: (86771) 280 6552

China International Trade Promotion Council—Sichuan Branch
Chenghua Street
Chengdu City
Sichuan Province 610081
PRC
Tel: (8628) 333 1406
Tel: (8628) 332 6884

China International Trade Promotion Council—Guizhou Branch
21 Beijing Road
Guiyang City
Guizhou Province 550004
PRC
Tel: (86851) 682 7109
Tel: (86851) 682 1225

China International Trade Promotional Council—Yunnan Branch
576 Beijing Road
Kunming City
Yunnan Province 650041
PRC
Tel: (86871) 313 4706
Tel: (86871) 314 0323

China International Trade Promotion Council—Shaanxi Branch
Xicheng Compound
Xian City
Shaanxi Province 710004
PRC
Tel: (8629) 729 1983
Tel: (8629) 729 2767

China International Trade Promotion Council—Gansu Branch
Dingxi Road
Lanzhou City
Gansu Province 730000
PRC
Tel: (86931) 888 6466

China International Trade Promotion Council—Ningxia Branch
Jiefang West Street
Yinchan City
Ningxia Region 750001
PRC
Tel: (86951) 504 3377

China International Trade Promotion Council—Xinjiang Branch
Wulumuqi City
Xinjiang Region 830000
PRC
Tel: (86991) 286 1902
Tel: (86991) 286 0456

Trade Promotion Office of Inner Mongolia
Zhongshan West Road
Huhehoute City
Inner Mongolia 010020
PRC
Tel: (86471) 696 5404

Hong Kong Trade Development Center Beijing Branch Office
Bright China Chang An Building Tower 2, Rm. 917–918
7 Jianguomen Nei Avenue
Dong Cheng District
Beijing 100005
PRC
Tel: (8610) 651 01700
Fax: (8610) 651 01760
Web Page: http://www.tdc.org.hk/

China Chamber of Commerce for Import and Export of Machinery and Electronic Products
95, Beiheyan Street
Beijing 100006
PRC
Tel: (8610) 651 25114
Tel: (8610) 651 36677
Fax: (8610) 651 25112
Fax: (8610) 652 33830

China Chamber of Commerce for Import and Export of Foodstuffs, Native Produce and Animal By-Products
95, Beiheyan Street
Beijing 100006
PRC
Tel: (8610) 651 32567
Tel: (8610) 651 36677
Fax: (8610) 651 39064

China Chamber of Commerce for Import and Export of Textile

A33, Dongdan Santiao
Beijing 100005
PRC
Tel: (8610) 652 31707
Fax: (8610) 651 36202

China Chamber of Commerce for Import and Export of Light Industrial Products & Arts & Crafts
11, Xinghua Road
Hepingli
Beijing 100013
PRC
Tel: (8610) 642 04150
Fax: (8610) 642 04154

China Chamber of Commerce of Metals, Minerals & Chemicals Import and Export
5/F, Langang Building, A1, Nanshoupokou
Guanganmemwai
Beijing 100055
PRC
Tel: (8610) 634 88942
Fax: (8610) 634 88940

China Chamber of Commerce of Medicines & Health Products Import and Export
11/F, 12, Jianguomenwai Street
Beijing 100022
PRC
Tel: (8610) 650 62352
Fax: (8610) 650 62353

China International Contractors Association
28, Donghouxiang
Andingmenwai
Beijing 100710
PRC
Tel: (8610) 642 11159
Tel: (8610) 642 16661
Fax: (8610) 650 13959

China Association of Enterprises with Foreign Investment
8/F, Part A, Poly Plaza, 14 Dongzhimennan Street
Beijing 100027
PRC
Tel: (8610) 650 01188
Fax: (8610) 650 13959

WEB PAGE ADDRESSES

http://www.aweto.com/china/
The Complete Reference to
China/Chinese-Related Web
Sites

http://www.chinavista.com/
hyper-c/hyper-c.html
The Ultimate China Search
Tool

http://www.wp.com/EASTNET
Business resources and business opportunities

http://www.new-century-
co.com/
Century Co., a California,
USA-based international
trade company
World-wide web site—Marco
Polo

http://www.yahoo.com/
Regional/Countries/China/
Business/Directories/
Business China Websites in
Yahoo

http://www.feer.com/
The Far Eastern Economic
Review

http://coombs.anu.edu.au/
WWWVLAsian/China.html
Australian National University's index of China-related
topics

http://iconovex.com/
WEBANCHOR/DEMOS/
GATT.HTM
GATT/WTO issues: Iconovex
Corp. / 1994 Uruguay
Round Agreements, includ-
ing the World Trade Organi-
zation Agreement

http://www.rand.org/
RAND, Los Angeles-based,
China-related publications

http://www.worldbank.org/
The World Bank

http://www.amcham.-
org.hk/
The American Chamber of
Commerce (AmCham) in
Hong Kong's website

http://www.redfish.com/
BRENT_CONSULTING/
Brent's China Entertainment
Network (CEN)

e-mail: jhendryx@doc.gov
The U.S. Department of Commerce—To receive the China
Commercial Daily Brief,
send message with your
return e-mail address in the
text of the message, and you
will automatically be added
to the mailing list.

COLOMBIA

GEOGRAPHY
Area:
Total Area: 1,138,910 sq km
Land Area: 1,038,700 sq km
Comparative Area: slightly less than three times the size of Montana
Natural Resources: petroleum, natural gas, coal, iron ore, nickel, gold, copper, emeralds

PEOPLE
Population: 36,813,161 (July 1996 est.)
Age Structure:
0–14 years: 32% (female 5,806,450; male 5,948,599)
15–64 years: 64% (female 11,890,875; male 11,496,931)
65 years and over: 4% (female 928,518; male 741,788) (July 1996 est.)
Population Growth Rate: 1.66% (1996 est.)
Ethnic Divisions: mestizo 58%, white 20%, mulatto 14%, black 4%, mixed black-Indian 3%, Indian 1%
Religions: Roman Catholic 95%
Languages: Spanish
Labor Force: 12 million (1990)

GOVERNMENT
Type: Republic; executive branch dominates government structure
Capital: Bogota

ECONOMY
National Product: GDP—purchasing power parity—$192.5 billion (1995 est.)
National Product Per Capita: $5,300 (1995 est.)
Exports: $10.5 billion (f.o.b., 1995 est.)
Commodities: petroleum, coffee, coal, bananas, fresh cut flowers
Partners: US 39%, EC 25.7%, Japan 2.9%, Venezuela 8.5% (1992)
Imports: $13.5 billion (c.i.f., 1995)
Commodities: industrial equipment, transportation equipment, consumer goods, chemicals, paper products
Partners: US 36%, EC 18%, Brazil 4%, Venezuela 6.5%, Japan 8.7% (1992)
Industries: textiles, food processing, oil, clothing and footwear, beverages, chemicals, cement, gold, coal, emeralds

TRANSPORTATION
Railroads: Total of 3,386 km
Highways: Total of 107,200 km
Merchant Marine: Total of 19 ships
Airports: Total of 989

COMMUNICATIONS
Telephone System: 1.89 million telephones (1986 est.); modern system in many respects

DEFENSE FORCES
Branches: Army (Ejercito Nacional), Navy (Armada Nacional, includes Marines and Coast Guard), Air Force (Fuerza Aerea Colombiana), National Police (Policia Nacional)

COLOMBIA SOURCES

RESEARCH SOURCES

Demographic Data Sources

DANE (National Administrative Department of Statistics)
A. Eldorado CAN
Bogotá
Colombia
Tel: (571) 222 1100
Tel: (571) 222 3298
Tel: (571) 222 3035

Trade Data Sources and Trade Associates

Cámara de Comercio Colombo-Americana
Transv. 19 # 122-63
Bogotá
Colombia
Tel: (571) 215 8716
Fax: (571) 215 8514

Cámara de Comercio Colombo-Británica
Avda 39 # 13-62
Bogotá
Colombia
Tel: (571) 285 2929
Fax: (571) 338 2813

Cámara de Comercio Colombo-Europea
Calle 129A # 10-14
Bogotá
Colombia
Tel: (571) 627 0082
Fax: (571) 258 7539

Cámara de Comercio Colombo-Mexicana
Calle 72 # 9-55 Of. 702
Bogotá
Colombia
Tel: (571) 354 3306
Fax: (571) 211 1879

Cámara de Comercio Colombo Suiza
Cra 7 # 33-81 Piso 2
Bogotá
Colombia
Tel: (571) 288 5479
Fax: (571) 218 5459

Cámara de Comercio Colombo-Venezolana
Cra 20 # 82-77

Bogotá
Colombia
Tel: (571) 610 8269
Fax: (571) 218 9064

Columbian Institute of Foreign Trade—Incomex
Edificio Centro de Comercio International
Calle 28 # 13-15 P1 L1 Ps 2 to 5
Bogotá
Colombia
Tel: (571) 281 2200
Fax: (571) 281 2560

Fedesarrollo
Calle 78 #9-91
Bogotá
Colombia
Tel: (571) 312 5300

Federación Nacional de Comerciantes
Cra 4 # 19-85 Piso 7
Bogotá
Colombia
Tel: (571) 286 0600
Fax: (571) 282 7573

Proexport
Edificio de Comercio Internacional
Cl 28 # 13-15 PS 1-35–36
Bogotá
Colombia
Tel: (571) 241 2066
Fax: (571) 282 8130
Fax: (571) 282 8230

Company Data Sources

Byington Colombia S.A.
Cra 7A # 69-99
Bogotá
Colombia
Tel: (571) 310 0200
Fax (571) 345 6636

Confederación Colombiana de Cámaras de Comercio
Cra 13 # 27-47 Of. 502
Bogotá
Colombia
Tel: (571) 288 1200
Fax: (571) 288 4228

RESEARCH AND CONSULTANCY FIRMS

Centro Nacional de Consultoria
Diagonal 34 # 5-27
Bogotá
Colombia
Tel: (571) 288 3100
Tel: (571) 287 2670
E-mail: cconsul@impsat.net.co

AC Nielson de Colombia S.A.
Calle 80 # 5-81
Bogotá
Colombia
Tel: (571) 211 9100
Tel: (571) 211 8894

Yankelovich Acevedo y Asociados
Avda 39. # 14-32
Bogotá
Colombia
Tel: (571) 288 7027
Tel: (571) 288 7575
E-mail: Yankelo3@openway.com.co

Econometria
Calle 94 # 13-59 Piso 5
Bogotá
Colombia
Tel: (571) 623 7717
Tel: (571) 623 7514

Booz-Allen & Hamilton de Colombia Ltda
Cra 12 # 79-43 Piso 4
Bogotá
Colombia
Tel: (571) 313 0060
Tel: (571) 313 0093

Andersen Consulting
Cra 7 # 74-09 Piso 8
Bogotá
Colombia
Tel: (571) 345 3300
Tel: (571) 313 0508

Universidad de los Andes / CEDE
Centro de Estudios de Desarrollo Económico
Cra 1 # 18A-11
Bogotá
Colombia

Tel: (571) 341 2240
Tel: (571) 281 5771

GOVERNMENTAL SOURCES

Chamber of Commerce of
    Bogota
Cra. 9 # 16-2
Aparlado Aereo 29824
Bogotá
Colombia
Tel: (571) 334 7900
Tel: (571) 334 7799
Fax: (517) 284 7735
Calle 94 #9-84
Tel: (571) 621 7093
Calle 116 Cra. 15
Tel: (571) 215 1489

National Planning
Calle 26 No. 13-19 17th Floor
Bogotá
Colombia
Tel: (571) 336 3415

Ministry of Foreign Relations
Calle 10 # 5-51
Bogotá
Colombia
Tel: (571) 282 7811
Tel: (571) 287 6800
Fax: (571) 341 677

FONADE—Fondo Financiero
    de Proyectos de Desarrollo
Calle 26 # 13-19 Pisos 1 al 20
Bogotá
Colombia
Tel: (571) 282 9400
Tel: (571) 282 6018

Departamento Nacional de
    Planeación

Calle 26 # 13-19 Piso 1 al 19
Bogotá
Colombia
Tel: (571) 336 1600
Tel: (571) 281 3348

**BUSINESS DEVELOPMENT
FIRMS AND BROKERS**

Banco de Comercio Exterior.
    Bancoldex
Cl 28 # 13-15 P 38-42
Bogotá
Colombia
Tel: (571) 341 0677
Tel: (9800) 15300
Fax: (571) 284 0056
Fax: (571) 282 5071

Banco de República
Estudios Económicos
Cra 7 #14-78
Bogotá
Colombia
Tel: (571) 342 1035
Fax: (571) 281 8531
http: www.banrep.gov.co

Finca Raiz Abril Cia. Ltda.
Av 19 # 16-21 P8
Bogotá
Colombia
Tel: (571) 281 7291

Finca Taiz Hernando Duran y
    Cia.
Cr 28 # 11-65 L 356
Bogotá
Colombia
Tel: (571) 201 7913

Finca Raiz Las Palmas Ltda.
Bogotá Cl 68 # 21-10 L202

Colombia
Tel: (571) 217 2919

Finca Raiz Pulido y Cia. Ltda.
Calle 18x # 20-40 Of. 201
Bogotá
Colombia
Tel: (571) 272 5089

Finca Raiz Urbanismo Ltda.
Calle 100 # 19-61 Of. 402
Bogotá
Colombia
Tel: (571) 635 3681

Finca Raiz Zulizni y Asociados
    Ltda.
Cl 77 # 16-38 Ap 404
Bogotá
Colombia
Tel: (571) 256 7887

Luque Carulla y Asociados S.A.
Diagonal 127A # 17-54 Of. 603
Bogotá
Colombia
Tel: (571) 615 2300
Tel: (571) 615 6261

Moralco Consultores Geren-
    ciales
Cra # 72-67
Bogotá
Colombia
Tel: (571) 313 3832
Tel: (571) 313 3824

CZECH REPUBLIC

GEOGRAPHY
Area:
Total Area: 78,703 sq km
Land Area: 78,645 sq km
Comparative Area: slightly smaller than South Carolina
Natural Resources: hard coal, soft coal, kaolin, clay, graphite

PEOPLE
Population: 10,432,774 (1995 est.)
Age Structure:
0–14 years: 19% (female 981,918; male 1,030,003)
15–64 years: 68% (female 3,529,411; male 3,530,112)
65 years and over: 13% (female 848,599; male 512,731) (July 1995 est.)
Population Growth Rate: 0.26% (1995 est.)
Ethnic Divisions: Czech 94.4%, Slovak 3%, Polish 0.6%, German 0.5%, Gypsy 0.3%, Hungarian 0.2%, other 1%
Religions: atheist 39.8%, Roman Catholic 39.2%, Protestant 4.6%, Orthodox 3%, other 13.4%
Languages: Czech, Slovak
Labor Force: 5.389 million (1990)

GOVERNMENT
Type: Parliamentary Democracy
Capital: Prague

ECONOMY
National Product: GDP—purchasing power parity—$76.5 billion (1994 est.)
National Product Per Capita: $7,350 (1994 est.)
Exports: $13.4 billion (f.o.b., 1994 est.)
Commodities: manufactured goods, machinery and transport equipment, chemicals, fuels, minerals, metals, agricultural products (January–November 1994)
Partners: Germany 28.7%, Slovakia 15.5%, Austria 7.9%, Italy 6.4%, France 3.2%, Russia 3.2%, Poland 3.1%, UK 2.9%, Netherlands 2.4%, Hungary 2.2%, US 2.1%, Belgium 1.3% (January–June 1994)
Imports: $13.3 billion (f.o.b., 1994 est.)
Commodities: machinery and transport equipment, manufactured goods, chemicals, fuels and lubricants, raw materials, agricultural products (January–November 1994)
Partners: Germany 24.1%, Slovakia 15.6%, Russia 9.8%, Austria 7.6%, Italy 4.9%, France 3.6%, US 3.2%, Netherlands 2.9%, UK 2.8%, Poland 2.7%, Switzerland 2.2%, Belgium 2.0% (January–June 1994)
Industries: fuels, ferrous metallurgy, machinery and equipment, coal, motor vehicles, glass, armaments

TRANSPORTATION
Railroads: Total of 9,434 km
Highways: Total of 55,890 km
Merchant Marine: Total of 14 ships
Airports: Total of 116

COMMUNICATIONS
Telephone System: NA

DEFENSE FORCES
Branches: Army, Air and Air Defense Forces, Civil Defense, Railroad Units

CZECH REPUBLIC SOURCES

RESEARCH SOURCES

Demographic Data Sources

Czech Statistical Office
Sokolovska 142
186 04 Praha 8
Czech Republic
Tel: (4202) 6604 1111
Fax: (4202) 6631 1243

Manufacturing Data Sources

Confederation of Industry of
the Czech Republic
Mikulandska 7
113 61 Praha 1
Czech Republic
Tel: (4202) 2491 5679
Fax: (4202) 2491 5253

Automotive Industry Association
Opletalova 29
110 00 Praha 1
Czech Republic
Tel: (4202) 8590 0505
Fax: (4202) 261 501

Confederation of Manufacturers and Suppliers of Engineering Technology
Politickych veznu 11
113 42 Praha 1
Czech Republic
Tel: (4202) 2421 1284
Fax: (4202) 2421 4963

Association of Plastics Processing Companies of the CR
Mikulandska 7
113 61 Praha 1
Czech Republic
Tel: (4202) 299 251
Fax: (4202) 297 896

Confederation of Chemical Industry of the CR
Kodanska 46
100 10 Praha 10
Czech Republic
Tel: (4202) 6715 4131
Fax: (4202) 6715 4130

Association of Glass and Ceramic Industries of the CR
Mikulandska 7
113 61 Praha 1
Czech Republic
Tel: (4202) 2491 5679
Fax: (4202) 297 896

Association of Textile-Clothing-Leather Products Manufacturers of the CR
nam. Hrdin (4202) u 3 budova Centrotex
140 61 Praha 4
Czech Republic
Tel: (4202) 6115 2873
Fax: (4202) 6115 2874

Trade Data Sources and Trade Associates

Ministry of Trade and Industry
Na Frantisku 32
110 15 Praha 1
Czech Republic
Tel: (4202) 2485 1111
Fax: (4202) 2481 1089

Czech-German Chamber of Trade and Industry
Masarykovo nabrezi 30
110 00 Praha 1
Czech Republic
Tel: (4202) 2980 51
Fax: (4202) 2491 3827

Company Data Sources

Association (4202) of Czech Enterpreneurs
Skretova 6
120 00 Praha 2
Czech Republic
Tel: (4202) 2421 5373
Fax: (4202) 2421 0434

Association of Suppliers of Investment Assemblies
Pocernicka 96
108 03 Praha 10
Czech Republic
Tel: (4202) 6702 1111
Fax: (4202) 77 41 24

Czech-Moravian Electrotechnical Association
Pobrezni 46
186 00 Praha 8
Czech Republic
Tel: (4202) 2421 8648
Fax: (4202) 2421 8648

Databases

Resources
Stepanska 15
120 00 Praha 2
Czech Republic
Tel: (4202) 299 205
Fax: (4202) 298 024

Inform Katalog
Sumavska 31
612 54 Brno
Czech Republic
Tel: (4205) 4121 1428
Fax: (4205) 4121 3658
http://www.inform.cz

Agroregister
Agrodat
Dlouha tr. 13
116 78 Praha 1
Czech Republic
Tel: (4202) 2315 106
Fax: (4202) 2323 349

Edit
Drtinova 2
150 00 Praha 5
Czech Republic
Tel: (4202) 5710 6111
Fax: (4202) 5468 11

RESEARCH AND CONSULTANCY FIRMS

Czech Agency for Foreign Investment (CzechInvest)
Politickych veznu 20
112 49 Praha 1
Czech Republic
Tel: (4202) 2422 1504
Fax: (4202) 2422 1804
http://www.czechinvest.com

Society of Science and Technology Parks
Novotneho lavka 5
116 68 Praha 1
Czech Republic
Tel: (4202) 2108 2275
Fax: (4202) 2108 2276

Association of Marketing Agencies
28. rijna 19
112 79 Praha 1
Czech Republic
Tel: (4202) 2419 5481
Fax: (4202) 2419 5349

Czech Managers Association
Podolska 50
147 40 Praha 4
Mikulandska 7
113 61 Praha 1
Czech Republic
Tel: (4202) 6121 14 111
Fax: (4202) 6122 5560

Chamber of Auditors of the CR
Opletalova 55/57
111 21 Praha 1
Czech Republic
Tel: (4202) 2421 2670
Fax: (4202) 2421 1905

Chamber of Tax Advisors of
the CR
Kozi 4
657 21 Brno
Czech Republic
Tel: (4202) 4232 1306
Fax: (4202) 4221 0328

Czech Chamber of Solicitors
Narodni 16
111 00 Praha 1
Czech Republic
Tel: (4202) 2491 3606
Fax: (4202) 2491 0162

GOVERNMENTAL SOURCES

Office of the Government of
the Czech Republic
Nabrezi Eduarda Benese 4
118 01 Praha
Czech Republic
Tel: (4202) 2400 2111
Fax: (4202) 2481 0231

Ministry of Finance
Letenská 15
118 10 Praha 1
Czech Republic
Tel: (4202) 2454 1111
Fax: (4202) 2454 2788

National Property Fund
Rasinovo nabrezi 42
128 00 Praha 2
Czech Republic
Tel: (4202) 2491 1907
Fax: (4202) 2491 4388

General Customs Office
Budejovicka 7
140 96 Praha 4
Czech Republic
Tel: (4202) 6133 1111
Fax: (4202) 6133 2100

Center of External Economic
Relations-Infocenter
Politickych veznu 20
112 49 Praha 1
Czech Republic
Tel: (4202) 2406 2424
Fax: (4202) 2406 2862

National Information Center of
the Czech Republic (NIS)
Havelkova 22
130 00 Praha 3
Czech Republic
Tel: (4202) 2422 1624
Fax: (4202) 2423 1488
e-mail: nlmraz@dec.nis.cz

American Chamber of Com-
merce
Mala Stupartska 7
110 00 Praha 1
Czech Republic
Tel: (4202) 2481 4280
Fax: (4202) 2481 3067

Canadian-Czech Chamber of
Commerce
Celetna 19
116 22 Praha 1
Czech Republic
Tel: (4202) 2321 247
Fax: (4202) 2321 247

The Netherlanden Chamber of
Commerce
Belohradska 110
120 00 Praha 2
Czech Republic
Tel: (4202) 6273 220
Fax: (4202) 6270 474

Swedish-Czech Chamber
Stepanska 54
110 00 Praha 1
Czech Republic
Tel: (4202) 2421 3318
Fax: (4202) 2421 3026

Arabic-Czech Chamber of
Commerce
Legerova 42
120 00 Praha 2
Czech Republic
Tel: (4202) 2979 55
Fax: (4202) 2979 54

Economic Chamber of the
Czech Republic
Argentinska 38
170 05 Praha 7
Czech Republic
Tel: (4202) 6679 4899
Fax: (4202) 87 53 68

Chamber of Agriculture of the
CR
Blaniska 3
772 00 Olomouc

Czech Republic
Tel: (42068) 5228 530
Fax: (42068) 523 0670

**BUSINESS DEVELOPMENT
FIRMS AND BROKERS**

Czech National Bank
Na Prikope 28
110 03 Praha 1
Czech Republic
Tel: (4202) 2441 2061
Fax: (4202) 2441 2179

Association of Real Property
Bureaus
Na Chodovci 2880/3
141 00 Praha 4
Czech Republic
Tel: (4202) 764 622
Fax: (4202) 762 953

Banking Association
Vodickova 30
111 21 Praha 1
Czech Republic
Tel: (4202) 2421 5679
Fax: (4202) 2422 5956

Czech Association of Insurance
Companies
Na Porici 12
115 30 Praha 1
Czech Republic
Tel: (4202) 2487 5611
Fax: (4202) 2487 5612

Association of Czech Insurance
Brokers
Voctarova 3/2145
180 00 Praha 8
Czech Republic
Tel: (4202) 6833 568

Czech Stock Exchange
Rybna 14
111 00 Praha 1
Czech Republic
Tel: (4202) 2183 2116
Fax: (4202) 2183 3031

Association of Security and
Stock Brokers
Na Pankraci 11
140 00 Praha 4
Czech Republic
Tel: (4202) 421 829

DENMARK

GEOGRAPHY
Area:
Total Area: 43,070 sq km
Land Area: 42,370 sq km
Comparative Area: slightly more than twice the size of Massachusetts
Natural Resources: petroleum, natural gas, fish, salt, limestone

PEOPLE
Population: 5,249,632 (July 1996 est.)
Age Structure:
0–14 years: 17% (female 446,907; male 469,672)
15–64 years: 67% (female 1,738,870; male 1,789,552)
65 years and over: 16% (female 474,235; male 330,396) (July 1996 est.)
Population Growth Rate: 0.38% (1996 est.)
Ethnic Divisions: Scandinavian, Eskimo, Faroese, German
Religions: Evangelical Lutheran 91%, other Protestant and Roman Catholic 2%, other 7% (1988)
Languages: Danish, Faroese, Greenlandic (an Eskimo dialect), German (small minority)
Labor Force: 2,553,900

GOVERNMENT
Type: Constitutional Monarchy
Capital: Copenhagen

ECONOMY
National Product: GDP—purchasing power parity—$112.8 billion (1995 est.)
National Product Per Capita: $21,700 (1995 est.)
Exports: $ 39.6 billion (f.o.b., 1994)
Commodities: meat and meat products, dairy products, transport equipment (shipbuilding), fish, chemicals, industrial machinery
Partners: EU 49.4% (Germany 22.4%, UK 8.2%), Sweden 10.4%, Norway 6.5%, US 5.5%, Japan 4.1%, FSU 1.7% (1994)
Imports: $34 billion (c.i.f., 1994 est.)
Commodities: petroleum, machinery and equipment, chemicals, grain and foodstuffs, textiles, paper
Partners: EU 51% (Germany 22%, UK 6.5%), Sweden 11.6%, Norway 5.1%, US 5.2%, Japan 3.5%, FSU 1.7% (1994)
Industries: food processing, machinery and equipment, textiles and clothing, chemical products, electronics, construction, furniture, and other wood products, shipbuilding

TRANSPORTATION
Railroads: Total of 2,848 km
Highways: Total of 71,042 km
Merchant Marine: Total of 334 ships
Airports: Total of 109

COMMUNICATIONS
Telephone System: 4.005 million telephones (1985 est.); excellent telephone and telegraph services

DEFENSE FORCES
Branches: Royal Danish Army, Royal Danish Navy, Royal Danish Air Force, Home Guard

DENMARK SOURCES

RESEARCH SOURCES

Demographic Data Sources

Danmarks Statistik
Sejerogade 11
DK-2100 Copenhagen O
Denmark
Tel: (4539) 17 39 17
Fax: (4531) 95 10 12

Manufacturing Data Sources

Dansk Standardiseringsraad
Baunegaardsvej 73
DK-2900 Hellerup
Denmark
Tel: (4539) 77 01 01
Fax: (4539) 77 02 02

Bureau Veritas Quality International (BVQI)
Denmark A/S Regional Office
Osterfaelled Torv 3
2100 Copenhagen O
Denmark
Tel: (4535) 42 34 54
Fax: (4535) 43 73 34

Trade Data Sources and Trade Associates

Danish Customs—Customs and Tax Region 1
Strandgade 100
DK-1401 Copenhagen O
Denmark
Tel: (4532) 88 93 00
Fax: (4531) 95 10 12

Confederation of Danish Industries
H.C. Andersens Boulevard 18
DK-1787 Copenhagen V
Denmark
Tel: (4533) 77 33 77
Fax: (4533) 77 33 00

The Danish Chamber of Commerce
Borsen
DK-1217 Copenhagen K.

Denmark
Tel: (4533) 95 05 00
Fax: (4533) 32 52 16

Company Data Sources

ERVMERVS-OG Selskabsstyrelsen (Central Registry)
Kampmannsgade 1
1604 Copenhagen
Denmark
POL info
Radhuspladsen
1785 Copenhagen
Denmark
Tel: (4533) 47 14 10
Fax: (4533) 12 99 81

Databases

Ministry of Agriculture / IT Division
Slotsholmsgael 10
DK-1216 Copenhagen K
Denmark
Tel: (4533) 293 301
Fax: (4533) 145 042

RESEARCH AND CONSULTANCY FIRMS

Federation of Danish Industries
H.C. Andersens Bv 18
DK-1790 Copenhagen V
Denmark
Tel: (4533) 152 233
Fax: (4533) 323 281

SONAR—Instituttet for Markeds—og Opinionsanalyser
Christianshusvej 193
2970 Hørsholm
Denmark
Tel: (4542) 86 20 40
Fax: (4545) 76 52 12

PA Research & Marketing—PA Consulting Group
Øster Allé 42

2100 Copenhagen Ø
Denmark
Tel: (4535) 25 50 00
Tel: (4535) 25 50 67
Fax: (4535) 25 51 00

DMA/Dansk Markedsanalyse A/S
Sct. Clemens Torv 15
8000 Arthus C
Denmark
Tel: (4586) 13 86 22
Fax: (4586) 13 85 52
E-mail: dma@aix1.danadata.dk

GOVERNMENTAL SOURCES

Ministry of Foreign Affairs
Asiatisk Plads 2
DK-1448 Copenhagen K
Denmark
Tel: (4533) 92 00 00
Fax: (4531) 54 05 33

Ministry of Business and Industry
Slotsholmsgade 12
DK1216 Copenhagen K
Denmark
Tel: (4533) 92 33 50
Fax: (4533) 12 37 78

Patentdirektoratet (The Patent Agency)
Helgeshoj Alle 81
DK-1433 Copenhagen K
Denmark
Tel: (4543) 71 71 71
Fax: (4543) 71 71 70

BUSINESS DEVELOPMENT FIRMS AND BROKERS

Nielsen Marketing Research A/S
Strandvoulevarden 89
DK-2100 Copenhagen O
Denmark
Tel: (4535) 43 35 43
Fax: (4535) 43 13 31

FINLAND

GEOGRAPHY
Area:
Total Area: 337,030 sq km
Land Area: 305,470 sq km
Comparative Area: slightly smaller than Montana
Natural Resources: timber, copper, zinc, iron ore, silver

PEOPLE
Population: 5,105,230 (July 1996 est.)
Age Structure:
0–14 years: 19% (female 471,736; male 492,616)
15–64 years: 67% (female 1,687,974; male 1,725,113)
65 years and over: 14% (female 451,864; male 275,927) (July 1996 est.)
Population Growth Rate: 0.1% (1996 est.)
Ethnic Divisions: Finn, Swede, Lapp, Gypsy, Tatar
Religions: Evangelical Lutheran 89%, Greek Orthodox 1%, none 9%, other 1%
Languages: Finnish 93.5% (official), Swedish 6.3% (official), small Lapp- and Russian-speaking minorities
Labor Force: 2.533 million

GOVERNMENT
Type: Republic
Capital: Helsinki

ECONOMY
National Product: GDP—purchasing power parity—$92.4 billion (1995 est.)
National Product Per Capita: $18,200 (1995 est.)
Exports: $29.7 billion (f.o.b., 1994)
Commodities: paper and pulp, machinery, chemicals, metals, timber
Partners: EU 46.5% (Germany 13.4%, UK 10.3%), Sweden 11%, US 7.2%, Japan 2.1%, FSU 8.6% (1994)
Imports: $23.2 billion (c.i.f., 1994)
Commodities: foodstuffs, petroleum and petroleum products, chemicals, transport equipment, iron and steel, machinery, textile yarn and fabrics, fodder grains
Partners: EU 44% (Germany 15%, UK 8.3%), Sweden 10.4%, US 7.6%, Japan 6.5%, FSU 10.3% (1994)
Industries: metal products, shipbuilding, pulp and paper, copper refining, foodstuffs, chemicals, textiles, clothing

TRANSPORTATION
Railroads: Total of 5,895 km
Highways: Total of 76,755 km
Merchant Marine: Total of 92 ships
Airports: Total of 157

COMMUNICATIONS
Telephone System: 2.78 million telephones (1986 est.); good service from cable and microwave radio relay network

DEFENSE FORCES
Branches: Army, Navy, Air Force, Frontier Guard (includes Sea Guard)

FINLAND SOURCES

RESEARCH SOURCES

Demographic Data Sources

Statistics Finland
Tyopajankatu 13 (mail: 00022
STATISTIKCENTRALEN)
FIN-00580 Helsinki
Finland
Tel: (3580) 173 41
Fax: (3580) 1734 2750

Ministry of Labour, Occupa-
tional Safety and Health
Division (ori)
Tyoministerio Tyosuojeluosasto
Uimalankatu 1
33100 Tampere
Finland
Tel: (35831) 608111
Fax: (35831) 530201

Manufacturing Data Sources

Finnish Standardization Associ-
ation (SFS)
Maistraatinportti 2
FIN-00240 Helsinki
Finland
Tel: (3580) 149 9331
Fax: (3580) 146 4925

Trade Data Sources and Trade Associates

Federation of Finnish Com-
merce and Trade
Mannerheimintie 76 A
FIN-00250 Helsinki
Finland
Tel: (3580) 441 651
Fax: (3580) 496 142

Tullihalliltus (Customs Infor-
mation Service)
Neuvonta PL 512
00101 Helsinki
Finland
Tel: (3589) 614 2153
Fax: (3589) 614 2256

Central Chamber of Com-
merce
Aleksanterinkatu 17

WTC Helsinki
FIN-00100 Helsinki
Finland
Tel: (3580) 696 969
Fax: (3580) 650 303

Company Data Sources

Confederation of Finnish
Industry and Employers
Etel"ranta 10
FIN-00130 Helsinki
Finland
Tel: (3580) 686 81
Fax: (3580) 6868 2316

National Board of Patents and
Registration
Albertinkatu 25 A
FIN-00180 Helsinki
Finland
Tel: (3580) 6939 500
Fax: (3580) 6939 5322

Databases

Dantek Informations-
systemer
Vertergade 41
8600 Silkeborg
Finland
Tel: (358) 8680 3099
Fax: (358) 8680 3094

Tekes
Malminkatu 34—P.O. Box 69
00101 Helsinki
Finland
Tel: (3589) 105 2151
Fax: (3589) 694 9196

RESEARCH AND CONSULTANCY FIRMS

Marketing Development Cen-
ter Ltd.
Itätuulenkuja 10
02100 Espoo
Finland
Tel: (3580) 61350 0
Fax: (3580) 61350 510

Taloustutkimus Oy
Susitie 11
00800 Helsinki

Finland
Tel: (3580) 755 6511
Fax: (3580) 788 939

Marketing Radar Ltd.
Lauttasaarentie 28–30
00200 Helsinki
Finland
Tel: (3580) 61545 11
Fax: (3580) 61545 200

GOVERNMENTAL SOURCES

Ministry of Foreign Affairs of
Finland
PO Box 103
00161 Helsinki
Finland
Tel: (3589) 134 151
Fax: (3589) 134 15901

National Board of Patents and
Registration
Albertinkatu 25 A
FIN-00180 Helsinki
Finland
Tel: (3580) 6939 500
Fax: (3580) 6939 5322

Ministry of Trade and Industry
Lastenkodinkatu 5
FIN-00180 Helsinki
Finland
Tel: (3580) 160 5850
Fax: (3580) 160 5866

BUSINESS DEVELOPMENT FIRMS AND BROKERS

Invest in Finland Bureau
Aleksanterinkatu 17
FIN-00100 Helsinki
Finland
Tel: (3580) 6969 125
Fax: (3580) 6969 2530

Research International
It"lahdenkatu 18A
FIN-00210 Helsinki
Finland
Tel: (3580) 348 6112
Fax: (3580) 348 61312

FRANCE

GEOGRAPHY
Area:
Total Area: 547,030 sq km
Land Area: 545,630 sq km
Comparative Area: slightly more than twice the size of Colorado
Natural Resources: coal, iron ore, bauxite, fish, timber, zinc, potash

PEOPLE
Population: 58,317,450 (July 1996 est.)
Age Structure:
0–14 years: 19.04% (female 5,417,355; male 5,688,505)
15–64 years: 65.62% (female 19,120,935; male 19,147,369)
65 years and over: 15.34% (female 5,354,186; male 3,589,100) (July 1996 est.)
Population Growth Rate: 0.34% (1996 est.)
Ethnic Divisions: Celtic and Latin with Teutonic, Slavic, North African, Indochinese, Basque minorities
Religions: Roman Catholic 90%, Protestant 2%, Jewish 1%, Muslim (North African workers) 1%, unaffiliated 6%
Languages: French 100%, rapidly declining regional dialects and languages (Provencal, Breton, Alsatian, Corsican, Catalan, Basque, Flemish)
Labor Force: 24.17 million

GOVERNMENT
Type: Republic
Capital: Paris

ECONOMY
National Product: GDP—purchasing power parity—$1.173 trillion (1995 est.)
National Product Per Capita: $20,200 (1995 est.)
Exports: $235.5 billion (f.o.b., 1994)
Commodities: machinery and transportation equipment, chemicals, foodstuffs, agricultural products, iron and steel products, textiles and clothing
Partners: Germany 17.1%, Italy 9.3%, Spain 7.1%, Belgium-Luxembourg 8.7%, UK 9.9%, Netherlands 4.6%, US 7.0%, Japan 2.0%, Russia 0.5%
Imports: $ 229.3 billion (c.i.f., 1994)
Commodities: crude oil, machinery and equipment, agricultural products, chemicals, iron and steel products
Partners: Germany 17.8%, Italy 10.1%, US 8.5%, Netherlands 4.9%, Spain 8.8%, Belgium-Luxembourg 9.1%, US 7.9%, Japan 3.7%, Russia 1.2%
Industries: steel, machinery, chemicals, automobiles, metallurgy, aircraft, electronics, mining, textiles, food processing, tourism

TRANSPORTATION
Railroads: Total of 33,891 km
Highways: Total of 1,511,200 km
Merchant Marine: Total of 55 ships
Airports: Total of 460

COMMUNICATIONS
Telephone System: 35 million telephones (1987 est.); highly developed

DEFENSE FORCES
Branches: Army, Navy (includes Naval Air), Air Force and Air Defense, National Gendarmerie

FRANCE SOURCES

RESEARCH SOURCES

Demographic Data Sources

Institut National de la Statistique et des Etudes Economiques (INSEE)
18 boulevard Adolphe-Pinard
75675 Paris Cedex 14
France
Tel: (331) 41 17 50 50
Fax: (331) 41 17 66 66

Institut National d'Etudes Demographics (INED)
27, rue du Commandeur
75675 Paris Cedex 14
France
Tel: (331) 42 18 20 00
Fax: (331) 42 18 21 99

Manufacturing Data Sources

Federation Francaise de l'Industrie des Produits de Parfumerie, de Beaute et de Toilette
8, place du General Catroux
75017 Paris
France
Tel: (331) 44 15 83 83

Chambre syndicale des constructeurs automobiles
2, rue de Presbourg
75008 Paris
France
Tel: (331) 49 52 51 00

Federation National des Industries Electriques et Electroniques
11, rue Hamelin
75783 Paris cedex 16
France
Tel: (331) 45 05 70 70

Trade Data Sources and Trade Associates

le Club des Exportateurs de la Charente
27 place Bouillard
16021 Angouleme Cedex
France
Tel: (335) 45 20 55 23
Fax: (335) 45 20 55 53

Company Data Sources

SCRL SA
5 quai Jayr - P.B. 9063

69255 Lyon Cedex 09
France
Tel: (334) 72 85 10 63
Fax: (334) 78 47 14 49

Bottin S.A.
4 rue Andre Boulle
94961 Creteil Cedex 09
France
Tel: (331) 49 81 56 00
Fax: (331) 49 81 56 76

Databases

DAFSA
11, rue Robert de Flers
75737 Paris cedex 15
France
Tel: (331) 44 37 26 00
Fax: (331) 44 37 26 35

O.R. Telematique (ORT)
28, Boulevard de Port Royal
F-75005 Paris
France
Tel: (331) 44 08 56 56
Fax: (331) 44 08 56 57

KOMPASS France
66, quai du Marechal Joffre
92415 Courbevoie Cedex
France
Tel: (331) 41 16 51 00
Fax: (331) 41 16 51 19

Agence France-Presse
13 place de la Bourse
75002 Paris
France
Tel: (331) 40 41 46 46
Fax: (331) 42 33 09 50

RESEARCH AND CONSULTANCY FIRMS

Francois Jakobiak
Strategic Information Consulting
9, Alee Raoul Follereau
69230 Saint-Genis-Laval
France
Tel: (3372) 39 95 60
Fax: (3372) 39 94 51

SOFRES GROUP
16 rue Barbès
92129 Montrouge Cedex
France

Tel: (331) 40 92 40 92
Fax: (331) 42 53 91 16
E-mail: dcomm01@sofres.worldnet.net

MV2 CONSEIL
Immeuble MV2
89/100 avenue Aristide Briand
92120 Montrouge
France
Tel: (331) 46 73 31 31
Fax: (331) 46 73 31 60

MOTIVACTION International
191 avenue du Général Leclerc
78220 Viroflay
France
Tel: (331) 39 24 53 00
Fax: (331) 30 24 15 18

INTERLINK
AES
32 rue Mortinat
92600 Asnieres
France
Tel: (331) 47 93 38 38
Fax: (331) 47 90 67 98

CEGMA TOPO
Conseil et Etudes en Gestion et Marketing
49 rue Albert Samain
59665 Villeneuve-d'Ascq Cedex
France
Tel: (3320) 91 33 33
Fax: (3320) 91 66 33

GOVERNMENTAL SOURCES

Chambre de Commerce et d'Industrie de Paris
189, av. Paul Vaillant Couturier
93000 Bobigny
France
Tel: (331) 48 95 25 25

Institut National de la Propriete Industrielle
32 Rue de Trois Fontanets
92016 Nanterre Cedex
France
Tel: (331) 42 94 52 60
Fax: (331) 42 94 01 16

Centre National de la Recherche Scientifique
Campus Michel-Ange-Paris
3, rue Michel Ange

75794 Paris Cedex 16
France
Tel: (331) 44 96 40 00
Fax: (331) 44 96 50 00

**BUSINESS DEVELOPMENT
FIRMS AND BROKERS**

Agency for Corporate Development

Ile de France Paris
16, boulevard Raspail
75007 Paris
France
Tel: (331) 45 44 34 87
Fax: (331) 45 48 43 59

SBF—La Bourse de Paris
39, rue Cambon

75001 Paris
France
Tel: (331) 49 27 10 00
Fax: (331) 49 27 11 71

GERMANY

GEOGRAPHY
Area:
Total Area: 356,910 sq km
Land Area: 349,520 sq km
Comparative Area: slightly smaller than Montana
Natural Resources: iron ore, coal, potash, timber, lignite, uranium, copper, natural gas, salt, nickel

PEOPLE
Population: 83,536,115 (July 1996 est.)
Age Structure:
0–14 years: 16.15% (female 6,563,026; male 6,928,750)
15–64 years: 68.52% (female 27,902,549; male 29,339,780)
65 years and over: 15.33% (female 8,143,996; male 4,658,014) (July 1996 est.)
Population Growth Rate: 0.67% (1996 est.)
Ethnic Divisions: German 95.1%, Turkish 2.3%, Italians 0.7%, Greeks 0.4%, Poles 0.4%, other
1.1% (made up largely of people fleeing the war in the former Yugoslavia)
Religions: Protestant 45%, Roman Catholic 37%, unaffiliated or other 18%
Languages: German
Labor Force: 36.75 million

GOVERNMENT
Type: Federal Republic
Capital: Berlin

ECONOMY
National Product: GDP—purchasing power parity—$1.4522 trillion (1995 est.)
National Product Per Capita: $17,900 (1995 est.)
Exports: $437 billion (f.o.b., 1994)
Commodities: manufactures 89.3% (including machines and machine tools, chemicals, motor vehicles, iron and steel products), agricultural products 5.5%, raw materials 2.7%, fuels 1.3%
Partners: EC 47.9% (France 11.7%, Netherlands 7.4%, Italy 7.5%, UK 7.7%, Belgium-Luxembourg 6.6%), EFTA 15.5%, US 7.7%, Eastern Europe 5.2%, OPEC 3.0% (1993)
Imports: $362 billion (f.o.b., 1994)
Commodities: manufactures 75.1%, agricultural products 10%, fuels 8.3%, raw materials 5%
Partners: EC 46.4% (France 11.3%, Netherlands 8.4%, Italy 8.1%, UK 6.0%, Belgium-Luxembourg 5.7%), EFTA 14.3%, US 7.3%, Japan 6.3%, Eastern Europe 5.1%, OPEC 2.6% (1993)
Industries: (western) among world's largest and technologically advanced producers of iron, steel, coal, cement, chemicals, machinery, vehicles, machine tools, electronics, food and beverages; (eastern) metal fabrication, chemicals, brown coal, shipbuilding, machine building, food and beverages, textiles, petroleum refining

TRANSPORTATION
Railroads: Total of 43,966 km
Highways: Total of 636,282 km
Merchant Marine: Total of 452 ships
Airports: Total of 617

COMMUNICATIONS
Telephone System: 44 million telephones; Germany has one of the world's most technologically advanced telecommunications systems; as a result of intensive capital expenditures since reunification, the formerly backward system of the eastern part of the country is being rapidly modernized and integrated with that of the western part

DEFENSE FORCES
Branches: Army, Navy (includes Naval Air Arm), Air Force, Border Police, Coast Guard

GERMANY SOURCES

RESEARCH SOURCES

Demographic Data Sources

Statistisches Bundesamt
Gustav-Stresemann-Ring 11
D-65180 Wiesbaden
Germany
Tel: (49) 611 75 1
Fax: (49) 611 724 000

Manufacturing Data Sources

Fachinformationszentrum
 (FIZ) Karlsruhe
Gesellschaft fur wissen-
 schaftlich-technisch Infor-
 mation mbH
P.O. Box 2465
6012 Karlsruhe
Germany
Tel: (49) 72 47 8 080
Fax: (49) 72 47 8 08 6 66

Beuth Verlag GmbH (DIN)
Burggrafenstr. 6
10787 Berlin
Germany
Tel: (49) 30 2601 2260

Umweltbundesamt
Postfach 33 00 22
14191 Berlin
Germany
Tel: (49) 30 89 03-0
Fax: (49) 30 89 03-2285

Klaus Gebhardt
Quality-Datenbank
Luruper Weg 15
20257 Hamburg
Germany
Tel: (49) 40 490 0577

CERTQUA GmbH
Der Bildungszertifizier der Spit-
 zenorganisationen der
 Deutschen Wirtschaft
Adenaueralle 12-14
53113 Bonn
Germany
Tel: (49) 228 104 480
Fax: (49) 228 104 482

Deutscher Industrie-und Han-
 delstag
Adenauerallee 148
Postfach 1446
53004 Bonn
Germany
Tel: (49) 228 104 0
Fax: (49) 228 104 158

Trade Data Sources and Trade Associates

Bundesminsterium fuer
 Wirtschaft
Villemombler Strasse 76
D-53123 Bonn
Germany
Tel: (49) 228 615 2158
Fax: (49) 228 615 2652

Company Data Sources

FINN
Verband der Vereine
 Creditreform E.V.
Hellersbergstrasse 12
41460 Neuss
Germany

BDIE
Verlag W. Sachon GmbH +
 Co.
Postfach 1213
Schloss Mindelburg
Germany

ABC der Deutschen Wirtschaft
 Verlags-
 gesellschaft mbH
Postfach 100262—Berliner
 Allee 8
D-64202 Darmstadt
Germany
Tel: (49) 6151 38920
Fax: (49) 6151 33164

Aachen, Industrie-und Handel-
 skammer
Theaterstr. 6,
52062 Aachen, DEU
Germany
Tel: (49) 241 44600
Fax: (49) 241 446 02 59

Databases

Agence France Presse GmbH
Adenaueralle 266
53113 Bonn
Germany
Tel: (49) 228 917 25 17
Fax: (49) 228 917 24 39

Datenbank-Informationsdienst
Wingertsheide 30
51427 Bergisch Gladbach
Germany
Tel: (49) 2203 23504
Fax: (49) 2204 63469

RESEARCH AND CONSULTANCY FIRMS

Dr.Hofner & Partner
Baierbrunner StraBe 33
81379 Munchen
Germany
Tel: (49) 89 78 0030
Fax: (49) 89 78 003 222

IRIS—Germany
SINUS
Ezanvillestrasse 59
69118 Heidelberg I
Germany
Tel: (49) 6221 80 89 0
Fax: (49) 6221 80 89 25

GfK Marktforschung GmbH
Nordwestring 101
90319 Nürnberg
Germany
Tel: (49) 911 395 0
Fax: (49) 911 395 4029

Dr. Reimund Muller
Uhlandstrasse 68
D-22 087 Hamburg
Germany
Tel: (49) 40 251 58200
Fax: (49) 40 251 5822

Reyes, Gloria
P.O. Box 104221
40033 Dusseldorf
Germany
Tel: (49) 211 938 5490
Fax: (49) 211 938 5491
E-mail: 106107,3366x
 compuserv.com

GOVERNMENTAL SOURCES

Deutsches Patentamt
80297 Munchen
Germany
Tel: (49) 89 2195 0
Fax: (49) 89 2195 2221

Ministry of Environment, Pro-
 tection of Nature & Reactor
 Safety
PF 12 06 29
53048 Bonn
Germany
Tel: (49) 228 3050
Fax: (49) 228 05 3225

Ministry of Education,
 Science, Research &
 Technology

Postfach 20 02 40
53170 Bonn
Germany
Tel: (49) 228 57 0
Fax: (49) 228 57 3601

Bundesminsterium fur
  Wirtschaft
Villemombler Str. 76
D-53123 Bonn
Germany

Tel: (49) 228 615 0
Fax: (49) 228 615 4436

**BUSINESS DEVELOPMENT
FIRMS AND BROKERS**

Wirtschaftsregion Offenburg/
  Mittelbaden (WRO)
In der Spoeck 10
D-77656 Offenburg
Germany

Tel: (49) 781 52125
Fax: (49) 781 52126

Multicom
Muthesiusstrasse 38
D-12163 Berlin
Germany
Tel: (49) 30 7 93 45 79
Fax: (49) 30 7 93 46 81

HONG KONG

GEOGRAPHY
Area:
Total Area: 1,040 sq km
Land Area: 990 sq km
Comparative Area: six times the size of Washington, DC
Natural Resources: outstanding deep water harbor, feldspar

PEOPLE
Population: 6,305,413 (July 1996 est.)
Age Structure:
0–14 years: 19% (female 593,687; male 609,493)
15–64 years: 70% (female 2,094,156; male 2,312,141)
65 years and over: 11% (female 388,750; male 307,186) (July 1996 est.)
Population Growth Rate: 1.77% (1996 est.)
Ethnic Divisions: Chinese 95%, other 5%
Religions: eclectic mixture of local religions 90%, Christian 10%
Languages: Chinese (Cantonese), English
Labor Force: 2,915,400 (1994)

GOVERNMENT
Type: dependent territory of the UK scheduled to revert to China on July 1, 1997
Capital: Victoria

ECONOMY
National Product: GDP—purchasing power parity—$152.4 billion (1995 est.)
National Product Per Capita: $27,500 (1995 est.)
Exports: $177.1 billion (f.o.b., 1995 est.)
Commodities: clothing, textiles, yarn and fabric, footwear, electrical appliances, watches and clocks, toys
Partners: China 33%, US 22%, Germany 5%, Japan 5%, UK 3% (1993)
Imports: $195.4 billion (c.i.f., 1995)
Commodities: foodstuffs, transport equipment, raw materials, semimanufactures, petroleum; a large share is re-exported
Partners: China 38%, Japan 17%, Taiwan 9%, US 7% (1993)
Industries: textiles, clothing, tourism, electronics, plastics, toys, watches, clocks

TRANSPORTATION
Railways: Total of 35 km
Highways: Total of 1,661 km
Merchant Marine: Total of 238 ships
Airports: Total of 2

COMMUNICATIONS
Telephone System: 4.13 million telephones (1995 est.); modern facilities provide excellent domestic and international services

DEFENSE FORCES
Branches: Headquarters of British Forces, Army, Royal Navy, Royal Air Force, Royal Hong Kong Auxiliary Air Force, Royal Hong Kong Police Force

HONG KONG SOURCES

RESEARCH SOURCES

Demographic Data Sources

Hong Kong Government, Census & Statistic Dept.
16th–22nd and 25th Floors,
Wanchai Tower
12 Harbour Road
Wanchai
Hong Kong
Tel: (852) 2582 4807
Fax: (852) 2802 4000

Manufacturing Data Sources

Chinese Manufacturers Association
3rd Floor, CMA Bldg.
64 Connaught Road C
Sheung Wan
Hong Kong
Tel: (852) 2545 6166
Fax: (852) 2541 4541

Federation of Hong Kong Industry
4th Floor, Hankow Centre
5-15 Hankow Road
Tsim Sha Tsui
Hong Kong
Tel: (852) 2732 3188
Fax: (852) 2721 3494

Trade Data Sources & Trade Associates

Hong Kong Trade Development Council
38/F, Office Tower
Convention Plaza
1 Harbour Road
Wanchai
Hong Kong
Tel: (852) 2584 4333
Fax: (852) 2824 0249
e-mail: hktdc@tdc.org.hk

Company Data Sources

Dun & Bradstreet Hong Kong Limited
12/F., K. Wah Centre
191 Java Road
North Point
Hong Kong
Tel: (852) 2516 1111
Fax: (852) 2562 6149

Hong Kong Retail Management Association

23B, United Centre
95 Queensway
Hong Kong
Tel: (852) 2866 8311
Fax: (852) 2866 8380

AGA Information Ltd.
Unit B1, 1st Floor
Sincere Insurance Building
No. 4–6 Hennessy Road
Wanchai
Hong Kong
Tel: (852) 2866 6438
Fax: (852) 2866 0816

RESEARCH AND CONSULTANCY FIRMS

Asian Strategies Ltd.
Rm 4401, China Resources Bldg.
26 Harbour Road
Wanchai
Hong Kong
Tel: (852) 2827 4627
Fax: (852) 2827 6097
e-mail: paul@mfasia.com.hk

Kroll & Associates
Rm 906–911, Mount Parker House
1111 King's Road
Taikoo City
Hong Kong
Tel: (852) 2884 7788
Fax: (852) 2568 8505

Pacific Rim Consulting Group
California Tower, 8/F
30–32 D'Aguilar St.
Central
Hong Kong
Tel: (852) 2526 4061
Fax: (852) 2810 4845

GOVERNMENTAL SOURCES

American Chamber of Commerce in Hong Kong
1904 Bank of America Tower
12 Harcourt Road
Central
Hong Kong
Tel: (852) 2526 0165
Fax: (852) 2537 8824

British Chamber of Commerce in Hong Kong

1401 Tung Wai Commercial Bldg.
111 Gloucester Road
Wanchai
Hong Kong
Tel: (852) 2824 2211
Fax: (852) 2824 1333

Hong Kong General Chamber of Commerce
United Centre, 22nd Floor
95 Queensway
Hong Kong
Tel: (852) 2529 9229
Fax: (852) 2527 9843

Hong Kong Government Information Services Department
5th–8th Floors, Murray Building
Garden Road
Hong Kong
Tel: (852) 2842 8777
Fax: (852) 2845 9078

Hong Kong Government Companies Registry
12th–15th, 17th and 29th Floors
Queensway Government Offices
66 Queensway
Hong Kong
Tel: (852) 2867 2712
Fax: (852) 2869 6817

Hong Kong Government Industry Dept.
14th Floor, Ocean Centre
5 Canton Road
Kowloon
Hong Kong
Tel: (852) 2737 2208
Fax: (852) 2730 4633

Hong Kong Government Inland Revenue Dept.
Revenue Tower
5 Gloucester Road
Wanchai
Hong Kong
Tel: (852) 187 8088

Hong Kong Government Trade Dept.
Basements 1 and 2, Ground, Mezzanine

1st–8th and 17th–19th Floors
Trade Department Tower
700 Nathan Road
Kowloon
Hong Kong
Tel: (852) 2789 7555
Fax: (852) 2789 2491

Hong Kong Productivity
    Council
HKPC Building
78 Tat Chee Avenue
Yau Yat Chuen

Kowloon
Hong Kong
Tel: (852) 2788 5678
Fax: (852) 2788 5900

US Department of Commerce,
    Foreign & Commercial
    Service
American Consulate General
26 Garden Road
Central
Hong Kong
Tel: (852) 2521 1467

Fax: (852) 2845 9800
e-mail: OHongkon@doc.gov

US Department of Commerce,
    Foreign & Commercial
    Service
Herbert C. Hoover Bldg.
14 Constitutional Ave., NW
Washington, DC 20230
USA
Tel: (202) 482 6228
Fax: (202) 482 3159

HUNGARY

GEOGRAPHY
Area:
Total Area: 93,030 sq km
Land Area: 92,340 sq km
Comparative Area: slightly smaller than Indiana
Natural Resources: bauxite, coal, natural gas, fertile soils

PEOPLE
Population: 10,318,838 (July 1995 est.)
Age Structure:
0–14 years: 18% (female 918,281; male 958,027)
15–64 years: 68% (female 3,534,218; male 3,440,036)
65 years and over: 14% (female 914,221; male 554,055) (July 1995 est.)
Population Growth Rate: 0.02% (1995 est.)
Ethnic Divisions: Hungarian 89.9%, Gypsy 4%, German 2.6%, Serb 2%, Slovak 0.8%, Romanian 0.7%
Religions: Roman Catholic 67.5%, Calvinist 20%, Lutheran 5%, atheist and other 7.5%
Languages: Hungarian 98.2%, other 1.8%
Labor Force: 5.4 million

GOVERNMENT
Type: Republic
Capital: Budapest

ECONOMY
National Product: GDP—purchasing power parity—$58.8 billion (1994 est.)
National Product Per Capita: $5,700 (1994 est.)
Exports: $10.3 (f.o.b., 1994 est.)
Commodities: raw materials and semi-finished goods 30.0%; machinery and transport equipment 20.1 %, consumer goods 25.2%, food and agriculture 21.4%, fuels and energy 3.4% (1993)
Partners: Germany 25.3%, Italy 8.3%, Austria 10.5%, the FSU 14.0%, US 4.3% (1993)
Imports: $14.2 billion (f.o.b., 1994 est.)
Commodities: fuels and energy 12.6%, raw materials and semi-finished goods 27.3%, machinery and transport equipment 33.0%, consumer goods 21.2%, food and agriculture 5.9% (1993)
Partners: Germany 21.5%, Italy 6.1%, Austria 11.8%, the FSU 20.9%, US 4.3% (1993)
Industries: mining, metallurgy, construction materials, processed foods, textiles, chemicals (especially pharmaceuticals), busses, automobiles

TRANSPORTATION
Railroads: Total of 7,785 km
Highways: Total of 158,711 km
Merchant Marine: Total of 10 ships
Airports: Total of 78

COMMUNICATIONS
Telephone System: 1,520,000 telephones; 14.7 phones per 100 inhabitants (1993); 14,213 telex lines; automatic telephone network based on microwave radio relay system; 608,000 phones on order; 12–15 year wait for a phone; 49% of all phones are in Budapest (1991)

DEFENSE FORCES
Branches: Ground, Air, and Air Defense Forces, Border Guard, Territorial Defense

HUNGARY SOURCES

RESEARCH SOURCES

Demographic Data Sources

Central Statistical Office
1024 Keleti Karoly u 5–7
Hungary
Tel: (361) 212 6212
Fax: (361) 212 6378

Manufacturing Data Sources

Association of Pharmaceutical
  Manufactures
1145 Amerikai ut 96
Hungary
Tel: (361) 251 3337
Fax: (361) 251 3677

Ipari Beruhazasi Informacio
Szolgaltato Piackutato Iroda
(Industrial Investment & Mar-
keting Service Ltd)
1082 Baross u. 115.
Hungary
Tel: (361) 114 1089
Fax: (361) 114 1089

Produkt Marketing Service Kft.
1119 Andor u. 13.
Hungary
Tel: (361) 205 6368
Fax: (361) 205 6368

Trade Data Sources and Trade Associates

Hungarian Chamber of Com-
merce and Industry
1055 Kossuth ter 6–8
Hungary
Tel: (361) 153 3333
Fax: (361) 111 1843

Association of Hungarian
  Agricultural Producers
1054 Akademia u. 1/3
Hungary
Tel: (361) 153 4444
Fax: (361) 153 0880

ITD (Investment & Trade
  Development Association)
1051 Dorottya u. 4.
Hungary
Tel: (361) 266 7034
Fax: (361) 118 3732

Company Data Sources

CEGINFO
1139 Petnchazi u. 21

Hungary
Tel: (361) 270 0479
Fax: (361) 140 7038

Association of Industial Entre-
preneurials
1021 Huvosvogyi ut 54
Hungary
Tel: (361) 176 3733
Fax: (361) 248 0411

KERSZOV
1027 Bem rkp. 51
Hungary
Tel: (361) 212 4249
Fax: (361) 212 4437

Ministry of Justice
1055 Szalay u. 16
Hungary
Tel: (361) 332 6170
Fax: (361) 331 8753

RESEARCH AND CONSULTANCY FIRMS

Ad Hoc Plus Piackutato Kft.
1029 Boleny u. 16.
Hungary
Tel: (361) 275 7190
Fax: (361) 275 7190

AGB Hungary Mediakutato
1146 Hermina ut 57–59
Hungary
Tel: (361) 351 5316
Fax: (361) 351 5316

Air Luck Marketing es Ker-
eskedelmi Kft.
1025 Kulpa u. 3.
Hungary
Tel: (361) 325 6995
Fax: (361) 325 6995

Amer Piac- es Kozvelemenyku-
tato Kft.
1037 Csatarka u. 5.
Hungary
Tel: (361) 188 7858
Fax: (361) 188 7858

Andersen Consulting (Hungar-
ian Branch)
1088 Rakoczl ut 1/3
Hungary
Tel: (361) 266 7707
Fax: (361) 266 7709

Argumentum-Mix Marketing
  Tanacsado Bt
1036 Nagyszombat u. 1.
Hungary
Tel: (361) 188 2337
Fax: (361) 188 2337

ASSIO Marketing Kommuni-
kacios Kft.
1145 Torokor u. 69
Hungary
Tel: (361) 266 6417
Fax: (361) 266 6417

B es SZ Marketing Kommuni-
kacios Tanacsado Iroda
1121 Hangya u. 5.
Hungary
Tel: (361) 393 1734
Fax: (361) 393 1734

Borgius Marketing Bt
1126 Edvl Illes. A. u. 10.
Hungary
Tel: (361) 246 4594
Fax: (361) 246 4594

CEG-INFO Direkt Marketing
  Kft.
1139 Petnehazy u. 21.
Hungary
Tel: (361) 140 7038
Fax: (361) 140 7038

Conservice Marketing Tanac-
sado Bt
1029 Zsiroshegyl ut 5/b.
Hungary
Tel: (361) 393 0381
Fax: (361) 393 0381

Co-Partners Marketing Kft.
1052 Semmelweis u. 8.
Hungary
Tel: (361) 137 9102
Fax: (361) 137 9102

Cowerb Kft
1052 Vaci u. 12.
Hungary
Tel: (361) 266 2470
Fax: (361) 266 2470

Creative Marketing Team
1037 Toronya u. 3.
Hungary
Tel: (361) 168 8334
Fax: (361) 168 8334

Direkt Piackutato Gmk
1023 Level u. 2.
Hungary
Tel: (361) 212 2701
Fax: (361) 212 2701

Dono Direct Marketing Kft
1092 Raday u.5.
Hungary
Tel: (361) 218 0542
Fax: (361) 218 0542

Domsodl es Friderikusz Kft.
1051 Vorosmarty ter 1.
Hungary
Tel: (361) 266 7798
Fax: (361) 266 7803

Euromarketing Kft
1124 Gebics u. 17/2
Hungary
Tel: (361) 319 8430
Fax: (361) 319 8423

Fokusz Marketing Kommuni-
  kacio Kft.
1026 Pasareti ut 31.
Hungary
Tel: (361) 213 0712
Fax: (361) 202 2893

Gallup Ltd
1033 Foter 1
Hungary
Tel: (361) 250 0999
Fax: (361) 250 0650

Gameorg Kft
1132 Vaci ut 60/62
Hungary
Tel: (361) 140 1370
Fax: (361) 120 9876

GFK—Hungaria Piackutato
  Interet
(Market Research Co.)
1132 Visegradi u. 31.
Hungary
Tel: (361) 120 1776
Fax: (361) 120 1776

GKI Gazdasagkutato Rt
1052 Gerloczyu. u. 11.
Hungary
Tel: (361) 117 6232
Fax: (361) 117 6232

Gordius Marketing Iroda Gmk
1125 Sarospatak ut 30/d

Hungary
Tel: (361) 393 0014
Fax: (361) 393 0014

GT Marketing Kft
1153 Czirakl u. 26/32.
Hungary
Tel: (361) 403 0879
Fax: (361) 403 0879

Hazex Piackutato Kft
1023 Level u. 2.
Hungary
Tel: (361) 212 2701
Fax: (361) 212 2701

Himok-Marketing Szovetkezet
1146 Olof Palme setany 1.
Hungary
Tel: (361) 343 9028
Fax: (361) 343 9028

House of Marketing Budapest
  Kft
1054 Hold u. 29.
Hungary
Tel: (361) 112 6498
Fax: (361) 112 6498

ImS Idegenforgalmi Marketing
  Szolgaltatasok Budapest Kft
1027 Csalogany u. 13/19
Hungary
Tel: (361) 157 6647
Fax: (361) 157 6647

Innografika Marketing Szer-
  vezo Gmk
1063 Osvat u. 11.
Hungary
Tel: (361) 122 0902
Fax: (361) 122 0902

Intermark Marketing Tanac-
  sado Szervezo Kft
1052 Parisi u. 3
Hungary
Tel: (361) 117 4119
Fax: (361) 118 5392

Intervill Villert Piackutato Lea-
  nyvallalat
1065 Revay u. 3.
Hungary
Tel: (361) 112 2430
Fax: (361) 112 2430

Investair Marketing Szolgaltato
  Kft.

1051 Vorosmarty ter 1.
Hungary
Tel: (361) 266 7250
Fax: (361) 266 7250

Investorg Piackutato es Beruha-
  zaselokeszito Kft
1055 Falk M. u. 12.
Hungary
Tel: (361) 111 5825
Fax: (361) 111 5258

Ipari Beruhazasi Informacio
  Szolgaltato Piackutato Iroda
1082 Baross u. 115.
Hungary
Tel: (361) 114 1089
Fax: (361) 114 1089

Kalnoky Bt.
1051 Zrinyl u. 16.
Hungary
Tel: (361) 269 4411
Fax: (361) 269 4411

KoD Kozvelemeny-es Piacku-
  tato Kft.
1135 Lehel ut 52.
Hungary
Tel: (361) 129 4225
Fax: (361) 129 4051

Kopint-Datorg Konjunktura-,
  Piackutato es Szamitastech-
  nikai Rt
1081 Csokonal u. 3.
Hungary
Tel: (361) 210 1550
Fax: (361) 266 6483

Kozlekedesi Marketing Egye-
  sules
(Transportation Marketing
  Association)
1062 Andrassy ut 98.
Hungary
Tel: (361) 131 9548
Fax: (361) 131 9548

Landimex Kereskedelml es
  Piackutato Kft
1065 Hajos u. 31.
Hungary
Tel: (361) 112 0001
Fax: (361) 112 0001

LICO Piackutato, Beruhazasi es
  Vezetesi Szaktanacsado Bt
1125 Vilma ut 3.

Hungary
Tel: (361) 274 4127
Fax: (361) 274 4127

M & S Marketing es Software
Kft.
1136 Pannonia u. 17/a
Hungary
Tel: (361) 112 4459
Fax: (361) 132 4598

Macro Marketing Informacios
es Szerviz Iroda
1115 Etele ut 68
Hungary
Tel: (361) 203 0277
Fax: (361) 203 0341

Mark-Cont Marketing, Tanac-
sado es Vallalkozasi Kft
1037 Gyogyszergyar u. 58.
Hungary
Tel: (361) 362 8283
Fax: (361) 326 8283

Market-Consult Piackutato es
Tanacsado Kft.
1025 Szerena ut 53.
Hungary
Tel: (361) 212 3145
Fax: (361) 212 4192

Marketing Centrum Orszagos
Piackutato Kft.
1065 Nagymezo u. 21.
Hungary
Tel: (361) 153 1366
Fax: (361) 131 6343

Interker-Direct-Mail Kft
1054 Zoltan u.8.
Hungary
Tel: (361) 311 1497
Fax: (361) 131 3143

Matrix-70 Marketing es Oziet-
viteli Tanacsado Bt
1089 Orczy ut 39
Hungary
Tel: (361) 303 0294
Fax: (361) 303 0294

Mecenas Kft.
1138 Parkany u. 11.
Hungary
Tel: (361) 270 0373
Fax: (361) 270 0373

Median Ltd
1034 Scregely u 21

Hungary
Tel: (361) 250 4334
Fax: (361) 250 4346

Medikal Prevention and Mar-
keting Kft.
1112 Koerberki ut 1/3
Hungary
Tel: (361) 166 9176
Fax: (361) 166 9176

MEMBER Hungary Ltd
Magyar Piackutato Iroda Kft
1054 Hold u. 8.
Hungary
Tel: (361) 131 0967
Fax: (361) 131 0967

Mester Marketing Muhely Kft.
1051 Arany J. u. 33.
Hungary
Tel: (361) 302 4279
Fax: (361) 302 4279

MMD Marketing-
Kommunikaclos Iroda
1077 Rottenbiller u. 35.
Hungary
Tel: (361) 351 2718
Fax: (361) 351 2718

MODUS Gazdasogi es Tarsa-
dalml Marketing Tanacsado
Kft.
1053 Szep u.2.
Hungary
Tel: (361) 117 4449
Fax: (361) 117 3240

Modusz Kft
1107 Mazso ter 2/6
Hungary
Tel: (361) 260 5916
Fax: (361) 260 5916

Molnar Marketing Muhely Kft
1023 Veronika u. 2.
Hungary
Tel: (361) 325 0712
Fax: (361) 325 0712

Motiva Reklam es Piakutato
Gmk
1142 Dorozsma koz 8/10
Hungary
Tel: (361) 363 4897
Fax: (361) 363 4897

Multikon Piackutato Kft.
1026 Julla u. 4.
Hungary

Tel: (361) 175 27740
Fax: (361) 202 5784

OMIKK (Orszagos Muszaki
Konyvtar)
1088. Muzeum u 17
Hungary
Tel: (361) 138 2300
Fax: (361) 118 0109

Orszagos Szechenyi Konyvtar
1014. Diaz ter 1
Hungary
Tel: (361) 175 7533
Fax: (361) 202 0804

OSB DM Kft.
1107 Mazsa ter 2–6
Hungary
Tel: (361) 261 8100
Fax: (361) 262 7655

Pro Marketing Kereske-
deimi es Szolgaltato Bt
1139 Roppentyu u. 5.
Hungary
Tel: (361) 129 4200
Fax: (361) 129 4200

Produkt Marketing Service Kft.
1119 Andor u. 13.
Hungary
Tel: (361) 205 6368
Fax: (361) 205 6368

Pro-Hunital Kereskedelmi Kft.
1055 Falk M. u. 16.
Hungary
Tel: (361) 132 3159
Fax: (361) 132 3159

Quo Vadis Marketing Kft
1072 Rakoczi ut 4.
Hungary
Tel: (361) 267 8863
Fax: (361) 267 8863

Ratkay es Tarsai Marketing
Kommunikacios Ogynokseg
1137 Katona J. u. 21.
Hungary
Tel: (361) 302 2908
Fax: (361) 302 2908

Seja Marketing Kkt
1054 Akademia u. 7.
Hungary
Tel: (361) 111 8288
Fax: (361) 112 4607

Sinus Szolgaltato Bt
1068 Szalmas P. u. 4.
Hungary
Tel: (361) 351 1849
Fax: (361) 351 1849

Summa Marketing Bt
1092 Radat u. 34.
Hungary
Tel: (361) 215 2333
Fax: (361) 215 2333

Szonda Ipsos Ltd
1012. Attila ut 93
Hungary
Tel: (361) 156 8211
Fax: (361) 175 3846

Tajfun Plackutato es Termelo
Kareskedelmi Bt
1202 Nagysandor J. u. 124.
Hungary
Tel: (361) 283 0473
Fax: (361) 283 0473

Talita Media Kft
1025 Napvirag u. 17.
Hungary
Tel: (361) 275 0226
Fax: (361) 275 0226

Teletel Media Kft
1092 Raday u. 32.
Hungary
Tel: (361) 217 3400
Fax: (361) 217 3400

Dr. Telkes Consulting Co.
1055 Falk Miksa u 4
Hungary
Tel: (361) 131 3350
Fax: (361) 131 1553

Testhall Piackutato Studio
1066 Terez krt. 12.
Hungary
Tel: (361) 351 2013
Fax: (361) 351 2013

TREND-Hungaria Marketing
es Piackutato Bt
1068 Kiraly u. 54
Hungary
Tel: (361) 268 0492
Fax: (361) 268 0492

Uno Piacszuervezesi Kft
1054 Ferenciek tere 7/8
Hungary
Tel: (361) 117 6539
Fax: (361) 117 6539

USA Sustems Kft
1111 Kende u. 13/17.
Hungary
Tel: (361) 186 8005
Fax: (361) 188 9724

Vizual Marketing Bt
1133 Bessenyei u. 23/b
Hungary
Tel: (361) 129 8742
Fax: (361) 129 8742

V-Sz Kereskedelmi es Piacku-
tato Bt
1054 Szechenyi u. 1/a.
Hungary
Tel: (361) 331 7915
Fax: (361) 331 7915

GOVERNMENT SOURCES

Central Statistical Office
1024 Keleti Karoly u 5–7
Hungary
Tel: (361) 212 6212
Fax: (361) 212 6378

Privatisation and State Holding
Co.
1133 Pozsonyi ut 56
Hungary
Tel: (361) 269 8600
Fax: (361) 149 5745

Ministry of Industry and Trade
1055 Honved u. 13/15
Hungary
Tel: (361) 302 2355
Fax: (361) 302 2384

Ministry of Agriculture
1055 Kossuth Lajos ter 11
Hungary
Tel: (361) 302 0000
Fax: (361) 302 1039

Ministry of Justice
1055 Szalay u. 16
Hungary
Tel: (361) 332 6170
Fax: (361) 332 8753

Office of Property Registration
1052 Varoshaz u. 9/11
Hungary
Tel: (361) 327 1000
Fax: (361) 117 5885

**BUSINESS DEVELOPMENT
FIRMS AND BROKERS**

Joint Venture Association
1012 Kuny Domokos u. 13/15
Hungary
Tel: (316) 212 2506
Fax: (316) 156 0728

Industrial and Trade Develop-
ment Hungary Ltd.
1051 Dorottya u. 4.
Hungary
Tel: (361) 266 7034
Fax: (361) 118 3732

Dun & Bradstreet (US- Hun-
garian)
1052 Varmegye u. 3/5
Hungary
Tel: (361) 267 4190
Fax: (361) 267 4198

Kopint—Datorg
1081 Csokonal u 3.
Hungary
Tel: (361) 210 1550
Fax: (361) 266 6483

International Marketing Insti-
tute Kft.
1086 Erdelyi u. 19
Hungary
Tel: (361) 303 0624
Fax: (361) 303 0624

Euromarketing Kft
1124 Gebics u. 17/2
Hungary
Tel: (361) 319 8430
Fax: (361) 319 8423

GKI Gazdasagkutato Rt
(Co. Of Economy Research)
1052 Gerloczy u. 11
Hungary
Tel: (361) 117 6232
Fax: (361) 117 6232

INDIA

GEOGRAPHY
Area:
Total Area: 3,287,590 sq km
Land Area: 2,973,190 sq km
Comparative Area: slightly more than one-third the size of the US
Natural Resources: coal (fourth largest reserves in the world), iron ore, manganese, mica, bauxite, titanium ore, chromite, natural gas, diamonds, petroleum, limestone

PEOPLE
Population: 952,107,694 (July 1996 est.)
Age Structure:
0–14 years: 34% (female 159,283,151; male 168,030,766)
15–64 years: 62% (female 281,311,834; male 304,805,787)
65 years and over: 4% (female 19,527,771; male 19,148,385) (July 1996 est.)
Population Growth Rate: 1.64% (1996 est.)
Ethnic Divisions: Indo-Aryan 72%, Dravidian 25%, Mongoloid and other 3%
Religions: Hindu 80%, Muslim 14%, Christian 2.4%, Sikh 2%, Buddhist 0.7%, Jains 0.5%, other 0.4%
Languages: English (associate status); Hindi 30%, Bengali, Telugu, Marathi, Tamil, Urdu, Gujarati, Malayalam, Kannada, Oriya, Punjabi, Assamese, Kashmiri, Sindhi, Sanskrit (all official)
Labor Force: 314.751 million (1990)

GOVERNMENT
Type: Federal Republic
Capital: New Delhi

ECONOMY
National Product: GDP—purchasing power parity—$1.4087 trillion (1995 est.)
National Product Per Capita: $1,500 (1995 est.)
Exports: $29.96 billion (f.o.b., 1995)
Commodities: clothing, gems and jewelry, engineering goods, chemicals, leather manufactures, cotton yarn, fabric
Partners: US, Japan, Germany, UK, Hong Kong
Imports: $33.5 billion (c.i.f., 1995)
Commodities: crude oil and petroleum products, machinery, gems, fertilizer, chemicals
Partners: US, Germany, Saudi Arabia, UK, Belgium, Japan
Industries: textiles, chemicals, food processing, steel, transportation equipment, cement, mining, petroleum, machinery

TRANSPORTATION
Railroads: Total of 62,462 km
Highways: Total of 2.037 million km
Merchant Marine: Total of 310 ships
Airports: Total of 288

COMMUNICATIONS
Telephone System: 9.8 million telephones (1995); probably the least adequate telephone system of any industrialized country; three of four villages have no telephone service with only 5% having long-distance service; poor telephone service significantly impedes commercial and industrial growth and penalizes India in global markets; slow improvement is taking place, but demand for communication services is growing rapidly

DEFENSE FORCES
Branches: Army, Navy, Air Force, various security or paramilitary forces (includes Border Security Force, Assam Rifles, and Coast Guard)

INDIA SOURCES

RESEARCH SOURCES

Trade Data Sources and Trade Associates

All India Shippers Council
Federation House
Tansen Marg
New Delhi 110001
India
Tel: (9111) 331 9251

Associated Chambers of Commerce and Industry (ASSOCHAM)
Allahabad Bank Building 17
Parliament Street
New Delhi 110001
India
Tel: (9111) 310 749
Tel: (9111) 310 77
Fax: (9111) 312 193

Confederation of Indian Industry (CII)
23-26 Institutional Area
Lodi Road
New Delhi 110003
India
Tel: (9111) 615 693
Tel: (9111) 462 1874
Fax: (9111) 694 298

Directorate-General of Commercia Intelligence and Statistics
1 Council House Street
Calcutta 700001
India
Tel: (9133) 283 111

Federation of Indian Chambers of Commerce and Industry (FICCI)
Federation House
Tansen Marg
New Delhi 110001
India
Tel: (9111) 331 9251
Fax: (9111) 332 0714

Federation of Indian Export Organizations (FIEO)
PHD House
Opp. Asian Games Village
New Delhi 110016
India
Tel: (9111) 686 4524
Tel: (9111) 685 1310
Fax: (9111) 686 3087

Indian Council of Arbitration
Federation House
Tansen Marg
New Delhi 110001
India
Tel: (9111) 331 9251

Indian Investment Centre
Jeevan Vihar Building
Sansad Marg
New Delhi 110001
India
Tel: (9111) 373 3673
Fax: (9111) 373 2245

India Trade Promotion Organization (ITPO)
Pragati Bhawan
Pragati Maidan
New Delhi 110001
India
Tel: (9111) 331 8143
Fax: (9111) 331 8143
Fax: (9111) 332 0855
Fax: (9111) 331 7896

RESEARCH AND CONSULTANCY FIRMS

Tifaclin
E-6, Qutab Hotel
Mehrauli Road
New Delhi, 110016
India
Tel: (9111) 686 3877
Fax: (9111) 686 3866

Dun & Bradstreet
Free Press House
Free Press Marg
Nariman Point
Mumbai 400021
India
Tel: (9122) 284 1898
Fax: (9122) 284 6280
Fax: (9122) 284 6380

Itvasline
New Ganjawalla Building
Tardeo
Mumbai 400034
India
Tel: (9122) 493 1611
Tel: (9122) 495 4718
Tel: (9122) 494 4741
Fax: (9122) 494 7502
Fax: (9122) 262 4027
Fax: (9122) 262 4064

KPMG
Centre Point
Centre 1, 30th Floor, World Trade Center
Cuffe Parade
Mumbai 400005
India
Tel: (9122) 218 0290
Fax: (9122) 218 8002
Fax: (9122) 218 8175

Arthur Anderson
66, Maker Towers "F"
Cuffe Parade
Mumbai 400005
India
Tel: (9122) 218 0683
Fax: (9122) 218 0290

Coopers & Lybrands
Shas House
Annie Besant Road
Mumbai 400018
India
Tel: (9122) 493 3672
Fax: (9122) 495 0329

GOVERNMENT SOURCES

Islamic Republic of Pakistan
G 5, Diplomatic Enclave
Islamabad
Pakistan
Tel: (9251) 814 371 through
Tel: (9251) 814 375
Fax: (9251) 820 742

Agricultural and Processed Food Products Export Development Authority
Ansal Chambers II
4th Floor, Bhikaji Cama Place
Ring Road
New Delhi 110066
India
Tel: (9111) 687 2159
Tel: (9111) 687 2141
Fax: (9111) 687 5016

Marine Products Export Development Authority
MPEDA House
Panampilly Nagar Avenue
Cochin 682015
India
Tel: (91484) 311 979
Fax: (91484) 313 361

Trade Promotion Office
101 Nirmal Tower
Barakhamda Road
New Delhi 110001
India
Tel: (9111) 371 9126
Fax: (9111) 331 0582

Basic Chemical Pharmaceuticals & Cosmetics Export Promotion Council
Jhansi Castle 7, 4th Floor
Cooperage Road
Bombay 400039
India
Tel: (9122) 202 1288
Tel: (9122) 202 1330
Tel: (9122) 202 6549
Fax: (9122) 202 6684

Cashew Export Promotion
Council
P.B.No. 1709, Chittoor Road
Ernakulam South
Cochin 682016
India
Tel: (91484) 351 973
Tel: 91484) 361 459
Fax: (91484) 351 973

Chemicals and Allied Products
Export Promotion Council
14/1B, 2nd Floor, Ezara Street
Calcutta 700001
India
Tel: (9133) 267 733
Tel: (9133) 267 734
Tel: (9133) 267 735
Fax: (9133) 261 204

Electronics and Computer Software Export Promotion
Council
PHD House, 3rd Floor
Opp. Asaid Village Complex
New Delhi 110016
India
Tel: (9911) 655 206
Tel: (9911) 655 103
Tel: (9911) 654 463
Fax: (9911) 662 427

Engineering Export Promotion
Council
World Trade Centre
14/1B, 3rd Floor, Ezra Street
Calcutta 700001
India
Tel: (9133) 263 080 through

Tel: (9133) 263 085
Fax: (9133) 266 302

Gem and Jewellery Export Promotion Council
Diamond Plaza, 391-A
Mumbai 400004
India
Tel: (9122) 387 1135
Tel: (9122) 388 8004
Fax: (9122) 386 8752

Council for Leather Exports
53 Sydendhams Road
Madras 600003
India
Tel: (9144) 589 098
Tel: (9144) 582 041
Fax: (9144) 588 713

Overseas Construction Council
of India
23 Kasturba Gandhi Marg
11th Floor, Himalaya House
New Delhi 110001
India
Tel: (9111) 331 2936
Tel: (9111) 332 7550
Fax: (9111) 331 2936

Plastic and Linoleums Export
Promotion Council
World Trade Centre
Centre 1, 11th Floor, Cuffe
Parade
Mumbai 400005
India
Tel: (9122) 218 4474
Tel: (9122) 218 4569
Fax: (9122) 218 4810

Shellac Export Promotion
Council
World Trade Centre
14/1B, 2nd Floor, Ezara Street
Calcutta 700001
India
Tel: (9133) 265 288
Tel: (9133) 260 010

Sports Goods Export Promotion Council
2nd Floor, 1E/6, Jhandewalan
Extension
New Delhi 110055
India
Tel: (9111) 525 695
Tel: (9111) 529 255
Fax: (9111) 753 2147

Export Inspection Council
Pragati Tower, 11th Floor,
Rajendra Place
New Delhi 110008
India
Tel: (9111) 571 0523
Tel: (9111) 571 8768
Tel: (9111) 572 9990
Fax: (9111) 571 4783

The Minerals & Metals Trading
Corporation of India Ltd.
(MMTC)
Scope Complex, 7, Lodi Road
New Delhi 110003
India
Tel: (9111) 436 3300
Tel: (9111) 436 0101
Tel: (9111) 436 2200
Fax: (9111) 436 2224
Fax: (9111) 436 0688

The State Trading Corporation
of India Ltd. (STC)
Tolstoy Marg
New Delhi 110001
India
Tel: (9111) 332 7930
Tel: (9111) 332 2495
Tel: (9111) 332 3002
Tel: (9111) 331 3177
Fax: (9111) 332 6741
Fax: (9111) 332 6459

Export Credit Guarantee Corporation of India Ltd.
(ECGC)
Express Towers
10th Floor, Nariman Point
Mumbai 400021
India
Tel: (9122) 202 3023
Tel: (9122) 202 3046
Fax: (9122) 204 5253

Coffee Board
P.O. Box No. 359, No. 1
Vidhana Veedh
Bangalore 560001
India
Tel: (91812) 28 917
Tel: (91812) 75 266

Spices Board
K.C. Avenue, St. Vincent Cross
Road
P.B. No. 1909
Ernakulam Cochin 682018
India
Tel: (91885) 353 837

Tel: (91885) 353 209
Tel: (91885) 353 632
Tel: (91885) 353 578
Tel: (91885) 360 767
Fax: (91885) 364 429

Tea Board
14, Biplabi Trilokya Maharaj
Sarani
P.O. Box 2172
Calcutta 700001
India
Tel: (9133) 260 210
Tel: (9133) 266 125
Fax: (9133) 260 218

Tobacco Board
P.O. Box No. 322, G.T. Road
Gunter 522004
India
Tel: (91863) 23 399
Tel: (91863) 22 434

Rubber Board
Shastri Road
P.B. No. 280
Kottayam 686001
India
Fax: (91481) 18 317

Indian Institute of Foreign
Trade (IIFT)
B-21, Mehrauli Institutional
Area
New Delhi 110016
India
Tel: (9111) 655 124
Tel: (9111) 663 009
Fax: (9111) 685 3956

Indian Institute of Packaging
E-2, MIIDC Area
P.B. No. 9432
Andheri (E)
Mumbai 400093
India
Tel: (9122) 832 4670
Fax: (9122) 837 5302

The Groundnut Extraction
Export Development Associ-
ation
A-142, Mittal Tower, Nariman
Point
Mumbai 400021
India
Tel: (9122) 230 089
Tel: (9122) 231 812

Soyabeen Processers Associa-
tion of India
Scheme No. 53, Near Malviya
Nagar
AB Road
Indore 452008 (M.P.)
India
Tel: (91731) 38 554

All India Cotton Seed Curshers
Association
198, Jamshedji Tata Road
Mumbai 400020
India
Tel: (9122) 221 935
Tel: (9122) 221 962

Apparel Export Promotion
Council
NBCC Towers 15
Bhikaji Cama Place
New Delhi 110066
India
Tel: (9111) 688 3351
Tel: (9111) 688 8505
Tel: (9111) 688 8656
Tel: (9111) 688 8300
Fax: (9111) 688 8584

Carpet Export Promotion
Coucil
110-A1, Kirishna Nagar Safdar-
jung Enclave
New Delhi 110029
India
Tel: (9111) 602 742
Tel: (9111) 601 024
Fax: (9111) 601 024

Cotton Textile Export Promo-
tion Council
Engineering Centre
5th Floor, 9 Mathew Road
Mumbai 400004
India
Tel: (9122) 363 2910 through
Tel: (9122) 363 2913
Fax: (9122) 363 2914

Export Promotion Council for
Handicrafts
6, Community Centre, Basant
Lok, Vasant Vihar
New Delhi 110057
India
Tel: (9111) 687 5377
Tel: (9111) 600 871
Fax: (9111) 606 144

Handloom Export Promotion
Council
18, Cathedral Garden Road
Nunagambakkam
Madras 600034
India
Tel: (9144) 827 6043
Tel: (9144) 827 8879

Office of the Development
Commissioner for
Handloom
Udyog Bhavan
New Delhi 110011
India
Tel: (9111) 301 2945
Tel: (9111) 301 6397
Fax: (9111) 379 2429

The Indian Silk Export Promo-
tion Council
62, Mittal Chambers, 6th Floor,
Narimal Point
Mumbai 400021
India
Tel: (9122) 202 5866
Tel: (9122) 202 7662
Fax: (9122) 287 4606

Synthetic and Rayon Textiles
Export Promotion Council
Resham Bhavan 78, Veer Nari-
man Road
Mumbai 400020
India
Tel: (9122) 204 8797
Tel: (9122) 204 8690
Fax: (9122) 204 8358

Wool & Woollens Export Pro-
motion Council
612/714, Ashoka Estate, 24 Bar-
akhamba Road
New Delhi 110001
India
Tel: (9111) 331 5512
Tel: (9111) 331 5205
Fax: (9111) 331 4626

Jute Manufacturers Develop-
ment Council
3A, Park Plaza
71, Park Street
Calcutta 700016
India
Tel: (9133) 299 240
Tel: (9133) 297 136
Tel: (9133) 293 437
Tel: (9133) 293 438
Fax: (9133) 297 136

Central Cottage Industries Corporation
West Block No. 7, RK Puram
New Delhi 110066
India
Tel: (9111) 332 8506
Tel: (9111) 332 1909
Tel: (9111) 332 1931
Fax: (9111) 332 8534

Handicrafts & Handlooms Exports Corporation Jawahar Viapar Bhavan, Annexe 1
Tolstoy Marg
New Delhi 110001
India
Tel: (9111) 331 1086
Fax: (9111) 331 5351

Central Silk Board
United Mansions, 2nd Floor, 39, M.G. Road
Bangalore 560001
India
Tel: (9180) 28 917
Tel: (9180) 70 250

Coir Board
P.B. No. 1752
Ernakulam South M.G. Road
Cochin 682016
India
Tel: (91484) 351 807
Tel: (91484) 351 788
Tel: (91484) 351 954
Tel: (91484) 354 397
Fax: (91484) 360 676

Bureau of Indian Standards
Manak Bhavan 9
Bahadur Shah Zafar Marg
New Delhi 110002
India
Tel: (9111) 331 1375
Fax: (9111) 331 0131

BUSINESS DEVELOPMENT FIRMS AND BROKERS

Financial Institutions

Reserve Bank of India
(The Central Banking Authority)
Central Office Building
Shahid Bhagat Singh Road
Mumbai 400023
India
Tel: (9122) 266 1602

Tel: (9122) 266 0604
Fax: (9122) 266 2105

Export Credit & Guarantee Corporation of India Ltd.
Express Towers, 10th Floor
Nariman Point
Mumbai 400021
India
Tel: (9122) 202 3023
Tel: (9122) 202 3046
Fax: (9122) 204 5253

Export-Import Bank of India
Centre One, 21st Floor, World Trade Centre
Cuffe Parade
Mumbai 400005
India
Tel: (9122) 218 5272
Fax: (9122) 218 8075

General Insurance Corporation of India
Suraksha, 170, J T Road
Churchgate
Mumbai 400020
India
Tel: (9122) 283 3046
Tel: (9122) 285 2041
Fax: (9122) 287 4129

Industrial Credit & Investment Corp. of India Ltd.
ICICI Building, 163, Backbay Reclamation
Churchgate
Mumbai 400020
India
Tel: (9122) 202 2535
Fax: (9122) 204 6582

Industrial Reconstruction Bank of India
19, N.S. Road
Calcutta 700001
India
Tel: (9133) 209 941
Tel: (9133) 209 945
Fax: (9133) 207 1182

Industrial Development Bank of India
IDBI Tower, Cuffe Parade
Mumbai 400005
India
Tel: (9122) 218 9111

Tel: (9122) 218 9121
Fax: (9122) 218 0411
Fax: (9122) 218 1294

Industrial Finance Corporation of India
Bank of Baroda Building, 16
Sansad Marg
New Delhi 110001
India
Tel: (9111) 332 2052
Tel: (9111) 332 1013
Fax: (9111) 332 0425

Life Insurance Corporation of India
Yogakshema, Jeevan Bima Marg
Mumbai 400021
India
Tel: (9122) 202 8267
Tel: (9122) 202 2151

National Bank for Agriculture & Rural Development
Sterling Centre, Dr. Annie Besant Road
Worli
Mumbai 400018
India
Tel: (9122) 493 8627
Fax: (9122) 493 1621

National Housing Bank
Hindustan Times House 18-20
Kasturba Gandhi Marg
New Delhi 110001
India
Tel: (9111) 371 2036
Tel: (9111) 371 2037
Fax: (9111) 371 5619

Security and Exchange Board of India
1st Floor, Mittal Court, B-Wing
24 Nariman Point
Mumbai 400005
India
Tel: (9122) 282 3886
Fax: (9122) 202 1073

Shipping Credit Investment Corporation of India
141, Maker Towers F
Cuffe Parade
Bombay 400005
India

Tel: (9122) 218 0800
Fax: (9122) 218 1539

Small Industries Development
  Bank of India
Nariman Bhavan, 227 Vinay K.
  Shah Marg

Nariman Point
Bombay 400021
India
Tel: (9122) 202 7716
Tel: (9122) 202 7012
Fax: (9122) 204 4448

Unit Trust of India
13, New Marine Lines, Sir
Vithaldas Thackersey Marg
Bombay 400020
Tel: (9122) 206 8468
Fax: (9122) 266 3673

INDONESIA

GEOGRAPHY
Area:
Total Area: 1,919,440 sq km
Land Area: 1,826,440 sq km
Comparative Area: slightly less than three times the size of Texas
Natural Resources: petroleum, tin, natural gas, nickel, timber, bauxite, copper, fertile soils, coal, gold, silver

PEOPLE
Population: 206,611,600 (July 1996 est.)
Age Structure:
0–14 years: 32% (female 32,414,363; male 33,354,840)
15–64 years: 64% (female 66,827,085; male 66,385,852)
65 years and over: 4% (female 4,248,893; male 3,380,567) (July 1996 est.)
Population Growth Rate: 1.53% (1996 est.)
Ethnic Divisions: Javanese 45%, Sundanese 14%, Madurese 7.5%, coastal Malays 7.5%, other 26%
Religions: Muslim 87%, Protestant 6%, Roman Catholic 3%, Hindu 2%, Buddhist 1%, other 1% (1985)
Languages: Bahasa Indonesia (official, modified form of Malay), English, Dutch, local dialects the most widely spoken of which is Javanese
Labor Force: 67 million

GOVERNMENT
Type: Republic
Capital: Jakarta

ECONOMY
National Product: GDP—purchasing power parity—$710.9 billion (1995 est.)
National Product Per Capita: $3,500 (1995 est.)
Exports: $39.9 billion (f.o.b., 1994)
Commodities: manufactures 51.9%, fuels 26.4%, foodstuffs 12.7%, raw materials 9.0%
Partners: Japan 27.4%, US 14.6%, Singapore 10.1%, South Korea 6.5%, Taiwan 4.1%, Netherlands 3.3%, China 3.3%, Hong Kong 3.3%, Germany 3.2%
Imports: $32 billion (f.o.b., 1994)
Commodities: manufactures 75.3%, raw materials 9.0%, foodstuffs 7.8%, fuels 7.7%
Partners: Japan 24.2%, US 11.2%, Germany 7.7%, South Korea 6.8%, Singapore 5.9%, Australia 4.8%, Taiwan 4.5%, China 4.3%
Industries: petroleum and natural gas, textiles, mining, cement, chemical fertilizers, plywood, food, rubber

TRANSPORTATION
Railroads: Total of 6,458 km
Highways: Total of 283,516 km
Merchant Marine: Total of 457 ships
Airports: Total of 414

COMMUNICATIONS
Telephone System: 1,276,600 telephones (1993 est.); domestic service fair, international service good

DEFENSE FORCES
Branches: Army, Navy, Air Force, National Police

INDONESIA SOURCES

RESEARCH SOURCES

Demographic Data Sources

Statistical Yearbook of Indonesia
Statistical Pocketbook of Indonesia
Jalan Dr Sutomo 8
P.O. Box 1003
Jakarta
Indonesia 10010
Tel: (6221) 381 0291
Fax: (6221) 385 7046

RESEARCH AND CONSULTANCY FIRMS

Arthur Anderson
Prasetio Utomo & Company
Wisma 46, Kota BNI
Jalan Jend Sudirman Kav 1
Jakarta
Indonesia
Tel: (6221) 575 7999
Fax: (6221) 574 4521

Coopers & Lybrand
32nd Floor, Wisma GKBI Kav 28
Jalan Jend Surinam 28
Jukarta
Indonesia 10210
Tel: (6221) 574 2888
Fax: (6221) 574 1777

Ernst & Young / Sarwoko & Sandiara
Jakarta Stock Exchange Building, 23rd Floor
Jalan Jend Sudirman Kav 52–53
Jakarta, Indonesia 12190
Tel: (6221) 515 1960
Fax: (6221) 515 1920

KPMG Peat Marwick / Hanadi Sudjecdro & Rekan
Wisma Dharmala Sakti, 10th Floor
Jalan Jend Sudirman No. 32
Jakarta
Indonesia 10220
Tel: (6221) 570 6111
Fax: (6221) 573 3003

Price Waterhouse
Price Waterhouse Centre, 6th Floor
Jalan HR Rasuna Said Kav, C-3
Kunigan, Jakarta

Indonesia 12940
Tel: (6221) 521 2901
Fax: (6221) 521 2911

Deloitte Touche Tomatsu International / Hans Tuanakotta & Mustofa
Wisma Antara 4th, 12th, 14th and 17th Floors
Jalan Medan Merdeka Selatan, No. 17
Jakarta
Indonesia 10110
Tel: (6221) 231 2829

GOVERNMENTAL SOURCES

Directorate of Foreign Information Services
Jalan Merdeka Barat 9
P.O. Box 1585
Jakarta
Indonesia 10015
Tel: (6221) 377 408

The National Development Information Office
Wisma Antara
Jalan Medan Merdeka Selatan 17
Jakarta
Indonesia 10110
Tel: (6221) 384 7412
Fax: (6221) 384 7603

BUSINESS DEVELOPMENT FIRMS AND BROKERS

Bank of Indonesia
Jalan M H Thamrin 2
Jakarta
Indonesia
Tel: (6221) 384 8888
Fax: (6221) 381 7000

Al / Drs. Andi, Iskandar & Rekan
Jalan Alaydrus, No. 16
Jakarta
Indonesia 10130
Tel: (6221) 363 224

BDO Binder
Bukit Duri Permai Estate Block B-1
Jalan Jatinegara Barat 54E
Jakarta
Indonesia 13320

Tel: (6221) 520 5564
Fax: (6221) 520 5569

Kantor Akuntan Publik
Jalan Prof. Dr. Supomo SH No. 3
Jakarta
Indonesia 12870
Tel: (6221) 830 3060
Fax: (6221) 820 5575

Hendrawinata & Rekan
Bank Bali Tower, 6th Floor
Jalan Jend Suriman Kav 27
Jakarta Selatan
Indonesia 12920
Tel: (6221) 523 7151
Fax: (6221) 523 7152

Salaki & Salaki
Plaza Mashill, Suite 1602
Jalan Jend Sudirman Kav 25
Jakarta
Indonesia 12920
Tel: (6221) 520 3482
Fax: (6221) 520 3483

Drs. Kantosantoso Tony & Company
Jalan Musi No. 3
Jakarta
Indonesia 10150
Tel: (6221) 351 9416
Fax: (6221) 351 9418

AAJ Amir Abadi Jusaf & Rekan
Samudera Indonesia Building, Floors No. 3 and 3A
Jalan Letjen S. Parmen Kav 35
Jakarta
Indonesia 11480
Tel: (6221) 530 7889
Fax: (6221) 530 7867

PT. Tomidpajow Konsultama
Pusat Niaga Roxy Mas
Block E-2, No. 16
Jalan K.H. Hasyim, Ashari
Jakarta
Indonesia 10150
Tel: (6221) 385 6535
Fax: (6221) 385 6536

HSG Indonesia / Drs. Heryanto S. Gani
Perkantoran Tamen Kebon Jeruk
A IV / 18–19 (Intercon)—Kebon Jeruk

Jakarta Barat
Indonesia 11650
Tel: (6221) 549 0319
Fax: (6221) 548 6138

Paul Imam Prodono / Drs. &
  Rekan
Perwakilan Semarang

Jalan Pringgading No. 46
Jakarta
Indonesia 13330
Tel: (6221) 819 0192
Fax: (6221) 819 5746

Stephanus Junianto &
  Company

Jalan Kelapa Gading Blvd.
Kelapa Gading Permal
Jakarta
Indonesia 14240
Tel: (6221) 452 8407
Fax: (6221) 452 0370

ISRAEL

GEOGRAPHY
Area:
Total Area: 20,770 sq km
Land Area: 20,330 sq km
Comparative Area: slightly larger than New Jersey
Natural Resources: copper, phosphates, bromide, potash, clay, sand, sulfur, asphalt, manganese, small amounts of natural gas and crude oil

PEOPLE
Population: 5,433,134 (July 1995 est.)
Age Structure: 0–14 years: 29%
15–64 years: 61%
65 years and over: 10%
Population Growth Rate: 1.4% (1995 est.)
Ethnic Divisions: Jewish 82% (Israel born 50%, Europe/Americas/Oceania born 20%, Africa born 7%, Asia born 5%), non-Jewish 18% (mostly Arab)(1993 est.)
Religions: Judaism 82%, Islam 14% (mostly Sunni Muslim), Christian 2%, Druze and other 2%
Languages: Hebrew (official), Arabic used officially for Arab minority, English most commonly used foreign language
Labor Force: 1.9 million (1992)

GOVERNMENT
Type: Republic
Capital: Jerusalem

ECONOMY
National Product: GDP—purchasing power parity—$70.1 billion (1994 est.)
National Product Per Capita: $13,880 (1994 est.)
Exports: $16.2 billion (f.o.b., 1994 est.)
Commodities: machinery and equipment, cut diamonds, chemicals, textiles and apparel, agricultural products, metals
Partners: US, EU, Japan
Imports: $22.5 billion (c.i.f., 1994 est.)
Commodities: military equipment, investment goods, rough diamonds, oil, other productive inputs, consumer goods
Partners: EU, US, Japan
Industries: food processing, diamond cutting and polishing, textiles and apparel, chemicals, metal products, military equipment, transport equipment, electrical equipment, miscellaneous machinery, potash mining, high-technology electronics, tourism

TRANSPORTATION
Railroads: Total of 520 km
Highways: Total of 13,461 km
Merchant Marine: Total of 32 ships
Airports: Total of 57

COMMUNICATIONS
Telephone System: 1,800,000 telephones; most highly developed in the Middle East although not the largest

DEFENSE FORCES
Branches: Israel Defense Forces (includes ground, naval, and air components), Pioneer Fighting Youth (Nahal), Frontier Guard, Chen (women)

417

ISRAEL SOURCES

RESEARCH SOURCES

Demographic Data Sources

Central Bureau of Statistics
P.O. Box 13015
Jerusalem 91130
Israel
Tel: (9722) 655 3364
Fax: (9722) 655 3573
e-mail: cbs@cbs.gov.il

Hebrew University Library
Mount Scopus
Jerusalem
Israel
Tel: (9722) 588 2313
Fax: (9722) 588 1302

Israel Yearbook and Almanac
IBRT
8 Ha'taasiya Street
Jerusalem 93420
Israel
Tel: (9722) 673 7251
Fax: (9722) 673 7252
e-mail: info@iyba.-
    virtual.co.il

Kav Mancheh
12 Yad Harutzim Street
Tel Aviv 67778
Israel
Tel: (9723) 638 8222
Fax: (9723) 638 8288
e-mail: 75300.3244@compu-
serve.com

Malam
P.O. Box 13016
Jerusalem 91130
Israel
Tel: (9722) 670 7648
Fax: (9722) 652 3025
e-mail: Yoram@mail.clal.com-
p.co.il

Ronen Publishing
P.O. Box 36665
Tel Aviv
Israel
Tel: (9723) 687 5912
Fax: (9723) 537 5719

Tel Aviv University Library
P.O. Box 39654
Tel Aviv 61396
Israel
Tel: (9723) 640 7984

Fax: (9723) 640 7840
e-mail: hmt@taulib.tau.ac.il

Manufacturing Data Sources

Manufacturer's Association of
    Israel
Industry House
29 Hamered Street
Tel Aviv 68125
Israel
Tel: (9723) 519 8787
Fax: (9723) 516 2026

The Kibbutz Industries Associ-
ation
P.O. Box 40012
Tel Aviv 61400
Israel
Tel: (9723) 695 5413
Fax: (9723) 695 1464

Israel Export Institute
29 Hamered Street
Tel Aviv 68125
Israel
Tel: (9723) 514 2830
Fax: (9723) 514 2902
e-mail: Bloch@export.gov.il

Business Data Israel
2 Habonim Street
Ramat Gan 52117
Israel
Tel: (9723) 575 1433
Fax: (9723) 575 1499

Trade Data Sources and Trade Associates

Israel Association of Electron-
    ics Industries
P.O. Box 50026
Tel Aviv 61500
Israel
Tel: (9723) 516 3986
Fax: (9723) 516 2026
e-mail: elec_har@
    netvision.net.il

General Federation of Labor
    (Histadrut)
93 Arlozorov Street
Tel Aviv 62098
Israel
Tel: (9723) 692 1111
Fax: (9723) 686 9906

Israel Software Association
29 Hamered Street

Tel Aviv 68125
Israel
Tel: (9723) 519 8787
Fax: (9723) 516 2026

Association of Contractors and
    Builders
10 Mikve Israel Street
Tel Aviv 65115
Israel
Tel: (9723) 560 4701
Fax: (9723) 560 8091

Advertisers Association of
    Israel
P.O. Box 20440
Tel Aviv 61204
Israel
Tel: (9723) 561 5310
Fax: (9723) 561 5281
e-mail: Igud@inter.net.il

Israel Diamond Exchange
P.O. Box 3222
Ramat Gan
Israel
Tel: (9723) 576 0211
Fax: (9723) 575 0652

Company Data Sources

A.B. Data
32 Habarzel Street
Tel Aviv 69710
Israel
Tel: (9723) 648 3212
Fax: (9723) 647 5001

Business Data Israel
2 Habonim Street
Ramat Gan 52117
Isreal
Tel: (9723) 575 1433
Fax: (9723) 575 1499

Kompass—GBI
P.O. Box 53814
Tel Aviv 61530
Israel
Tel: (9723) 647 0033
Fax: (9723) 647 0242

Databases

Golden Pages
40 Hanamal Street
Tel Aviv 63506
Israel
Tel: (9723) 543 3777
Fax: (9723) 544 4199

e-mail:
noam_y@netvision.net.il

Tel Dan
7 Derech Hashalom
Tel Aviv 67892
Israel
Tel: (9723) 695 0073
Fax: (9723) 695 6359

Ifat
93 Derech Petach Tikva
Tel Aviv 67138
Israel
Tel: (9723) 562 6996
Fax: (9723) 563 5065
e-mail: Ifat_on@netvision,net.il

Israel Export Institute
29 Hamered Street
Tel Aviv 68125
Israel
Tel: (9723) 514 2830
Fax: (9723) 514 2902
internet: WWW.Export.Gov.IL

Globes
127 Igal Alon Street
Tel Aviv 67443
Israel
Tel: (9723) 697 9797
Fax: (9723) 695 1994
internet: WWW.Globes.
  Co.Il

Interage
81 Hagalil Street
Givat Savion 55900
Israel
Tel: (9723) 534 0684
Fax: (9723) 535 2856
internet: WWW.interage.co.il/

**RESEARCH AND
CONSULTANCY FIRMS**

Amcon Marketing Strategy
  International
P.O. Box
Tel Aviv
Israel
Tel: (972)
Fax: (972)
e-mail: amcon@ibm.net

Dahaf
2 Ben Zvi Street
Jaffa 68181
Israel

Tel: (9723) 512 7744
Fax: (9723) 512 7756

Edna Pasher & Associates
31 Zohar Street
Herziliya B' 40741
Israel
Tel: (9729) 955 1512
Fax: (9729) 954 6184

Gallup
22 Baruch Hirsh St.
Bnei Brak 51202
Israel
Tel: (9723) 577 3111
Fax: (9723) 570 1335

Giza Advisory and Financial
  Consulting
2 Kaufman Street
Tel Aviv 68012
Israel
Tel: (9723) 516 3302
Fax: (9723) 516 3305

Geocartography
57 Hovevei Zion
Tel Aviv 63346
Israel
Tel: (9723) 528 3773
Fax: (9723) 528 3771

Yecholet Ltd.
17 Kaplan Street
Tel Aviv 64734
Israel
Tel: (9723) 691 5858
Fax: (9723) 691 5750

GOVERNMENTAL SOURCES

Chief Scientist's Office
4 Mevo Matmid Street
Jerusalem
Israel
Tel: (9722) 622 0597
Fax: (9722) 624 8159

Federation of Israel Chambers
  of Commerce
84 Hahashmonaim Street
Tel Aviv
Israel
Tel: (9723) 563 1010
Fax: (9723) 561 2614

Israel Federation of Bi-
  National Chambers of Com-
  merce and Industry
P.O. Box 50196

Tel Aviv 61501
Israel
Tel: (9723) 517 3261
Fax: (9723) 517 3283

Matimop
29 Hamered Street
Tel Aviv 68125
Israel
Tel: (9723) 517 0150
Fax: (9723) 510 6724

Ministry of Industry and Trade
30 Agron Street
Jerusalem 84190
Israel
Tel: (9722) 622 0220
Fax: (9722) 624 5110

Ministry of Science
P.O. Box 18195
Jerusalem 91181
Israel
Tel: (9722) 684 7096
Fax: (9722) 687 5581

Ministry of Agriculture
8 Arania Street
Hakirya
Tel Aviv 61070
Israel
Tel: (9723) 697 1444
Fax: (9723) 686 8899

Ministry of Defense
Kaplan Street
Hakirya
Tel Aviv 67659
Israel
Tel: (9723) 697 5144

Representative of the European
  Union in Israel
3 Daniel Frish Street
Tel Aviv 64731
Israel
Tel: (9723) 696 4166
Fax: (9723) 695 1983

**BUSINESS DEVELOPMENT
FIRMS AND BROKERS**

Agrexco
121 Hahashmonaim Street
Tel Aviv 67133
Israel
Tel: (9723) 563 0940
Fax: (9723) 563 0918

Bobrow Marketing Israel
4 Lechi Street
Ramat Hasharon 47224
Israel
Tel: (9723) 549 7233
Fax: (9723) 549 7233
e-mail: gideon@attmail.com

Dun and Bradstreet (Israel)
27 Hamered Street
Tel Aviv 68152
Israel
Tel: (9723) 510 3355
Fax: (9723) 510 3397

Israex
5 Drouyanov Street
Tel Aviv 61110

Israel
Tel: (9723) 620 0611
Fax: (9723) 528 3280

Koor Trade
6 Kreminsky Street
Tel Aviv
Israel
Tel: (9723) 565 4300
Fax: (9723) 562 7898

Mehav Group
33 Havatzelet Hasharon
Heriliya Pituch
Israel
Tel: (9729) 950 1735
Fax: (9729) 950 1733

Ronen Wolf Ltd.
10 Hazfira Street

Tel Aviv 67779
Israel
Tel: (9723) 380 8213
Fax: (9723) 373 4660

Tel Aviv Stock Exchange
54 Ahad Ha'am Street
Tel Aviv 65543
Israel
Tel: (9723) 567 7411
Fax: (9723) 510 5379

Toam Import
27 Soutine Street
Tel Aviv 64684
Israel
Tel: (9723) 521 2232
Fax: (9723) 524 8140

ITALY

GEOGRAPHY
Area:
Total Area: 301,230 sq km
Land Area: 294,020 sq km
Comparative Area: slightly larger than Arizona
Natural Resources: mercury, potash, marble, sulfur, dwindling natural gas and crude oil reserves, fish, coal

PEOPLE
Population: 57,460,274 (July 1996 est.)
Age Structure:
0–14 years: 15% (female 4,167,860; male 4,419,636)
15–64 years: 68% (female 19,629,291; male 19,656,546)
65 years and over: 17% (female 5,684,515; male 3,902,426) (July 1996 est.)
Population Growth Rate: 0.13% (1996 est.)
Ethnic Divisions: Italian (includes small clusters of German-, French-, and Slovene-Italians in the north and Albanian-Italians and Greek-Italians in the south), Sicilians, Sardinians
Religions: Roman Catholic 98%, other 2%
Languages: Italian, German (predominantly in parts of Trentino-Alto Adige region), French (small minority in Valle d'Aosta region), Slovene (minority in the Trieste-Gorizia area)
Labor Force: 23.988 million

GOVERNMENT
Type: Republic
Capital: Rome

ECONOMY
National Product: GDP—purchasing power parity—$1.0886 trillion (1995 est.)
National Product Per Capita: $18,700 (1995 est.)
Exports: $190.8 billion (f.o.b., 1994)
Commodities: metals, textiles and clothing, production machinery, motor vehicles, transportation equipment, chemicals
Partners: EU 53.4%, US 7.8%, OPEC 3.8% (1994)
Imports: $168.7 billion (c.i.f., 1994)
Commodities: industrial machinery, chemicals, transport equipment, petroleum, metals, food, agricultural products
Partners: EU 56.3%, OPEC 5.3%, US 4.6% (1994)
Industries: tourism, machinery, iron and steel, chemicals, food processing, textiles, motor vehicles, clothing, footwear, ceramics

TRANSPORTATION
Railroads: Total of 18,961 km
Highways: Total of 305,388 km
Merchant Marine: Total of 419 ships
Airports: Total of 132

COMMUNICATIONS
Telephone System: 25.6 million telephones (1987 est.); modern, well-developed, fast; fully automated telephone, telex, and data services

DEFENSE FORCES
Branches: Army, Navy, Air Force, Carabinieri

ITALY SOURCES

RESEARCH SOURCES

Demographic Data Sources

Instituto Naziale di Stistica (ISTAT)
Via Depretis 74/b
00184 Roma
Italy
Tel: (396) 4673 5150
Fax: (396) 4673 3221

Manufacturing Data Sources

General Confederation of the Italian Industry
Viale dell'Astronomia 30
00144 Roma
Italy
Tel: (396) 59031
Fax: (396) 591 9615

ISO Central Secretariat
1, rue de Varembe—Case postale 56
CH-1211 Geneve 20
Switzerland
Tel: (4122) 749 0111
Fax: (4122) 733 3430

Instituto per la Ricerca Scientifica e Technologica (IRST)
Via Sommarive 1
I-38050 Trento Povo
Trento
Italy
Tel: (39461) 314444
Fax: (39461) 314591

Associazione Industriali Mugnai e Pastai d'Italia (ITALMOPA)
Via dei Crociferi 44
00187 Roma
Italy
Tel: (396) 679 4768
Fax: (396) 678 3054

Ente Nazionale Italiano di Unificazione (UNI)
Piazza Armando Diaz-2
20123 Milano
Italy
Tel: (392) 876 914

Trade Data Sources and Trade Associates

Istituto Nazionald per il Commercio Estero (ICE)
Via Liszt 21,

00144 Roma
Italy
Tel: (396) 59921
Fax: (396) 5992

Federal Trade S.pA
Via L. da Vinci 23
20090 Seagrate
Milano
Italy
Tel: (392) 213 4034
Fax: (392) 213 3970

Company Data Sources

EMPORION s.r.l.
V.G.B. Morgagni 30/H
00161 Roma
Italy
Tel: (396) 4425 1894
Fax: (396) 4425 1331

Unioncamere
Piazzza Sallustio 21
00187 Roma
Italy
Tel: (396) 4704 1
Fax: (396) 4704 222

Assocamerestero
Via Flaminia 21
00196 Roma
Italy
Tel: (396) 321 5660
Fax: (396) 321 0253

Databases

CERVED
Via Aristide Staderini 93
00155 Roma
Italy
Tel: (396) 2277 4010
Fax: (396) 2277 4008

ETI SpA
Viale Mazzini 25
00195 Rome
Italy
Tel: (396) 3217 578
Fax: (396) 3217 808

Kompass Italia SpA
Via G. Servals 125
10146 Turin
Italy
Tel: (3911) 7792 337
Fax: (3911) 7792 380

SARIN Telematica—SpA (SARITEL)

SS 148 Pontina Km 29,100
1-00040 Pomezia
Roma
Italy
Tel: (396) 9119 71
Fax: (396) 9119 7600

RESEARCH AND CONSULTANCY FIRMS

B & C Marketing Research
Piazza S. Giovanni in Laterano 26
Rome 00184
Italy
Tel: (396) 700 4674
Tel: (396) 700 4368
Fax: (396) 700 5982

CIRM Market Research
Via B. Cellini 2
20129 Milan
Italy
Tel: (392) 551 2405
Fax: (392) 551 80489
Fax: (392) 545 9774
E-mail: cirmmr@mbox.vol.it

Demoskopea Spa
Via Battistotti Sassi 13
20133 Milan
Italy
Tel: (392) 7012 5941
Fax: (392) 7012 5059

MCS International
Via Albani 52
20148 Milano
Italy
Tel/Fax: (392) 327 0689

S & I—Strategy & Innovazione
Via G.B. Pergolesi
20124 Milan
Italy
Tel: (392) 670 9699
Fax: (392) 669 1921

GOVERNMENTAL SOURCES

Ministero Del Commercio Con L'Estero
Viale America 341
00144 Roma
Italy
Tel: (396) 5993 1
Fax: (396) 5964 7494

Dipartimento della Dogana
(customs)
Viale Liszt, 21
00144 Roma
Italy
Tel: (396) 427 1043

Ministero dell'Industria e Commercio
Ufficio Centrale Brevetti per
Invenzioni
Modelli e Marchi
Via Molise, 19
00187 Roma
Italy
Tel: (396) 488 4450

**BUSINESS DEVELOPMENT
FIRMS AND BROKERS**

DataBank Consulting SpA
Corso Italia 8
I-20122 Milano
Italy
Tel: (392) 7210 71
Fax: (392) 7210 7402

JAPAN

GEOGRAPHY

Area:
Total Area: 377,835 sq km
Land Area: 374,744 sq km
Comparative Area: slightly smaller than California
Natural Resources: negligible mineral resources, fish

PEOPLE

Population: 125,449,703 (July 1996 est.)
Age Structure:
0–14 years: 16% (female 9,644,243; male 10,121,414)
15–64 years: 55% (female 43,359,249; male 43,624,464)
65 years and over: 2% (female 10,962,552; male 7,737,781) (July 1996 est.)
Population Growth Rate: 0.21% (1996 est.)
Ethnic Divisions: Japanese 99.4%, other 0.6% (mostly Korean)
Religions: observe both Shinto and Buddhist 84%, other 16% (including Christian 0.7%)
Languages: Japanese
Labor Force: 65.87 million (December 1994)
By occupation: trade and services 54%, manufacturing, mining, and constructions 33%, agriculture, forestry, and fishing 7%, government 3%, other 3% (1998)

GOVERNMENT

Type: constitutional monarchy
Capital: Tokyo

ECONOMY

National Product: GDP—purchasing power parity—$2.6792 trillion (1995 est.)
National Product Per Capita: $21,300 (1995 est.)
Exports: $4442.84 billion (f.o.b., 1995 est.)
Commodities: manufactures 97%, (including machinery 46%, motor vehicles 20%, consumer electronics 10%)
Partners: Southeast Asia 38%, US 27%, Western Europe 17%, China 5%
Imports: $336.09 billion (f.o.b., 1995 est.)
Commodities: manufactures 52%, fossil fuels 20%, foodstuff and raw materials 28%
Partners: Southeast Asia 25%, US 22%, Western Europe 16%, China 11%
Industries: among world's largest and technologically advanced producers of steel and non-ferrous metallurgy, heavy electrical equipment, construction and mining equipment, motor vehicles and parts, electronic and telecommunication equipment, machine tools, automated production systems, locomotives and railroad rolling stock, ships, chemicals; textiles, processed foods

TRANSPORTATION

Railroads: Total of 26,506 km
Highways: Total of 1,112,844 km
Merchant Marine: Total of 796 ships
Airports: Total of 164

COMMUNICATIONS

Telephone System: 64 million (1987 est.)

DEFENSE FORCES

Branches: Japan Ground Self-Defense (Army), Japan Maritime Self-Defense Force (Navy), Japan Air Self-Defense Force (Air Force)

JAPAN SOURCES

RESEARCH SOURCES

Demographic, Manufacturing, and Trade Data Sources

Statistical Information Institute for Consulting and Analysis
6-3-9 Minami Aoyama
Minato-ku
Tokyo 107
Japan
Tel: (813) 5467 0481
Fax: (813) 5467 0482

Company Data Sources and Databases

Teikoku Databank
2-5-20 Minami Aoyama
Tokyo 107
Tel: (813) 3404 5235
Fax: (813) 3404 2164

Tokyo Shoko Research
Shinichi Building, 1-9-6
Shinbashi, Minato-ku
Tokyo
Japan
Tel: (813) 3574 2111
Fax: (813) 3573 5094

Databases

Nikkei Telecon
c/o Nihon Keizai Shimbun
(Nikkei)
195 Olemachi
Chiyoda-ku
Tokyo 100-66
Japan
Tel: (813) 5255 2808
Fax: (813) 5255 2809

JOIS
Japan Science and Technology
  Corporation, Information
  Center
5-3 Yobancho
Chiyoda-ku
Tokyo 102
Japan
Tel: (813) 5214 8413
Fax: (813) 5214 8410

COSMOS
Teikoku Databank
2-5-20 Minami Aoyama
Tokyo 107
Japan

Tel: (813) 3404 5235
Fax: (813) 3404 2164

QUICK
1-6-1 Otemachi
Chiyoda-ku
Tokyo 100
Japan
Tel: (813) 3216 5911
Fax: (813) 5632 9046

TSR-VAN
Tokyo Shoko Research (Tokyo
  Commerce and Industry
  Research)
Shinichi Building
1-9-6 Shinbashi
Minato-ku
Tokyo 105
Japan
Tel: (813) 3574 2268
Fax: (813) 3573 5094

NEEDS-IR
Nihon Keizai Shimbun
NTT Data Communication
1-9-5 Otemachi
Chiyoda-ku
Tokyo 100-66
Japan
Tel: (813) 5255 2808
Fax: (813) 5255 2809

PATOLIS—Japan Patent Infor-
  mation Organization
Sato Dia Building
4-1-7 Toyo
Koto-ku
Tokyo 135
Japan
Tel: (813) 5690 5555
Fax: (813) 5690 3501

RESEARCH AND CONSULTANCY FIRMS

Japan Market Research Bureau,
  Inc.
Crystal Tower
2-14-5 Kami-Osaki
Shinagawa-ku
Tokyo 141
Japan
Tel: (813) 3449 8711
Fax: (813) 3473 4029

Mitsubishi Research Institute,
  Inc.
3-6 Otemachi 2-Chome

Chiyoda-ku
Toyko 100
Japan
Tel: (813) 3270 9211
Fax: (813) 3277 0524

Nikkei Research, Inc.
Park Side 1 Building
2-2-7 Kanda Tsukasa-cho
Chiyoda-ku
Tokyo 101
Japan
Tel: (813) 5296 5155
Fax: (813) 5296 5228

Nomura Research Institute Ltd.
1-10-1 Nihonbashi
Chuo-ku
Tokyo 103
Japan
Tel: (813) 5255 1800
Fax: (813) 5255 9301

R&D—Research and Develop-
  ment, Inc.
Ningyocho Center Building
1-4-10 Nihonbashi
Ningyocho, Chuo-ku
Tokyo 103
Japan
Tel: (813) 5642 7711
Fax: (813) 5642 7731

GOVERNMENTAL SOURCES

Management and Coordina-
  tion Agency
3-1-1 Kasumigaseki
Chiyoda-ku
Tokyo 100
Japan
Tel: (813) 3581 6361

Ministry of Health and Welfare
1-2-2 Kasumigaseki
Chiyoda-ku
Tokyo 100–45
Japan
Tel: (813) 3503 1711

Ministry of Agriculture, Forest
  and Fisheries
1-2-1 Kasumigaseki
Chiyoda-ku
Tokyo 100
Japan
Tel: (813) 3502 8111

Ministry of International Trade
    and Industry
1-3-1 Kasumigaseki
Chiyoda-ku
Tokyo 100
Japan
Tel: (813) 3501 1511

Ministry of Transport
2-1-3 Kasumigaseki
Chiyoda-ku
Tokyo 100
Japan
Tel: (813) 3580 3111

Ministry of Posts and Telecom-
    munications
1-3-2 Kasumigaseki
Chiyoda-ku
Tokyo 100–90
Japan
Tel: (813) 3504 4411

Ministry of Construction
2-1-3 Kasumigaseki
Chiyoda-ku
Tokyo 100
Japan
Tel: (813) 3580 4311

National Diet Library
2-1-2 Nagata-cho

Chiyoda-ku
Tokyo 100
Japan
Tel: (813) 3581 2331

**BUSINESS DEVELOPMENT
FIRMS AND BROKERS**

JETRO
2-5 Toranomon 2-Chome
Minato-ku
Tokyo 105
Japan
Tel: (813) 3582 5561
Fax: (813) 3505 5747

MIPRO
World Import Mart Building
    6F
1-3 Higashi-Ikebukuro
    3-Chome
Toshima-ku
Tokyo 107
Japan
Tel: (813) 3988 2791
Fax: (813) 3988 1629

Japan Small Business Corpo-
    ration
37th Mori Building
5-1 Toranomon 3-Chome

Minato-ku
Tokyo 105
Japan
Tel: (813) 5470 1522
Fax: (813) 5470 1527

FIND
6th Floor, Akasaka Annex
2-17-42 Akasaka
Minato-ku
Tokyo 107
Japan
Tel: (813) 3224 1203
Fax: (813) 3224 9871

LBS
IBM Building
2-12 Roppongi 3-Chome
Minato-ku
Tokyo 106
Japan
Tel: (813) 5563 4335
Fax: (813) 5563 4886

Kokusai Marketing, Inc.
2-18-1-611 Sumiyoshi-cho
Fuchu City
Tokyo 183
Japan
Tel: (814) 2362 7262
Fax: (814) 2362 7296

KUWAIT

GEOGRAPHY
Area:
Total Area: 17,820 sq km
Land Area: 17,820 sq km
Comparative Area: slightly smaller than New Jersey
Natural Resources: petroleum, fish, shrimp, natural gas

PEOPLE
Population: 1,950,047 (July 1996 est.)
Age Structure:
0–14 years: 33% (female 317,241; male 334,778)
15–64 years: 65% (female 507,064; male 757,535)
65 years and over: 2% (female 14,970; male 18,459) (July 1996 est.)
Population Growth Rate: 6.65% (1996 est.)
Ethnic Divisions: Kuwaiti 45%, other Arab 35%, South Asian 9%, Iranian 4%, other 7%
Religions: Muslim 85% (Shi'a 30%, Sunni 45%, other 10%), Christian, Hindu, Parsi, and other 15%
Languages: Arabic (official), English widely spoken
Labor Force: 1 million

GOVERNMENT
Type: Nominal Constitutional Monarchy
Capital: Kuwait

ECONOMY
National Product: GDP—purchasing power parity—$30.8 billion (1995 est.)
National Product Per Capita: $17,000 (1995 est.)
Exports: $11.9 billion (f.o.b., 1994)
Commodities: oil
Partners: US 23%, Japan 13%, Germany 8%, UK 9%, France 8%
Imports: $6.7 billion (f.o.b., 1994)
Commodities: food, construction materials, vehicles and p arts, clothing
Partners: US 14%, Japan 12%, Germany 8%, UK 7%, France 6% (1994 est.)
Industries: petroleum, petrochemicals, desalination, food processing, construction materials, salt, construction

TRANSPORTATION
Railroads: N/A
Highways: Total of 4,273 km
Merchant Marine: Total of 46 ships
Airports: Total of 4

COMMUNICATIONS
Telephone System: 548,000 telephones (1991 est.); the civil network suffered some damage as a result of the Gulf war, but most telephone exhanges were left intact and, by the end of 1994, domestic and international telecommunications had been restored to normal operation; the quality of service is excellent

DEFENSE FORCES
Branches: Army, Navy, Air Force, National Guard, Ministry of Interior Forces, Coast Guard

KUWAIT SOURCES

RESEARCH AND CONSULTANCY FIRMS

Amer Research
P.O. Box 6243
Hawalli
Kuwait
Tel: (965) 245 4938
Fax: (965) 246 7853

MEMRB
P.O. Box 20231
Safat 13063
Kuwait
Tel: (965) 246 7154
Fax: (965) 246 7179

Gulf National Consultants
  Management & Finance
P.O. Box 3479
Safat 13035
Kuwait
Tel: (965) 244 4535
Fax: (965) 244 4543

Tariq Ramadan Marketing
  Consultant

P.O. Box 6211
Hawalli 32037
Kuwait
Tel: (965) 534 2637
Fax: (965) 534 2639

GOVERNMENTAL SOURCES

Kuwait Chamber of Com-
  merce & Industry
P.O. Box 775
Safat 13008
Chamber's Building, Ali Sales
  Street
Kuwait City
Kuwait
Tel: (965) 243 3864
Fax: (965) 240 4110

Ministry of Commerce &
  Industry
P.O. Box 2944
Safat 13151
Kuwait
Tel: (965) 246 3600
Fax: (965) 241 1089

Ministry of Information
P.O. Box 193
Safat 13030
Kuwait
Tel: (965) 241 5301

Ministry of Justice & Legal &
  Administrative Affairs
P.O. Box 6
Safat 13001
Kuwait
Tel: (965) 246 5600

Ministry of Social Affairs &
  Labour
P.O. Box 6634
Safat 32041
Kuwait
Tel: (965) 246 4500
Fax: (965) 247 7444

LAOS

GEOGRAPHY
Area:
Total Area: 236,800 sq km
Land Area: 230,800 sq km
Comparative Area: slightly larger than Utah
Natural Resources: timber, hydropower, gypsum, tin, gold, gemstones

PEOPLE
Population: 4,975,722 (July 1996 est.)
Age Structure: 0–14 years: 45% (female 1,114,628; male 1,142,825)
15–64 years: 51% (female 1,316,591; male 1,237,660)
65 years and over: 4% (female 88,320; male 75,748) (July 1996 est.)
Population Growth Rate: 2.81% (1996 est.)
Ethnic Divisions: Lao Loum (lowland) 68%, Lao Theung (upland) 22%, Lao Soung (highland) including the Hmong ("Meo") and the Yao (Mien) 9%, ethnic Vietnamese/Chinese 1%
Religions: Buddhist 60%, animist and other 40%
Languages: Lao (official), French, English, and various ethnic language
Labor Force: 1 million–1.5 million

GOVERNMENT
Type: Communist state
Capital: Vientiane

ECONOMY
National Product: GDP—purchasing power parity—$5.2 billion (1995 est.)
National Product Per Capita: $1,100 (1995 est.)
Exports: $278 million (f.o.b., 1994)
Commodities: electricity, wood products, coffee, tin, garments
Partners: Thailand, Japan, France, Germany, Netherlands
Imports: $486 million (c.i.f., 1994)
Commodities: food, fuel oil, consumer goods, manufactures
Partners: Thailand, China, Japan, France, US
Industries: tin and gypsum mining, timber, electric power, agricultural processing, construction

TRANSPORTATION
Railroads: Total of 0 km
Highways: Total of 14,130 km
Merchant Marine: Total of 1 cargo ship
Airports: Total of 39

COMMUNICATIONS
Telephone System: 6,600 (1991 est.); service to general public very poor; radiotelephone communications network provides generally erratic service to government users

DEFENSE FORCES
Branches: Lao People's Army (LPA; includes riverine naval and militia elements), Air Force, National Police Department

LEBANON

GEOGRAPHY
Area:
Total Area: 10,400 sq km
Land Area: 10,230 sq km
Comparative Area: about 0.8 times the size of Connecticut
Natural Resources: limestone, iron ore, salt, water-surplus state in a water-deficit region

PEOPLE
Population: 3,776,317 (July 1996 est.)
Age Structure:
0–14 years: 36% (female 662,100; male 687,631)
15–64 years: 59% (female 1,163,255; male 1,049,689)
65 years and over: 5% (female 115,236; male 98,406) (July 1996 est.)
Population Growth Rate: 2.16% (1996 est.)
Ethnic Divisions: Arab 95%, Armenian 4%, other 1%
Religions: Islam 70% (5 legally recognized Islamic groups—Alawite or Nusayri, Druze, Isma'ilite, Shi'a, Sunni), Christian 30% (11 legally recognized Christian groups—4 Orthodox Christian, 6 Catholic, 1 Protestant), Judaism NEGL%
Languages: Arabic (official), French (official), Armenian, English
Labor Force: 650,000

GOVERNMENT
Type: Republic
Capital: Beirut

ECONOMY
National Product: GDP—purchasing power parity—$18.3 billion (1995 est.)
National Product Per Capita: $4,900 (1995 est.)
Exports: $1 billion (f.o.b., 1995 est.)
Commodities: agricultural products, chemicals, textiles, precious and semiprecious metals and jewelry, metals and metal products
Partners: Saudi Arabia 13%, Switzerland 12%, UAE 11%, Syria 9%, US 5%
Imports: $7.3 billion (c.i.f., 1995 est.)
Commodities: consumer goods, machinery and transport equipment, petroleum products
Partners: Italy 14%, France 9%, US 8%, Turkey 5%, Saudi Arabia 3%
Industries: banking, food processing, textiles, cement, oil refining, chemicals, jewelry, some metal fabricating

TRANSPORTATION
Railroads: Total of 222 km
Highways: Total of 7,370 km
Merchant Marine: Total of 58 ships
Airports: Total of 7

COMMUNICATIONS

Telephone System: 150,000 telephones (1990 est.); telecommunications system severely damaged by civil war; rebuilding still underway

DEFENSE FORCES
Branches: Lebanese Armed Forces (LAF; included Army, Navy and Air Force)

LEBANON SOURCES

RESEARCH SOURCES

Manufacturing Data Sources

Association of Lebanese Industrialists
Chamber of Industry & Commerce Building
P.O. Box 11-1520
Sanayeh, Beirut
Lebanon
Tel: (9611) 350 280
Tel: (9611) 350 281
Tel: (9611) 350 282
Fax: (9611) 351 167

Trade Data Sources and Trade Associates

Beirut Traders Association
Ashrafieh—Sofil Center
Charles Malek Avenue
Beirut
Lebanon
Tel: (9611) 354 640
Fax: (9611) 351 167

Databases

ARAB Business Net
P.O. Box 830184
Anman 11183
Jordan
Tel: (9626) 648 573
Fax: (9626) 613 194

GOVERNMENTAL SOURCES

Union of Arab Chambers of
Commerce, Industry & Agriculture

P.O. Box 2837-11
Beirut
Lebanon
Tel: (9611) 814 269
Fax: (9611) 804 860

Beirut Chamber of Commerce & Industry
Chamber of Commerce & Industry Building
Justinien Street
P.O. Box 11-8081
Beirut
Lebanon
Tel: (9611) 354 640
Fax: (9611) 602 050
Fax: (9611) 865 802

Ministry of Industry and Petroleum
Sami Solh Street
Beirut
Lebanon
Tel: (9611) 427 114
Tel: (9611) 427 115
Tel: (9611) 427 985
Tel: (9611) 427 986
Tel: (9611) 427 004

Ministry of Trade & Economy
Tel: (9611) 427 114
Tel: (9611) 427 114

Ministry of Tourism of
Lebanon
550 Central Bank Street

P.O. Box 11/5344
Beirut
Lebanon
Tel: (9611) 340 940
Fax: (9611) 343 279

BUSINESS DEVELOPMENT FIRMS AND BROKERS

Beirut Stock Exchange
Sadat Street—Sadat Tower,
2nd Floor
Beirut
Lebanon
Tel: (9611) 807 552
Fax: (9611) 807 331

Banque Du Liban
P.O. Box 11-5544
Beirut
Lebanon
Council for Development and
Reconstruction
Tallet Al Saray
P.O. Box 116/5351
Beirut
Lebanon
Tel: (9611) 643 980
Fax: (9611) 647 947
Fax: (9611) 864 494

Investment Development
Authority of Lebanon
(IDAL)
Tel: (9611) 344 394
Fax: (9611) 344 463

MALAYSIA

GEOGRAPHY
Area:
Total Area: 329,750 sq km
Land Area: 328,550 sq km
Comparative Area: slightly larger than New Mexico
Natural Resources: tin, petroleum, timber, copper, iron ore, natural gas, bauxite

PEOPLE
Population: 19,962,893 (July 1996 est.)
Age Structure:
0–14 years: 36% (female 3,483,893; male 3,684,510)
15–64 years: 60% (female 6,017,327; male 5,996,369)
65 years and over: 4% (female 438,052; male 342,742) (July 1996 est.)
Population Growth Rate: 2.07% (1996 est.)
Ethnic Divisions: Malay and other indigenous 59%, Chinese 32%, Indian 9%
Religions: (Peninsular Malaysia) Muslim (Malays), Buddhist (Chinese), Hindu (Indians); (Sabah) Muslim 38%, Christian 17%, other 45%; (Sarawak) tribal religion 35%, Buddhist and Confucianist 24%, Muslim 20%, Christian 16%, other 5%
Languages: (Peninsular Malaysia) Malay (official), English, Chinese dialects, Tamil; (Sabah) English, Malay, numerous tribal dialects, Chinese (Mandarin and Hakka dialects predominate); (Sarawak) English, Malay, Mandarin, numerous tribal languages
Labor Force: 7.627 million (1993)

GOVERNMENT
Type: Constitutional Monarchy
Capital: Kuala Lumpur

ECONOMY
National Product: GDP—purchasing power parity—$193.6 billion (1995 est.)
National Product Per Capita: $9,800 (1995 est.)
Exports: $72 billion (1995)
Commodities: electronic equipment, petroleum and petroleum products, palm oil, wood and wood products, rubber, textiles
Partners: Singapore 21%, US 20%, Japan 12%, UK 4%, Thailand 4%, Germany 3% (1994)
Imports: $72.2 billion (1995)
Commodities: machinery and equipment, chemicals, food, petroleum products
Partners: Japan 26%, US 17%, Singapore 14%, Taiwan 5%, Germany 4%, UK 3%, South Korea 3% (1993)
Industries: (Peninsular Malaysia) rubber and oil palm processing and manufacturing, light manufacturing industry, electronics, tin mining and smelting, logging and processing timber; (Sabah) logging, petroleum production; (Sarawak) agriculture processing, petroleum production and refining, logging

TRANSPORTATION
Railroads: Total of 1806 km
Highways: Total of 92,545 km
Merchant Marine: Total of 248 ships
Airports: Total of 105

COMMUNICATIONS
Telephone System: 2,550,957 (1992 est.); international service good

DEFENSE FORCES
Branches: Malaysian Army, Royal Malaysian Navy, Royal Malaysian Air Force, Royal Malaysian Police Force, Marine Police, Sarawak Border Scouts

MALAYSIA SOURCES

RESEARCH SOURCES

Trade Data Sources and Trade Associates

Consulate General of Malaysia
Malaysian Trade Commission
630 Third Avenue, 11th Floor
New York, NY 10017-6757
USA
Tel: (212) 682 0232
Fax: (212) 983 1987

Company Data Sources

Dialog Marketing Communication SDN. BHD.
22nd Floor Menara Multi Purpose, Capital Square
No. 8 Jalan Munshi AbDullah
Kuala Lumpur
Malaysia 50100
Tel: (603) 294 0139
Fax: (603) 294 6404

Databases

Internet Executive Service
(International / Interactive
Service, office services, etc.)
54A, Jalan SS2/67, Petaling Jaya
Selangor
Malaysia 47300
Tel: (603) 774 8179
Fax: (603) 775 4111

RESEARCH AND CONSULTANCY FIRMS

Coopers & Lybrand
22nd Floor, 16B, The Plaza
Jalan Kampar
Kuala Lumpur
Malaysia 50400
Tel: (603) 443 4188
Fax: (603) 441 0880

Ernst & Young
1st Floor, Kompleks Antara-
bangsa
Jalan Sultan Ismail
Kuala Lumpur
Malaysia 50250400

KPMG Peat Marwick
4th Floor, Wisma Pereana
Jalan Dungun Tamsara Heights
Kuala Lumpur
Malaysia 50490
Tel: (603) 255 3388
Fax: (603) 255 0971

Price Waterhouse
Wisma Sime Darby, 11th Floor
Jalan Raja Laut
Kuala Lumpur
Malaysia 50350
Tel: (603) 293 1077
Fax: (603) 293 0997

Arthur Anderson
Level 1, Block C South, Busap
    Bandar Daman Sara
Kuala Lumpur
Malaysia 50490
Tel: (603) 255 7000
Fax: (603) 255 5332

Anderson Consulting
26th Floor, Menara Tun Razak
Jalan Raja Laut
Kuala Lumpur
Malaysia 50350
Tel: (603) 293 5133
Fax: (603) 293 5360

Research Pacific (M) Sdn BHD.
28-C Lorong Medan Tuanku
    Satu
Kuala Lumpur
Malaysia 50300
Tel: (603) 291 7315
Fax: (603) 291 1753

MIHR Consulting SDN. BHD.
26th Floor, Menara Tan & Tan'
Jalan Tun Razak
Kuala Lumpur
Malaysia
Tel: (603) 264 8600
Fax: (603) 264 7001

Business Trends
Lot 13.02, 13th Floor, MCB
    Plaza
6 Changkat Raja Chulan
50200 Kuala Lumpur
Malaysia
Tel: (603) 238 8833
Fax: (603) 230 4740

Ecco Personnel Services SDN
    Bhd.
Wisma Lim Foo Young
Kuala Lumpur
Malaysia
Tel: (603) 244 8386
Fax: (603) 244 8464

P-J Point Business Services
    Center

31A Jalan S52/64
Petaling Jaya
Malaysia
Tel: (603) 776 8850
Fax: (603) 776 1234

Professional Services Center
76-B Jalan SS22/25
Petaling Jaya
Malaysia
Tel: (603) 717 8093
Fax: (603) 717 8093 (same)

Abdullah Sani ABD Karim
55-A Jalan SS22/19
Petaling Jaya
Malaysia
Tel: (603) 719 5688
Fax: (603) 719 5664

Acer Consultants SDN BHD
Plaza Pengkalan
Kuala Lumpur
Malaysia
Tel: (603) 442 1622
Fax: (603) 443 8677

IWB Engineering (M) SDN.
    BHD
12-3-3 Jalan 8/70 A S. Har-
    tamas
Kuala Lumpur
Malaysia
Tel: (603) 254 5339
Fax: (603) 254 5258

Perundig Aziz Sehu Sdn Bhd.
Consulting Engineers
50150 Jalan Maharajaleta
Kuala Lumpur
Malaysia
Tel: (603) 242 9022
Fax: (603) 242 9583

Ambang-Hrd Svc.
10-3 Jalan 1/82B Bangsar
    Utama
Kuala Lumpur
Malaysia
Tel: (603) 282 1588
Fax: (603) 282 1859

Anavee Management
Goon Institute
Kuala Lumpur
Malaysia
Tel: (603) 292 8142
Fax: (603) 292 8027

Antheneum Communications
SDN BHD.
Plaza Ampang
Kuala Lumpur
Malysia
Tel: (603) 453 3526
Fax: (603) 453 3528

Brooks Business Institute
17-A Lrg Rahim Kajai 13
Kuala Lumpur
Malaysia
Tel: (603) 716 0991
Fax: (603) 716 0953

Business Trends Corporate
Consultants
25 M Jalan Thamby Abdullah 1
Kuala Lumpur
Malaysia
Tel: (603) 274 6577
Fax: (603) 274 1075

C&A Industrial Consultants
2E Jalan Giam TMN Majidee
Jahor Bahru
Malaysia
Tel: (607) 335 0992
Fax: (607) 223 0997

BTI Consultants
Lot 12 12.04, 12th Floor
MCB Plaza

6 Changkat Raja Chulan 50200
Kuala Lumpur
Malaysia
Tel: (603) 238 8832
Fax: (603) 201 2331

Vital Factor Consulting
30M Jalan SS 21/58 Damansara
Utama
Kuala Lumpur
Malaysia
Tel: (603) 718 0248
Fax: (603) 718 7248

EML Associates
Suite 22.02, 22nd Floor
Plaza Atrium
Lorong P. Ramlee 50250
Kuala Lumpur
Malaysia
Tel: (603) 232 9255
Fax: (603) 232 9259

Korn Ferry International
12th Floor, UBN Tower
Kuala Lumpur
Malaysia
Tel: (603) 238 1655

GOVERNMENTAL SOURCES

US Embassy in Malaysia
376 Jalan Tun Razak

P.O. Box 10035
50400 Kuala Lumpur
Malaysia
Tel: (603) 248 9011
Fax: (603) 242 2207

American Business Council of
Malaysia /
American Chamber of Com-
merce
Unit 15-01, Level 15, Amoda
22 Jalan Imbi
55100 Kuala Lumpur
Malaysia
Tel: (603) 248 2407
Fax: (603) 242 8540

**BUSINESS DEVELOPMENT
FIRMS AND BROKERS**

AcmeSoft Accounting Systems
57-1 Jalan 3/93 Taman Miharja
Cheras
Kuala Lumpur
Malaysia 55200
Tel: (603) 981 9329
Fax: (603) 983 2779

All Consult (M) SDN. BHD.
54D Jalan SS1/22, Petaling Jaya
Selangor
Malaysia
Tel: (603) 774 4502
Fax: (603) 774 4498

MEXICO

GEOGRAPHY
Area:
Total Area: 1,972,550 sq km
Land Area: 1,923,040 sq km
Comparative Area: slightly less than three times the size of Texas
Natural Resources: petroleum, silver, copper, gold, lead, zinc, natural, gas, timber

PEOPLE
Population: 95,772,462 (July 1996 est.)
Age Structure:
0–14 years: 36% (female 17,125,562; male 17,732,725)
15–64 years: 59% (female 29,165,138; male 27,562,285)
65 years and over: 5% (female 2,274,784; male 1,911,968) (July 1996 est.)
Population Growth Rate: 1.87% (1996 est.)
Ethnic Divisions: mestizo (Indian-Spanish) 60%, Amerindian or predominantly Amerindian 30%, Caucasian or predominantly Caucasian 9%, other 1%
Religions: nominally Roman Catholic 89%, Protestant 6%
Languages: Spanish, various Mayan dialects
Labor Force: 33.6 million (1994)

GOVERNMENT
Type: Federal Republic operating under a centralized government
Capital: Mexico

ECONOMY
National Product: GDP—purchasing power parity—$721.4 billion (1995 est.)
National Product Per Capita: $7,700 (1995 est.)
Exports: $80 billion (f.o.b., 1995 est.)
Commodities: crude oil, oil products, coffee, silver, engines, motor vehicles, cotton, consumer electronics
Partners: US 85%, Japan 1.6%, EU 4.6% (1994 est.)
Imports: $72 billion (f.o.b., 1995 est.)
Commodities: metal-working machines, steel mill products, agricultural machinery, electrical equipment, car parts for assembly, repair parts for motor vehicles, aircraft, and aircraft parts
Partners: US 69%, Japan 6%, EU 12% (1994 est.)
Industries: food and beverages, tobacco, chemicals, iron and steel, petroleum, mining, textiles, clothing, motor vehicles, consumer durables, tourism

TRANSPORTATION
Railroads: Total of 20,567 km
Highways: Total of 245,433 km
Merchant Marine: Total of 51 ships
Airports: Total of 1,411

COMMUNICATIONS
Telephone System: 11,890,868 (1993 est.); highly developed system with extensive microwave radio relay links; privatized in December 1990

DEFENSE FORCES
Branches: National Defense (includes Army and Air Force), Navy (includes Naval Air and Marines)

MEXICO SOURCES

RESEARCH SOURCES

Demographic Data Sources

Governmental Information
Baja California 272 esquina
Culiacán
Col Hipódromo Condesa
Mexico, D.F.
Tel: (527) 22 55 00

Buro de Investigación de Mercados , S.A. de C.V. (BIMSA)
Sófocles 18
Col. Polanco entre Ejército Nacional y Homero
Mexico, D.F.
Tel: (525) 80 02 885
Tel: (525) 80 02 89
Tels: (525) 80 70 21 through
(525) 80 70 33

Manufacturing Data Sources

Anuncios en Directorios, S.A. de C.V.
Classification of Commerce, Industry, Professionalists and Services
Río Pánuco 38
C.P. 06500
México, D.F.
Tel: (525) 66 84 99

Mercametrica of México Cities
Av. Universidad 1621, nivel 3-A
Col.Hacienda de Guadalupe Chimalistac
C.P. 01050
Mèxico, D.F.
Tel: (525) 661 62 93
Tel: (525) 661 92 86
Tel: (525) 663 30 04
Fax.: (525) 662 33 08
E-mail: mercame@infosel.
net.mx

National Chamber of Match Industry
Cámara Nacional de la Industria Cerillera
Viena 26–501.A
C.P. 06600
México, D.F.
Tel: (525) 535 88 77

National Chamber of Chemical Laboratories
Cámara Nacional de la Industria de Laboratorios Químicos

Cuauthémoc 1481
C.P. 03310
México, D.F.
Tel: (526) 88 94 77
Fax: (526) 88 97 04

National Chamber of Perfume Industry
Cámara Nacional de la Industria de Perfumería
G. Mancera 1134
C.P. 03100
México, D.F.
Tel: (525) 75 18 83
Tel: (525) 75 21 11
Tel: (525) 75 21 21
Fax: (525) 59 90 18

National Chamber of Silver and Jewelry Industry
Cámara Nacional de la Industria de la Platería y Joyería
Reynosa 13. Z.P.11 CP-11
México, D.F.
Fax: (525) 16 10 67

National Chamber of the Transformation Industry
Cámara Nacional de la Industria de la Transformación (CANACINTRA)
San Antonio 256
C.P 03849
México, D.F.
Tel: (525) 63 34 00
Tel: (525) 6 11 62 38
Tel: (525) 6 11 32 27

National Commerce Chamber Union
Confederación de Cámaras Nacionales de Comercio (CONCANACO)
Balderas 144, Piso 2
C.P. 06070
México, D.F.
Tel: (527) 09 00 34
Tel: (527) 09 19 19
Tel: (527) 09 01 01

Industrial Chamber Union
Confederación de Cámaras Industriales
Manuel Ma. Contreras 133
Piso 2
Col Cuauthémoc
C.P. 06500

México, D.F.
Tel: (525) 66 79 72
Tel: (525) 66 78 22
Fax: (525) 35 68 71

National Chamber of Cloth Industry
Cámara Nacional de la Industria del Vestido A.C.
M.Tolsa 54
C.P. 06040
México, D.F.
Tel: (525) 78 07 88
Tel: (525) 88 06 98
Tel: (525) 88 07 53
Tel: (525) 88 39 34
Tel: (525) 78 72 10

National Chamber of Cellulose Industry
Cámara Nacional de la Industria de la Celulosa
Privada San Isidro 30
C.P. 11650
México, D.F.
Tel: (522) 02 86 75
Tel: (522) 02 86 03
Fax: (522) 02 13 49

National Council of Multure Industry
Consejo Nacional de la Industria Maquiladora
San Antonio 256 Piso 7
C.P. 03810
México, D.F.
Tel: (526) 11 65 66
Tel: (526) 11 65 23

Chamber of Footwear Industry
Cámara de la Industria de Calzado
Durango 245 Piso !1 y 12
Col. Roma
México, D.F.
Tels: (525) 25 49 60 through
(525) 25 49 63
Fax: (525) 11 50 54

National Chamber of Tanner Industry
Cámara Nacional de la Industria de la Curtiduría
Tehuantepec 225 1er. Piso
Col. Roma Sur
C.P. 06160
México, D.F.
Tel: (525) 64 66 00
Tel/Fax: (525) 74 25 55

National Rubber Industry
Chamber
Cámara Nacional de la Indu-
stria Hulera
Manual Ma. Contreras 133-115
Col. Cuauthémoc
C.P. 06500
México, D.F.
Tel: (525) 35 22 66
Tel: (525) 66 61 99
Fax: (525) 35 89 17

National Oil Industry Chamber
Asociación Nacional de la Indu-
stria de Aceites
(antes Cámara Nacional de la
Industria de Aceites)
Praga 39 Piso 3
Col. Juárez
C.P. 06600
México, D.F.
Tel: (525) 25 75 46
Tel: (525) 33 28 47

Trade Data Sources

Mexican Workers General
Union
Confederación Nacional de Tra-
bajadores de México
Río de la Loza No. 6-11
Col. Doctores
C.P. 06720
México, D.F.
Tel: (525) 78 73 17
Tel: (527) 61 33 49

National Chamber of Trade in
Mexico City
Cámara Nacional de Comercio
de la Ciudad de México
Reforma 42
Col Centro
C.P. 06010
México, D.F.
Gerencia de Registro: (525) 46
00 05
Conmutador: (525) 92 26 77

Mexican Chambers of Indus-
trial Relations
Cámara Méxicana de Asociaci-
ones de Relaciones Indus-
triales
Protacio Tagle 104
San Miguel Chapultepec
C.P. 11850

Mexico, D.F.
Tel: (525) 74 90 56

Company Data Sources

National Chamber of Graphic
Arts
Cámara Nacional de la Indu-
stria de Artes Gráficas
Río Churubusco No. 428, Piso
2
México, D.F.
Tel: (526) 59 27 50
Tel: (526) 59 35 00
Fax: (526) 59 15 20

National Construction
Chamber
Cámara Mexicana de la Con-
strucción
Periférico Sur No. 4839
Col. Parques del Pedregal
Mexico
Tel: (524) 24 74 00
Fax: (526) 06 67 20

National Chamber of Radio
and Television Industry
Cámara Nacional de la Indu-
stria de Radio y Televisión
Horacio No. 1013 Col. Polanco
C.P. 11550
México, D.F.
Tel: (527) 26 99 09
Fax: (525) 45 41 65

Centro de Capacitación: (522)
54 18 36
National Chamber or Pharma-
ceutical Industry
Cámara Nacional de la Indu-
stria Farmacéutica
Av. Cuauhtémoc No. 1481
C.P. 03310
México, D.F.
Tel: (526) 88 96 16
Fax: (526) 88 97 04

National Chamber of Publish-
ing Industry
Cámara Nacional de la Indu-
stria Editorial
Calle de Holanda No. 13
Col. San Diego Churubusco
C.P. 04120
México, D.F.
Tel: (526) 88 22 21
Tel: (526) 88 24 34

Data Bases

Products Catalog of the
National Statistic, Geogra-
phy and Informatic Institute
(INEGI)
Catálogo de Productos del
Instituto Nacional de Estadís-
tica, Geografia E Informática
Publications, Cartographie,
Information
Francisco Sosa No. 3873
Col. Coyoacán,
C.P. 04000
México, D.F.
Tel: (526) 58 48 14

IBCON, S.A.
Information Centers Directory
Governmental Directory
Gutenberg No. 224 Col.
Anzures
C.P. 11590
México, D.F.
Tel: (522) 55 45 77 (Conmuta-
dor y Fax)

INFOFIN
Library of the Newspaper "EL
FINANCIERO"
Lago Bolsena No. 176
Col. Anáhuac
C.P. 11320
México, D.F.
Tel: (522) 27 76 00

México Data Bank
Economic Financial Bank
Felix Cuevas No. 301–304
Col. del Valle
C.P. 03100
Tel: (525) 24 31 31
Tel: (525) 24 22 97

**RESEARCH AND
CONSULTANCY FIRMS**

A.M.A.I (23 Agencies)
Mexican Marketing Research
Agencies Asociation
Homero No. 223 5to Desp. 501
Col. Polanco
C.P. 11560
Del. M. Higalgo
México, D.F.
Tel: (525) 45 14 65
Tel: (522) 54 42 57
E-mail: 74173.2654@
compuserve.com

Directory of Business Services in Mexico American Chamber of Commerce
Lucerna 78
Col. Juárez
C.P. 06600
Mexico
Tel: (527) 24 38 00
Fax: (527) 03 29 11

Asesoría e Investigaciónes Gamma, S.A. DE C.V.
Bruno Traven 60
Col. General Pedro Ma. Anaya
C.P. 03810
México, D.F.
Tel: (526) 88 44 44
Tel: (526) 05 03 42
Fax: (526) 88 43 31

Touristic Developments Consulting Firm
Consultores en Desarrollos Turísticos y Hoteles
HB FACTO
Proyecto, Coordinación y Supervisión
Monte Athos 113
Lomas de Chapultepec
C.P. 11000
México, D.F.
Tel: (525) 20 74 90
Tel: (525) 02 68 54

Real State Location Studies Consulting Firm
Consultores en Estudios de Ubicación de Terrenos e Inmuebles
Grupo DECOSI
Tehuantepec 125
Col. Roma
C.P. 06160
México, D.F.
Tel: (525) 74 79 32

AFICE, S.A. DE C.V.
Administración-Finanzas Comercio Exterior
Reforma 9
Col. Centro
C.P. 06010
México, D.F.
Tel: (523) 61 61 54

ICA INGENIERIA
Empresa de Ingeniería y Consultoría

Calz. Legaria 251
Col. Pensil
C.P. 11430
México, D.F.
Tel: (523) 99 69 22

PROSUCO, S.A. DE C.V.
Proyecto, Supervisión Coordinación de Obras
Av. Coyoacán 1878–502
Col. del Valle
C.P. 03240
México, D.F.
Tel: (525) 34 80 23
Tel: (525) 24 90 42

GOVERNMENTAL SOURCES

American Chamber of Commerce (México-USA)
Cámara de Comercio México-Estados Unidos
Lucerna No. 78
Col. Juárez
C.P. 06600
Mexico
Tel: (527) 24 38 00
Fax: (527) 03 29 11

Library of Mexican Bank
Biblioteca Banco de México
Yearbook of the Mexican Bank
Direction of Economic Research
Information Office
Av. Emilio Cárdenas 211
Col. Industrial Tlanepantla
C.P. 54030
Mexico
Tel: (525) 65 98 86
Tel: (525) 65 92 55
Tel: (525) 65 53 40

Local Government Representations in México City
Oficinas de Representaciones de los Gobiernos de los Estados, En El D.F.
(29 States Representatives)

AGUASCALIENTES
Homero 109 Col. Polanco México, D.F.
Tel: (525) 250 03 50
Tel: (525) 254 52 66
Tel: (525) 250 03 86

BAJA CALIFORNIA NORTE
Rio Tane 229 Piso 5

Col. Cuauhtémoc
C.P. 11560
México, D.F.
Tel: (525) 31 97 96

BAJA CALIFORNIA SUR
Tokio 35
Col. Juárez
C.P. 06605
México
Tel: (522) 08 59 44
Tel: (522) 08 71 07
Tel: (522) 08 61 82

CAMPECHE
Santa Rosalia 114
Sección Insurgente
San Borja
C.P. 03100
Mexico
Tel: (525) 75 18 69
Tel: (525) 75 29 02
Fax: (525) 75 24 83

COAHUILA
Lebintz 14, Piso 12
Col. Nueva Anzurez
C.P. 11590
Mexico
Tel: (522) 54 73 92
Tel: (522) 54 74 32
Tel: (522) 54 73 24

COLIMA
Paseo de la Reforma 444, Piso 8
C.P. 06600
Mexico
Tel: (522) 14 17 74
Tel: (522) 08 08 05
Tel: (525) 33 04 23

CHIAPAS
Toledo 22
C.P. 06600
Mexico
Tel: (522) 07 49 02
Tel: (522) 07 26 52
Tel: (522) 07 42 60
Fax: (522) 08 07 24

CHIHUAHUA
Río Pánuco 108
C.P. 06500
Mexico
Tel: (522) 08 01 18
Tel: (522) 08 02 95
Fax: (522) 08 05 45

DURANGO
Amstedam 108
C.P. 06170
Mexico
Tel: (522) 86 02 51
Tel: (522) 86 86 86
Fax: (522) 86 03 32

GUANAJUATO
Arquímedes 3, Piso 8
C.P. 11560
Mexico
Tel: (522) 80 28 70
Tel: (522) 80 36 47

GUERRERO
Arquímedes 147
Col. Polanco
C.P. 11560
México, D.F.
Tel: (522) 54 11 45
Tel: (522) 54 18 28
Tel: (522) 54 12 88

HIDALGO
Ruben Dario 281, Ofna. 1 Piso
13
Col. Las Lomas
C.P. 11580
México, D.F.
Tel: (522) 82 08 41
Fax: (522) 82 10 91

ESTADO DE MEXICO
Explanada 916
Lomas de Chapultepec
C.P. 11000
México D.F.
Tel: (522) 02 51 57
Tel: (522) 02 12 89
Fax: (522) 20 14 02

MICHOACAN
Kansas 48
Col. Nápoles
C.P. 03810
México, D.F.
Tel: (525) 23 09 03
Tel: (525) 23 09 14

MORELOS
Montecitos 38, Piso 17, Ofna.
25
Col. Nápoles
C.P. 03810
Mexico, D.F.
Tel: (524) 88 07 40

Tel: (524) 88 07 41
Tel: (524) 88 07 42

NAYARIT
Prolongación Uxmal 1006
Col. Santa Cruz Atoyac
C.P. 03310
México, D.F.
Tel: (526) 04 97 83
Tel: (526) 04 96 89
Tel: (526) 88 10 07
Tel: (525) 45 30 50

NUEVO LEON
F. Mata 12
México D.F.
C.P. 06000
Mexico
Tel: (525) 21 42 40
Tel: (525) 21 42 41
Fax: (525) 10 21 40

PUEBLA
Insurgentes Sur 421
Conjuno Aristos
Edificio 8 desp. 100 primer
piso
C.P. 06100
Mexico, D.F.
Tel: (525) 84 20 34
Tel: (525) 84 84 71

QUERETARO
León de los Aldamas 26
Col. Roma Sur
C.P. 06760
México, D.F.
Tel: (522) 64 02 11
Tel: (522) 64 02 71

QUINTANA ROO
5 de Mayo 32
Col Centro
C.P. 06010
México, D.F.
Tel: (525) 21 08 70
Tel: (525) 12 51 85

SAN LUIS POTOSI
Lago estefanía 40
Col. Granada
C.P. 11520
México D.F.
Tel: (522) 50 06 22
Tel: (522) 50 08 94
Fax: (525) 45 22 15

SINALOA
Santa Rosalía 116

México D.F.
C.P. 03100
Tel: (525) 59 11 62
Tel: (525) 75 04 42
Tel: (525) 75 38 07
Fax: (525) 75 63 39

SONORA
Julio Verne 39
Col. Polanco
C.P. 11560
Mexico
Tel: (522) 80 08 53
Tel: (522) 80 59 96
Tel: (522) 81 42 26
Tel: (522) 80 62 36

TABASCO
P. Díaz 102
C.P 03720
México, D.F.
Tel: (525) 98 93 18
Tel: (522) 80 60 26

TAMAULIPAS
Reforma 195 piso 4
C.P. 06500
Mexico
Tel: (525) 66 30 27
Tel: (525) 66 34 47
Tel: (525) 66 30 55

TLAXCALA
San Idelfonso 40
Col. Centro
Del. Cuauthémoc
C.P. 06200
Mexico
Tel: (527) 02 97 46
Tel: (527) 02 91 10
Tel: (527) 02 97 46
Fax: (527) 02 81 81

VERACRUZ
Marsella 77 esquina Havre
Col Juárez
C.P. 06600
Mexico
Tel: (522) 08 76 33
Tel: (522) 08 74 79
Fax: (522) 08 79 07

YUCATAN
Rio Atoyac 9
Col. Cuauthémoc
C.P. 06500
Mexico
Tel: (522) 07 20 41

Tel: (522) 07 77 83
Fax: (522) 08 72 67

ZACATECAS
Bahía Coqui 73
Col Verónica Anzures
C.P 11300
México D.F.
Tel: (522) 60 35 85
Tel: (522) 60 39 39
Fax: (522) 60 37 34

UNITED NATIONS ORGANI-
ZATION
Organización de la Naciones
Unidas

(ONU) México
Mazarik 29, Piso 6
Col. Polanco
C.P. 11570
Mexico, D.F.
Tel: (522) 50 15 55
Fax: (525) 31 11 51

**BUSINESS DEVELOPMENT
FIRMS AND BROKERS**
El Inversionista
(Mexican Financial Advisory
Service)
Economic/Financial Analysis
Felix Cuevas No. 301–304

Col. del Valle
P. 03100
Mexico
Tel: (525) 24 31 31
Tel: (525) 24 22 97

Technological Information
INFOTEC (Información Tecno-
lógica)
San Fernando No. 37
Col. Toriello Guerra
Del. Tlalpan
C.P. 14000
Mexico
Tel: (526) 24 28 00

NETHERLANDS

GEOGRAPHY
Area:
Total Area: 37,330 sq km
Land Area: 33,920 sq km
Comparative Area: slightly less than twice the size of New Jersey
Natural Resources: natural gas, petroleum, fertile soil

PEOPLE
Population: 15,568,034 (July 1996 est.)
Age Structure:
0–14 years: 18% (female 1,393,402; male 1,457,694)
15–64 years: 68% (female 5,228,579; male 5,412,402)
65 years and over: 14% (female 1,239,023; male 836,934) (July 1996 est.)
Population Growth Rate: 0.56% (1996 est.)
Ethnic Divisions: Dutch 96%, Moroccans, Turks, and other 4% (1988)
Religions: Roman Catholic 34%, Protestant 25%, Muslim 3%, other 2%, unaffiliated 36% (1991)
Languages: Dutch
Labor Force: 6.4 million (1993)

GOVERNMENT
Type: Constitutional Monarchy
Capital: Amsterdam; The Hague is the seat of government

ECONOMY
National Product: GDP—purchasing power parity—$301.9 billion (1995 est.)
National Product Per Capita: $19,500 (1995 est.)
Exports: $146 billion (f.o.b., 1995)
Commodities: metal products, chemicals, processed food and tobacco, agricultural products
Partners: EU 73%, (Germany 28%, Belgium-Luxembourg 13%, UK 9%), Central and Eastern Europe 2%, US 5% (1994)
Imports: $133 billion (c.i.f., 1995)
Commodities: raw materials and semifinished products, consumer goods, transportation equipment, crude oil, food products
Partners: EU 56% (Germany 21%, Belgium-Luxembourg 11%, UK 8.5%), US 8.6% (1994)
Industries: agroindustries, metal and engineering products, electrical machinery and equipment, chemicals, petroleum, fishing, construction, microelectronics

TRANSPORTATION
Railroads: Total of 2,891 km
Highways: Total of 104,831 km
Merchant Marine: Total of 352 ships
Airports: Total of 28

COMMUNICATIONS
Telephone System: 8.272 million telephones (1983 est.); highly developed and well maintained; extensive redundant system of multi conductor cables, supplemented by microwave radio relay

DEFENSE FORCES
Branches: Royal Netherlands Army, Royal Netherlands Navy (includes Naval Air Service and Marine Corps), Royal Netherlands Air Force, Royal Constabulary

NETHERLANDS SOURCES

RESEARCH SOURCES

Demographic Data Sources

Centraal Bureau voor de Statistiek
Afdeling Verkoop
Kamer J116—Postbus 4481
6401 CZ Neerlen
Netherlands
Tel: (3145) 570 79 70
Fax: (3145) 570 62 68

Statistics Netherlands (CBS)
Statistical Informatics
Department
Prinses Beatrixlaan 428—P.O.
Box 4000
2270 JM Voorburg
Netherlands
Tel: (3170) 337 5050
Fax: (3170) 337 5990

Manufacturing Data Sources

ESTEC/QB, ECSS Secretariat
Keperlaan 1
NL 2200 AG Noordwijk
Netherlands
Tel: (3171) 565 3952
Fax: (3171) 565 6839

The Dutch Council for Accreditation (RvA)
Radboudkwartier 223—P.O.
Box 2768
3511 DN, Utrecht
Netherlands
Tel: (3130) 239 4500
Fax: (3130) 239 45 39

Nederlands Meetinstituut B.V.
Schoemakerstraat 97—P.O.
Box 654
Delft
Netherlands
Tel: (31) 269 1800
Fax: (31) 261 2971

Trade Data Sources and Trade Associates

HISWA Export Group
P.O. Box 98
1135 ZJ Edam
Netherlands
Tel: (31299) 372 620
Fax: (31299) 371 528

Netherlands Foreign Investment Agency

Bezuidenhoutseweg 2—P.O.
Box 20101
2500 EC Den Haag
Netherlands
Tel: (3170) 379 8818
Fax: (3170) 379 6322

Company Data Sources

Information Desk Senter
Agency for Technology, Energy
and Environment
Postbus 30732
2500 GS Den Haag
Netherlands
Tel: (3170) 361 0311
Fax: (3170) 361 0355

Information Desk NWO
Postbus 93138
2509 AC Den Haag
Netherlands
Tel: (3170) 344 0714
Fax: (3170) 384 0971

Bedrijven Informatie Informatie Centrum (B.I.C.)
Rotterdam School of
Management / Faculteit
Bedrijfskunde
Burgemeester Oudlaan 50
3062 PA Rotterdam
Netherlands
Tel: (3110) 408 2014
Tel: (3110) 408 1903

Databases

Redactie InfoServices—
Koninklijke Bibliotheek
Prins Willem Alexanderhof 5
2595 BE DEN HAAG
Netherlands
Tel: (3170) 314 0501
Fax: (3170) 314 0615

SURFnet bv
Hoog Catharijne—P.O. Box
19035
NL 3501 DA Utrecht
Netherlands
Tel: (3130) 230 5305
Fax: (3130) 230 5329

Adviesraad voor het Wetenschaps- en Technologiebeleid (AWT)
Javastraat 42
2582 AP Den Haag

Netherlands
Tel: (3170) 3639922
Fax: (3170) 360 8992

ABC voor handel en industrie
c.v.
Koningin Wilhelminalaan 16
2012 JK Haarlem
Netherlands
Tel: (3123) 532 7033
Fax: (3123) 531 9031

RESEARCH AND CONSULTANCY FIRMS

Adriaan H. Koppens &
Partners
Spoorstraat 2
P.O. Box 262
3740 AG Baarn
Netherlands
Tel: (3121) 541 1741
Fax: (3121) 542 3744

Rodenberg Tillman Associates
Spoorstraat 2
P.O. Box 482
3740 Al Baarn
Netherlands
Tel: (3135) 543 1144
Fax: (3135) 542 5533
E-mail: tillman@-
knoware.nl.

MRC Onderzoek & Advies BV
Houttuinlaan 16a
3447 GM Woerden
Netherlands
Tel: (31348) 420550
Fax: (31348) 425431

Strateq—Market Oriented
Strategic Research
Balistraat 60
2585 XV's Gravenhage
Netherlands
Tel: (3170) 346 9548
Fax: (3170) 363 3984

NIPO, The Market Research
Institute
Grote Bickersstraat 74
1013 KS Amsterdam
Netherlands
Tel: (3120) 522 5444
Fax: (3120) 522 5333
E-mail: info@nipo.nl

GOVERNMENTAL SOURCES

Ministry for Economic Affairs
Postbus 20101
2500 EC Den Haag
Netherlands
Tel: (3170) 379 8911
Fax: (3170) 347 4081

Ministerie van Landbouw,
  Natuurbeheer en Visserij
Bezuidenhoutseweg 73

Postbus 20401
2500 EK Den Haag
Netherlands
Tel: (3170) 379 3911
Fax: (3170) 381 5153

**BUSINESS DEVELOPMENT
FIRMS AND BROKERS**

Media Development Europe
Luchthavenweg 59
5657 EA Eindhoven

Netherlands
Tel: (3140) 257 1935
Fax: (3140) 257 2098

GfK Nederland bv
Schaepmanlaan 55
5103 BB Dongen
Netherlands
Tel: (31) 1623 844000
Fax: (31) 1623 22337

NORWAY

GEOGRAPHY
Area:
Total Area: 324,220 sq km
Land Area: 307,860 sq km
Comparative Area: slightly larger than New Mexico
Natural Resources: petroleum, copper, natural gas, pyrites, nickel, iron ore, zinc, lead, fish, timber, hydropower

PEOPLE
Population: 4,383,807 (July 1996 est.)
Age Structure:
0–14 years: 19% (female 411,668; male 434,848)
15–64 years: 65% (female 1,396,150; male 1,446,746)
65 years and over: 16% (female 405,606; male 288,789) (July 1996 est.)
Population Growth Rate: 0.48% (1996 est.)
Ethnic Divisions: Germanic (Nordic, Alpine, Baltic), Lapps (Sami) 20,000
Religions: Evangelical Lutheran 87.8% (state church), other Protestant and Roman Catholic 3.8%, none 3.2%, unknown 5.2% (1980)
Languages: Norwegian (official)
Labor Force: 2.13 million

GOVERNMENT
Type: Constitutional Monarchy
Capital: Oslo

ECONOMY
National Product: GDP—purchasing power parity—$106.2 billion (1995 est.)
National Product Per Capita: $24,500 (1995 est.)
Exports: $34.7 billion (f.o.b., 1994)
Commodities: petroleum and petroleum products 43%, metals and products 11%, foodstuffs (mostly fish) 9%, chemicals and raw materials 25%, natural gas 6.0%, ships 5.4%
Partners: EU 77.8% (UK 20.8%, Germany 12.4%, France 8.12%), Sweden 9.4%, US 6.7%, Japan 1.9% (1994)
Imports: $27.3 billion (c.i.f., 1994)
Commodities: machinery and equipment and manufactured consumer goods 54%, chemicals and other industrial inputs 39%, foodstuffs 6%
Partners: EU 68.9% (Germany 13.9%, UK 10.4%, Denmark 7.4%), Sweden 15%, US 7.4%, Japan 6.0% (1994)
Industries: petroleum and gas, food processing, shipbuilding, pulp and paper products, metals, chemicals, timber, mining, textiles, fishing

TRANSPORTATION
Railroads: Total of 4,027 km
Highways: Total of 88,922 km
Merchant Marine: Total of 712 ships
Airports: Total of 102

COMMUNICATIONS
Telephone System: 2.39 million telephones (1986 est.); high-quality domestic and international telephone, telegraph, and telex services

DEFENSE FORCES
Branches: Norwegian Army, Royal Norwegian Navy (includes Coast Artillery and Coast Guard), Royal Norwegian Air Force, Home Guard

NORWAY SOURCES

RESEARCH SOURCES

Demographic Data Sources

Statistisk Sentralbyra (CEBA)
Skipprgata 15
P.O. Box 8131 Dep.
N-0033 Oslo
Norway
Tel: (4722) 864 500
Fax: (4722) 864 988

Manufacturing Data Sources

Bureau Veritas Quality International (BVQI)
P.O. Box 1765 Vika
0122 Oslo
Norway
Tel: (4722) 417 620
Fax: (4722) 412 503

Trade Data Sources and Trade Associates

Naeringslivets Hovedorganisasjon (NHO)
Confederation of Norwegian
  Business & Industry
Middelthunsgate 27
P.O. Box 5250 Majorstua
0303 Oslo 3
Norway
Tel: (4722) 95 50 00
Fax: (4722) 69 55 93

Norwegian Trade Council
Drammensveien 40
0243 Oslo
Norway
Tel: (4722) 92 63 00
Fax: (4722) 92 64 00

Company Data Sources

Bronnoysundregistrene
Register of Business Enterprises
P.O. Box 1400
N-8901 Bronnoysund
Norway
Tel: (4775) 00 75 00
Fax: (4775) 00 75 05

Databases

UNINETT A/S
Pb 6883—Elgeseter
7002 Trondheim
Norway
Tel: (4773) 59 29 80

The Norwegian EMBnet node
The Biotechnology Centre of
  Oslo
University of Oslo
Gaustadallen 21
0317 Oslo
Norway
Tel: (4722) 95 87 56
Fax: (4722) 69 41 30

RESEARCH AND CONSULTANCY FIRMS

Markeds—og Mediainstituttet
  A/S (MMI)
Chr. Krohgsgt. 2
0186 Oslo
Norway
Tel: (4722) 95 47 00
Fax: (4722) 17 12 81

SCAN-FACT Marketing
  A/S
Kongensgate 15
0128 Oslo 1
Norway
Tel: (4722) 47 35 00
Fax: (4722) 47 35 01

Yankelovich InfoJobs AS
Fornebuveien 37
1324 Lysaker Oslo
Norway
Tel: (4767) 12 74 00
Fax: (4767) 12 73 65

GOVERNMENTAL SOURCES

Naeringsdepartementet
Royal Norwegian Ministry of
  Industry and Energy
Ploensgate 8

P.O. Box 8148
0033 Oslo
Norway
Tel: (4722) 34 90 90
Fax: (4722) 34 95 25

Utenriksdepartementet
Royal Norwegian Ministry of
  Foreign Affairs
7 Juni Plass 1
P.O. Box 8114 Dep
0032 Oslo
Norway
Tel: (4722) 34 36 00
Fax: (4722) 34 95 80

Miljoverndepartementet
The Ministry of Environmental
  Affairs
Myntgata 2
P.O. Box 8013
0030 Oslo
Norway
Tel: (4722) 34 90 90
Fax: (4722) 34 95 60

BUSINESS DEVELOPMENT FIRMS AND BROKERS

Statens Naerings & Distriktutviklingsfond
The Regional Development
  Fund
Akersgaten 13
P.O. Box 448 Sentrum
0104 Oslo
Norway
Tel: (4722) 00 25 00
Fax: (4722) 42 96 11

Nilsen Norge A/S
Kjelsasveien 160
0411 Oslo
Norway
Tel: (4722) 95 09 20
Fax: (4722) 95 07 29

OMAN

GEOGRAPHY
Area:
Total Area: 212,460 sq km
Land Area: 212,460 sq km
Comparative Area: slightly smaller than Kansas
Natural Resources: petroleum, copper, asbestos, some marble, limestone, chromium, gypsum, natural gas

PEOPLE
Population: 2,186,548 (July 1996 est.)
Age Structure:
0–14 years: 46% (female 493,369; male 511,664)
15–64 years: 51% (female 513,042; male 609,423)
65 years and over: 3% (female 32,427; male 26,623) (July 1996 est.)
Population Growth Rate: 3.53% (1996 est.)
Ethnic Divisions: Arab, Baluchi, South Asian (Indian, Pakistani, Sri Lankan, Bangladeshi), African
Religions: Ibadhi Muslim 75%, Sunni Muslim, Shi'a Muslim, Hindu
Languages: Arabic (official), English, Baluchi, Urdu, Indian dialects
Labor Force: 454,000

GOVERNMENT
Type: Monarchy
Capital: Muscat

ECONOMY
National Product: GDP—purchasing power parity—$19.1 billion (1995 est.)
National Product Per Capita: $10,800 (1995 est.)
Exports: $4.8 billion (f.o.b., 1994 est.)
Commodities: petroleum 87%, reexports, fish, processed copper, textiles
Partners: Japan 35%, South Korea 15.8%, US 9%, China 8%, Thailand 5% (1994)
Imports: $4 billion (c.i.f., 1994 est.)
Commodities: machinery and equipment, chemicals, foodstuff, motor vehicles, textiles
Partners: UAE 27% (largely reexports), Japan 20%, UK 15%, US 5%, Germany 4% (1993)
Industries: crude oil production and refining, natural gas production, construction, cement, copper

TRANSPORTATION
Railroads: N/A
Highways: Total of 25,948 km
Merchant Marine: Total of 3 ships
Airports: Total of 129

COMMUNICATIONS
Telephone System: 150,000 telephones (1994 est.); modern system consisting of open wire, microwave, and radiotelephone communication stations; limited coaxial cable

DEFENSE FORCES
Branches: Army, Navy, Air Force, paramilitary (includes Royal Oman Police)

OMAN SOURCES

**RESEARCH AND
CONSULTANCY FIRMS**

Amer Research
P.O. Box 2655
Ruwi 112
Sultanate of Oman
Tel: (968) 701 063
Fax: (968) 701 064

Arthur Anderson & Co.
P.O. Box 3482
Ruwi 112
4th Floor, Citibank Building
  MBD
Sultanate of Oman
Tel: (968) 796 983
Fax: (968) 797 403

Oman Management Consul-
tants
P.O. Box 233
Muscat 113

Sultanate of Oman
Tel: (968) 540 497
Fax: (968) 705 789

GOVERNMENTAL SOURCES

Oman Chamber of Com-
merce & Industry
P.O. Box 1400
Ruwi 112
Sultanate of Oman
Tel: (968) 707 674
Fax: (968) 708 497

Ministry of Commerce &
  Industry
P.O. Box 550
PC 112
Sultanate of Oman
Tel: (968) 707 728
Fax: (968) 707 215

Ministry of Finance
P.O. Box 506

PC 112
Sultanate of Oman
Tel: (968) 738 201
Fax: (968) 738 140

Ministry of Information
P.O. Box 600
PC 113
Sultanate of Oman
Tel: (968) 603 222
Fax: (968) 601 638

Ministry of Legal Affairs
P.O. Box 578
PC 112
Sultanate of Oman
Tel: (968) 605 802
Fax: (968) 605 697

Ministry of National Economy
P.O. Box 506
PC 113
Sultanate of Oman
Tel: (968) 738 201

PERU

GEOGRAPHY
Area:
Total Area: 1,285,220 sq km
Land Area: 1,280,000 sq km
Comparative Area: slightly smaller than Alaska
Natural Resources: copper, silver, gold, petroleum, timber, fish, iron ore, coal, phosphate, potash

PEOPLE
Population: 24,087,372 (July 1995 est.)
Age Structure:
0–14 years: 35% (female 4,152,000; male 4,296,293)
15–64 years: 61% (female 7,280,287; male 7,378,227)
65 years and over: 4% (female 535,156; male 444,889) (July 1995 est.)
Population Growth Rate: 1.8% (1995 est.)
Ethnic Divisions: Indian 45%, mestizo (mixed Indian and European ancestry) 37%, white 15%, black, Japanese, Chinese, and other 3%
Religions: Roman Catholic
Languages: Spanish (official), Quechua (official), Aymara
Labor Force: 8 million (1992)

GOVERNMENT
Type: Republic
Capital: Lima

ECONOMY
National Product: GDP—purchasing power parity—$73.6 billion (1994 est.)
National Product Per Capita: $3,110 (1994 est.)
Exports: $4.1 billion (f.o.b., 1994 est.)
Commodities: copper, zinc, fishmeal, crude petroleum and byproducts, lead, refined silver, coffee, cotton
Partners: US 19%, Japan 9%, Italy, Germany
Imports: $5.1 billion (f.o.b., 1994 est.)
Commodities: machinery, transport equipment, foodstuffs, petroleum, iron and steel, chemicals, pharmaceuticals
Partners: US 21%, Colombia, Argentina, Japan, Germany, Brazil
Industries: mining of metals, petroleum, fishing, textiles, clothing, food processing, cement, auto assembly, steel, shipbuilding, metal fabrication

TRANSPORTATION
Railroads: Total of 1,801 km
Highways: Total of 69,942 km
Merchant Marine: Total of 10 ships
Airports: Total of 236

COMMUNICATIONS
Telephone System: 544,000 telephones; fairly adequate for most requirements

DEFENSE FORCES
Branches: Army ((Ejercito Peruano), Navy (Marina de Guerra del Peru), Air Force (Fuerza Aerea del Peru), National Police

PERU SOURCES

RESEARCH SOURCES

Demographic Data Sources

Consejo Nacional de Población (CONAPO)
Jr Carabaya 442
Lima
Peru
Tel: (511) 426 2947
Fax: (511) 426 2716

Instituto Nacional de Estadística e Informática (INEI)
Av. Gral. Garzón 654
Jesús Maria
Peru
Tel: (511) 433 4223
Tel: (511) 433 3865
Fax: (511) 433 3159
e-mail: Postmast@
inei.gob.pe

Ministerio de Trabajo y Promoción Social
Av. Salaverry Cdra. 7
Jesúa Maria
Peru
Tel: (511) 433 7814
Fax: (511) 431 4906
Fax: (511) 433 0606

Organización Internacional del Trabajo (OIT)
Las Flores 295
San Isidro
Peru
Tel: (511) 421 5286
Fax: (511) 421 5292
e-mail: oit@ilolim.org.pe

Naciones Unidas
Centro de información de Naciones Unidas (CINUS)
Jacinto Lara 320
San Isidro
Peru
Tel: (511) 441 8745
Fax: (511) 441 8735

Manufacturing Data Sources

Cámara Peruana de la Construcción (CAPECO)
Av. Paseo de la República
4297 Piso 5
Surquillo
Peru
Tel: (511) 428 7480
Tel: (511) 432 9217
Fax: (511) 433 0188

Confederación Nactional de Instituciones Empresariales Privadas (CONFIEP)
Vanderghen 595
San Isidro
Peru
Tel: (511) 442 9122
Tel: (511) 441 5070
Fax: (511) 440 7702

Federación Nacional de Asociaciones de Pequeñas Empresas Industriales del Perú (FENAPI)
Jr Zepita 423 Of. 209
Lima
Peru
Tel: (511) 423 4381

Fundación Fondo de Garantía para Préstamos a la Pequeña Industria (FOGAPI)
Av. Central 671 Piso 10
San Isidro
Peru
Tel: (511) 462 4334

Instituto de Desarrollo del Sector Informal (IDESI)
Las Perdices 122. Piso 2
San Isidro
Peru
Tel: (511) 441 4768
Te: (511) 221 7232
Fax: (511) 441 4768
Fax: (511) 221 7284

Ministerio de Industria, Turismo, Integración y Negociaciones Comerciales Internacionales (MITINCI)
Urb Corpac
Calle 1 oeste s/n
Planta Baja
Peru
Tel: (511) 224 3121
Fax: (511) 224 3144

Sociedad Nacional de Industrias (SNI)
Los Laureles 3654
San Isidro
Peru
Tel: (511) 421 8830
Fax: (511) 442 2573

Trade Data Sources and Trade Associates

Asociación de Pequeños y Medianos Comerciantes del Perú (APEMIPE)
Av. Arequipa 4155
Miraflores
Peru
Tel: (511) 442 4192
Cámara de Comercio de Lima
Gregorio Escobedo 396
Peru
Tel: (511) 463 3434
Tel: (511) 463 3435
Tel: (511) 463 3436
Fax: (511) 463 2820
Fax: (511) 463 9813

Cámara de Comercio e Industria Peruano—Alemana
Av. Camino Real 348 of. 1502
Peru
Tel: (511) 441 8616

Cámara de Comercio e Industria Peruano—Argentina
Av. Javier Prado Este 2875 Piso 4
Peru
Tel: (511) 346 2530
Fax: (511) 346 1879

Cámara de Comercio e Industria Peruano—Brasilena
Federico Recavarren 624
Peru
Tel: (511) 241 2589
Tel: (511) 446 0502
Fax: (511) 241 2589

Cámara de Comercio e Industria Peruano—Ecuatoriana
Av. Javier Prado Este 2875 Piso 4
Peru
Tel: (511) 346 2530
Fax: (511) 346 2530

Cámara de Comercio e Industria Peruano—Francesa
Los Nogales 326
Peru
Tel: (511) 421 4050
Fax: (511) 421 9093

Cámara de Comercio e Industria Peruano—Japonesa
Av. Gregorio Escobedo 803

Peru
Tel: (511) 261 3992
Fax: (511) 463 0453
Fax: (511) 463 0455

Cámara de Comercio Hispano
Peruana
Los Naranjos 319 / 323
Peru
Tel: (511) 422 2135
Tel: (511) 440 1367

Cámara de Comercio Italiana
del Peru
Porras Osores 280
San Isidro
Peru
Tel: (511) 441 0849
Tel: (511) 441 1133
Fax: (511) 441 0849

Cámara de Comercio Industria
y Turismo Peruano—Polaca
Av. Aramburu 836-E
Peru
Tel: (511) 441 2824
Fax: (511) 441 2828

Cámara de Comercio Internaci-
onal Comite Nacional del
Peru
Gregorio Escobedo 396
Jesus Maria
Peru
Tel: (511) 463 4263
Fax: (511) 463 9629
e-mail: Postmast@cci.com.pe

Cámara de Comercio Peru-
ano—Americana
Av. Camino Real 111
San Isidro
Peru
Tel: (511) 421 4414

Cámara de Comercio Peru-
ano—Britanica
2210453
Av. Lynch 110
Peru
Tel: (511) 221 0453

Cámara de Comercio Peru-
ano—Ecuatoriana
Av. Javier Prado Este 2875
Peru
Tel: (511) 346 4177
Fax: (511) 346 2530

Cámara de Comercio Suiza en
el Peru
Av. Central 717
Peru
Tel: (511) 442 2345

Cámara de Comercio Peru-
ano—Holandesa
Lord Nelson 419
Peru
Tel: (511) 221 6066
Tel: (511) 441 6170
Fax: (511) 221 6066

Cámara de Comercio y Produc-
ción del Callao
Mrcal. Miller 450
Peru
Tel: (511) 429 5970

Confederación General de Tra-
bajadores del Peru (CGTP)
Pza. 2 de Mayo s/n
Peru
Tel: (511) 424 2357
Tel: (511) 432 6819

Confederación Nacional de
Comerciantes (CONACO)
Av. Abancay 210
Peru
Tel: (511) 427 8258
Tel: (511) 427 0647
Tel: (511) 427 2527
Fax: (511) 427 2567

Confederación Nacional de
Instituciones Empresariales
Privades (CONFIEP)
Vanderghen 595
San Isidro
Peru
Tel: (511) 442 9122
Tel: (511) 441 5070
Fax: (511) 440 7702

Empresa de Mercados Mayoris-
tas (EMMSA)
Husares de Junin 893
Jesus Maria
Peru
Tel: (511) 471 5425
Fax: (511) 472 3849

Instituto de Desarrollo del Sec-
tor Informal (IDESI)
Las Perdices 122
San Isidro
Peru

Tel: (511) 441 4768
Fax: (511) 441 4768
Fax: (511) 221 7284

**RESEARCH AND
CONSULTANCY FIRMS**

Apoyo Opinión y Mercado S.A.
Av. Republica de Panama 6380
Peru
Tel: (511) 446 9668
Tel: (511) 446 9076
Fax: (511) 447 9556

Analistas y Consultores (A&C)
Julio Becerra 252
Miraflores
Peru
Tel: (511) 445 1862
Tel: (511) 446 7474
Fax: (511) 446 7474

Cuánto S.A.
Plaza del Ovalo 203 B
San Isidro
Peru
Tel: (511) 442 3421
Tel: (511) 422 4932
Tel: (511) 241 8084
Tel: (511) 241 8135
Fax: (511) 442 3421
Fax: (511) 442 5460

Compañia Peruana de Investi-
gación de Mercados S.A.
(CPI)
Rio de Janeiro 154
Jesus Maria
Peru
Tel: (511) 221 2909
Tel: (511) 440 2985
Tel: (511) 440 3517
Fax: (511) 421 5320

Consumer & Communication
Research Latin America S.A.
(CCR)
Av. Santa Cruz 348
San Isidro
Peru
Tel: (511) 442 6713
Tel: (511) 440 2144
Fax: (511) 442 6719

IBOPE Time
Av. Santa Cruz 1521
Miraflores
Peru

Tel: (511) 241 2340
Fax: (511) 242 4203

Imasén
Manuel Bañon 430
San Isidro
Peru
Tel: (511) 442 5980
Fax: (511) 422 0821

Mayéutica
Los Laureles 305
San Isidro
Peru
Tel: (511) 421 3266
Tel: (511) 441 7681
Fax: (511) 440 2159
Fax: (511) 441 7681

Nielsen
Av. Salaverry 3240
San Isidro
Peru
Tel: (511) 264 0221
Tel: (511) 264 0218
Tel: (511) 264 2383
Fax: (511) 264 0151

Servicios de Asesoria y Marketing e Investigación de Mercados y Producciones
S.R.Ltda (SAMIMP S.R. Ltda)
Av. Guardia Civil 260
San Isidro
Peru
Tel: (511) 476 6880
Tel: (511) 475 2945
Fax: (511) 476 6870

Supervisión Nacional de Comerciales S.R.ltda
Av. Arnaldo Márquez 1359 Of. 203
Jesus Maria
Peru
Tel: (511) 423 5270

GOVERNMENTAL SOURCES

Banco Central De Reserva del Peru (BCR)
Sub Gerencia del Sector Publico
Jr. Miró Quesada 441
Lima
Peru
Tel: (511) 427 6250
Tel: (511) 427 3940

Fax: (511) 427 5888
Fax: (511) 431 4703

Biblioteca Nacional
Av. Abancay cdra. 4 s/n
Peru
Tel: (511) 428 7690
Fax: (511) 427 7331

Comisión de Promoción de la Inversión Privada (COPRI)
Av. las Artes 260
San Borja
Peru
Tel: (511) 475 6253
Tel: (511) 221 7008
Fax: (511) 221 2942

Comisión Nacional de Inversión y Tecnologia Extranjera (CONITE)
Jr. Antonio Miro Quesada 320
Lima
Peru
Tel: (511) 428 9358
Fax: (511) 427 7696

Comisión Nacional Supervisora de Empresas y Valores (CONASEV)
Av. Santa Cruz 315
Miraflores
Peru
Tel: (511) 447 0925
Fax: (511) 475 0189

Congreso de la República
Plaza Bolivar s/n
Peru
Tel: (511) 426 0769
Fax: (511) 432 2027

Instituto de Investigación de la Amazonia Peruana
Independencia 648
Peru
Tel: (511) 446 9155

Instituto del Mar del Peru (IMARPE)
Gamarra esq. Gral. Valle s/n
Callao
Peru
Tel: (511) 429 7630
Tel: (511) 420 2000
Fax: (511) 462 6023
e-mail: imarpe+@amauta.-rcp.net.pe

Instituto Geofisico del Peru
Calatrava 216. Urb. Camino Real
La Molina
Peru
Tel: (511) 437 0244
Tel: (511) 437 0258
Tel: (511) 437 0244

Instituto Geográfico Nacional del Peru
Av. Aramburu 1190
Surquillo
Peru
Tel: (511) 475 9960

Instituto Geológico, Minero y Metalúrgico (INGEMMET)
Av. Canada 1470
San Borja
Peru
Tel: (511) 224 2965

Instituto Nacional de la Administración Publica (INAP)
Guzmán Blanco 296
Lima
Peru
Tel: (511) 431 0559
Tel: (511) 441 5070

Instituto Nacional de Recursos Naturales (INRENA)
Los Petirrojos 355 Urb El Palomar
San Borja
Peru
Tel: (511) 224 3298

Instituto Nacional de Investigación Agraria
Av. Universidad s/n
Peru
Tel: (511) 437 0393
Fax: (511) 436 1282

Instituto Nacional de Investigación y Normalización de Vivienda
Alfredo Mendiola 4203
Los Olivos
Peru
Tel: (511) 485 1989
Fax: (511) 485 0035

Instituto Nacional de Recursos Humanos
Calle 17 n°355. Urb
El Palomar

Peru
Tel: (511) 224 3037
Tel: (511) 225 3286

Instituto Peruano de Energia
Nuclear
Av. Canada 1470. Urb. Santa
Catalina
La Victoria
Peru
Tel: (511) 224 8960
Tel: (511) 224 8845
Fax: (511) 224 8991

Jurado Nacional de Elecciones
(JNE)
Secretaria General
Av. Nicolás de Pierola 1070
Lima
Peru
Fax: (511) 428 0323

Ministerio de Agricultura
Pje. Francisco de Zela s/n Piso
9
(espalda del Ministerio de
Trabajo)
Jesus Maria
Peru
Tel: (511) 433 2271
Fax: (511) 432 2343

Ministerio de Economia y
Finanzas (MEF)
Jr Junin 319
Lima
Peru
Tel: (511) 427 3930
Fax: (511) 428 2999
Fax: (511) 432 7887

Ministerio de Educación
Dirección de Estadistica
Jr Van De Velde 160
San Borja
Peru
Tel: (511) 436 8831
Tel: (511) 436 2352
Fax: (511) 436 6610
Fax: (511) 436 6386

Ministerio de Energia y Minas
Dirección de Hidrocarburos
Av. Las Artes s/n
San Borja
Peru
Tel: (511) 475 0546
Tel: (511) 475 0065
Fax: (511) 475 0689

Ministerio de Energia y Minas
(MEM)
Dirección General de Elec-
tricidad
Av. Las Artes 260
San Borja
Peru
Tel: (511) 475 0546
Fax: (511) 475 0065

Ministerio de Industria, Turi-
smo, Integración y Negocia-
ciones Comerciales
Internacionales
(MITINCI)
Urb Corpac
Calle 1 oeste s/n
Planta Baja
Peru
Tel: (511) 224 3121
Tel: (511) 224 3347
Fax: (511) 224 3144

Ministerio de la Presidencia
Av. Paseo de la República 4297
Peru
Tel: (511) 447 6986
Fax: (511) 447 4135

Ministerio de Transportes,
Comunicaciones, Vivienda y
Construcción
Av. 28 de Julio 800
Lima
Peru
Tel: (511) 433 7800
Tel: (511) 433 7223
Fax: (511) 433 6622

Oficina Nacional de Procesos
Electorales (ONPE)
Jr. Nazca 598
Jesus Maria
Peru
Tel: (511) 330 2616
Fax: (511) 330 2616

Superintendencia de Admin-
istradora Privada de Fondo
de Pensiones (SAFP)
Av. Paseo de la República 3285
San Isidro
Peru
Tel: (511) 471 3430
Tel: (511) 471 5150
Fax: (511) 221 2229
Fax: (511) 440 6125

Superintendencia de Banca y
Seguros (SBS)
Los Laureles 214
San Isidro
Peru
Tel: (511) 421 9273
Fax: (511) 441 7839
e-mail: jabad@sbs.gob.pe

Superintendencia Nacional de
Administración Tributaria
(SUNAT)
Av. Garcilaso de la Vega 1472
Lima
Peru
Tel: (511) 432 9535
Tel: (511) 432 3169
Fax: (511) 432 2530

Superintendencia Nacional de
Aduanas (ADUANAS)
Av. Gamarra 680
La Punta
Callao
Peru
Tel: (511) 465 5885
Tel: (511) 469 0058

**BUSINESS DEVELOPMENT
FIRMS AND BROKERS**

Apoyo Consultoria
Gonzales Larrañaga 265
Miraflores
Peru
Tel: (511) 241 4030
Tel: (511) 241 4031
Tel: (511) 241 4028
Fax: (511) 241 4032

Banco de Crédito
Centenario 156 Urb. Santa
Patricia
La Molina
Peru
Tel: (511) 349 0606
Tel: (511) 349 0808
Fax: (511) 349 0638

Banco Wiese Ltdo.
Jr. Cuzco 245 Piso 2
Lima
Peru
Tel: (511) 427 6000
Fax: (511) 426 5133

Citibank N.A.
Av. Camino Real 456
Torre Real Piso 6

San Isidro
Peru
Tel: (511) 421 4000
Tel: (511) 441 1034
Fax: (511) 440 9044
Fax: (511) 440 4996

Corporación de Inversiones
Latinoamericanas S.A.
(CORIL S.A.B.)
Av. República de Panama 3420
San Isidro
Peru
Tel: (511) 442 1888
Tel: (511) 442 1890
Fax: (511) 421 8888
Fax: (511) 441 7745

Ingeniería Financiera
Miguel Dasso 144 of. 6b
Peru
Tel: (511) 442 9164
Tel: (511) 440 8058
Fax: (511) 440 8058
Fax: (511) 442 9164

Interinvest S.A.
Pardo y Aliaga 634
San Isidro
Peru
Tel: (511) 422 7785
Fax: (511) 422 8065

Macroconsult S.A.
General Borgoño 1156
Miraflores
Peru
Tel: (511) 221 2692
Tel: (511) 221 2693
Fax: (511) 221 2696

Macroinvest S.A.
General Borgoño 1156
Miraflores
Peru
Tel: (511) 422 2142
Tel: (511) 422 6467
Fax: (511) 422 6467

Norandina Ingenieria Finan-
ciera
Av. República de Panama 3545
San Isidro
Peru
Tel: (511) 222 8011
Tel: (511) 222 8012
Tel: (511) 222 8013
Fax: (511) 222 1214

Prisma Sociedad Agente de
Bolsa S.A.
Las Begonias 475 of. 502
San Isidro
Peru

Tel: (511) 221 8393
Tel: (511) 221 8294
Fax: (511) 421 0804

Santander Investment S.A.B.
Juan de Arona 830 Piso 9
San Isidro
Peru
Tel: (511) 442 2930
Tel: (511) 442 3838
Fax: (511) 441 8347

Sociedad Agente de Bolsa Peru-
val S.A.
Av. Los Incas 172 Piso 7
San Isidro
Peru
Tel: (511) 421 4527
Tel: (511) 421 9018
Fax: (511) 421 8824

½ de Cambio
Av. República de Panama 6445
San Antonio
Miraflores
Peru
Tel: (511) 444 6805
Tel: (511) 445 2109
Fax: (511) 446 9888

POLAND

GEOGRAPHY
Area:
Total Area: 312,680 sq km
Land Area: 304,510 sq km
Comparative Area: slightly smaller than New Mexico
Natural Resources: coal, sulfur, copper, natural gas, silver, lead, salt

PEOPLE
Population: 38,792,442 (July 1995 est.)
Age Structure:
0–14 years: 23 % (female 4,349,467; male 4,559,536)
15–64 years: 66% (female 12,849,300; male 12,698,179)
65 years and over: 11% (female 2,693,407; male 1,642,553) (July 1995 est.)
Population Growth Rate: 0.36% (1995 est.)
Ethnic Divisions: Polish 97.6%, German 1.3%, Ukrainian 0.6%, Byelorussian 0.5% (1990 est.)
Religions: Roman Catholic 95% (about 75% practicing), Eastern Orthodox, Protestant, other 5%
Languages: Polish
Labor Force: 17.321 million (1993 annual average)

GOVERNMENT
Type: Democratic state
Capital: Warsaw

ECONOMY
National Product: GDP—purchasing power parity—$191.1 billion (1994 est.)
National Product Per Capita: $4,920 (1994 est.)
Exports: $16.3 billion (f.o.b., 1994 est.)
Commodities: intermediate goods 26.5%, machinery and transport equipment 18.1%, miscellaneous manufactures 16.7%, foodstuffs 9.4%, fuels 8.4% (1993)
Partners: Germany 33.4%, Russia 10.2%, Italy 5.3%, UK 4.3% (1993)
Imports: $18.1 billion (f.o.b., 1994 est.)
Commodities: machinery and transport equipment 29.6%, intermediate goods 18.5%, chemicals 13.3%, fuels 12.5%, miscellaneous manufactures 10.1%
Partners: Germany 35.8%, Italy 9.2%, Russia 8.5%, UK 6.6% (1993)
Industries: machine building, iron and steel, extractive industries, chemicals, shipbuilding, food processing, glass, beverages, textiles

TRANSPORTATION
Railroads: Total of 25,528 km
Highways: Total of 367,000 km (excluding farm, factory and forest roads)
Merchant Marine: Total of 152 ships
Airports: Total of 134

COMMUNICATIONS
Telephone System: 4.9 million telephones; 12.7 phones per 100 residents (1994); severely underdeveloped and outmoded system; exchanges are 86% automatic (1991)

DEFENSE FORCES
Branches: Army, Navy, Air and Air Defense Forces

POLAND SOURCES

RESEARCH SOURCES

Demographic Data Sources

GUS
Central Statistical Office
al. Niepodleglosci 208
00-925 Warsaw
Poland
Tel: (4822) 25 2431
Fax: (4822) 25 1525

Statistical Data Information
Center
(Centralne Informatorium
Statystrczne)
REGON Register
(enterprises information)
Tel: (4822) 608 3161
Tel: (4822) 608 3168
Tel: (4822) 608 3280
Fax: (4822) 608 3187

Manufacturing Data Sources

Industry Development Agency
Agencja Rozwoju Przemyseu
S.A.
Ul. Wspolna 4
00-926 Warsaw
Poland
Tel: (4822) 628 4114
Tel: (4822) 628 6570

Trade Data Sources and Trade Associates

Ministry of Industry and Trade
Ministerstwo Rozwoju Przemyseu S.A.
ul. Wspolna 4
00-926 Warsaw
Poland
Tel: (4822) 661 8111

Company Data Sources

Industry and Science Informa-
tion Center
Centrum Informacji Naukowj I
Przemyslowej
ul. Wspolna 2
Warsaw
Poland
Tel: (4822) 621 6818

RESEARCH AND CONSULTANCY FIRMS

ANR Amer Nielson Research
Sp. z o.o.

Main Office
ul. Zgoda 6
00-018 Warsaw
Poland
Tel: (4822) 827 0081
Tel: (4822) 827 1044
Tel: (4822) 827 2585
Fax: (4822) 827 2978
Fax: (4822) 625 6709

DEMOSKOP
Marketing and Social Research
ul. Dubois 9
00-182 Warsaw
Poland
Tel: (4822) 831 0116
Fax: (4822) 831 0126

GFK Polonia Sp. z o.o.
Ul. Swietokryzska 14
00-050 Warsaw
Poland
Tel: (4822) 26 1073
Fax: (4822) 26 6933

IQS and Quant Group
ul. Lekarska 7
00-610 Warsaw
Poland
Tel: (4822) 622 0080
Tel: (4822) 25 0933
Fax: (4822) 25 4870

SMG/KRC Poland
ul. Okopowa 47
01-059 Warsaw
Poland
Tel: (4822) 38 8218
Tel: (4822) 38 8706
Tel: (4822) 636 3330
Fax: (4822) 38 4196

OBOP
ul. Derenlowa 11
02-766 Warszawa
Poland
Tel: (4822) 644 9995
Tel: (4822) 644 9973
Tel: (4822) 644 1105
Tel: (4822) 644 2017
Fax: (4822) 644 9947

Andersen Consulting Sp. z o.o.
Atrium Business Center
al. Jana Pawla 11 23
00-854 Warszawa
Poland

Tel: (4822) 653 9200
Fax: (4822) 653 9201

Coopers & Lybrand Consulting
Sp. z o.o.
ul. Mokotowska 49
00-950 Warszawa
Poland
Tel: (4822) 660 0666
Fax: (4822) 660 0572

Deloitte & Touche Sp. z o.o
ul. Grzybowska 80/82
00-844 Warsaw
Poland
Tel: (4822) 661 5300
Fax: (4822) 661 5350

Ernst & Young Management
Consulting Services Sp. z o.o.
ul. Solec 22
00-410 Warsaw
Poland
Tel: (4822) 625 5477
Fax: (4822) 629 4263

GOVERNMENTAL SOURCES

CBOS
Social, Political and Marketing
Studies
ul. Zurawia 4a
00-503 Warszawa
Poland
Tel: (4822) 629 3569
Tel: (4822) 628 3704
Tel: (4822) 629 4089

PESEL
Government Informative
Center
Rzadowe Centrum Informa-
tyczne
ul. Pawinskiego 17/21
Warsaw
Poland
Tel: (4822) 25 6081

National Chamber of Com-
merce
Krajowa Izba Gospodarcza
ul. Trebacka 4
Warsaw
Poland
Tel: (4822) 26 0221
Tel: (4822) 630 9600
Fax: (4822) 827 4673

QATAR

GEOGRAPHY
Area:
Total Area: 11,000 sq km
Land Area: 11,000 sq km
Comparative Area: slightly smaller than Connecticut
Natural Resources: petroleum, natural gas, fish

PEOPLE
Population: 547,761 (July 1996 est.)
Age Structure:
0–14 years: 30% (female 83,552; male 82,147)
15–64 years: 68% (female 109,177; male 263,107)
65 years and over: 2% (female 3,169; male 6,609) (July 1996 est.)
Population Growth Rate: 2.39% (1996 est.)
Ethnic Divisions: Arab 40%, Pakistani 18%, Indian 18%, Iranian 10%, other 14%
Religions: Muslim 95%
Languages: Arabic (official), English commonly used as a second language
Labor Force: 233,000 (1993 est.)

GOVERNMENT
Type: Traditional Monarchy
Capital: Doha

ECONOMY
National Product: GDP—purchasing power parity—$10.7 billion (1994 est.)
National Product Per Capita: $20,820 (1994 est.)
Exports: $2.9 billion (f.o.b., 1994 est.)
Commodities: petroleum products 75%, steel, fertilizers
Partners: Japan 61%, Australia 5%, UAE 4%, Singapore 4% (1994)
Imports: $2 billion (c.i.f., 1994 est.)
Commodities: machinery and equipment, consumer goods, food, chemicals
Partners: Germany 14%, Japan 12%, UK 11%, US 9%, Italy 5% (1994)
Industries: crude oil production and refining, fertilizers, petrochemicals, steel reinforcing bars, cement

TRANSPORTATION
Railroads: N/A
Highways: Total of 1,191 km
Merchant Marine: Total of 19 ships
Airports: Total of 3

COMMUNICATIONS
Telephone System: 160,717 telephones (1992 est.); modern system centered in Doha

DEFENSE FORCES
Branches: Army, Navy, Air Force, Public Security

QATAR SOURCES

RESEARCH SOURCES

Demographic Data Sources

The Central Statistical Organization (CSO)
P.O. Box 7283
Doha
Qatar
Tel: (974) 491 497

Manufacturing Data Sources

Qatar University
P.O. Box 2713
Doha
Qatar
Tel: (974) 832 222

Trade Data Sources and Trade Associates

Qatar Chamber of Commerce & Industry
P.O. Box 402
Doha
Qatar
Tel: (974) 425 131

Intramas W.L.L.
P.O. Box 3471
Doha
Qatar
Tel: (974) 670 020
Fax: (974) 671 214

Al-Sumeity Trading & Services GRP
P.O. Box 15578
Doha
Qatar

Tel: (974) 432 660
Fax: (974) 412 822

Company Data Sources

Gulf Explorer
P.O. Box 13085
Doha
Qatar

InterGulf/Arabian Yellow Pages
P.O. Box 8731
Doha
Qatar
Tel: (974) 420 523
Fax: (974) 437 280

Databases

Hieros Gamos/Law Firms Directory
1800 West Loop
Suite 1880
Houston, TX 77027

RESEARCH AND CONSULTANCY FIRMS

Amer Research
P.O. Box 15804
Doha
Qatar
Tel: (974) 421 382
Fax: (974) 421 387

GOVERNMENTAL SOURCES

Qatar Chamber of Commerce & Industry

P.O. Box 402
Doha
Qatar
Tel: (974) 425 131
Fax: (974) 324 338

Ministry of Finance, Economy & Commerce
P.O. Box 83
Doha
Qatar
Tel: (974) 461 444

Ministry of Foreign Affairs
P.O. Box 232
Doha
Qatar
Tel: (974) 415 000

Ministry of Information & Culture
P.O. Box 1836
Doha
Qatar
Tel: (974) 831 333

Department of Publications & Foreign Information
P.O. Box 5147
Doha
Qatar
Tel: (974) 427 333

BUSINESS DEVELOPMENT FIRMS AND BROKERS

Gulf Cooperation Council
P.O. Box 7153
Riyadh 11462
Saudi Arabia
Tel: (966) 1 482 7777
Fax: (966) 1 482 9089

RUSSIA

GEOGRAPHY
Area:
Total Area: 17,075,200 sq km
Land Area: 16,995,800 sq km
Comparative Area: slightly more than 1.8 times the size of US
Natural Resources: wide natural resources base including major deposits of oil, natural gas, coal, and many strategic minerals, timber

PEOPLE
Population: 148,178,487 (July 1996 est.)
Age Structure:
0–14 years: 21% (female 15,213,854; male 15,792,573)
15–64 years: 67% (female 51,125,902; male 48,145,679)
65 years and over: 12% (female 12,497,413; male 5,403,066) (July 1996 est.)
Population Growth Rate: −0.07% (1996 est.)
Ethnic Divisions: Russian 81.5%, Tatar 3.8%, Ukrainian 3%, Chuvash 1.2%, Bashkir 0.9%, Byelorussian 0.8%, Moldavian 0.7%, other 8.1%
Religions: Russian Orthodox, Muslim, other
Languages: Russian, other
Labor Force: 85 million (1993)

GOVERNMENT
Type: Federation
Capital: Moscow

ECONOMY
National Product: GDP—purchasing power parity—$796 billion (1995 estimate as extrapolated from World Bank estimate for 1994)
National Product Per Capita: $5,300 (1995 est.)
Exports: $77.8 billion (f.o.b., 1995)
Commodities: petroleum and petroleum products, natural gas, wood and wood products, metals, chemicals, and a wide variety of civilian and military manufactures
Partners: Europe, North America, Japan, Third World countries, Cuba
Imports: $57.9 billion (c.i.f., 1995)
Commodities: machinery and equipment, consumer goods, medicines, meat, grain, sugar, semifinished metal products
Partners: Europe, North America, Japan, Third World countries, Cuba
Industries: range of mining and extractive industries producing coal, oil, gas, chemicals, and metals; all forms of machine building from rolling mills to high-performance aircraft and space vehicles; shipbuilding; road and rail transportation, communications, construction, and electric power generating and transmitting equipment; agricultural machinery and tractors; medical and scientific instruments; consumer durable, textiles, foodstuffs, handicrafts

TRANSPORTATION
Railroads: Total of 154,000 km
Highways: Total of 934,000 km
Merchant Marine: Total of 745 ships
Airports: Total of 2,517

COMMUNICATIONS
Telephone System: 25.4 million (1993 est.); enlisting foreign help to speed up the modernization of its telecommunications system; expanded access to international electronic mail service available via Sprint network; the inadequacy of Russian telecommunications is a severe handicap to the economy, especially with respect to international connections

DEFENSE FORCES
Branches: Ground Forces, Navy, Air Forces, Air Defense Forces, Strategic Rocket Forces

Russia Sources

RESEARCH SOURCES

AK&M
3G Gubkina St
Moscow 117924
Russia
Tel: (7095) 132 6130
Fax: (7095) 132 6026

Economic News Agency Prime-Tass
10 Tverskoy bulvard
103009 Moscow
Russia
Tel: (7095) 290 0990
Fax: (7095) 243 9506
http://prime.itar-tass.com

Finmarket Ltd
building 1
4 Alymov Lane
Moscow 107329
Russia
Tel: (7095) 963 2380
Tel: (7095) 964 3319
Fax: (7095) 964 3337
Fax: (7095) 964 3365
E-Mail: agency@finmarket.ru
http:www.finmarket.ru

Itar-Tass Agency
10-12 Tverskoy bulvard
Moscow 103009
Russia
Tel: (7095) 229 7925

Kommersant-Rating Magazine
4 Vrubelya St
Moscow
Russia
Tel: (7095) 943 9125
Fax: (7095) 943 9126
http://www.kommersant.ru

MBIT
80/2 Leningradsky Prospect
Moscow 125190
Russia
Tel: (7095) 158 8080
Fax: (7095) 158 9681

Posfactum Agency
Office 10
21b 5th Donskoy Lane
Moscow 117926
Russia
Tel: (7095) 958 5900

Russian Information Agency
Novosti
4 Zubobsky Bulvard
Moscow 119021
Russia
Tel: (7095) 201 8383

Russika-Izvestia
18/1 Tverskaya St.
Moscow 103791
Russia
Tel: (7095) 209 2083
Fax: (7095) 209 3744
E-mail: root@russika.-
rusnet.sovam.com

Sovam-Teleport / Russian On
Line
12 Krasnokazarmennaya St.
Moscow 111250
Russia
Tel: (7095) 258 0464
E-mail: mosmarkt@
sovam.com
http://www.roline.ru/

Skate Press
8 2nd Frunzenskaya St.
Moscow 119146
Russia
Tel: (7095) 291 2533

RESEARCH AND CONSULTANCY FIRMS

Arthur Andersen
14 Staraya Basmannaya St.
Moscow 103064
Russia
Tel: (7095) 262 5077
Fax: (7095) 262 7336
Fax: (7095) 262 7338
Int'l Tel: (7502) 222 1600
Int'l Fax: (7502) 222 4603
Telex: 41193 PSB SU

Association of Independent
Lawyers
Office 15
12 Obydensky Lane
Moscow 119034
Russia
Tel: (7095) 291 1875
Fax: (7095) 203 1063

Baker & McKenzie
22/25 B.Strochenovsky Lane
Moscow 113054
Russia

Tel: (7095) 230 6036
Fax: (7095) 230 6047
Telex: 413671 BAKER SU

Business Intelligence Consultancy
8/7 Bolshoy Zlatoustinsky Lane
Moscow
Russia
Tel: (7095) 722 3019
Fax: (7095) 206 8824
E-mail: igor@versia.msk.ru

Coopers & Lybrand
5 Belinskogo St., 6th Floor
Moscow 103009
Russia
Tel: (7095) 564 8600
Fax: (7095) 564 8619
Int'l Tel: (7502) 225 8600
Int'l Fax: (7502) 225 8619
Telex: 413258 NWBMO SU

Ernst & Young
20/12 Podsosensky Lane
Moscow 103062
Russia
Tel: (7095) 925 0569
Fax: (7095) 917 3607
Telex: 612130 VNESH SU

KPMG
3th Floor
37 Novaya Basmannaya St.
Moscow 107066
Russia
Tel: (7095) 926 5444
Int'l Tel: (7502) 222 4030
Int'l Fax: (7502) 222 4024

Mosvneshinform
2/1 Pavla Korchagina St.
Moscow 129278
Russia
Tel: (7095) 205 6434
Fax: (7095) 205 7873
E-mail: pavosh@mosinf.msk.su

Price Waterhouse
13 Ulyanovskaya St.
Moscow 109240
Russia
Tel: (7095) 967 6000
Telex: 413866 PW MOS

Russaudit Dornhof, Evseyev &
Partners, Ltd.
95 Prospect Mira
Moscow 129085

Russia
Tel: (7095) 217 2329
Fax: (7095) 217 2389

GOVERNMENTAL SOURCES

Foreign Trade Ministry
18/1 Ovchinnikovskaya
Embankment
Russia
Tel: (7095) 207 4882

State Statistics Committee
39 Myasnitskaya St
Moscow
Russia
Tel: (7095) 207 4882

State Customs Committee
1A Komsomolskaya Sq.
Moscow 107842
Russia
Tel: (7095) 975 4200

Center for Monitoring of Markets and Investments of Economics Mininstry
26 7th PArkovaya St.
Moscow 105264
Russia
Tel: (7095) 163 3812

Moscow Registration Chamber
23/43 Zeleny Prospect
111401 Moscow
Russia
Tel: (7095) 301 1418

Moscow Chamber of Commerce & Industry
22 Academica Pilugina St.
Moscow 117393
Russia
Tel: (7095) 132 7510

Russian Chamber of Commerce and Industry
6 Ilyinka St
Moscow K-5 103684
Russia
Tel: (7095) 929 0009
Telex: 411126

BUSINESS DEVELOPMENT FIRMS AND BROKERS

PR-Impact
4 Komsomolskaya Square
Moscow 107140
Russia
Tel: (7095) 262 6053
Fax: (7095) 975 4744

State Investment Corporation
GOSINCOR
35 Myasntskaya Street
Moscow
Russia
Tel: (7095) 208 9944

Russian Union For Trade & Finance
8/7 Bolshoy Zlatoustinsky Lane
Moscow
Russia
Tel: (7095) 206 8645
Fax: (7095) 206 8829
E-mail: RTFS@RTFS.MSK.RU

Sovincenter
12 Krasnopresnenskaya Emb.
Moscow 123610
Russia
Tel: (7095) 256 6303
Fax: (7095) 253 2481

Security Company Mentalitet
3 Nemirovicha Danchenko St.
Moscow 103808
Russia
Fax: (7095) 292 9811

SAUDI ARABIA

GEOGRAPHY
Area:
Total Area: 1,960,582 sq km
Land Area: 1,960,582 sq km
Comparative Area: slightly less than one-fourth the size of the US
Natural Resources: petroleum, natural gas, iron ore, gold, copper

PEOPLE
Population: 18,729,576 (July 1995 est.)
Age Structure:
0–14 years: 43% (female 3,952,573; male 4,065,224)
15–64 years: 55% (female 4,078,001; male 6,219,737)
65 years and over: 2% (female 203,372; male 210,669) (July 1995 est.)
Population Growth Rate: 3.68% (1995 est.)
Ethnic Divisions: Arab 90%, Afro-Asian 10%
Religions: Muslim 100%
Languages: Arabic
Labor Force: 5 million–6 million

GOVERNMENT
Type: Monarchy
Capital: Riyadh

ECONOMY
National Product: GDP—purchasing power parity—$173.1 billion (1994 est.)
National Product Per Capita: $9,510 (1994 est.)
Exports: $39.4 billion (f.o.b., 1993 est.)
Commodities: petroleum and petroleum products 92%
Partners: US 20%, Japan 18%, Singapore 5%, France 5%, South Korea 5% (1992)
Imports: $28.9 billion (f.o.b., 1993 est.)
Commodities: machinery and equipment, chemicals, foodstuff, motor vehicles, textiles
Partners: US 21%, Japan 14%, UK 11%, Germany 8%, Italy 6%, France 5% (1992)
Industries: crude oil production, petroleum refining, basic petrochemicals, cement, two small steel-rolling mills, construction, fertilizer, plastics

TRANSPORTATION
Railroads: Total of 1,390 km
Highways: Total of 151,530 km
Merchant Marine: Total of 71 ships
Airports: Total of 211

COMMUNICATIONS
Telephone System: 1,624,000 telephones; modern system

DEFENSE FORCES
Branches: Land force (Army), Navy, Air Force, Air Defense Force, National Guard, Coast Guard, Frontier Forces, Special Security Force, Public Security Force

SAUDI ARABIA SOURCES

RESEARCH AND CONSULTANCY FIRMS

Middle Office for Studies
Nejmat Al Tahlyah Building 6,
Flat 4
Al Tahlyah Street, Corner
Seteen Street
Al Azizeyah District, 2nd Floor
Jeddah
Saudi Arabia
Tel: (9662) 670 1879
Tel: (9662) 673 3128
Fax: (9662) 673 448

Middle Office for Studies
Khazzan Commercial Center
Khazzan Street, 2nd Floor
Offices
Office No. 40209 & 40210
Riyadh
Saudi Arabia
Tel: (9661) 405 3790
Tel: (9661) 403 2887
Fax: (9661) 403 7491

Amer Saudi Research Asso-
ciates
Al Dabal Building, Flat 208

10th Street
P.O. Box 5592
Dammam
Saudi Arabia
Tel: (9663) 827 4681
Fax: (9663) 827 1580

National Management Consul-
tancy & Translation Center
P.O. Box 40719
Jeddah 21511
Saudi Arabia
Tel: (9662) 653 1945
Fax: (9662) 651 0549

GOVERNMENTAL SOURCES

Federation of GCC Chambers
(FGCCC)
P.O. Box 2198
Dammam 31451
Saudi Arabia
Tel: (9663) 826 5943
Fax: (9663) 826 6794

Council of Saudi Chambers of
Commerce & Industry
P.O. Box 16683
Riyadh 11474

Saudi Arabia
Tel: (9661) 403 3200
Fax: (9661) 402 4747

Ministry of Commerce
Riyadh 11162
Saudi Arabia
Tel: (9661) 401 2222
Fax: (9661) 403 8421

Ministry of Finance & National
Economy
Riyadh 11177
Saudi Arabia
Tel: (9661) 405 0000
Fax: (9661) 403 3190

Ministry of Information
P.O. Box 570
Riyadh 11161
Saudi Arabia
Tel: (9661) 406 8888
Fax: (9661) 405 5218

Ministry of Labour & Social
Affairs
Riyadh 11157
Saudi Arabia
Tel: (9661) 477 8888

SINGAPORE

GEOGRAPHY
Area:
Total Area: 632.6 sq km
Land Area: 622.6 sq km
Comparative Area: slightly more than three times the size of Washington, DC
Natural Resources: fish, deep water ports

PEOPLE
Population: 3,396,924 (July 1996 est.)
Age Structure:
0–14 years: 22% (female 358,739; male 379,076)
15–64 years: 72% (female 1,219,412; male 1,220,131)
65 years and over: 6% (female 121,684; male 97,882) (July 1996 est.)
Population Growth Rate: 1.9% (1996 est.)
Ethnic Divisions: Chinese 76.4%, Malay 14.9%, Indian 6.4%, other 2.3%
Religions: Buddhist (Chinese), Muslim (Malays), Christian, Hindu, Sikh, Taoist, Confucianist
Languages: Chinese (official), Malay (official and national), Tamil (official), English (official)
Labor Force: 1.649 million (1994)

GOVERNMENT
Type: Republic within Commonwealth
Capital: Singapore

ECONOMY
National Product: GDP—purchasing power parity—$66.1 billion (1995 est.)
National Product Per Capita: $22,900 (1995 est.)
Exports: $119.6 billion (1995)
Commodities: computer equipment, rubber and rubber products, petroleum products, telecommunications equipment
Partners: Malaysia 20%, US 19%, Hong Kong 9%, Japan 7%, Thailand 6% (1994)
Imports: $125.9 billion (1995)
Commodities: aircraft, petroleum, chemicals, foodstuffs
Partners: Japan 22%, Malaysia 16%, US 15%, Taiwan 4%, Saudi Arabia 4% (1994)
Industries: petroleum refining, electronics, oil drilling equipment, rubber processing and rubber products, processed food and beverages, ship repair, entrepot trade, financial services, biotechnology

TRANSPORTATION
Railroads: Total of 38.6 km
Highways: Total of 2,989 km
Merchant Marine: Total of 646 ships
Airports: Total of 8

COMMUNICATIONS
Telephone System: 1.23 million telephones (1993 est.); good domestic facilities; good international service

DEFENSE FORCES
Branches: Army, Navy, Air Force, People's Defense Force, Police Force

SINGAPORE SOURCES

RESEARCH SOURCES

Trade Development Board
230 Victoria Street, #07-00
Bugis Junction Office Tower
Singapore 188024
Tel: (65) 337 6628
Fax: (65) 337 6898

Registries of Companies and
Business
International Plaza Building
10 Anson Toad #05-01/15
Singapore 079903
Tel: (65) 227 8551
Fax: (65) 225 1676

Registry of Trade Marks and
Patents
31 Exeter Road, 02-00
Singapore 239732
Tel: (65) 330 2700
Fax: (65) 339 0252

Ministry of Labor
18 Havelok Road
Singapore 059764
Tel: (65) 538 3033
Fax: (65) 534 4840

National Science and Technol-
ogy Board
16 Science Park Drive
#01-03 The Pasteur Singapore
Science Park
Singapore 118227
Tel: (65) 779 7066
Fax: (65) 777 1711

Telecommunications Board of
Singapore
TAS Building
35 Robinson Road
Singapore 068876
Tel: (65) 323 3888
Fax: (65) 323 1486

RESEARCH AND
CONSULTANCY FIRMS

Acorn Marketing and Research
Consultants
241 River Valley Road
Singapore 238298
Tel: (65) 733 6565
Fax: (65) 732 6128

Forbes Research PTE LTD
585 North Bridge Road
#14-12 Blanco Court

Singapore 188770
Tel: (65) 291 9496
Fax: (65) 292 5301

Research International
150 Beach Road
Gateway West, #20-07
Singapore 189720
Tel: (65) 291 7003
Fax: (65) 291 7486

Asia Market Intelligence (AMI)
10 Anson Road, #21-14 Inter-
national Plaza
Singapore 079903
Tel: (65) 324 2228
Fax: (65) 324 1380

MMS Consultancy (ASIA) Pte
Ltd
140 Cecil Street, #08-02 Pil
Building
Singapore 069540
Tel: (65) 223 3122
Fax: (65) 223 2022

Applied Research Corporation
Engineering Block E-4-04
National University of Sin-
gapore
Kent Ridge, Singapore 119260

7-SRS-Survey Research Singa-
pore PTE Ltd
51 Newton Road, #09-01-12
Goldhill Plaza
Singapore 308900
Tel: (65) 252 8595
Fax: (65) 253 4287

Arthur Anderson
10 Hoe Chiang Street
#18-00
Singapore 089315
Tel: (65) 220 4377
Fax: (65) 223 4795

Coopers & Lybrand
9 Penang Rd., #12-00 Park Mall
Singapore 238459
Tel: (65) 336 2344
Fax: (65) 336 2539

Ernest & Young
10 Collyer Quay, #21-01 Ocean
Building
Singapore 049315
Tel: (65) 535 7777
Fax: (65) 532 7662

KPMG Peat Marwick
16 Raffles Quay, #22-00
Singapore 048581
Tel: (65) 220 7411
Fax: (65) 225 0984

Price Waterhouse
Standard Chartered Bank
Building
6 Battery Road, #32-00
Singapore 049909
Tel: (65) 225 6066
Fax: (65) 225 2366

Frank Small and Associates
510 Thomson Road #15-03,
SLF Building
Singapore 298135
Tel: (65) 258 9911
Fax: (65) 258 2672

GOVERNMENTAL SOURCES

Inland Revenue Authority of
Singapore
Fullerton Building
Singapore 049212
Tel: (65) 535 4244
Fax: (65) 535 5393

Port Authority of Singapore
PSA Building
460 Alexandra Road
Singapore 119964
Tel: (65) 274 7111
Fax: (65) 274 4677

Economic Development Board
250 North Bridge Road
#24-00 Raffles City Tower
Singapore 179101
Tel: (65) 336 2288
Fax: (65) 339 6077

Economic Development
Board / North American
Office
East 59th Street
New York, New York 10022-
1112
USA
Tel: (212) 421 2206

Economic Development
Board / European Office
Norfolk House
30 Charles II Street
London SW1Y4AE
United Kingdom

Tel: (71) 839 6688
Fax: (71) 839 6162

**BUSINESS DEVELOPMENT
FIRMS AND BROKERS**

Adam & Associates
1 Columbo Court, #06-23A
Singapore 179742
Tel: (65) 336 0819

Asia Business Consultants Ltd
28B Smith Street

Singapore 058942
Tel: (65) 225 0656
Fax: (65) 225 3531

Euroconsultants Pte Ltd
Hong Leong Building
16 Raffles Quay #B1-14A
Singapore 048581
Tel: (65) 227 6100
Fax: (65) 221 0259

Latinasian Business Services
10 Anson Road, #33-17

Singapore 079903
Tel: (65) 324 2657

Risk Consultantcy Pte Ltd
111 North Bridge Road #03-46
Singapore 179098
Tel: (65) 339 6500
Fax: (65) 338 5128

SOUTH AFRICA

GEOGRAPHY
Area:
Total Area: 1,219,912 sq km
Land Area: 1,219,912 sq km
Comparative Area: slightly less than twice the size of Texas
Natural Resources: gold, chromium, antimony, coal, iron ore, manganese, nickel, phosphates, tin, uranium, gem diamonds, platinum, copper, vanadium, salt, natural gas

PEOPLE
Population: 41,743,459 (July 1996 est.)
Age Structure:
0–14 years: 36% (female 7,428,123; male 7,578,639)
15–64 years: 60% (female 12,516,467; male 12,356,753)
65 years and over: 4% (female 1,118,671; male 744,806) (July 1996 est.)
Population Growth Rate: 1.76% (1996 est.)
Ethnic Divisions: black 75.2%, white 13.6%, Colored 8.6%, Indian 2.6%
Religions: Christian (most whites and Coloreds and about 60% of blacks), Hindu (60% of Indians), Muslim 2%.
Languages: 11 official languages, including Afrikaans, English, Ndebele, Pedi, Sotho, Swazi, Tsonga, Tswana, Venda, Xhosa, Zulu
Labor Force: 14.2 million economically active (1996)

GOVERNMENT
Type: Republic
Capital: Pretoria

ECONOMY
National Product: GDP—purchasing power parity—$215 billion (1995 est.)
National Product Per Capita: $4,800 (1995 est.)
Exports: $27.9 billion (f.o.b., 1995)
Commodities: gold 27%, other minerals and metals 20%-25%, food 5%, chemicals 3% (1994)
Partners: Italy, Japan, US, Germany, UK, other EU countries, Hong Kong
Imports: $27 billion (f.o.b., 1995)
Commodities: machinery 32%, transport equipment 15%, chemicals 11%, oils, textiles, scientific instruments (1994)
Partners: Germany, US, Japan, UK, Italy
Industries: mining (world's largest producer of platinum, gold, chromium), automobile assembly, metalworking, machinery, textile, iron and steel, chemical, fertilizer, foodstuffs

TRANSPORTATION
Railroads: Total of 21,431 km
Highways: Total of 182,329 km
Merchant Marine: Total of 4 ships
Airports: Total of 667

COMMUNICATIONS
Telephone System: 5,306,235 (1993 est.); the system is the best developed, most modern, and has the highest capacity in Africa

DEFENSE FORCES
Branches: South African National Defense Force (SANDF; includes Army, Navy, Air Force, and Medical Services), South African Police Services (SAPS)

SOUTH AFRICA SOURCES

RESEARCH SOURCES

Demographic Data Sources

Central Statistical Services (CSS)
274 Schoeman Street
Steyns Arcade
Pretoria
South Africa
Tel: (2712) 310 8911
Fax: (2712) 310 8500
Fax: (2712) 310 8501
Fax: (2712) 310 8502

National Productivity Institute
P.O. Box 3971
Pretoria 0001
South Africa
Tel: (2712) 341 1470
Fax: (2721) 44 1866

Manufacturing Data Sources

Industrial Development Corporation of South Africa
P.O. Box 784055
Sandton 2146
South Africa
Tel: (2711) 883 1600
Fax: (2711) 883 1655

Building Industries Federation South Africa
P.O. Box 1619
Halfway House 1685
South Africa
Tel: (2711) 315 1010
Fax: (2711) 315 1644

Clothing Federation of South Africa
Van der Linde Street
Bedfordview 2008
South Africa
Tel: (2711) 622 8125
Fax: (2711) 622 8316

Industrial Rubber Manufacturers Association of South Africa
P.O. Box 91267
Auckland Park 2006
South Africa
Tel: (2711) 482 2524
Fax: (2711) 726 1344

Motor Industries' Federation
P.O. Box 2940
Randburg 2125
Tel: (2711) 789 2542
Fax: (2711) 789 4525

National Textile Manufacturers' Association
P.O. Box 1506
Durban 4000
Tel: (2731) 301 3692
Fax: (2731) 304 5255

Plastics Federation of South Africa
18 Gazelle Road
Corporate Park
Old Pretoria Road
Midrand
South Africa
Tel: (2711) 314 4021
Fax: (2731) 314 3764

Steel and Engineering Industries Federation of South Africa (SEIFSA)
P.O. Box 1338
Johannesburg 2000
South Africa
Tel: (2711) 833 6033
Fax: (2711) 838 1522

Trade Data Sources and Trade Associates

Department of Trade and Industry
House of Trade and Industry
226 Prinsloo Street
Pretoria
South Africa
Tel: (2712) 310 9791
Fax: (2712) 322 0298

SA Foreign Trade Organization (SAFTO)
5 Esterhuyzen Street
Sandton
South Africa
Tel: (2711) 883 3737
Fax: (2711) 883 6569

Congress of South African Trade Unions (COSATU)
P.O. Box 1019
Johannesburg 2000
South Africa
Tel: (2711) 339 4911
Fax: (2711) 339 4060

National Council of Trade Unions (NACTU)
P.O. Box 10928
Johannesburg 2000
South Africa
Tel: (2711) 336 8031
Fax: (2711) 333 7625

Company Data Sources

Armaments Corporation of SA Ltd (ARMSCOR)
Private Bag X337
Pretoria 0001
South Africa
Tel: (2712) 428 1911
Fax: (2712) 428 5635

Printing Industries Federation of South Africa
Printech Avenue
Laser Park
Honeydew
South Africa
Tel: (2711) 794 3810
Fax: (2711) 794 3964

South African Federation of Civil Engineering Contractors
P.O. Box 644
Bedfordview 2008
South Africa
Tel: (2711) 455 1700
Fax: (2711) 455 1153

South African Fruit and Vegetable Canners' Association (Pty) Ltd
258 Main Street
Paarl 7622
South Africa
Tel: (27221) 61 1308
Fax: (27221) 25 930

RESEARCH AND CONSULTANCY FIRMS

Zero Foundation
9 Churchdown Lane
Bergvliet
Cape Town
South Africa
Tel: (2721) 72 3024
Fax: (2721) 72 6897

OMEGA Investment Research (Pty) Ltd
50 Barnet Street
Gardens
Cape Town
South Africa
Tel: (2721) 45 1905
Fax: (2721) 45 2374

CSIR
Meiring Naude Road
Brummeria

Pretoria
South Africa
Tel: (2712) 841 3809
Fax: (2712) 841 2051

Investment Surveys (Pty) Ltd
P.O. Box 5868
Halfway House
Johannesburg
South Africa
Tel: (2711) 805 0923
Fax: (2711) 805 1303

Telkom Marketing
Corner of Bosman and Ver-
meulen Street
5th Floor TTS
Room # 525
Pretoria
South Africa
Tel: (2712) 311 1170
Fax: (2712) 323 7377

Mintek (Mineral Research)
200 Hans Strydom Drive,
Randburg
Tel: (2711) 709 4111
Fax: (2711) 793 2413

GOVERNMENTAL SOURCES

Bureau of Information
Midtown Building, Corner of
Vermeulen and Pretorius
Streets
Pretoria
South Africa
Tel: (2712) 314 2911
Fax: (2712) 323 3831

Bureau for Economic Research
(BER)
Private Bag 5050
Stellenbosch 7599
South Africa
Tel: (2721) 887 2810
Fax: (2721) 883 9225

Chamber of Mines
5 Hollard Street, Crn. Mar-
shall and Main Street
Johannesburg
South Africa
Tel: (2711) 498 7100
Fax: (2711) 834 1884

Council for Scientific & Industrial Research (CSIR)
South Africa

Tel: (2712) 841 4076
Fax: (2712) 804 2679

Department of Mineral &
Energy Affairs
234 Finodale Centre, Corner
Andries & Visagie Street
Pretoria
South Africa
Tel: (2712) 317 9157
Fax: (2712) 320 210

South African Institute for
Medical Research (SAIMR)
Corner of Hospital and De
Korte Street
Johannesburg
South Africa
Tel: (2711) 489 9000
Fax: (2711) 489 9001

South African Institute of Race
Relations (SAIRR)
68 Gekorte Street
Braamfontein
South Africa
Tel: (2711) 403 3600
Fax: (2711) 399 2061

South African Institute of Inter-
national Affairs (SAIIA)
Jan Smuts House, East Cam-
pus, Wits University
South Africa
Tel: (2711) 339 2021
Fax: (2711) 339 2154

South African Bureau of Stan-
dards (SABS)
1 Dr. Lategan Road
Groenkloof, Pretoria
South Africa
Tel: (2712) 428 7911
Fax: (2712) 344 1568

Transnet Ltd.
P.O. Box 72501
Parkview 2122
South Africa
Tel: (2711) 488 7000
Fax: (2711) 488 7010

Spoornet
Paul Kruger Building
30 Wolmarans Street
Johannesburg 2001
South Africa
Tel: (2711) 773 5090
Fax: (2711) 773 3033

South African Roads Board
Private Bag X193
Pretoria 0001
South Africa
Tel: (2712) 328 3094
Fax: (2712) 328 3194

Chief Directorate of Shipping
Private Bag X193
Pretoria 0001
South Africa
Tel: (2712) 290 2904
Fax: (2712) 323 7009

**BUSINESS DEVELOPMENT
FIRMS AND BROKERS**

Investec Bank Ltd.
5 Fox Street
Johannesburg
South Africa
Tel: (2711) 498 2000
Fax: (2711) 498 2100

Discount House Merchant
Bank Ltd
66 Marshall Street
Johannesburg
South Africa
Tel: (2711) 836 7451
Fax: (2711) 836 9636

Interbank Ltd
108 Fox Street
Johannesburg
South Africa
Tel: (2711) 834 4831
Fax: (2711) 834 5357

The National Discount House
of South Africa Ltd.
Loveday House, 1st Floor
15 Loveday Street
Johannesburg
South Africa
Tel: (2711) 832 3151

Institute of Bankers in South
Africa
P.O. Box 61420
Marshalltown 2107
South Africa
Tel: (2711) 832 1371
Fax: (2711) 834 6592

The South African Insurance
Association
P.O. Box 2163
Johannesburg 2000

South Africa
Tel: (2711) 838 4881
Fax: (2711) 838 6140

South African Chamber of
  Business (SACOB)
P.O. Box 91267

Aukland Park 2006
South Africa
Tel: (2711) 482 2524
Fax: (2711) 726 1344

The Independent Development
  Trust

129 Bree Street
Cape Town
South Africa
Tel: (2721) 23 8030
Fax: (2721) 23 4512

SOUTH KOREA

GEOGRAPHY
Area:
Total Area: 98,480 sq km
Land Area: 98,190 sq km
Comparative Area: slightly larger than Indiana
Natural Resources: coal, tungsten, graphite, molybdenum, lead, hydropower

PEOPLE
Population: 45,482,291 (July 1996 est.)
Age Structure:
0–14 years: 23% (female 4,962,915; male 5,531,032)
15–64 years: 71% (female 15,910,846; male 16,374,678)
65 years and over: 6% (female 1,688,171; male 1,014,649) (July 1996 est.)
Population Growth Rate: 1.02% (1996 est.)
Ethnic Divisions: homogeneous (except for about 20,000 Chinese)
Religions: Christianity 48.6%, Buddhism 47.4%, Confucianism 3%, pervasive folk religion (shamanism), Chondogyo (Religion of the Heavenly Way) 0.2%
Languages: Korean, English widely taught in high school
Labor Force: 20 million

GOVERNMENT
Type: Republic
Capital: Seoul

ECONOMY
National Product: GDP—purchasing power parity—$590.7 billion (1995 est.)
National Product Per Capita: $13,000 (1995 est.)
Exports: $125.4 billion (f.o.b., 1995)
Commodities: electronic and electrical equipment, machinery, steel, automobiles, ships, textiles, clothing, footwear, fish
Partners: US 19%, Japan 14%, EU 13%
Imports: $135.1 billion (c.i.f., 1995)
Commodities: machinery, electronics and electronic equipment, oil, steel, transport equipment, textiles, organic chemicals, grains
Partners: Japan 24%, US 22%, EU 13%
Industries: electronics, automobile production, chemicals, shipbuilding, steel, textiles, clothing, footwear, food processing

TRANSPORTATION
Railroads: Total of 3,101 km
Highways: Total of 61,296 km
Merchant Marine: Total of 428 ships
Airports: Total of 105

COMMUNICATIONS
Telephone System: 16.6 million telephones (1993); excellent domestic and international services

DEFENSE FORCES
Branches: Army, Navy, Air Force, Marine Corps, National Maritime Police (Coast Guard)

SOUTH KOREA SOURCES

RESEARCH SOURCES

Demographic Data Sources

1990 Population & Housing
Census Report
Vol. 1, Full Country
National Statistical Office
647-15 Yoksam-dong Kang-
nam-gu
Seoul 135-723
Korea
Tel: (822) 222 1901 through
1905
Fax: (822) 538 3874
e-mail: kkyoung@nsohp.
nso.go.kr

Business Korea Year Book
Business Korea Co.Ltd.
Yoido P.O. Box 273
Seoul 150-602
Korea
Tel: (822) 784 4010
Fax: (822) 784 1915

Korea Business & Industry Year
Book
Hahns PR. Ltd.
Yoido C.P.O. Box 923
Seoul 150-609
Korea
Fax: (822) 785 5340

Manufacturing Data Sources

Small & Medium Industry Pro-
motion Corporation
27-2 Youido dong Yong Dung
Po gu, Seoul
Tel: (822) 783 9611
Tel: (822) 783 9618
Fax: (822) 784 9230

EIAK (Korea Electronics Directory & Catalog (Annually)
Electronic Industries Association of Korea
Electronics Building
648, Yeogsamdong, Kang-
namku
Seoul
Korea

Directory of Electrical & Electronic Manufacturers in
Korea (Annually)
Electronic Industries Association of Korea
Electronics Building
648, Yeogsamdong, Kang-
namku

Seoul
Korea

**Trade Data Sources and Trade
Associates**

Korea International Trade Asso-
ciation (KITA)
Korea World Trade Center
C.P.O. Box 100
Seoul
Korea
Tel: (822) 551 5114
Fax: (822) 551 5100
e-mail: feedback@kotis.net
homepage: http://
www.kita.or.kr/

Korea Trade Promotion Corpo-
ration (KOTRA)
C.P.O. Box 1621
Seoul
Korea
Tel: (822) 551 4181

Korea Exhibition Center
(KOEX)
159, Samsung Dong Kangnam-
gu
Seoul 135-731
Korea
Tel: (822) 551 0114
Fax: (822) 555 7414
e-mail: webmaster@star.
koex.co.kr
hompage: http://www.-
koex.co.kr/e_index.html

Korea Traders Association
C.P.O. Box 1117
Seoul
Korea
Tel: (822) 551 5114

Association of Foreign Trading
Agents of Korea
C.P.O. Box 3138
Seoul
Korea
Tel: (822) 782 4411
Fax: (822) 785 4373

Korean Trade Directory
(Annually)
Korea International Trade Asso-
ciation
Trade Center
C.P.O. Box 100
Seoul
Korea 2

Trade Today of Korea
(Annually)
Overseas Media Corporation
C.P.O. Box 6494
Seoul
Korea

Directory of Korean Trading
Agents (Annually)
Association of Foreign Trading
Agents of Korea
45-14, Yoidodong
Youngdungpoku
Seoul
Korea

Korea Export Buying Offices
Directory (Annually)
Korea Export Buying Offices
Association
159-1, Samsungdong
Kangnamku
Seoul
Korea

Company Data Sources

The Korea Directory Company
C.P.O. Box 3955
Seoul
Korea

Directory of the Korean Small
Business (Annually)
Korea Federation of Small
Business
16-2, Yoidodong
Seoul
Korea

Business Korea Yearbook
(Annually)
Business Korea Co.,Ltd.
Yoido P.O. Box 273
Seoul
Korea

Korea Banking & Finance Year-
book (Annually)
Doory International, Inc.
Yoido, P.O. Box 1167
Seoul
Korea

Databases

Korea Institute of Industry &
Technology Information
Tel: (822) 962 6211
Fax: (822) 962 7199

Korean: CODI, KPTN, DIGS
English: DIALOG, LEXIS/
NEXIS, JOIS

**RESEARCH AND
CONSULTANCY FIRMS**

Pacific Consultants Corpo-
ration
Korea World Trade Center
35 Floor, 159 Samsung-dong
Gangnam-gu
Seoul 135-719
Korea
Tel : (822) 551 3351
Tel : (822) 551 3354
Fax : (822) 551 3360
e-mail : PccPark@chollian.
dacom.co.kr

A.C. Nielsen Company—Korea
Branch
Young Dong
C.P.O. Box 170
Seoul
Korea
Tel: (822) 546 1181
Tel: (822) 546 1184
Fax: (822) 544 8101

Korea Survey (Gallup) Polls
LTD
221, Sajik Dong
Chnag no
Seoul
Korea
Tel: (822) 736 8448
Fax: (822) 739 9696

Han Kook Research, Inc.
829, Yeogsam dong
Kangnam Ku
Seoul
Korea
Tel: (822) 562 9731
Tel: (822) 562 9733
Fax: K23989 HANRE

Korea Development Institute
(KDI)
270-41, Chong Nyang ni-dong
Tongdaemun-gu
Seoul
Korea
Tel: (822) 960 4811
Tel: (822) 960 4816
Fax: (822) 961 5092

Korea Institute for Econom-
ics & Technology (KIET)
206-9 Chong Nyang ni-dong
Tongdaemun-gu
Seoul
Korea
Tel: (822) 960 6211
Tel: (822) 960 6216
Fax: (822) 960 8540

Korea Institute of Science &
Technology (KIST)
39-1 Hawol gok-dong
Songbukgu
Seoul
Korea
Tel: (822) 962 8801
Fax: (822) 963 4013

Korea Productivity Center
(KPC)
122-1, Chok song Dong
Seoul
Korea
Tel: (822) 739 5868
Fax: (822) 736 0322

KMA Consulting Inc.
544 Tohwa Dong Mapo-gu
Seoul
Korea
Tel: (822) 719 8225

KPC Consulting Group
122-1 Chokson Dong
Chongno-gu
Seoul
Korea
Tel: (822) 739 5863
Fax: (822) 736 0322

KTDC Consulting, Inc.
60, Youido dong Young Dung
Po gu
Seoul
Korea
Tel: (822) 786 4900
Fax: (822) 786 4805

Sei Hwa Consulting Co.,Ltd.
C.P.O. Box 4986
Seoul
Korea
Tel: (822) 745 8500
Fax: (822) 738 0447

GOVERNMENTAL SOURCES

Korea Institute for International Economic Policy

157-21, Samsung dong Kang
nam gu
Seoul
Korea
Tel: (822) 561 2999
Fax: (822) 561 2688

Korea Institute for Human Set-
tlement
Tel: (822) 784 2560
Fax: (822) 785 4519

Korean Industrial Property
Office
823-1, Yeoksam-Dong Kang-
nam-Ku
Seoul 135-784
Korea
e-mail: w3master@kipo.go.kr
homepage: http://www.
kipo.go.kr/index-e.html

**BUSINESS DEVELOPMENT
FIRMS AND BROKERS**

Korea Development Bank
Seoul
Korea
Tel: (822) 398 6114

Dacom Korea
Seoul
Korea
Tel: (822) 220 1114
Fax: (822) 220 8177

Export/Import Bank of Korea
C.P.O. Box 4009
Seoul
Korea
Tel: (822) 784 1021

Korea Business Directory
(Annually)
The Korea Chamber of Com-
merce & Industry
45, Namdaemunro 4ga
Chungku
Seoul
Korea

The Bank of Korea
110, Namdaemoonro 3ka
Chungku
Seoul
Korea

SPAIN

GEOGRAPHY
Area:
Total Area: 504,750 sq km
Land Area: 499,400 sq km
Comparative Area: slightly more than twice the size of Oregon
Natural Resources: coal, lignite, iron ore, uranium, mercury, pyrites, fluorspar, gypsum, zinc, lead, tungsten, copper, kaolin, potash, hydropower

PEOPLE
Population: 39,181,114 (July 1996 est.)
Age Structure:
0–14 years: 16% (female 3,055,881; male 3,237,942)
15–64 years: 68% (female 13,352,582; male 13,380,956)
65 years and over: 16% (female 3,587,025; male 2,566,728) (July 1996 est.)
Population Growth Rate: 0.16% (1996 est.)
Ethnic Divisions: composite of Mediterranean and Nordic types
Religions: Roman Catholic 99%, other sects 1%
Languages: Castilian Spanish, Catalan 17%, Galician 7%, Basque 2%
Labor Force: 11.837 million (1993 est.)

GOVERNMENT
Type: Parliamentary Monarchy
Capital: Madrid

ECONOMY
National Product: GDP—purchasing power parity—$565 billion (1995 est.)
National Product Per Capita: $14,300 (1995 est.)
Exports: $85 billion (f.o.b., 1995)
Commodities: cars and trucks, semifinished manufactured goods, foodstuffs, machinery
Partners: EU 68.7%, US 4.9%, other developed countries 7.9% (1994)
Imports: $110 billion (c.i.f., 1995)
Commodities: machinery, transport equipment, fuels, semifinished goods, foodstuffs, consumer goods, chemicals
Partners: EU 60.9%, US 7.3%, other developed countries 11.5%, Middle East 6.2% (1994)
Industries: textiles and apparel (including footwear), food and beverages, metals and metal manufactures, chemicals, shipbuilding, automobiles, machine tools, tourism

TRANSPORTATION
Railroads: Total of 14,343 km
Highways: Total of 331,961 km
Merchant Marine: Total of 147 ships
Airports: Total of 96

COMMUNICATIONS
Telephone System: 12.6 million telephones (1990 est.); generally adequate, modern facilities

DEFENSE FORCES
Branches: Army, Navy, Air Force, Marines, Civil Guard, National Police, Coastal Civil Guard

SPAIN SOURCES

RESEARCH SOURCES

Demographic Data Sources

Instituto Nacional de Estadistica
Paseo de la Castellana, 183
28071 Madrid
Spain
Tel: (341) 583 94 38
Fax: (341) 579 27 13

La Libreria Del Boe
Trafalgar, 29
28010 Madrid
Spain
Tel: (341) 583 22 95
Fax: (341) 583 23 48

Instituto de Estadistica de la
Comunidad de Madrid
Consejeria de Hacienda
Principe de Vezgara 132, 6ª
planta
28002 Madrid
Spain
Tel: (341) 580 23 67

Manufacturing Data Sources

Instituto de Automatica Industrial
Carretera de Campo Real Km
0.200
La Proveda—Arganda del
Rey—Apartado, 56
28500 Madrid
Spain
Tel: (341) 871 1900
Fax: (341) 871 7050

ASCER/Association of Ceramic
Tile Manufacturers of Spain
(ITSE)
Camino Caminas, s/n
12003 Castellon
Spain
Tel: (3464) 727200
Fax: (3464) 727212

Spanish Machine Tool Builders
Association
Avenida de Zarautz, 82
Oficinas Lorea San Sebastian
Spain
Tel: (934) 219011
Fax: (934) 218036

Trade Data Sources and Trade Associates

Ministry of Foreign Affairs
Plaza de la Provincia 1
28070 Madrid
Spain
Tel: (341) 537 11 11

*Prodei. Catalogo de la Produccion, Exportacion e
Importacion Espanola;*
CEDISA
C/Almirante, 21
28004 Madrid
Spain
Tel: (341) 308 0644
Fax: (341) 310 5141

Confederacion Espanola de
Organizaciones Empresariales (CEOE)
Diego de Leon, 50
28006 Madrid
Spain
Tel: (341) 563 9641
Fax: (341) 562 8023

SECIMPEX
PO Box 78
08190 Sant Cugat del Valles
Barcelona
Spain
Tel: (343) 721 8962
Tel/Fax: (343) 674 2091

Company Data Sources

DICODI S.A.
Doctor Castelo, 10, 4º
28009 Madrid
Spain
Tel: (341) 573 7002
Fax: (341) 504 0134

Dun & Bradstreet
C/Salvador de Maradiaga, 1, 2º
28027 Madrid
Spain
Tel: (341) 377 9100
Fax: (341) 377 9165

Directorios Industriales IMPI
IMPI. Instituto de la Pequana y
Mediana Empresa Industrial.
Ps.
De la Castellana, 141
28046 Madrid
Spain
Tel: (341) 582 9392

Kompass
Ibericom, SA,
Julian Camarillo, 29
28037 Madrid
Spain
Tel: (341) 304 7106
Fax: (341) 327 3605

Espana 30.000 (Fomento)
Fomento de la Produccion, SL
Casanova, 57
08011 Barcelona
Spain
Tel: (343) 451 1246
Fax: (343) 323 3885

Registro Mercantil Central
Principe de Vergara, 71
28006 Madrid
Spain
Tel: (341) 564 5253
Fax: (341) 563 6926

Databases

Camerdata S.A.
Av. Diagonal 452–454, 3º pl.
08006 Barcelona
Spain
Tel: (343) 416 9493
Fax: (341) 415 6165

Telefonica Publicidade
Informacion
Av. Manoteras, 12
28050 Madrid
Spain
Tel: (341) 900 131 131

RESEARCH AND CONSULTANCY FIRMS

DAD
Vallvidrera 21–23
08017 Barcelona
Spain
Tel: (343) 205 5716
Fax: (343) 205 6740

SIGMA DOS, S.A.
Flora 1, 2a plta.
28013 Madrid
Spain
Tel: (341) 559 6410
Fax: (341) 547 5715
E-mail: 100524,3470@compuserve.com

Demoscopia S.A.
Investigación de Opinión y
  Mercado
Pza. Carlos Trias Bertrán 7 4°
Edificiio Sollube
28020 Madrid
Spain
Tel: (341) 596 9600
Fax: (341) 555 7232

CIMEI—Centro de Investiga-
  ción de Mercados Españoles
  e Internacionales S.A.
C/Alberto Aguilera, 7 50 Izq.
28015 Madrid
Spain
Tel: (341) 594 4793
Tel: (341) 594 4799
Fax: (341) 594 5223

Sofres, A.M.
Plaxa de Carlos Tias Bertrán 7
Edificio Sollube 4a planta
28020 Madrid
Spain
Tel: (341) 596 9606
Fax: (341) 597 4077

GOVERNMENTAL SOURCES

Ministry of Industry and
  Energy
Paseo de la Castellana 160
28071 Madrid
Spain
Tel: (341) 349 4801
Fax: (341) 349 4802

Officina Espanola de Patentes y
  Marcas
Panama 1
E-28071 Madrid
Spain
Tel: (341) 349 5300
Fax: (341) 457 2280

Servicio de Informacion
  Administrativa
C/ Alcala, 9
28071 Madrid
Spain
Tel: (341) 522 64 51

Instituto Espanol de Comercio
  Exterior (ICEX)
Direccion General de Informa-

cion. Division de Formacion
  y Publicaciones
Paseo de la Castellana, 14
28071 Madrid
Spain
Tel: (341) 349 6100

**BUSINESS DEVELOPMENT
FIRMS AND BROKERS**

INCRESA Madrid
Villanueva, 35
28001 Madrid
Spain
Tel: (341) 577 7216
Fax: (341) 577 9200

CIDEM
Avda. Diagonal 449, 7e
08036 Barcelona
Spain
Tel: (343) 405 1104
Fax: (343) 419 8823

Euro Info Centre IMADE
(ES215) Gran Via, 42
E-28013 Madrid
Spain
Tel: (341) 580 2600
Fax: (341) 580 2589

SWEDEN

GEOGRAPHY
Area:
Total Area: 449,964 sq km
Land Area: 410,928 sq km
Comparative Area: slightly smaller than California
Natural Resources: zinc, iron ore, lead, copper, silver, timber, uranium, hydropower potential

PEOPLE
Population: 8,900,954 (July 1996 est.)
Age Structure:
0–14 years: 19% (female 815,967; male 860,940)
15–64 years: 64% (female 2,794,593; male 2,884,687)
65 years and over: 17% (female 890,328; male 654,439) (July 1996 est.)
Population Growth Rate: 0.56% (1996 est.)
Ethnic Divisions: white, Lapp (Sami), foreign-born or first-generation immigrants 12% (Finns, Yugoslavs, Danes, Norwegians, Greeks, Turks)
Religions: Evangelical Lutheran 94%, roman Catholic 1.5%, Pentecostal 1%, other 3.5% (1987)
Languages: Swedish
Labor Force: 4.552 million (84% unionized, 1992)

GOVERNMENT
Type: Constitutional Monarchy
Capital: Stockholm

ECONOMY
National Product: GDP—purchasing power parity—$177.3 billion (1995 est.)
National Product Per Capita: $20,100 (1995 est.)
Exports: $61.2 billion (f.o.b., 1994)
Commodities: machinery, motor vehicles, paper products, pulp and wood, iron and steel products, chemicals, petroleum and petroleum products
Partners: EU 59.1% (Germany 13.2%, UK 10.2%, Denmark 6.9%, France 5.1%), Norway 8.1%, Finland 4.8%, US 8.0% (1994)
Imports: $51.8 billion (c.i.f., 1994)
Commodities: machinery, petroleum and petroleum products, chemicals, motor vehicles, foodstuffs, iron and steel, clothing
Partners: EU 62.6% (Germany 18.4%, UK 9.5%, Denmark 6.6%, France 5.5%), Finland 6.3%, Norway 6.1%, US 8.5% (1994)
Industries: iron and steel, precision equipment (bearings, radio and telephone parts, armaments), wood pulp and paper products, processed foods, motor vehicles

TRANSPORTATION
Railroads: Total of 12,624 km
Highways: Total of 135,859 km
Merchant Marine: Total of 169 ships
Airports: Total of 251

COMMUNICATIONS
Telephone System: 7.41 million telephones (1986 est.); excellent domestic and international facilities; automatic system

DEFENSE FORCES
Branches: Swedish Army, Royal Swedish Navy, Swedish Air Force

SWEDEN SOURCES

RESEARCH SOURCES
Demographic Data Sources
Statistics Sweden
SCB—Box 24 300
S-104 51 Stockholm
Sweden
Tel: (468) 783 40 00
Fax: (468) 66 52 61

Manufacturing Data Sources
CHAMPS
Chalmers Teknikpark
S-412 80 Goteborg
Sweden
Tel: (4631) 772 4222
Fax: (4631) 772 4171

Trade Data Sources and Trade Associates
Tradeline AB
Hamng. 1
S-211 22 Malmoe
Sweden
Tel: (4640) 23 65 65
Fax: (4640) 30 69 31

Swedish Trade Council
Box 5513
11485 Stockholm
Sweden
Tel: (4687) 83 85 00

Tullverket
The Swedish Board of Customs
 and Excises
Box 2267
S-103 17 Stockholm
Sweden
Tel: (468) 789 7300
Fax: (468) 20 80 12

Grossistforbundet Svenska
 Handel
Swedish Federation of Com-
 merce and Trade
Box 5512
S-114 85 Stockholm
Sweden
Tel: (468) 663 5280
Fax: (468) 662 7457

Sveriges Handelsagenters
 Forbund
The Federation of Swedish
 Commercial Agents
Hantverkargatan 46
S-112 21 Stockholm

Sweden
Tel: (468) 654 0975
Fax: (468) 650 3517

The National Board of Trade
Drottininggatan 89—Box 6803
113 86 Stockholm
Sweden
Tel: (468) 690 48 00
Fax: (468) 30 67 59

Company Data Sources
WireWorks AB
Brahegatan 9
114 37 Stockholm
Sweden
Tel: (468) 660 59 19
Fax: (468) 662 02 85

Algonet AB
Oca Brogatan 9—Box 1160
111 91 Stockholm
Sweden
Tel: (468) 587 587 00
Fax: (468) 587 587 30

The Federation of Swedish
 Industries
Industriforbundet
Box 5501
S-114 85 Stockholm
Sweden
Tel: (468) 783 8000
Fax: (468) 662 3595

Patent-Och Registreringsverket
 (PRV)
Swedish Patent and Registra-
 tion Office
Trade and Industry Register
PRV Bolag
S-851 81 Sundsvall
Sweden
Tel: (4660) 18 40 00

Stockholm Stock Exchange
Kallargrand 2—P.O. Box 1256
S-111 82 Stockholm
Sweden
Tel: (468) 613 88 00
Fax: (468) 10 81 10

Databases
AKTUELLProdukt Infor-
 mation
PO Box 5137
S-426 05 VF Goteborg
Sweden

Tel: (4631) 690 180
Fax: (4631) 690 370

Wennergren-Williams Informa-
 tionsservice AB
Box 1305
S-171 Solna
Sweden
Tel: (468) 705 9750
Fax: (468) 270 071

SICOMP
Swedish Institute of Com-
 posites
P.O. Box 271
SE-941 26 Pitea
Sweden
Tel: (460) 911 935 80
Fax: (460) 911 657 64

RESEARCH AND CONSULTANCY FIRMS
Stevan Dedijer
Integrated Intelligence Con-
 sulting
Business Administration
 Department
Lund University
Sweden
Fax: (4646) 222 4437

GfK Sverige AB
St Lars Väg 46
221 00 Lund
Sweden
Tel: (4646) 18 16 00
Fax: (4646) 18 16 09
E-mail: gfk-info@gfksve.
 postnet.se

IMAB Industriell Marknadsa-
 nalys AB
Artillerigatan 53
114 45 Stockholm
Sweden
Tel: (468) 667 0025
Fax: (468) 662 8724

Demoskop AB
Sköldungagatan 9
Stockholm
Sweden
Tel: (468) 723 4230
Fax: (468) 723 4240

GOVERNMENTAL SOURCES

Swedish Environmental Protection Agency
S-106 48 Stockholm
Sweden
Tel: (468) 698 10 00
Fax: (468) 20 29 25

BUSINESS DEVELOPMENT FIRMS AND BROKERS

NUTEK
Swedish National Board for
Industrial and Technical
Development

Liljeholmsvagen 32
S-117 886 Stockholm
Sweden
Tel: (468) 681 91 00
Fax: (468) 19 68 26

TAIWAN

GEOGRAPHY
Area:
Total Area: 35,980 sq km
Land Area: 32,260 sq km
Comparative Area: slightly smaller than Maryland and Delaware combined
Natural Resources: small deposits of coal, natural gas, limestone, marble, and asbestos

PEOPLE
Population: 21,465,881 (July 1996 est.)
Age Structure:
0–14 years: 23% (female 2,436,864; male 2,605,495)
15–64 years: 69% (female 7,252,188; male 7,505,344)
65 years and over: 8% (female 758,680; male 907,310) (July 1996 est.)
Population Growth Rate: 0.89% (1996 est.)
Ethnic Divisions: Taiwanese 84%, mainland Chinese 14%, aborigine 2%
Religions: mixture of Buddhist, Confucian, and Taoist 93%, Christian 4.5%, other 2.5%
Languages: Mandarin Chinese (official), Taiwanese (Min), Hakka dialects
Labor Force: 8.874 million

GOVERNMENT
Type: multiparty democratic regime; opposition political parties legalized in March 1989
Capital: Taipei

ECONOMY
National Product: GDP—purchasing power parity—$290.5 billion (1995 est.)
National Product Per Capita: $13,510 (1995 est.)
Exports: $93 billion (f.o.b., 1994)
Commodities: electrical machinery 19.7%, electronic products 19.6%, textiles 10.9%, footwear 3.3%, foodstuff 1.0%, plywood and wood products 0.9% (1993 est.)
Partners: US 27.6%, Hong Kong 21.7%, EU countries 15.2%, Japan 10.5% (1994 est.)
Imports: $85.1 billion (c.i.f., 1994)
Commodities: machinery and equipment 15.7%, electronic products 15.6%, chemicals 9.8%, iron and steel 8.5%, crude oil 3.9%, foodstuffs 2.1% (1993 est.)
Partners: Japan 30.1%, US 21.7%, EU countries 17.6% (1993 est.)
Industries: electronics, textiles, chemicals, clothing, food processing, plywood, sugar milling, cement, shipbuilding, petroleum refining

TRANSPORTATION
Railroads: Total of 4,600 km
Highways: Total of 19,860 km
Merchant Marine: Total of 198 ships
Airports: Total of 38

COMMUNICATIONS
Telephone System: 10,253,773 million telephones (1993 est.); best developed system in Asia outside of Japan

DEFENSE FORCES
Branches: Army, Navy (includes Marines), Air Force, Coastal Patrol and Defense Command, Armed Forces Reserve Command, Combined Service Forces

TAIWAN SOURCES

RESEARCH SOURCES

Demographic Data Sources

World Bank Headquarters
Public Information Center
1818 H Street, NW—Room
GC1-300
Washington, DC 20433
USA
Tel: (202) 458 5454

UNICEF House
3 United Nations Plaza
New York, NY 10017
USA

Macro International, Inc.
Demographic and Health
Surveys
11785 Beltsville Drive, Suite
300
Calverton, MD 20705
USA
Tel: (301) 572 0200

Manufacturing Data Sources

Chinese National Association
of Industry & Commerce
13F 390 Fuhsing S. Road, Section 1
Taipei
Taiwan
Tel: (8862) 707 0111

Chinese National Federation of
Industries
12F 390 Fuhsing S. Road, Sec-
tion 1
Taipei
Taiwan
Tel: (8862) 703 3500

Taiwan Garment Industry Asso-
ciation
Tapei
Taiwan
Tel: (8662) 391 9113

Trade Data Sources and Trade Associates

China External Trade Organiza-
tion (CETRA)
Taiwan Trade Center
8491, NW 17th Street, Suite
107
Miami, FL 33126
USA
Tel: (305) 477 9696

American Institute in Taiwan
Commercial Section, Suite
3207
Keelung Road, Section 1
Taipei
Taiwan
Tel: (8862) 709 2000

China External Trade Development Council
4-8F, 333 Keelung Road, Section I
Taipei
Taiwan
Tel: (8862) 725 5200

Taiwan Floriculture Exports
Association
901 Room 41, Section 1
Chung Hsiao West Road
Taipei
Taiwan
Tel: (8862) 331 3146

Company Data Sources

Asia Market Intelligence
Taiwan
Tel: (8522) 881 5388
e-mail: ami-tr@tr@hk.super.net

Trade Point USA
41 South High Street, Suite
1660
Columbus, OH 43215
USA
Tel: (614) 645 1710

IBI Corporation
P.O. box 46–220
Taipei
Taiwan
Fax: (8862) 508 4318

Universal Commerce Informa-
tion Company, Ltd.
12F-1, No. 262, Honan Road
Taichung
Taiwan
Tel: (8864) 255 1887

17F, No. 22 Chunghua Road
Sanchung City
Tapei
Taiwan
Tel: (8862) 971 0909

Databases

Asia Information Resources,
Ltd.

Hong Kong
Tel: (8522) 549 7209
e-mail: achang@lawhk.
hku.hk

Law-On-Line
Hong Kong
Tel: (8522) 858 9150
e-mail: lol@lawhk.hku.hk

Edward International Commer-
cial Company, Ltd.
No. 188, Section 2, Fuhsing S.
Road
Taipei
Taiwan
Tel: (8862) 709 8981

Taiwan Products
A1 14F, No. 130 Chung Te
Road, Section 2
Taichung
Taiwan
Tel: (8864) 237 4077

Trade Winds, Inc.
P.O. Box 7-129
Taipei
Taiwan
Tel (8862) 396 4022

RESEARCH AND CONSULTANCY FIRMS

Coopers & Lybrand Consul-
tants
3F, 367 Fu Hsing North Road
Taipei
Taiwan
Tel: (8862) 715 2822
Fax: (8862) 545 1185

Deloitte & Touche
12F, 102 Kuang Fu South Road
Taipei
Taiwan
Tel: (8862) 741 0258
Fax: (8862) 774 3833

Price Waterhouse
27F, Internation Trade Building
333 Keelung Road, Section 1
Taipei
Taiwan, R.O.C.
Tel: (8862) 729 6666
Fax: (8862) 757 6371

Diwan Ernst & Young
9th Floor, Taipei World Trade
Center

International Trade Building
333 Keelung Road, Section 1
Taipei
Taiwan
Tel: (8862) 720 4000

InterMatrix Taiwan
5F, 156-1, Sung Chiang Road
Taipei
Taiwan
Tel: (8862) 567 0159

A.C. Nielson Company
8F-2, 87 Sung Chiang Road
Taipei
Taiwan
Tel: (8862) 506 6823

Investec-Coopers Lybrand Consulting Ltd.
3F, 367 Fu Hsing North Road
Taipei
Taiwan
Tel: (8862) 715 2822

Global Industry Analysis, Inc.
210 Feil Street
San Francisco, CA 94102
USA
Tel: (415) 255 9333

Clock & Co.
Certified Public Accountants
14F, 111, Section 2, Nanking East Road
Taipei 104
Taiwan R.O.C.
Tel: (8862) 516 5255 (5 lines)
Tel: (8862) 515 0343 (3 lines)
Fax: (8862) 516 1995
Fax: (8862) 516 0312

GOVERNMENTAL SOURCES

Ministry of Economic Affairs
15 Foochow Street
Taipei

Taiwan
Tel: (8862) 321 9273

Board of Foreign Trade
1 Hukou Street
Taipei
Taiwan
Tel: (8862) 321 0717

Director General of Telecommunications
31 Aikuo East Road
Taipei
Taiwan
Tel: (8862) 341 5123

BUSINESS DEVELOPMENT FIRMS AND BROKERS

Morgan Stanley Asia (Taiwan) Ltd.
Room 1503, Chia Hsin Building
96 Chung Shan North Road, Section 2
Taipei
Taiwan R.O.C.
Tel: (8862) 561 5125

Salomon Brothers Taiwan, Ltd.
9F, Wasin Financial Building
No. 117, Min Sheng East Road, Section 3
Taipei
Taiwan R.O.C.
Tel: (8862) 719 6647
Fax: (8862) 718 0582

Goldman, Sachs & Co.
7F, Hung Kuo Building
No. 167, Tun Hua North Road
Taipei
Taiwan R.O.C.
Tel: (8862) 718 8713

China External Trade Development Council (CETRA)

4–8th Floor, 333, Keelung Road, Section 1
Taipei
Taiwan
Fax: (8862) 757 6653

China/USA Business Development & Network
473 Boardway 4th Floor
New York, NY 10013
USA
Tel: (212) 606 3739

MKC Customs Brokers International
P.O. Box 91042
Los Angeles, CA 90009-1042
Tel: (310) 645–0100

American Institute in Taiwan (AIT)
No. 7, Lane 134, Hsin Yi Road, Section 3
Taipei
Taiwan
Tel: (8862) 709 2000
Fax: (8862) 702 7675

AIT Commercial Section
Room 3207, International Trade Building
333 Keelung Road, Section 1
Taipei
Taiwan
Tel: (8862) 720 1550
Fax: (8862) 757 7162

American Chamber of Commerce in Taiwan
Room 1012, No. 96, Chung Shan N. Road, Section 2
Taipei
Taiwan
Tel: (8862) 581 7089
Fax: (8862) 542 3376

THAILAND

GEOGRAPHY
Area:
Total Area: 514,000 sq km
Land Area: 511,770 sq km
Comparative Area: slightly more than twice the size of Wyoming
Natural Resources: tin, rubber, natural gas, tungsten, tantalum, timber, lead, fish, gypsum, lignite, fluorite

PEOPLE
Population: 58,851,357 (July 1996 est.)
Age Structure:
0–14 years: 25% (female 7,351,264; male 7,627,916)
15–64 years: 69% (female 20,576,141; male 19,994,884)
65 years and over: 6% (female 1,832,338; male 1,468,814) (July 1996 est.)
Population Growth Rate: 1.03% (1996 est.)
Ethnic Divisions: Thai 75%, Chinese 14%, other 11%
Religions: Buddhism 95%, Muslim 3.8%, Christianity 0.5%, Hinduism 0.1%, other 0.6% (1991)
Languages: Thai, English (the secondary language of the elite, ethnic and regional dialects)
Labor Force: 32,152,600 (1993 est.)

GOVERNMENT
Type: Constitutional Monarchy
Capital: Bangkok

ECONOMY
National Product: GDP—purchasing power parity—$416.7 billion (1995 est.)
National Product Per Capita: $6,900 (1995 est.)
Exports: $45.1 billion (f.o.b., 1994)
Commodities: manufactures 73%, agricultural products and fisheries 21%, raw materials 5%, fuels 1%
Partners: US 21.0%, Japan 17.1%, Singapore 13.6%, Hong Kong 5.3%, Germany 3.5%, UK 3.0%, Netherlands 2.8%, Malaysia 2.4%
Imports: $53.9 billion (c.i.f., 1994)
Commodities: Manufactures 80%, fuels 6.9%, raw materials 6.6%, foodstuffs 4.3%
Partners: Japan 30.4%, US 11.9%, Singapore 6.3%, Germany 5.8%, Taiwan 5.1%, Malaysia 4.9%, South Korea 3.7%, China 2.6%
Industries: tourism, textiles and garments, agricultural processing, beverages, tobacco, cement, light manufacturing (e.g. jewelry), electric appliances and components, integrated circuits, furniture, plastics; world's second-largest tungsten producer and third-largest tin producer

TRANSPORTATION
Railroads: Total of 4,623 km
Highways: Total of 54,388 km
Merchant Marine: Total of 259 ships
Airports: Total of 98

COMMUNICATIONS
Telephone System: 1,553,200 telephones (1994 est.); service to general public inadequate; bulk of service to government activities provided by multichannel cable and microwave radio relay network

DEFENSE FORCES
Branches: Royal Thai Army, Royal Thai Navy (includes Royal Thai Marine Corps), Royal Thai Air Force, Paramilitary Forces

THAILAND SOURCES

RESEARCH SOURCES
Trade Development Board
230 Victoria Street #07-00
Bugis Junction Office Tower
Singapore 188024
Tel: (65) 337 6628
Fax: (65) 337 6898

RESEARCH AND CONSULTANCY FIRMS
Advanced Business Consultants
Co. Ltd.
496 Rachadapisek Rd.
Bangkok
Thailand
Tel: (662) 541 4240
Tel: (662) 541 4241
Tel: (662) 513 9783

Anderson Consultant Group
Co. Ltd.
514/1 Larnluang Rd., Dusit
Bangkok
Thailand
Tel: (662) 280 1645
Tel: (662) 280 1648
Fax: (662) 280 1649

B.E. Consultant Co. Ltd.
12 Ladproa Rd. Soi 115
Bangkok
Thailand
Tel: (662) 375 8904
Tel: (662) 375 8905

J.P. Rooney and Associates Ltd.
(Stanford Research Institute)
Panunee Bldg.
Ploenchit Rd.
Bangkok
Thailand
Tel: (662) 251 2323
Tel: (662) 251 9832
Fax: (662) 652 0788

Thai Business Consultants Co.
Ltd.
54 Sukhumvit Rd. Soi 21
Bangkok
Thailand
Tel: (662) 260 7310
Tel: (662) 260 7314
Tel: (662) 260 7322

Ventures International Consultants Co. Ltd.

5/19–20 Witthayu Rd.
Bangkok
Thailand
Tel: (662) 255 3555
Tel: (662) 238 4104
Tel: (662) 238 4109
Fax: (662) 255 3699

GOVERNMENT SOURCES
Thai Ministry of Commerce
Bangkok
Thailand
Tel: (662) 221 9872
Tel: (662) 221 2851

BUSINESS DEVELOPMENT FIRMS AND BROKERS
Boyden Associates (Thailand)
Ltd.
Sinn Sathorn Tower
Krungthonburi Rd.
Bangkok
Thailand
Tel: (662) 440 0140 to 440 0159
(all numbers inclusive)
Fax: (662) 440 0179

Century 25 Co. Ltd.
89 Soi Nathong
Rachadapisek Rd.
Bangkok
Thailand
Tel: (662) 248 7635
Tel: (662) 248 7636

Coopers & Lybrand Associates
Co. Ltd.
90/14-6 North Sathorn Rd.
Bangkok
Thailand
Tel: (662) 236 7814
Tel: (662) 236 7819
Tel: (662) 237 1202
Tel: (662) 237 1206
Fax: (662) 236 5226

Deloitte Touche Tohmatsu Jai-
yos Co. Ltd.
Rajanakarn Bldg. 26th Floor
183 South Sathorn Rd.
Yannawa
Bangkok
Thailand 10120
Fax: (662) 676 5747

Frank Small and Associates
Ltd.
Unico House 14 Floor
29/1 Soi Langsuan
Ploenchit Rd.
Pathumwan
Bangkok
Thailand 10330
Tel: (662) 254 9390
Tel: (662) 254 9394
Tel: (662) 255 4271
Tel: (662) 255 4274
Fax: (662) 254 9389

KPMG Peat Marwick
92/18 North Sathorn Rd.
Bangkok
Thailand
Tel: (662) 236 6161
Tel: (662) 236 6164
Fax: (662) 236 6165

Legal Consultants Co. Ltd.
2098/98–9 Preecha Village
Ramamhang Rd.
Bangkok
Thailand
Tel: (662) 718 3078

Independent Marine Consul-
tants & Surveyors Co. Ltd.
373/3 New Rd. Soi 45
Bangkok
Thailand
Tel: (662) 266 4906
Tel: (662) 266 4907

Projects Asia Group
52/53 Soi Nananua
Sukhumvit 3
Bangkok
Thailand 10110
Tel: (662) 254 6819
Fax: (662) 254 4849

VA Management and Legal
Consultant Co. Ltd.
Phaholyothin Place Building,
9th Floor
408-34 Phaholyothin Rd.
Samsennai, Phraya
Bangkok
Thailand 10400
Tel: (662) 619 0100
Fax: (662) 619 0108

| Business Improvement Consultants Co. Ltd. & Asian Business Consultants Co. Ltd. Oriflame Asoke Tower | 253 Asoke Rd. Sukumvit Rd. Soi 21 Klongtoey Bangkok | Thailand 10110 Tel: (662) 261 8747 Tel: (662) 261 8748 Fax: (662) 261 8749 |

UNITED ARAB EMIRATES (UAE)

GEOGRAPHY
Area:
Total Area: 75,581 sq km
Land Area: 75,581 sq km
Comparative Area: slightly smaller than Maine
Natural Resources: petroleum, natural gas

PEOPLE
Population: 3,057,337 (July 1996 est.)
Age Structure:
0–14 years: 35% (female 519,952; male 542,848)
15–64 years: 64% (female 683,282; male 542,848)
65 years and over: 1% (female 11,180; male 22,246) (July 1996 est.)
Population Growth Rate: 4.33% (1996 est.)
Ethnic Divisions: Emiri 19%, other Arab and Iranian 23%, South Asian 50%, other expatriates (includes Westerners and East Asians) 8% (1992)
Religions: Muslim 96% (Shi'a 16%), Christian, Hindu, and other 4%
Languages: Arabic (official), Persian, English, Hindi, Urdu
Labor Force: 794,400 (1993 est.)

GOVERNMENT
Type: Federation with specified powers delegated to the UAE central government and other powers reserved to member emirates
Capital: Abu Dhabi

ECONOMY
National Product: GDP—purchasing power parity—$7019.1 billion (1995 est.)
National Product Per Capita: $24,000 (1995 est.)
Exports: $25.3 billion (f.o.b., 1994 est.)
Commodities: crude oil 66%, natural gas, reexports, dried fish, dates
Partners: Japan 45%, India 6%, Oman 6%, South Korea 5%, Iran 5% (1994)
Imports: $21.7 billion (f.o.b., 1994 est.)
Commodities: manufactured goods, machinery and transport equipment, food
Partners: Japan 11%, UK 8%, Germany 8%, US 8%, Italy 7% (1994)
Industries: petroleum, fishing, petrochemicals, construction materials, some boat building, handicrafts, pearling

TRANSPORTATION
Railroads: N/A
Highways: Total of 3,000 km
Merchant Marine: Total of 57 ships
Airports: Total of 36

COMMUNICATIONS
Telephone System: 677,793 telephones (1993 est.); modern system consisting of microwave radio relay and coaxial cable; key centers are Abu Dhabi and Dubai

DEFENSE FORCES
Branches: Army, Navy, Air Force, paramilitary (includes Federal Police Force)

UNITED ARAB EMIRATES (UAE) SOURCES

RESEARCH AND CONSULTANCY FIRMS

Amer Research
P.O. Box 22525
Sharjah
UAE
Tel: (9716) 391 086
Tel: (9716) 598 324
Fax: (9716) 31271
Fax: (9716) 597 490

MEMRB
P.O. Box 6097
Sharjah
UAE
Tel: (9716) 596 919
Fax: (9716) 592 040

MERAC
P.O. Box 60992
Dubai
UAE
Tel: (9714) 822 688
Fax: (9714) 822 711

Booz Allen & Hamilton Inc.
P.O. Box 43754
Abu Dhabi
UAE
Tel: (9714) 270 882
Fax: (9714) 275 154

GOVERNMENTAL SOURCES

Federation of the UAE Chambers of Commerce & Industry
P.O. Box 3014
Abu Dhabi
UAE
Tel: (9714) 214 144
Fax: (9714) 339 210

Ministry of Economy & Commerce
P.O. Box 901
Abu Dhabi
UAE
Tel: (9714) 215 455
Fax: (9714) 215 339
P.O. Box 3625
Dubai
Tel: (9714) 284 151
Fax: (9714) 225 685

Ministry of Information & Culture
P.O. Box 17
Abu Dhabi
UAE
Tel: (9714) 453 000
Fax: (9714) 452 504
P.O. Box 5053

Dubai
Tel: (9714) 615 500
Fax: (9714) 615 648

Ministry of Justice
P.O. Box 753
Abu Dhabi
UAE
Tel: (9714) 625 224
Fax: (9714) 664 944
P.O. Box 1682
Dubai
Tel: (9714) 825 999
Fax: (9714) 825 557

Ministry of Labour & Social Affairs
P.O. Box 809
Abu Dhabi
UAE
Tel: (9714) 651 890
Fax: (9714) 665 889
P.O. Box 5025
Dubai
Tel: (9714) 691 666
Fax: (9714) 668 967

UNITED KINGDOM

GEOGRAPHY
Area:
Total Area: 244,820 sq km
Land Area: 241,590 sq km
Comparative Area: slightly smaller than Oregon
Natural Resources: coal, petroleum, natural gas, tin, limestone, iron ore, salt, clay, chalk, sypsum, lead, silica

PEOPLE
Population: 58,489,975 (July 1996 est.)
Age Structure:
0–14 years: 20% (female 5,565,153; male 5,853,545)
15–64 years: 65% (female 18,797,406; male 19,050,420)
65 years and over: 15% (female 5,470,090; male 3,753,361) (July 1996 est.)
Population Growth Rate: 0.22% (1996 est.)
Ethnic Divisions: English 81.5%, Scottish 9.6%, Irish 2.4%, Welsh 1.9%, Ulster 1.8%, West Indian, Pakistani, and other 2.8%
Religions: Anglican 27 million, Roman Catholic 9 million, Muslim 1 million, Presbyterian 800,000, Methodist 760,000, Sikh 4000,000, Hindu 350,000, Jewish 300,000 (1991 est.)
Languages: English, Welsh (about 26% of the population of of Wales), Scottish form of Gaelic (about 60,000 in Scotland)
Labor Force: 28.048 million (June 1992)

GOVERNMENT
Type: Constitutional monarchy
Capital: London

ECONOMY
National Product: GDP—purchasing power parity—$1.1384 trillion (1995 est.)
National Product Per Capita: $19,500 (1995 est.)
Exports: $200.4 billion (f.o.b., 1994)
Commodities: manufactured goods, machinery, fuels, chemicals, semifinished goods, transport equipment
Partners: EU countries 56.4% (Germany 12.7%, France 9.9%, Netherlands 7.0%), US 13.1%
Imports: $221.9 billion (c.i.f., 1994)
Commodities: manufactured goods, machinery, semifinished goods, foodstuffs, consumer goods
Partners: EU countries 54.9% (Germany 14.6%, France 10.0%, Netherlands 6.7%), US 12.2%
Industries: production machinery including machine tools; electric power, automation, railroad, and electronics and communications equipment; shipbuilding; aircraft; motor vehicles and parts; metals; chemicals; coal; petroleum; paper and paper product; food processing, textiles, clothing

TRANSPORTATION
Railroads: Total of 17,561 km
Highways: Total of 386,243 km
Merchant Marine: Total of 151 ships
Airports: Total of 388

COMMUNICATIONS
Telephone System: 29.5 million telephones (1987 est.); technologically advanced domestic and international system

DEFENSE FORCES
Branches: Army, Royal Navy (includes Royal Marines), Royal Air Force

UNITED KINGDOM SOURCES

RESEARCH SOURCES

Demographic Data Sources

UK Office for National Statistics
Horseguards Road
London SW1
United Kingdom
Tel: (441171) 270 3000

Manufacturing Data Sources

Department of Trade and Industry
1 Victoria Street
SW1H 0ET
London
United Kingdom
Tel: (441171) 215 5000

The Economist Intelligence Unit
15 Regent Street
London SW1Y 4LR
United Kingdom
Tel: (441171) 830 1000
Fax: (441171) 499 9767

Trade Data Sources and Trade Associates

British Chambers of Commerce
22 Carlisle Place
London SW1
United Kingdom
Tel: (441171) 565 2000
Fax: (441171) 565 2049

Company Data Sources

Companies Registration Office (Companies House)
55 City Road
London EC1
United Kingdom
Tel: (441171) 253 9393

ELC International
109 Uxbridge Road
Ealing
London W5 5TL
United Kingdom
Tel: (441181) 566 2288
Fax: (441181) 566 4931

ICC Information Group Ltd.
64 St Paul Street
London EC2A 4NA
United Kingdom

Tel: (441171) 251 4941
Fax: (441171) 251 4616

RESEARCH AND CONSULTANCY FIRMS

BMRB International
Hadley House
79–81 Uxbridge Road
Ealing
London W5 5SU
United Kingdom
Tel: (441181) 566 5000
Fax: (441181) 579 9208

Research International Group Ltd.
6/7 Grosvenor Place
London
SW1X 7SH
United Kingdom
Tel: (441171) 235 1588
Fax: (441171) 235 0202

Marketing Intelligence Services
109 Uxbridge Road
Ealing
London W5 5TL
United Kingdom
Tel: (441181) 579 9400
Fax: (441181) 566 4931

Taylor Nelson AGB
Taylor Nelson House
44–46 Upper High Street
Epsom
Surrey KT17 4QS.
United Kingdom
Tel: (4411372) 729688
Fax: (4411372) 744100

Mintel International Group
18 Long Lane
London, EC
United Kingdom
Tel: (441171) 606 6000
Fax: (441171) 606 5932

Euromonitor PLC
60 Britton St.
London
EC1
United Kingdom
Tel: (441171) 251 8024
Fax: (441171) 638 3149

Management Horizons Europe
Waverley House
Lower Square

Isleworth
London TW7 6RL
United Kingdom
Tel: (441181) 560 9393
Fax: (441181) 568 6900

MPA International
Chesterton Tower
Chapel Street
Cambridge CB4 1DY
United Kingdom
Tel: (4411223) 518851
Fax: (4411223) 518850

MEDISTAT
MDIS Publications Ltd.
8 Eastgate Square
Chichester
West Sussex PO19 1JN
United Kingdom
Tel: (4411243) 533322
Fax: (4411243) 532124

Nielsen
Nielsen House
London Road
Headington
Oxford OX3 9RX
United Kingdom
Tel: (4411865) 742742
Fax: (4411865) 742222

IAL Consultants Ltd.
109 Uxbridge Road
Ealing
London W5 5TL
United Kingdom
Tel: (441181) 810 0919
Fax: (441181) 566 4931

Marketing Improvements
17 Ulster Terrace
Outer Circle
Regents Park
London NW1 4PJ
United Kingdom
Tel: (441171) 487 5811
Fax: (441171) 935 4839

BUSINESS DEVELOPMENT FIRMS AND BROKERS

Dun & Bradstreet Ltd.
Holmers Farm Way
High Wycombe
Bucks. HP12 4UL
United Kingdom
Tel: (4411494) 422 000
Fax: (4411494) 422 2600

UNITED STATES

GEOGRAPHY
Area:
Total Area: 9,372,610 sq km
Land Area: 9,166,600 sq km
Comparative Area: about one-half the size of Russia; about three-tenths the size of Africa
Natural Resources: coal, copper, lead, molybdenum, phosphates, uranium, bauxite, gold, iron, mercury, nickel, potash, silver, tungsten, zinc, petroleum, natural gas, timber

PEOPLE
Population: 266,476,278 (July 1996 est.)
Age Structure:
0–14 years: 22% (female 28,335,934; male 29,718,390)
15–64 years: 65% (female 87,411,573; male 86,225,056)
65 years and over: 13% (female 20,021,655; male 13,850,234) (July 1996 est.)
Population Growth Rate: 0.91% (1996 est.)
Ethnic Divisions: white 83.4%, black 12.4%, Asian 3.3%, Native American 0.8% (1992)
Religions: Protestant 56%, Roman Catholic 28%, Jewish 2%, other 4%, none 10% (1989)
Languages: English, Spanish (spoken by a sizable minority)
Labor Force: 132.304 million (includes unemployed)(1995)

GOVERNMENT
Type: Federal Republic; strong democratic tradition
Capital: Washington, DC

ECONOMY
National Product: GDP—purchasing power parity—$7.2477 trillion (1995 est.)
National Product Per Capita: $27,500 (1995 est.)
Exports: $578 billion (f.o.b., 1995 est.)
Commodities: capital goods, automobiles, industrial supplies and raw materials, consumer goods, agricultural products
Partners: Western Europe 24.3%, Canada 22.1%, Japan 10.5% (1993)
Imports: $751 billion (c.i.f., 1995 est.)
Commodities: crude oil and refined petroleum products, machinery, automobiles, consumer goods, industrial raw materials, food and beverages
Partners: Canada 19.3%, Western Europe 18.1%, Japan 18.1% (1993)
Industries: leading industrial power in the world, highly diversified and technologically advanced; petroleum, steel, motor vehicles, aerospace, telecommunications, chemicals, electronics, food processing, consumer goods, lumber, mining

Transportation
Railroads: Total of 240,000 km (mainline routes; nongovernment owned)
Highways: Total of 6,284,488 km
Merchant Marine: Total of 322 ships
Airports: Total of 13,387

COMMUNICATIONS
Telephone System: 182.558 million telephones (1987 est.)

DEFENSE FORCES
Branches: Department of the Army, Department of the Navy (includes Marine Corps), Department of the Air Force

USA Sources

RESEARCH SOURCES

Demographic Data Sources

American Statistical Association
1429 Duke Street
Alexandria, VA 22314
USA
Tel: (703) 684 1221
Fax: (703) 684 2036

American Demographics
127 West State Street
Ithaca, NY 14850
USA
Tel: (607) 273 6343
Fax: (607) 273 3196
e-mail: www.demographics.com

Bureau of the Census
Public Information Office
Washington, DC 20233-0900
USA
Tel: (301) 457 2794
Fax: (301) 457 3670

Center for Demographic Studies
Duke University
P.O. Box 90408
2117 Campus Drive
Durham, NC 90408
USA
Tel: (919) 684 6126
Fax: (914) 684 3861

Center for Demography
University of Wisconsin
1180 Observatory Drive, Rm 4412
Madison, WI 53706-1393
USA
Tel: (608) 262 1537
Fax: (608) 262 8400

Futures Group
1050 17th Street, NW—Suite 1000
Washington, DC 20036
USA
Tel: (202) 775 9680
Fax: (202) 775 9694

LEXIS-NEXIS, div. Reed Elsevier, Inc.
9393 Springboro Pike
PO Box 933
Dayton, OH 45401
USA
Tel: (937) 865 6800

W.E.R. The Information Connection, Inc.
P.O. Box 107—160 North 1st Street
Mill City, OR 97360-0110
USA
Tel: (503) 897 2300
Fax: (503) 897 2335

Manufacturing Data Sources

Center for Manufacturing Information Technology
1575 Northside Drive—Bldg. 400, Suite 435
Atlanta, GA 30318
USA
Tel: (404) 894 4472
Fax: (404) 894 4157

Electronic Industries Association
2500 Wilson Boulevard
Arlington, VA 22201-3834
USA
Tel: (703) 907 7500
Fax: (703) 907 7501

James J. Hill Reference Library
80 West Fourth Street
Saint Paul, MN 55102
USA
Tel: (612) 227 9531
Fax: (612) 222 4139

Market Share Reporter
Gale Research Company
BookTower
Detroit, MI 48226
USA
Tel: (313) 961 2242

National Association of Manufacturers
Manufacturers' Institute
1331 Pennsylvania Avenue, NW
Washington, DC 20004
USA
Tel: (202) 637 3108
Fax: (202) 637 3182

National Center for Manufacturing Sciences
3025 Boardwalk
Ann Arbor, MI 48108-3266
USA
Tel: (313) 995 0300
Fax: (313) 995 4004

Trade Data Sources and Trade Associates

American Association of Exporters and Importers
11 West 42nd Street, 30th Floor
New York, NY 10036
USA
Tel: (212) 944 2230
Fax: (212) 382 2606

Bankers' Association for Foreign Trade
1600 M. Street, NW, Suite 700
Washington, DC 20036
USA
Tel: (202) 452 0013
Fax: (202) 452 0959

Federation of International Trade Associations
1851 Alexander Bell Drive
Reston, VA 22091
USA
Tel: (703) 620 1588
Fax: (703) 391 0159
e-mail: www.fita.org

National Association of Export Companies
P.O. Box 1330, Murray Hill Station
New York, NY 10156
USA
Tel: (212) 725 3311
Fax: (212) 725 3312
e-mail: www.imex.com/nexco/nexcohom.html

National Customs Brokers and Forwarders Association of America
One World Trade Center, Suite 1153
New York, NY 10048
USA
Tel: (202) 466 0222
Fax: (202) 466 0226
e-mail: www.neb-faa.org

U.S. Council for International Business
1212 Avenue of the Americas
New York, NY 10036

USA
Tel: (212) 354 4480
Fax: (212) 575 0327
e-mail: www.uscib.org

World Trade Centers Association
One World Trade Center, Suite 7701
New York, NY 10048
USA
Tel: (800) 937 8886

Company Data Sources
American National Standards Institute
11 West 42nd Street, 13th Floor
New York, NY 10036
USA
Tel: (212) 642 4900
Fax: (212) 398 0023

Corporate Technology Directory (CorpTech)
12 Alfred Street, Suite 200
Woburn, MA 01801-1915
USA
Tel: (617) 932 3939
Fax: (617) 932 6335
e-mail: www.corptech.com

Dun & Bradstreet Information Services
3 Sylvan Way
Parsippany, NJ 07054-3896
USA
Tel: (800) 526 0651
Fax: (201) 605 6980
e-mail: www.dbisna.com

Thomas Publishing Company
One Penn Plaza
New York, NY 10001
USA
Tel: (212) 695 0500
Fax: (212) 290 7373
e-mail: www.thomasregister.com

International Strategies, Inc.
Export Hotline/TradeBank
11 Beacon Street, Suite 1100
Boston, MA 02108
USA
Tel: (617) 723 6430
Fax: (617) 292 7788
e-mail: www.exporthotline.com

Databases
ABI Inform/Proquest
UMI
300 North Zeeb Road
Ann Arbor, MI 48106
USA
Tel: (313) 761 4700

Business Periodicals Index
H.W. Wilson Company
950 University Avenue
Bronx, NY 10452-8400
USA
Tel: (718) 588 8400

Dialog
Knight-Ridder Information, Inc.
2440 Camino Real
Mountain View, CA 94040
USA
Tel: (415) 254 7000

National Trade Data Bank / US Department of Commerce
National Technical Information Service
5285 Port Royal Road
Springfield, VA 22161
USA
Tel: (703) 487 4650
e-mail: www.fedworld.gov/ntis/ntishome

RESEARCH AND CONSULTANCY FIRMS
Applied Decision Analysis, Inc.
2710 Sand Hill Road
Menlo Park, CA 94025
USA
Tel: (415) 854 7101
Fax: (415) 854 6233

Audits and Surveys Worldwide
The Audits & Surveys Building
650 Avenue of the Americas
New York, NY 10011
USA
Tel: (212) 627 9700
Tel: (800) 274 3577
Fax: (212) 627 2034
Fax: (212) 627 1433

Arthur Anderson LLP
1150 17th Street, NW #901
Washington, DC 20036
USA
Tel: (202) 833 5500

BAI International (Division of BAI)
580 White Plains Road
Tarrytown, NY 10591
USA
Tel: (914) 332 5545
Fax: (914) 631 8300
e-mail: kpermut@behavioralanalysis.com

BASES International Research (Division of BASES)
55 Greens Farms Road
Westport, CT 06880
USA
Tel: (203) 222 2100
Fax: (203) 222 5792
e-mail: info@bases.com

Boston Bay Brokers, Inc.
85 Merrimac Street, 4th Floor
Boston, MA 02114
USA
Tel: (617) 227 5851
Fax: (617) 227 0473

CLT Research Associates
345 Park Avenue South
New York, NY 10010
USA
Tel: (212) 779 1990
Fax: (212) 779 8533
e-mail: info@cltresearch.com
internet: www.cltresearch.com

Custom Research, Inc.
10301 Wayzata Boulevard
P.O. Box 26695
Minneapolis, MN 55426-0695
USA
Tel: (612) 542 0800
Fax: (612) 542 0864
e-mail: brounds@cresearch.com

Diagnostic Research International
7474 North Figueroa Street
Los Angeles, CA 90041
USA
Tel: (213) 254 4326
Fax: (213) 254 8756
e-mail: dri@diagnostic.com

Ernst and Young LLP
1225 Connecticut Ave. NW

Washington, DC 20036
USA
Tel: (202) 327 6000
Fax: (202) 327 6200

Friedman Marketing Services
566 East Boston Post Road
Mamaroneck, NY 10543
USA
Tel: (914) 698 9591
Fax: (914) 698 2769

Gallup & Robinson, Inc.
575 Ewing Street
Princeton, NJ 08540
USA
Tel: (609) 924 3400
Fax: (609) 921 2748

Goldstein/Krall Marketing
Resources, Inc.
25 Third Street
P.O. Box 3321, Ridgeway
  Station
Stamford, CT 06905
USA
Tel: (203) 359 2820
Fax: (203) 327 9061
e-mail: wxhc99a@
  prodigy.com

IMPEX Logistics, Inc.
6969 Alum Creek Drive
Columbus, OH 43217
USA
Tel: (614) 491 5900
Fax: (614) 491 6262

Lieberman Research Inc.
245 Fifth Avenue
Suite 1503
New York, NY 10016
USA
Tel: (212) 532 0277
Fax: (212) 532 0710

M/A/R/C Marketing Research
  Counselors
7850 North Belt Line Road
Irving, TX 75063
USA
Tel: (972) 506 3400
Fax: (972) 506 3505

Macro International Inc.
100 Avenue of the Americas
New York, NY 10013
USA

Tel: (888) MACRO US (622
  7687)
Fax: (212) 941 7031
e-mail: levitt@macroint.
  com

Market Facts Inc.
3040 West Salt Creek Lane
Arlington Heights, IL 60005
USA
Tel: (708) 590 7000
Fax: (708) 590 7010

McCollum Spielman World-
  wide (MSW)
235 Great Neck Road
Great Neck, NY 11021
USA
Tel: (516) 482 0310
Fax: (516) 482 5180

Millward Brown, International
1245 East Diehl Road
Naperville, IL 60553
USA
Tel: (630) 505 0066
Fax: (630) 505 0077

M.O.R.-PACE, Inc.
31700 Middlebelt Road, Suite
  200
Farmington Hills, MI 48334
USA
Tel: (810) 737 5300
Fax: (810) 737 5326

NFO Research, Inc.
Executive Offices
2 Pickwick Plaza
Greenwich, CT 06830
USA
Tel: (203) 629 8888
Fax: (203) 629 8885
internet: www.nfor.com

Price Waterhouse International
  Trade Consulting Services
1251 Avenue of the Americas
New York, NY 10020
USA
Tel: (212) 819 5000

Research International—USA
466 Lexington Avenue
New York, NY 10017
USA
Tel: (212) 973 2300
Fax: (212) 973 3414

e-mail: d.struse@research
  int.com

Response Analysis Corporation
1060 State Road
P.O. Box 158
Princeton, NJ 08542
USA
Tel: (609) 921 3333
Fax: (609) 921 2611
e-mail: info@response
  analysis.com
internet: www.response
  analysis.com

Roper Starch Worldwide Inc.
566 East Boston Post Road
Mamaroneck, NY 10543
USA
Tel: (914) 698 0800
Fax: (914) 698 0485

Ross-Cooper-Lund, Inc.
Glenpointe Center East
Teaneck, NJ 07666-6769
USA
Tel: (201) 836 0040
Fax: (201) 836 1654

SIL: Sweeney International Ltd.
7601 North Federal Highway
Suite 205-B
Boca Raton, FL 33487
USA
Tel: (800) 626 5421
Fax: (800) 599 5688
e-mail: sil@siltd.com
internet: www.siltd.com

SIS International Research
6219 Constitution Drive
Fort Wayne, IN 46804
USA
Tel: (219) 432 2348
Fax: (219) 432 3031
e-mail: sisfwa@ctlnet.com

SRG International Ltd.
427 Bedford Road
Pleasantville, NY 10570
USA
Tel: (914) 769 4444
Fax: (914) 769 7760
Fax: (914) 769 7725

Walker Information
3939 Priority Way South Drive
Indianapolis, IN 46240
USA

Tel: (317) 843 3939
Fax: (317) 843 8897
internet: www.walker
net.com

GOVERNMENT SOURCES

Department of Agriculture
Foreign Agricultural Informa-
tion Service
14th & Independence Avenue
Washington, DC 20250
USA
Tel: (202) 690 3424
e-mail: www.fas.usda.gov

Department of Agriculture
Agricultural Marketing Service
14th & Independence Avenue
Washington, DC 20250
USA
Tel: (202) 720 3193

Department of Commerce /
Bureau of the Census
Federal Office Building—3 Sil-
ver Hill and Suitland Roads
Suitland, MD 20746
USA
Tel: (301) 457 4100

Department of Commerce /
Bureau of Export Adminis-
tration
Export Counseling Service
Washington, DC 20230

USA
Tel: (202) 482 4811
e-mail: www.ita.doc.gov

Department of Commerce /
International Trade Adminis-
tration
Trade Information Center
Washington, DC 20230
USA
Tel: (800) 872 8723
e-mail: www.ita.doc.gov

Department of Commerce /
International Trade Adminis-
tration
U.S. and Foreign Commercial
Service
Washington, DC 20230
USA
Tel: (202) 482 0543

Department of Treasury / U.S.
Customs Service
1301 Constitution Avenue
Washington, DC 20229
USA
Tel: (202) 927 6724
Fax: (202) 482 3322

Export / Import Bank
811 Vermont Avenue, NW
Washington, DC 20571
USA
Tel: (202) 565 3900

Fax: (202) 565 3380
e-mail: www.exim.com.gov

US Small Business Adminis-
tration
International Trade
409 Third Street, SW
Washington, DC 20416
USA
Tel: (202) 205 6720
Fax: (202) 205 7272

**BUSINESS DEVELOPMENT
FIRMS AND BROKERS**

Hamilton Consultants
124 Mt. Auburn Street, Suite
101 North
Cambridge, MA 02138
USA
Tel: (617) 661 2000
Fax: (617) 661 2001

Kamden International
Shipping
195 Cottage Street
Chelsea, MA 02150
USA
Tel: (617) 887 2717
Fax: (617) 887 2735

The Schraff Group
3158 Redhill
Costa Mesa, CA 92626
Tel: (714) 556 6800
Fax: (714) 556 1739

VENEZUELA

GEOGRAPHY
Area:
Total Area: 912,050 sq km
Land Area: 882,050 sq km
Comparative Area: slightly more than twice the size of California
Natural Resources: petroleum, natural gas, iron ore, gold, bauxite, other minerals, hydropower, diamonds

PEOPLE
Population: 21,983,188 (July 1996 est.)
Age Structure:
0–14 years: 35% (female 3,704,561; male 3,946,196)
15–64 years: 61% (female 6,666,626; male 6,702,404)
65 years and over: 4% (female 520,742; male 442,659) (July 1996 est.)
Population Growth Rate: 1.89% (1996 est.)
Ethnic Divisions: mestizo 67%, white 21%, black 10%, Amerindian 2%
Religions: nominally Roman Catholic 96%, Protestant 2%
Languages: Spanish (official), native dialects spoken by about 200,000 Amerindians in the remote interior
Labor Force: 7.6 million

GOVERNMENT
Type: Republic
Capital: Caracas

ECONOMY
National Product: GDP—purchasing power parity—$195.5 billion (1995 est.)
National Product Per Capita: $9,300 (1995 est.)
Exports: $18.3 billion (f.o.b., 1995)
Commodities: petroleum 72%, bauxite and aluminum, steel, chemicals, agricultural products, basic manufactures
Partners: US and Puerto Rico 55%, Japan, Netherlands, Italy
Imports: $11.6 billion (f.o.b., 1995)
Commodities: raw materials, machinery and equipment, transport equipment, construction materials
Partners: US 40%, Germany, Japan, Netherlands, Canada
Industries: petroleum, iron ore mining, construction materials, food processing, textiles, steel, aluminum, motor vehicle assembly

TRANSPORTATION
Railroads: Total of 584 km
Highways: Total of 93,472 km
Merchant Marine: Total of 32 ships
Airports: Total of 377

COMMUNICATIONS
Telephone System: 1.44 million telephones (1987 est.); modern and expanding

DEFENSE FORCES
Branches: National Armed Forces (Fuerzas Armadas Nacionales or FAN) includes Ground Forces or Army (Fuerzas Terrestres or Ejercito), Naval Forces (Fuerzas Navales or Armada), Air Force (Fuerzas Aereas or Aviacion), Armed Forces of Cooperation or National Guard (Fuerzas Armadas de Cooperacion or Guardia Nacional)

Venezuela Sources

RESEARCH SOURCES

Demographic Data Sources

Oficina Central de Estadistica e
 Informática (OCEI)
Official Census Office
Av. Boyaca, Edf. Fundación
La Salle, Caracas
Venezuela
Tel: (582) 793 7863
Tel: (582) 782 2243
Fax: (582) 782 2243

Fundacredesa
Foundation for Growth and
 Development
Av. N° 8 entre 6a y 7a
Transversal, Qta. Caley
Altamira, Caracas 1060
Venezuela
Tel: (582) 261 1717
Tel: (582) 261 3735
Fax: (582) 261 5813

Manufacturing Data Sources

Fedecamaras
Federación de Cámaras y Asoci-
 aciones de Comercio y Pro-
 ducción
Urb. El Bosque, Av. El
Empalme, Edf. Fedecamaras
Caracas
Venezuela
Tel: (582) 731 1711
Tel: (582) 731 1845
Fax: (582) 74 2097

Fedeindustria
Federación de Industriales
Parque Central, Edf. Catuche
Nivel Mezzanina, Ofc. 20
Caracas
Venezuela
Tel: (582) 578 2253
Tel: (582) 578 3470
Fax: (582) 578 3470

Consecomercio
Consejo Nacional de Comercio
Av. Andres Eloy Blanco, Edf.
Camara de Comercio
Los Caobos, Caracas
Venezuela
Tel: (582) 576 5060
Tel: (582) 571 2331
Fax: (582) 576 5066

Company Data Sources

Venezuela Competitiva
Centro de Arte Integral, Colina
 Creativa
Módulo 3, Zona Rental, Uni-
 versidad
Metropolitana, Terrasas del
 Avila
Caracas
Venezuela
Tel: (582) 242 1250
Tel: (582) 242 1642
Fax: (582) 242 3353

Promexport
Urb. El Bosque, Av. El
 Empalme, Edf.
Fedecamaras, Caracas
Venezuela
Tel: (582) 74 6903
Tel: (582) 74 5687
Fax: (582) 731 3053

Databases

Infoguia
Av. Principal de Las Mercedes
Edf. Irune, Mezzanina B.
Las Mercedes, Caracas
Venezuela
Tel/Fax: (582) 993 4057
Tel/Fax: (582) 993 4580

RESEARCH AND CONSULTANCY FIRMS

StatMark
Av. Francisco de Miranda,
 Torre Bazar
Bolivar, Piso 2
Boleita Sur, Caracas
Venezuela
Tel: (582) 235 0930
Tel: (582) 235 0982
Fax: (582) 235 0796

Mizrahi & Maduro
Av. Rio Caura, Centro Empre-
 sarial Torre
Humbolt, Ofc. 103
Prados del Este, Caracas
Venezuela
Tel: (582) 975 2414
Tel: (582) 975 3125
Fax: (582) 977 1976

Mercedes Hercules y Asociados
Av. Libertador, Edf. Folgana,
 Piso 4, Ofc. 4C

Chacao, Caracas
Venezuela
Tel: (582) 952 6430
Tel: (582) 953 4492
Fax: (582) 953 6240

Consultores 21
Calle 10 de La Urbina, Edf., Viz-
 caya, Piso 2
La Urbino, Caracas
Venezuela
Tel: (582) 243 5905
Tel: (582) 243 6605
Fax: (582) 242 5342

Datos Information Resources
Avenida José Maria Vargas
Torre del Colegio de Medicos
Santa Fe Norte, Caracas
Venezuela
Tel: (582) 979 5166

Data Analysis
Torre La Previsora
Piso 17 Sabana
Grande, Caracas
Venezuela
Tel: (582) 781 9569

GOVERNMENTAL SOURCES

Ministerio de Industria y Com-
 ercio
Av. Libertador, Centro Com-
 ercial Los Cedros
Pent House
La Florida, Caracas
Venezuela
Tel: (582) 761 1593
Tel: (582) 761 2442
Fax: (582) 762 9303

Instituto de Comercio Exterior
Av. Libertador, Centro Com-
 ercial Los Cedros
nivel, PH
La Florida, Caracas
Venezuela
Tel: (582) 731 0336
Tel: (582) 762 3881
Fax: (582) 731 2343

Venamcham
Venezuelan American Chamber
 of Commerce

Torre Credival, 10th Floor 2a
Avenida de Campo alegre
P.O. Box 5181
Caracas 1010-A
Venezuela
Tel/Fax: (582) 263 1829
Tel/Fax: (582) 263 0833

E-mail: venam@-
    venamcham.org

**BUSINESS DEVELOPMENT
FIRMS AND BROKERS**

Bolsa de Valores de Caracas
Avenida Venezuela con Sora-
    caima

Edificio Atrium P.1
El Rosal, Caracas
Venezuela
Tel: (582) 952 5668
Fax: (582) 905 5829

VIETNAM

GEOGRAPHY
Area:
Total Area: 329,560 sq km
Land Area: 325,360 sq km
Comparative Area: slightly larger than New Mexico
Natural Resources: phosphates, coal, manganese, bauxite, chromate, offshore oil deposits, forests

PEOPLE
Population: 73,976,973 (July 1996 est.)
Age Structure:
0–14 years: 36% (female 12,988,929; male 13,739,304)
15–64 years: 59% (female 22,448,944; male 20,956,735)
65 years and over: 5% (female 2,294,548; male 1,548,513) (July 1996 est.)
Population Growth Rate: 1.57 % (1996 est.)
Ethnic Divisions: Vietnamese 85%–90%, Chinese 3%, Muong, Thai, Meo, Khmer, Man, Cham
Religions: Buddhist, Taoist, Roman Catholic, indigenous beliefs, Islam, Protestant
Languages: Vietnamese (official), French, Chinese, English, Khmer, tribal languages (Mon-Khmer and Malayo-Polynesian)
Labor Force: 32.7 million

GOVERNMENT
Type: Communist state
Capital: Hanoi

ECONOMY
National Product: GDP—purchasing power parity—$97 billion (1995 est.)
National Product Per Capita: $1,300 (1995 est.)
Exports: $5.3 billion (f.o.b., 1995 est.)
Commodities: crude oil, rice, marine products, coffee, rubber, tea, garments
Partners: Japan, Singapore, Taiwan, Hong Kong, France, South Korea
Imports: $7.5 billion (f.o.b., 1995 est.)
Commodities: petroleum products, machinery and equipment, steel products, fertilizer, raw cotton, grain
Partners: Singapore, South Korea, Japan, France, Hong Kong, Taiwan
Industries: food processing, textiles, machine building, mining, cement, chemical fertilizer, glass, tires, oil

TRANSPORTATION
Railroads: Total of 2,835 km
Highways: Total of 105,000 km
Merchant Marine: Total of 112 ships
Airports: Total of 48

COMMUNICATIONS
Telephone System: 800,000 telephones (1995 est.); while Vietnam lags far behind other countries in Southeast Asia, Hanoi has made considerable progress since 1991 in upgrading the system; 100% of provincial switch boards have been digitized, and fiber optic and microwave transmission systems have been extended to all provinces; the density of telephone receivers nationwide doubled from 1993 to 1995, but is still far behind other countries in the region; telecommunications strategy aims to increase telephone density to 30 per 1,000 inhabitants by the year 2000; approximately $2.7 billion has been estimated to be spent on upgrades in the decade

DEFENSE FORCES
Branches: People's Army of Vietnam (PAVN) (includes Ground Forces, Navy, and Air Force)

VIETNAM SOURCES

RESEARCH SOURCES

Trade Data Sources and Trade Associates

Technical Development and
Trading Company
103 Pasteur Street District
Ho Chi Minh City
Vietnam
Tel: (848) 230 291
Fax: (848) 297 431

Trade Fair and Exibition
Company
97–101 Nguyen Cong Tru
Street, District 1
Ho Chi Minh City
Vietnam
Tel: (848) 294 565
Fax: (848) 294 248

Trading Investments Company
Number 9 Room, 3rd floor,
Hom Market
Hai Ba Trung District
Hanoi City
Vietnam
Tel: (844) 226 636
Fax: (844) 226 696

Company Data Sources

Fine Arts Advertisement
Company
43 Trang Tien Street, Hoan
Kiem District
Hanoi City
Vietnam
Tel: (844) 253 045

**RESEARCH AND
CONSULTANCY FIRMS**

Ernst and Young
61 Trang Thi
Hanoi
Vietnam
Tel: (844) 265 595
Fax: (844) 265 596

Price Waterhouse
88 Nguyen Du Street
District 1
Ho Chi Minh City
Vietnam
Tel: (848) 230 796
Fax: (848) 251 947

38A Trieu Viet Vuong
Hai Ba Trung District

Hanoi
Vietnam
Tel: (844) 228 985
Tel: (844) 228 986
Fax: (844) 228 992

Coopers and Lybrand
142, Nguyen Dhi Minh Khai
District 3
Ho Chi Minh City
Vietnam
Tel: (848) 829 2389
Fax: (848) 829 2392

Arthur Anderson
LTD 12, nam Ky Khoi Nghia
Q1
Ho Chi Minh City
Vietnam
Tel: (848) 821 0033
Fax: (848) 821 0026

KPMG Peat Marwick
256 Ba Trieu Street
Hanoi
Vietnam
Tel: (844) 822 8128
Fax: (844) 822 6355

64 Pham Ngoc Thach
Ho Chi Minh City
Vietnam
Tel: (848) 820 0159
fax: (848) 820 0158

Asia Pacific Engineering Consultants
278 Ton Duc Thang
Hanoi City
Vietnam
Tel: (844) 513 529
Fax: (844) 513 409

Viet Consult International
Corp.
Hanoi City
Vietnam
Tel: (844) 281 208
Fax: (844) 243 028

Information and Advertising
Company of Sea Products
Ministry of Fisheries
2 Dong Khoi Street, District 1
Ho Chi Minh City
Vietnam
Tel: (848) 224 951

Investment and Development
Consulting Center for Technology of Glass and Ceramic
43B Hoang Hoa Tham
Hanoi
Vietnam
Tel: (844) 256 982
Fax:(844) 254 485

Maison Consultancy and
Financial Services
34 Quang Trung Street
Hanoi City
Vietnam
Tel: (844) 250 862
Fax: (844) 250 860

Javidec International
Hanoi
Vietnam
Tel: (844) 253 093
Fax: (844) 253 093

Malavina Company, LTD
28 Thanh Nien Street
Hanoi City
Vietnam
Tel: (844) 257 105
Fax: (844) 232 658

CDC Corp. Consultants
Designers Contractors
Hanoi
Vietnam
Tel: (844) 266 935
Fax: (844) 258 122

Ha Noi Juridal and Commercial Consultancy Service
Company
8 Ho Xuan Huong Street, Hai
Ba Trung District
Hanoi City
Vietnam
Tel: (844) 226 093

Investment Consultancy and
Technology Transfer Corporation
Vietnam General General Institute of Sciences- 260 ba
Trieu Street,
Hai Ba Trung District
Hanoi
Vietnam
Tel: (844) 226 268
Fax: (844) 252 282

GOVERNMENTAL SOURCES

Cement Development and
Investment Consult
Company
Ministry Of Construction
Le Duan Street, Hai Ba Trung
District
Hanoi
Vietnam
Tel: (844) 260 545
Fax: (844) 269 889

Design Consultant Company
Ministry of Light Labor
30 Nguyen Du Street, Hai Ba
Trung District
Hanoi
Vietnam
Tel: (844) 255 511
Fax: (844) 265 303

Electric Engineering Investment and Consultancy
Company
Ministry of Agriculture and
Food Industry
10A-55 Tran Nhat Duat Street,
District 1
Ho Chi Minh City
Vietnam
Tel: (848) 442 947
Fax: (848) 440 437

Vietnam Central Information
and Consumers Affairs
Giang Vo Exibitionward, Ba
Dinh District
Hanoi City
Vietnam
Tel: (844) 345 948
Fax: (844) 267 418

Vietnam Overseas Labor Service Company

Ministry of Labor and Disabled
Soldiers
34 Dai Co Viet Road
Hanoi
Vietnam
Tel: (844) 260 098

Vietnam Scientific Production
Union Of Geodesy and Cartography
Lang Trung Street, Dong Da
District
Hanoi City
Vietnam
Tel: (844) 344 066
Fax: (844) 267 398

Labor Cooperation with Foreign Countries Company
Ministry of Communication
and Transport
28 Tran Hung Dao Street,
Hoan Kiem District
Hanoi City
Vietnam
Tel: (844) 259 794
Fax: (844) 268 704

International Labor Cooperation Service Company
55 Lang Road, Dong Da District
Hanoi City
Vietnam
Tel: (844) 244 098
Fax: (844) 534 165

BUSINESS DEVELOPMENT FIRMS AND BROKERS

Vinh Hanh Investment / Development Company
Bao Khanh Street, Hoan Kiem
District
Hanoi City

Vietnam
Tel: (844) 233 397
Fax: (844) 257 317

Youth Advertising Company
4a Pham Ngoc Thach Street
District 1
Ho Chi Minh City
Vietnam
Tel: (848) 231 028
Fax: (848) 296 735

Youth Economic Development
Consultant Office
33 Nguyen Thi Minh Khai
District 1
Ho Chi Minh City
Vietnam
Tel: (848) 225 123

Services for Foreign Organizations Company
124 Nguyen Dinh Chieu Road
District 3
Ho Chi Minh City
Vietnam
Tel: (848) 443 134
Tel: (848) 295 794

Technology Development Supporting Company/ Vietnam
Institute of Sciences
65 Nguyen Du Street, Hai Ba
Trung District
Hanoi
Vietnam
Tel: (844) 256 612
Fax: (844) 268 842

The Vietnamese Legal Advisory
Company
9 Hang Chuoi Street, Hai Ba
Trung District
Hanoi City
Vietnam
Tel: (844) 268 624
Fax: (844) 261 943

INTERNATIONAL INTERNET SOURCES

General Trade Information and Support

U.S. Council for International Business
http://www.uscib.org

Small Business Exporters Association
http://web.miep.org/sbfa/

National Association of Export Companies (NEXCO)
http://www.imex.com/nexco/nexcohom.html

Export Today
http://www.enews.com:80/magazines/export/

Government Support

U.S. Department of Commerce
http://www.doc.gov/

NAFTA, Eastern Europe and Asia
http://www.ita.doc.gov/ita_home/itacnreg.html

Trade Information Center
http://www.ita.doc.gov/ita_home/itatic.html

U.S. Agency for International Development
http://www.info.usaid.gov/

The U.S. Department of State
http://www.usda.gov/

U.S. Customs Department
http://www.ustreas.gov/treasury/bureaus/customs/customs.htm

State of Ohio
http://natp.iftea.com/ooed/home.html

State of Alaska
http://www.alaska.net:80/~itd/ITD/index.html

State of Texas
http://www.texas.gov/TDOC_homepage.html

Australian Trade Organizations
http://www.austrade.gov.au/

Japanese Trade Organizations
http://www.jetro.go.jp/

Searchable Directories and Databases

Trade Research and Data Exchange
http://www.tradeinfo.com

Worldwide Marketplace
http://www.inetbiz.com/market/

Asia-Pacific Manufacturers & Traders
http://apple.ia.com.hk/jk/jk.html

EUROPAGES
http://www.europages.com/

World Importers Directory
http://teletron.com/buyersguide.html

International Trade Law Home Page
http://ananse.irv.uit.no/trade_law/nav/trade.html

The Global LawNet
http://www.lawnet.net

Internet On-Line Legal Directory
http://www.iigi.com/~iig/ild.html

Financing Exports and Receivables

Small Business Administration
http://www.sbaonline.sba.gov/business_finance

Export Credits Guarantee Department of the U.K.
http://www.expo.co.uk/ecgd.html

Commercial Finance Online
http://www.cfonline.com/cfo/opps/opps.htm

Actrade International
http://actrade.interse.com/index.html

"Save the U.S. Department of Commerce"
http://www.mdle.com/commerce.htm

Insurance Guidelines for the Exporter
http://www.imex.com/goexport/nyeac/export/ex_forum/insuranc

Understanding Letters of Credit
http://www.imex.com/goexport/nyeac/export/ex_forum/lcredit
http://www.imex.com/goexport/nyeac/export/ex_forum/forms/or
http://www.imex.com/goexport/nyeac/export/ex_forum/telecom

How to Export
http://www.dbisna.com/dbis/global/hglobal.htm

Marketing Your Products / Services

Trade Point USA
http://www.tpusa.com

Internet Tradelines
http://www.intrade.com

Trade Compass
http://www.tradecompass.com